Georgia Real Estate
An Introduction to the Profession

9th Edition

Charles J. Jacobus and
Thomas E. Gillett

Georgia Real Estate: An Introduction to the Profession, 9th Edition

Charles J. Jacobus and Thomas E. Gillett

Executive Editor: Sara Glassmeyer

Product Specialist: Deborah Miller

Project Manager: Elizabeth King and Randy Baldini, KnowledgeWorks Global Ltd.

Typesetting: KnowledgeWorks Global Ltd.

Cover Design: Nicholas Kindt

Front Cover Image: novikat, Getty Images

Back Cover Image: Sean Pavone, Getty Images

Copyright © 2021 Mbition LLC

ALL RIGHTS RESERVED. No part of this work covered by the copyright herein may be reproduced, transmitted, stored, or used in any form or by any means graphic, electronic, or mechanical, including but not limited to photocopying, recording, scanning, digitizing, taping, web distribution, information networks, or information storage and retrieval systems, except as permitted under Section 107 or 108 of the 1976 United States Copyright Act, without the prior written permission of the publisher.

> For product information and technology assistance, contact us at
> **Mbition Customer Support, 800-532-7649.**
>
> For permission to use material from this text or product, please contact publishingsupport@mbitiontolearn.com.

Library of Congress Control Number: 2021902252
ISBN-13: 978-1-62980-971-7
ISBN-10: 1-62980-971-3

Mbition, LLC
18500 W Corporate Drive, Suite 250
Brookfield, WI 53045
USA

Visit us at **www.mbitiontolearn.com**

Printed in the United States of America
1 2 3 4 5 6 26 25 24 23 22 21

BRIEF CONTENTS

Preface xxxi
About the Authors xxxv
Dedication xxxvii

PART 1: OWNERSHIP

1 Introduction to Real Estate 3
2 Nature and Description of Real Estate 28
3 Rights and Interests in Land 52
4 Forms of Ownership 75

PART 2: FEDERAL LAWS, ALTERNATIVE FORMS OF OWNERSHIP, AND LAND USE

5 Fair Housing, ADA, Equal Credit, and Community Reinvestment 89
6 Condominiums, Cooperatives, PUDs, and Timeshares 107
7 Land-Use Control 127

PART 3: AGENCY AND CONTRACTS

8 The Principal–Broker Relationship: Agency 139
9 Contract Law 164
10 The Principal–Broker Relationship: Employment 182
11 Real Estate Sales Contracts 197

PART 4: FINANCE, TAXES, AND VALUATION

12 Lending Practices 221
13 The Loan and the Consumer 244
14 Sources of Financing 258
15 Types of Financing 278
16 Notes and Security Documents 299
17 Taxes and Assessments 321
18 Real Estate Appraisal 338

PART 5: CLOSING, TRANSFER, AND LEASES

19	Closing the Transaction	371
20	Transferring Title	397
21	Recordation, Abstracts, and Title Insurance	415
22	Real Estate Leases	436

PART 6: GEORGIA-SPECIFIC LICENSE LAW, RULES AND REGULATIONS, AND GEORGIA PRACTICE

23	Georgia License Law	449
24	Georgia Rules and Regulations	478
25	Georgia Practice	500

Appendix A: Solutions to Student Calculations from Chapter 19	535
Appendix B: Real Estate Math Review	538
Appendix C: Measurement Conversion Table	547
Appendix D: Answers to Chapter Review Questions	548
Appendix E: Documents for Review	555
Index & Glossary	636

CONTENTS

Preface — xxxi
About the Authors — xxxv
Dedication — xxxvii

PART 1: OWNERSHIP

1 Introduction to Real Estate — 1
- How to Read This Book — 4
- Career Opportunities — 5
  - *Residential Brokerage* — 5
  - *Commercial Brokerage* — 5
  - *Industrial Brokerage* — 6
  - *Farm Brokerage* — 6
  - *Property Management* — 7
  - *Rental Listing Services* — 7
  - *Real Estate Appraising* — 7
  - *Government Service* — 8
  - *Land Development* — 8
  - *Urban Planning* — 8
  - *Mortgage Financing* — 8
  - *Securities and Syndications* — 9
  - *Consulting* — 9
  - *Research and Education* — 9
  - *Full-Time Investor* — 9
- Licensing Laws and Professional Affiliation — 10
  - *License Requirements* — 10
  - *Rationale for Licensing* — 10
  - *Loyalty, Honesty, and Truthfulness* — 11
  - *People Required to Be Licensed* — 11

Real Estate Broker	12
Salesperson	12
Associate Broker	13
Qualifications for Licensing	13
Examination	13
Education Requirements	14
Continuing Education	14
Licensing Procedure	14
Renewal	15
Nonresident Licensing	15
License Reciprocity	16
Notice of Consent	16
Moving to Another State	16
Licensing The Business Firm	17
Fictitious Business Name	17
Branch Offices	17
Real Estate Regulation	17
Real Estate Commission	18
Real Estate Department	18
License Suspension and Revocation	18
Securities License	19
Affiliating with a Broker	19
Training	20
Compensation	20
Broker Support	21
Finding a Broker	21
Employment Contract	22
Independent Contractor Status	22
Franchised Offices	23
National Real Estate Firms	23
Professional Real Estate Associations	24
National Association of REALTORS®	24
REALTOR®	25
Code of Ethics	25
Realtist	26
GRI Designation	26
Review Questions	26

2 Nature and Description of Real Estate   28
  Land   29
  Improvements   30
  Physical Characteristics of Land   30
    Indestructible   30
    Immovable   30
    Nonhomogeneous   31
  Economic Characteristics of Land   31
    Situs   31
    Improvability   31
    Scarcity   31
    Fixity (Investment Permanence)   32
  Fixtures   32
    Modification   32
    Attachment   33
    Relationship of the Parties   33
    Intentions of the Annexing Party   33
    Agreement   34
    Prior Liens Against Fixtures   34
    Ownership of Plants, Trees, and Crops   34
  Appurtenances   35
  Water Rights   35
  Land Descriptions   36
    Metes and Bounds   36
    Rectangular Survey System   40
    Recorded Plat   44
    Reference to Documents Other Than Maps   46
    Informal Reference: Street Numbers and Common Names   46
    Assessor's Parcel Number   46
  Vertical Land Descriptions   48
  Lot Types   49
  Review Questions   50

3 Rights and Interests in Land   52
  Government Rights in Land   53
    Police Power   53
    Eminent Domain   53
    Taxation   54
    Escheat   55

Protecting Ownership	55
Fee Simple	55
Encumbrances	56
Easements	58
Encroachments	61
Deed Restrictions	61
Liens	62
Qualified Fee Estates	64
Life Estates	65
Prohibition of Waste	65
Statutory Estates	66
Dower	66
Curtesy	66
Community Property	67
Homestead Protection	67
Freehold Estates	67
Leasehold Estates	68
Estate for Years	68
Periodic Estate	69
Estate at Will	69
Tenancy at Sufferance	69
Rights and Interests in Land: A Review	69
License	71
Chattel	71
Law Sources	71
Common Law	71
Statutory Law	71
Review Questions	72

4 Forms of Ownership — 75

Sole Ownership	76
Tenants in Common	76
Wording of Conveyance	77
No Right of Survivorship	77
Co-Owner Responsibilities	77
"What Ifs"	78
Joint Tenancy	78
Four Unities	78

Right of Survivorship	79
"Poor Man's Will"	79
Tenancy by the Entirety	80
Advantages and Disadvantages	83
Effect of Divorce	83
Community Property	83
Separate Property	84
Philosophy	84
Caveat to Agents	84
Review Questions	85

PART 2: FEDERAL LAWS, ALTERNATIVE FORMS OF OWNERSHIP, AND LAND USE

5 Fair Housing, ADA, Equal Credit, and Community Reinvestment — 89

Fair Housing Constitutional Concepts	90
Fair Housing Laws	91
1988 Amendments to the Fair Housing Act	92
Steering	94
Blockbusting	95
Housing Covered by the 1968 Fair Housing Act	95
Acts Not Prohibited by the 1968 Fair Housing Act	95
Fair Housing Enforcement	96
Agent's Duties	97
Testers	97
State Laws	97
The Americans with Disabilities Act	97
Scope	98
Defenses and Challenges	99
Equal Credit Opportunity Act	99
Prohibited Requests	99
Evaluating Credit Applications	100
Sex	101
Credit Denial	102
Penalties	102
Copies of Appraisal Reports	102
Community Reinvestment Act	103
CRA Notice	103
Review Questions	104

6 Condominiums, Cooperatives, PUDs, and Timeshares — 107

- The Desire for Land-Use Efficiency — 108
- The Amenities of Multifamily Living — 108
- Dividing the Land of an Estate — 110
- Condominiums — 110
  - *Separate and Common Elements* — 111
  - *Owners' Association* — 111
  - *Bylaws* — 111
  - *CC&Rs* — 112
  - *Deed* — 112
  - *Voting Rules* — 112
  - *Board of Directors* — 112
  - *Annual Meetings* — 113
  - *Condominium Management* — 113
  - *Maintenance Fees* — 113
  - *Reserves* — 114
  - *Property Taxes and Insurance* — 114
  - *Condominium Financing* — 114
  - *Condominium Conversions* — 115
  - *Advantages of Condominium Living* — 116
  - *Disadvantages of Condominium Living* — 117
  - *Before Buying* — 117
- Cooperative Apartments — 118
  - *Financing* — 119
  - *Default* — 119
  - *Resale* — 120
  - *Government* — 120
- Comparison of Condominiums and Cooperatives — 120
- Planned Unit Development — 120
- Resort Timesharing — 121
  - *Right-to-Use* — 121
  - *Fee Simple* — 122
  - *Costs* — 122
  - *Benefits* — 122
  - *Commitment* — 123
  - *State Regulation* — 124
- Review Questions — 124

7 Land-Use Control   **127**

- Zoning   128
  - *Zoning Symbols*   128
  - *Land-Use Restrictions*   129
  - *Enforcement*   129
  - *Nonconforming Use*   129
  - *Amendment*   129
  - *Variance*   130
  - *Conditional-Use Permit*   130
  - *Spot Zoning*   130
  - *Downzoning*   130
  - *Taking*   130
  - *Buffer Zone*   131
  - *Legality and Value*   131
- Subdivision Regulations   131
- Building Codes   132
- Deed Restrictions   132
- Planning Ahead for Development   133
  - *Master Plan*   133
- Long-Run Continuity   134
- Review Questions   134

PART 3: AGENCY AND CONTRACTS

8 The Principal–Broker Relationship: Agency   **139**

- Agency   140
- Establishing the Agent's Authority   140
- Broker's Obligations to the Principal   141
  - *Loyalty to the Principal*   142
  - *Obedience*   143
  - *Treat Information Confidentially*   144
  - *Full Disclosure*   144
  - *Accountability for Actions and Funds Received*   145
  - *Reasonable Care*   146
  - *Honesty, Fairness, and Integrity*   146
- Broker's Obligations to Third Parties   147
  - *Lead-Based Paint*   148
  - *Red Flags*   148

Owner Disclosure Statement 149
   As Is 150
   Puffing 151
Buyer Agency 151
Principal's Obligations 152
Broker's Sales Staff 153
Cooperating Broker 153
   The Complicating Issues 153
   Agency Disclosure 155
Termination of Agency 156
   Death 157
   Expiration 157
   Agreement 157
   Revocation or Renunciation 157
   Incapacity 157
   Extinction of the Subject Matter 157
Interstate Land Sales Disclosure Statements 158
   Property Report 158
   Not an Approval 159
Antitrust Laws 159
   Price Fixing 159
   Boycotting 160
   Monopolies 160
   Tie-in (Tying) Agreement 160
   Penalties 161
   Errors and Omission Insurance 161
Review Questions 161

9 Contract Law **164**
How a Contract Is Created 165
   Bilateral Contract 165
   Unilateral Contract 165
   Forbearance 166
Essentials of a Valid Contract 166
   Competent Parties 167
   Mutual Agreement 168
   Lawful Objective 172
   Consideration 172

Contract in Writing	174
Executory, Executed, Execute	175
Performance and Discharge of Contracts	175
Novation	175
Deceased Party	176
Property Damage	176
Breach of Contract	176
Partial Performance	176
Unilateral Rescission	177
Lawsuit for Money Damages	177
Lawsuit for Specific Performance	177
Monetary Damages Versus Specific Performance	177
Liquidated Damages	178
Mutual Rescission	178
Statute of Limitations	179
Implied Obligations	179
Review Questions	180

10 The Principal–Broker Relationship: Employment — 182

Listing Agreement	183
Exclusive Right-to-Sell Listing	185
Exclusive Agency Listing	185
Open Listing	185
Net Listing	186
Advance Fee and Advance Cost Listings	186
Buyer Brokerage Engagement Agreement	187
Multiple Listing Service	188
Market Exposure	188
Computerized MLS	189
Visual Tours	190
Broker Compensation	190
Procuring Cause	191
Terminating the Employment Contract	192
Mutual Agreement	192
Abandonment	193
Alternative Business Models	193
Review Questions	194

11 Real Estate Sales Contracts — 197

- Purpose of Sales Contracts — 197
- Purchase Contracts — 198
  - *Purchase and Sale* — 198
  - *Purchase Price* — 199
  - *Amount and Deposit of Earnest Money* — 199
  - *Date of Closing and Transfer of Possession* — 199
  - *Seller's Contributions at Closing* — 199
  - *Method of Payment* — 200
  - *Closing Attorney* — 200
  - *Inspection* — 200
  - *Property Sold Subject to Due Diligence Period, or "As Is"* — 201
  - *Lead-Based Paint* — 201
  - *Warranty* — 202
  - *Taxes and Prorations* — 202
  - *Risk of Damage to Property* — 202
  - *Entitlement to and Disbursement of Earnest Money* — 202
  - *Agency and Brokerage* — 203
  - *Disclaimer* — 203
  - *Notices* — 203
  - *Other Provisions* — 204
  - *Exhibits and Addenda* — 204
- Federal Clauses — 205
  - *Preprinted Clauses* — 205
  - *Riders* — 206
- Negotiation — 206
- The Binder — 206
- Letter of Intent — 207
- Practicing Law — 207
- Installment Contracts — 208
  - *Vendor, Vendee* — 209
  - *Public Criticism* — 209
  - *Protections* — 209
- Equitable Title — 210
- Option Contracts — 211
  - *Option Contracts on Multiple Properties* — 211
  - *Lease with Option to Buy* — 212
- Right of First Refusal — 214

The E-Sign Act	215
Review Questions	216

PART 4: FINANCE, TAXES, AND VALUATION

12 Lending Practices — 221

Term Loans	222
Loan Renewal	222
Amortized Loans	223
Repayment Methods	223
Monthly Payments	224
Loan Size	225
Change in Maturity Date	226
Budget Mortgage	227
Balloon Loan	227
Partially Amortized Loan	227
Earlier Payoff	229
15-Year Loan	229
Biweekly Payments	229
Existing Loans	229
Loan-to-Value Ratio	230
Equity	230
Loan Points	231
Origination Fee	231
Discount Points	231
FHA Insurance Programs	232
Current FHA Coverage	233
Assumability	233
Mortgage Insurance	233
Floating Interest Rates	234
Loan Qualification	234
Construction Regulations	235
Department of Veterans Affairs	236
No Down Payment	236
VA Certificates	237
Financial Liability	238
Funding Fee	238
Interest Rates	239
Assumption Requirements	240
Adjustable-Rate Mortgages	240

Private Mortgage Insurance   240
    Approval Procedure   241
Rural Housing Service   241
Review Questions   242

13   The Loan and the Consumer   244

Truth in Lending Act   244
    Advertising   245
    Trigger Terms   245
    Annual Percentage Rate   246
    Lending Disclosures   246
    Who Must Comply?   247
    Exempt Transactions   247
    Failure to Disclose   247
    Right to Rescind   248
Loan Application and Approval   248
    Settlement Funds   249
    Purpose of Loan   249
    Borrower Analysis   250
    Monthly Income   250
    Assets and Liabilities   251
    Declarations   252
    Redlining   252
    Loan-to-Value Ratios   252
    Credit Report   253
Predatory Lending   255
Review Questions   256

14   Sources of Financing   258

Primary Market   259
Savings and Loan Associations   259
    Disintermediation   260
    Restructuring the System   260
Commercial Banks   261
    Life Insurance Companies   262
Mortgage Companies   262
Mortgage Brokers   263
Computerized Loan Origination   264
Municipal Bonds   264

Other Lenders	265
Secondary Market	265
Traditional Delivery System	266
Secondary Market Delivery Systems	267
Standardized Loan Procedures	267
Federal National Mortgage Association (FNMA)	268
Commitments	268
FNMA Pooling	269
Revised Lending Practices	269
Government National Mortgage Association (GNMA)	269
Ginnie Mae Procedures	270
Federal Home Loan Mortgage Corporation	270
The Future of the Government Secondary Market	270
Farmer Mac	271
Federal Housing Finance Agency (FHFA)	272
Private Conduits	272
Computerization	272
Automated Underwriting Systems	273
Character Loans	273
Availability and Price of Mortgage Money	274
Usury	275
Price to the Borrower	275
Due-on-Sale	275
Prepayment	276
Review Questions	276

15 Types of Financing — 278

Adjustable Rate Mortgages	279
Current Format	279
Interest Rate	280
Margin	280
Adjustment Period	281
Interest Rate Cap	281
Payment Cap	281
Negative Amortization	281
Disclosures	282
Choosing Wisely	282
Graduated Payment Mortgage	283
Equity Sharing	283

	"Rich Uncle" Financing	284
	Package Mortgage	284
	Blanket Mortgage	284
	Reverse Mortgage	285
	Construction Loan	285
	Blended-Rate Loan	286
	Equity Mortgage	286
	Affordable Housing Loans	287
	Credit Criteria	288
	Consumer Education	288
	Seller Financing	288
	Wraparound Mortgage	289
	Subordination	290
	Contract for Deed	291
	Option	291
	Overly Creative Financing?	292
	Mortgage Fraud	292
	Illegal Flipping	293
	Silent Second	293
	Chunking	293
	Identity Theft	293
	Debt Cancellation/Deed Transfer	294
	Red Flags of Mortgage Fraud	294
	Reporting Mortgage Fraud	294
	Investing in Mortgages	295
	Rental	296
	Land Leases	296
	Financing Overview	297
	Review Questions	297
16	**Notes and Security Documents**	**299**
	Promissory Note	300
	Provisions and Terminology in the Note	300
	Obligee and Obligor	300
	Interest Conveyance	300
	Prepayment Rights	301
	Default	302
	Security	302

The Mortgage Instrument	302
Deed of Trust	303
Parties to a Deed of Trust	303
Reconveyance	303
Default	304
Trustee	304
Security Deed (Deed to Secure Debt)	304
Provisions of the Security Deed	305
Satisfaction of the Security Deed	307
Foreclosure on a Security Deed	307
"Subject To"	308
Assumption	309
Assumption with a Release of Liability	309
Estoppel	309
Debt Priorities	309
First and Second Mortgages	310
Subordination	310
Chattel Liens	311
The Foreclosure Process	311
Delinquent Loan	311
Foreclosure Routes	312
Judicial Foreclosure	312
Surplus Money Action	312
Notice of Lis Pendens	313
Public Auction	313
Equity of Redemption	313
Deficiency Judgment	314
Statutory Redemption	314
Strict Foreclosure	315
Nonjudicial Foreclosure (Power of Sale)	315
Entry and Possession	316
Deed in Lieu of Foreclosure	316
Equitable Mortgage	318
Choice of Security Instrument	318
Review Questions	318

17 Taxes and Assessments — 321

- Property Taxes — 322
  - *Budget and Appropriation* — 322
  - *Appraisal and Assessment* — 322
  - *Tax Rate Calculation* — 323
  - *Applying the Rate* — 323
- Unpaid Property Taxes — 324
- Assessment Appeal — 325
- Property Tax Exemptions — 325
- Property Tax Variations — 326
- Special Assessments — 327
  - *Forming an Improvement District* — 327
  - *Confirmation* — 328
  - *Bond Issues* — 328
  - *Apportionment* — 329
- Income Taxes on the Sale of One's Residence — 329
  - *Calculating a Home's Basis* — 329
  - *Calculating the Amount Realized* — 330
  - *Calculating Gain on the Sale* — 330
  - *Income Tax Exclusion* — 331
  - *Capital Gains* — 331
- Installment Method — 332
- Property Tax and Interest Deductions — 333
- Interest Deduction Limitations — 333
- Impact on Real Estate — 333
- Agent's Liability for Tax Advice — 334
- Conveyance Taxes — 334
- Review Questions — 335

18 Real Estate Appraisal — 338

- Purpose and Use of Appraisals — 339
- The Real Property Valuation Process — 340
- Characteristics of Value — 340
- Principles of Value — 340
- Multiple Meanings of the Word *Value* — 342
  - *Plottage Value* — 342
  - *Rental Value* — 342
  - *Replacement Value* — 342

Buyer's and Seller's Markets	343
Value Approaches	343
Market Comparison Approach	343
Comparables	344
Sales Records	344
Verification	345
Number of Comparables	345
Adjustment Process	345
Time Adjustments	346
House Size	346
Garage and Patio	347
Building Age, Condition, and Quality	347
Landscaping	348
Lot Features and Location	348
Terms and Conditions of Sale	348
Adjusted Market Price	348
Correlation Process	349
Unique Issues	349
Gross Rent Multipliers	353
Cost Approach	354
Estimating New Construction Costs	355
Estimating Depreciation	356
Final Steps in the Cost Approach	359
Income Approach	359
Income and Expense Forecasting	359
Operating Expenses	360
Reserves	361
Net Operating Income	361
Operating Expense Ratio	361
Capitalizing Income	361
Depreciation	362
Choice of Approaches	363
Reconciliation	364
Appraiser's Best Estimate	364
Review Questions	365

PART 5: CLOSING, TRANSFER, AND LEASES

19 Closing the Transaction — 371
- Buyer's Walk-Through — 372
- Closing — 372
- Closing or Settlement Meeting — 373
  - *Seller's Responsibilities at Closing* — 373
  - *Buyer's Responsibilities at Closing* — 374
  - *Real Estate Agent's Duties* — 374
  - *The Transaction* — 375
  - *Dry Closing* — 375
- Delays and Failure to Close — 376
- Reporting Requirements — 376
- Prorating at the Closing — 377
  - *Property Taxes* — 378
  - *Hazard Insurance* — 379
  - *Accrued Interest* — 380
  - *New Loans and Down Payments* — 382
  - *Interest Adjustment* — 383
  - *Rent Proration* — 384
  - *Mortgage Insurance* — 385
  - *Tax Escrows* — 386
  - *Insurance* — 386
  - *Transfer Tax* — 387
  - *Intangibles Tax* — 388
- Buyer and Seller Worksheets — 389
- Real Estate Settlement Procedures Act — 389
  - *Restrictions* — 389
  - *Consumer Financial Protection Bureau (CFPB)* — 392
  - *TILA-RESPA Integrated Disclosures (TRID)* — 392
  - *Penalties* — 394
- Review Questions — 394

20 Transferring Title — 397
- Deeds — 398
  - *Essential Elements of a Deed* — 398
  - *Covenants and Warranties* — 401
  - *General Warranty Deed* — 403
  - *Special Warranty Deed* — 403

Bargain and Sale Deed		404
Quitclaim Deed		404
Other Types of Deeds		405
Conveyance After Death		406
Intestate		406
Testate		406
Probate or Surrogate Court		407
Protecting the Deceased's Intentions		407
Holographic Will		408
Oral Will		408
Codicil		408
Adverse Possession		408
Color of Title		409
Easement by Prescription		410
Ownership by Accession		411
Public Grant		411
Dedication		412
Forfeiture of Title		412
Alienation of Title		413
Review Questions		413
21	**Recordation, Abstracts, and Title Insurance**	**415**
	Need for Public Records	416
	Constructive Notice	416
	Inquiry Notice	416
	Actual Notice	417
	Recording Acts	417
	Mortgage Electronic Registration System	417
	Unrecorded Interests	418
	Summary	419
	Requirements for Recording	419
	Witnesses	419
	Acknowledgment	419
	Public Records Organization	420
	Tract Indexes	421
	Grantor and Grantee Indexes	421
	Example of Title Search	422
	The Next Step	422

	Chain of Title	422
	Abstract of Title	424
	"What Ifs"	425
	Title Insurance	425
	Title Commitment	426
	Policy Premium	427
	Lender's Policy	428
	Claims for Losses	428
	The Growth of Title Insurance	429
	Quiet Title Suit	430
	The Torrens System	430
	Torrens Certificate of Title	431
	Adoption	431
	Marketable Title Acts	432
	Review Questions	433
22	**Real Estate Leases**	**436**
	The Leasehold Estate	437
	Creating a Valid Lease	437
	The Lease Document	438
	Provisions of the Lease	438
	Landlord–Tenant Laws	439
	Setting Rents	440
	Option Clauses	441
	Assignment and Subletting	441
	Lease Termination	441
	Eviction	442
	Eminent Domain	442
	Foreclosure	443
	Job Opportunities	443
	Training Programs	443
	Review Questions	444

PART 6: GEORGIA-SPECIFIC LICENSE LAW, RULES AND REGULATIONS, AND GEORGIA PRACTICE

23	**Georgia License Law**	**449**
	43-40-1 Definitions	450
	43-40-2 Creation of the Commission	451
	43-40-3 Determination of Fees	451

43-40-4 Office of Commissioner	451
43-40-5 Status of the License of Commission Employees	451
43-40-6 Seal and Records	452
43-40-7 Application for Licenses and Confidentiality	452
43-40-8 Qualifications of Licensees; Courses; Continuing Education; Reinstatement and Renewal	452
43-40-9 Nonresident Licensees	453
43-40-10 Granting of a Broker's License	455
43-40-11 Form of License	455
43-40-12 Fees; Inactive Status; Penalty Fees	455
43-40-13 Disposition of Fees	457
43-40-14 Power of the Commission to Issue, Revoke, Suspend, and Censure	457
43-40-15 Granting, Revoking, and Suspending Licenses	457
43-40-16 Refusal to Issue	458
43-40-18 Management of Firms and Licensed Affiliates	458
43-40-19 Change of Place of Business and Transferring Licensees	459
43-40-20 Trust Accounts	460
43-40-21 Violations Involving Trust Accounts	461
43-40-22 Real Estate Education, Research, and Recovery Fund	461
43-40-23 County or Municipality Occupational Tax	463
43-40-24 Requirements to Bring Action under this Chapter	463
43-40-25 Unfair Trade Practices and Violations	464
43-40-26 Hearings	470
43-40-27 Investigation of Complaints	470
43-40-28 Injunctive Actions	470
43-40-29 Exceptions	470
43-40-30 Acting without a License	473
43-40-31 Penalty	473
Review Questions	473
24 Georgia Rules and Regulations	**478**
520-1-.01 Organization of the Commission	479
520-1-.02 Definitions	480
520-1-.03 Commission Operations	481
520-1-.04 Obtaining a License	481

520-1-.05 Maintaining a License		483
520-1-.06 Brokerage Relationships		485
520-1-.07 Management Responsibilities of Firms		486
520-1-.08 Managing Trust Accounts and Trust Funds		489
520-1-.09 Advertising		492
520-1-.10 Handling Real Estate Transactions		494
520-1-.11 Licensees Acting as Principals		495
520-1-.12 Business Brokerage		495
520-1-.13 Fair Housing		495
520-1-.14 Citations		496
Review Questions		497

25 Georgia Practice — 500

Working with Clients; Working with Customers	501
Brokerage Relationships in Real Estate Transactions Act (BRRETA) 10-6A	501
Single Agency Seller Agency	506
Single Agency Buyer Agency	506
Single Agency Co-op	506
Dual Agency	507
Designated Agency	507
Subagency Co-op	508
Transaction Brokerage	508
Working with Sellers	509
Listing Presentations	509
Seller's Property Disclosure Form	511
Commercial Real Estate Broker Lien Act	512
Working with Buyers	513
Contract to Closing	518
Property Management	520
Functions of a Property Manager	520
Property Maintenance	520
Marketing	521
Market Analysis	521
Budgeting	522
Tenant Selection	523
Negotiating the Lease	523
Rent Collection	523
Retaining Tenants	524

Georgia Real Estate Finance	524
Community Association Management	527
Antitrust Laws	528
Sherman Antitrust Act	528
Price Fixing	529
Boycotting	529
Monopolies	529
Tie-in (or Tying) Agreements	530
Fair Business Practices Act of 1975 (FBPA) O.C.G.A. 10-1-390, et seq.	530
Uniform Deceptive Trade Practices Act (UDTPA)	530
Timeshares	531
Review Questions	532
Appendix A: Solutions to Student Calculations from Chapter 19	535
Appendix B: Real Estate Math Review	538
Appendix C: Measurement Conversion Table	547
Appendix D: Answers to Chapter Review Questions	548
Appendix E: Documents for Review	555
Index & Glossary	636

PREFACE

THE FOUNDATION

Is your goal to have a full-time or part-time career in real estate? Do you own or plan to own your own home or an investment property? Are you a student of real estate who desires to broaden your knowledge of this subject? If you answered "Yes" to one or more of these questions, this book will be of immense help to you. After all, real estate is part of the Great American Dream. It touches all of our lives. We share stories about it, invest in it, live in it and on it, sell it, and hire people to advise us about it. The subject of real estate has always been fun and interesting, but often complex.

In this book you will learn about:

- real estate brokerage
- appraisal
- financing
- contracts
- closing
- investment
- land descriptions
- rights and interests
- fair housing
- taxes
- leases
- condominiums
- zoning
- licensing
- the use of computers in real estate

You will find particularly valuable the attention given to such timely topics as water rights, variable rate commissions, alternative business models, investments agency law, real estate contract law, financing (with an emphasis on financing in

Georgia,) Georgia license law, Georgia practice, and Federal National Mortgage Association (FNMA) affordable housing programs.

NEW TO THIS EDITION

It has always been the goal to present the material in this text in a logical and practical sequence. After we listened to students, schools, instructors, and practitioners, it became evident that there was an even more practical way to present the material in this edition. The most logical way to learn the material is to present such in context, in the order one would need to know the information if in the field. For that reason, this edition in presented in six parts:

Part 1 is the foundation. Here the basics of ownership of real estate, the rights to land, and the description of land are discussed.

Part 2 is a discussion of federal laws that impact the ownership and use of real estate.

Part 3 is where we begin to build on our foundation of knowledge and apply what we have learned. Representation of the interests of the public (agency) is what real estate brokerage is about.

Part 4 digs deep into the financing principles. The fact is, one can sell property all day long, but if this person does not have the knowledge, ability, and contacts to obtain financing for the buyer, the closing does not occur. Closing is when we get paid.

Part 5 is the closing. Again, this is where we get paid. We drill down into the process, the legal aspects, and transfer of title.

Part 6 covers Georgia-specific information. Here is a thorough discussion of Georgia license law, Georgia rules and regulations, and practices specific to Georgia.

We are confident that you will agree that this change in the order of presentation offers the student the most solid of foundations!

THIS IS WHY

This book was written by teachers. The original manuscript was written by Dr. Bruce Harwood, and, after his untimely death, updating this text became a passion for Charles J. Jacobus. The manuscript was rewritten and modified specifically for the Georgia practitioner by Thomas E. Gillett. This book is written in a clear and easily readable style to help you understand and apply the important information contained in these chapters. The book's explanations combine how things are done with why they are done. Figures and tables will help you to visualize real estate rights and interests, financing techniques, appraisal methods, closing statements, and map reading. The basics of real estate have stayed the same for hundreds of years, since they are based on the English common law. These fundamentals are discussed in different ways in different chapters, each reinforcing what was learned in prior topics. Ownership and estates in land, for instance, can be revisited when discussing contracts and mortgages. All of this information, then, is again revisited when learning about the more complicated topics of recording, appraising, financing, fair housing, and land-use control. Most of those who read this book will move on to become licensed as real estate professionals, so we've tried to cover all pertinent topics to prepare the reader for the license examination and to provide a good base for further education.

HERE'S HOW

The special features of this book include:

- **Practical Application:** For those students anticipating a career in real estate, "In the Field" comments are included throughout the text to give the student some practical suggestions from a teacher with an active broker's license.
- **Additional Study Material:** At the end of each chapter are multiple choice questions for further review. These are designed to help readers focus on the chapter's important concepts and pinpoint areas that may need more study when preparing for the licensing examination. Answers to these questions are found in Appendix D, making this a self-contained study tool.
- **Easy Review:** Each chapter offers a list of key terms and their definitions in the margins. Key terms are also boldfaced when first discussed in a chapter. To aid students in reviewing terms and topics, this book combines the glossary with the index, allowing the reader to look up a term and find not only the definition, but also page references that show where the topic is discussed throughout the book.
- **Useful Appendices:** These appendices offer the reader comprehensive study tools for the field of real estate. They include:
    - **A** Solutions to Student Calculations from Chapter 19
    - **B** Real Estate Math Review
    - **C** Measurement Conversion Table
    - **D** Answers to Chapter Review Questions
    - **E** Documents for Review

WE CAN HELP

This product has a number of supplemental instructor resources included, please contact publishingsupport@mbitiontolearn.com for access and more information. Resources include:

- an instructor's manual with suggested guidelines and schedule;
- a 100-question midterm;
- final exams; and
- a PowerPoint presentation for each chapter.

LOOKING AHEAD

As a publisher, we understand that learning does not stop after the pre-license exam, and neither do our products. From pre-license to brokerage, and from principles to graduate degrees, we provide learning solutions that address continuing education, professional development, and advanced study needs. To learn more about Mbition LLC's complete list of real estate education resources, visit **www.mbitiontolearn.com.**

ABOUT THE AUTHORS

Charles J. Jacobus is an attorney with law offices in Bellaire, Texas, and is an executive vice president of Charter Title Company in Houston, Texas. He is board-certified by the State Bar of Texas Board of Legal Specialization in both residential and commercial real estate law.

He is a member of the Houston Real Estate Lawyer's Council, served as co-chair of the Broker-Lawyer Committee of the Texas Real Estate Commission, and was on the Texas Real Estate Center's MCE Writing Committee. He is listed in Woodward/White's "The Best Lawyers in America," Martindale-Hubbell's "Bar Registry of Preeminent Lawyers," and Marquis "Who's Who in the World." He served on the Council of the Real Estate, Probate, and Trust Law Section of the State Bar of Texas from 2003 to 2006, and he chaired the Title Insurance Committee for the State Bar of Texas from 2005 to 2007. He is an adjunct professor at the University of Houston Law Center and the University of Houston Bauer School of Business. He has served as president of the Real Estate Educators Association (REEA), as president of the Texas Real Estate Teachers Association, and as mayor of his hometown of Bellaire, Texas. He was named REEA's Educator of the Year, is a recipient of REEA's Jack Wiedemer Distinguished Career Award, TRETA's Don Roose Award of Excellence in real estate education, the Texas Land Title Association's Peggy Hayes Teaching Excellence Award, and the TRETA Lifetime Achievement Award. He was the State Bar of Texas Recipient of the Distinguished Texas Real Estate Lawyer Lifetime Achievement Award in 2012. In May of 2013, he was honored by the Boy Scouts of America as a Distinguished Eagle Scout, a rarely given and very prestigious award.

He has been voted a Superlawyer by the Texas Monthly magazine every year since 2003; he was listed as one of the Top 100 Lawyers in Texas in 2011, and given a Best Law Firm Tier One Ranking by U.S. News & World Report in 2018.

He is the author of *Texas Real Estate*; *Texas Real Estate Law*; *Real Estate: An Introduction to the Profession*; *Real Estate Principles*; and *Texas Title Insurance*. He is the editor-in-chief of the *Texas Forms Manual: A Guide for Real Estate and Title Documentation* and coauthor of *Texas Real Estate Brokerage and Law of Agency*.

Thomas E. Gillett has been a real estate and appraisal licensee and educator for over 30 years. Beginning his real estate career after military service in the early 1970s, he has become well respected in education for his ability to explain complex concepts in simple and practical terms that students can both understand and apply. He has developed a presentation style that involves playful interaction with his students, which is both educationally dynamic and entertaining. He continues to conduct in excess of 200 classes per year for both candidates for real estate and appraisal licensure and those already practicing in the profession. He is a primary instructor for the popular Georgia Association of REALTORS® Partners in Education program. He is a three-time recipient of the Georgia Instructor of the Year Award (2003, 2012, and 2013), and in 2006 he was presented with the Career Achievement Award by the Georgia Real Estate Educators Association. He has been recognized as a Captain of Industry by his local REALTOR® Association, and in 2016 he was humbled to be recognized by the Atlanta Business Chronicle as one of the most influential people in residential real estate in Georgia.

DEDICATION

There are many who deserve recognition for whatever accomplishments I may have achieved in my life. I am forever grateful and indebted to my family, friends, coworkers, and clients for their continued support.

There is one, however, who deserves to be mentioned individually. He did not teach me about real estate, but he taught me about life. He did not teach me to sell, but he demonstrated to me integrity and character. He did not teach me how to instruct, but he taught me the importance of people in your life. She demonstrated daily the importance of not just gathering, but scattering; to serve others and find victory in their accomplishments. She was my hero, my best friend, and my wife. Pam Gillett passed from this life in June, 2020, but the goodness of who she was and the lessons she taught me with the way she lived and the way she died live within me. While I will continue to grieve, I will do what she taught me: be incredibly thankful that I can grieve because I had her in my life. I love you baby girl. Keep sending the butterflies and rainbows! …I will see you later!!

Tom Gillett

PART 1
OWNERSHIP

It is my desire to present the material in this textbook, for your study of the real estate business, in a concise, relevant, and logical manner. Not unlike constructing a new home on a vacant parcel of land, it begins with the foundation. The foundation must be strong, sturdy, and square for the new building to rest upon. Likewise with Part 1. The information studied in these first four chapters will be the foundation of your real estate knowledge. Everything forward will be built on this foundation. The first four chapters are:

Chapter 1:   Introduction to Real Estate

Chapter 2:   Nature and Description of Real Estate

Chapter 3:   Rights and Interests in Land

Chapter 4:   Forms of Ownership

CHAPTER 1
INTRODUCTION TO REAL ESTATE

KEY TERMS

associate broker
independent contractor
license reciprocity
license revocation
license suspension

licensee
principal broker
real estate broker
real estate commission
real estate department

real estate salesperson
realtist
REALTOR®

OBJECTIVES

After successful completion of this chapter, you should be able to:

1. understand the career opportunities available in real estate;
2. define a broker, salesperson, franchise office, and real estate inspector;
3. describe major licensing procedures and requirements in Georgia;
4. explain the role of a state real estate commission or department;
5. describe nonresident licensing, business firm licensing, and real estate inspector licensing;
6. list and explain those violations that could lead to license suspension or license revocation;
7. describe the affiliation one may have with a broker;
8. discuss the independent contractor issue;
9. explain the purpose and role of franchised offices; and
10. describe the role of the various professional real estate associations.

OVERVIEW

Real estate is a unique subject, and because it is unique, it has spawned complex legal theories and very unusual situations. No two situations are ever exactly alike, and the subject never ceases to be intellectually stimulating. Everyone has a favorite story about real estate, and it has remained a fascinating topic for centuries.

This fascination is what makes real estate such a fun, interesting business. As a new real estate student, one must be prepared to learn a lot of new concepts and be willing to commit time and effort to that end. There are some who say that the only way to learn real estate is by experience. Many years ago, this was the traditional concept. Real estate was then considered to be a "marketing" or "salesmanship" business, and experience was the best teacher. Recent years, however, have seen the development of extensive academic applications in real estate education. Real estate has come to the academic forefront; undergraduate degrees in real estate are becoming more common, and graduate-level degree programs are proliferating. There is also a resulting emphasis on the professionalism and ethics of these new real estate professionals. Unlike many other academic subjects, however, real estate continues to emphasize experience in the people-oriented aspects of the business. Experience has a high correlation with success in the real estate business. This book has been written with those factors in mind to provide you with an understanding of the basic principles and business fundamentals of real estate. Emphasis is placed on an easily readable presentation that combines explanations of the basic principles of the subject, along with why things are done and how these principles apply to everyday activities.

HOW TO READ THIS BOOK

At the beginning of each chapter, there is a list of the new key terms that you will learn and a brief introduction of topics to be covered. Read these before starting the chapter. In the body of the chapter, these terms are set in boldface type, defined in the margin, and given a more in-depth discussion. Additional terms important to real estate are set in italics. There are questions and problems at the end of each chapter. These are designed to help you test yourself on your comprehension of the material in the chapter you've just read. The answers are given in Appendix D in the back of the book. Also at the back of this book is a combined index and glossary, meant to reinforce your familiarity with the language of real estate. Terms in this index and glossary, usually with a short definition, are followed by page references for more detailed discussion. Periodically, the textbook will reference interest rates or other technical data. Information such as interest rates are very fluid and potentially change on a daily basis. There is no intent to represent current market conditions. If you are asked to compute the daily interest on a loan, the exercise is to measure your competence in completing the calculation; it is immaterial whether the interest rate used is 2% or 18%. Another feature of this book is its simplified documents, which are combined with examples of contracts similar to what you can expect to use in the field. Deeds and title policies, for example, are sometimes written in legal language, which may be confusing to anyone except a lawyer. In the chapters ahead, you will find simplified versions of these documents, written in plain English and set in standard-size type. The intention is to give you a clearer understanding of these important real estate documents. It's commonly the duty of the agent to be familiar with contracts and fill them out for the consumer. These field documents are available to all licensees in Georgia from the Georgia Association of REALTORS®.

CAREER OPPORTUNITIES

The contents and organization of this book are designed for people who are interested in real estate because they now own or plan to own real estate, and for people who are interested in real estate as a career. It is to those who are considering real estate as a profession that the balance of this chapter is devoted. Most people who are considering a career in real estate think of becoming a real estate agent who specializes in selling homes. This is quite natural because home selling is the most visible segment of the real estate industry. It is the area of the business most people enter, and the one in which most practicing real estate licensees make their living. Selling residential property is good experience. Entry-level positions are more readily available, and residential property selling can help you to decide whether a career in real estate sales appeals to you.

Residential Brokerage

Residential brokerage requires a broad knowledge of the community and its neighborhoods; an understanding of real estate principles, law, and practice; and an ability to work well with people. Working hours will often include nights and weekends, as these times are usually most convenient to buyers and sellers. A residential agent must also have an automobile that is suitable for taking clients to see property. Some real estate offices are now giving new residential salespersons a minimum guaranteed salary or a draw against future commissions. However, a newcomer should have enough capital to survive until the first commissions are earned—and that can take four to six months. Additionally, the salesperson must be capable of developing and handling a personal budget that will withstand the feast-and-famine cycles that can occur in real estate selling. A person who is adept at interpersonal relations, and who can identify clients' motives and find the property to fit those motives, will probably be quite successful in this business.

Commercial Brokerage

Commercial brokers specialize in income-producing properties such as apartment and office buildings, retail stores, and warehouses. In this specialty, the salesperson is primarily selling monetary benefits. These benefits are the income, appreciation, mortgage reduction, and tax shelter that a property can reasonably be expected to produce. To be successful in income property brokerage, one must be very competent in mathematics, know how to finance transactions, and keep abreast of current tax laws. One must also have a sense for what makes a good investment, what makes an investment salable, and what the growth possibilities are in the neighborhood where a property is located. Commission income from commercial brokerage is likely to be less frequent, but in larger amounts than from residential brokerage. The time required to break into the business is longer, but once an agent is in the business, turnover is low. The working hours for a commercial broker are much closer to regular business hours than for those in residential selling, although appearances can be deceiving. Commercial brokers often spend evenings and weekends networking, as that is a primary source of their business. One almost always finds commercial brokers actively involved in charitable activities, fundraisers, golf tournaments, and similar activities, as it gives them a lot of time to work with community leaders and expand these networks.

Industrial Brokerage

Similar to commercial brokers, industrial brokers specialize in finding suitable land and buildings for industrial concerns. This task includes leasing and developing industrial property, as well as listing and selling it. An industrial broker must be familiar with industry requirements such as proximity to raw materials, water and power, labor supplies, and transportation. An industrial broker must also know about local building, zoning, and tax laws as they pertain to possible sites, and about the schools, housing, and cultural and recreational facilities that would be used by future employees of the plant. Commissions are irregular, but they are usually substantial. Working hours are regular business hours, and sales efforts are primarily aimed at locating facts and figures and presenting them to clients in an orderly fashion. Industrial clients are usually sophisticated businesspeople. Gaining entry to industrial brokerage and acquiring a client list can take a long time.

Farm Brokerage

With the rapid disappearance of the family farm, the farm broker's role is changing. Today, a farm broker must be equally capable of handling the 160-acre spread of Farmer Jones and the 10,000-acre operation owned by an agribusiness corporation. College training in agriculture is an advantage, and on-the-job training is a must. Knowledge of soils, seeds, plants, fertilizers, production methods, new machinery, government subsidies, and tax laws is vital to success. Farm brokerage offers as many opportunities to earn commissions and fees from leasing and property management as from listing and selling property.

Property Management

For an investment property, the property manager's job is to supervise every aspect of a property's operation so as to produce the highest possible financial return over the longest period of time. The manager's tasks include renting, tenant relations, building repair and maintenance, accounting, advertising, and supervision of personnel and tradespeople. The expanding development of condominiums has resulted in a growing demand for property managers to maintain them. In addition, large businesses that own property for their own use hire property managers.

In the Field

Property managers are usually paid a salary and, if the property is a rental, a bonus for keeping the building fully occupied. To be successful, a property manager should be not only a public relations expert and a good bookkeeper, but also a person who is at ease with tenants, handy with tools, and knowledgeable about laws applicable to rental units.

Rental Listing Services

In some cities, there are rental listing services that help tenants find rental units and landlords find tenants. Most compile lists of available rentals and sell this information to persons looking for rentals. A few also charge the landlord for listing the property. The objective is to save a person time and gasoline by providing pertinent information on a large number of rentals. Each property on the list is accompanied by information regarding location, size, rent, security deposit, pet policy, and so on. Especially popular in cities with substantial numbers of single persons are roommate listing services. These maintain files on persons with space to share (such as the second bedroom in a two-bedroom apartment) and those looking for space. The files contain such information as location, rent, gender, smoking preference, etc. A majority of states now require a real estate license for rental listing services.

Real Estate Appraising

The job of the real estate appraiser is to gather and evaluate all available facts affecting a property's value. Appraisal is a real estate career opportunity that does not require property selling; however, it does demand a special set of skills of its own. The job requires practical experience, technical education, and good judgment. If you have an analytical mind and like to collect and interpret data, you might consider becoming a real estate appraiser. The job combines office work and field work, and the income of an expert appraiser can match that of a top real estate salesperson. One can be an independent appraiser or take advantage of the numerous opportunities to work as a salaried appraiser for local tax authorities or lending institutions. The appraisal process is now becoming more complex, however. Most lenders and taxing authorities require that their appraisers have some advanced credential designation or special state certification to ensure an adequate level of competence.

Government Service

Approximately one third of the land in the United States is government-owned. This includes vacant and forested lands, office buildings, museums, parks, zoos, schools, hospitals, public housing, libraries, fire and police stations, roads and highways, subways, airports, and courthouses. All of these are real estate, and all of these require government employees who can negotiate purchases and sales, as well as appraise, finance, manage, plan, and develop. City, county, and state governments all have extensive real estate holdings. At the federal level, the Forest Service, Park Service, Department of Agriculture, Army Corps of Engineers, Bureau of Land Management, and General Services Administration are all major landholders. In addition to outright real estate ownership, government agencies such as the Federal Housing Administration, Department of Veterans Affairs, and Federal Home Loan Banks employ thousands of real estate specialists to operate their real estate lending programs.

Land Development

Most new homes in the United States are built by developers who, in turn, sell them to homeowners and investors. Some homes are built by small-scale developers who produce only a few a year. Others are part of 400-home subdivisions and 40-story condominiums that are developed and constructed by large corporations that have their own planning, appraising, financing, construction, and marketing personnel. There is equal opportunity for success in development whether you build four houses per year or work for a firm that builds 400 per year.

Urban Planning

Urban planners work with local governments and civic groups to anticipate future growth and land-use changes. The urban planner makes recommendations for new streets, highways, sewer and water lines, schools, parks, and libraries. Emphasis on environmental protection and controlled growth has made urban planning one of real estate's most rapidly expanding specialties. An urban planning job is usually a salaried position and does not emphasize sales ability.

Mortgage Financing

Specialists in mortgage financing have a dual role: (1) to find economically sound properties for lenders, and (2) to locate money for borrowers. A mortgage specialist can work independently, receiving a fee from the borrower for locating a lender, or as a salaried employee of a lending institution. The ease with which mortgages can be bought and sold has encouraged many individuals to open their own mortgage companies in competition with established lending institutions. Some mortgage specialists also offer real estate loan consulting for a fee. They will help a borrower choose from among the numerous mortgage loan formats available today, find the best loan for the client, and assist in filling out and processing the loan application.

Securities and Syndications

Numbering in the thousands, limited partnerships and other forms of real estate syndications combine the investment capital of a number of investors to buy large properties. The investment opportunities and professional management offered by syndications are eagerly sought out by people with money to invest in real estate. As a result, there are job opportunities in creating, promoting, and managing real estate syndications.

Consulting

Real estate consulting involves giving others advice about real estate for a fee. A consultant must have a very broad knowledge about real estate, including financing, appraising, brokerage, management, development, construction, investing, leasing, zoning, taxes, title, economics, and law. To remain in business as a consultant, one must develop a good track record of successful suggestions and advice.

Research and Education

A person interested in real estate research can concentrate on such matters as improved construction materials and management methods or on finding answers to economic questions such as, "What is the demand for active adult communities going to be in the next five years in Georgia?" Opportunities abound in real estate education. Nearly all states require the completion of specified real estate courses before a real estate license is issued. Georgia also requires continuing education for license renewal. As a result, persons with experience in the industry and an ability to effectively teach the subject are much sought after as instructors. Georgia requires a state-approved instructor for teaching classes that lead to licensure.

Full-Time Investor

One of the advantages of the free enterprise system is that you can choose to become a full-time investor solely for yourself. A substantial number of people have quit their jobs to work full-time with their investment properties and have done quite well at it. A popular and successful route for many has been to purchase, inexpensively and with a low down payment, a small apartment building that has not been maintained but is in a good neighborhood. The property is then thoroughly reconditioned, and rents are raised. This process increases the value of the property. The increase is parlayed into a larger building—often through a tax-deferred exchange—and the process is repeated. Alternatively, the investor can increase the mortgage loan on the building and take the cash received as a "salary" or use it as a down payment on another not-too-well-maintained apartment building in a good neighborhood. This can also be done with single-family houses. It is not unusual for an investor to acquire several dozen rental houses over a period of years. Other individual investors have done well financially by searching newspaper ads and regularly visiting real estate brokerage offices looking for underpriced properties that can be sold at a markup. A variation of this is to write to out-of-town property owners in a given neighborhood to see if there is any wish to sell at a bargain price. Another approach is to become a small-scale developer and contractor. (No license is needed if you work with your own property.) Through your own personal efforts, you create value in your projects and then hold them as investments.

LICENSING LAWS AND PROFESSIONAL AFFILIATION

License Requirements

As previously stated, property owners who deal only with their own property are not required to hold a real estate license. However, any person who, for compensation or the promise of compensation, lists or offers to list, sells or offers to sell, buys or offers to buy, negotiates or offers to negotiate, either directly or indirectly for the purpose of bringing about a sale, purchase, or option to purchase, exchange, auction, lease, or rental of real estate, or any interest in real estate, is required to hold a valid real estate license.

Rationale for Licensing

Does the public have a vested interest in seeing that real estate salespersons and brokers have the qualifications of honesty, truthfulness, a good reputation, and real estate knowledge before they are allowed to negotiate real estate transactions on behalf of others? It was this concern that brought about real estate licensing laws as we know them today. Until 1917, no state required real estate agents to be licensed. Anyone who wanted to be an agent could simply hang up an agent's sign. In larger cities, there were persons and firms that specialized in bringing buyers and sellers together. In smaller towns, a local banker, attorney, or barber would know who had what for sale and be the person a buyer would ask for property information. The first attempt to require that persons acting as real estate agents be licensed was made by the California legislature in 1917. That law was declared unconstitutional, with the main opposition being that the state was unreasonably interfering with the right of every citizen to engage in a useful and legitimate occupation. Two years later, in 1919, the California legislature passed a second real estate licensing act. This time, it was upheld by the U.S. Supreme Court. That same year, Michigan, Oregon, and Tennessee also passed real estate licensing acts. Today, all 50 states and the District of Columbia require that persons who offer their services as real estate agents be licensed.

Loyalty, Honesty, and Truthfulness

The first license laws did not require examinations for competency, nor did they require real estate education. Those came later. The first laws were aimed at weeding out persons who placed loyalty to themselves above loyalty to those whom they were representing. By requiring persons to be licensed, the state had the power to refuse to issue a license to someone with a record of dishonesty and untruthfulness. Additionally, the state could temporarily or permanently take away a license once it had been issued. To help make licensing laws work, the state refused to allow its courts to enforce claims for commissions by unlicensed people. That a real estate license applicant has a good reputation for honesty and truthfulness is still an important part of real estate licensing today. If you apply for a license, you may be asked to provide a photograph, credit report, fingerprints, and/or personal character references. The state licensing agency will check for links to any criminal convictions or other significant infractions of the law. Inquiry may be made of your character references to learn more about your reputation. In the 1930s and 1940s, states began adding the requirement of a license examination in an attempt to determine whether the license applicant also had some level of technical ability in real estate. Then, beginning in the 1950s, states began adding the requirement that a person take a certain number of hours of real estate education before being licensed. Thus, what we see today is that a person who plans to be a real estate agent must qualify both ethically and technically before being issued a license.

People Required to Be Licensed

In what situations does a person need a real estate license? A person who, for another, and for compensation or the promise of compensation, lists or offers to list, sells or offers to sell, buys or offers to buy, negotiates or offers to negotiate, either directly or indirectly, for the purpose of bringing about a sale, purchase or option to purchase, exchange, auction, lease, or rental of real estate, or any interest in real estate, is required to hold a valid real estate license. Some states also require persons offering their services as real estate appraisers, property managers, mortgage bankers, apartment locators, or rent collectors to hold real estate licenses. Property owners dealing with their own property, and licensed attorneys conducting a real estate transaction as an incidental part of their duties as an attorney for a client, are exempt from holding a license. Also exempt are trustees and receivers in bankruptcy, legal guardians, administrators and executors handling a deceased's estate, officers and employees of a government agency dealing in real estate, and persons holding power of attorney from an owner. However, the law does not permit a person to use these exemptions as a means of conducting a brokerage business without the proper license. That is to say, an unlicensed person may not take a listing under the guise of power of attorney and then act as a real estate broker.

REAL ESTATE BROKER

Before the advent of licensing laws, there was no differentiation between real estate brokers and real estate salespersons. People who brought about transactions were simply called real estate agents or whatever else they wanted to be called. With licensing laws came two classes of **licensees**: real estate brokers and real estate salespersons. A **real estate broker** is a person licensed to act independently in conducting a real estate brokerage business. A broker brings together those with real estate to be marketed and those seeking real estate and negotiates a transaction. For those services, the broker receives a fee, usually in the form of a commission based on the selling price or lease rent. The broker may represent the buyer or the seller or, upon full disclosure, both at the same time. The role is more than that of a middleman who puts two interested parties in contact with each other, for the broker usually takes an active role in negotiating price and terms acceptable to both the buyer and seller. A broker can be an actual person or a legal entity—that is, a business firm. If the broker is a business firm, the person in charge must be a broker. The laws of all states permit a real estate broker to hire others for the purpose of bringing about real estate transactions. These persons may be other licensed associate brokers, or they may be licensed real estate salespersons.

licensees: those who hold licenses

real estate broker: one who acts as an agent for others in negotiating contracts or sales

SALESPERSON

real estate salesperson: a person employed by a broker to list, negotiate, sell, or lease real property for others

A **real estate salesperson**, within the meaning of the license laws, is a person working for a real estate broker to list and negotiate the sale, exchange, lease, or rental of real property for others for compensation, under the direction, guidance, and responsibility of the employing broker. In Georgia, only an actual person can be licensed as a salesperson (i.e., a business firm cannot be licensed as a salesperson). A salesperson must be employed by a broker; a salesperson cannot operate independently. Thus, a salesperson who takes a listing on a property does so in the name of the broker and is typically empowered through the engagement agreement with the broker to sign on behalf of the firm. In the event of a legal dispute caused by a salesperson, the dispute would be between the principal and the broker. Therefore, some brokers take considerable care to oversee the documents that their salespeople prepare and sign. Other brokers do not, relying instead on the knowledge and sensibility of their salespeople, and accepting a certain amount of risk in the process. The salesperson is a means by which a broker can expand a sales force. Presumably, the more salespeople that a broker employs, the more listings and sales that are generated, and thus the more commissions that are earned by the broker. Against this, the broker must pay enough to keep the sales force from leaving, provide sales facilities and personnel management, and take ultimate responsibility for any mistakes the salespersons make.

ASSOCIATE BROKER

An **associate broker** is a licensee who meets the age, education, testing, and experience requirements to be a broker but chooses to work for a brokerage firm rather than be the broker of the firm. There is little an associate broker can do on a day-to-day basis that a person with a sales license would be restricted from doing. One main advantage to obtaining the broker status is, while this person may view working for a firm rather than having the responsibility of being the broker as best in the moment, if the opportunity arises to start his/her own firm or broker one for someone else, the ability to do so would not be delayed until the proper license was obtained. Some clients may also perceive a licensee who has achieved broker status to have more credibility.

associate broker: a licensee who meets all the requirements to be a broker of a firm but chooses to work for the brokerage firm

QUALIFICATIONS FOR LICENSING

Of the two license levels, the salesperson's license is regarded as the entry-level license and, as such, requires no previous real estate sales experience. The minimum age is 18 years. By comparison, the broker's license in nearly all states requires one to five years of licensed experience (two or three years is most common), with the minimum requirements in Georgia being three years of licensed experience and having obtained the age of 21.

Examination

Examination of the license applicant's knowledge of real estate law and practices, mathematics, valuation, finance, and the like is required for license granting in all states. Salesperson exams in Georgia currently consist of 152 multiple choice questions with a minimum of 109 correct required for passing. Broker exams consist of 11 exercises, which are computer simulations. Nine of these exercises are graded, and the remaining two are pretest simulations for the testing service to create statistics. Usually, four hours is allowed to complete the exam. Salesperson exams cover the basic aspects of license law, contracts and agency, real property ownership, transfer and use, subdivision map reading, fair housing laws, real estate mathematics, financing, leases, valuation, and the ability to follow written instructions. Broker exams cover the same topics in more depth, with an emphasis on office management. The computer simulations test the broker candidate's ability to gather appropriate information for a situation and subsequently make decisions.

Education Requirements

Nearly all states require that license applicants take real estate education courses at private real estate schools or colleges or through adult education programs at high schools. Currently, to qualify for a license in Georgia, a salesperson must complete a 75-hour course, and a broker candidate must complete—in addition to the sales course—a 60-hour course. Both of these courses require that the candidate pass a school exam to graduate. For up-to-the-minute information on education and experience requirements, you should contact the real estate licensing department of the state in which you are interested.

Continuing Education

Licensing authorities in a growing number of states require additional coursework each time a license is renewed. This is called *continuing education*, and its purpose is to force licensees to stay up to date in their field as a prerequisite to license renewal. Georgia's continuing education requirement is six hours per license year upon renewal. Currently, the requirement is 36 hours of continuing education each license period with at least 3 hours of the 36 in a dedicated and Commission-approved course on license law update. In that Georgia has a four-year license period, this requires all licensees licensed after 1979 to show proof that they have completed a minimum of 36 hours of education each license period. (Those licensed prior to 1980 are exempt from continuing education.)

LICENSING PROCEDURE

Having completed the educational requirements to become licensed, a candidate will contact PSI, which has been contracted by the Georgia Real Estate Commission (GREC) to supply testing for real estate and appraisal licensing. Contact may be made either by telephone or via the internet (www.goamp.com). There are four exam sites in Georgia: two in the Atlanta area—Duluth and Marietta—one in Savannah, and one in Macon. The exams are typically available every day except Sundays and holidays at one or all of the sites.

Once the candidate has completed the exam, grading is instantaneous. Both salesperson and broker exams are given by computer and graded immediately. Literally, by the time you can get up from your seat, clear your area, and walk across the room, the proctor is waiting for you with your results printed out. If the proctor is smiling, congratulations!

If the candidate fails the written examination, the usual procedure is to repeat the exam until passed. A fee is charged to retake the exam, and the candidate must wait until the next testing date.

If you would like to become licensed as soon as possible as a salesperson or associate broker, be sure to follow all procedures. To become licensed, you will need a certified check for the license (currently $170), a GCIC report (Georgia Crime Information Center; the report can be obtained for a small fee from most police stations or sheriff's offices), a broker's affidavit from the broker who will hold your license stating that s/he agrees to be responsible for you, and the passing results from your exam. PSI has the authority to act as an agent for the GREC in issuing licenses. Once you take the license to your broker, you are legal.

Renewal

Once licensed, a person who remains active in real estate and meets any continuing education requirements may renew the license by paying the required renewal fee. If a license is not renewed before it expires, the license will lapse and it will be necessary to pay additional fees to be reinstated. If the license has been lapsed for more than two years, the licensee will also be required to complete educational courses. This is covered more in a later chapter. If a licensee wishes to be temporarily inactive from the business but does not wish to let the license lapse, Georgia will permit the license to be placed on inactive status. The inactive license must be renewed every four years, just like the active license, and the fees must be paid. If licensees want to activate their license at a later date, they may do so by applying with the GREC and making sure all continuing education is current.

Nonresident Licensing

The general rule regarding license requirements is that a person must be licensed in the state within which that person negotiates. Thus, if a broker or one of the broker's sales associates sells an out-of-state property but conducts the negotiations entirely within the borders of his/her own state, a license is not needed in the state where the land is located. State laws also permit a broker in one state to split a commission with a broker in another state, provided each conducts negotiations only within the state where s/he is licensed. Therefore, if Broker B, licensed in State B, takes a listing at his/her office on a parcel of land located in State B, and Broker C in State C sells it, conducting the sale negotiations within State C, then Brokers B and C can split the commission. If, however, Broker C comes to State B to negotiate a contract, then a license in State B is necessary. Many states will issue a *nonresident license* to out-of-state brokers. This is particularly helpful when a broker is located near a state border. In issuing a nonresident license, a state will usually require substantially the same examination and experience requirements as demanded of resident brokers. Some states will give the out-of-state broker credit for the uniform part of a license test already taken, requiring only passage of a test on local law, custom, and practice. Others require a complete examination. Many states have reciprocal licensing agreements with other states (especially bordering states) that allow resident licensees of one state to obtain a nonresident license in another state without taking an examination.

License Reciprocity

In recent years, there has been considerable effort to design real estate licensing systems that permit a broker and the broker's sales staff to conduct negotiations in other states without having to obtain a nonresident license. The result is **license reciprocity**, and it applies when one state honors another's license. In permitting reciprocity, state officials are primarily concerned with a nonresident's knowledge of real estate law and practice as it applies to the state in which the applicant wishes to operate. A few states accept real estate licenses issued by other states. This is called *full reciprocity*. It means that a licensee can operate in another state without having to take that state's examination and meet its education and experience requirements. More commonly, states have *partial reciprocity* that gives credit to the licensees of another state for experience, education, and examination. Georgia has differing agreements of reciprocity with other states. If you have a specific circumstance in which you are interested, you should contact the real estate department of the state in which you are interested or the GREC.

license reciprocity: when one state honors another's license

Notice of Consent

When brokers operate outside of their home state, they may be required to file a notice of consent in each state in which they intend to operate, usually with the secretary of state. This enables the secretary of state to receive legal summonses on behalf of the nonresident broker, and provides a state resident an avenue by which to sue a broker who is a resident of another state.

Moving to Another State

When a broker or salesperson moves a place of business from one state to another, a license is required in the new state. Many states will give credit for experience and part or all of the examination that was passed in the previous state. This can be particularly helpful for two-income families when one spouse is transferred to another state. Details of what a state will allow as credit are too complex and too changeable to include here. If negotiating across state lines or moving to another state as a real estate agent is of interest to you, you should contact that state's real estate licensing authority.

LICENSING THE BUSINESS FIRM

When a real estate broker wishes to establish a brokerage, the simplest method is to form a sole proprietorship under the broker's own name, such as Hannah Lee, Real Estate Broker. Some states permit brokers to operate out of their residence. However, operating a business in a residential neighborhood can be bothersome to neighbors, and most states require brokers to maintain a place of business in a location that is zoned for businesses.

Fictitious Business Name

When persons operate under a name other than their own, they must register that name by filing a *fictitious business name statement* or *assumed name certificate* with both the county clerk and the state real estate licensing authority. This statement must also be published in a local newspaper. Thus, if Hannah Lee wishes to call her brokerage business ABC Realty, her business certificate would show "Hannah Lee, doing business as ABC Realty." (Sometimes, the phrase *doing business as* is shortened to dba or d/b/a.) A real estate broker can operate as a sole proprietorship under either the broker's own name or a fictitious name. A broker can also operate in partnership with other brokers or as a corporation. Since a corporation is an artificial being (not an actual person), it cannot take a real estate examination. Therefore, there must be a person who is licensed as a broker, known as the qualifying broker, who accepts responsibility for the management of the firm. Other officers and stockholders may include brokers, salespersons, and non-licensed persons. However, only those actually licensed may represent the corporation in activities requiring a real estate license.

Branch Offices

If a broker expands by establishing branch offices that are geographically separate from the main or home office, it is not required that those offices have their own qualifying brokers. It is required, however, that the company provide adequate supervision for the staff, so each office will typically have a managing broker. This person is really a sales manager or office manager and may be a salesperson, broker, or associate broker.

REAL ESTATE REGULATION

Thus far, we have discussed why and when a real estate license is required and how to obtain one. Now we will address these questions: "Who makes these rules, and how are they enforced?" The starting point is the state legislature. The legislature of each state has the authority to enact laws to promote the safety, health, morals, order, and general welfare of its population. This includes the licensing and regulation of real estate brokers and salespersons. The legislature establishes general requirements. For example, the legislature enacts laws requiring that real estate agents be licensed, that there will be two classes of licenses, that there will be a prelicense education requirement, that there will be a license examination, and that continuing education will be required. The legislature also establishes two bodies to carry out the requirements: the real estate commission and the real estate department.

Real Estate Commission

The **real estate commission** deals primarily with adopting rules and regulations to implement the license law as established by the legislature. In Georgia, the real estate commission has six members. Five of these members are licensees from the real estate community, and the other one is a non licensed member of the general public. Commission members are volunteers selected by the governor to represent all geographical parts of the state. Meetings are usually held monthly, at which time members provide input to the state on such matters as the needs of real estate licensees, state policies regarding real estate, and the welfare of the general public in dealing with licensees. In addition, the commission hires a commissioner to oversee real estate regulation. This person's responsibility is to carry out the wishes of the legislature and the real estate commission on a day-to-day basis. To assist in this, the commissioner hires and supervises a staff, referred to here as the real estate department. Although we commonly refer to the six-member body, the regulatory office, and the staff interchangeably as the real estate commission, this almost creates a "Who's on first?" routine when trying to explain the distinction.

real estate commission: a state board that advises and sets policies regarding real estate licensees and transaction procedures

Real Estate Department

Staffed by full-time civil service employees, the **real estate department** answers correspondence, sends out application forms, arranges for examinations, collects fees, issues licenses, approves subdivision reports, and so forth. Staff members are also available for the investigation of alleged malpractices and for audits of broker trust fund accounts. The department produces a periodic newsletter, which is available on the GREC website at www.grec.state.ga.us, to keep licensees informed about changes in real estate law and rules. In short, it is the real estate department with which licensees have the most contact, but it is the commission, the commissioner, and the legislature that set license requirements and tell licensees what they may and may not do in real estate transactions.

real estate department: civil service employees who handle paperwork, arrange for examinations, collect fees, and issue licenses

LICENSE SUSPENSION AND REVOCATION

The most important control mechanism a state has over its real estate salespeople and brokers is that it can *suspend* (temporarily make ineffective) or *revoke* (recall and make void) a real estate license. It is unlawful for a person without a real estate license to engage in real estate activities for the purpose of earning a commission or fee. Unless an agent has a valid license, a court of law will not uphold an agent's claim for a commission from a client. Reasons for **license suspension** and **license revocation** include any violation of the state's real estate act, misrepresentation or false promises, undisclosed dual agency, commingling, and acting as an undisclosed principal. Licenses can also be revoked or suspended for false advertising, obtaining a license by fraud, negligence, incompetence, failure to supervise salespeople, failure to properly account for clients' funds, practicing law without a license, paying commissions to unlicensed persons, conviction of a felony or certain types of misdemeanors, dishonest conduct in general, and, in many states, failure to have a fixed termination date on an exclusive listing. When the real estate commissioner or department receives a complaint from someone who feels wronged by a licensee, the real estate department staff will conduct an investigation. Statements are received from witnesses. Title company records, public records, and the licensee's bank records are checked as necessary. The commissioner or director may call an informal conference and invite all parties involved to attend. If it appears that the complaint is serious enough and that a violation of the law has occurred, a formal hearing is held in the presence of the full commission. The licensee, the party bringing the complaint, and any necessary witnesses appear. Testimony is taken under oath, and a written record is made of the proceedings. If the commissioner or director decides to suspend or revoke the respondent's license, the respondent has the right of appeal to the courts.

license suspension: to temporarily make a license ineffective

license revocation: to recall and make void a license

SECURITIES LICENSE

Be aware that there may be times when a real estate salesperson or broker also needs a securities license. This occurs when the property being sold is an investment contract in real estate rather than real estate itself. This investment contract is classified as a *security*. Examples of securities include real estate limited partnerships, rental pools where condominium owners put their units into a pool for a percentage of the pool's income, and some timeshares. Securities licenses are issued by the Financial Industry Regulatory Authority (FINRA, which replaced the National Association of Securities Dealers), based on successful completion of its examination. Legal counsel is advised if there is the possibility that you may be selling securities. Counsel will also advise on state and federal laws requiring the registration of real estate securities before they are sold.

AFFILIATING WITH A BROKER

If you plan to enter real estate sales, selecting a broker to work for is one of the most important decisions you must make. The best way to approach it is to carefully consider what you have to offer the real estate business and what you expect in return. And look at it in that order. It is easy to become captivated by the big commission income you visualize coming your way. But if that is your only perspective, you will meet with disappointment. The reason people will pay you money is to receive some product or service in return. Your clients are not concerned with your income goal; it is only incidental to their goals. If you help them reach their goals, you will reach yours. Before applying for a real estate license, ask yourself whether the working hours and conditions of a real estate agent are suitable to you. Specifically, are you prepared to work on a commission-only basis? Evenings and weekends? On your own? With people you've never met before? If you can comfortably answer "yes" to these questions, then start looking for a broker to sponsor you. (Salesperson license educational requirements can be completed and the examination taken without broker sponsorship, but a salesperson must have a broker to work for before the actual license is issued.)

Training

Your next step is to look for those features and qualities in a broker that will complement, enhance, and encourage your personal development in real estate. If you are new to the industry, training and education will most likely be at the top of your list. Therefore, in looking for a broker, you will want to find one that will offer you some on-the-job training. (What you have learned to date from books, classes, and license examination preparation will be helpful, but you will need additional specific training.) Real estate franchise operations and large brokerage offices usually offer extensive training. In smaller offices, the broker in charge is usually responsible for seeing that newcomers receive training. An office that offers no training to a newcomer should be avoided.

Compensation

Another decision-making factor high on your list will be compensation. Very few offices provide a newcomer with a guaranteed minimum wage or even a draw against future commissions. Most brokers feel that one must produce to be paid, and the hungrier the salesperson, the quicker the production. A broker who pays salespersons regardless of sales produced simply must siphon the money from those who are producing. The old saying "There's no such thing as a free lunch" applies to sales commissions. Compensation for salespeople is usually a percentage of the commissions they earn for the broker. How much each receives is open to negotiation between the broker and each salesperson working for that broker. A broker who provides office space, extensive secretarial help, a large advertising budget, a mailing program, and generous long-distance telephone privileges might take 40% to 50% of each incoming commission dollar for office overhead. A broker who provides fewer services might take 25% or 30%. Salespeople with proven sales records can usually reduce the portion of each commission dollar that must go to the broker. This is because the broker knows that with an outstanding sales performer, a high volume of sales will offset a smaller percentage for overhead. Conversely, a new and untried salesperson, or one with a mediocre sales record, may have to give up a larger portion of each dollar for the broker's overhead. When one brokerage agency lists a property and another locates the buyer, the commission is split according to any agreement the two brokers wish to make. The most common arrangement is a 50-50 split. After splitting, each broker pays a portion of the money received to the salesperson involved in accordance with the brokers' commission agreement. While investigating commission arrangements, one should also inquire about incentive and bonus plans, automobile expense reimbursement, health insurance, life insurance, errors and omission insurance, and retirement plans. An alternative commission arrangement is the *100% commission*, wherein the salesperson does not share the commission with the broker. Instead, the salesperson is charged a fee for office space, advertising, telephone, multiple listing, and any other expenses the broker incurs on behalf of the salesperson. Generally speaking, 100% arrangements are more popular with proven performers than with newcomers.

Broker Support

Broker support will have an impact on success. Specifically: Does each salesperson have a desk to work from? Are office facilities efficient and modern? Does the broker provide secretarial services? What is the broker's advertising policy, and who pays for ads? Who pays for signs, business cards, franchise fees, and realty board dues? Does the broker have sources of financing for clients? Does the broker allow the salespeople to invest in real estate? Does the broker have a good reputation in the community?

Finding a Broker

Many licensees associate with a particular broker as a result of friendship or word-of-mouth information. However, there are other ways to find a suitable position. An excellent way to start your search is to decide what geographical area you want to work in. If you choose the same community or neighborhood in which you live, you will already possess a valuable sense and feel for that area.

Having selected a geographical area, you should look in the Sunday newspaper real estate advertisements section, in the yellow pages, and on websites for names of brokers. Hold interviews with several brokers, and, as you do, remember that you are interviewing them just as intensively as they are interviewing you. At your visits with brokers, be particularly alert to your feelings. Intuition can be as valuable a guide to a sound working relationship as a list of questions and answers regarding the job. As you narrow your choices, revisit the offices of brokers who particularly impressed you. Talk with some of the salespeople who have worked or are working there. They can be valuable sources of information. Be wary of individuals who are extreme in their opinions; rely instead on the consensus opinion. Locate clients who have used the firm's services and ask them their opinions of the firm. You might also talk to local appraisers, lenders, and escrow agents for candid opinions. If you do all this advance work, the benefits to you will be greater enjoyment of your work, more money in your pocket, and less likelihood of wanting to quit or move to another office.

Employment Contract

Having selected a broker with whom to associate, your next step is to make an employment contract. An *employment contract* formalizes the working arrangement between the broker and salespersons. This agreement must be in writing and must stipulate how the agent will be compensated while s/he is with the broker and after leaving the broker for transactions that have been started but not yet completed. Not only is a written agreement required by Georgia law, but it also greatly reduces the potential for future controversy and litigation. The employment contract will typically cover such matters as compensation (how much and under what circumstances), training (how often and if required), hours of work (including assigned office hours and open houses), company identification (distinctive articles of clothing and name tags), fees and dues (license and realty board), expenses (automobile, advertising, telephone), fringe benefits (health and life insurance, pension, and profit-sharing plans), withholding (income taxes and Social Security), territory (assigned area of the community), termination of employment (quitting and firing), and general office policies and procedures (office manual).

INDEPENDENT CONTRACTOR STATUS

Is the real estate sales associate an employee of the broker or an independent contractor? The answer is both. On one hand, the sales associate acts like an employee because the associate works for the broker, usually at the broker's place of business; prepares listings and sales documents on forms specified by the broker; and, upon closing, receives payment from the broker. On the other hand, the sales associate acts like an **independent contractor** because the associate is typically paid only if the associate brings about a sale that produces a commission. An important distinction between the two is whether the broker must withhold income taxes and Social Security from the associate's commission checks. If the sales associate is considered by the Internal Revenue Service (IRS) to be an employee for tax purposes, the broker must withhold. If classed as an independent contractor for tax purposes, the sales associate is responsible for the income taxes and Social Security. The IRS prefers employee status because it is easier to collect taxes from an employer than from an employee. The IRS will treat real estate sales associates as independent contractors if they meet all of the following requirements. First, the associate must be a licensed real estate agent. Second, a large percentage (90%) of the associate's payment

independent contractor: one who contracts to do work according to his/her own methods and is responsible to employer only for the results of that work

for services as a real estate agent must be directly related to sales, not to hours worked. Third, a written agreement must exist between the associate and the broker stating that the associate will be treated as an independent contractor for tax purposes. If an agent and the sponsoring broker do not comply with this statute, they run the risk of losing their independent contractor status. If this occurs, the sponsoring broker becomes subject to the same filing requirements as any other employer in the normal course of business. These are the highlights of the issue. If you plan to work for a broker, you may find it valuable to have this matter, as well as your entire employment contract, reviewed by an attorney before you sign it.

FRANCHISED OFFICES

Prior to the early 1970s, real estate brokerage was a small business industry. Most brokerages were one-office firms. A large brokerage was one having four or five offices and selling 200 properties a year. Then real estate franchise organizations entered the real estate business in a big way. *Franchisers*, such as Century 21, Prudential, RE/MAX, and ERA, offered brokerage firms national identification, large-scale advertising, sales staff training programs, management advice, customer referrals, financing help for buyers, and guaranteed sales plans. In return, the brokerage firm (the franchisee) paid a fee of from 3% to 8% of gross commission income. The idea became popular, and by the mid-1990s, approximately half of the real estate licensees affiliated with the National Association of REALTORS® were working in franchised offices, and their numbers have continued to grow. Meanwhile, the number of franchisers grew to over 60, and new franchisers continue to be established, offering attractive franchise opportunities to small firms.

Statistics show that franchising appeals mostly to firms with 10 to 50 sales associates. Larger firms are more capable of providing the advantages of a franchise for themselves. Smaller firms tend to occupy market niches and often consist of one or two licensees who do not bring in additional sales associates. For a newly licensed salesperson wishing to affiliate with a firm, a franchised firm offers immediate public recognition, extensive training opportunities, established office routines, regular sales meetings, and access to a nationwide referral system. Franchise affiliation is not magic, however; success still depends on the individual to make sales calls, value property, get listings, advertise, show property, qualify, negotiate, and close transactions.

National Real Estate Firms

During the late 1970s, a large real estate firm in California—Coldwell Banker—began an expansion program by purchasing multibranch real estate firms in other states. Today, a number of national firms have offices across the United States. Among them are Cushman & Wakefield; RE/MAX; Long & Foster; Marcus & Millichap; GMAC (Ally Financial); Weichert, Realtors; and Prudential Rubloff Inc. For a newcomer, affiliating with a national or regional real estate firm offers benefits like those of a franchised firm (recognition, training, routines, etc.). The main difference is in who owns the firm. A franchised firm will be locally owned and managed (i.e., an independent firm). Regional and national firms are locally managed, but the sales associate will only occasionally, if ever, meet the owner(s).

PROFESSIONAL REAL ESTATE ASSOCIATIONS

Even before laws required real estate agents to have licenses, there were professional real estate organizations. These real estate boards joined agents together within a city or county on a voluntary basis. The push to organize came from real estate people who saw the need for some sort of controlling organization that could supervise the activities of individual agents and elevate the profession's status in the public's mind. Next came the gradual grouping of local boards into state associations, and, finally, in 1908, the National Association of Real Estate Brokers (NAREB) was formed. In 1914, NAREB developed a model license law that became the basis for real estate license laws in many states.

National Association of REALTORS®

Today, the local boards are still the fundamental units of the National Association of REALTORS® (NAR). Local board membership is open to anyone holding a real estate license. Called boards of REALTORS®, real estate boards, realty boards, or Associations of REALTORS®, they promote fair dealing among their members and with the public, and they protect members from dishonest and irresponsible licensees. They also promote legislation that protects property rights, offer short seminars to keep members up to date with current laws and practices, and, in general, do whatever is necessary to build the dignity, stability, and professionalization of the industry. Local boards often operate the local multiple listing service, although in some communities, it is a privately owned and operated business. State associations are composed of the members of local boards plus sales associates and brokers who live in areas where no local board exists. The purposes of the state associations are to unite members statewide, to encourage legislation that benefits and protects the real estate industry and safeguards the public in real estate transactions, and to promote economic growth and development in the state. State associations also hold conventions to educate members and foster contacts among them.

REALTOR®

NAR is made up of local boards and state associations in the United States. The term **REALTOR**® is a registered trade name that belongs to NAR. REALTOR® is not synonymous with real estate agent. It is reserved for the exclusive use of members of the National Association of REALTORS® who, as part of their membership, pledge themselves to abide by the association's code of ethics. The term *REALTOR*® may not be used by nonmembers, and in some states, the unauthorized use of the term is a violation of real estate law. Before 1974, the use of the term REALTOR® was primarily reserved for **principal brokers**. Then, by a national membership vote, the decision was made to create an additional membership class, the *REALTOR-ASSOCIATE*®, for salespeople and broker licensees working for members.

REALTOR®: a registered trademark owned by the National Association of REALTORS® for use by its members

principal brokers: the brokers in charge of real estate offices

Code of Ethics

One of the most important features of the National Association of REALTORS® is its *code of ethics*. First adopted in 1913, the code of ethics has been revised numerous times and now contains 17 articles that pertain to REALTORS® in relation to clients, to other real estate agents, and to the public as a whole. The full code is reproduced in Appendix E. Although a complete review of each article is beyond the scope of this chapter, it can be seen that some articles parallel existing laws. For example, Article 10 speaks against racial discrimination, and Article 2 speaks for full disclosure. However, the bulk of the code addresses the aspirations and obligations of a REALTOR® that may be beyond the written law. In other words, to be recognized as a REALTOR®, one must not only comply with the letter of the law, but also observe the ethical standards by which the industry operates. In some states, ethical standards such as those in the NAR code of ethics have been made into law. Called *canons* or *standards of conduct*, their intent is to promote ethical practices by all real estate licensees, not just by those who join the National Association of REALTORS®. Additionally, the National Association of REALTORS® publishes the *Standards of Practice*. These interpret various articles in the code of ethics.

The National Association of REALTORS® reserves exclusively unto itself the right to officially comment on and interpret the code and particular provisions thereof. For the National Association's official interpretations of the code, see "Interpretations of the Code of Ethics; National Association of REALTORS®" at www.Realtor.org.

In addition to its emphasis on real estate brokerage, the National Association of REALTORS® also contains a number of specialized professional groups within itself. These include the REALTORS® Land Institute, the Institute of Real Estate Management, the Society of Industrial and Office REALTORS®, Counselors of

Real Estate, and the Women's Council of REALTORS®. Membership is open to REALTORS® interested in these specialties.

Realtist

The National Association of Real Estate Brokers (NAREB) is a national trade association representing real estate professionals of color actively engaged in the industry. Founded in 1947, its 5,000 members use the trade name **realtist**. The organization extends through 14 regions across the country, with more than 60 active local boards. NAREB education and certification programs include the Real Estate Management Brokers Institute, the National Society of Real Estate Appraisers, and the United Developers Council. The organization's purposes are to promote high standards of service and conduct and to protect the public against unethical, improper, or fraudulent real estate practices.

realtist: trade name for a member of the National Association of Real Estate Brokers (NAREB)

GRI Designation

To help encourage and recognize professionalism in the real estate industry, state boards of REALTORS® sponsor education courses leading to the Graduate, *REALTOR® Institute (GRI)* designation. Course offerings typically include real estate law, finance, appraisal, investments, office management, and salesmanship. Upon completion of the prescribed curriculum, the designation Graduate, REALTOR® Institute is awarded.

Review Questions

Answers to these questions can be found in Appendix D at the end of this book.

1. Which of the following can independently conduct real estate business on the behalf of others for compensation?
   A. a licensed practicing attorney
   B. a licensed real estate salesperson
   C. a licensed real estate associate broker
   D. a licensed real estate broker

2. People who sell real estate for others:
   A. must be licensed in order to collect compensation
   B. need not be licensed if no more than $1,000 in compensation is involved
   C. need not be licensed if they are involved in no more than one transaction per year
   D. have no obligation to become licensed, but may do so voluntarily

3. Which of the following could be licensed as a real estate broker?
   A. a corporation
   B. a partnership
   C. an actual person
   D. all of the above

4. Which of the following is NOT a real estate license category?
   A. salesperson
   B. broker
   C. attorney-in-fact
   D. associate broker

5. A real estate listing is a contract between:
   A. the owner and the listing broker
   B. the owner, the broker, and the listing salesperson
   C. the owner and the listing salesperson
   D. the broker and the listing salesperson

6. The ultimate responsibility for a mistake in a document prepared by a real estate salesperson rests:
   A. equally on the salesperson and the employing broker
   B. on the employing broker
   C. with the lead associate broker
   D. with the salesperson

7. Continuing education requirements exist for the purpose of:
   A. ensuring that only competent license applicants are granted real estate licenses
   B. requiring licensees to stay up to date in their field
   C. making sure the public is properly educated
   D. creating jobs for educators

8. Before being granted an original salesperson's license, an applicant must:
   A. pass the examination for salesperson licensure
   B. name the broker with whom the applicant will be associated
   C. complete any state-mandated education requirements
   D. do all of the above

9. Brokers who wish to operate outside their home state will usually be required to file a notice of consent with the secretary of state in:
   A. their home state
   B. each state in which they wish to operate
   C. Washington, D.C.
   D. any state

10. Real estate brokers may operate a business as a sole proprietorship under:
    A. their own name only
    B. a fictitious name only
    C. a trade name
    D. a corporate charter

NATURE AND DESCRIPTION OF REAL ESTATE

CHAPTER 2

KEY TERMS

acre
appurtenance
fixture
improvement
legal description
littoral rights

meridians
metes and bounds
monuments
personal property
real property
recorded plat

rectangular survey system
riparian right
section
township

OBJECTIVES

After successful completion of this chapter, you should be able to:

1. define real estate, land, improvements, fixtures, and water rights;
2. apply the tests of a fixture;
3. define water table, riparian rights, littoral rights, and other such terms dealing with water rights;
4. describe land using the metes and bounds method, the rectangular survey system, or a recorded plat;
5. explain the use of assessor's parcel numbers; and
6. describe the land in terms of vertical measurements.

OVERVIEW

In this chapter, you will be introduced to the terminology used to define and describe real estate. The term *real estate* is defined, and rights in land are also described. Other topics include fixtures, appurtenances, water rights, and land descriptions. The metes and bounds description of land and the rectangular survey system of describing land are covered, as well as other land descriptive survey systems. These

and other defined terms within this chapter should be studied thoroughly to enhance your understanding of material in subsequent chapters.

What is real estate? **Real estate**, or **real property**, is land and the improvements made to land, and the rights to use them. Let us begin this chapter by looking more closely at what is meant by land and improvements. In the next chapter we shall focus our attention on the various rights one may possess in land and improvements.

real property: land and improvements in a physical sense, as well as the rights to own or use them

LAND

Often, we think of land as only the surface of the earth. But it is substantially more than that. As shown in Figure 2-1, land starts at the center of the earth, passes through the earth's surface, and continues on into space. An understanding of this concept is important because, given a particular parcel of land, it is possible for one person to own the rights to use its surface (*surface rights*), another to own the rights to drill or dig below its surface (*subsurface rights*), and still another to own the rights to use the airspace above it (*air rights*).

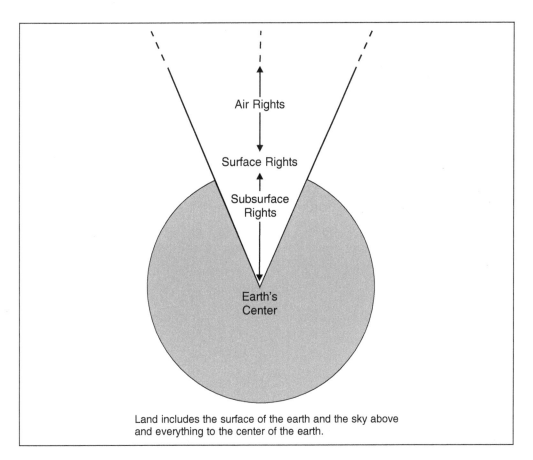

Land includes the surface of the earth and the sky above and everything to the center of the earth.

FIGURE 2-1 Land, from a real estate perspective
Source: © 2021 Mbition LLC

IMPROVEMENTS

Anything affixed to land with the intent of being permanent is considered to be part of the land and, therefore, real estate. Thus houses, schools, factories, barns, fences, roads, pipelines, and landscaping are real estate. As a group, these are referred to as **improvements** because they improve or develop land. Being able to identify what is real estate and what is not is important. For example, in conveying ownership to a house, the deed describes only the lot. Items that permanently become part of the land and pass with the ownership are known as appurtenances. An **appurtenance** could be defined as an improvement, right, or privilege that is part of the land and passes with the ownership. The word *appurtenance* comes from the word *appurtenant*, which means to "run with or belong to." It is not necessary to describe the dwelling unit itself, or the landscaping, driveways, sidewalks, wiring, or plumbing. They are all part of the lot being conveyed. Items that are not a part of the land, such as tables, chairs, beds, desks, automobiles, farm machinery, and the like, are classified as **personal property** or *personalty* (these items are alternatively known as *chattel*); if the right to use them is to be transferred to the buyer, the seller should sign a separate bill of sale in addition to the deed.

> **improvements:** any form of land development, such as buildings, roads, fences, and pipelines
>
> **appurtenance:** an improvement, right, or privilege that is part of the land and passes with the ownership
>
> **personal property:** a right or interest in things of a temporary or movable nature; anything not classified as real property; also known as personalty or chattel

PHYSICAL CHARACTERISTICS OF LAND

Land can be broken into two distinct categories: physical characteristics and economic characteristics. Physical characteristics are those that refer to the tangible makeup of the land. Let's explore these further.

Indestructible

Indestructible refers to the fact that land does not typically wear out over time. Although the improvements to the property must periodically be replaced, an owner would not expect to replace the land. If you have previously purchased real estate, you most likely considered the age of the building, carpet, heating and air conditioning systems, appliances, roof, and paint. In making a purchase decision, the consumer should consider when and at what cost these items must be replaced.

Immovable

Land cannot be moved from one location to another. You may have heard someone lament, "If I could only have this house on the lot I had in the Georgia mountains . . . ." Land is where it is. This is one of the reasons land (real estate) is such a popular security for debt. If a car were to be used as security, lenders could repossess on defaulting purchasers, but the purchaser could keep the car moving for a while. Not true with land.

Nonhomogeneous

No two parcels of real estate are the same, because each has a unique location. It has been said many times before: The three most important considerations in real estate investment are location, location, and location. While there may be a property that is similar in size, zoning, topography, and shape, each location is unique to itself.

ECONOMIC CHARACTERISTICS OF LAND

The second way to describe land is economic characteristics. The economic characteristics refer to items that affect the value of the land.

Situs

This refers to location preference. People will pay more to live in one area than they will to live in another. This decision may be induced by transportation, schools, convenience, or perceived benefit. Sometimes, having one address rather than another will affect the value. If people believe their children will receive a better education in one system versus another, they will pay a premium.

Improvability

This is sometimes referred to as modification. Improvability recognizes that changing a property can change the value, not only of the property in question, but also of surrounding areas. The classic example of this is Disney World in Florida. Walt Disney assembled much of the land that now is Disney World in the 1950s for less than $200 per acre. To a large extent, the land was swampy and worn-out farmland. It had no access to drinkable water or sewage waste facilities. Once all the land was developed, the area has obviously changed and benefited economically because of that parcel being modified. More local but less dramatic examples occur when a developer purchases land and builds a shopping mall, or the government builds a road providing access to an area that was previously difficult to reach.

Scarcity

The supply of land in relationship to the demand for land defines scarcity. There is an inverse relationship between supply and price. When supply is down, price is up; when supply is up, price is down. This assumes there is no change in demand. Scarcity of land can happen naturally (such as when all available land has been developed) or artificially (such as when government intervenes to reduce permission for development). Historically, there have been areas for which the government has issued moratoriums on building permits, sewer permits, or water meters to slow down development. This results in a scarcity of available building lots, thereby increasing the prices of those lots and slowing down growth (i.e., inflation).

Fixity (Investment Permanence)

Land is not typically a short-term investment, and takes a long time to pay for itself. When one purchases buildings, while there is risk, the buildings will typically produce rent, which will assist in paying the operating expenses and debt service on the property. Undeveloped land typically produces very little, if any, cash flow. Although investing in land can produce large future returns, the investor must have the ability to pay cash and/or make the payments until the property can be sold or developed.

FIXTURES

When an object that was once personal property becomes part of the real property, it is called a **fixture**. As a rule, a fixture is the property of the landowner, and when the land is conveyed to a new owner, it is automatically included with the land. The question of whether an item is a fixture also arises with regard to property taxes, mortgages, lease terminations, and hazard insurance policies. Specifically, real estate taxes are based on real property valuation. Real estate mortgages are secured by real property. Objects attached to a building by a tenant may become real property and, hence, belong to the building's owner. Hazard insurance policies treat real property differently from personal property.

While items such as carpet, built-in appliances, drywall, and kitchen cabinets clearly are real property, and items such as clothing, furniture, dishes, and electronic equipment are personal property, there are items that could fall into either category, depending on circumstances. Items in this third category could include a microwave oven, gas logs in a fireplace, a child's play set in the backyard, a hot tub on the deck, or a gas grill. There are tests that can be used to determine if the items are real or personal property. These tests can be remembered with the acronym MARIA.

Modification

Attachment

Relationship of the parties

Intentions of the annexing party

Agreement

Modification

This test refers to the alteration of the article for the building or the building for the article. For example, if an owner purchased a window air conditioning unit at an appliance store and simply placed it in a window, this unit would be treated as personal property. If the owner cut a hole in an exterior wall just large enough to accept the unit, installed the unit in the hole, and then neatly trimmed around the unit, it would be real property and would pass with the sale of the home. Another example would be a microwave oven that is installed in a cabinet that has been adapted to fit the microwave rather than the same unit sitting on a counter.

---

fixture: an object that has been attached to land physically so as to become real estate

Attachment

The second test, *attachment*, refers to how the object is affixed to the land. Ordinarily, when an object that was once personal property is attached to land by virtue of its being embedded in the land or affixed to the land by means of cement, nails, bolts, and so on, it becomes a fixture. When considering attachment, one must consider both physical attachment and legal attachment. For instance, concrete that has been poured to create a driveway, lumber that has been used to frame the building, and a garage door and garage door opening mechanism that have been bolted to the house all are physically attached and become fixtures.

A problem often is created with the idea of "legally attached" items. Examples would be the remote control device for the garage door opener, the keys to the house, or a framed, beveled glass mirror with a gold inlay installed in an ornate gold leaf frame (read into this "expensive") hanging above the pedestal sink in a powder room. Although these items are not physically installed, it could be argued that they are part of the property by their use. The door (which is real) can't be unlocked without the key, the garage door cannot be remotely operated (as it is designed to do) without the remote control, and people cannot groom themselves when using the restroom without the mirror. These items are constructively attached. When you see the word *constructive* used as an adjective in this context, think "for all intents and purposes." Constructive attachment means that, for all intents and purposes, the item has been attached to the building.

Relationship of the Parties

The third test in determining whether an item of personal property has become a fixture is to look at the *relationship of the parties*. For example, a supermarket moves into a rented building, then buys and bolts to the floor various *trade fixtures* (hereby defined as items that are purchased and installed by the tenant for use in a business) such as display shelves, meat and dairy coolers, frozen food counters, and checkout stands. When the supermarket later moves out, do these items, by virtue of their attachment, become the property of the building owner? Modern courts rule that tenant-purchased and installed trade fixtures do not become the property of the landlord. However, they must be removed before the expiration of the lease, and the tenant is responsible for repairing any damage caused by the installation or removal.

Intentions of the Annexing Party

Our fourth, and possibly weakest, test has to do with the intentions of the annexing party. When the owner installed the item, was it his/her intention to leave it and let ownership pass to the buyer, or was it his/her intention to remove the item before leaving? For example, a seller has a beautiful crystal chandelier in the dining room, which the buyer admires, but there is no discussion specifically about this chandelier. The day of closing, the purchaser comes by to do the final walk-through, and the seller is removing the light fixture. When questioned about this, the seller responds that it is a family heirloom and will be replaced with the original light fixture, which is far inferior in quality and value. The seller's position is that the action is proper since it was always his/her intention to remove and replace. You may now anticipate a dispute, in which the agent too often acquiesces and pays all or part of the cost of replacing with an appropriate chandelier. This scenario gets old, fast. Such a situation would be eliminated by our final test.

Agreement

The fifth, final, and most effective test is the *agreement* between the parties involved. For example, a seller can clarify in advance and in writing to the broker what is considered personal property, and thus will be removed, and what is not considered personal property, and thus will transfer to the buyer. Common items that can cause confusion are garage door openers, satellite dishes, remote controls, swimming pool equipment, keyless entry systems, and controls for burglar alarm systems. Many of these items can be uniquely adapted to the premises, but the seller considers them personal property, as they might be able to be recoded or utilized for another residence. Although a party might argue that many of these items are constructively attached, as previously discussed, the point is, don't put yourself into a position that you must argue.

Prior Liens Against Fixtures

In addition to the misunderstandings that often arise between buyer and seller in determining the intention of the parties regarding fixtures, there are also priorities given in the law that can create a lien on fixtures if that lien is timely and properly recorded. For instance, if one finances a new air conditioning unit from a vendor, the vendor has a right to file a lien on that item, which will become a fixture and will show up as a lien on the real estate in the real property records. Many homeowners are surprised when they have a lien from a department store on an item that they thought they put on their charge account, when, in fact, it was a lien created for a home improvement (air conditioners, roofs, gutters, or other major repairs that had been financed through a local department store).

Ownership of Plants, Trees, and Crops

Trees, cultivated perennial plants, and uncultivated vegetation of any sort are considered part of the land. For example, landscaping is included in the sale or rental of a house. If a tenant plants a tree or plant in the ground while renting, the tree or plant stays when the lease expires unless both landlord and tenant agree otherwise. Plants and trees in movable pots are personal property and are not generally included in a sale or lease. Annual cultivated crops are called *emblements*, and most courts of law regard them as personal property even though they are attached to the soil. For example, tenant farmers are entitled to the fruits of their labor even if the landlord terminates the lease partway through the growing season. When property with harvestable plants, trees, or crops is offered for sale or lease, it is good practice to make clear in any listing, sale, or lease agreement who will have the right to harvest the crop that season. This is particularly true of farm property, where the value of the crop can be quite substantial.

APPURTENANCES

The conveyance of land carries with it any appurtenances to the land. An *appurtenance* is a right or privilege or improvement that belongs to and passes with land but is not necessarily a part of the land. Examples of appurtenances are easements and rights-of-way (which will be discussed in Chapter 3), condominium parking stalls, and shares of stock in a mutual water company that services the land.

WATER RIGHTS

Water rights vary greatly across the country. Some have noted the "30-inch" rule. This concept divides the country from north to south between the eastern areas that receive more than 30 inches of annual rainfall and the western areas that receive less than 30 inches of annual rainfall (roughly paralleling Interstate Highway 35, from Texas to Minnesota). Eastern areas generally have an ample supply of water, so their water laws are largely the law of surface waters and are modeled after the English riparian system. Western areas regularly experience varying degrees of water shortages and drought conditions, resulting in water laws based on the concept that the state is the owner of the water (in fee or in trust for the public) and allowing a person to establish a state-permitted right to use the water by putting it to beneficial use.

The ownership of land that borders on a river or stream carries with it the right to use that water in common with the other landowners whose lands border the same watercourse. This is known as a **riparian right**. The landowner does not have absolute ownership of the water that flows past his land but may use it in a reasonable manner. In western states, riparian rights have been modified by the *doctrine of prior appropriation*: the first owner to divert water for personal use may continue to do so, even though it is not equitable to the other landowners along the watercourse. Some estates have a right to the use of property as a prior appropriation. Where land borders on a lake or sea, it is said to carry **littoral rights** rather than riparian rights. Littoral rights allow landowners to use and enjoy the water touching their land provided they do not alter the water's position by artificial means. A lakefront lot owner would be an example of this.

Ownership of land normally includes the right to drill for and remove water found below the surface. The first to use the water (even underground water) has a prior right to its use. This is called the *doctrine of capture*. Where water is not confined

riparian right: the right of a landowner whose land borders a river or stream to use and enjoy that water

littoral rights: right of landowners to use and enjoy a lake or sea touching their land

to a defined underground waterway, it is known as *percolating water*. In some states, landowners have the right, in conjunction with neighboring owners, to draw their share of percolating water. Other states subscribe to the doctrine of prior appropriation. With underground water, the term *water table* refers to the upper limit of percolating water below the earth's surface. It is also called the *groundwater level*. This may be only a few feet below the surface or hundreds of feet down.

LAND DESCRIPTIONS

There are six commonly used methods of describing the location of land, some of which may not be acceptable as a **legal description**:

1. metes and bounds
2. rectangular survey system
3. recorded plat
4. reference to documents other than maps
5. informal reference
6. assessor's parcel number

legal description: a method of identifying a property geographically exclusive of any other property on the face of the earth

Methods (1) through (4) are generally considered to be *legal descriptions*. That is, they sufficiently identify the land so that it cannot be confused with another tract. A legal description is defined as a method of identifying a property geographically exclusive of any other property on the face of the earth. Methods (5) and (6) are informal references. While commonly used, they are not sufficient for legally identifying the land. For instance, if a home is located on Pine, it could be Pine Street, Pine Avenue, Pine Lane, or Pine Court. They are often confused with each other when a person lives "on Pine." Finally, some houses have one address but are located on two lots; some single-family lots have two houses with different addresses; or tax assessors misidentify tracts (i.e., their employees identify tracts for tax purposes only and can make mistakes). This is why a proper legal description is so important. Let's look at each in detail.

Metes and Bounds

monuments: iron pipes, stones, trees, or other fixed points used in making a survey

Early land descriptions in America depended heavily on convenient natural or manmade objects called **monuments**. A stream might serve to mark one side of a parcel, an old oak tree to mark a corner, a road another side, a pile of rocks a second corner, a fence another side, and so forth. This survey method was handy, but it had two major drawbacks: There might not be a convenient corner or boundary marker where one was needed, and, over time, oak trees died, stone heaps were moved, streams and rivers changed course, stumps rotted, fences were removed, and unused roads became overgrown with vegetation. The following description, excerpted from the Hartford, Connecticut, Probate Court records for 1812, illustrates just how difficult it can be to try to locate a parcel's boundaries precisely using only convenient natural or manmade objects:

Commencing at a heap of stone about a stone's throw from a certain small clump of alders, near a brook running down off from a rather high part of said ridge; thence, by a straight line to a certain marked white birch tree, about two or three times as far from a jog in a fence going around a ledge nearby; thence by another straight line in a different direction, around said ledge, and the Great Swamp, so called; thence . . . to the "Horn," so called, and passing around the same as aforesaid, as far as the "Great Bend," so called, and . . . to a stake and stone not far off from the old Indian trail; thence, by another straight line . . . to the stump of the big hemlock tree where Philo Blake killed the bear; thence, to the corner begun at by two straight lines of about equal length, which are to be run by some skilled and competent surveyor, so as to include the area and acreage as herein before set forth.

The metes and bounds method of description is used in Georgia and is a common way to identify an irregularly shaped parcel of property. Regardless of how complex the shape may be, it can be described geometrically using this method.

Permanent Monuments

The drawbacks of the previous outmoded method of land description are resolved by setting a permanent, manmade *monument* at one corner of the parcel. This monument will typically be an iron pin or pipe, 1 to 2 inches in diameter, driven several feet into the ground. Sometimes concrete or stone monuments are used. To guard against the possibility that the monument might later be destroyed or removed, it is referenced by means of a connection line to a nearby permanent reference mark established by a government survey agency. Other parcels in the vicinity will also be referenced to the same permanent reference mark. The surveyor then describes the parcel in terms of distance and direction from that point. This is called **metes and bounds** surveying, which means distance (metes) and direction (bounds). From the monument, the surveyor runs the parcel's outside lines by compass and distance so as to take in the land area being described. Distances are measured in feet, usually to the nearest 1/10th to 1/100th of a foot. Direction is shown in degrees, minutes, and seconds. There are 360 degrees (°) in a circle, 60 minutes (') in each degree, and 60 seconds (") in each minute. The abbreviation 29°14'52" would be read as 29 degrees, 14 minutes, and 52 seconds.

Figure 2-2 illustrates a simple modern metes and bounds land description. Note that, at each corner, there is superimposed a coordinate system. This may help you better understand how the bounds are set from each point. Note in Figure 2-2 that, with a metes and bounds description, you start from a permanent reference mark and travel to the nearest corner of the property. This is where the parcel survey begins and is called the point of beginning. From this point in Figure 2-2, we travel clockwise along the parcel's perimeter, reaching the next corner by going in the direction 80 degrees east of south for a distance of 180 feet.

metes and bounds: a detailed method of land description that identifies a parcel by specifying its shape and boundaries

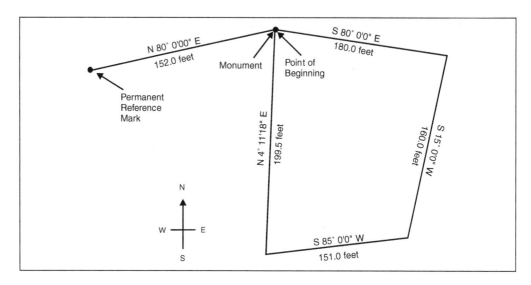

FIGURE 2-2 Describing land by metes and bounds
Source: © 2021 Mbition LLC

We then travel in a direction 15 degrees west of south for 160 feet, thence 85 degrees west of south for 151 feet, and thence 4 degrees, 11 minutes, and 18 seconds east of north for 199.5 feet back to the point of beginning. In mapping shorthand, this parcel would be described by first identifying the monument, then the county and state within which it lies, and "thence S80°0'0"E, 180.0'; thence S15°0'0"W, 160.0'; thence S85°0'0"W, 151.0'; thence N4°11'18"E, 199.5' back to the p.o.b."

Although one can successfully describe a parcel by traveling around it either clockwise or counterclockwise, it is customary to travel clockwise. The job of taking a written land description (such as the one just described) and locating it on the ground is done by a two-person survey team. The survey team drives a wooden or metal stake into the ground at each corner of the parcel. If a corner lies on a sidewalk, a nail through a brass disc about 3 to 4 inches wide is used. (Look closely for these the next time you are out walking. At construction sites, you will see that corner stakes often have colored streamers on them.) The basic equipment of a survey team includes a compass, a transit, a sight pole or rod, a steel tape, and a computation book. A transit consists of a very accurate compass plus a telescope with crosshairs that can be rotated horizontally and vertically. It will measure angles accurately to one second of a degree. The sight pole is about 8 feet high and held by the rodman, the second member of the survey team. The surveyor aligns marks on the sight pole with the crosshairs in the telescope. A 100-foot steel tape, made of a special alloy that resists expansion on hot days, is used to measure distances. For longer distances, and especially distances across water, canyons, heavy brush, and so on, surveyors use laser beam equipment. The beam is aimed at a mirror on the sight pole, bounced back, and electronically converted to a digital readout that shows the distance to the pole. Handheld computers now perform many of the angle and distance computations necessary to a survey.

Compass Directions

The compass in Figure 2-3A shows how the direction of travel along each side of the parcel in Figure 2-2 is determined. Note that the same line can be labeled two ways, depending on which direction you are traveling. To illustrate, look at the line from P to Q. If you are traveling toward P on the line, you are going N45°W. But if you are traveling toward point Q on the line, you are going S45°E. Curved boundary lines are produced by using arcs of a circle. The length of the arc is labeled L or A; the radius of the circle producing the arc is labeled R. The symbol Δ (delta) indicates the angle used to produce the arc (see Figure 2-3B). Where an arc connects to a straight boundary or another arc, the connection is indicated by a small circle or by a dot, as shown in Figure 2-3B.

Benchmarks are commonly used as permanent reference marks. A *benchmark* is a fixed mark of known location and elevation. It may be as simple as an iron post or as elaborate as an engraved 3-inch brass disc set into concrete. The mark is usually set in place by a government survey team from the U.S. Geological Survey (USGS) or the National Geodetic Survey (formerly the U.S. Coast & Geodetic Survey). Benchmarks are referenced to each other by distance and direction. The advantages of this type of reference point (compared to stumps, trees, rocks, and the like) are permanence and accuracy to within a fraction of an inch. Additionally, even though it is possible to destroy a reference point or monument, it can be replaced in its exact

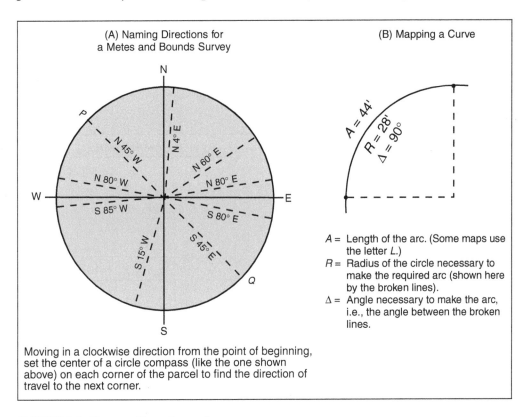

FIGURE 2-3 Metes and bounds mapping
Source: © 2021 Mbition LLC

former position because the location of each is related to other reference points. In states using the rectangular survey system or a grid system (discussed shortly), a section corner or a grid intersection is often used as a permanent reference mark. As a convenience to surveyors, it will be physically marked with an iron post or a brass disc set in concrete. With improvements in the ability of surveyors to accurately pinpoint the corners of land, and with land always changing due to the actions of wind and water, it is not uncommon that the measurements as stated in the deed will not be the same as those measured by a surveyor. In these instances, the surveyed measurement will typically control. So if a distance stated in the legal description is 300 feet from the road to the center of the creek, and a surveyor measures the same distance as 308 feet, the 308-foot measurement will supersede.

Rectangular Survey System

rectangular survey system: also known as the government survey or U.S. public land survey, describes land based on longitude and latitude

meridians: imaginary lines running north and south, used as references in mapping land

The **rectangular survey system** was authorized by Congress in 1785. It was designed to provide a faster and simpler method than metes and bounds for describing land in newly annexed territories and states. Rather than using available physical monuments, the rectangular survey system, also known as the *government survey* or *U.S. public land survey*, is based on imaginary lines. These lines are the east-west latitude lines and the north-south longitude lines that encircle the earth, as shown in Figure 2-4. A helpful way to remember this is that longitude lines (**meridians**) run the long way around the earth.

While this system is not used in Georgia, it is prudent and beneficial to a student to have a basic awareness of this system as two-thirds of the exam for a real estate sales license is generic and national in scope. A brief study of this system

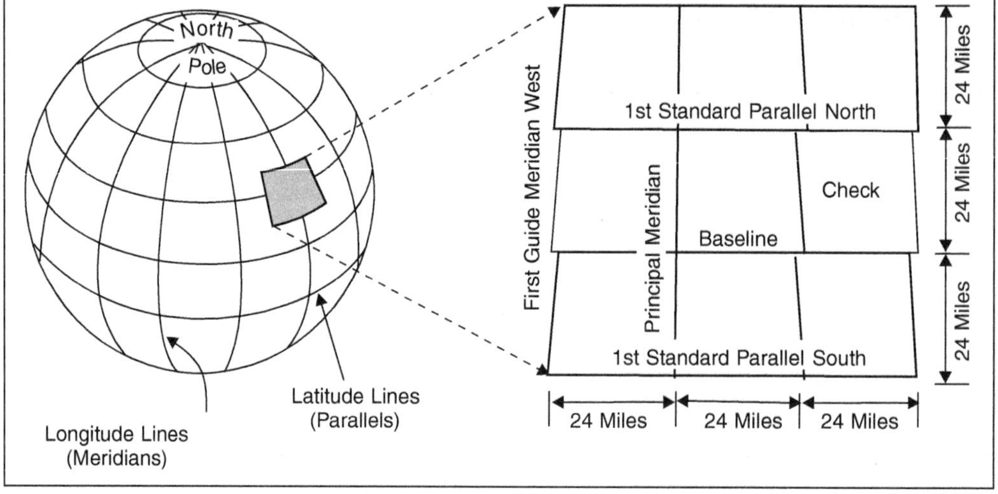

FIGURE 2-4 Select latitude and longitude lines serve as baselines and meridians
Source: © 2021 Mbition LLC

also introduces a discussion of other information, such as the number of square feet in an acre, the number of linear feet in a mile, and the number of acres in a square mile, which may be useful later. Georgia, being one of the original 13 colonies, developed its own form of mass land description before the rectangular survey system was invented. While similar in results, it is unique. The Georgia system uses districts and land lots instead of townships and sections. The state is further divided into 159 counties, and legal descriptions from there are commonly the metes and bounds or reference to a recorded plat.

Certain longitude lines were selected as *principal meridians*. For each of these, an intercepting latitude line was selected as a baseline. Every 24 miles north and south of a baseline, *correction lines* or *standard parallels* were established. Every 24 miles east and west of a principal meridian, guide meridians were established to run from one standard parallel to the next. These are needed because the earth is a sphere, not a flat surface. As one travels north in the United States, longitude (meridian) lines come closer together—that is, they converge. Figure 2-4 shows how guide meridians and correction lines adjust for this problem. Each 24-by-24-mile area created by the guide meridians and correction lines is called a *check* or *quadrangle*. There are 36 principal meridians and their intersecting baselines in the U.S. public land survey system. Figure 2-5 shows the states in which this system is used and the land area for which each principal meridian and baseline

FIGURE 2-5 The public land survey system of the United States
Source: © 2021 Mbition LLC

act as a reference. For example, the sixth principal meridian is the reference point for land surveys in Kansas, Nebraska, and portions of Colorado, Wyoming, and South Dakota. In addition to the U.S. public land survey system, a portion of western Kentucky was surveyed into townships by a special state survey. Also, the state of Ohio contains eight public land surveys that are rectangular in design but use state boundaries and major rivers rather than latitude and longitude as reference lines.

Range

Figure 2-6 shows how land is referenced to a principal meridian and a baseline. Every six miles east and west of each principal meridian, parallel imaginary lines are drawn. The resulting 6-mile-wide columns are called ranges and are numbered consecutively east and west of the principal meridian. For example, the first range west is called Range 1 West and abbreviated R1W; the next range west is R2W, and so forth. The fourth range east is R4E.

Township

Every six miles north and south of a baseline, township lines are drawn. They intersect with the range lines and produce 6-by-6-mile imaginary squares called **townships** (not to be confused with the word *township*, as applied to political subdivisions). Each tier or row of townships thus created is numbered with respect to the

township: a 6-mile square made up of 36 square miles or sections

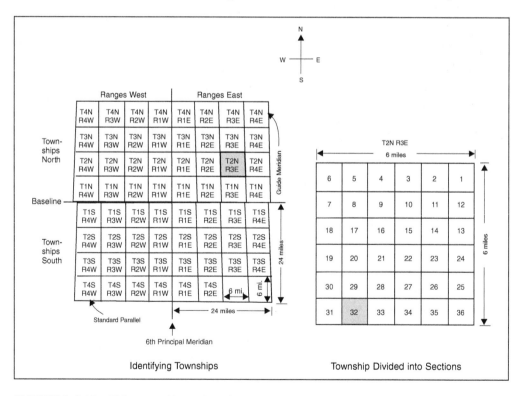

FIGURE 2-6 Identifying townships and sections
Source: © 2021 Mbition LLC

baseline. Townships lying in the first tier north of a baseline all carry the designation Township 1 North, abbreviated T1N. Townships lying in the first tier south of the baseline are all designated T1S, and in the second tier south, T2S. By adding a range reference, an individual township can be identified. Thus, T2S, R2W would identify the township lying in the second tier south of the baseline and the second range west of the principal meridian. T14N, R52W would be a township 14 tiers north of the baseline and 52 ranges west of the principal meridian.

Section

Each 36-square-mile township is divided into 36 units of 1 square mile each called **sections**. When one flies over farming areas, particularly in the Midwest, the checkerboard pattern of farms and roads that follow section boundaries can be seen. Sections are numbered 1 through 36, starting in the upper-right corner of the township. With this numbering system, any two sections with consecutive numbers share a common boundary. The section numbering system is illustrated in the right half of Figure 2-6 where the shaded section is described as Section 32, T2N, R3E, 6th Principal Meridian.

section: 1 square mile (A township is made up of 36 sections.)

Acre

Each square-mile section contains 640 acres, and each **acre** contains 43,560 square feet. Any parcel of land smaller than a full 640-acre section is identified by its position in the section. This is done by dividing the section into quarters and halves, as shown in Figure 2-7. For example, the shaded Parcel A is described as the NW1/4 of the SW1/4 of Section 32, T2N, R3E, 6th P.M. Additionally, it is customary to name the county and state in which the land lies. How much land does the NW1/4 of the SW1/4 of a section contain? A section contains 640 acres; therefore, a *quarter-section* contains 160 acres. Dividing a quarter-section again into quarters results in four 40-acre parcels. Thus, the northwest quarter of the southwest quarter contains 40 acres. The rectangular survey system is not limited to parcels of 40 or more acres. To demonstrate this point, the SE1/4 of Section 32 is exploded in the right half of Figure 2-7. Parcel B is described as the SE1/4 of the SE1/4 of the SE1/4 of the SE1/4 of Section 32 and contains 2½ acres. Parcel C is described as the west 15 acres of the NW1/4 of the SE1/4 of Section 32. Parcel D would be described in metes and bounds using the northeast corner of the SE1/4 of Section 32 as the starting point. When locating or sketching a rectangular survey on paper, many people find it helpful to start at the end of the description and work to the beginning; that is, work backwards. Try it.

acre: 43,560 square feet

Not all sections contain exactly 640 acres. Some are smaller because the earth's longitude lines converge toward the North Pole. Also, a section may be larger or smaller than 640 acres due to historical accommodations or survey errors dating back a hundred years or more. For the same reason, not all townships contain exactly 36 square miles. Between 1785 and 1910, the U.S. government paid

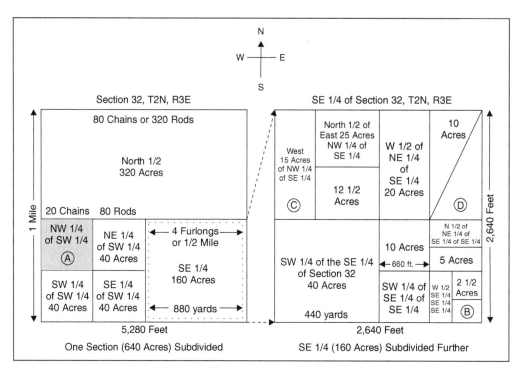

FIGURE 2-7 Subdividing a section
Source: © 2021 Mbition LLC

independent surveyors by the mile. The job was often accomplished by tying a rag to one spoke of the wheel of a buckboard wagon. A team of horses was hitched to the wagon and the surveyor, compass in hand, headed out across the prairie. Distance was measured by counting the number of wheel turns and multiplying by the circumference of the wheel. Today, large area surveys are made with the aid of aerial photographs, sophisticated electronic equipment, and earth satellites. In terms of surface area, more land in the United States is described by the rectangular survey system than by any other survey method.

Recorded Plat

When a tract of land is ready for subdividing into lots for homes and businesses, reference by **recorded plat** provides the simplest and most convenient method of land description. A plat is a map that shows the location and boundaries of individual properties. Also known as the *lot-block-tract system, recorded map*, or *recorded survey*, this method of land description is based on the filing of a surveyor's plat in the public recorder's office of the county where the land is located.

Figure 2-8 shows a plat. Notice that a metes and bounds survey has been made and a map prepared to show in detail the boundaries of each parcel of land. Each parcel is then assigned a lot number. Each block in the tract is given a block number, and the tract itself is given a name or number. A plat showing all the blocks in the tract is delivered to the county recorder's office, where it is placed in

recorded plat: a subdivision map filed in the county recorder's office that shows the location and boundaries of individual parcels of land

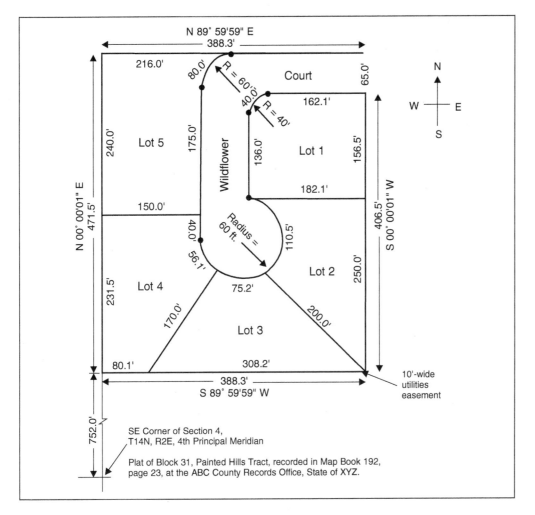

FIGURE 2-8 Land description by recorded plat
Source: © 2021 Mbition LLC

map books or *survey books*, along with plats of other subdivisions in the county. Each plat is given a book and page reference number, and all map books are available for public inspection. From that point on, it is no longer necessary to give a lengthy metes and bounds description to describe a parcel. Instead, one need only provide the lot and block number, tract name, map book reference, county, and state. To find the location and dimensions of a recorded lot, one simply looks in the map book at the county recorder's office.

Note that the plat in Figure 2-8 combines both of the land descriptions just discussed. The boundaries of the numbered lots are in metes and bounds. These, in turn, are referenced to a section corner in the rectangular survey system. In Georgia, instead of referencing the rectangular survey system, the district, land lot, and county would be stated.

Reference to Documents Other Than Maps

Land can also be described by referring to another publicly recorded document, such as a deed or a mortgage that contains a full legal description of the parcel in question. For example, suppose that several years ago, Baker received a deed from Adams that contained a long and complicated metes and bounds description. Baker recorded the deed in the public records office, where a photocopy was placed in Book 1089, page 456. If Baker later wants to deed the same land to Cooper, Baker can describe the parcel in his deed to Cooper by saying, "All the land described in the deed from Adams to Baker recorded in Book 1089, page 456, county of ABC, state of XYZ, at the public recorder's office for said county and state." Since these books are open to the public, Cooper (or anyone else) could go to Book 1089, page 456, and find a detailed description of the parcel's boundaries. The key test of a land description is: "Can another person, reading what I have written or drawn, understand my description and go out and locate the boundaries of the parcel?"

Informal Reference: Street Numbers and Common Names

Street numbers and place names are informal references: the house located at 7216 Maple Street; the apartment identified as Apartment 101, 875 First Street; the office identified as Suite 222, 3570 Oakview Boulevard; or the ranch known as the Rocking K Ranch—in each case followed by the city (or county) and state where it is located. The advantage of an informal reference is that it is easily understood. The disadvantage from a real estate standpoint is that it is not a precise method of land description. A street number or place name does not provide the boundaries of the land at that location, and these numbers and names change over the years. Consequently, in real estate, the use of informal references is limited to situations in which convenience is more important than precision. Thus, in a rental contract, Apartment 101, 875 First Street, city and state, may be sufficient for a tenant to find the apartment unit. However, if you were buying the apartment building, you would want a more precise land description. Please note, however, that according to Georgia License Law (which governs real estate licensees), most documents created with the assistance of a licensee, including leases, must include a sufficient legal description.

Assessor's Parcel Number

In many counties in the United States, the tax assessor assigns an *assessor's parcel number* to each parcel of land in the county. The primary purpose is to aid in the assessment of property for tax collection purposes. These parcel numbers are public information, and real estate brokers, appraisers, and investors can and do use them extensively to assist in identifying real properties. A commonly used system is to divide the county into map books. Each book is given a number and covers a given portion of the county. On every page of the map book are parcel maps, each with its own number. For subdivided lots, these maps are based on the plats submitted by the subdivider to the county records office when the subdivision was made. For unsubdivided land, the assessor's office prepares its own maps. Each parcel of land on the map is assigned a parcel number by the assessor. The assessor's parcel number may or may not be the same as the lot number assigned by the subdivider. To reduce confusion, the assessor's parcel number is either circled or underlined. Figure 2-9 shows a page out of an assessor's map book. The assessor also produces an assessment roll that lists every parcel in the county by its assessor's parcel number. Stored and printed by computer now, this roll shows the current owner's name and address and the assessed value of the land and buildings.

The assessor's maps are open to viewing by the public at the assessor's office. In many counties, private firms reproduce the maps and the accompanying list of property owners and make them available to real estate brokers, appraisers, and lenders for a fee. Before we leave the topic of assessor's maps, a word of caution is in order. These maps should not be relied on as the final authority for the legal description of a parcel. That can come only from a title search that includes looking at the current deed to the property and the recorded copy of the subdivider's plat. Note also that an assessor's parcel number is never used as a legal description in a deed.

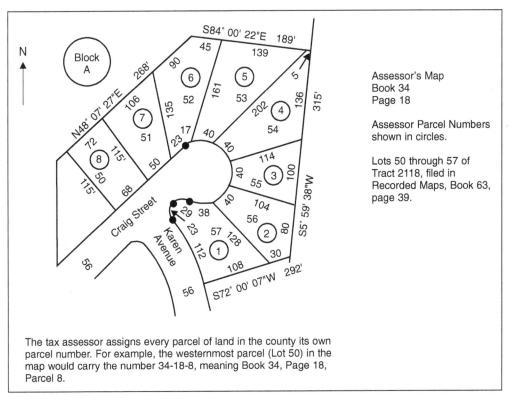

The tax assessor assigns every parcel of land in the county its own parcel number. For example, the westernmost parcel (Lot 50) in the map would carry the number 34-18-8, meaning Book 34, Page 18, Parcel 8.

FIGURE 2-9 Assessor's map
Source: © 2021 Mbition LLC

VERTICAL LAND DESCRIPTIONS

In addition to surface land descriptions, land may also be described in terms of vertical measurements. This type of measurement is necessary when air rights or subsurface rights need to be described—as for multistory condominiums or oil and mineral rights. A point, line, or surface from which a vertical height or depth is measured is called a *datum*. The most commonly used datum plane in the United States is mean sea level, although a number of cities have established other datum surfaces for use in local surveys. Starting from a datum, government survey teams set benchmarks at calculated intervals; thus, a surveyor need not travel to the original datum to determine an elevation. These same benchmarks are used as reference points for metes and bounds surveys. When subsurface drilling or mineral rights are sold, the chosen datum is often the surface of the parcel. For example, an oil lease may permit the extraction of oil and gas from a depth greater than 500 feet beneath the surface of a parcel of land. (Subsurface rights are discussed in a future chapter.) An air lot (a space over a given parcel of land) is described by identifying both the parcel of land beneath the air lot and the elevation of the air lot above the parcel (see Figure 2-10A). Multistory condominiums use this system of land description. *Contour maps* (topographic maps) indicate elevations. On these maps, contour lines connect all points having the same elevation. The purpose is to show hills and valleys, slopes, and water runoff. If the land is to be developed, the map shows where soil will have to be moved to provide level building lots. Figure 2-10B shows how vertical distances are shown using contour lines.

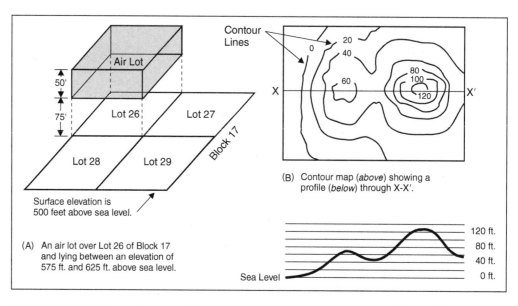

FIGURE 2-10 Air lot and contour lines
Source: © 2021 Mbition LLC

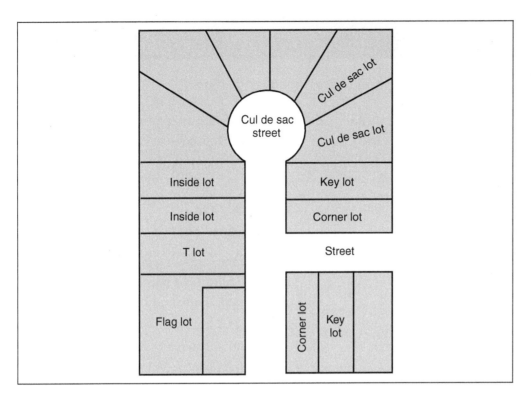

FIGURE 2-11 Lot types
Source: © 2021 Mbition LLC

LOT TYPES

In talking about subdivisions, you should be familiar with several terms. All of these are shown in Figure 2-11. A *cul-de-sac* is a street that is closed at one end with a circular turnaround. The pie-shaped lots fronting on the turnaround are called *cul-de-sac* lots. A flag lot is a lot shaped like a flag on a flagpole. This is a popular method of creating a buildable lot out of the land at the back of a larger lot. A *corner lot* is a lot that fronts on two or more streets. An *inside lot* is a lot with only one side on a street. A *key lot* is a lot that adjoins the side or rear property line of a corner lot. The key lot has added value if it is needed by the corner lot for expansion but may also be less desirable in a residential situation with loss of privacy. A *T lot* is a lot at the end of a T *intersection*, as shown in Figure 2-11.

Review Questions

Answers to these questions can be found in Appendix D at the end of this book.

1. In determining whether an article of personal property has become a fixture, which of the following tests would NOT be applied?
   A. the manner of attachment
   B. the cost of the article
   C. the adaptation of the article to the land
   D. the existence of an agreement between the parties

2. The term *real estate* includes all EXCEPT:
   A. the right to use land
   B. anything affixed to land with the intent of being permanent
   C. rights to the air above the land
   D. a hot tub on a deck

3. Which of the following is an economic characteristic of land?
   A. indestructability
   B. mortgaged
   C. immovable
   D. scarcity

4. In remodeling their home, the Wades put the following items in the home. Once in place, all would be fixtures EXCEPT:
   A. an oriental throw rug in the front entry hall
   B. the built-in kitchen range
   C. the built-in dishwasher
   D. custom-fitted wall-to-wall carpet installed over plywood subflooring

5. Which of the following are NOT classified as real property?
   A. fixtures
   B. emblements
   C. a shrub planted in the ground
   D. air rights

6. The right of an owner to use water from a stream for personal use is called:
   A. an emblement right
   B. a riparian right
   C. a littoral right
   D. a percolated right

7. Which of the following land description methods identifies a parcel of land by specifying its shape and boundaries?
   A. metes and bounds
   B. government survey
   C. recorded plat
   D. assessor's parcel number

8. Which of the following is best used as a monument to designate the corner of a parcel of land in the metes and bounds description of the land?
   A. an outcropping of rock
   B. a tree
   C. a fence corner
   D. an iron rod driven into the ground

9. The term *point of beginning* refers to:
   A. a permanent reference marker
   B. the first corner of the parcel to be surveyed
   C. a benchmark
   D. the intersection of a principal meridian with its baseline

10. 1/60th of 1/360th of a circle is known as a/an:
    A. second
    B. minute
    C. degree
    D. hour

11. An acceptable form of legal description that identifies a property but does not physically describe the property is best known as:
    A. metes and bounds
    B. government survey
    C. rectangular survey
    D. reference to a recorded plat

12. East-west lines in the government rectangular survey system are known as:
    A. baselines
    B. guide meridians
    C. meridians
    D. quadrangles

13. In a metes and bounds description, if there is discrepancy between a measurement stated in the legal description and a measurement in a survey:
    A. the measured distance will control
    B. the distance in the legal description will control
    C. the discrepancy is divided in two
    D. the survey follows the legal description because there is never a discrepancy

14. A township is:
    A. six miles square
    B. one mile square
    C. six square miles
    D. one square mile

15. The amount 43,560 is the number of square feet in:
    A. an acre
    B. a section
    C. a township
    D. a tier

16. The NW1/4 of the NW1/4 of the NW1/4 of a section of land contains:
    A. 80 acres
    B. 10 acres
    C. 20 acres
    D. 40 acres

17. An assessor's parcel number is:
    A. the final authority for the legal description of a parcel of land
    B. often used as a legal description in a deed
    C. not a preferred method of legal description, though it is acceptable
    D. not recognized as an acceptable form of legal description

RIGHTS AND INTERESTS IN LAND

CHAPTER 3

KEY TERMS

chattel
easement
eminent domain
encroachment
encumbrance
escheat
estate
fee simple
police power
qualified fee estate
title

OBJECTIVES

After successful completion of this chapter, you should be able to:

1. distinguish between the feudal and allodial systems of land ownership;
2. explain the rights that government has in land;
3. explain the fee simple bundle of rights;
4. understand such terms as fee simple, encumbrances, easements, encroachments, deed restrictions, and liens;
5. define and explain the various types of liens;
6. explain the various types of estates and understand their usage;
7. distinguish between freehold and leasehold estates; and
8. define such terms as license and chattel.

OVERVIEW

This chapter provides general and legal information concerning rights and interest in land. It begins with a brief discussion of government rights in land, individual rights, easements, encroachments, deed restrictions, and types of liens. Other topics covered in this chapter include various types of estates, homestead rights, chattels, and subsurface rights.

GOVERNMENT RIGHTS IN LAND

Under the feudal system, all land was owned to the benefit of the government, and the king was responsible for organizing defense against invaders, making decisions on land use, providing services such as roads and bridges, and the general administration of the land and his subjects. In the allodial system, land is owned to the benefit of the people. An important aspect of the transition from feudal to allodial ownership was that the need for these services did not end. Consequently, even though private citizens could now hold ownership, it became necessary for the government to retain the rights of police power, eminent domain, taxation, and escheat. The acronym PETE can be used to help remember these government rights in real estate. Let us look at each of these more closely.

Police Power

The right of government to enact laws and enforce them for the order, safety, health, morals, and general welfare of the public is called **police power**. Examples of police power applied to real estate include zoning laws; planning laws; building, health, and fire codes; and rent control. A key difference between police power and eminent domain is that, although police power restricts how real estate may be used, there is no legally recognized "taking" of property. Consequently, there is no payment to an owner who suffers a loss of value through the exercise of police power. A government may not utilize police power in an offhand or capricious manner; any law that restricts how an owner may use real estate must be deemed in the public interest and applied evenhandedly to be valid. The breaking of a law based on police power results in either a civil or criminal penalty rather than the seizing of real estate, as in the case of unpaid property taxes. Of the various rights government holds in land, police power has the most impact on land value.

police power: the right of government to enact laws and enforce them for the order, safety, health, morals, and general welfare of the public

Eminent Domain

The right of government to take ownership of privately held real estate, regardless of the owner's wishes, is called **eminent domain**. There are two legal requirements when property is taken from the public by the government:

1. The property taken MUST be for public purpose (defined as use OR benefit).
2. The property owner MUST be paid a fair and just compensation.

Land for schools, freeways, streets, parks, urban renewal, public housing, public parking, and other social and public purposes is obtained this way. Quasi-public organizations, such as utility companies and railroads, are also permitted to obtain land needed for utility lines, pipes, and tracks by state and federal laws. The legal proceeding involved in eminent domain is *condemnation*, and property owners must be paid the fair market value of the property taken from them. The actual condemnation is usually preceded by negotiations between the property

eminent domain: the right of government to take privately held land for public use, provided fair compensation is paid

owner and an agent of the public body wanting to acquire ownership. If the agent and the property owner can arrive at a mutually acceptable price, the property is purchased outright. If an agreement cannot be reached, a formal proceeding in eminent domain is filed against the property owner in a court of law. The court hears expert opinions from appraisers brought by both parties and then sets the price the property owner must accept in return for the loss of ownership.

When only a portion of a parcel of land is being taken, *severance damages* may be awarded in addition to payment for land actually being taken. For example, if a new highway requires a 40-acre strip of land through the middle of a 160-acre farm, the farm owner will not only be paid for the 40 acres, but will also receive severance damages to compensate for the fact that the farm will be more difficult to work because it is no longer in one piece.

An *inverse condemnation* is a proceeding brought about by property owners demanding that their land be purchased from them. In a number of cities, homeowners at the end of airport runways have forced airport authorities to buy their homes because of the deafening noise of jet aircraft takeoffs. Damage awards may also be made when land itself is not taken, but when its usefulness is reduced because of a nearby condemnation. These are also *consequential damages* that might be awarded—for instance, when land is taken for a sewage treatment plant and privately owned land downwind from the plant suffers a loss in value owing to foul odors.

It appears to many that the government has, over the years, expanded its concept of eminent domain, and the courts have supported this "land grab." In *Kelo v. City of New London*, a 2005 landmark case involving economic development in New London, Connecticut, the U.S. Supreme Court essentially confirmed the government's constitutional right to take property from the public to increase tax revenue. This very controversial split decision by the Court left the door open for states to create legislation limiting the rights of eminent domain for state and local governments. Georgia was one of the first to create such legislation in the 2006 legislative session.

Taxation

Under the feudal system, governments financed themselves by requiring lords and vassals to share a portion of the benefits they received from the use of the king's lands. With the change to private ownership, the need to finance governments did not end. Thus, the government retained the right to collect property taxes from landowners. Before the advent of income taxes, the taxes levied against land were the main source of government revenues. Taxing land was a logical method of raising revenue for two reasons: (1) until the Industrial Revolution, which started in the mid-18th century, land and agriculture were the primary sources of income—i.e., the more land one owned, the wealthier one was considered to be, and, therefore, the better able to pay taxes to support the government; and (2) land is impossible to hide, making it easily identifiable for taxation. This is not true of other valuables such as gold or money.

The real property tax has endured over the centuries, and today it is still a major source of government revenue. There has been a major change in real estate taxation: Initially, real estate taxes were used to support all levels of government, including defense; today, defense is supported by the income tax, and real estate taxes are sources of city, county, and, in some places, state revenues. At state and local government levels, the real property tax provides money for such things as schools, fire and police protection, parks, and libraries.

In the Field

To encourage property owners to pay their taxes in full and on time, the right of taxation also enables the government to seize ownership of real estate upon which taxes are delinquent and to sell the property to recover the unpaid taxes.

Escheat

When a person dies and leaves no heirs and no instructions as to how to dispose of real and personal property, or when property is abandoned, the ownership of that property reverts to the state. This reversion to the government (state or county) is called **escheat**, from the Anglo-French word meaning to *fall back*. Escheat solves the problem of property becoming ownerless.

escheat: when ownership of abandoned property reverts to the state

PROTECTING OWNERSHIP

It cannot be overemphasized that, to have real estate, there must be a system or means of protecting rightful claims to the use of land and the improvements thereon. In the United States, the federal government is given the task of organizing a defense system to prevent confiscation of those rights by a foreign power. The federal government, in combination with state and local governments, also establishes laws and courts within the country to protect the ownership rights of one citizen in relation to another citizen. Whereas the armed forces protect against a foreign takeover within a country, deeds, public records, contracts, and other documents have replaced the need for brute force to prove and protect ownership of real estate.

FEE SIMPLE

The concept of real estate ownership can be more easily understood when viewed as a collection or bundle of rights. Under the allodial system, the rights of taxation, eminent domain, police power, and escheat are retained by the government. The remaining bundle of rights, called **fee simple**, is available for private ownership. The fee simple bundle of rights can be held by a person and his/her heirs

fee simple: the largest, most complete bundle of rights one can hold in land; land ownership forever, or until the government can no longer protect those rights. Figure 3-1 demonstrates the fee simple bundle of rights concept.

estate: one's legal interest or rights in land

The word **estate** is synonymous with bundle of rights. Stated another way, estate refers to one's legal interest or rights in land, not the physical quantity of land as shown on a map. Simply put, "title" = "rights" and "rights" = "estate." A fee simple is the largest estate one can hold in land. Most real estate sales are for the fee simple estate. When a person is said to "own" or have "title" to real estate, it is usually the fee simple estate that is being discussed. **Title** refers to the ownership of something. All other lesser estates in land, such as life estates and leaseholds, are created from the fee estate. Real estate is concerned with the "sticks" in the bundle: how many there are, how useful they are, and who possesses the sticks not in the bundle. With that in mind, let us describe what happens when sticks are removed from the bundle.

title: the right to or ownership of something; also the evidence of ownership, such as a deed or bill of sale

ENCUMBRANCES

encumbrance: any impediment to a clear title, such as a lien, lease, or easement

Whenever a stick is removed from the fee simple bundle, it creates an impediment to the free and clear ownership and use of that property. These impediments to title are called encumbrances. An **encumbrance** is defined as any claim, right, lien, estate, or liability that limits the fee simple title to property. An encumbrance is, in effect, a stick that has been removed from the bundle. Commonly found encumbrances are easements, encroachments, deed restrictions, liens, leases, and air and subsurface rights. In addition, qualified fee estates are encumbered estates, as are life estates.

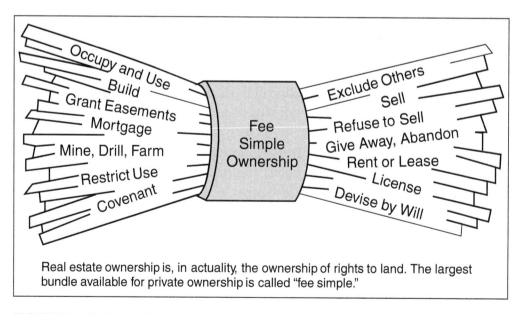

FIGURE 3-1 The fee simple bundle of rights

Source: © 2021 Mbition LLC

The party holding a stick from someone else's fee simple bundle is said to hold a claim, a right to, or an interest in that land. In other words, what is one person's encumbrance is another person's claim or right or interest. For example, a lease is an encumbrance from the standpoint of the fee simple owner. But from the tenant's standpoint, it is an interest in land that gives the tenant the right to the exclusive use of land and buildings. A mortgage is an encumbrance from the fee owner's viewpoint but a right to foreclose from the lender's viewpoint. A property that is encumbered with a lease and a mortgage is called "a fee simple subject to a lease and a mortgage." Figure 3-2 shows how a fee simple bundle shrinks as rights

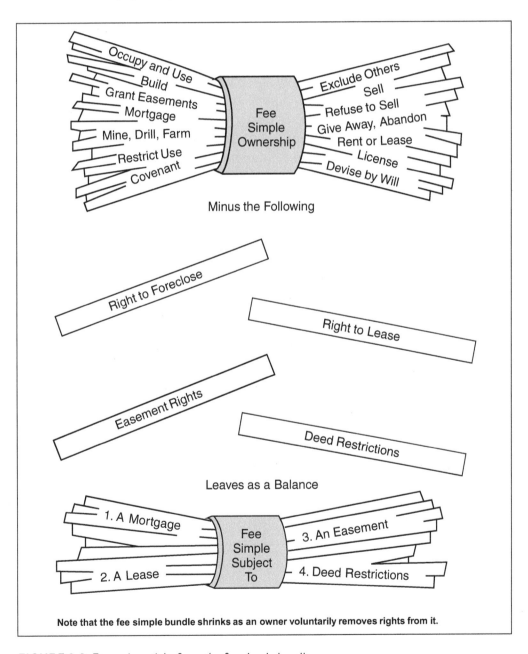

FIGURE 3-2 Removing sticks from the fee simple bundle
Source: © 2021 Mbition LLC

easement: the right or privilege one party has to use land belonging to another for a special purpose not inconsistent with the owner's use of the land

are removed from it. Meanwhile, let us turn our attention to a discussion of individual sticks found in the fee simple bundle.

EASEMENTS

An **easement** is a right or privilege one party has to the use of land of another for a special purpose consistent with the general use of the land. The landowner is not dispossessed from the land but, rather, coexists side by side with the holder of the easement. Examples of easements are those given to telephone and electric companies to erect poles and run lines over private property, easements given to people to drive or walk across someone else's land, and easements given to gas and water companies to run pipelines to serve their customers. Figure 3-3 illustrates several examples of easements.

There are several different ways an easement can come into being. One is for the landowner to use a written document to specifically grant an easement to another party. A second way is for an owner to reserve (withhold) an easement in the deed when granting the property to another party. For example, a land developer may reserve easements for utility lines when selling the lots, and then grant the easements to the utility companies that will service the lots. Another

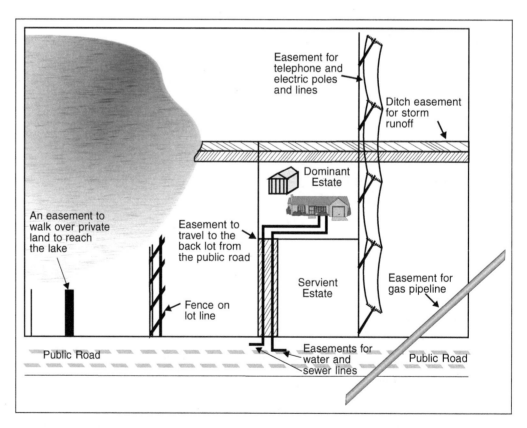

FIGURE 3-3 Commonly found easements
Source: © 2021 Mbition LLC

way for an easement to be created is by government condemnation, such as when a government flood control district purchases an easement to run a drainage pipe under someone's land.

It is also possible for an easement to arise without a written document. For example, a parcel of land fronts on a road, and the owner sells the back half of the parcel. If the only access to the back half is by crossing over the front half, even if the seller did not expressly grant an easement, the law will generally protect the buyer's right to travel over the front half to get to the back half. The buyer must not be landlocked by the seller. This is known as an *easement by necessity*. Another method of acquiring an easement without a written document is by constant use, or *easement by prescription*. If a person acts as though s/he owns an easement long enough, and the use is open, obvious, and without permission of the property owner, that person will have a legally recognized easement. A person using a private road without permission for a long enough time can acquire a legally recognized easement by this method.

In review, the five ways an easement can be created are:

1. Grant
2. Reservation
3. Condemnation
4. Necessity
5. Prescription

Easement Appurtenant—In Figure 3-3, the driveway from the road to the back lot is called an easement appurtenant. The word *appurtenant* means "to belong to" or "is a part of." This driveway is automatically included with the back lot whenever the back lot is sold or otherwise conveyed. This is so because this easement is legally connected (appurtenant) to the back lot. Please note that just as the back lot benefits from this easement, the front lot is burdened by it. Whenever the front lot is sold or otherwise conveyed, the new owners must continue to respect the easement to the back lot. The owner of the front lot owns all the front lot but may not put a fence across the easement, plant trees on it, grow a garden on it, or otherwise hamper access to the back lot. The key to an easement appurtenant is that it always requires at least two properties, servient and dominant. Because the front lot serves the back lot, the front lot is called the *servient estate*, and the back lot is called the *dominant estate*. Although the law may protect the first purchaser through the doctrine of easement by necessity, it is nonetheless critical that any subsequent purchaser of back lots and back acreage carefully inspect the public records and the property to make certain there are both legal and actual means of access from a public road to the parcel. It is also important for anyone purchasing land to inspect the public records and the property for evidence of the rights of others to pass over that land, such as a driveway or private road to a back lot, or a pathway used by the public to get from a road to a beach.

Easement In Gross—An *easement in gross* differs from an easement appurtenant because there is a servient estate but no dominant estate. Some examples will illustrate this. Telephone, electricity, and gas line easements are all easements in gross. These easements belong to the telephone, electric, and gas companies, respectively, not to a parcel of land. The servient estate is the parcel on which the telephone, electric, and gas companies have the right to run their lines. All future owners of the parcel are bound by these easements. While most easements in gross are commercial in nature (power line, drainage, utility), there are also personal easements. An example of a personal easement in gross would be development of an easement on the property of another to hunt or fish. The significant differences between commercial and personal gross easements are that personal easements in gross terminate with the death of a party or with the transfer of the property, while commercial easements in gross do not; and that commercial easements in gross may be assigned to another, while personal easements cannot. Although utility easements are the most common examples of easements in gross, the ditch easement for storm runoff in Figure 3-3 is another example. It will most likely be owned by a flood control district. Note that utility and drainage easements, although legally a burden on a parcel, are consistent with the use of a parcel if the purpose of the easement is to provide utility service or flood control for the parcel. In fact, without these services, a parcel would be less useful and hence less valuable.

Party Wall Easement—*Party wall easements* exist when a single wall is located on the lot line that separates two parcels of land. The wall may be either a fence or the wall of a building. In either case, the lot owners own that portion of the wall on their land, plus an easement in the other half of the wall for physical support. Party walls are common where stores and office buildings are built right up to the lot line. Such a wall can present an interesting problem when the owner of one lot wants to demolish a building. Since the wall provides support for the building next door, the wall must be left and special supports provided for the adjacent building during demolition and until such time as another building is constructed on the lot. A party wall is an easement appurtenant.

Easement Termination—Easements may be terminated when the necessity for the easement no longer exists (for example, when a public road is built adjacent to the back half of the lot mentioned earlier), when the dominant and servient estates are combined (merged) with the intent of extinguishing the easement, by release from the easement holder to the servient estate, or by lack of use (abandonment). Again, to review, easements may be terminated by:

1. End of necessity
2. Merger
3. Release
4. Abandonment

Encroachments

The unauthorized intrusion of a building or other form of real property onto another person's land is called an **encroachment**. A tree that overhangs a neighbor's yard and a building or eave of a roof that crosses a property line are examples of encroachments. The owner of the property being encroached upon has the right to force the removal of the encroachment. Failure to do so may eventually injure his/her title and make the land more difficult to sell. Ultimately, inaction may result in the encroaching neighbor claiming a legal right to continue the use. Figure 3-4 illustrates several commonly found encroachments.

encroachment: the unauthorized intrusion of a building or other improvement onto another person's land

Deed Restrictions

Private agreements that govern the use of land are known as *deed restrictions* or *deed covenants*. For example, a land subdivider can require that persons who purchase lots build only single-family homes containing 1,200 square feet or more. The purpose is to protect those who have already built houses from an erosion in property value due to the construction of nearby buildings not compatible with the neighborhood. Where scenic views are important, deed restrictions may limit the height of buildings and trees. Buyers would still obtain fee simple ownership but, at the same time, would voluntarily give up some rights to do as they please. Such a buyer is said to receive a fee simple title subject to deed restrictions.

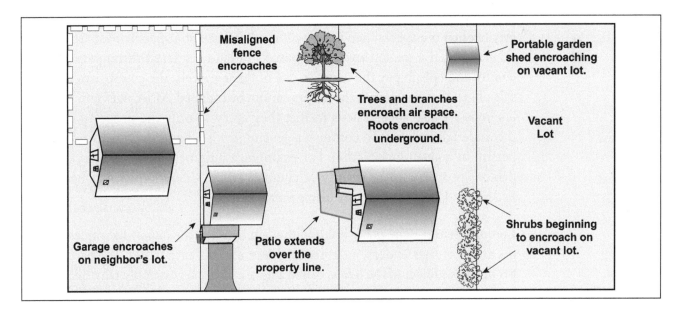

FIGURE 3-4 Commonly found encroachments
Source: © 2021 Mbition LLC

> **In the Field**
>
> The right to enforce the restrictions is usually given by the developer to the subdivision's homeowners association. Violation of a deed restriction can result in a civil court action brought by other property owners who are bound by the same deed restriction.

Liens

A hold or claim that one person has on the property of another to secure payment of a debt or other obligation is called a lien. Common examples are property tax liens, mechanic's liens, judgment liens, and mortgage liens. From the standpoint of the property owner, a lien is an encumbrance on a title. Note that a lien does not transfer title to property. In most states, the debtor retains title unless the lien is foreclosed. When there is more than one lien against a property, the lien that was recorded first usually has the highest priority in the event of foreclosure (exceptions to this rule are mechanic's liens, property tax liens, and subordination agreements). Property tax liens are always superior to other liens.

Voluntary and Involuntary Liens—A *voluntary lien* is a lien created by the property owner. A mortgage lien is an example of a voluntary lien; the owner voluntarily creates a lien against property to borrow money. An *involuntary lien* is created by operation of law. Examples are property tax liens, judgment liens, and mechanic's liens.

Special and General Liens—A *special lien* is a lien on a specific property. A property tax lien is a special lien because it is a lien against a specific property and no other. Thus, if a person owns five parcels of land scattered throughout a given county and fails to pay the taxes on one of those parcels, the county can force the sale of just that one parcel; the others cannot be touched. Mortgages and mechanic's liens are also special liens in that they apply to only the property receiving the materials or labor. In contrast, a *general lien* is a lien on all the property of a person in a given jurisdiction. For example, a judgment lien is a lien on all the debtor's property in the county or counties where the judgment has been filed. Federal and state tax liens are also general liens.

Lienor, Lienee—The party holding the lien is called the *lienor*. Examples of lienors are mortgage lenders, judgment holders, and tax authorities. The party whose property is subject to the lien is called a *lienee*. These terms apply whether the lien is voluntary or involuntary, specific or general.

Property Tax Liens—*Property tax liens* result from the right of government to collect taxes from property owners. At the beginning of each tax year, a tax lien is placed on taxable property. It is removed when the property taxes are paid. If they are not paid, the lien gives the government the right to force the sale of the property to collect the unpaid taxes.

Mechanic's Liens—*Mechanic's lien* laws give anyone who has furnished labor or materials for the improvement of land the right to place a lien against those improvements and the land if payment has not been received. A sale of the property can then be forced to recover the money owed. To be subject to a mechanic's lien, the work or materials must have been provided pursuant to a contract with the landowner or the landowner's representative. If a landowner hires a contractor to build a house or add a room to an existing house and then fails to pay the contractor, the contractor may file a mechanic's lien against the land and its improvements.

> ### In the Field
>
> If the landowner pays the contractor but the contractor does not pay the subcontractors, the subcontractors are entitled to file a mechanic's lien against the property. In this situation, the owner may have to pay twice.

The legal theory behind mechanic's lien rights is that the labor and materials supplied enhance the value of the property. Therefore, the property should be security for payment. If the property owner does not pay voluntarily, the lien can be enforced with a court-supervised foreclosure sale. Mechanics (contractors), materialmen, architects, surveyors, and engineers are among those who may be entitled to the protection of mechanic's lien laws. All mechanic's liens attach and take effect at the time the first item of labor or material is furnished, even though no document has been filed with the county recorder. To preserve the rights, a lien statement (affidavit) must be filed in the county where the property is located within 90 days of the last date labor or material was furnished. The person filing the lien must then file suit against the responsible party within one year. This is called *perfecting the lien*. Whenever improvements are made to the land, all persons (including landlords and sellers under a contract for deed) may be held to have authorized the improvements. As protection, an owner can serve or post notice that the improvements are being made without the owner's authority. A lender planning to finance a property will be particularly alert to the possibility of mechanic's liens. If work has commenced or material has been delivered before the mortgage is recorded, the mechanic's lien may be superior to the mortgage in the event of foreclosure. The owner's affidavit, signed by the owner of property at closing, states that no material or labor has been supplied to the property within the previous 90 days that has not been paid.

Judgment Liens—Judgment liens arise from lawsuits for which money damages are awarded. The law permits a hold to be placed against the real and personal property of the debtor until the judgment is paid. Usually, the lien created by the judgment covers only property in the county where the judgment was awarded. However, the creditor can extend the lien to property in other counties by filing a notice of lien in each of those counties. If the debtor does not repay the lien voluntarily, the creditor can (although this can vary from state to state) ask the court to issue a writ of execution that directs the county sheriff to seize and sell a sufficient amount of the debtor's property to pay the debt and expenses of the sale.

Mortgage Liens—A mortgage lien is created when property is offered by its owner as security for the repayment of a debt. If the debt secured by the mortgage lien is not repaid, the creditor can foreclose and sell the property. If this is insufficient to repay the debt, some states allow the creditor to petition the court for a judgment lien for the balance due. (Mortgage law is covered in more detail in Chapter 9.)

QUALIFIED FEE ESTATES

qualified fee estate: a fee estate that is subject to certain limitations imposed by the person creating the estate

A **qualified fee estate** (also known as *defeasible fee estate*) is a fee estate that is subject to certain limitations imposed by the person creating the estate. Qualified fee estates fall into three categories: determinable, condition subsequent, and condition precedent. They will be discussed only briefly, as they are rather uncommon.

A *fee simple determinable estate* indicates that the duration of the estate can be determined from the deed itself. For example, Mr. Smith donates a parcel of land to a church so long as the land is used for religious purposes. The key words are "so long as": so long as the land is used for religious purposes, the church has all the rights of fee simple ownership. But if some other use is made of the land, it reverts back to the grantor (Mr. Smith) or someone else named by Mr. Smith (called a *remainderman* or *remainderperson*). Note that the termination of the estate is automatic if the land is used contrary to the limitation stated in the deed.

A *fee simple subject to condition subsequent* gives the grantor the right to terminate the estate. Continuing the previous example, Mr. Smith would have the right to re-enter the property and take it back if it was no longer being used for religious purposes.

With a *fee simple upon condition precedent*, title will not take effect until a condition is performed. For example, Mr. Smith could deed his land to a church with the condition that the deed will not take effect until a religious sanctuary is built.

Occasionally, land developers have used qualified fees in lieu of deed restrictions or zoning. For example, the buyer has fee title as long as the land is used for a single-family residence. In another example, a land developer might use a condition precedent to encourage lot purchasers to build promptly. This would enhance the value of unsold lots. From the standpoint of the property owner, a qualification is an encumbrance to a title.

LIFE ESTATES

A *life estate* conveys an estate for the duration of someone's life. The duration of the estate can be tied to the life of the *life tenant* (the person holding the life estate) or to a third party. In addition, someone must be named to acquire the estate upon its termination. The following example will illustrate the life estate concept. Suppose you have an aunt who needs financial assistance and you have decided to grant her, for the rest of her life, a house to live in. When you create the life estate, she becomes the life tenant. This is commonly referred to as an *ordinary life estate* and was created by grant (conveyed or transferred to). Additionally, you must decide who gets the house upon her death. If you want it back, you would want a reversion for yourself. This way, the house reverts back to you or, if you predecease her, to your heirs. If you want the house to go to someone else—your son or daughter, for example—you could name him/her as the remainderperson. Alternatively, you could name a friend, relative, or charity as the remainderperson.

Sometimes a life estate is used to avoid the time and expense of probating a will and to reduce estate taxes. For example, an aging father could deed his real estate to his children but retain a life estate for himself. This is known as a life estate created by *reservation*. A life estate can also be created for the life of another. In legal terms, this is called a life estate *pur autre vie* (*for the life of another*). For example, I will deed this property to Jim Bob for the life of his mother (anticipating that Jim Bob will maintain control over the property for the purpose of taking care of his mother—perhaps given the opportunity to live there at no cost). Then, upon the death of the mother, the life estate would revert to the grantor or vest in the remainderman, depending on the terms that created the life estate.

Prohibition of Waste

Since a life estate arrangement is temporary, the life tenant must not commit *waste* by destroying or harming the property. Furthermore, the life tenant is required to keep the property in reasonable repair and to pay any property taxes, assessments, and interest on debt secured by the property. The life tenant is entitled to income generated by the property and may sell, lease, rent, or mortgage the interest in the property.

Although the life estate concept offers intriguing gift and estate planning possibilities, the uncertainty of the duration of the estate makes it rather unmarketable. Thus, you will rarely see a life estate advertised for sale in a newspaper or listed for sale at a real estate brokerage office.

STATUTORY ESTATES

Statutory estates are created by state law. They include dower, which gives a wife rights in her husband's real property; curtesy, which gives a husband rights in his wife's real property; and community property, which gives each spouse a one-half interest in marital property. Additionally, there is homestead protection, which is designed to protect the family's home from certain debts and, upon the death of one spouse, provide the other with a home for life.

Dower

Historically, *dower* came from old English common law in which the marriage ceremony was viewed as merging the wife's legal existence into that of her husband's. From this viewpoint, property bought during marriage belongs to the husband, with both husband and wife sharing the use of it. As a counterbalance, the dower right recognizes the wife's efforts in marriage and grants her legal ownership to one-third (or in some states, one-half) of the family's real property for the rest of her life. This prevents the husband from conveying ownership of the family's real estate without the wife's permission and protects her even if she is left out of her husband's will. In real estate sales, the effect of dower laws is such that when a husband and wife sell their property, the wife must relinquish her dower rights. This is usually accomplished by the wife signing the deed with her husband or by signing a separate quitclaim deed. If she does not relinquish her dower rights, the buyer (or even a future buyer) may find that, upon the husband's death, the wife may return to legally claim an undivided ownership in the property. This is important if you buy real estate. Have the property's ownership researched by an abstracter and the title insured by a title insurance company. The state of Georgia does not recognize the rights of dower.

Curtesy

Roughly the opposite of dower, *curtesy* gives the husband benefits in his deceased wife's property as long as he lives. However, unlike dower, the wife can defeat those rights in her will. Furthermore, state law may require the couple to have had a child in order for the husband to qualify for curtesy. Because dower and curtesy rights originally were unequal, some states interpret dower and curtesy so as to give equal rights, while other states have enacted additional legislation to protect spousal rights. To summarize, the basic purpose of dower and curtesy (and community property laws) is to require both spouses to sign any deed, mortgage, or other document affecting title to their lands and to provide legal protection for the property rights of a surviving spouse. The state of Georgia does not recognize the rights of curtesy.

Community Property

Ten states (Alaska, Arizona, California, Idaho, Louisiana, Nevada, New Mexico, Texas, Washington, and Wisconsin) recognize the legal theory that both spouses have an equal interest in all property acquired by their joint efforts during the marriage. This jointly produced property is called *community property*. Upon the death of one spouse, the community property passes to the heirs and/or the surviving spouse. When community property is sold or mortgaged, both spouses must sign the document. Community property rights arise upon marriage (either formal or common law) and terminate upon divorce or death. Community property is discussed at greater length in a future chapter. The state of Georgia does not recognize community property.

Homestead Protection

Nearly all states have passed *homestead protection* laws, usually with two purposes in mind: (1) to provide some legal protection for the homestead claimants from debts and judgments against them that might result in the forced sale and loss of the home, and (2) to provide a home for a widow, and sometimes a widower, for life. Homestead protection laws essentially keep people from being kicked to the curb and left penniless and homeless because they cannot pay personal debts. However, homestead protection laws do not protect people from being foreclosed on and sent packing because they do not pay their mortgage payments or property tax payments. Homestead protection laws are usually a limited protection, but Florida has become infamous because of its unlimited homestead protection rights. For this reason, you hear of people who have had large judgments placed against them moving to Florida and sinking all of their money in their personal home. As referred to here, homestead is not the acquiring of title to state-owned or federally owned lands by filing and establishing a residence. Additionally, *homestead protection* should not be confused with the *homestead exemption* that some states grant to homeowners to reduce their property taxes. A homeowner is also protected by the Federal Bankruptcy Reform Act of 1978. While more protective state statutes may control this protection, the Reform Act provides that persons who seek protection under this act are entitled to an exemption of up to $7,500 of the equity in their residence. Also exempt is any household item that does not exceed $200 in value.

FREEHOLD ESTATES

In a carryover from the old English court system, estates in land are classified as either freehold estates or leasehold estates. Typically, the main difference is that freehold estate cases are tried under real property laws, whereas leasehold (also called non-freehold or less-than-freehold) estates are tried under personal property laws. Georgia is unique in that leasehold estates are defined by law as being real property. The two distinguishing features of a *freehold estate* are: (1) there must be actual ownership of the land, and (2) the estate must be of unpredictable duration. Fee estates, life estates, and estates created by statute are freehold estates.

> ## In the Field
>
> The distinguishing features of a leasehold estate are: (1) although there is possession of the land, there is no ownership, and (2) the estate is of definite or indefinite duration. Stated another way, freehold means ownership, and leasehold means nonownership.

LEASEHOLD ESTATES

As previously noted, the user of a property need not be its owner. Under a leasehold estate, the user is called the *lessee* or *tenant*, and the person from whom it is leased is the *lessor* or *landlord*. As long as the tenant has a valid lease, abides by it, and pays the rent on time, the owner, even though owning the property, may not occupy it until the lease has expired. During the lease period, the freehold estate owner is said to hold a *reversion*. This is the right to recover possession at the end of the lease period. Meanwhile, the lease is an encumbrance against the property.

There are four categories of leasehold estates: estate for years, periodic estate, estate at will, and tenancy at sufferance. Note that in this chapter, we will be examining leases primarily from the standpoint of estates in land. Leases as financing tools and lease contracts are covered in future chapters.

Estate for Years

Also called a tenancy for years, the *estate for years* is somewhat misleadingly named, as it implies that a lease for a number of years has been created. Actually, the key criterion is that the lease have a specific starting time and a specific ending time. It can be for any length of time, ranging from less than a day to many years. An estate for years does not automatically renew itself. Neither the landlord nor the tenant must act to terminate it, as the lease agreement itself specifies a termination date.

Usually, the lessor is the freehold estate owner. However, the lessor could also be a lessee. To illustrate, a fee owner leases to a lessee, who, in turn, leases to another person. By doing this, this first lessee has become a *sublessor*. The person who leases from that person is a *sublessee*. It is important to realize that in no case may a sublessee acquire from the lessee any more rights than the lessee has. Thus, if a lessee has a five-year lease with three years remaining, only the remaining three years or a portion of them may be assigned to a sublessee.

Periodic Estate

Also called an estate from year to year or a periodic tenancy, a *periodic estate* has an original lease period with fixed length; when it runs out, unless the tenant or the landlord acts to terminate it, renewal is automatic for another like period of time. A month-to-month apartment rental is an example of this arrangement. To avoid last-minute confusion, rental agreements usually require that advance notice be given if either the landlord or the tenant wishes to terminate the tenancy.

Estate at Will

Also called a tenancy at will, an *estate at will* is a landlord-tenant relationship with all the normal rights and duties of a lessor-lessee relationship, except that the estate may be terminated by either the lessor or the lessee at any time. The key ingredient in an estate at will is that it is for an indefinite period of time. It is usually not in writing, though it could be; it is typically vague and informal. Because of the lack of definition in the estate at will, the rights and obligations of the parties terminate automatically with a transfer of the property or the death of one of the parties. Georgia requires the tenant to provide a 30-day notice of intent to terminate and the landlord to provide a 60-day notice.

Tenancy at Sufferance

A *tenancy at sufferance* occurs when a tenant stays beyond the legal tenancy without the consent of the landlord. In other words, this occurs when the tenant wrongfully holds the property against the owner's wishes. In a tenancy at sufferance, the tenant is commonly called a *holdover tenant*, although once the stay exceeds the terms of the lease or rental agreement, the person is not actually a tenant in the normal landlord-tenant sense. The landlord is entitled to evict that person and recover possession of the property, provided the landlord does so in a timely manner. A tenant at sufferance differs from a trespasser in that the original entry was rightful. Another major difference is that a tenant, even one at sufferance, has legal rights and would have to be removed by going through proper court procedures. Trespassers are just that and have no legal rights. To remove them, call the police. If, during the holdover period, the tenant pays and the landlord accepts rent, the tenancy at sufferance changes to a tenancy at will.

RIGHTS AND INTERESTS IN LAND: A REVIEW

Figure 3-5 provides an overview of the various rights and interests in land that are discussed in this chapter and the previous chapter. This chart is designed to give you an overall perspective of what real estate includes.

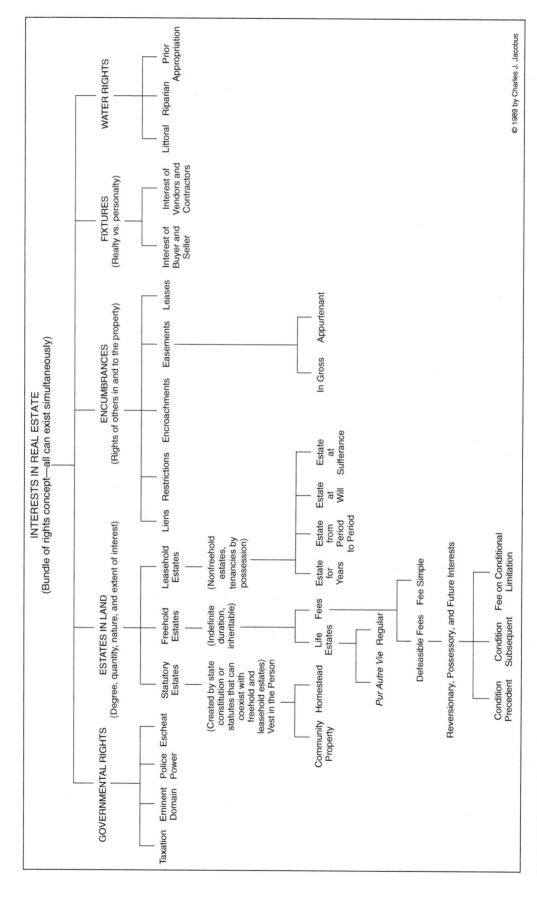

FIGURE 3-5 Rights and interests in land

Source: © 2021 Mbition LLC

License

A license is not a right or an estate in land, but a personal privilege given to someone to use land (the *license*). A license is similar to a personal easement in gross in that it is nonassignable; however, a license can be given orally (unlike a personal easement in gross), and a license can be revoked by the person who issues it. A license to park is typically what an automobile parking lot operator provides for persons parking in the lot. The contract creating the license is usually written on the stub that the lot attendant gives the driver or is posted on a sign in the lot. Tickets to theaters and sporting events also fall into this category. Because it is a personal privilege, a license is not an encumbrance against land.

Chattel

A **chattel** is an article of personal property. The word comes from the old English word for cattle, which, of course, were (and still are) personal property. Chattel is a word more often heard in a law office than in a real estate office. Occasionally, you will see it used in legal documents, such as in the case of a *chattel mortgage*, which is a mortgage against personal property.

chattel: an article of personal property

Law Sources

You will better understand real estate law when you understand its roots. Most American law originally came from early English law through English colonization of America. Additionally, Spanish law, via Spain's colonization of Mexico, can be found in Arizona, California, Idaho, Nevada, New Mexico, Texas, and Washington. Lastly, old French civil law, by way of the French ownership of Louisiana, is the basis for that state's law. In all three of these, the law that took root in America originated in predominantly agricultural economies. Consequently, there has been a great deal of legal modifications over the years by legislatures and courts.

Common Law

You will also find it helpful to understand the difference between common law and statutory law. *Common law* derives its authority from usage and custom over long periods of time. Thus, the concepts of fee simple estates, qualified fee estates, life estates, leasehold estates, mortgages, air rights, and subsurface rights, for example, grew out of usage over hundreds of years. Individual court decisions (called *case law*) also contributed to the development of common law in England and the United States.

Statutory Law

Statutory law is created by the enactment of legislation. Examples of statutory laws are laws enacted by state legislatures that require the licensing of real estate agents. Zoning laws and building codes are also statutory laws, as they have their source in legislative enactment. Federal and state income tax and local property tax laws are statutory laws.

Sometimes common law concepts are enacted into statutory law. For example, many statutory laws pertaining to leasehold estates and the rights and obligations of landlords and tenants have come directly from common law. Additionally, statutory laws have been passed where common law was held to be unclear or unreasonable. For example, old English law did not provide equality in property rights for both spouses. Modern statutory laws do provide equality.

Review Questions

Answers to these questions can be found in Appendix D at the end of this book.

1. The system under which individuals are given the right to own land is known as the:
   A. feudal system
   B. allodial system
   C. chattel system
   D. fee system

2. By which of the following processes may a government acquire ownership of privately held land?
   A. condemnation
   B. taxation
   C. police power
   D. eminent domain

3. The right of the government to place reasonable restrictions on the use of privately held land is known as:
   A. a restrictive covenant
   B. police power
   C. escheat
   D. estate

4. Which of the following is NOT an example of a government's exercise of its police powers?
   A. rent controls
   B. building codes
   C. zoning laws
   D. restrictive covenants

5. Property owned by a person who dies intestate and without heirs will escheat to the:
   A. city
   B. city or county
   C. state or county
   D. federal government

6. A property owner who holds fee simple title to land will have all of the following "sticks" in the bundle of rights EXCEPT the right to:
   A. occupy and use it
   B. restrict the use of the land
   C. devise it by will
   D. violate building, health, and safety codes

7. The term *estate* refers to:
   A. the quantity of land as shown on a plat of the property
   B. one's legal rights in the land
   C. properties over $1 million
   D. residential properties over 25 acres

8. All of the following constitute an encumbrance on the fee simple title to real property EXCEPT:
   A. the will conveying the property to the owner's heirs upon death of the owner
   B. a restrictive covenant in the deed to the property
   C. a mortgage
   D. a lease

9. Which of the following easements could be created without a written document?
   A. an easement by grant
   B. an easement by reservation
   C. an easement by prescription
   D. an easement by abandonment

10. An easement is:
    A. a burden to the holder of the dominant estate
    B. an encumbrance to the holder of the dominant estate
    C. a benefit to the holder of the dominant estate
    D. a burden to the holder of the dominant estate

11. Morris sold the back half of his lot to Katz and gave Katz a permanent easement across his land for Katz to have access to the road. Which of the following statements is TRUE?
    A. The easement is an easement in gross.
    B. The easement is an easement appurtenant.
    C. The servient estate is held by Katz.
    D. The dominant estate is held by Morris.

12. An easement appurtenant may NOT be terminated:
    A. by combination of the dominant and servient tenements
    B. when the purpose for the easement no longer exists
    C. by lack of use
    D. unilaterally by the holder of the servient tenement

13. All of the following may constitute a lien on real property EXCEPT:
    A. a mortgage
    B. unpaid real property taxes
    C. a restrictive covenant in a deed
    D. a judgment against the owner

14. Which of the following is an example of a general lien?
    A. mechanic's liens
    B. judgment liens
    C. mortgage liens
    D. property tax liens

15. Which of the following is NOT classified as a freehold estate?
    A. an estate created by statute
    B. a life estate
    C. a fee simple estate
    D. a leasehold estate

16. Real estate held as a leasehold:
    A. is used by the owner rather than the tenant
    B. reverts to the tenant upon termination of the lease
    C. gives the lessor possessory rights
    D. is usually considered to be real property

17. Unless the landlord or tenant acts to terminate it, an estate from period to period:
    A. can be terminated by either party unilaterally
    B. continues only if renewed
    C. automatically renews itself
    D. becomes an estate at will

18. Which of the following is classified as a non-freehold estate in real estate?
    A. life estate
    B. fee simple estate
    C. estate at will
    D. qualified fee estate

19. A tenant at sufferance is a:
    A. legal tenant
    B. holdover tenant
    C. licensee
    D. guest

20. A chattel is a/an:
    A. item of personal property
    B. item of real property such as a building
    C. freehold estate in land
    D. term that refers to land used for cattle ranching

CHAPTER 4
FORMS OF OWNERSHIP

KEY TERMS

community property
concurrent ownership
estate in severalty
four unities
joint tenancy
right of survivorship
tenancy by the entirety
tenants in common
undivided interest

OBJECTIVES

After successful completion of this chapter, you should be able to:

1. explain the characteristics and benefits of sole ownership;
2. understand the advantages and disadvantages of community property;
3. explain the benefits and disadvantages of tenancy by the entirety;
4. define and explain the significance of the four unities; and
5. explain the different aspects of community and separate property.

OVERVIEW

In a previous chapter we looked at land from a physical standpoint: the size and shape of a parcel, where it is located, and what is affixed to it. We then explored various legal rights and interests that can be held in land. This chapter will look at how a given right or interest in land is held by one or more individuals. It covers such topics as sole ownership, tenants in common, joint tenancy, tenancy by the entirety, and community property.

SOLE OWNERSHIP

When title to property is held by one person, it is called an **estate in severalty** or *sole ownership*. Although the word *severalty* seems to imply that several persons own a single property, the correct meaning can be easily remembered by thinking of "severed" ownership. Sole ownership is available to single and married persons, although the nature of ownership can vary, depending on an individual state's marital property laws. Businesses usually hold title to property in severalty. It is from the estate in severalty that all other tenancies are created.

The major advantage of sole ownership for an individual is flexibility. As a sole owner, you can make all the decisions regarding a property without having to get the agreement of co-owners. You can decide what property or properties to buy, when to buy, and how much to offer. You can decide whether to pay all cash or to seek a loan by using the property as collateral. Once bought, you control (within the bounds of the law) how the property will be used, how much will be charged if it is rented, and how it will be managed. If you decide to sell, you alone decide when to offer the property for sale, and at what price and terms.

But freedom and responsibility go together. For example, if you purchase a rental property, you must determine the prevailing rents, find tenants, prepare contracts, collect the rent, and keep the property in repair—or you must hire and pay someone else to manage the property. Another deterrent to sole ownership is the high entry cost. This form of real estate ownership is usually not possible for someone with only a few hundred dollars to invest.

Let us now turn to methods of **concurrent ownership**—that is, ownership by two or more persons at the same time.

TENANTS IN COMMON

When two or more people wish to share the ownership of a single property, they may do so as **tenants in common**. As tenants in common, each owns an **undivided interest** in the whole property. This is commonly known as the unity of possession and means that each owner has a right to possession of the entire property. No individual can exclude the others or claim any specific portion of the property for his/her own exclusive possession. In a tenancy in common, the interests need not be the same, and each owner can independently sell, mortgage, give away, or devise an individual interest. This independence is possible because each tenant in common has a separate legal title to an undivided interest.

Suppose that you invest $20,000 along with two of your friends, who invest $30,000 and $50,000, respectively; together, you buy 100 acres of land as tenants in common. Presuming that everyone's ownership interest is proportional to his/her cash investment, you will hold a 20% interest in the entire 100 acres, and your two friends will hold 30% and 50%, respectively. You may not pick out 20 acres and exclude the other co-owners from them, nor may you pick out 20 acres and say, "These are mine and I'm going to sell them," nor may they do that

---

estate in severalty: owned by one person; sole ownership

concurrent ownership: ownership by two or more persons at the same time

tenants in common: shared ownership of a single property among two or more persons; interests need not be equal, and no right of survivorship exists

undivided interest: ownership by two or more persons that gives each the right to use the entire property

to you. You do, however, have the legal right to sell or otherwise dispose of your 20% interest (or a portion of it) without the permission of your two friends. Your friends have the same right. If one of you sells, the purchaser becomes a new tenant in common with the remaining co-owners.

Wording of Conveyance

As a rule, a tenancy in common is indicated by naming the co-owners in the conveyance and adding the words *as tenants in common*. For example, a deed might read, "Samuel Smith, John Jones, and Robert Miller, as tenants in common . . . ." If nothing is said regarding the size of each co-owner's interest in the property, the law presumes that all interests are equal. Therefore, if the co-owners intend their interests to be unequal, the size of each co-owner's undivided interest must be stated as a percentage or a fraction, such as 60% and 40%, or 1/3 and 2/3.

> **In the Field**
>
> In Georgia, if two or more persons are named as owners, and there is no specific indication as to how they are taking title, they are presumed to be tenants in common with an equal ownership interest. Thus, if a deed is made out to "Donna Adams and Barbara Kelly," the law would consider them to be tenants in common, each holding an undivided one-half interest in the property. An important exception to this presumption is when the co-owners are married to each other.

No Right of Survivorship

When a tenancy in common exists, if a co-owner dies, the co-owner's interest passes to his/her heirs or devisees, who then become tenants in common with the remaining co-owners. There is no **right of survivorship**; that is, the remaining co-owners do not acquire the deceased's interest unless they are named in the deceased's last will and testament to do so. When a creditor has a claim on a co-owner's interest and forces its sale to satisfy the debt, the new buyer becomes a tenant in common with the remaining co-owners. A co-owner who wants to sell (or give away) only a portion of the co-owner's undivided interest may do so; the new owner then becomes a tenant in common with the other co-owners.

right of survivorship: a feature of joint tenancy whereby the surviving joint tenants automatically acquire all the rights, title, and interest of the deceased joint tenant

Co-Owner Responsibilities

Any income generated by the property belongs to the tenants in common in proportion to the size of their interests. Similarly, each co-owner is responsible for paying a proportionate share of property taxes, repairs, upkeep, and so on, plus interest and debt repayment, if any. If any co-owner fails to contribute a proportionate share, the other co-owners can pay that sum and then sue for that amount. If co-owners find that they cannot agree as to how the property is to be run and cannot agree on a plan for dividing or selling it, it is possible to request a court-ordered partition. A *partition* divides the property into distinct portions so that each person can hold a proportionate interest in severalty. If this is physically impossible, such as when three co-owners all have a one-third interest in a house, the court will order the property sold and the proceeds divided among the co-owners.

"What Ifs"

The major advantage of tenancy in common is that it allows two or more persons to achieve goals that one person could not accomplish alone. However, prospective co-owners should give advance thought as to what they would do (short of going to court) if: (1) a co-owner fails to pay the rightful share of ownership expenses, (2) differences arise regarding how the property is to be operated, (3) agreement cannot be reached as to when to sell, for how much, and on what terms, or (4) a co-owner dies and those who inherit that interest have little in common with the surviving co-owners. The counsel of an attorney experienced in property ownership can be very helpful when considering the co-ownership of property.

JOINT TENANCY

Another form of concurrent ownership is **joint tenancy**. The most distinguishing characteristic of joint tenancy is the right of survivorship. Upon the death of a joint tenant, that interest does not descend to the heirs or pass by the will. Rather, the entire ownership remains with the surviving joint tenant(s). In other words, there is simply one less owner.

joint tenancy: a form of property co-ownership that features the right of survivorship

Four Unities

To create a joint tenancy, **four unities** must be present. They are the unities of possession, interest, title, and time. To assist in remembering these unities of title, consider using the acronym PITT.

Unity of possession means that the joint tenants must enjoy the same undivided possession of the whole property. All joint tenants have the use of the entire property, and no individual owns a particular portion of it. By way of contrast, unity of possession is the only unity essential to a tenancy in common.

Unity of interest means that the joint tenants own one interest together and that each joint tenant has exactly the same right in that interest. If there are two owners, they each own one-half; if there are three owners, they each own one-third; and so on. (This, by the way, is the foundation upon which the survivorship feature rests.) If the joint tenants list individual interests, they lack unity of interest and will be treated as tenants in common. Unity of interest also means that, if one joint tenant holds a fee simple interest in the property, the others cannot hold anything but a fee simple interest.

four unities: for joint tenancy, unities of possession, interest, title, and time must be present; represented by the acronym PITT

Unity of title means that the joint tenants acquire their interests from the same source (i.e., the same deed or will). Georgia will allow property owners to create a valid joint tenancy by conveying to themselves and another without going through a third party.

Unity of time means that each joint tenant must acquire his/her ownership interest at the same moment. Once a joint tenancy is formed, it is not possible to add new joint tenants later unless an entirely new joint tenancy is formed among the existing co-owners and the new co-owner. To illustrate, suppose that A, B, and C own a parcel of land as joint tenants. If A sells interest to D, then B, C, and D must sign documents to create a new joint tenancy among them. If this is not done, D automatically becomes a tenant in common with B and C, who, between themselves, remain joint tenants. D will then own an undivided one-third interest in common with B and C, who will own an undivided two-thirds interest as joint tenants.

Right of Survivorship

The feature of joint tenancy ownership that is most widely recognized is its right of survivorship. Upon the death of a joint tenant, that interest in the property is extinguished. In a two-person joint tenancy, when one person dies, the other immediately becomes the sole owner. With more than two persons as joint tenants, when one dies, the remaining joint tenants are automatically left as owners. Ultimately, the last survivor becomes the sole owner. The legal philosophy is that the joint tenants constitute a single owning unit. The death of one joint tenant does not destroy that unit—it only reduces the number of persons owning the unit. For the public record, a copy of the death certificate and an affidavit of death of the joint tenant is recorded in the county where the property is located. The property must also be released from any estate tax liens.

It is the right of survivorship that has made joint tenancy a popular form of ownership among married couples. Married couples often want the surviving spouse to have sole ownership of the marital property. Any property held in joint tenancy goes to the surviving spouse without the delay of probate, and usually with less legal expense.

"Poor Man's Will"

Because of the survivorship feature, joint tenancy has loosely been labeled a "poor man's will." However, it cannot replace a properly drawn will because it affects only that property held in joint tenancy. Moreover, a will can be changed if the persons named therein are no longer in one's favor. But once a joint tenancy is formed, title is permanently conveyed and there is no further opportunity for change. As a joint tenant, you may not will your joint tenancy interest to someone because your interest ends upon your death. Ownership in joint tenancy may result in additional estate taxes.

Another important aspect of joint tenancy ownership is that it can be used to defeat dower or curtesy rights. If a married man forms a joint tenancy with someone other than his wife (such as a business partner) and then dies, his wife has no dower rights in that joint tenancy. As a result, courts have begun to look with disfavor upon the right of survivorship. The states of Louisiana, Ohio, and Oregon either do not recognize joint tenancy or have abolished it. Of the remaining states that recognize joint tenancy ownership (see Table 4-1), 14 have abolished the automatic presumption of survivorship. In these states, if the right of survivorship is desired in a joint tenancy, it must be clearly stated in the conveyance. For example, a deed might read, "Karen Carson and Judith Johnson, as joint tenants with the right of survivorship and not as tenants in common." Even in those states not requiring it, this wording is often used to ensure that the right of survivorship is intended. In community property states, one spouse may not take community funds and establish a valid joint tenancy with a third party. As stated in an earlier chapter, Georgia does not recognize dower, curtesy, or community property rights. Georgia does recognize joint tenancy, but, as discussed, the deed must clearly state that it is a joint tenancy coupled with the right of survivorship.

There is a popular misconception that a debtor can be protected from creditors' claims by taking title to property as a joint tenant. It is generally true that in a joint tenancy, the surviving joint tenant(s) acquire(s) the property free and clear of any liens against the deceased. However, this can happen only if the debtor dies before the creditor seizes the debtor's interest.

Only a human being can be a joint tenant. A corporation may not be a joint tenant. This is because a corporation is an artificial legal being and can exist in perpetuity—that is, never die. Joint tenancy ownership is not limited to the ownership of land; any estate in land and any chattel interest may be held in joint tenancy.

TENANCY BY THE ENTIRETY

tenancy by the entirety: a form of joint ownership reserved for married persons; right of survivorship exists and neither spouse has a disposable interest during the lifetime of the other

Tenancy by the entirety (also called *tenancy by the entireties*) is a form of joint tenancy specifically for married persons. To the four unities of a joint tenancy is added a fifth: *unity of person*. The basis for this is the legal premise that a husband and wife serve as an indivisible legal unit. Two key characteristics of a tenancy by the entirety are: (1) the surviving spouse becomes the sole owner of the property upon the death of the other, and (2) neither spouse has a disposable interest in the property during the lifetime of the other. Thus, while both are alive and married to each other, both signatures are necessary to convey title to the property. With respect to the first characteristic, tenancy by the entirety is similar to joint tenancy because both feature the right of survivorship. They are quite different, however, with respect to the second characteristic. Whereas a joint tenant can convey his/her proportionate interest to another party without the approval of the other joint tenant(s), a tenancy by the entirety can be terminated only by joint action of (or joint judgment against) husband and wife.

TABLE 4-1 Concurrent ownership by states

	LLP.*	LLC.**	Tenancy in common	Joint tenancy	Tenancy by the entirety	Community property
Alabama	X	X	X	X		
Alaska		X	X	X	X	
Arizona	X	X	X	X		X
Arkansas		X	X	X	X	
California		X	X	X		X
Colorado		X	X	X		
Connecticut		X	X	X		
Delaware	X	X	X	X	X	
District of Columbia	X	X	X	X	X	
Florida		X	X	X	X	
Georgia	X	X	X	X		
Hawaii		X	X	X	X	
Idaho	X	X	X	X		X
Illinois		X	X	X		
Indiana		X	X	X		
Iowa	X	X	X	X		
Montana		X	X	X	X	
Nebraska		X	X	X		
Nevada		X	X	X		X
New Hampshire		X	X	X		
New Jersey	X	X	X	X	X	
New Mexico		X	X	X		X
New York	X	X	X	X	X	
North Carolina		X	X	X	X	
North Dakota		X	X	X		
Ohio	X	X	X		X	
Oklahoma		X	X	X	X	
Oregon		X	X		X	
Pennsylvania		X	X	X	X	
Rhode Island		X	X	X	X	
South Carolina		X	X	X		
South Dakota		X	X	X		
Tennessee		X	X	X	X	

(Continued)

TABLE 4-1 (Continued)

	LLP*	LLC.**	Tenancy in common	Joint tenancy	Tenancy by the entirety	Community property
Kansas	X	X	X	X		
Kentucky		X	X	X	X	
Louisiana	X	X				X
Maine		X	X	X		
Maryland	X	X	X	X	X	
Massachusetts		X	X	X	X	
Michigan	X	X	X	X	X	
Minnesota		X	X	X		
Mississippi	X	X	X	X	X	
Missouri		X	X	X	X	
Texas	X	X	X	X		X
Utah	X	X	X	X	X	
Vermont		X	X	X	X	
Virginia	X	X	X	X	X	
Washington		X	X	X		X
West Virginia		X	X	X	X	
Wisconsin		X	X	X		X
Wyoming		X	X	X	X	

*Limited Liability Partnership **Limited Liability Company
In Ohio and Oregon, other means are available to achieve rights of survivorship between nonmarried persons. When two or more persons own property together in Louisiana, it is termed an "ownership in indivision" or a "joint ownership." Louisiana law is based on an old French civil law.
Source: © 2021 Mbition LLC

States that recognize tenancy by the entirety are listed in Table 4-1. Notice that Georgia does not recognize tenancy by the entirety. Also understand that while we discuss information in this text that is not specifically recognized in Georgia, it is still of importance because we routinely interact with people who have experiences in other states and we must have some ability to properly counsel them. Some of these states automatically assume that a tenancy by the entirety is created when married persons buy real estate. However, it is best to use a phrase such as "John and Mary Smith, husband and wife as tenants by the entirety with the right of survivorship" on deeds and other conveyances. This avoids later questions as to whether their intention might have been to create a joint tenancy or a tenancy in common.

Advantages and Disadvantages

There are several important advantages to tenancy by the entirety ownership: (1) it protects against one spouse conveying or mortgaging the couple's property without the consent of the other; (2) it provides in many states some protection from the forced sale of jointly held property to satisfy a debt judgment against one of the spouses, and (3) it features automatic survivorship. Disadvantages are that: (1) tenancy by the entirety provides for no one except the surviving spouse; (2) it may create estate tax problems, and (3) it does not replace the need for a will to direct how the couple's personal property shall be disposed.

Effect of Divorce

In the event of divorce, the parting spouses become tenants in common. This change is automatic, as tenancy by the entirety can exist only when the co-owners are husband and wife. If the ex-spouses do not wish to continue co-ownership, either can sell his/her individual interest. If a buyer cannot be found for a partial interest and an amicable agreement cannot be reached for selling the interests of both ex-spouses simultaneously, either may seek a court action to partition the property.

Note that severalty, tenancy in common, joint tenancy, and tenancy by the entirety are called English common law estates because of their roots in English common law.

COMMUNITY PROPERTY

Laws and customs acquired from Spain and France when vast areas of the United States were under their control are the basis for the **community property** system of ownership for married persons. Table 4.1 identifies the 10 states that recognize community property. Notice that Georgia is not a community property state. The laws of each community property state vary slightly, but the underlying concept is that the husband and wife contribute jointly and equally to their marriage and thus should share equally in any property purchased during marriage. Whereas English law is based on the merging of husband's and wife's interests

community property: spouses are treated as equal partners, with each owning one-half interest

upon marriage, community property law treats husband and wife as equal partners, with each owning a one-half interest.

Separate Property

Property owned before marriage and property acquired after marriage by gift, inheritance, or purchase with separate funds can be exempted from the couple's community property. Such property is called *separate property* and can be conveyed or mortgaged without the signature of the owner's spouse. The owner of a separate property also has full control over naming someone in his/her will to receive the property. All other property acquired by the husband or wife during marriage is considered community property and requires the signature of both spouses before it can be conveyed or mortgaged. Each spouse can name in his/her will the person to receive his/her one-half interest; it does not have to go to the surviving spouse. If death occurs without a will, in six states (California, Idaho, Nevada, New Mexico, Texas, and Washington), the deceased spouse's interest goes to the surviving spouse. In Arizona and Louisiana, the descendants of the deceased spouse are the prime recipients. Texas also allows community property to be held with a right of survivorship. Neither dower nor curtesy exists in community property states.

Philosophy

The major advantage of the community property system is found in its philosophy: It treats the spouses as equal partners in property acquired through their mutual efforts during marriage. Even if the wife elects to be a full-time homemaker and all the money brought into the household is the result of her husband's job (or vice versa), the law treats them as equal co-owners in any property bought with that money. This is true even if only one spouse is named as the owner.

In the event of divorce, if the parting couple cannot amicably decide how to divide community property, the courts will do so. If the courts do not, the ex-spouses will become tenants in common with each other. If it later becomes necessary, either can file suit for partition.

Caveat to Agents

Often, while preparing a real estate purchase contract, the buyers will ask the real estate agent how to take title. This is an especially common question posed by married couples purchasing a home. If the agent attempts to answer with a specific recommendation, the agent is practicing law, and a license is required to practice law. The agent can describe the ownership methods available in the state, but should then refer the buyers to their lawyer for a specific recommendation. This is important because the choice of ownership method cannot be made in the vacuum of a single purchase. It must be made in light of the buyers' total financial picture and estate plans by someone well versed in federal and state tax and estate laws.

Review Questions

Answers to these questions can be found in Appendix D at the end of this book.

1. Abel, Baker, and Charles are going to purchase an investment property as co-owners and will take title as joint tenants. Which of the following statements is INCORRECT?
   A. All will acquire their interests at the same moment in time.
   B. Each will receive a separate deed for his share.
   C. All may have equal interest in the property.
   D. All will enjoy equal rights of possession.

2. In a community property state, a married person can hold as separate property:
   A. only property bought by that person before marriage
   B. only property inherited by that person after marriage
   C. property bought before marriage and property inherited after marriage
   D. no real property, only personal property

3. A tenant in common may NOT:
   A. claim a portion of the property for personal use
   B. convey his/her interest by will
   C. use his/her share of the property as collateral for a mortgage loan
   D. sell his/her share without the agreement of the other tenants

4. Which of the following is NOT true of joint tenancy?
   A. Unities of time, title, interest, and possession must be present.
   B. New joint tenants may be added without forming a new joint tenancy.
   C. Survivorship exists among joint tenants.
   D. A husband and wife may hold title as joint tenants.

5. Which of the following is NOT a requirement of joint tenancy?
   A. Interest is gained at the same time.
   B. Interest is gained from the same source.
   C. Interest is provided in the same instrument.
   D. Interest is in equal or unequal quantities.

6. If any unity of joint tenancy is broken, the law will regard the estate as:
   A. a tenancy by the entireties
   B. community property
   C. a tenancy in common
   D. an estate in severalty

7. If tenants by the entireties divorce, barring any other agreement:
   A. they become tenants in common with each other
   B. the status of the title to the property is not affected
   C. the ex-wife takes title in severalty
   D. the ex-husband takes title in severalty

8. Community property laws are derived from legal concepts that have their origin in:
   A. Spanish and French law
   B. English common law
   C. American statutory law
   D. English parliamentary law

9. Mr. and Mrs. Marvin live in a community property state. Which of the following would most likely be considered their community property?
   A. property that is inherited by either spouse
   B. property conveyed as a gift to either spouse
   C. property purchased after they were married
   D. property owned by either spouse prior to their marriage

10. Which interest is shared in both the tenancy in common and the joint tenancy?
    A. time
    B. title
    C. interest
    D. possession

PART 2

FEDERAL LAWS, ALTERNATIVE FORMS OF OWNERSHIP, AND LAND USE

Now that the foundation of your study is complete, it is time to continue with the construction of your real estate knowledge. Part 2 is a study of the laws that impact our rights associated with the ownership of the American dream. We will also explain the less common forms of ownership and then do a little deeper dive into the private and public methods of limitation on the use of the land. In this part we will complete the following chapters:

Chapter 5: Fair Housing, ADA, Equal Credit, and Community Reinvestment

Chapter 6: Condominiums, Cooperatives, PUDs, and Timeshares

Chapter 7: Land-Use Control

CHAPTER 5
FAIR HOUSING, ADA, EQUAL CREDIT, AND COMMUNITY REINVESTMENT

KEY TERMS

Americans with Disabilities Act (ADA)
blockbusting
Civil Rights Act of 1866
Community Reinvestment Act (CRA)
Equal Credit Opportunity Act (ECOA)
Fair Housing Act
familial status
handicapped
protected class
steering
tester

OBJECTIVES

After successful completion of this chapter, you should be able to:

1. explain how the U.S. Constitution affects property rights;
2. explain the impact of the Fair Housing Act;
3. discuss the effect of the Americans with Disabilities Act on commercial properties;
4. know the credit requirements of the Equal Credit Opportunity Act; and
5. describe the Community Reinvestment Act's effect on lenders.

OVERVIEW

This chapter concentrates on federal legislation that has had a strong impact on expanding the ability of individuals to own real estate. The concept of fair housing prohibits illegal discrimination in the sale or leasing of real property. Equal credit has made lending sources available for thousands who could not previously qualify for loans. The Community Reinvestment Act encourages lenders to make loans in disadvantaged areas.

It is almost impossible to fully explain the effects of federal legislation on real estate over the last 50 years. The scope and effect of the changes resulting from federal legislation are felt daily and have touched virtually every aspect of the real estate business. The federal government's emphasis on protection of individual rights was imposed because many states found this goal politically difficult to pursue and, in many cases, a long history of prejudice was an overwhelming obstacle.

FAIR HOUSING CONSTITUTIONAL CONCEPTS

The federal legislation has been liberally applied to virtually all areas of discrimination: race, color, religion (creed), national origin, alienage, sex, marital status, age, familial status, and handicapped status. The theories supporting these federal laws are applied differently, depending on the source of the law and enforcement of the applicable statute. Let's review these theories in greater detail.

The most fundamental rights in real property are found in the U.S. Constitution. These rights are so firmly established and so broadly affect real estate that they deserve discussion at the outset. The Declaration of Independence declared that all men are created equal and set the stage for an attitude of the government that we enjoy in the United States. It was with this forethought that our founders wrote the U.S. Constitution, which instilled in all citizens certain inalienable rights. As far as real property ownership is concerned, the most significant of these rights are the Fifth, Thirteenth, and Fourteenth Amendments to the Constitution.

To date, the types of discrimination that have been deemed "suspect" by the U.S. Supreme Court have included discrimination on the basis of race, color, religion, national origin, and alienage. This is logical in that a citizen of the United States cannot alter race, color, national origin, or alienage, and is entitled to practice his/her religion of choice. Therefore, very strict constitutional prohibitions have been established by the courts to eliminate this type of discrimination for any citizen in the United States. It should be emphasized that there is no *constitutional* prohibition of discrimination on the basis of sex, age, or marital status, although the Supreme Court has ruled that the Fourteenth Amendment applies. One of the most significant areas of litigation has been based on racial discrimination. This has been applied to all federal activity through the Fifth Amendment, and to state and individual actions through the Thirteenth and Fourteenth Amendments to the Constitution.

The *Fifth Amendment* clearly states that no person shall ". . . be deprived of life, liberty, or property without due process of law . . . ." It was from this fundamental statement that we have developed the inherent right that no one can have property taken away without court proceedings. This concept has been expanded over the last 40 years or so to include the prohibition of certain types of discrimination, creating certain protected classes of people who may not be discriminated against.

The *Thirteenth Amendment* to the U.S. Constitution prohibits slavery and involuntary servitude. This amendment formed the basis for the most significant case on discrimination, *Jones v. Alfred H. Mayer Company*. That case basically held that any form of racial discrimination, even by individuals, creates a "badge of slavery," which, in turn, results in the violation of the Thirteenth Amendment. The Supreme Court stated that in enforcing the *Civil Rights Act of 1866*, which prohibits discrimination in housing, Congress is empowered under the Thirteenth Amendment to secure to all citizens the right to buy whatever a white man may buy and the right to live wherever a white man may live. The Court further stated, "If Congress cannot say that being a free man means at least this much, then the Thirteenth Amendment has a promise the Nation cannot keep." This case effectively prohibits racial discrimination and is applicable to real estate transactions.

The *Fourteenth Amendment* prohibits any state (as distinguished from the federal government) from depriving a person of life, liberty, or property without due process of law, and it prohibits any state from denying any person within its jurisdiction the equal protection of the laws. The significant case in interpreting the Fourteenth Amendment as it applies to the states was *Shelley v. Kraemer*. In this Supreme Court case, some white property owners were attempting to enforce a deed restriction that required all property owners to be Caucasian. The state courts granted the relief sought. The Supreme Court, however, reversed the case, stating that the action of state courts in imposing penalties deprived parties of their substantive right, without providing due process of law, to have access to housing. The opportunity to defend against discrimination has long been regarded as a denial of due process of law as guaranteed by the Fourteenth Amendment. The Court stated that equality and the enjoyment of property rights were regarded by the framers of the Fourteenth Amendment as an essential precondition to realization of other basic civil rights and liberties that the Fourteenth Amendment was intended to guarantee. Therefore, it was concluded that the "equal protection" clause of the Fourteenth Amendment should prohibit the judicial enforcement by state courts of restrictive covenants based on race or color.

FAIR HOUSING LAWS

In addition to the constitutional issues, two major federal laws prohibit discrimination in housing. The first is the **Civil Rights Act of 1866**. It says that all citizens of the United States shall have the same right in every state and territory as white citizens to inherit, purchase, lease, sell, hold, and convey real and personal property. In 1968, the Supreme Court affirmed that the 1866 Act prohibits "all racial discrimination, private as well as public, in the sale of real property."

The second is the **Fair Housing Act,** officially known as *Title VIII of the Civil Rights Act of 1968*, as amended. This law creates **protected classes** of people, making it illegal to discriminate on the basis of race, color, religion, sex (gender), national origin, physical handicap, or familial status in connection with the sale or rental of housing and any vacant land offered for residential construction or use.

Civil Rights Act of 1866: federal law that prohibits discrimination in buying, holding, or inheriting real estate

Fair Housing Act: federal law that specifies protected classes who are protected from discrimination; also called Title VIII

protected class: a class of people that by law is protected from discrimination

There are three ways that a Fair Housing Act violation can be proven. The first is obvious: an intentional discrimination against someone in a protected class, such as: "I refuse to sell to the Irish." The second requires that a regulation, while appearing neutral, results in a discriminatory impact. For instance, a "one person per bedroom" restriction that effectively eliminates occupancy by families or children has a discriminatory impact, even though it isn't specifically set out in the restriction. The third way a fair housing violation can be proven is if the owner fails to "reasonably accommodate" members of a protected class. For instance, if an occupant develops a disability, the owner or landlord must attempt to reasonably accommodate that occupant's needs. Once a fair housing violation has been demonstrated, the burden shifts to the defendant to produce evidence that shows the defendant's conduct was for a legitimate, nondiscriminatory purpose. If the owner can prove that, which may be difficult, there is no fair housing violation.

1988 Amendments to the Fair Housing Act

Understanding that one must not discriminate on the basis of race, color, religion, national origin, and sex (gender) seems fundamental today. The first four were the original protected classifications in 1968, and "sex" was added with an amendment in 1974. In 1988, the Civil Rights Act of 1968 was expanded to provide for housing for the handicapped and for people with children under the age of 18. The act now provides protection from any form of discrimination based on race, color, religion, national origin, sex, familial status, or handicapped status. The 1988 law's application may be very broad and needs to be discussed in more detail.

Handicapped

handicapped: having a physical or mental impairment that substantially limits one or more life activities, or having a record of such impairment

The 1988 amendment defines **handicapped** in three ways:

1. having a physical or mental impairment that substantially limits one or more major life activities;
2. having a record of having such an impairment; and
3. being regarded as having such an impairment.

The Act apparently includes recovered mental patients, as well as those who are suffering from a mental handicap. The legislation has definitely changed our attitude about certain restrictions. It is assumed, for instance, that a blind person may live with a guide dog in a housing project that prohibits pets. The handicapped are also allowed to make reasonable modifications to existing units, as long as it is at the handicapped person's expense. The landlord may require the tenant to restore the unit to its original condition upon termination of occupancy if the changes to the unit would not be conducive to renting to another tenant. An example would be if a tenant in a wheelchair had countertops lowered so s/he could reach them from the chair. In this case, the landlord could require the tenant, at his/her expense, to return the lowered countertops to their original position. The law also makes it unlawful for a landlord or owner to refuse to make reasonable accommodations, rules, policies, practices, or services when it is necessary to afford a handicapped person an equal opportunity to use and enjoy the dwelling.

In addition, all new multifamily dwellings with four or more units must be constructed to allow access and use by handicapped persons. If the building has no elevators, only first-floor units are covered by this provision. Doors and hallways in the buildings must be wide enough to accommodate wheelchairs. Light switches and other controls must be in convenient locations. Most rooms and spaces must be on an accessible route, and special accommodations, such as grab bars in the bathrooms, must be provided.

There are some exceptions under the handicapped-person provision. The term *handicapped*, for instance, does not include current illegal use of or addiction to a controlled substance, but it *does* include recovering drug addicts (halfway houses). Handicapped status also does not include any person whose tenancy imposes a direct threat to the health, safety, and property of others. Since the statute was enacted, some cases have held that recovering drug addicts and alcoholics are handicapped, as are people infected with HIV. Therefore, they must not be discriminated against, and denial of housing as a result of this "handicap" is a violation of the Fair Housing Act. This may result in unusual situations where recovering drug addicts (perhaps criminals) could be moving into a neighborhood, and the neighbors are prohibited from discriminating against them or denying them housing (by enforcing deed restrictions or zoning ordinances) because it would have a discriminatory effect on the handicapped.

Familial Status

Familial status is defined as one or more individuals (who have not obtained the age of 18 years) living with a parent or legal custodian, or, with the written permission of the parent or legal custodian, are living with a designee. These protections also apply to any person who is pregnant or is in the process of securing legal custody of any individual who has not obtained the age of 18 years. The most significant effect of this amendment is that all homeowners association property, apartment projects, and condominiums now have to have facilities adapted for children and cannot discriminate against anyone on the basis of familial status when leasing, selling, or renting property.

There are specific exemptions to this portion of the Act. A building can qualify for an exemption if: (1) it provides housing under the state or federal program that the secretary of Housing and Urban Development determines is specifically designed and operated to assist elderly persons; (2) it provides housing intended for, and generally occupied only by, persons 62 years of age or older; or

familial status: occurs when one or more individuals under the age of 18 are living with a parent or other person having custody

(3) it provides housing of which at least 80% of the units are occupied by at least one person 55 years of age or older and meets certain regulations that are adopted by the secretary of Housing and Urban Development. The penalties for violation of the Act are severe and change annually. The first violation results in a fine exceeding $20,000; for subsequent violations, the fine exceeds $100,000. The fines are in addition to other civil damages, potential injunctions, reasonable attorney's fees, and costs.

These amendments to the Fair Housing Act have a significant impact for all licensees attempting to sell, list, lease, or rent real estate. It is unlawful to refuse to sell or rent, or to refuse to negotiate the sale or rental of, any property based on familial status or handicapped status. Printing and advertising must not make any reference to preference based on handicapped or familial status. As stated previously, the landlord must not deny the right of a handicapped tenant to make any changes in the physical structure of the building, provided that the tenant agrees to reinstate the building to its original form upon departure.

It is safe to say that there are many more situations and circumstances that will occur that have not been specifically addressed by the statute. It is critically important that licensees recognize these prohibitions against discrimination and deem them just as serious a violation of an individual's civil rights as the more traditional areas of race, color, religion, national origin, and sex. Specifically, what do these two federal statutes prohibit, and what do they allow? The 1968 Fair Housing Act provides protection against the following acts if they discriminate against one or more of the protected classes:

- refusing to sell or rent to, deal with, or negotiate with any person;
- discriminating in the terms or conditions for buying or renting housing;
- discriminating by advertising that housing is available only to persons of a certain race, color, religion, sex, or national origin, those who are not handicapped, or adults;
- denying that housing is available for inspection, sale, or rent when it really is available;
- denying or making different terms or conditions for home loans by commercial lenders;
- denying to anyone the use of or participation in any real estate services, such as brokers' organizations, multiple listing services, or other facilities related to the selling or renting of housing; and
- steering or blockbusting.

Steering

steering: practice of directing home seekers to particular neighborhoods based on race, color, religion, sex, national origin, handicapped status, or adults-only status

Steering is the practice of directing home seekers to or from particular neighborhoods or properties based on race, color, religion, sex, national origin, nonhandicapped status, or adults-only status. Steering includes efforts to exclude people from one area of a city based on a protected classification as well as to direct them to specific or changing areas relating to a protected classification. Examples include showing only certain neighborhoods, slanting property descriptions, and downgrading neighborhoods. Steering is often subtle, sometimes no more than a word, phrase, or facial expression. Nonetheless, steering accounts for the bulk of the complaints filed against real estate licensees under the Fair Housing Act.

Blockbusting

Blockbusting is the illegal practice of inducing panic selling in a neighborhood for financial gain. Blockbusting typically starts when one person induces another to sell property cheaply by stating that an impending change in the racial or religious composition of the neighborhood will cause property values to fall, school quality to decline, and crime to increase. The first home thus acquired is sold (at a markup) to a member of a protected class. This event is used to reinforce fears that the neighborhood is indeed changing. The process quickly snowballs as residents panic and sell at progressively lower prices. The homes are then resold at higher prices to incoming residents. Note that blockbusting is not limited to fears about people moving into a neighborhood. In a Virginia case, a real estate firm attempted to gain listings in a certain neighborhood by playing upon residents' fears regarding an upcoming expressway project.

blockbusting: the illegal practice of inducing panic selling in a neighborhood for financial gain

Housing Covered by the 1968 Fair Housing Act

The 1968 Fair Housing Act applies to the following types of housing:

- single-family houses owned by private individuals when: (a) a real estate broker or other person in the business of selling or renting dwellings is used, and/or (b) discriminatory advertising is used;
- single-family houses not owned by private individuals;
- single-family houses owned by a private individual who owns more than three such houses or who, in any two-year period, sells more than one in which the individual was not the most recent resident;
- multifamily dwellings of five or more units; and
- multifamily dwellings containing four or fewer units, if the owner does not reside in one of the units

Acts Not Prohibited by the 1968 Fair Housing Act

Not covered by the 1968 Fair Housing Act are the sale or rental of single-family houses owned by a private individual who owns three or fewer such single-family houses if:

- a broker is not used;
- discriminatory advertising is not used; and

- no more than one house in which the owner was not the most recent resident is sold during any two-year period.

Not covered by the 1968 Act are rentals of rooms or units in owner-occupied multifamily dwellings for two to four families, if discriminatory advertising is not used. The Act also does not cover the sale, rental, or occupancy of dwellings that a religious organization owns or operates for other than a commercial purpose to persons of the same religion, if membership in that religion is not restricted on account of race, color, or national origin. It also does not cover the rental or occupancy of lodgings that a private club owns or operates for its members for other than a commercial purpose. Housing for the elderly may also allow discrimination in not permitting children or young adult occupants in the development or building, provided that the housing is primarily intended for the elderly, has minimum age requirements (55 or 62), and meets certain HUD guidelines. Note, however, that the above listed acts *not* prohibited by the 1968 Fair Housing Act *are* prohibited by the 1866 Civil Rights Act when discrimination based on race occurs in connection with such acts.

Fair Housing Enforcement

Adherence to the 1968 Act can be enforced in any of three ways by someone who feels discriminated against. The first is to file a written complaint with the U.S. Department of Housing and Urban Development (HUD) in Washington, D.C. The second is to file court action directly in a U.S. district court or state or local court. The third is to file a complaint with the U.S. attorney general. If a complaint is filed with HUD, HUD may investigate to see if the law has been broken; may attempt to resolve the problem by conference, conciliation, or persuasion; may refer the matter to a state or local fair housing authority; or may recommend that the complaint be filed in court. If HUD finds that a fair housing violation has occurred, it will schedule a hearing before a HUD administrative law judge, where the defendant is given the opportunity to explain the justification for the discrimination charge. Either party, the complainant or the defendant, can cause the HUD-scheduled administrative proceeding to be terminated if s/he elects to have the matter litigated in federal court instead. HUD has a "complaints" section on its website (hud.gov/program_offices/fair_housing_equal_opp/online-complaint). A person seeking enforcement of the 1866 Act must file a suit in a federal court.

No matter which route is taken, the burden of proving illegal discrimination under the 1968 Act is the responsibility of the person filing the complaint. If successful, the following remedies are available: (1) an injunction to stop the sale or rental of the property to someone else, making it available to the complainant; (2) money for actual damages caused by the discrimination; (3) punitive damages; and (4) court costs. There are also criminal penalties for those who coerce, intimidate, threaten, or interfere with a person's buying, renting, or selling of housing.

Enforcement by Private Persons

A person may also file a civil action in district court within one year of the occurrence or the termination of an alleged discriminatory housing practice; or the breach of a conciliation agreement entered into with a state housing law, whichever occurs last; or to obtain relief of the breach or discriminatory housing practice. If the court finds that a discriminatory practice has occurred or is about to occur, the court may award to the plaintiff actual and punitive damages, reasonable attorney's fees and court costs, and any permanent or temporary injunction.

Agent's Duties

It is a real estate agent's duty to uphold the 1968 Fair Housing Act and the 1866 Civil Rights Act. If a property owner asks an agent to discriminate, the agent must refuse to accept the listing. An agent is in violation of fair housing laws by giving a minority buyer or seller less than favorable treatment or by ignoring or referring him/her to an agent of the same minority. Violation also occurs when an agent fails to use best efforts or does not submit an offer because of race, color, religion, sex, national origin, handicap, or familial status.

Testers

From time to time, a licensee may be approached by fair housing **testers**. These are individuals or organizations that respond to advertising and visit real estate offices to test for compliance with fair housing laws. The tester does not announce this status or ask if the office follows fair housing practices. Rather, the tester plays the role of a person looking for housing to buy or rent and observes whether fair housing laws are being followed. If not followed, the tester lodges a complaint with the appropriate fair housing agency.

tester: an individual or organization that responds to advertising and visits real estate offices to test for compliance with fair housing laws

State Laws

When a state has laws substantially the same as the federal Fair Housing Act, prosecutors may elect to prosecute in state rather than federal court. Georgia has a fair housing law that essentially mimics the federal legislation. This gives the government some flexibility in deciding the venue for prosecution. In addition to federal and state laws, counties and cities may have ordinances that expand the protected classes under Fair Housing Act. Licensees must always be aware of the laws and ordinances where they practice, and adopting a policy of fair treatment for all is a good immunization from liability for violation.

THE AMERICANS WITH DISABILITIES ACT

The **Americans with Disabilities Act (ADA)** was enacted on July 26, 1990, and deals primarily with commercial property. Generally stated, it provides access

Americans with Disabilities Act (ADA): a federal law giving disabled individuals the right to access commercial facilities open to the public

requirements and prohibits discrimination against people with disabilities in public accommodations, state and local government, transportation, telecommunications, and employment. Anyone who has had a physical or mental handicap, or who is "perceived" as having such, that interferes with a "major life activity" is covered by the Act. The Act specifically affects the real estate brokerage industry in that real estate licensees need to determine whether the product the licensee is selling, managing, or leasing is in compliance with the Act. A licensee should always be cautioned, however, that the statute is very detailed, and there are a number of gray areas that still lack clear interpretation.

Scope

The antidiscrimination and removal of barrier requirements of the ADA apply to "places of public accommodations," and the accessibility requirements of the ADA with respect to new construction and alterations apply to public accommodations and "commercial facilities." The term "places of public accommodations" encompasses 12 categories of retail and service businesses, including places of lodging; food and drink establishments; places of exhibitionary entertainment; places of public gathering; sales and rental establishments; service establishments such as law firms, accounting firms, and banks; public transportation stations; places of public display or collection; places of recreation; educational facilities; social service center establishments; and exercise clubs. It is presumed that this definition includes brokerage offices, even if they are located in private homes. "Commercial facility" is defined as a facility: (1) whose operations affect commerce; (2) that is intended for nonresidential use; and (3) that is not expressly exempted from coverage under the Fair Housing Act of 1968.

The ADA contains a broad prohibition affecting public accommodations and discriminating against those with disabilities by denying them the full and equal enjoyment of goods, services, facilities, privileges, advantages, and accommodations of any place of public accommodation. Facilities need to be usable by those with disabilities. All commercial facilities must also be accessible to the maximum extent feasible whenever alterations are being performed on the facility.

Alteration is defined as any change that affects the usability of a facility. If the alterations are made to a lobby or work area of the public accommodation, a path of travel to the altered area and to the bathrooms, telephones, and drinking fountains serving that area must be made accessible to the extent that the added accessibility costs are not disproportionate to the overall cost of the original alteration. Disproportionate cost is defined for the purposes of the Act as cost that exceeds 20% of the original alteration. The cost of alteration means all costs and renovating in particular proportion to the facility in a three-year period.

The Act requires modifications to procedures so that disabled individuals are not excluded from regular programs. Places of public accommodations must make reasonable modifications to the policies and procedures in order to accommodate individuals with disabilities and not create restrictions that tend to screen out individuals with disabilities, such as requiring a person to produce a driver's license or not allowing more than one person in a clothes-changing area when a disabled person needs the assistance of another. The act also requires auxiliary aids and services to ensure effective communication with individuals with hearing, vision, or speech impairments. These requirements include interpreters, listening headsets, television closed caption decoders, telecommunication devices for the deaf, video tech displays, Braille materials, and large-print materials.

Defenses and Challenges

There are several defenses and exclusions available under the Act, but most are extremely narrow in scope. In addition, there are few court precedents to help us with interpretation of the Americans with Disabilities Act. Problems in compliance will occur; for example, if a water fountain is placed low enough for someone in a wheelchair to use it, what happens to the tall person who has difficulty in bending?

Lowering a fire extinguisher for easier access to the person in the wheelchair also gives easier access to small children. Something that is "childproof" will also be inaccessible to those with limited use of their hands. Both the Department of Justice and private individuals may maintain a cause of action to enforce Title III against commercial building owners. The Department may seek monetary damages or injunctive relief, but private individuals are entitled only to seek injunctive relief under the statute. Apparently, a tort claim may create a cause of action for monetary damages.

EQUAL CREDIT OPPORTUNITY ACT

The **Equal Credit Opportunity Act (ECOA)** was originally passed to make way for equal credit for borrowers by making it unlawful to discriminate against an applicant for credit based on sex or marital status. In 1976, the Act was amended to prohibit discrimination in any credit transaction based on race, color, religion, national origin, sex, marital status, age (not including minors), receipt of income from a public assistance program, and the good faith exercise of rights under the ECOA or other federal consumer protection laws.

Equal Credit Opportunity Act: federal law that provides for equal credit to borrowers

Prohibited Requests

To effect this prohibition on discrimination, a creditor is prohibited from requiring certain information from the borrower, including:

- information concerning a spouse or former spouse, except when that spouse will be contractually obligated for repayment or if the spouse resides in a community property state.

- information regarding the applicant's marital status, unless the credit requested is for an individual's unsecured account, or unless the applicant resides in a community property state and the community property is to be relied upon to repay the credit. Inquiries as to the applicant's marital status are limited, however, to categories of "married," "unmarried," and "separated." "Unmarried" includes single, divorced, and widowed persons and may be specified in the application.
- information concerning the source of an applicant's income without disclosing that information regarding alimony, child support, or separate maintenance. This information is to be furnished only at the option of the applicant. The big exception to the rule is when the applicant expects to use any of those sources of income for repayment. If so, the lender may request this information.
- information regarding an applicant's birth control practices or any intentions concerning the bearing or rearing of children, although a lender still has the right to ask an applicant about the number and ages of any dependents or about dependent-related financial obligations.
- questions regarding race, color, religion, or national origin of the applicant. There are minor exceptions when a real estate loan is involved. These exceptions are allowed in order to provide certain information that may be used by the federal government for the purposes of monitoring conformance with the Equal Credit Opportunity Act. When the information is requested, the lender is required to advise the applicants that the furnishing of the specific information is for purposes of monitoring the lender's compliance and is requested on a voluntary basis only. If the applicant does not wish to answer the questions, the lender simply notes the refusal on the application form. The refusal to give the information requested may not be used in any way in considering whether or not credit is granted to the applicant. If the applicant agrees to provide the information on a voluntary basis, the following information can be furnished:
    - race or national origin
    - sex, relating to gender only (not sexual orientation)
    - marital status (using the categories of married, unmarried, or separated)

Evaluating Credit Applications

As previously stated, the lender must not use information obtained from an applicant that might be considered to be illegally discriminatory. Each applicant has to be evaluated on the same basic information as any other individual. Lenders may not refuse credit based on an individual category, such as newlywed status, being recently divorced, and so on. The lender's rules must be applied uniformly to all applicants. The areas in which there must be be no discrimination have already been discussed (sex, marital status, race, color, religion, national origin, age, public assistance), but some of these areas need to be discussed in greater detail.

Age

A lender is prohibited from taking an applicant's age into account in determining ability to repay. Neither may income from any public assistance program be taken into account. The only exception to this prohibition is minors, who lack full contractual capacity to enter into real estate transactions.

Children

As discussed in the previous sections on fair housing, the Equal Credit Opportunity Act has always provided that there be no assumptions or statistics relating to the likelihood that a group of persons may bear children. In prior years, lenders required non-pregnancy affidavits and other indications that a young, newly married couple would not endanger the income-producing capacity of the wife.

Part-Time Income

Income from part-time employment or retirement income must not be discounted because of its source. However, the creditor may still consider the amount and probability of continuance of such income.

Alimony and Child Support

Alimony and child support and separate maintenance may not be considered in evaluating a loan application unless the creditor determines that such payments are not likely to be made consistently. In such cases, the lender has the right to determine whether the applicant has the ability to compel payment, and to determine the creditworthiness of the party who is obligated to make such payments.

Credit History

The Equal Credit Opportunity Act requires a creditor to consider the separate record of the applicant. This prohibits the lender from tying the applicant's credit history to the record of the spouse or former spouse.

Immigration Residency

A creditor may consider an applicant's immigration status and whether the applicant is a permanent resident of the United States.

Sex

A lender may not ask about the sex of an applicant, but may ask an applicant to designate a title on the application form (Ms., Miss, Mrs., or Mr.) if the form indicates that the designation of the title is optional.

Marital Status

If an applicant applies for individual credit, the lender may not ask the applicants their marital status unless the applicant resides in a community property state or is relying on property located in a community property state to repay the loan. Similarly, a lender may not seek information about a spouse or former spouse unless a spouse will be permitted to use the account, the spouse is contractually liable on the account, or the borrower is relying on the spouse's income as a basis for repayment of the loan.

Credit Denial

If an applicant is denied credit, the lender must give a written notice of denial, also referred to as "Notice of Adverse Action," to the applicant and advise the rejected applicant of the federal agency that administers compliance with the Equal Credit Opportunity Act for that particular loan transaction. The statement of specific reasons must give the precise reason or reasons for the denial of credit. There are suggested guidelines for giving reasons for credit denial, including:

- inability to verify credit references
- temporary or irregular employment
- insufficient length of employment
- insufficient income
- excessive obligations
- inadequate collateral
- too short a period of residency
- delinquent credit obligation

An application can also be declined if it is incomplete.

Penalties

Failure to comply with the Equal Credit Opportunity Act or the accompanying federal regulations makes a creditor subject to a civil liability fine for damages, which is limited to $10,000 in individual actions and the lesser of $500,000 or 1% of the creditor's net worth in class actions. The court may also award court costs and reasonable attorney's fees to an aggrieved applicant.

Copies of Appraisal Reports

A lender or loan broker must make available a copy of an appraisal report to an applicant for a loan to be secured by a lien on the dwelling. The report may be provided either routinely as a part of the lender's standard process or when the loan applicant requests a copy. If the lender decides to provide the appraisal only upon request, it must notify the applicant in writing of the right to receive a copy of the appraisal report. The lender must promptly (generally within 30 calendar days) mail or deliver the copy of the appraisal report after the borrower's request is received.

COMMUNITY REINVESTMENT ACT

The **Community Reinvestment Act (CRA)** expands the concept that regulated financial institutions must serve the needs of their communities. Whenever a financing institution regulated by the federal government applies for a charter, branch facility, office relocation, or acquisition of another financing institution, the record of the institution's help in meeting local credit needs must be one of the factors considered by the supervising agencies of the federal government.* Federal regulators are required to evaluate each financial institution's actual performance in meeting the credit needs of its community, using lending, investment, and service tests to review an institution's performance. Some financial institutions may choose to adopt a strategic plan that sets forth specific goals that must be achieved.

For larger institutions and some smaller institutions, the lending, investment, and service tests are measured by home mortgage loan originations, small business and small firm loans, community development loans, and consumer loans. The investment test evaluates the extent to which an institution has been meeting community needs through qualified investment. A service test reviews the availability and responsiveness of an institution's system for delivering retail banking and community development of services. In addition, the retail institution must delineate an assessment area consisting of one or more metropolitan statistical areas or contiguous subdivisions, such as counties, cities, and towns, focusing on the location where the lender has its main office, branches, and automatic teller machines.

Community Reinvestment Act: a federal statute encouraging federally regulated lenders to increase their participation in low-income areas

CRA Notice

The institution must post in the public lobby of its main office and each branch office a "Community Reinvestment Act" notice, which informs consumers that they are entitled to certain information about the operations of the lender and its performance under the CRA. This notice also informs consumers of the schedules for the CRA examination and the availability of any federal regulatory report covered by the CRA.

---

*The supervising agencies include the Office of the Comptroller of the Currency, the Board of Governors of the Federal Reserve System, the Federal Deposit Insurance Corporation, and the Office of Thrift Supervision.

It is very difficult to ascertain what impact the Community Reinvestment Act has on lending institutions and on practices of lenders generally. Many areas of the statute are vague, and it is difficult for federal regulators to establish hard-and-fast rules because of the variety of needs that the lending institutions generally serve in different communities. As with a lot of other federal legislation, it may take some time before the full impact of this act is felt.

Review Questions

Answers to these questions can be found in Appendix D at the end of this book.

1. Discrimination in the availability of housing on the basis of religion is prohibited by the:
   A. Civil Rights Act of 1866
   B. Equal Credit Opportunity Act
   C. Civil Rights Act of 1968
   D. Americans with Disabilities Act

2. Vera, a real estate broker, was offered a rental listing by a homeowner who stated that he would not rent the property to a person of certain religious beliefs. Vera should:
   A. refuse to accept the listing on these terms
   B. accept the listing and leave it up to the owner to refuse any offers received from persons of that religion
   C. accept the listing and steer persons of that religion to other properties
   D. file a complaint of discrimination against the owner

3. Under federal law, the owner of one single-family dwelling in which the owner has resided for 10 years, who does not employ an agent and does not use discriminatory advertising, may discriminate in the sale or rental of the property on any of the following bases EXCEPT:
   A. religion
   B. race
   C. color
   D. national origin

4. State and local laws that restrict or prohibit discrimination in the availability of rental housing:
   A. are not allowed because of federal law
   B. may not conflict with federal law
   C. may be more restrictive than federal statutes
   D. are created to empower federal laws

5. The Civil Rights Act of 1866 prohibits:
   A. racial discrimination
   B. steering
   C. blockbusting
   D. discrimination for any reason

6. All of the following are prohibited by the Fair Housing Act of 1968, as amended, EXCEPT:
   A. discrimination in advertising
   B. denial of availability of housing on the basis of religion
   C. discrimination in terms or conditions for sale or rent
   D. discrimination on the basis of age

7. Amendments to the Fair Housing Act of 1968, signed by the president in 1988, prohibit:
   A. discrimination on the basis of physical handicap
   B. the offering of different loan terms by commercial lenders based on race or religion of the loan applicant
   C. refusal to sell, rent, or negotiate with any person
   D. steering and blockbusting

8. The practice of directing home seekers to particular neighborhoods based on race, color, religion, sex, or national origin:
   A. is known as steering
   B. is prohibited by the Civil Rights Act of 1866
   C. constitutes blockbusting
   D. is not illegal if requested by the buyer

9. Which of the following is NOT true of the inducement of panic selling in a neighborhood for financial gain?
   A. It is prohibited by the Fair Housing Act of 1968.
   B. It is limited to fear of loss of value because of the changing racial composition of a neighborhood.
   C. It is known as blockbusting.
   D. The prohibition applies to licensed real estate agents.

10. The Fair Housing Act of 1968 applies to:
    A. single-family housing only
    B. multiple-family dwellings only
    C. residential properties
    D. all real estate

11. A church that operates housing for the elderly may restrict occupancy to members of the church if:
    A. it follows guidelines as set by HUD
    B. the units are to be rented, but not if they are being offered for sale
    C. it advertises in a discriminatory way
    D. it wishes to violate the Fair Housing Act

12. A victim of discrimination in housing may seek enforcement of the 1968 Fair Housing Act by any of the following means EXCEPT:
    A. filing a complaint with the Department of Housing and Urban Development
    B. filing action in federal court
    C. filing a complaint with the U.S. attorney general
    D. filing a complaint with the state real estate department

13. A person seeking enforcement of the Civil Rights Act of 1866 may do so by filing:
    A. an action in federal court
    B. a complaint with the U.S. attorney general
    C. an action in county court
    D. a complaint with HUD

14. A licensed real estate agent is offered a listing by an owner who will not sell to any person of a certain national origin. The agent should:
    A. accept the listing and leave it up to the owner to reject offers from these persons
    B. refuse to accept the listing
    C. report the owner to the real estate department
    D. file a complaint against the owner with HUD

15. The Sunset Hills Country Club has several guest bedrooms that are made available to members and guests for a nominal charge, but are not available to the general public. Does this constitute a violation of the federal fair housing laws?
    A. Yes, because rental housing of this nature must be open to the public.
    B. Yes, because the charging of a fee constitutes a commercial purpose.
    C. No, because the club is exempt under the provisions of the Fair Housing Act of 1968.
    D. No, because this does not constitute steering or blockbusting.

CHAPTER 6
CONDOMINIUMS, COOPERATIVES, PUDs, AND TIMESHARES

KEY TERMS

bylaws
common elements
condominium
cooperative
covenants, conditions, and restrictions (CC&Rs)
planned unit development (PUD)
proprietary lease
resort timesharing
separate elements

OBJECTIVES

After successful completion of this chapter, you should be able to:

1. explain the concepts of land division and land-use efficiency;
2. describe the features of the condominium declaration;
3. explain the advantages and disadvantages of condo living;
4. describe condo financing and conversions;
5. explain the features of both timesharing and cooperative apartments;
6. define PUD and explain its purpose;
7. describe the key features of resort timesharing; and
8. describe the unique character of condominium financing.

OVERVIEW

This chapter covers the methods of dividing land. The **condominium** declaration is covered in some detail. Other topics include management, maintenance fees, taxes, insurance, and financing. The advantages and disadvantages of condominium living are discussed, along with a list of things to check before buying. Other condo topics include a discussion of legislation, condo conversions, and physical appearance. Cooperative apartments, planned unit developments (PUDs), and timesharing are also covered.

condominium: individual ownership of a particular airspace plus undivided ownership of the common elements

The idea of combining community living with community ownership is not new. Two thousand years ago, the Roman Senate passed condominium laws that permitted Roman citizens to own individual dwelling units in multiunit buildings. This form of ownership resulted because land was scarce and expensive in Rome. After the fall of the Roman Empire, condominium ownership was used in the walled cities of the Middle Ages. Here, it was primarily a defensive measure since residing outside the walls was dangerous because of roving bands of raiders. With the stabilization of governments after the Middle Ages, the condominium concept became dormant. Then in the early 20th century, in response to land scarcity in cities, the idea was revived in Western Europe. From there, the concept spread to several Latin American countries and, in 1951, to Puerto Rico. Puerto Rican laws and experience in turn became the basis for passage by Congress in 1961 of Section 234 of the National Housing Act. Designed as a legal model that condominium developers could follow in order to obtain Federal Housing Administration (FHA) loan insurance, Section 234 also served as a model for state condominium laws now in effect across the United States. In this chapter, we'll discuss condominiums, in particular an overview of their organization, operation, benefits, and drawbacks. Then we'll turn our attention to cooperatives, PUDs, and timesharing.

THE DESIRE FOR LAND-USE EFFICIENCY

Of the forces responsible for creating the need for condominiums, cooperatives, and planned unit developments (PUDs), the most important are land scarcity in desirable areas, continuing escalation of construction costs, disenchantment with the work of maintaining the grounds around a house, and the desire to own rather than rent. When constructing single-family houses on separate lots, a builder can usually average four to five houses per acre of land. In a growing number of cities, the sheer physical space necessary to continue building detached houses either does not exist or, if it does, it is a long distance from employment centers or is so expensive as to eliminate all but a small portion of the population from building there. As in ancient Roman times, the solution is to build more dwellings on the same parcel of land. Instead of four or five dwellings, build 25 or 100 on an acre of land. That way, not only is the land more efficiently used, but the cost is divided among more owners. From the standpoint of construction costs, the builder does not have the miles of streets, sewers, or utility lines that would be necessary to reach every house in a subdivision. Furthermore, the facts that there are shared walls, that one dwelling unit's ceiling is often another's floor, and that one roof can cover many vertically stacked units can produce savings in construction materials and labor.

THE AMENITIES OF MULTIFAMILY LIVING

For some householders, the lure of "carefree living," wherein such chores as lawn mowing, watering, weeding, snow shoveling, and building maintenance are provided, is the major attraction. For others, it is the security often associated with clustered dwelling or the extensive recreational and social facilities that are not economically possible on a single-dwelling-unit basis. It is commonplace to find swimming pools, recreation halls, tennis and volleyball courts, gymnasiums, and even social directors at some condominium, cooperative, and PUD projects. A large rental apartment project can also produce the same advantages of land and construction economy and amenities. Nevertheless, we must not overlook the preference of most American households to own rather than rent their dwellings. This preference is typically based on a desire for a savings program, observation of inflation in real estate prices, and advantageous income tax laws that allow owners, but not renters, to deduct property taxes and mortgage interest.

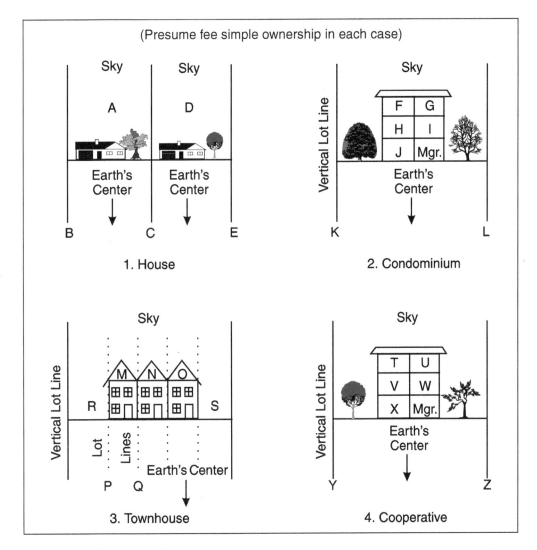

FIGURE 6-1 Comparison of estates
Source: © 2021 Mbition LLC

DIVIDING THE LAND OF AN ESTATE

Figure 6-1 demonstrates the estate in land created by a condominium, cooperative, and planned unit development, and compares each with the estate held by the owner of a house. Notice in Figure 6-1 that the ownership of house A extends from lot line B across to lot line C. Except where limited by zoning or other legal restrictions, the owner of house A has full control over and full right to use the land between the lot lines from the center of the Earth to the limits of the sky. Within the law, the owner can choose how to use the land, what to build on it or add to it, what color to paint the house and garage, how many people and animals will live there, what type of landscaping to have, from whom to purchase property insurance, and so on. The owner of house D has the same control over the land between lot lines C and E.

The owner of A may not dictate to a neighbor what color to paint the neighbor's house, what kind of shrubs and trees to grow, or from whom to buy hazard insurance, if any at all. (Occasionally, one will find deed restrictions in housing subdivisions that give the owners a limited amount of control over each other's land uses in the subdivision.)

CONDOMINIUMS

The first step in creating a condominium is for the state to pass laws that create the legal framework for condominium ownership. All states have passed them, and they are variously known as a state's horizontal property act, strata titles act, condominium act, or a similar name. They all follow the FHA model plus each state's particular refinements. As the names suggest, these laws address the problem of subdividing the airspace over a given parcel of land. Prior to these acts, the legal framework that made it possible for people to own a cubicle of airspace plus an undivided interest in the shell of the building and the land under and around the building did not exist. Moreover, condominium acts had to be designed to be acceptable to lenders who would be asked to make loans on condominiums, property tax authorities who would have to assess them, and income tax authorities who would allow owners to deduct loan interest and property taxes. The lawmakers were successful, and today millions of people live in condominiums. Physically, a condominium can take the shape of a 2-story garden apartment building, a 40-story tower with several living units on each floor, row houses, clustered houses, or even detached houses sharing a single parcel of land.

Condominiums are not restricted to residential uses. In recent years, a number of developers across the nation have built office buildings and sold individual suites to doctors, dentists, and lawyers. The same idea has been applied to shopping centers and industrial space. A condominium does not have to be a new building: Many existing apartment houses have been converted from rental status to condominium ownership with only a few physical changes to the building.

Separate and Common Elements

The distinguishing features of a condominium are its separate and common elements and its system of self-government. The **separate elements**, called separate property, are those areas in the condominium that are exclusively owned and used by the individual condominium owners. These are the individual dwelling units in the building. More precisely, the separate property is the airspace occupied by a unit. This is the space lying between the interior surfaces of the unit walls and between the floor and the ceiling. Everything else is a common element in which each unit owner holds an undivided interest. Thus, the land and the shell of the building are common elements owned by all. **Common elements** include, for example, the manager's office, lobby, hallways, stairways, elevators, recreation areas, landscaping, and parking lot. Sometimes, you will hear the term *limited common element*. This is a common element the use of which is restricted to a specific unit owner. Examples are assigned parking stalls and individual storage units.

separate elements: areas in the condominium that are exclusively owned and used by the individual owners; also called separate property

common elements: those parts of a condominium that are owned by all the unit owners

Owners' Association

When a developer wants to create a condominium (either built from the ground up or converted from an existing building to condominium ownership), the developer prepares and records with the public recorder what is variously known as an enabling declaration, master deed, plan of condominium ownership, or condominium subdivision plan. This document, usually 50 to 150 pages long, converts a parcel of land held under a single deed into a number of individual separate property estates (the condominium units) and an estate composed of all the common elements.

Survey maps are included to show the location of each condominium unit plus all the common elements. The developer also creates a legal framework so that the unit owners can govern themselves. This is the condominium owners' association, of which each unit purchaser automatically becomes a member. Although the association can be organized as a trust or unincorporated association, most often it will be organized as a corporation in order to provide the legal protections normally afforded by a corporation to its owners. Additionally, it will be organized as not-for-profit so as to avoid income taxes on money collected from members. The main purpose of the owners' association is to control, regulate, and maintain the common elements for the overall welfare and benefit of its members. The owners' association is a mini-government by and for the condominium owners.

Bylaws

The rules by which an owners' association operates are called its **bylaws**. They are prepared by the developer's attorney and recorded with the master deed. The bylaws provide the rules by which the association's board of directors

bylaws: rules that govern how an owners' association will be run

is elected and set the standards by which the board must rule. The bylaws set forth how association dues (maintenance fees) will be established and collected; how contracts will be let for maintenance, management, and repair work; and how personnel will be hired.

CC&Rs

Finally, the developer must file a list of regulations by which anyone purchasing a unit in the condominium must abide. These are known as **covenants, conditions, and restrictions (CC&Rs)**. They tell a unit owner such things as not to store personal items on balconies or driveways, what color the exterior of the living room drapes should be, to what extent an owner may alter the exterior of the unit, and whether an owner may install a satellite television dish on the roof, for example. Additional regulations may be embodied in a set of house rules. Typically, these govern such things as when the swimming pool and other recreation facilities will be open for use and when quiet hours will be observed in the building.

CC&Rs: covenants, conditions, and restrictions by which a property owner agrees to abide

Deed

Each purchaser of a condominium unit receives a deed from the developer. The deed describes the location of the unit, both in terms of the unit number in the building and its surveyed airspace. The deed will also describe the common elements and state the percentage interest in the common elements that the grantee is receiving. The deed is recorded upon closing just like a deed to a house. Upon selling, the owner has a new deed prepared that describes the unit and the common element interest and delivers it to the purchaser at closing. If the condominium is on leased land, the developer will deliver a lease (or sublease) to the unit buyer. Upon resale, that lease is assigned to the buyer.

Voting Rules

Once the units in the building have been sold and the association turned over to the unit owners, the unit owners can change the rules. Generally, the bylaws require a three-fourths vote and the CC&Rs require a two-thirds vote from the association members for a change. House rules can be changed with a simple majority or, in some cases, by the board of directors without a vote of the association.

Board of Directors

Condominium bylaws provide that a board of directors be elected by the association members. The board is authorized to administer the affairs of the condominium, including purchasing of hazard and liability insurance for the common elements, arranging for maintenance and repair of common elements, enforcing CC&Rs and house rules, assessing and collecting a sufficient amount of monthly homeowner fees and special assessments, and listening to complaints and suggestions from unit owners as to how the condominium should be run.

Board members are usually elected at the annual meeting of the association, are unit owners, and serve for one year. Typically, there will be five to seven members on the board, and one will be elected as president, one as vice president, one as secretary, and one as treasurer. Meetings are held monthly unless added business requires more frequent meetings. Board meetings are usually open to all association members, who can then watch the proceedings and provide input. To help spread out the work, the board will appoint committees on which owners are asked to serve. Examples are landscaping, architectural, security, clubhouse, and social committees. Directors and committee members are not usually paid for their time.

Annual Meetings

Once a year, the owners' association as a whole will meet for an annual meeting. Besides the election of board members for the following year, this is an opportunity for association members to vote on major issues such as changes in the CC&Rs and bylaws, monthly maintenance fee increases, special assessments, and any other matters the board feels should be put to a general ownership vote rather than handled at a board meeting. Owners also receive an annual report of the fiscal health of the association and other information pertinent to their ownership.

Condominium Management

Most condominium associations will employ a condominium management company to advise the board and take care of day-to-day tasks. The management company is usually responsible for finding, hiring, and paying gardeners, trash haulers, janitors, repair personnel, and a pool maintenance firm. The management company collects maintenance fees and special assessments from unit owners, accounts for condominium expenses, handles the payroll, and pays for contracted services.

If the association chooses to hire an on-site manager, that person is usually responsible for enforcing the house rules, handling complaints or problems regarding maintenance, making daily security checks, and supervising the swimming pool and recreation areas. The extent of the duties and responsibilities is set by the owners' association. The association should also retain the right to fire the resident manager and the management firm if their services are not satisfactory.

Maintenance Fees

The costs of maintaining the common elements in a condominium are allocated among the unit owners in accordance with percentages set forth in the master deed. These are called maintenance fees or association dues and are collected monthly. Failure to pay creates a lien against the delinquent owner's unit.

The amount collected is based on the association's budget for the coming year. This is based on the board of directors' estimate of the cost of month-to-month maintenance, insurance, legal and management services, plus reserves for expenses that do not occur monthly.

Reserves

The importance of setting aside reserves each month is illustrated by the following example. Suppose it is estimated that the exterior of a 100-unit building will have to be painted every seven years and that the cost is expected to be $25,200. To avoid a special painting assessment of $252 per unit, the association instead collects $3 per month from each unit owner for 84 months. The reserves should be kept in a separate, interest-bearing savings account.

Property Taxes and Insurance

Since condominium law recognizes each condominium dwelling unit as a separate legal ownership, property taxes are assessed on each unit separately. Property taxes are based on the assessed value of the unit, which is based on its market value. As a rule, it is not necessary for the taxing authority to assess and tax the common elements separately. The reason is that the market value of each unit reflects not only the value of the unit itself, but also the value of the fractional ownership in the common elements that accompany the unit.

The association is responsible for purchasing hazard and liability insurance covering the common elements. Each dwelling unit owner is responsible for purchasing hazard and liability insurance for the interior of the dwelling. Thus, if a visitor slips on a banana peel in the lobby or a hallway of the building, the association is responsible. If the accident occurs in an individual's unit, the unit owner is responsible. In a high-rise condominium, if the roof is damaged during a heavy rainstorm and floods several apartments below, the association is responsible. If a unit owner's dishwasher overflows and soaks the apartments below, the owner is responsible. If patio furniture is stolen from the swimming pool area, the association is responsible. If patio furniture (or any personal property, for that matter) is stolen from an individual's unit, that is the unit owner's responsibility. Policies designed for associations and policies for condominium owners are readily available from insurance companies. If a condominium unit is being rented, the owner will want to have landlord insurance, and the tenant, for personal protection, will want a tenant's hazard and liability policy.

Condominium Financing

Because each condominium unit can be separately owned, each can be separately financed, similar to a detached single-family residential property. Thus, condominium purchasers can choose whether to borrow against their unit. If they borrow, they can choose a large or small down payment and a long or short amortization period. If they want to repay early or refinance, that is their option, too. Upon resale, the buyer can elect to assume the loan, pay it off, or obtain new financing. In other words, while association bylaws, restrictions, and house rules may regulate the use of a unit, in no way does the association control how a unit may be financed. Since each unit is a separate ownership, if a lender needs to foreclose against a delinquent borrower in the building, the remaining unit owners are not involved. They are neither responsible for the delinquent borrower's mortgage debt nor are they parties to the foreclosure.

Loan Terms

Loan terms offered to condominium buyers are quite similar to those offered on houses, although most lenders will require that at least 50% of the condominiums in the development are owner-occupied. Typically, lenders will make conventional uninsured loans for up to 80% of value. With private mortgage insurance, this can be raised to 90% or 95%. On FHA-approved buildings, the FHA offers insurance terms similar to those for detached dwellings. Financing can also be in the form of an installment contract or a seller carryback.

Deposit Practices

If a project is not already completed and ready for occupancy when it is offered for sale, it is common for the developer to require a substantial deposit. The best practice is to place this in an escrow account payable to the developer upon completion. Without this precaution, some developers will use deposits to help pay the expenses of construction while the building is being built. Unfortunately, if the deposits are spent by a developer who goes bankrupt before the project is completed, the buyer receives neither a finished unit nor the return of the deposit. If the deposits are held in escrow, the buyers do not receive a unit, but they do get their deposits back.

Condominium Conversions

During the late 1970s, the idea of condominium ownership became very popular in the United States. Builders constructed new condominiums at a rapid pace, but there still were not enough to meet the demand. Soon, enterprising developers found that existing apartment buildings could be converted to condominiums and sold to the waiting public. Compared to new construction, a condominium conversion is often simpler, faster, and more profitable for the developer. The procedure involves finding an attractively built existing building that is well located and has good floor plans. The developer does a face-lift on the outside, adds more landscaping, paints the interior, and replaces carpets and appliances. The developer also files the necessary legal paperwork to convert the building and land into condominium units and common elements.

A potential problem area with condominium conversions, and one that a prospective buyer should be aware of, is that converted buildings are used buildings that were not intended to become condominiums when built. As used buildings, there may be considerable deferred maintenance, and the building may have thermal insulation suitable to a time when energy costs were lower. If the building was originally built for rental purposes, sound-deadening insulation in the walls, floors, and ceilings may be inadequate. Fire protection between units may also be less than satisfactory. In contrast, newly built condominiums must meet current building code requirements regarding thermal and sound insulation, firewall construction, and so forth.

It is worth noting that not all condominium conversions are carried out by developers. Enterprising tenants have successfully converted their own buildings and saved considerable sums of money. It is not uncommon for the value of a building to double when it is converted to a condominium. Tenants who are willing to hire the legal, architectural, and construction help they need can create valuable condominium homes for themselves in the same building where they were previously renters.

Advantages of Condominium Living

Compared to detached dwellings, condominium living offers a number of advantages and some disadvantages. On the advantage side, instead of four or five detached dwellings on an acre of land, a condominium builder can place 25 or even 100 living units. This spreads the cost of the site among more dwellings, and the builder does not have the miles of streets, sewers, or utility lines that would be necessary to reach every house in a spread-out subdivision. Furthermore, the use of shared walls and foundations, the fact that one dwelling unit's ceiling is another's floor, and the fact that one roof can cover many vertically stacked units can produce savings in construction materials and labor. In central city districts where a single square foot of vacant land can cost $100 or more, only a high-rise condominium can make housing units possible. In the suburbs, where land is cheaper, a condominium is often the difference between buying and renting for some people.

Other advantages are the lure of "carefree living" wherein such chores as lawn mowing, watering, weeding, snow removal, and building maintenance are provided. For some people, it is the security that is often associated with clustered dwellings and nearby neighbors. Other advantages are extensive recreational and social facilities that are not economically feasible on a single-dwelling basis. It is commonplace to find swimming pools, recreation halls, tennis and volleyball courts, gymnasiums, and even social directors at condominiums. Lastly, we cannot overlook the psychological and financial advantages of ownership. Many large rental apartment projects produce the same economies of scale and amenities just described. Nonetheless, most Americans prefer to own rather than rent their dwellings. Part of this is the pride of owning something. Part comes from a desire for a savings program, the potential for capital appreciation, and income tax laws that favor owners over renters.

Disadvantages of Condominium Living

A major disadvantage of condominium living is the close proximity of one's neighbors and the extra level of government. In other words, buying into a condominium means buying into a group of people whose lifestyles may differ from yours and whose opinions as to how to run the association will differ from yours. By way of contrast, if you buy a single-family detached house on a lot, you will have sole control (subject to zoning and legal restrictions) over the use of it. You may be able to choose to remodel or add on. You may be able to choose what color to paint your house and garage, how many people and animals will live there, what type of landscaping to have, from whom to purchase property insurance, whether to rent it out or live in it, and so on. Your next-door neighbors will have the same rights over their land.

In a condominium, the owners have a considerable degree of control over each other in matters that affect the common good of the association. Moreover, certain decisions must be made as a group, such as what kinds of common element hazard and liability insurance to carry, how much to carry, and from whom to purchase it. If there is an outdoor swimming pool, a decision must be made as to what months it should be heated and how warm it should be kept. The group as a whole must decide on how the landscaping is to be maintained, who will do it, and how much should be spent. If there is to be security service, again, there must be a group decision as to how much, when, and who should be hired. If a large truck runs into a unit on one end of the building, it's an association problem because each owner has an undivided interest in the whole building.

All matters affecting the condominium must be brought to the attention of the board of directors, often by way of a committee. All committee and board positions are filled by volunteers from the association. Thus, owning a condominium is not entirely carefree, and there will be times when the board of directors will do things differently from what an individual owner would like. Another possibility is that there may be a lack of interested and talented people to serve as directors and on committees. Consequently, things that need to be done may be left undone, possibly posing a hazard to the association. Individual unit owners may be unaware of the management and maintenance requirements for a multimillion-dollar building and may have hired a management firm that knows (or does) even less.

Before Buying

If you are considering the purchase of a condominium unit, consider the above points with care. Also, look closely at the association's finances. The association may not have adequate reserves for upcoming maintenance work, such as painting the building and putting on a new roof. If so, existing owners and new buyers will be in for a rude surprise in the form of a special assessment. Check the budget to see if it covers everything adequately, and ask about lawsuits against the association that might drain its finances.

Although articles of incorporation, CC&Rs, and bylaws make boring reading, if you offer to buy a condominium unit, you should make the offer contingent on your reading and approving them. These are the rules you agree to live by, and it's better to read them before committing to buy than after. You may find prohibitions against your pet cat or dog or against renting your unit while you are temporarily transferred overseas. (At the closing, the seller must give you a current set of these documents along with the deed and keys to the unit. When you sell, you must give a current set to your buyer.)

Before buying, pay special attention to construction quality. Will ongoing maintenance be expensive? Is there deferred maintenance? Ask if the clubhouse and recreation facilities are owned by the association or by the developer, who will continue to charge you for their use year after year. Is soundproofing between units adequate, or will you hear your neighbor's piano, drums, and arguments? What is the owner-tenant mix? The most successful condominiums are predominantly owner–occupied rather than renter-occupied. Owners usually take more interest and care in their properties, and this in turn boosts resale values. The list of things to look for and ask about when buying into a condominium is longer than there is space for here, and bookstores have good books that will help you. But before moving on, the following two thoughts apply to any purchase of a condominium, cooperative, planned unit development, or timeshare. First, keep a balance between your heart and your head. It is easy to be enchanted to the point that no further investigation is made, perhaps knowing in advance it would sour the deal. Second, ask those who have already bought if they would buy again.

COOPERATIVE APARTMENTS

Now that you have just read about condominiums, take yourself back to the year 1900 in New York City. You've been renting an apartment unit in Manhattan for several years and would like to own it. Your neighbors in the building have expressed the same desire, but condominium legislation is more than half a century in the future. How would you and your neighbors accomplish this, given existing legal frameworks? Your answer is the corporate form of ownership, a form of multiperson ownership well established in America by that time. To carry out your collective desires, you form a not-for-profit corporation. Shares in the corporation are sold to the building's tenants and the money used as a down payment to buy the building. Title to the building is placed in the name of the corporation, and shareholders receive from the corporation a lease to their apartments. Thus, the shareholders own the corporation, the corporation owns the building, and the corporation gives its shareholders leases to their apartments. Each month, each shareholder makes a payment to the corporation to enable it to make the required monthly payment on the debt against the building and to pay for maintenance and repairs. Government of the building is handled by a board of directors that meets monthly and at an annual meeting of all the shareholders. This form of residential ownership, which can be found in significant numbers in New York City, Miami, Chicago, San Francisco, and Honolulu, is called a **cooperative**.

The individual shareholders are called cooperators, and the lease that the corporation gives to a shareholder is called a **proprietary lease**. When a cooperator wishes to sell, the cooperator does not sell the apartment but, rather, the shares of stock that carry with them a proprietary lease on that apartment. Although for all practical purposes the transaction looks like a sale of real estate, from a legal standpoint, it is a sale of corporate stock. As such, the listing and selling forms that are used for houses and condominiums are not suitable, and special cooperative forms must be used.

cooperative: land and building owned or leased by a corporation that, in turn, leases space to its shareholders

proprietary lease: a lease issued by a cooperative corporation to its shareholders

Financing

Financing a cooperative is different from financing a house or condominium. When a cooperative apartment building is first organized, the entire property is in the name of the cooperative corporation, and there is one mortgage loan on all of it. To illustrate, suppose a 10-unit building will cost the cooperators $1 million, and all of the units are considered equal in desirability. A lender will finance 70% of the purchase if the cooperators raise the remaining 30%. This requires the cooperators to sell 10 shares of stock, each share for $30,000 and good for one apartment unit in the building. The lender provides the remaining $700,000 to complete the purchase, and the corporation gives the lender a note for $700,000 secured by a mortgage against the building. Suppose the monthly payments on this loan are $7,000; this means that each month, each cooperator must contribute $700 toward the mortgage plus money to maintain and operate the building, pay the property taxes on it, and keep it insured.

Default

What happens if one of the cooperators fails to make the monthly payment to the cooperative? If the cooperative sends the lender anything less than the required $7,000 per month, the loan will be in default. To stay out of default, the remaining cooperators must make up the difference. Meanwhile, they can seek voluntary reimbursement by the tardy cooperator, or, if that does not work, terminate that cooperator as a shareholder and resell the share to someone who will make the payments.

Resale

What happens if a shareholder in good standing wants to sell the unit? Since the underlying mortgage is against the entire building, it is impossible to refinance a portion of the building. Only the whole building can be refinanced, and that requires approval by the cooperators as a whole. Traditionally, this has forced the cooperator to sell the share for all cash or on an installment sale plan. This is a handicap where the value of the share has increased substantially due to property value increase and reduction of the building's mortgage loan.

Government

A cooperative apartment is governed by its articles of incorporation, bylaws, CC&Rs, and house rules. The governing body is a board of directors elected by the cooperators. The board hires the services needed to maintain and operate the building, just as in a condominium. Annual meetings are also held, just as in a condominium.

COMPARISON OF CONDOMINIUMS AND COOPERATIVES

Now that the condominium format is available, relatively few cooperatives are being organized. This is largely because, in a condominium, the individual apartment unit can be financed separately from the remainder of the building. Moreover, if one condominium unit owner fails to make loan payments, the remaining owners in the building are not responsible for that loan. The condominium unit owner also has the personal choice of whether to have no debt, a little debt, or a lot of debt against the unit.

Unpaid property taxes are another potential difference. In a condominium, each unit is taxed separately, and nonpayment brings a property tax foreclosure sale against just the delinquent unit, not the entire building.

A similarity exists between condominiums and cooperatives with respect to the money collected each month for the general maintenance and upkeep of the building. In either case, nonpayment will bring action against the tardy owner by the association that can result in foreclosure of that owner. Income tax rules effectively allow the same homeowner deductions on cooperatives as on condominiums and houses. However, a strict set of rules must be followed because, technically, a cooperator does not own real estate, but shares of stock.

PLANNED UNIT DEVELOPMENT

planned unit development (PUD): individually owned lots and houses with community ownership of common areas

If you buy into a condominium, you get a dwelling unit as separate property, plus an undivided interest in the land and other common elements. If you buy into a cooperative, you get stock in the corporation that owns the building and a lease on a particular apartment. If you buy into a **planned unit development (PUD)**, you get a house and lot as separate property, plus ownership in a community association that owns the common areas. Common areas may be as minimal as a few green spaces between houses or as extensive as parks, pools, clubhouse facilities, jogging trails, boat docks, horse trails, and a golf course. Although you own your lot and house as separate property in a PUD, there will be CC&Rs to follow. The PUD developer will establish an initial set of CC&Rs, then turn them over to the association for enforcement. Thus, your lot and home are not quite all yours to do with as you please because your association can dictate what color you can paint the exterior of your home, what you may and may not plant in your front yard, and how many people and pets may reside with you. As with condominiums and cooperatives, PUD CC&Rs are not meant to be burdensome for the sake of being burdensome, but, rather, to maintain the attractiveness and tranquility of the development, and in doing so support the investment made by the owners.

The dwellings in a planned unit development typically take the form of detached houses and houses that share a common wall, such as row houses, town houses, and cluster houses. Because each owner owns the land, vertical stacking of homes is limited to one owner and housing densities to 8 or 10 units per acre. Even though this is twice the density of a typical detached-house subdivision, by careful planning, a developer can give each owner the feeling of spaciousness. One way is by taking advantage of uneven terrain. If a parcel contains some flat land, some hilly land, some land covered with trees, and a stream, the dwellings can be clustered on the land best suited for building and thus preserve the stream, woods, and steep slopes in their natural state. With a standard subdivision layout, the developer would have to remove the groves of trees, fill in the stream, and terrace the slopes, and would still be able to provide homes for only half the number of families.

RESORT TIMESHARING

Resort timesharing is a method of dividing up and selling a living unit at a vacation facility for specified lengths of time each year. The idea started in Europe in the 1960s when groups of individuals would jointly purchase ski resort lodgings and summer vacation villas, with each owner taking a week or two of exclusive occupancy. Resort developers quickly recognized the market potential of the idea, and in 1969, the first resort timeshare opened in the United States. Since then, hotels, motels, condominiums, townhouses, lodges, villas, recreational vehicle parks, campgrounds, houseboats, and even a cruise ship have been timeshared.

resort timesharing: the exclusive use of a property for a period of time each year

Right-to-Use

Nearly all timeshares fall into one of two legal formats. The first is the right-to-use format. This gives the buyer a contractual right to occupy a living unit at a resort property for one week a year for a specific term of 20 to 40 years. The cost for the entire period is paid in advance. At the end of the contract term, all of the buyer's possessory rights terminate unless the contract contains a renewal clause or a right to buy. The developer creates these contracts by either buying or leasing a resort property and then selling 50 one-week-a-year right-to-use contracts on each living unit. (The other two weeks of the year are reserved for maintenance.) Approximately 30% of the timeshare market is right-to-use.

Fee Simple

The second format is fee simple ownership. Here, the timeshare purchaser obtains a fee ownership in the unit purchased. The purchaser owns the property for one week a year in perpetuity, and the sale is handled like a sale of real estate. There will be a formal closing, a title policy, execution of a mortgage and note, and delivery of a recordable deed that conveys the timeshare interest. A developer offers fee timeshares by either building or buying a resort property and then selling 50 one-week-a-year fee simple slices in each unit, with the remaining two weeks for maintenance. Approximately 70% of the timeshare market is fee simple.

Costs

The initial cost of a timeshare week at a resort in the United States is typically $6,000 to $25,000 or more, depending on the quality and location of the resort, the time of year (low season or high season), and form of ownership (right-to-use is usually less expensive). Additionally, there will be an annual maintenance fee of $140 to $500-plus per timeshare week. Buyers can purchase two or more timeshare weeks if they want a longer vacation. Some buyers purchase one week in the summer and one week in the winter.

Benefits

The appeal of timesharing to developers is that a resort or condominium complex that can be bought and furnished for $100,000 per unit can be resold in 50 timeshare slices at $6,000 each—that is, $300,000 a unit. The primary appeal of timesharing to consumers is having a resort to go to every year at a prepaid price. This is particularly appealing during inflationary times, although the annual maintenance fee can change. There may be certain tax benefits if the timeshare is financed, or for property taxes paid on fee simple timeshares. There may also be appreciation of the timeshare unit if it is in a particularly popular and well-run resort, but this is not common and should not be expected.

Then again, some or all of these benefits may not materialize. First, the lump sum paid for a timeshare week does look cheaper than hotel bills year after year. However, the timeshare must be paid for in full in advance (or financed with interest), whereas the hotel is paid as it is used each year. Also, there is a timeshare maintenance fee of $20 to $70 per day that goes for clerk and maid service, linen laundry and replacement, structural maintenance and repairs, swimming pool service, hazard and liability insurance, reservations, collections and accounting services, general management, and so on.

Second, going to the same resort for the same week every year for the next 40 years may become wearisome. Yet, that is what a timeshare buyer is agreeing to do. And if the week goes vacant, the maintenance fee must still be paid. To offset this, two large resort exchange services and several smaller ones exist, and some of the larger timeshare developers allow their buyers to exchange weeks among their various projects. There is a cost, however, to exchanging. There may be as many as three fees to pay: an initiation fee, an annual membership fee, and a fee when an exchange is made. These can amount to $100 or more for an exchange. Moreover, someone else with a timeshare week s/he doesn't want that you do want at the right time of the year must also be in the exchange bank. Satisfaction is usually achieved in exchanging by being flexible in accepting an exchange. Note, too, that if you own an off-season week at one resort, do not count on exchanging it for a peak-season vacation somewhere else. Exchange banks require members to accept periods of equal or lesser popularity. Another method of overcoming the "locked in" objection is points. With many timeshare developers, a person purchases a period of time, and that period of time represents a certain number of points. The purchaser may then reserve an available unit at any of the developer's resorts using the points.

Third, the interest paid on the loan may be tax-deductible. Timeshares have occasionally been touted as tax shelter vehicles; however, that has already met the ire of the Internal Revenue Service.

Fourth, although there have been several reported instances of timeshare appreciation, it is generally agreed in the timeshare industry and by consumer groups that the primary reason to purchase a resort timeshare is to obtain a vacation, not have a property appreciate. An industry rule-of-thumb is that one-third of the retail price of a timeshare unit goes to marketing costs. This acts as a damper on timeshare resale prices and even suggests that a buyer may be able to purchase a timeshare on the resale market for less than from a developer.

Commitment

Against the comfort of knowing that, as a timeshare owner, one has a long-term commitment to use a resort, one also has a long-term commitment to its maintenance, repair, refurbishing, and management. This is similar to ownership in a condominium; however, with ownership split among as many as 50 owners for each unit, will any owner have a large enough stake to want to take an active part in overseeing the management? As a result, management falls to the developer who, having once sold out the project, may no longer have as much incentive to oversee things as carefully as it did during the sales period. The developer can turn the job over to a management firm, but who oversees the firm to make certain the timeshare owners get good service at a fair price?

State Regulation

Many states, Georgia included, have adopted timeshare regulations. Many of these follow the Model Timeshare Act designed by the National Association of Real Estate License Law Officials and the National Timesharing Council and endorsed by the National Association of REALTORS®. Much timeshare legislation is in the form of consumer protection and disclosure (prospectus) requirements. Other legislation deals with how timeshares should be assessed for property taxation and what type of license a person employed to sell timeshares should hold, if any. Due to high-pressure sales techniques observed at some timeshare sales offices, Georgia has enacted mandatory "cooling-off" periods of seven days during which a buyer can rescind a contract. Because of multimillion-dollar consumer losses due to uncompleted timeshare projects, the sale of the same timeshare to more than one party, and money collected with deeds never sent, surety bonds and escrows are now required by some states. Meanwhile, any prospective timeshare purchaser or salesperson would do well to take plenty of time in deciding, have all paperwork reviewed by an attorney before signing, and spend time talking to existing purchasers to ask if they would buy again.

Review Questions

Answers to these questions can be found in Appendix D at the end of this book.

1. State laws that provide the legal framework for condominium ownership may be identified by any of the following terms EXCEPT:
   A. strata titles act
   B. cooperative housing act
   C. condominium act
   D. horizontal property act

2. Condominium developments are:
   A. restricted to residential dwelling units
   B. restricted to multiple-unit buildings
   C. restricted to residential detached units
   D. not restricted by property type

3. Which of the following is NOT true about condominiums?
   A. In a condominium, each property owner pays his/her own taxes.
   B. Condominiums can be detached residential.
   C. Condominiums are substantially the same as cooperatives.
   D. The common areas in a condominium are held as common property by all owners.

4. Individual units in a condominium development are classed as:
   A. separate property
   B. common elements
   C. cooperative elements
   D. limited common elements

5. Within a condominium development, common elements are owned by:
   A. the owners' association
   B. all unit owners, who hold undivided interests in the elements
   C. the condominium developer
   D. individual unit owners as community property

6. Which of the following would be classified as limited common elements in a condominium development?
   A. elevators
   B. hallways
   C. assigned parking spaces
   D. the manager's apartment

7. Which of the following is a disadvantage of condominium ownership?
   A. maintenance
   B. land cost per unit
   C. many decisions are made by a board rather than the individual
   D. security

8. The rules by which an owners' association operates are known as:
   A. bylaws
   B. covenants, conditions, and restrictions
   C. house rules
   D. ordinances

9. The purchaser of a condominium unit is NOT obligated to abide by the development's:
   A. covenants, conditions, and restrictions
   B. house rules
   C. unreasonable restrictions
   D. architectural controls

10. In a condominium, the authority to raise homeowner fees (association dues) rests with the:
    A. board of directors
    B. management company
    C. condominium act
    D. city and county

11. The guest of a unit owner was injured by stepping on broken glass in the swimming pool at the Sunset Hills condominiums. Liability for this injury would probably initially fall upon:
    A. the unit owner
    B. the condominium association
    C. the management company
    D. the developers

12. The owner of a specific unit in a cooperative is the:
    A. tenant
    B. lender
    C. cooperator
    D. lessee

13. Ownership of the interior space of your home and garage and an undivided interest in the building structures, common areas, and land area of the entire project describes a:
    A. condominium
    B. cooperative
    C. PUD
    D. corporate form of ownership

14. Traditionally, the resale of cooperative shares has been financed by means of:
    A. installment sales agreements
    B. second mortgages on the seller's unit
    C. bonds
    D. government securities

15. The governing body of a cooperative is called a:
    A. cooperation
    B. corporation
    C. CC&R
    D. board of directors

16. The owners of a unit in a planned unit development hold title to all of the following EXCEPT:
    A. the air above their unit
    B. the land beneath their unit
    C. a share of the common area
    D. fee simple title to their unit

17. In a planned unit development, the owners' association can dictate all of the following EXCEPT:
    A. exterior paint colors
    B. exterior landscaping
    C. use of common areas
    D. interior paint colors

18. Of the two principal forms of timeshare formats, which makes up the larger percentage of the market?
    A. right-to-use
    B. fee simple
    C. each holds an approximately equal market share
    D. statistics are not available

19. Under the right-to-use plan of timesharing, the purchaser:
    A. holds title to real property
    B. is a tenant in common with other users of the unit
    C. receives his/her interest in a deed
    D. is a tenant for years

20. The right of rescission on a timeshare contract in Georgia is:
    A. 3 days
    B. 7 days
    C. 10 days
    D. 12 days

CHAPTER

7 LAND-USE CONTROL

KEY TERMS

building codes
certificate of occupancy
downzoning
land-use control
master plan
nonconforming use
restrictive covenants
variance
zoning laws

OBJECTIVES

After successful completion of this chapter, you should be able to:

1. describe the many aspects and results of zoning, changes, and downzoning;
2. understand and discuss the application of subdivision regulations and building codes;
3. explain the use of deed restrictions;
4. explain the purpose of planning ahead and the need for master plans; and
5. define transferable development rights.

OVERVIEW

Land-use control describes any legal restriction that controls how a parcel of land may be used. There are both public controls and private controls. Public controls include zoning, building codes, subdivision regulations, and master plans. Private controls come in the form of deed restrictions. This chapter covers all those topics and concludes with a brief discussion of master plans.

All methods of land-use control are coming under some level of scrutiny. The U.S. Supreme Court has recently held that land may not be regulated such that it renders it totally valueless, and the Supreme Court has also held that any such regulation of one's private land must bear some "rough proportionality" to the benefit that the regulation gives to the public. There have been a number of recent cases that have prohibited the

land-use control: a broad term that describes any legal restriction that controls how a parcel of land may be used

enforcement of certain zoning ordinances or deed restrictions because they result in discrimination under the federal fair housing requirements, so the following discussion on land-use control must be tempered with the knowledge that these methods of land-use control are not absolute.

ZONING

zoning laws: public regulations that control the specific use of land

Zoning is based on the principle of use separation; some land uses are incompatible with others and should not be permitted in the same area. **Zoning laws** divide land into zones (districts) and, within each zone, regulate the purpose for which buildings may be constructed, the height and bulk of the buildings, the area of the lot that they may occupy, and the number of persons that they can accommodate.

Through zoning, a community can protect existing land users from encroachment by undesirable uses and ensure that future land uses in the community will be compatible with one another. Zoning also can control development so that each parcel of land will be adequately serviced by streets, sanitary and storm sewers, schools, parks, and utilities. The authority to control land use is derived from the basic police power of each state to protect the public health, safety, morals, and general welfare of its citizens. Through an enabling act passed by the state legislature, the authority to control land use is also given to individual towns, cities, and counties. These local government units then pass zoning ordinances that establish the boundaries of the various land-use zones and determine the type of development that will be permitted in each of them. By going to your local zoning office, you can learn how a parcel of land is zoned. By then consulting the zoning ordinance, you can see the permitted uses for the parcel.

Zoning Symbols

For convenience, zones are identified by code abbreviations such as R (residential), C (commercial), I or M (industrial-manufacturing), and A (agriculture). Within general categories are subcategories, such as single-family residences, two-family residences, low-rise apartments, and high-rise apartments. Similarly, there will usually be several subcategories of commercial, ranging from small stores to shopping centers, and several subcategories of manufacturing, ranging from light, smoke-free to heavy industry.

Additionally, there can be found overlay zoning categories such as RPD (residential planned development) and PUD (planned unit development). These are designed to permit a mixture of land uses within a given parcel. For example, a 640-acre parcel may contain open spaces plus clusters of houses, townhouses, and apartments, and perhaps a neighborhood shopping center. Another combination zone is RO (residential-office), which allows apartment buildings alongside or on top of office buildings.

Note that there is no uniformity to zoning classifications. A city may use A to designate apartments while the county uses A to designate agriculture. Similarly, one city might use I for industrial and another city might use I for institutional (hospitals and universities, for example).

Land-Use Restrictions

Besides telling a landowner the use to which the land may be put, the zoning ordinance imposes additional rules. For example, land zoned for low-density apartments may require 1,500 square feet of land per living unit, a minimum of 600 square feet of living space per unit for one bedroom, 800 square feet for two bedrooms, and 1,000 square feet for three bedrooms. The zoning ordinance may also contain a setback requirement that states that a building must be placed at least 25 feet back from the street, 10 feet from the sides of the lot, and 15 feet from the rear lot line. The ordinance may also limit the building's height to 2½ stories, require two parking spaces for each dwelling unit, and restrict the kinds of animals that may be kept on the property. As can be seen, zoning encourages uniformity.

Enforcement

Zoning laws are enforced by virtue of the fact that, in order to build, a person must obtain a building permit from the city or county government. Before a permit is issued, the proposed structure must conform to government-imposed structural standards and comply with the zoning on the land. If a landowner builds without a permit, the landowner can be forced to tear down the building.

Nonconforming Use

When an existing structure does not conform to a new zoning law, it is "grandfathered in" as a **nonconforming use**. Thus, the owner can continue to use the structure even though it does not conform to the new zoning. However, the owner is not permitted to enlarge or remodel the structure, or to extend its life. When the structure is ultimately demolished, any new use of the land must be in accordance with the zoning law. If you are driving through a residential neighborhood and see an old store or service station that looks very much out of place, it is probably a nonconforming use that was allowed to stay because it was built before the current zoning on the property went into effect.

nonconforming use: an improvement that is inconsistent with current zoning regulations

Amendment

Once a zoning ordinance has been passed, it can be changed by amendment. Thus, land previously zoned for agriculture may be changed to residential. Land along a city street that has become a major thoroughfare may change from residential to commercial. An amendment can be initiated by local government or a property owner in the area to be rezoned. Either way, notice of the proposed change must be given to all property owners in and around the affected area, and a public hearing must be held so that property owners and the public at large may voice their opinions on the matter.

Variance

variance: allows an individual landowner to vary from zoning requirements

A **variance** allows an individual landowner to deviate from current zoning requirements for a parcel. For example, a variance might be granted to the owner of an odd-shaped lot to reduce the setback requirements slightly so that a building can fit on it. Variances usually are granted where strict compliance with the zoning ordinance or code would cause undue hardship. A variance can also be used to change the permitted use of a parcel. However, the variance must not change the basic character of the neighborhood, and it must be consistent with the general objectives of zoning as they apply to that neighborhood.

Conditional-Use Permit

A *conditional-use permit* allows a land use that does not conform to existing zoning, provided the use is within the limitations that are specifically imposed by the city ordinance. A conditional-use permit is usually quite restrictive, and if the conditions of the permit are violated, the permit is no longer valid. For example, a neighborhood grocery store operating under a conditional-use permit may be only a neighborhood grocery. The structure may not be used as an auto parts store.

Spot Zoning

Spot zoning refers to the rezoning of a small area of land in an existing neighborhood. For example, a neighborhood convenience center (grocery, laundry, barbershop) might be allowed in a residential neighborhood, provided it serves a useful purpose for neighborhood residents and is not a nuisance.

Downzoning

downzoning: rezoning of land from a higher-density use to a lower-density use

Downzoning means that land previously zoned for higher-density uses (or more active uses) is rezoned for lower-density uses (or less active uses). Examples are downzoning from high-rise commercial to low-rise commercial, apartment zoning to single-family, and single-family to agriculture. Although a landowner's property value may fall as a result of downzoning, there is no compensation to the landowner as there is no taking of land, unlike with eminent domain.

Taking

Taking is a concept wherein the municipality regulates the property to where it has no value or, in some cases, has no remaining economic value. The U.S. Supreme Court, in several cases, has determined that a municipality may regulate land use to where it becomes a "taking" and results in condemnation. This is also sometimes referred to as an inverse condemnation. Some years ago, there was a lawsuit by a neighborhood located near an airport that was expanding. The suit claimed that the expansion caused a devaluation of the neighborhood and that it was the responsibility of the airport authority to compensate the owners. The neighborhood won this inverse condemnation action. This area of the law is clearly becoming more protective of the private landowner's rights.

Buffer Zone

A *buffer zone* is a strip of land that separates one land use from another. Thus, between a large shopping center and a neighborhood of single-family homes, there may be a row of garden apartments. Alternatively, between an industrial park and a residential subdivision, a developer may leave a strip of land in grass and trees rather than build homes immediately adjacent to the industrial buildings. Note that *buffer zone* is a generic term and not necessarily a zoning law category.

Legality and Value

A zoning law can be changed or struck down if it can be proven in court that it is unclear, discriminatory, or unreasonable; not for the protection of the public health, safety, and general welfare; or not applied to all property in a similar manner. A topical, but difficult, legal issue involves taking. When property is zoned so that its use is destroyed or severely limited, the act becomes condemnation, not zoning, because the property has been effectively taken.

Zoning alone does not create land value. For example, zoning 100 square miles of lonely desert or mountain land for stores and offices would not appreciably change its value. Value is created by the number of people who want to use a particular parcel of land for a specific purpose. To the extent that zoning channels that demand to certain parcels of land and away from others, it does have a powerful impact on property value.

SUBDIVISION REGULATIONS

Before a building lot can be sold, a developer must comply with government regulations concerning street construction, curbs, sidewalks, street lighting, fire hydrants, storm and sanitary sewers, grading and compacting of soil, water and utility lines, minimum lot size, and so on. In addition, the developer may be required to either set aside land for schools and parks or provide money so that land for that purpose may be purchased nearby. These are often referred to as mapping requirements, and until the developer has complied with all state and local regulations, the subdivision will not be approved. Without approval, the plan cannot be recorded, which, in turn, means that the lots cannot be sold to the public. If the developer tries to sell lots without approval, the developer can be stopped by a government court order and, in some states, may be fined. Moreover, permits to build will be refused to lot owners, and anyone who bought from the developer is entitled to a refund.

BUILDING CODES

building codes: local and state laws that set minimum construction standards

Recognizing the need to protect public health and safety against slipshod construction practices, state and local governments have enacted **building codes**. These codes establish minimum acceptable material and construction standards for such things as structural load and stress, windows and ventilation, size and location of rooms, fire protection, exits, electrical installation, plumbing, heating, and lighting. Before a building permit is granted, the design of a proposed structure must meet the building code requirements. During construction, local building department inspectors visit the construction site to make certain that the codes are being observed. Finally, when the building is completed, a **certificate of occupancy** is issued to the building owner to show that the structure meets the code. Without this certificate, the building may not be legally occupied.

certificate of occupancy: a government-issued document that states a structure meets local zoning and building code requirements and is ready for use

Traditionally, the establishment of building codes has been given by states to individual counties, cities, and towns. The result has been a lack of uniformity from one local government to the next, oftentimes adding unnecessary construction costs and occasionally leaving gaps in consumer protection. The trend today is toward statewide building codes that overcome these weaknesses and, at the same time, improve the uniformity of mortgage collateral for the secondary mortgage market. It is common in Georgia for local governments to follow the Southern Building Code.

DEED RESTRICTIONS

Although property owners tend to think of land-use controls as being strictly a product of government, it is possible to achieve land-use control through private means. In fact, some areas of the country, such as Houston, Texas, operate without zoning and rely almost entirely upon private land-use controls to achieve a similar effect.

Private land-use controls take the form of *deed* and *lease restrictions*. In the United States, it has long been recognized that the ownership of land includes the right to sell or lease it on whatever legally acceptable conditions the owner wishes, including the right to dictate to the buyer or lessee how to use or not use it. For example, a developer can sell the lots in a subdivision, subject to a restriction written into each deed that the land must not be used for anything but a single-family residence containing at least 1,200 square feet of living area. The legal theory is that if the buyers or lessees agree to the restrictions, they are bound by them. If the restrictions are not obeyed, any lot owner in the subdivision can obtain a court order to enforce compliance. The only limit to the number of restrictions that an owner may place on the land is economic. If there are too many restrictions, the landowner may find that no one wants the land.

Deed restrictions, also known as **restrictive covenants**, can be used to dictate such matters as the purpose of the structure to be built, architectural requirements, setbacks, size of the structure, and aesthetics. In neighborhoods with view lots, they are often used to limit the height to which trees may be permitted to grow. Deed restrictions may not be used to discriminate on the basis of race, color, religion, sex, or national origin, nor may they violate our allodial rights to ownership of property; if they do, they are unenforceable by the courts.

restrictive covenants: clauses placed in deeds and leases to control how future owners and lessees may or may not use the property

PLANNING AHEAD FOR DEVELOPMENT

When a community first adopts a zoning ordinance, the usual procedure is to recognize existing land uses by zoning according to what already exists. Thus, a neighborhood that is already developed with houses is zoned for houses. Undeveloped land may be zoned for agriculture or simply left unzoned. As a community expands, undeveloped land is zoned for urban uses and a pattern that typically follows the availability of new roads, the aggressiveness of developers, and the willingness of landowners to sell. All too often, this results in a hodgepodge of land-use districts, all conforming internally because of tightly enforced zoning, but with little or no relationship among them. This happens because they were created over a period of years without the aid of a long-range land-use plan that took a comprehensive view of the entire growth pattern of the city. Since uncoordinated land use can have a negative impact on both the quality of life and the economic vitality of a community, more attention is now being directed toward land-use master plans to guide the development of towns and cities, districts, coastlines, and even whole states.

Master Plan

To prepare a **master plan** (or *general plan* or *comprehensive plan*), a city or regional planning commission is usually created. The first step is a physical and economic survey of the area to be planned. The physical survey involves mapping existing roads, utility lines, developed land, and undeveloped land. The economic survey looks at the present and anticipated economic base of the region, its population, and its retail trade facilities. Together the two surveys provide the information upon which a master plan is built. The key is to view the region as a unified entity that provides its residents with jobs and housing as well as social, recreational, and cultural opportunities. In doing so, the master plan uses existing patterns of transportation and land use and directs future growth so as to achieve balanced development. For example, if agriculture is important to the area's economy, special attention is given to retaining the best soils for farming.

master plan: a comprehensive guide for the physical growth of a community

Waterfront property may also receive special planning protection. Similarly, if houses in an older residential area of town are being converted to rooming houses and apartments, that transition can be encouraged by planning apartment usage for the area. In doing this, the master plan guides those who must make day-to-day decisions regarding zoning changes and gives the individual property owner a long-range idea of what property may be used for in the future.

LONG-RUN CONTINUITY

To ensure long-run continuity, a master plan should look at least 15 years into the future, and, preferably, 25 years or more. It must also include provisions for flexibility in the event that the city or region does not develop as expected, such as when population grows more rapidly or more slowly than anticipated. Most importantly, the plan must provide for a balance between the economic and social functions of the community. For example, to emphasize culture and recreation at the expense of adequate housing and the area's economic base will result in the slow decay of the community because people must leave to find housing and jobs.

Review Questions

Answers to these questions can be found in Appendix D at the end of this book.

1. Through zoning, a community can protect existing land users from all of the following EXCEPT:
   A. encroachment by undesirable uses
   B. uncontrolled development
   C. incompatible uses of land
   D. competitive business establishments

2. Land-use controls may NOT be imposed:
   A. by state governments
   B. by local governments
   C. by subdivision developers
   D. to keep an owner from selling

3. Zoning laws may NOT be used to regulate which of the following?
   A. the purpose for which a building may be constructed
   B. the number of persons a building may accommodate
   C. the placement of interior partitions
   D. the height and bulk of a building

4. The basic authority for zoning laws is derived from a state's:
   A. powers of eminent domain
   B. right of taxation
   C. powers of escheat
   D. police power

5. Zoning laws:
   A. tell a landowner the use to which land may be put
   B. compensate an owner for loss of property value due to zoning
   C. are set by the state
   D. can be set by the county, but not by the city

6. Applied to land use, zoning laws may do all of the following EXCEPT:
   A. encourage uniformity in land usage
   B. set minimum square footage requirements for buildings
   C. determine the location of a building on a lot
   D. dictate construction standards for buildings

7. A use of property that is not in agreement with current zoning laws:
   A. is always illegal
   B. is always legal because of "grandfathering"
   C. is called a nonconforming use
   D. is referred to as a variance

8. Permission to use a building for a nonconforming use may be accomplished by:
   A. amendment of the zoning ordinance
   B. obtaining a zoning variance
   C. rezoning the property
   D. none of the above; nonconforming uses cannot be created with permission

9. A zoning variance:
   A. allows an owner to deviate from the existing zoning law
   B. involves a change in the zoning law
   C. does not require a public hearing
   D. is created by a 75% agreement of landowners within one mile

10. When a small area of land in an existing neighborhood is rezoned, this is known as:
    A. downzoning
    B. spot zoning
    C. conditional zoning
    D. a zoning variance

11. A garden apartment development is situated between an office park and a subdivision of single-family residences. These apartments are in a:
    A. buffer zone
    B. downzone
    C. spot zone
    D. commercial zone

12. Minimum standards for materials and construction of buildings are set by:
    A. zoning laws
    B. building codes
    C. deed restrictions
    D. subdivision regulations

13. Before a newly constructed building may be utilized by tenants, the owner must secure a certificate of:
    A. inspection
    B. utilization
    C. approval
    D. occupancy

14. Building codes:
    A. are voluntary
    B. guarantee quality construction
    C. are typically enforced by local government
    D. are required by Georgia law

15. A subdivider wants to limit the height to which trees may grow so as to preserve views. This would most likely be done with a:
    A. zoning amendment
    B. conditional-use permit
    C. buffer zone
    D. deed restriction

16. The effect of a proposed development on a community is determined by the preparation of:
    A. a property disclosure report
    B. an environmental impact statement
    C. a prospectus
    D. the community's master plan

17. An environmental impact statement will NOT reveal the effect of a planned development on:
    A. air quality
    B. automobile traffic
    C. property values
    D. school enrollments

PART 3

AGENCY AND CONTRACTS

At this point of our study, if we are to continue the analogy of house construction, we have put in a solid, level, and square foundation. In Part 2 we then framed up the skeletal building. It is now time to construct the roof and put drywall in the building. In Part 3, our knowledge really starts taking shape. The study of representation of clients as they pursue their real estate needs and dreams and the contracts that ensue is where the excitement really begins! In Part 3 we will continue our knowledge building by looking at the following chapters:

Chapter 8:   The Principal–Broker Relationship: Agency

Chapter 9:   Contract Law

Chapter 10: The Principal–Broker Relationship: Employment

Chapter 11: Real Estate Sales Contracts

CHAPTER

8 THE PRINCIPAL–BROKER RELATIONSHIP: AGENCY

KEY TERMS

agency
agent
boycotting
commingling
dual agency

latent defect
middleman
ostensible authority
patent defect
price fixing

principal
puffing
third parties

OBJECTIVES

After successful completion of this chapter, you should be able to:

1. discuss how an agency relationship can be created;
2. define the different types of agency authority;
3. list the duties of a licensee to the principal;
4. list the duties of a licensee to third parties;
5. discuss the pitfalls of dual agency;
6. explain the concept of buyer agency; and
7. explain the risks of federal antitrust laws.

OVERVIEW

Let's take a close look at the agency aspects of the principal–broker relationship—that is, the legal responsibilities of the broker toward the principal and vice versa. The concept of agency is changing dramatically and is being addressed on a state-by-state basis, so a working knowledge of Georgia's laws is going to be of primary importance in determining the scope of a real estate agency.

This chapter covers creation of the agency relationship and obligations of the broker, both to the principal and to third parties. Owner disclosure statements and buyer agency are also discussed. The final portions of the chapter deal with dual agency and antitrust laws. As we discuss agency, when the term "broker" is mentioned, unless the context is that of a specific person, the term is used in reference to the brokerage firm.

AGENCY

agency: created when the principal delegates to the agent the right to act on behalf of the principal

principal: a person who authorizes another to act

agent: the person empowered to act by and on behalf of the principal

An **agency** is created when one person (called the **principal**) delegates to another person (called the **agent**) the right to act on the principal's behalf. There are three levels of agent authority: universal, general, and special. In a *universal agency*, the principal gives the agent legal power to transact matters of all types on the principal's behalf on a continuing basis.

An example is an unlimited power of attorney. Universal agencies are rarely encountered in practice, and courts generally frown on them because they are so broad. In a *general agency*, the agent is given the power to bind the principal in a particular trade or business on a continuing basis. For example, a salesperson is a general agent of the sponsoring broker. Another example is that of a property manager for a property owner. In a *special agency*, the principal empowers the agent to perform a particular act or transaction with no continuity expected or agreed upon. One example is a real estate listing. Another is a power of attorney to sign a deed on behalf of someone who will be out of the country.

third parties: persons who are not parties to a contract but who may be affected by it

The principal in an agency relationship can be either a natural person or a legal entity such as a corporation. Likewise, an agent can be either a natural person or a corporation such as a real estate brokerage company. The persons and firms with whom the principal and agent negotiate are called **third parties**. When a broker represents a seller, the buyers are third parties, often referred to as customers. The seller is often referred to as the client. When a broker represents a buyer, the sellers become the third parties, and the buyer is the client. Sometimes you will see the phrase "principals only" in real estate advertisements. This means the owner wants to be contacted by persons who want to buy and not by real estate agents who want to list the property.

ESTABLISHING THE AGENT'S AUTHORITY

An agency relationship can be established through a contractual agreement (expressed) or by acts of the parties (implied). In a brokerage engagement contract, the engagement agreement outlines the agent's (broker's) authority to act on behalf of the principal (owner) and the principal's obligations to the agent. A written agreement is generally the preferred method of creating an agency because it provides a document to evidence the existence of the agency relationship. To create an agency in real estate in Georgia, a written agreement is not just good or preferred practice, it is required.

Agency authority may also arise from custom in the industry, common usage, and conduct of the parties involved. For example, the right of an agent to use a photograph of the listed property for advertising may not be expressly stated in the listing. However, if it is the custom in the industry to do so, and presuming there are no restrictions to the contrary, the agent has *implied authority* to use a photograph. A similar situation exists with regard to showing a listed property to prospects. The seller of a home can expect to have it shown on weekends and evenings, whereas a commercial property owner may expect showings only during business hours.

Ostensible authority is conferred when a principal gives a third party reason to believe that another person is the agent even though that person is unaware of the appointment. If the third party accepts this as true, the principal may well be bound by the acts of the agent. For example, you give your house key to a plumber with instructions that when s/he has finished unstopping the waste lines, s/he is to lock the house and give the key to your next-door neighbor. Even though you do not call and expressly appoint your neighbor as your agent to receive your key, once the plumber gives the key to your neighbor, your neighbor becomes your agent with regard to that key. Since you told the plumber to leave the key there, s/he has every reason to believe that you appointed your neighbor as your agent to receive the key. In that the plumber has reason to believe your neighbor is your agent, you would be prohibited (by estoppel) from claiming that the relationship does not exist. This is sometimes referred to as an *agency by estoppel*.

ostensible authority: an agency relationship created by the conduct of the principal

An *agency by ratification* is one established after the fact. For example, if an agent secures a contract on behalf of a principal and the principal subsequently ratifies or agrees to it, a court may hold that an agency was created at the time the initial negotiations started.

An *agency coupled with an interest* is said to exist when an agent holds an interest in the property the agent is representing. For example, a broker is a part owner in a property the broker has listed for sale.

Remember, all these methods of establishing agency apply to buyer's brokers as well as to seller's brokers. A licensee must be always vigilant to ensure that agency is not created without proper contracts and/or required agency disclosures.

BROKER'S OBLIGATIONS TO THE PRINCIPAL

When an agency is created, such as an attorney for a client, a property manager for an owner, or a broker for a principal, a *fiduciary relationship* is created. (This term is somewhat confusing in Georgia because, according to the Brokerage Relationships in Real Estate Transactions Act, which is discussed in another section of this textbook, the agency between a broker and a client is NOT fiduciary unless the parties agree that it is. The significance of this is to limit the legal liability of the broker. With that being said, for the purposes of our discussion on agency, the term *fiduciary* is used in the traditional and generic sense.) The agent (called the *fiduciary*) must be faithful to the principal, exhibit trust and honesty, and exercise good business judgment. For a real estate broker, this means the broker must be loyal to the principal, obey legal instructions, maintain confidentiality, make full disclosure, be accountable for monies and actions, act with reasonable care, and treat the client with honesty, fairness, and integrity. Due to the rapidly growing number of buyer's agents, you must keep in mind that the principal–agent relationship includes buyer's agents as well as seller's agents. Let's look at these various requirements more closely.

Loyalty to the Principal

Once an agency is created, the agent must be loyal to the principal. The law is clear in all states that, in an employment agreement, the broker and the broker's sales staff occupy a position of trust, confidence, and responsibility. As such, the broker is legally bound to keep the principal fully informed as to all matters that might affect the sale of the property and to promote and protect the principal's interests.

Unfortunately, greed and expediency sometimes get in the way. As a result, numerous laws have been enacted for the purpose of protecting the principal and threatening the agent with court action for misplaced loyalty. For example, an out-of-town landowner who is not fully up to date on the value of the land visits a local broker and wants to list it for $130,000. The broker is much more knowledgeable about local land prices and is aware of a recent city council decision to extend roads and utilities to the area of this property. As a result, the broker knows the land is now worth $200,000. The broker remains silent on the matter, and the property is listed for sale at $130,000. At this price, the broker can find a buyer before the day is over and have a commission on the sale. However, the opportunity for a quick $70,000 is too tempting to let pass. He buys the property (or, to cover up, buys the property in the name of his wife or a friend) and, shortly thereafter, resells it for $200,000.

Whether he sold the property to a buyer for $130,000 or bought it and resold it for $200,000, the broker did not exhibit loyalty to the principal. Laws and penalties for breach of loyalty are stiff. The broker can be sued for recovery of the price difference and the commission paid, the real estate license can be suspended or revoked, and the broker may be required to pay additional fines and money damages pursuant to various consumer protection statutes.

If a licensee intends to purchase a property listed for sale by the licensee's agency or through a cooperating broker, the licensee is under both a moral and a legal obligation to make certain that the price paid is the fair market value and that the seller knows both who the buyer is and that the buyer is a licensee.

> **In the Field**
>
> This is a good time to set the stage that a licensee should always disclose unless s/he is positive that disclosure is not required or relevant. Disclosure goes well beyond what is selectively being discussed here. It is recommended that an agent disclose knowledge of any defect, repairs, facts about the property or transaction which would cause a person to turn away from the transaction, and any other item of significance. Better to be accused of providing too much information rather than misrepresentation or fraud.

A genuine concern arises over how much information a real estate broker is free to disclose to other brokers or other industry members who rely on this information in determining statistical data, market values, and other pertinent real estate–related information. For instance, can a real estate agent maintain a confidential relationship with a principal, yet disclose pertinent details of sales prices and financial terms related to the principal's business? Most state license laws specifically relieve a broker from liability for providing information about real property sales prices or terms for the purposes of facilitating the listing, selling, leasing, financing, or appraisal of real property unless this disclosure is specifically prohibited by a state statute or written agreement. Any licensee would be well advised to make this provision clear to the principal so that the principal can make an informed decision as to whether to disclose certain information.

Obedience

Obedience (also referred to as *faithful performance*) means that the agent is to obey all legal instructions given by the principal and to apply best efforts and diligence to carry out the objectives of the agency. For a real estate broker, this means performance as promised in the listing contract. A broker who promises to make a "reasonable effort" or apply "diligence" in finding a buyer and then does nothing to promote the listing gives the owner legal grounds for terminating the listing.

Obedience also means not departing from the principal's instructions. If the agent does so (except in extreme emergencies not foreseen by the principal), it is at the agent's own risk. If the principal thereby suffers a loss, the agent is responsible for that loss. For example, a broker accepts a personal note from a buyer as an earnest money deposit but fails to tell the seller that the deposit is not in cash. If the seller accepts the offer and the note is later found to be worthless, the broker is liable for the amount of the note.

Another aspect of faithful performance is that the agent must personally perform the delegated tasks. This protects the principal, who has selected an agent on the basis of trust and confidence, from finding that the agent has delegated that responsibility to another person. However, a major question arises on this point in real estate brokerage, as a large part of the success in finding a buyer for a property results from the cooperative efforts of other brokers and their salespeople. Therefore, listing agreements usually include a statement that the listing broker is authorized to secure the cooperation of other brokers and pay them part of the commission from the sale.

Treat Information Confidentially

Our next requirement of agency is *confidentiality*. Arising from the relationship between client and agent is the assumption that the client may speak openly to the agent and not have his/her confidence violated. A client should feel free to discuss sensitive information with the agent, and the agent must not breach that trust. A simple example would be a seller-client sharing with the agent the urgency to sell. Sharing this urgency with a buyer would be damaging to the negotiating position of the seller.

Confidentiality means that when negotiating a sale, the broker must continue to protect the principal's financial interests. Suppose that an owner lists a home at $125,000 but confides in the broker, "If I cannot get $125,000, anything over $118,000 will be fine." The broker shows the home to a prospect who says, "125,000 is too much. What will the owner really take?" or "Will the owner take $120,000?" Confidentiality and loyalty to the principal require the broker to say that the owner will take $125,000, for that is the price in the listing agreement. If the buyer balks, the broker should attempt to overcome the buyer's objection and obtain a full-price offer. If this fails, the broker may induce an offer from the buyer for the seller's consideration.

Georgia law requires that all offers be submitted to the owner, no matter what the offering price and terms. This prevents the agent from rejecting an offer that the owner might have accepted if the owner had known about it. If the seller really intends for the broker to quote $118,000 as an acceptable price, the listing price should be changed; then the broker can say, "The property was previously listed for $125,000 but is now priced at $118,000." Similarly, if a broker represents a buyer and the buyer is willing to pay $125,000, and it is the highest price paid in the market, the buyer's agent should inform the buyer of that fact. If the broker knows the seller-customer is willing to accept less than the list price, this information must be disclosed to the buyer-client.

Full Disclosure

An agent has a duty to make *full disclosure* to the client. Essentially, this means tell the client everything. If you are not sure whether to disclose or not, disclose. If you are not sure whether the client would want to know or not, disclose. If you are not sure if the client would consider the information material or not, disclose. If you are going to miss it, miss it on the side of disclosure. Be accused of TMI (too much information) rather than failure to disclose when dealing with a client. If you have knowledge that a buyer-customer will pay more for the property than offered, give that information to the seller-client. If you know that the seller-customer is desperate to sell and needs this transaction to happen, inform the buyer-client.

A broker's duty to disclose includes keeping the principal informed of changes in market conditions during the employment period. If, after a listing is taken, an adjacent landowner is successful in rezoning his/her land to a higher use and the listed property becomes more valuable, the broker's responsibility is to inform the seller. Similarly, if a buyer is looking at a property priced at $80,000 and tells the listing broker, "I'll offer $75,000 and come up if need be," it is the duty of the broker to report this to the principal. The principal can then decide whether to accept the $75,000 offer or try for more. If the broker does not keep the principal fully informed, the broker is not properly fulfilling the duties of an agent.

Accountability for Actions and Funds Received

A broker is accountable not only for his/her actions on behalf of the client, but also for monies received on the client's behalf. The earnest money that accompanies an offer on a property does not belong to the broker, even if the broker's name is on the check. For the purpose of holding clients' and customers' money, a broker is required under Georgia laws to maintain a *trust account*. All monies received by a broker as agent for the principal are to be promptly deposited in this account or in the trust account of the attorney, escrow, or title company handling the transaction. Georgia laws require that a trust account be held in a bank, which is defined as a financial institution with federally insured checking. The law also allows brokers to deposit trust funds in bank accounts that earn interest. The broker's trust account must be separate from any personal bank account, and the broker is required by law to accurately account for all funds received into and paid out of the trust account. As a general practice, a broker will have one trust account for properties listed for sale and another trust account for rental properties managed by the broker; however, this is not required by law. State-conducted surprise audits are made on brokers' trust accounts to ensure compliance with the law. Failure to comply with trust fund requirements can result in the loss of one's real estate license.

If a broker places money belonging to a client or customer in a personal account, it is called **commingling** and is grounds for suspension or revocation of the broker's real estate license. The reason for such severe action is that from commingling it is a very short step to *conversion*—that is, the agent's personal use of money belonging to others. Also, clients' and customers' money placed in a personal bank account can be attached by a court of law to pay personal claims against the broker.

commingling: the mixing of clients' or customers' funds with an agent's personal funds

If a broker receives a check as an earnest money deposit along with instructions from the buyer that it remain uncashed, the broker may comply with the buyer's request as long as the seller is informed of this fact when the offer is presented (some state regulations may prohibit this—check your state's guidelines). Earnest money can take any form. The broker can accept a promissory note if the seller is informed. The objective is to disclose to the seller all material facts that might influence the decision to accept or reject the offer. The fact that the deposit accompanying the offer is not cash is a material fact. If the broker withholds this information, there is a violation of agency.

Reasonable Care

The duty of *reasonable care* implies competence and expertise on the part of the broker. It is the broker's responsibility to disclose all knowledge and material facts concerning a property to the principal. Also, the broker must not become a party to any fraud or misrepresentation likely to affect the sound judgment of the principal. Although the broker has a duty to disclose all material facts of a transaction, legal interpretations must be avoided. Giving legal interpretations of documents involved in a transaction can be construed as practicing law without a license, an act specifically prohibited by real estate licensing acts. Moreover, the broker can be held financially responsible for any incorrect legal information given to a client. The duty of reasonable care also requires an agent to take proper care of property entrusted to the agent by the principal. For example, if a broker is entrusted with a key to an owner's building to show it to prospects, it is the broker's responsibility to see that it is used for only that purpose and that the building is locked upon leaving. Similarly, if a broker receives a check as an earnest money deposit, the broker must properly deposit it in a bank and not carry it around for several weeks.

Honesty, Fairness, and Integrity

The duty of *honesty* states simply that we should be compelled to tell the truth. While puffing (the use of extravagant statements that a reasonable person would recognize as exaggeration) is not misrepresentation, a broker should make sure that the client is not only being "told" the truth, but that the client is also "perceiving" the truth. Speak to the client in such a way that the words cannot be misinterpreted; be careful in using industry slang and abbreviations.

The doctrine of *fairness* requires that we not take advantage. If a seller is not aware of the value of the property, it would be unfair to purchase the property for ourselves without first disclosing our knowledge of value. If our company is offering inducements to list, such as free home warranties, it would be unfair to not offer this to a seller who is not knowledgeable enough to ask.

Finally, we must treat people with *integrity*. In your mind, this may be the "Golden Rule": Treat others the way you would want to be treated. It may be the "Platinum Rule": Treat others the way they would want to be treated. It may be the "Mama's Rule": Treat people the way you would want your mama treated. Or it may be the "Kids' Rule": Act in such a way that your kids would not be disappointed or ashamed.

BROKER'S OBLIGATIONS TO THIRD PARTIES

A broker's primary and fiduciary obligations are to the principal. Georgia laws nonetheless make certain demands on the broker in relation to the third parties the broker deals with on behalf of the principal. Foremost among these are honesty, integrity, care, accountability, and fair business dealing.

Misrepresenting a property by omitting vital information is as wrong as giving false information. Disclosure of such misconduct usually results in a broker losing the right to a commission. Also possible are loss of the broker's real estate license and a lawsuit by any party to the transaction who suffered a financial loss because of the misrepresentation. In essence, everything a broker owes a customer, the broker also owes the client. The broker's relationships to the customer and the client are different. The broker owes the client—but not the customer—loyalty, obedience, confidentiality, and full disclosure.

In guarding against misrepresentation, a broker must be careful not to make statements not known to be true. For example, a prospect looks at a house listed for sale and asks if it is connected to the city sewer system. The broker does not know the answer but, sensing it is important to making a sale, says yes. If the prospect relies on this statement, purchases the house, and finds out that there is no sewer connection, the broker may be at the center of litigation regarding sale cancellation, commission loss, money damages, and state license discipline. The answer should be, "I don't know, but I will find out for you." Then do it! Suppose the seller has told the broker that the house is connected to the city sewer system, and the broker, having no reason to doubt the statement, accepts it in good faith and gives that information to prospective buyers. If this statement is not true, the owner is at fault and owes the broker a commission; both the owner *and* the broker may be subject to legal action for sale cancellation and money damages. When a broker must rely on information supplied by the seller, it is best to have it in writing and to verify its accuracy. However, relying on the seller for information does not completely relieve the broker's responsibility to third parties. If a seller says the house is connected to the city sewer system and the broker knows that is impossible because there is no sewer line on that street, the broker should make an effort to correct the erroneous statement.

Most people have a good sense of what constitutes intentional fraud and vigorously avoid it. Not quite so obvious, and yet equally dangerous from the standpoint of dissatisfaction and legal liability, is the area of ignorance. Ignorance results from not knowing all the pertinent facts about a property. This may result from the broker not taking the time to check the facts or from not knowing what to look for in the first place. This is called "what the agent should have known," and there has been some far-reaching litigation that is forcing real estate brokers and their salespeople to know more about the product they are selling. In addition to the traditional common law theory of disclosures to third parties, there is now at least one additional obligation imposed by the federal government involving lead-based paint.

Lead-Based Paint

The U.S. Department of Housing and Urban Development (HUD) requires FHA buyers to be notified and advised about the possibility of lead-based paint in homes built prior to the 1978 ban on such paint. The two-page notice must be given to the buyers and signed before the execution of the sales contract, which would seem to make it the duty of the real estate salesperson if there is one. HUD will not permit FHA financing without a signed form delivered to the lender. If a loan is to be refinanced on a home built before 1978, the notice must be signed before the refinancing is finalized, even if the refinancing is conventional and not HUD/FHA-insured.

In the Field

While lead-based paint disclosure is required on homes built prior to 1978, it is possible to have lead-based paint in a home that was built well after this date. It is currently common for new construction to feature repurposed materials. Imagine a new home constructed with a fireplace mantel from a 1930s' New England farmhouse. Lead-based paint has been introduced into new construction. It is recommended that a brokerage representing sellers encourage the seller to complete a lead-based paint exhibit at the time of hiring the brokerage in ALL situations. There is no penalty for including the lead-based paint exhibit stating the seller has no knowledge of lead when the exhibit is not required. The penalty for NOT including the exhibit with a contract when the disclosure is required can be in excess of $200,000.

Red Flags

For the real estate agent, this means a careful inspection of the property to determine obvious defects or red flags. A *red flag* is something that would warn a reasonably observant agent that there may be an underlying problem. The agent is then responsible for disclosing this to the seller and any prospective buyers. The agent is not responsible for knowing the underlying problem that produces the red flag. It is strongly suggested that a broker recommend to the seller and/or buyer that a specialist be hired to determine whether there is an underlying problem causing the red flag. The careful agent will also want to inspect such things as kitchen appliances, water heater (and it IS a water heater, not a HOT water heater, as is often stated—why in the world would one need a heater to heat HOT water?! ☒), water supply, swimming pool, sewer hookup, heating and air conditioning systems, electrical capacity, plumbing, roof, walls, ceiling, fireplace, foundation, garage, fences, sidewalks, and sprinklers. The broker may also want to have the seller purchase a home warranty for the buyer as a means of reducing legal liability for all involved. What we see in the courts today is that the legal system is pushing the real estate industry further toward professionalism. When instructing the jury in one case, the judge said, "A real estate broker is a licensed person or entity who holds himself out to the public as having particular skills and knowledge in the real estate field." In the future, you may expect to see more court cases on this issue, as well as legislation that defines the standard of care owed by a broker to a prospective purchaser.

OWNER DISCLOSURE STATEMENT

To assist in providing full disclosure and to shift some of the responsibility squarely where it should be, seller disclosure forms have become common in real estate transactions. You will find that some sellers—particularly sellers who are not familiar with the property, such as banks, investors, and corporations—will not complete the disclosure form because they are not familiar with the property and do not want to make statements that could be used against them. Refusal to fill out the form does not relieve the seller of disclosing knowledge of a latent defect. It would be prudent at this time to review the types of defects. A **latent defect** is one that is concealed, hidden, or could only be identified by a trained eye. A seller is always required to disclose if s/he has knowledge of a latent defect. A **patent defect** is one that is in the open and would not take training or specific expertise to recognize. For example, a badly stained carpet in the middle of the floor would be a patent defect. Cover that stain with a sofa, and it becomes latent. An electrical panel that is not properly grounded and is a fire hazard would be latent, as it would take specific training to identify. If in doubt, treat defects as latent and disclose. It is much better to be accused of TMI (too much information) than finding advantage by failure to disclose.

Seller disclosure statements are a detailed disclosure of property defects (or lack thereof). As a general rule, the seller fills out the form, which is then made available to the buyer as a representation of the seller's statement of condition of the property. The seller is the most likely person to fill out the disclosure because the seller simply knows more about the property than anyone else. A real estate licensee should NEVER complete this form for the seller. Doing so would put the licensee at unnecessary risk. The risks of using the form are nominal, and the benefits are great. In the last 10 years, there has been extensive litigation on the sales of real property based on misrepresentations and material omissions. When the buyer sues, the broker has often been a defendant because the seller is

latent defect: concealed, hidden, or could only be identified by a trained eye; a seller is always required to disclose if s/he has knowledge of a latent defect

patent defect: in the open and would not take training or specific expertise to recognize the problem

gone and the broker marketed the property. This creates an unfair burden on a broker who may have no knowledge of the defect, or the expertise to investigate the potential for defects.

For the seller's benefit, the seller disclosure form gives the opportunity for the seller to reinvestigate the house. Very few of us have perfect homes. Many sellers simply overlook the defects (we all learn to live with them or forget about them, particularly when it's our house). This failure to disclose, however, results in misrepresentation on the part of the seller either because of negligence or because of innocently overlooking defects. In the worst-case scenario, the seller may intentionally misrepresent or intentionally fail to mention a defect to induce the buyer to purchase. In all circumstances, the seller's disclosure form yields these benefits: (1) it informs the buyer as to which defects exist; (2) it provides a basis from which the buyer can conduct further investigation on the property; (3) it allows the buyer to make an informed decision as to whether to purchase; and (4) it may provide a more concrete basis for litigation if the buyer can determine that the seller filled out the disclosure statement incorrectly or failed to disclose a defect the seller knew was material.

Similarly, brokers can find the disclosure statement beneficial because they now have written proof as to what disclosures were made to them. The disclosure statement should be compared with their listing agreement and the MLS disclosures to ensure consistency in marketing their product. In addition, knowing that there is a defect allows the broker to effectively market the property "as is," disclosing the defects and therefore limiting liability for both the seller (who sometimes overlooks potential liability in his/her eagerness to sell) and the broker.

As Is

After reading broker liability cases, you may begin to think that selling a property "as is" is a safe way to avoid the liability to disclose. This is not so. In a case that found its way to the courts, a property had been condemned by local government authorities for building code violations. The broker listed and sold it, making it very clear and in writing to the buyer that the property was being sold "as is." Although "as is" indicates the seller does not intend to make repairs, courts here found that this statement did not excuse the broker from failing to disclose material information. Essentially, "as is" simply means "no warranty or guarantee." "As is" does not relieve the seller or broker from liability to disclose latent defects. If *caveat emptor* (let the buyer beware) is not dead in Georgia, it is on life support.

In general terms, an agreed "as is" provision can shift a burden from the seller to the buyer, provided that the buyer is given ample opportunity to inspect the premises and agrees to assume the liability as part of his/her contractual agreement.

Most of these "as is" provisions, however, will not protect the seller if the seller has engaged in fraud, misrepresentation, or similar deception.

Puffing

Puffing refers to subjective statements that are merely an opinion, or extravagant statements that a reasonable person would recognize as exaggeration. Thus, a buyer may have no legal complaint against a broker who told the buyer that a certain hillside lot had the most beautiful view in the world or that a listed property had the finest landscaping in the county. Usually reasonable buyers can see these things and make up their own mind. However, if a broker, in showing a rural property, says it has the world's purest well water, there had better be plenty of good water when the buyer moves in. If a consumer believes the broker and relies on the representation, the broker may have a potential liability. The line between puffing and misrepresentation is subjective. It is best to simply avoid puffing.

puffing: statements a reasonable person would recognize as nonfactual or extravagant

BUYER AGENCY

It has long been recognized that a real estate agent can represent the purchaser. Buyer's brokerage is a common topic in real estate seminars, and it is often touted as the solution to the dual agency/intermediary conflict of interest (discussed next). It gives the buyer representation, which some people feel the buyer is entitled to, or needs, in many circumstances. Buyer brokerage may even ease the duty of a listing broker because the buyer's broker can perform some duties for the buyer.

In cases of office building leasing and more sophisticated commercial property acquisitions, parties frequently seek the assistance of a real estate broker to represent them in making prudent purchases when they lack the expertise to do their own investigations. This has now become more common in residential real estate. Buyer representation shifts the entire agency theory in the opposite direction of traditional seller representation. When representing a seller, a real estate agent (and the resulting fiduciary duty) focuses on the marketing of the project for the benefit of the owner. This involves "getting the highest price in the marketplace," maintaining the confidentiality of information, and trying to effect a sale within the shortest period of time for the benefit of the seller. This is the same focus of the traditional MLS sub-agency concept for cooperating brokers. Historically, the MLS system and most state laws on agency encourage agents to be trained as seller's brokers or cooperating brokers, so few agents had training as a buyer's broker. Today, however, buyer's brokerage courses are available in virtually every real estate market. The courses are well attended, reflecting a need for this type of expanded education.

Let's talk about buyer's brokers in more detail. The buyer's broker has a different focus. The emphasis in buyer's brokerage is to help the buyer make informed decisions and to obtain the desired product at a fair price, giving the buyer's interests the highest priority. This emphasis includes getting the lowest price in the marketplace, or at least a "good deal" for the buyer, facilitating resale or investment potential (a main reason why relocation companies use buyer's brokers), and finding a "safe" purchase of a product without latent defects.

There is also a shift of focus away from effecting the sale of the property, because the buyer's broker is more concerned with a satisfactory purchase by the buyer, not just making a sale. Simply searching the MLS may not be enough. Buyer's brokers should also search newspaper advertisements, websites, and other information sources for potential sellers.

What are the duties of a buyer's broker? The same care of agency duties that apply to sellers as principals also apply to buyers as principals. However, the situations do differ dramatically. The buyer may request assistance in finding out certain information, or the buyer may need help in pursuing certain issues (homeowners associations, deed restrictions, financing, and final walk-through) in which the buyer's agent may take on additional duties. (Remember, the buyer's agent isn't trying to market the property, but is trying to obtain the requested product.) If this is the case, most state license acts impose a duty of diligence and competency in undertaking those additional duties. Most buyers who hire a buyer's broker want advice, or they wouldn't hire them. This situation may create a conflict between the seller's and buyer's brokers. The result may be the same, but the means to achieve the sale may vary from the "typical" transaction in the past. The buyer's broker is expected to be more protective of the buyer (the primary focus) than on effecting the sale (the main focus of the listing broker). Buyer brokerage has gained wide acceptance. A growing niche for buyer's brokers has been created in the agency marketplace by consumers moving into new areas and relocation companies whose services buyers might want to use. Brokers may perceive buyer representation and/or cooperation with buyer's brokers as both beneficial and cost-effective given that a home buyer may be a home seller in a few years.

PRINCIPAL'S OBLIGATIONS

The principal also has certain obligations to the agent. Although these do not receive much statutory attention, they are important when the principal fails to live up to those obligations. The principal's primary obligation is *compensation*. Additionally, the agent is eligible for *reimbursement* for expenses not related to the sale itself. For example, if an agent had to pay a plumber to fix a broken pipe for the principal, the agent could expect reimbursement from the principal over and above the sales commission. The other two obligations of the principal are *indemnification* and performance. An agent is entitled to indemnification upon suffering a loss through no personal fault, such as when a misrepresentation by the principal to the agent was passed on in good faith to the buyer. The duty of *performance* means the principal is expected to do whatever reasonably can be done to accomplish the purpose of the agency, such as referring inquiries by prospective buyers to the broker.

BROKER'S SALES STAFF

A broker's sales associates are general agents of the broker. A sales associate owes the broker the duties of competence, obedience, accounting, loyalty, and full disclosure. The broker's obligations to the sales associate are compensation, reimbursement, indemnification, and performance. In addition, the broker will authorize the extent to which the sales associate can bind the broker. For example, is the sales associate's signature by itself sufficient to bind the broker to a listing, or must the broker also sign it? With regard to third parties, the sales associate owes them honesty, integrity, and fair business dealings.

COOPERATING BROKER

The fiduciary obligation of the cooperating broker is one of the most difficult legal problems of real estate brokerage. In approximately 70% of all sales made through multiple listing services, the broker who locates the buyer is not the same broker who listed the property. This results in a dilemma: Is the broker who located the buyer (the *cooperating broker*) an agent of the buyer or the seller? The traditional view (Theory 1) is that everyone is an agent (or subagent) of the seller because the seller has an employment contract with the listing broker, the seller is paying the commission, and the cooperating broker has rights through that employment contract. Theory 2 is that since the cooperating broker has no contract with the seller (only an agreement to share commission and information with the listing broker) and none with the buyer, the cooperating broker is the agent of neither.

In the Field

Up until the early 1990s, it was assumed that the cooperating brokerage (the brokerage firm working with the buyer) represented the seller and so became a subagent of the seller. There were massive lawsuits in the late 1980s that caused the industry to change its practices. Today, subagency, while legal, is all but dead. The cooperating brokerage today either represents the interests of the buyer or represents no one.

The Complicating Issues

You will recall that the real estate broker has a fiduciary duty to the seller in our traditional employment relationship. Part of that duty is that the broker must make full disclosure of every known item concerning the real estate and the agency relationship. What, then, is an agent to do if a buyer shares confidential information? If the agent pretends to be a dual agent, may the agent represent both parties and disclose all information to both without violating confidential relationships? In many cases, what matters is not what the agent intends but what the consumer perceives as the agent's duty of care. That is, do buyers think that the cooperating broker represents them? A Federal Trade Commission (FTC) study found that 71% of buyers surveyed believe this to be the case. And buyers come to believe this because it is the cooperating broker who is spending time with them, *and* is taking them to see properties, *and* will write and present the offer, *and*, if needed, will come back with a counteroffer. Moreover, the cooperating broker hopes to make a good enough impression so that a sale will be made and the buyer, in the future, will return to that broker for more real estate dealings.

Middleman Principle

middleman: a person who brings two or more parties together but does not represent either party (known as a transaction broker in Georgia)

Under this legal theory, the broker operates as a **middleman** who represents neither party. The broker simply brings the parties together, and neither party expects the middleman's loyalty. In Georgia, the term for a licensee acting in this way is *transaction broker*. This *middleman principle* can work in some sophisticated real estate transactions. The problem with this theory is that if either party thinks that the broker is that party's representative, an agency relationship could be created and fiduciary duties established, resulting in potential liability for the broker. It is very difficult, in most situations, to represent neither party yet still be an effective agent.

Dual Agency

dual agency: representation of two or more principals in a transaction by the same agent

If a broker represents a seller, it is the broker's duty to obtain the highest price and the best terms possible for the seller. If a broker represents a buyer, the broker's duty is to obtain the lowest price and the best terms for the buyer. When the same broker represents two or more principals in the same transaction, it is a **dual agency** or divided agency, and a conflict of interest results. If the broker represents both principals in the same transaction, to whom is the broker loyal? Does the broker work equally hard for each principal? This is an unanswerable question; therefore, the law requires that each principal be told not to expect the broker's full allegiance, and thus both principals are responsible for looking after their own interests. If a broker represents more than one principal and does not obtain the informed consent of all principals, the broker may not claim a commission, and the defrauded principal(s) may be able to rescind the transaction. Moreover, the broker's real estate license may be suspended or revoked. This is true even though the broker does the utmost to be equally fair to each principal.

If the student truly understands the discussion presented in these pages relating to the duties of the agent to represent the principal and maintain loyalty, confidentiality, and make full disclosure, the student should also recognize the conflict. An agent cannot maintain his/her duty of full disclosure and also maintain a duty of confidentiality. If the seller has a property listed for $225,000 but has indicated a willingness to take $210,000, then under full disclosure, the agent is required to disclose this knowledge to the buyer-client—but the agent may not do this and also abide by a duty of confidentiality to the seller-client. If a buyer wants to offer $150,000 for a property but has expressed a willingness to pay $165,000 if needed, this information must be disclosed to the seller-client—but the agent may not disclose it and still maintain duty of confidentiality to the buyer-client. Most brokerage companies in Georgia recognize this conflict and make every attempt not to allow themselves to be in a position of dual agency.

Designated Agency

An alternative to the conflict of dual agency is *designated agency*. In this theory, which is allowed by Georgia law, while there are two clients (buyer and seller or landlord and tenant) and one broker, there are two salespeople designated by the broker to represent the individual interest of each client. Although the law says that this is not a dual agency for the brokerage company, most prudent people would agree that it is best for the company to treat this situation with the care of a dual agency to make sure it does not violate perceived duties. Care must also be taken by companies that allow designated agency to have policies in place to keep the confidences of clients before or during the designated agency period. Although designated agency is clearly better than a single-agent dual agency, caution should be used.

Agency Disclosure

One can easily see that the problem of agency representation, particularly with the complication of the cooperating broker, can be a difficult subject. Agency relationships can be created without written agreements (ostensible authority), consumers can misunderstand the broker's role in a transaction, and there are very few rules under the traditional laws of agency that give the agent or the consumer an easy understanding of how the agency relationships work in the real world.

In many cases, the brokers do not really understand which party they represent. If, on the one hand, a broker's best friend requests some help in acquiring property and wants to buy one of the broker's listings, it is easy to see the problem of divided loyalty a broker can encounter. The buyer, on the other hand, has requested the broker's help and, as previously discussed, often thinks the broker represents the buyer in these situations. The simplest solution to this complicated problem is education, both for the real estate licensees and for the consumer.

The solution has been developed through the National Association of REALTORS®, the Association of Real Estate License Law Officials, the Georgia legislature, and the Georgia Real Estate Commission. That solution is merely disclosure, to the extent that all parties to the transaction understand who the real estate licensee represents. Georgia law requires that the disclosure be made as soon as reasonably possible in the transaction, usually at the point of first significant contact with the buyer (i.e., obtaining specific information from the buyer as to financial capacity, the property desired to be purchased, or other information deemed to be confidential). While this initial disclosure should be made in writing, Georgia law does not require written disclosure until the time of an offer being made. A similar situation occurs in reverse when a broker is representing a buyer. When showing property to the client, a seller-customer may try to offer sensitive information, not fully understanding the duties of the agent. Care should be taken to properly disclose to the seller the role of the broker and to educate the unsuspecting seller-customer of the duties the broker has to the buyer-client. It cannot be said too often: If unsure, disclose. Disclose early. Disclose often.

Perhaps the most difficult problem is when you represent the buyer and the buyer requests that the broker submit an offer on one of the broker's listings. This clearly establishes a dual agency, where the licensee represents the buyer and also the seller. There is simply no way you can disclose to both parties all the confidences that the broker knows without breaching a fiduciary duty. Georgia has not outlawed dual agency, but this theory is still difficult to deal with in everyday practice. A licensee is better advised to disclose this conflict of interest to both parties or offer to withdraw from the transaction if either party complains of this conflict. Be knowledgeable of company policy, comply with the policy, and engage your manager/broker if unsure of how to proceed.

There are two key factors in this disclosure of dual agency. The first is that it is up to the principal to decide whether dual agency is acceptable, not the broker. It is the principal who stands to lose on a breach of confidential information and has the most at risk. The second key factor in this disclosure is that the principals must understand how serious the conflict of interest is. Georgia will allow dual agency when written consent by all parties has been obtained. The more important emphasis is *informed consent*. An agent should be very careful to make sure that the principals understand the ramifications of the dual agency. A broker who says, "Here is a disclosure you have to sign—it's a required standard form," may not be making an effective disclosure. The broker must be sure that the parties understand whom that broker represents and the nature of that confidential relationship. This should eliminate misplaced confidences.

TERMINATION OF AGENCY

An agency relationship may be terminated in several ways. The easiest way to remember the circumstances of agency termination is by using the acronym DEARIE.

Death

An agency is a personal service and, as such, is not binding upon the estate of the deceased. If Rodney appoints Sally as his attorney-in-fact under a properly executed power of attorney, the agency would terminate if Sally died.

Expiration

In many agencies, the agent is appointed for a specific period of time. Once the time has expired, the agency duties and responsibilities would expire, also. The agency may also expire because of a performance. If an owner engaged a broker for 180 days to market his home and the broker found a buyer and closed the sale in 120 days, the performance would cause the agency to expire.

Agreement

The parties to the agency may agree to a cancellation. If an owner listed a property with a broker because she was being transferred to another state by her employer and then the transfer was rescinded, the seller and broker could mutually agree to cancel the agency and listing contract.

Revocation or Renunciation

Revocation refers to the unilateral cancellation by the principal; renunciation refers to the unilateral cancellation by the agent. If a seller or buyer is unhappy with the representation, either may cancel the agency at any time. Understand, however, that cancellation of the agency is not the same as cancellation of the contractual liability. For instance, if a seller cancelled an agency with a listing broker before the time period expired and then sold the property without a broker, the seller might still be liable to pay a commission to the broker if the sale took place during the listing period. This is a point that is misunderstood by many practitioners, but it makes sense. If a person could simply terminate a contractual obligation without cause at any time, there would be no reason to have the contract in the first place. Contracts would be meaningless.

Incapacity

If one of the parties to the agency is unable to continue, the agency would terminate. For instance, if a buyer-client was adjudicated to be insane, the agency would end. If a brokerage company had its license revoked, the agency would end. If a party filed for bankruptcy, this might cause the agency to terminate.

Extinction of the Subject Matter

If the reason the agency was created is no longer in existence, the agency would terminate. For example, if an owner of property enters into a property management agreement with a broker and the broker is instructed to market the property and find a tenant, the agency would terminate if the house burned down.

Termination of agency can be further broken down into one of two categories: *act of the parties* or *operation of law*. Act of the parties refers to the one of the principals to the agency being proactive in terminating the relationship. This would include agreement and revocation/renunciation. Operation of law refers to the fact that the law dictates the termination. This would include death, expiration, incapacity, and extinction. A simple key to remembering this is that in DEARIE, the middle two terms (agreement and revocation/renunciation) are acts of the parties. The remaining terms are operations of law.

INTERSTATE LAND SALES DISCLOSURE STATEMENTS

The federal government, through the Department of Housing and Urban Development (HUD), has enacted legislation aimed at protecting purchasers of property in new subdivisions from misrepresentation, fraud, and deceit. The HUD requirements, administered by the Office of Interstate Land Sales Registration, apply primarily to subdivision lots located in one state and sold to residents of another state. The purpose of this legislation, which took effect in 1969 and was amended in 1979, is to require that developers give prospective purchasers extensive disclosures regarding the lots in the form of a property report.

Property Report

The requirement that a *property report* be prepared according to HUD specifications was the response of Congress to the concern that all too often buyers were receiving inaccurate or inadequate information. A color brochure might be handed to prospects picturing an artificial lake and boat marina within the subdivision, yet the developer has not obtained the necessary permits to build either, and may never do so. Or a developer implies that the lots being offered for sale are ready for building, when in fact there is no sewer system and the soil cannot handle septic tanks. Or prospects are not told that many roads in the subdivision will not be built for several years, and when they are, lot owners will face a hefty paving assessment followed by annual maintenance fees because the county has no intention of maintaining the roads as public roads.

In addition to addressing the above issues, the property report also discloses information concerning payment terms, defaults, any soil problems, distance to schools and stores, additional costs to expect, availability of utilities, restrictive covenants, oil and mineral rights, and so on. The property report must be given to each purchaser before a contract to purchase is signed. Failure to do so gives the purchaser the right to cancel any contract or agreement.

Not an Approval

The property report is *not* a government approval of the subdivision. It is strictly a disclosure of pertinent facts that the prospective purchaser is strongly encouraged to read before buying. In these reports, the developer is required to make a number of pertinent disclosures about the lot, structure, owners' association, neighborhood, financing terms, and so on, and this must be given to the prospective purchaser before a purchase contract can be signed. Once signed, HUD allows the buyer a "cooling-off" period of seven days, during which the buyer can cancel the contract and receive all money back. The property report is strictly a disclosure statement designed to help the prospective purchaser make an informed decision about buying.

ANTITRUST LAWS

Federal antitrust laws, particularly the Sherman Antitrust Act, have had a major impact on the real estate brokerage industry. The purpose of federal antitrust laws is to promote competition in an open marketplace and to regulate any activities that would endanger that competition. True antitrust violations involve interstate activities, so true antitrust laws are federal. While Georgia has laws that deal with antitrust-type activities, they are not true antitrust laws. These will be discussed in a later chapter. To people not familiar with the real estate business, it could appear that all real estate brokers charge the same fee. In fact and in practice, nothing is further from the truth. Real estate brokers establish their fees from a complex integration of market factors, and all real estate brokerage fees are a result of a negotiated agreement between the owner and the broker. A brokerage firm may have a policy of charging a percentage of the sales price, a flat fee, an hourly fee, or any combination thereof. The brokerage firm may negotiate a lesser fee when there is less risk or a higher fee for a complex property that may have a higher risk of not being successfully marketed.

Price Fixing

Price fixing in any industry is so grossly anticompetitive and contrary to the free enterprise form of government that it is construed to be *"per se" illegal*. This means that the conduct of price fixing is, in itself, so illegal that no series of mitigating circumstances can correct it. While a brokerage company can establish a policy on fees, it should be acutely aware that any hint, or any perceived hint, of price fixing between brokers can result in both civil and criminal penalties. That is, if the court determines that a broker has engaged in price fixing with another broker or group of brokers, the licensee could serve time in a federal penitentiary in addition to paying a substantial fine. Consequently, brokers are well advised never to discuss their fees, under any circumstances, except with the owner of the property.

price fixing: two or more people conspiring to charge a fixed fee, having an anticompetitive effect

Boycotting

boycotting: two or more people conspiring to restrain competition

Another aspect of antitrust laws that has affected brokers has been the **boycotting** of other brokers in the marketplace. This, too, is a violation of the Sherman Antitrust Act. In some circumstances, agent trade associations have established rules for membership that have resulted in some brokers being unfairly excluded (unreasonably high fees, part-time employment, "discount" brokers, etc.). Standards for membership are usually an attempt to upgrade the professionalism of the industry and to maintain high standards. The difficulty that is encountered, however, is that high-quality real estate brokers are excluded from competing with members of broker trade associations, which results in an unfair market advantage.

Antitrust cases involving boycotting have tended to recognize the pro-competitive efforts of associations of REALTORS®, MLS systems, and other similar trade associations, however. Therefore, associations of REALTORS® and other trade associations can establish reasonable fees, residency requirements, and other pertinent requirements for membership. However, no membership requirements can be established that may arbitrarily exclude licensed real estate brokers from participation.

Most boards or associations of REALTORS® have opened up their membership to eliminate arbitrary exclusion of licensees from other boards who may wish to access pertinent information. This area of law is constantly changing, as REALTORS® are concerned in protecting their rights but also want to accommodate the needs of consumers. Real estate is still a service business.

Monopolies

If a business becomes so dominant that no one can compete, it can be considered an illegal *monopoly*. Think of the board game we have all played: If one player corners the market on all of the real estate, as the game continues, all other players will have to pay the one holding the monopoly, and eventually all but the property owner will be forced into bankruptcy. In a free enterprise system, competition is a must. In the past, companies such as AT&T, Wal-Mart, Home Depot, Delta Airlines, and Microsoft have had to deal with threats of antitrust violation and regulation as a monopoly. These companies are mentioned simply as an illustration of known companies that have done well; it is not meant in any way by the author or publisher that these companies have ever been involved in any activity that is illegal or improper.

Tie-in (Tying) Agreement

A *tie-in agreement* is when one contract is tied to another. For example, if a developer is offering lots for sale but requires that any builder who purchases lots also enter into a listing agreement with the developer's real estate company, the developer is tying the listing contract to the purchase contract. If there is no competition in the marketplace (i.e., there are no other developers with lots for sale, so the builder must buy from this developer), this tie-in agreement may be considered to violate antitrust laws.

Penalties

The penalty for violating the Sherman Antitrust Act is up to 10 years in prison and up to a $1 million fine for an individual. For a corporation, the penalty is a fine up to $100 million.

Errors and Omissions Insurance

Because of the trend in recent years to a more consumer-oriented and more litigious society, the possibility of a broker being sued has risen to the point that errors and omission insurance (E&O) has become very popular. The broker pays an annual fee to an insurance company that, in turn, will defend the broker and pay legal costs and judgments. E&O does not cover intentional acts of a broker to deceive, punitive damages, or negligence or misrepresentation when buying or selling for one's own account. Other than that, E&O offers quite broad coverage. This includes defending so-called "nuisance cases" in which the broker may not be at fault but must defend, anyway. Moreover, E&O covers not only courtroom costs and judgments but also pretrial conferences, negotiations, and out-of-court settlements. Today, E&O is simply a cost of the real estate business, just like rent, telephone fees, and automobile expenses.

Review Questions

Answers to these questions can be found in Appendix D at the end of this book.

1. When an agent is given the right to transact all types of matters on behalf of the principal, the agent serves as a:
   A. notary public
   B. third party
   C. universal agent
   D. special agent

2. Agents who are authorized to bind their employer in a trade or business are:
   A. special agents
   B. general agents
   C. exclusive agents
   D. principal agents

3. The relationship of a real estate broker to the owner of property listed for sale with the broker is that of a:
   A. general agent
   B. universal agent
   C. limited agent
   D. special agent

4. Which of the following is NOT a termination by the operation of law?
   A. a house burning down
   B. a person being adjudicated insane by the courts
   C. revocation by the seller
   D. the fact that it is the 91st day of a 90-day listing agreement

5. When an agent's authority arises from custom in the industry, it is identified as:
   A. implied authority
   B. ostensible authority
   C. customary authority
   D. conventional authority

6. An agency is NOT created by:
   A. ratification
   B. estoppel
   C. adjudication
   D. written agreement

7. Broker Gomez was part-owner of an apartment building along with two co-owners. When they decided to sell the building, broker Gomez was named as the agent in the listing agreement. Broker Gomez thus held an agency:
   A. by ratification
   B. coupled with an interest
   C. by estoppel
   D. by implication

8. Brokers have fiduciary responsibilities to:
   A. the owner of property listed by them
   B. third parties with whom they deal
   C. buyer customers
   D. all parties in a real estate transaction

9. Fiduciary responsibilities of an agent to the principal include all of the following EXCEPT:
   A. faithful performance
   B. loyalty
   C. accounting for funds or property received
   D. provision of legal advice

10. A broker may act as an agent for both parties in a transaction only with the permission of:
    A. the property owner
    B. the real estate commission
    C. both parties
    D. the purchaser

11. Isaacs introduced owner DiVita to prospective buyer Park. DiVita and Park conducted negotiations between themselves without assistance from Isaacs. The role of Isaacs was that of a:
    A. dual agent
    B. middleman
    C. single agent
    D. cooperating broker

12. Any earnest money deposits paid by the purchaser to a broker:
    A. belong to the broker
    B. must be placed in a proper trust account
    C. may be held by anybody designated in the contract
    D. must be interest-bearing

13. The placing of funds belonging to others in a broker's personal bank account would NOT constitute:
    A. commingling
    B. grounds for revocation of the broker's license
    C. grounds to be fined by the attorney general
    D. grounds for suspension of the broker's license

14. A broker who misrepresents a property to a prospect may be subject to all of the following EXCEPT:
    A. loss of rights to a commission
    B. revocation of broker's license
    C. criminal prosecution
    D. civil action for damages

15. An owner who gives false information regarding the listed property would NOT be liable for:
    A. a commission to the broker
    B. misrepresentation
    C. money damages to the purchaser
    D. suspension of license by the real estate commission

16. A broker who intentionally misleads a prospect by making an incorrect statement known to be not true would NOT be:
    A. guilty of fraud
    B. subject to license revocation
    C. subject to litigation
    D. in violation of the statute of frauds

17. Agents who fail to investigate the cause of an apparent underlying defect in a property they are selling may be found:
    A. criminally liable
    B. liable for civil damages
    C. guilty of a felony
    D. civilly liable with imprisonment not to exceed seven years

18. Brokers can indemnify themselves against legal actions by those with whom they deal by purchasing:
    A. errors and omission insurance
    B. middleman insurance
    C. property insurance
    D. employee insurance

19. The obligations of a principal to an agent DO NOT include:
    A. compensation
    B. reimbursement
    C. indemnification
    D. obedience

20. The relationship of a sales associate to the employing broker is:
    A. that of a special agent
    B. subject to all laws and rules of agency
    C. an employer–employee relationship
    D. that of a universal agent

CHAPTER 9

CONTRACT LAW

KEY TERMS

bilateral contract
breach of contract
competent party
consideration
contract

counteroffer
expressed contract
fraud
implied contract
liquidated damages

power of attorney
specific performance
unilateral contract
void contract
voidable contract

OBJECTIVES

After successful completion of this chapter, you should be able to:

1. explain how a contract is created and its legal effect;
2. describe the essentials of a valid contract;
3. understand the use of the power of attorney;
4. explain the factors involved in mutual agreement, including the offer and acceptance, counteroffer, fraud, innocent misrepresentation, mistake, and duress;
5. explain the parol evidence rule;
6. describe breach of contract and unilateral or mutual rescission;
7. explain the purpose and application of the statute of limitations; and
8. describe an implied obligation.

OVERVIEW

A contract is an agreement to do (or not to do) a specific thing. This chapter will introduce you to contract law, how a contract is created, and what makes a contract legally binding.

The essentials of a valid contract are also covered in detail. While studying this chapter, be aware this is an introduction to basic contract law and is not specific to real estate contract law. Basic contract law could apply to hiring a caterer for a party to hiring a mechanic to repair your car. How this specifically applies to real estate will be studied in a future chapter. Other covered topics include offer and acceptance, fraud, mistake, lawful objective, consideration, performance, and breach of contract—all very important concepts.

HOW A CONTRACT IS CREATED

A **contract** may be either expressed or implied. An **expressed contract** occurs when the parties to the contract declare their intentions either orally or in writing. (The word *party* [plural, *parties*] is a legal term that refers to a person or group involved in a legal proceeding.) A lease or rental agreement, for example, is an expressed contract. The lessor (landlord) expresses the intent to permit the lessee (tenant) to use the premises, and the lessee agrees to pay rent in return. A contract to purchase real estate is also an expressed contract.

An **implied contract** is created by neither words nor writing but, rather, by actions of the parties, which indicate that they intend to create a contract. For example, when you step into a taxicab, you imply that you will pay the fare. The cab driver, by allowing you in the cab, implies that you will be taken where you want to go. The same thing occurs at a restaurant. The presence of tables, silverware, menus, waiters, and waitresses implies that you will be served food. When you order, you imply that you are going to pay when the bill is presented.

contract: an agreement to do (or not to do) a particular thing

expressed contract: an agreement in which the parties to the contract declare their intentions—either orally or in writing—to do a particular thing

implied contract: an agreement made by neither words nor writing but by actions of the parties, which indicate that they intend to create a contract

Bilateral Contract

A contract may be either bilateral or unilateral. A **bilateral contract** results when a promise is exchanged for a promise. For example, in a typical real estate sale, the buyer promises to pay the agreed price and the seller promises to deliver title to the buyer. In a lease contract, the lessor promises the use of the premises to the lessee and the lessee promises to pay rent in return. A bilateral contract is basically an "I will do this *and* you will do that" arrangement.

bilateral contract: a promise exchanged for a promise

Unilateral Contract

A **unilateral contract** results when a promise is exchanged for performance. For instance, during a campaign to get more listings, a real estate office manager announces to the firm's sales staff that a $100 bonus will be paid for each salable new listing. No promises or agreements are necessary from the salesperson. The offer is accepted by the salesperson's performance. Each time the salesperson performs by bringing in a salable listing, s/he is entitled to the promised $100 bonus. An option to purchase is also a unilateral contract. It is an offer by the optionor to sell his/her property in the future in return for an option fee. At the time the option is exercised (and the optionee has the obligation to close), it becomes

unilateral contract: a promise exchanged for performance

a bilateral contract for sale (i.e., the optionor has agreed to the conveyance and the optionee has agreed to purchase at some time in the very near future).

Similarly, a listing can be structured as a unilateral contract. The seller agrees to pay a commission if the broker finds a buyer. When the broker starts to perform, the contract becomes more bilateral, as the agent has expended time and money and would be entitled to reimbursement. When the broker produces the buyer, the broker has completed the performance. The commission is earned and the seller's promise to pay the commission is enforceable. The broker has accepted the offer (discussed later), and the agreement to pay the commission becomes a valid, binding contract because of the broker's performance.

A unilateral contract is basically an "I will do this *if* you will do that" arrangement. The offer is made, and it is accepted by performance.

Forbearance

Most contractual agreements are based on promises by the parties involved to act in some manner (pay money, provide services, or deliver title). However, a contract can contain a promise to *forbear* (not to act) by one or more of its parties. For example, a lender may agree not to foreclose on a delinquent mortgage loan if the borrower agrees to a new payment schedule.

ESSENTIALS OF A VALID CONTRACT

There are four essential elements of any contract. If *any* of these elements is not present, the contract is not valid. The four elements are:

1. legally competent parties
2. mutual agreement
3. lawful objective
4. consideration

With these four elements in mind, consider the following basic definitions:

valid—an agreement that contains all essential elements of a contract

void—an agreement that is missing at least one of the essential elements of a contract and has no legal effect

voidable—an agreement that contains all essential elements of a contract, but from which, because of a defect, one or more of the elements may be removed at the option of the injured party

invalid—an agreement between parties that once had validity, but for which the validity has ceased

enforceable—a contract that a court would allow and uphold

unenforceable—a contract that a court would not allow or would not uphold

We begin with a basic discussion about the fundamentals of contract law. We are not specifically talking about contracts involving real estate unless real estate is used as an example. Throughout this chapter, examples of contracts that are valid, void, voidable, invalid, enforceable, and unenforceable will be given. Let's turn our attention to having a better understanding of the four stated essential elements of a contract.

Competent Parties

For a contract to be legally enforceable, all parties entering into it must be legally **competent**. In deciding competency, the law provides a mixture of objective and subjective standards. The most objective standard is that of age. A person must reach the age of majority to be legally capable of entering into a fully valid contract. *Minors* may or may not have contractual capability. In Georgia, the age for entering into a legally binding contract is 18. The purpose of majority laws is to protect minors from entering into contracts that they may not be old enough to understand.

In some cases, a contract with a minor is **void**. For example, a minor does not have the capacity to appoint someone to sell property. Any contract to do so (called a power of attorney) is void from the outset, as a minor does not have the legal ability to issue a power of attorney. If a contract with a minor is required, it may still be possible to enter into the contract; however, the contract would be **voidable** at the option of the minor (the injured party).

Regarding intoxicated persons, if there was a deliberate attempt to intoxicate a person involuntarily for the purpose of approving a contract, the contract would be void. If the contracting party was voluntarily drunk to the point of incompetence, the contract is voidable. When the intoxicated party is sober, s/he may ratify or deny the contract, if s/he does so promptly. However, some courts look at the matter strictly from the standpoint of whether the intoxicated person had the capability of formulating the intent to enter into a contract did. Obviously, there are some fine and subjective distinctions here, and a judge may interpret them differently than the parties to the contract. The points made in this paragraph also apply to a person who contracts while under the influence of other legal or illegal drugs.

competent party: person considered legally capable of entering into a binding contract

void contract: a contract that is missing an essential element and has no binding effect on the parties

voidable contract: a contract with a defect that can be voided by one of its parties

In the Field

Most contracts made with minors, except those for necessities such as food and clothing, are voidable by the minor at the minor's option. For example, a real estate sales contract entered into by a minor is voidable at the option of the minor. A minor wishing to disaffirm a contract must do so while still a minor or within a reasonable time after reaching majority. If not, *laches* attaches, and the contract becomes valid. Laches is the loss of a legal right due to failure to assert that right within a reasonable period of time. Other contracts, such as notes and mortgages, require the parties to have full legal capacity to contract, and so any note signed by a minor would be void.

Persons of unsound mind who have been declared incompetent by a judge may not make a valid contract, and any attempt to do so results in a void contract. The solution is to contract through the person appointed to act on behalf of the incompetent. If a person has not been judged legally incompetent but nonetheless appears incapable of understanding the transaction in question, that person has no legal power to contract. In some states, persons convicted of felonies may not enter into valid contracts without the prior approval of the parole board.

Power of Attorney

Individuals can give another person the power to act on their behalf to do things such as buy or sell land or sign a lease. The document that accomplishes this is called a **power of attorney**. The person holding the power of attorney is called an *attorney-in-fact*. Any document signed with a power of attorney should be executed as follows: "Paul Jones, principal, by Samuel Smith, agent, his attorney-in-fact." If the attorney-in-fact is to convey title to land, then the power of attorney must be acknowledged by the principal and recorded. The attorney-in-fact is legally competent to the extent of the powers granted by the principal as long as the principal remains legally competent and as long as both of them are alive. The principal can, of course, terminate the power of attorney at any time. A recorded notice of revocation is needed to revoke a recorded power of attorney.

> **power of attorney:** a document by which one person authorizes another to act his/her behalf

Corporations

As an artificial person, a corporation is considered legally competent. However, the individual contracting on behalf of the corporation must have authority from the board of directors. Some states also require that the corporate seal be affixed to contracts. A partnership may contract either in the name of the partnership or in the name of any of its general partners. Executors and administrators with court authorization may contract on behalf of estates, and trustees on behalf of trusts.

Mutual Agreement

The requirement of *mutual agreement* (also called *mutual consent, mutual assent,* or *meeting of the minds*) means that there must be agreement to the provisions of the contract by the parties involved. In other words, there must be a mutual willingness to enter into a contract. The existence of mutual agreement is evidenced by the words and acts of the parties indicating that there is a valid offer and an unqualified acceptance. In addition, there must be no fraud, innocent misrepresentation, or mistake, and the agreement must be genuine and freely given. Let's consider each of these points in more detail.

Offer, Acceptance, and Communication

Offer and acceptance requires that one party (the *offeror*) make an offer to another party (the *offeree*). If the offer is acceptable, the offeree must then communicate the acceptance to the offeror. The means of communication may be spoken or written or an action that implies acceptance, depending on agreement between the parties.

To illustrate, suppose that you own a house and want to sell it. You tell your listing broker that you will accept $100,000, deliver a general warranty deed, and pay the normal closing costs for the area. Within a few days, the broker submits a signed document from a prospective buyer. This constitutes an offer, and the buyer (the offeror) has just presented it to you (the offeree). If you then accept the buyer's offer and direct your agent to properly communicate that decision back to the buyer, at the time of communication of your acceptance to the buyer, a valid contract exists.

One requirement of a valid offer is that the offer be specific in its terms. Mutual agreement cannot exist if the terms of the offer are vague or undisclosed and/or if the offer does not clearly state the obligations of each party involved. If the seller were to say to a prospective purchaser, "Do you want to buy this house?" without stating the price, and the prospective purchaser said, "Yes, I do," the law would not consider this to be a valid offer or result in a valid and enforceable contract.

Counteroffer

Upon receiving the offer, the offeree has three options: to agree to it, to reject it, or to make a counteroffer. If the offeree agrees, the offeree must agree to every item of the offer. An offer is considered by law to be rejected not only if the offeree rejects it outright, but also if any change is made in the terms. *Any* change in the terms is considered a **counteroffer**. Although it may appear that the offeree is only amending the offer before accepting it, the offeree has actually rejected it and is making a new offer. This now makes the seller the offeror.

counteroffer: an offer made in response to an offer

To illustrate, suppose the prospective purchaser submits an offer to the listing broker to purchase the property for $95,000, but instead of accepting the $95,000 offer, the seller amends the contract to reflect a selling price of $100,000. This is a rejection of the original offer and creates a counteroffer to the purchaser. The purchaser now has the right to accept or reject this counteroffer. If, however, the original $95,000 offer is agreeable to the offeree (seller), the offeree must communicate the acceptance to the purchaser. While a spoken, "Yes, I'll take it," may be legally adequate, prudent real estate brokers should obtain the signature of the seller on a contract, without any further changes.

It should also be pointed out that an offer can be revoked by the offeror at any time prior to the offeror's hearing of its acceptance. For example, if you tell a prospective tenant that she can rent the property for $495 per month and, while waiting for her response, you find another prospective tenant who is willing to pay more, you may revoke your first offer at any time prior to hearing of its acceptance, then make your contract with the second prospective tenant. An offer, whether an original offer or counteroffer, may be withdrawn at any time prior to communication of acceptance. The one minor exception to this rule would be if the offeree provided an additional consideration to the offeror to make the offer irrevocable for a period of time, and the offeror accepted. For instance, if a buyer makes an offer requesting the seller to carry financing and the seller is not currently in a position to do so, the seller may offer a separate consideration to the buyer to make the offer irrevocable for a period of time in order to negotiate with others to create the ability to accept the buyer's offer. If accepted during this period of time, the buyer has essentially "sold" his/her legal right to withdraw. An offeror should be strongly advised, however, not to initiate more than one offer at a time, since considerable confusion can be caused by multiple offers, revocations, and acceptances in one transaction.

Fraud

fraud: an act intended to deceive for the purpose of inducing another to give up something of value

Mutual agreement requires that there be no fraud, innocent misrepresentation, or mistake in the contract if it is to be valid. A **fraud** is an act intended to deceive for the purpose of inducing another to part with something of value. It can be as blatant as knowingly telling a lie or making a promise with no intention of performance. For example, you are showing your apartment and a prospective tenant asks if there is frequent bus service nearby. There isn't, but you say "yes" since you sense that this is important and you want to rent the apartment. The prospective tenant rents the apartment, relying on this information from you, and moves in. The next day, the tenant calls to say there is no public transportation and wants to break the rental agreement immediately. Because mutual agreement was lacking, the tenant may *rescind* (cancel) the contract and get the rent money back.

Fraud can also result from failing to disclose important information, thereby inducing someone to accept an offer. For example, the day you show your apartment to a prospective tenant, the weather is dry. But you know that during every rainstorm, the tenant's automobile parking stall becomes a lake of water 6 inches deep. This would qualify as a fraud if the prospective tenant was not made aware of the problem before agreeing to the rental contract. Once again, the law will permit the aggrieved party to rescind the contract. However, the tenant does not have to rescind the contract. If the tenant likes the other features of the apartment enough, the tenant can elect to live with the flooded parking stall.

If a real estate agent commits a fraud to make a sale and the deceived party later rescinds the sales contract, not only is the commission lost, but also explanations will be necessary to the other parties of the contract. Moreover, Georgia license law provides for suspension or revocation of a real estate license for fraudulent acts.

Innocent Misrepresentation

Innocent misrepresentation differs from fraud (intentional misrepresentation) in that the party providing the wrong information is not doing so to deceive another for the purpose of reaching an agreement. To illustrate, suppose that over the past year, you have observed that city buses stop near your apartment building. If you tell a prospective tenant that there is bus service, only to learn the day after the tenant moves in that service stopped last week, this is innocent misrepresentation. Although there was no dishonesty involved, the tenant still has the right to rescind the contract. If performance has not begun on the contract (in this case, the tenant has not moved in), the injured party may give notice to *disaffirm* (revoke) the contract. However, if the tenant wants to break the contract, the tenant must do so in a timely manner; otherwise, the law will presume that the situation is satisfactory to the tenant.

Mistake

As it is applied to contract law, the term *mistake* has a very narrow meaning. It does not include innocent misrepresentation, nor does it include ignorance, inability, or poor judgment. If persons enter into a contract that they later regret because they did not investigate it thoroughly enough, or because it did not turn out to be beneficial, the law will not grant relief to them on the grounds of mistake (even though they may now consider it was a "mistake" to have made the contract in the first place).

Mistake, as used in contract law, arises from ambiguity in negotiations and mistake of material fact. For example, you offer to sell your mountain cabin to an acquaintance. He has never seen your cabin, and you give him instructions on how to get there to look at it. He returns and accepts your offer. However, he made a wrong turn, and the cabin he looked at was not your cabin. A week later, he discovers his error. The law considers this ambiguity in negotiations. In this case, the buyer, in his mind, was purchasing a different cabin from the one the seller was selling; therefore, there is no mutual agreement, and any contract signed is void.

To illustrate a mistake of fact, suppose that you show your apartment to a prospective tenant and tell her that she must let you know by tomorrow if she wants to rent it. The next day, she visits you and together you enter into a rental contract. Although neither of you is aware of it, there has just been a serious fire in the apartment. Since a fire-gutted apartment is not what the two of you had in mind when the rental contract was signed, there is no mutual agreement.

Occasionally, *mistake of law* will be claimed as grounds for relief from a contract. However, mistake as to one's legal rights in a contract is not generally accepted by courts of law unless it is coupled with a mistake of fact. Ignorance of the law is not considered a mistake.

Contractual Intent

Mutual agreement also requires that the parties express *contractual intent*. This means that their intention is to be bound by the agreement, thus precluding jokes or jests from becoming valid contracts.

Duress

The last requirement of mutual agreement is that the offer and acceptance be genuine and freely given. *Duress* (use of force), *menace* (threat of violence), or *undue influence* (unfair advantage) may not be used to obtain agreement. The law permits a contract made under any of these conditions to be revoked by the aggrieved party.

Lawful Objective

To be enforceable, a contract must not call for the breaking of laws. This is because a court of law may not be called on to enforce a contract that requires that a law be broken. Such a contract is void, or, if already in operation, is unenforceable in a court of law. For example, a debt contract requiring an interest rate in excess of that allowed by state law would be void. If the borrower had started repaying the debt and then later stopped, the lender would not be able to look to the courts to enforce collection of the balance. Contracts contrary to general public policy are also unenforceable.

Consideration

For an agreement to be enforceable, it must be supported by consideration. The purpose of requiring consideration is to demonstrate that a bargain has been struck between the parties to the contract. The size, quantity, nature, or amount of what is being exchanged is irrelevant as long as it is present. **Consideration** is usually something of value, such as a promise to do something, money, property, or personal services. For example, there can be an exchange of a promise for a promise, money for a promise, money for property, or goods for services. Forbearance also qualifies as consideration.

consideration: the promise or payment of something good or valuable

Exchange of Promises

In a deed, the consideration requirement is usually met with a statement such as, "For ten dollars and other good and valuable consideration." Also, the purchase contract is part of the consideration and is legally merged into the deed. In a lease, the periodic payment of rent is the consideration for the use of the premises.

> ### In the Field
>
> In a typical offer to purchase a home, the consideration is the mutual exchange of promises by the buyer and seller to obligate themselves to do something they were not previously required to do. In other words, the seller agrees to sell on the terms agreed, and the buyer agrees to buy the property on those same terms. The earnest money the buyer may put down is not the consideration necessary to make the contract valid. Rather, earnest money is a tangible indication of the buyer's intent and may become a source of compensation (damages) to the seller in the event the buyer does not carry out the promises.

Valuable versus Good Consideration

The consideration required under general contract law can be valuable or good. Consideration that can be measured in dollars and cents is *valuable consideration.* Valuable consideration may be money, jewelry, goods, or services. Valuable consideration is required for a sales contract. As previously stated, the consideration in a $100,000 sales contract for real estate would be the buyer's promise to pay the $100,000 and the seller's promise to convey the property, which apparently is worth $100,000. The earnest money, which is common but not legally required, is not the consideration required in a sales agreement.

What about outright gifts, such as the gift of real property from a parent to a child based solely on love and affection? Although this is not valuable consideration, it is nonetheless *good consideration* and, as such, fulfills the legal requirement that consideration be present. The law generally will not inquire as to the adequacy of the consideration unless there is evidence of fraud, mistake, duress, threat, or undue influence. For instance, if a man gave away his property or sold it very cheaply to keep it from his creditors, the creditors could ask the courts to set aside those transfers.

Multiple Meanings of the Word Consideration

If the word *consideration* continues to be confusing to you, it is because the word has three meanings in real estate. The first is consideration from the standpoint of a legal requirement for a valid contract. You may wish to think of this form of consideration as *legal consideration,* or *cause.* The second meaning is money. For example, the consideration upon which conveyance taxes are charged is the amount of money exchanged in the transaction. The third meaning is acknowledgment. Thus, the phrase "in consideration of ten dollars" means "in acknowledgment of" or "in receipt of."

Contract in Writing

In each state, there is a law that is commonly known as a *statute of frauds*. Its purpose is to prevent frauds by requiring that most contracts for the sale of land, or an interest in land, be in writing and signed to be enforceable in a court of law. This includes such things as offers, acceptances, land contracts, deeds, and options to purchase. Mortgages and trust deeds (and their accompanying bonds and notes) and leases for more than one year must also be in writing to be enforceable. In addition, most states have adopted the *Uniform Commercial Code* that requires, among other things, that the sale of personal property with a value in excess of $500 be in writing. Most states also require that real estate listing contracts be expressed in writing. All of these statements are true not only in Georgia, but generally throughout the United States, as well.

> **In the Field**
>
> A written contract will supersede an oral one. Thus, if two parties orally promise one thing and then write and sign something else, the written contract will prevail. This has been the basis for many complaints against overzealous real estate agents who make oral promises that do not appear anywhere in the written sales contract.

Purpose

The legal purpose of requiring that a real estate sales contract (and some, but not all, others) be written and signed is to prevent perjury and fraudulent attempts to seek legal enforcement of a contract that never existed. It is not necessary that a contract be a single formal document. It can consist of a series of signed letters or memoranda as long as the essentials of a valid contract are present. Note that the requirement for a written contract relates only to the enforceability of the contract. Thus, if Ms. Colby orally agrees to sell her land to Mr. Conan and they carry out the deal, neither may come back after the contract was performed and ask a court to rescind the deal because the agreement to sell was oral.

A lease for one year or less does not need to be in writing to be enforceable. Nonetheless, most are in writing because people tend to forget oral promises. While the unhappy party can go to court, the judge may have a difficult time determining what oral promises were made, particularly if there were no witnesses other than the parties to the agreement. Hence, it is advisable to put all important contracts in writing and for each party to recognize the agreement by signing it. If a party is a corporation, most states require the signatures of two corporate officers plus the corporate seal. It is also customary to date written contracts, although most can be enforced without showing the date the agreement was reached.

Parol Evidence Rule

Under certain circumstances, the *parol evidence rule* permits oral evidence to complete an otherwise incomplete or ambiguous written contract. However, the application of this rule is quite narrow. If a contract is complete and clear in its intent, the courts presume that what the parties put into writing is what they agreed upon.

Executory, Executed, Execute

A contract that is in the process of being carried out is said to be *executory*—that is, in the process of being performed. Once completed, it is said to be *executed*—that is, performance has taken place. This may refer to the signing of the contract or to its completed performance, depending on what the contract requires. The word *execute,* a much more frequently used term, refers to the process of completing, performing, or carrying out something. Thus, you execute a document when you sign it, and this is the most common use of the term. Once signed, you execute the terms of the contract by carrying out its terms.

PERFORMANCE AND DISCHARGE OF CONTRACTS

Most contracts are discharged by being fully performed by the contracting parties in accordance with the contract terms. However, alternatives are open to the parties of the contract. One is to sell or otherwise assign the contract to another party. Unless prohibited by the contract, rights, benefits, and obligations under a contract may be assigned to someone else. The original party to the contract, however, remains ultimately liable for its performance. Note, too, that an assignment is a contract in itself and must meet all the essential contract requirements to be enforceable. A common example of an assignment occurs when a lessee wants to move out and sells the lease to another party. When a contract creates a personal obligation, such as a listing agreement with a broker, an assignment may not be made.

Novation

A contract can also be discharged by novation. *Novation* is the substitution of a new contract between the same or new parties. For example, novation occurs when a buyer assumes a seller's loan *and* the lender releases the seller from the loan contract. With novation, the departing party is released from the obligation to complete the contract.

If the objective of a contract becomes legally impossible to accomplish, the law will consider the contract discharged. For example, a new legislative statute may forbid what the contract originally intended. If the parties mutually agree to cancel their contract before it is executed, this, too, is a form of discharge.

For instance, you sign a five-year lease to pay $900 per month for an office. Three years later, you find a better location and want to move. Meanwhile, rents for similar offices in your building have increased to $1,000 per month. Under these conditions, the landlord might be happy to agree to cancel your lease.

Deceased Party

If one of the contracting parties dies, a contract is considered discharged if it calls for some specific act or personal service that only the dead person could have performed. For example, if you hired a freelance gardener to do your landscaping and the gardener died, the contract would be discharged. However, if your contract is with a firm that employs other gardeners who can do the job, the contract would still be valid.

If there is a valid purchase contract and one party dies, the contract is usually enforceable against the estate because the estate has the authority to carry out the deceased's affairs. Similarly, if a person mortgages property and then dies, the estate must continue the payments or lose the property.

Property Damage

Under the *Uniform Vendor and Purchaser Risk Act*, if neither possession nor title has passed and there is material destruction to the property, the seller may not enforce the contract and the purchaser is entitled to the money back. If damage is minor and promptly repaired by the seller, the contract would still be enforceable. If either title or possession has passed and destruction occurs, the purchaser is not relieved of the duty to pay the price, nor is the purchaser entitled to a refund of money already paid.

BREACH OF CONTRACT

When one party fails to perform as required by a contract and the law does not recognize the reason for failure to be a valid excuse, there is a **breach of contract**. The wronged or innocent party has six alternatives: (1) to accept partial performance; (2) to rescind the contract unilaterally; (3) to sue for money damages; (4) to sue for specific performance; (5) to accept liquidated damages, or (6) to mutually rescind the contract. Let us consider each of these.

breach of contract: failure, without legal excuse, to perform as required by a contract

Partial Performance

Partial performance may be acceptable to the innocent party because there may not be a great deal at stake or because the innocent party feels that the time and effort to sue would not be worth the rewards. Suppose that you contracted with a roofing repairman to fix your roof for $400. When he was finished, you paid him. A week later, you discover a spot that he had agreed to fix but missed. After many futile phone calls, you accept the breach and consider the contract discharged because it is easier to fix the spot yourself than to keep pursuing the repairman.

Unilateral Rescission

Under certain circumstances, the innocent party can *unilaterally rescind* a contract; that is, the innocent party can take the position that if the other party is not going to perform contractual obligations, then the innocent party will not, either. An example would be a rent strike in retaliation to a landlord who fails to keep the premises habitable. Unilateral rescission should be resorted to only after consulting an attorney.

Lawsuit for Money Damages

If the damages to the innocent party can be reasonably expressed in terms of money, the innocent party may sue for *money damages*. For example, you rent an apartment to a tenant. As part of the rental contract, you furnish the refrigerator-freezer unit. While the tenant is on vacation, the unit breaks down and $200 worth of frozen meat and other perishables spoil. Since your obligation under the contract is to provide the tenant with a working refrigerator-freezer, the tenant may sue you for $200 in money damages. The tenant may also recover interest on the money awarded to him from the day of the loss to the day you reimburse.

Lawsuit for Specific Performance

A lawsuit for **specific performance** is an action in court by the innocent party to force the breaching party to carry out the remainder of the contract according to the precise terms, price, and conditions agreed upon. For example, you make an offer to purchase a parcel of land and the seller accepts. A written contract is prepared and signed by both of you. If you carry out all your obligations under the contract, but the seller has a change of mind and refuses to deliver title to you, you may bring a lawsuit against the seller for specific performance. In reviewing your suit, the court will determine whether the contract is valid and legal, whether you have carried out your duties under the contract, and whether the contract is just and reasonable. If you win your lawsuit, the court will force the seller to deliver title to you as specified in the contract.

specific performance: contract performance according to the precise terms agreed upon

Monetary Damages Versus Specific Performance

Note the difference between suing for money damages and suing for specific performance. When money can be used to restore one's position (as in the case of the tenant who can buy $200 worth of fresh food), a suit for money damages is appropriate. In situations in which money cannot provide an adequate remedy—which is often the case in real estate because no two properties are exactly alike (previously defined as nonhomogeneity)—specific performance is appropriate. Notice, too, that the mere existence of the legal rights of the wronged party is often enough to gain cooperation. In the case of the spoiled food, you would give the tenant the value of the lost food before spending time and money in court to hear a judge tell you to do the same thing. A threat of a lawsuit will often bring the desired results if the defendant knows that the law will side with the wronged party. The cases that do go to court are usually those in which the identity of the wronged party and/or the extent of the damages is not clear.

Liquidated Damages

The parties to a contract may decide in advance the amount of damages to be paid in the event either party breaches the contract. An example is an offer to purchase real estate that includes a statement to the effect that, once the seller accepts the offer, if the buyer fails to complete the purchase, the seller may keep the buyer's deposit (the earnest money) as **liquidated damages**. If a broker is involved, seller and broker usually agree to divide the damages, thus compensating the seller for damages and the broker for time and effort. Another case of liquidated damages occurs when a builder promises to finish a building by a certain date or pay the hiring party a certain number of dollars per day until it is completed. This impresses upon the builder the need for prompt completion and compensates the property owner for losses due to the delay. Georgia courts have specific requirements for liquidated damages to be enforceable. A real estate licensee should not attempt to write such stipulations without legal assistance.

liquidated damages: an amount of money specified in a contract as compensation to be paid if the contract is not satisfactorily completed

Mutual Rescission

Specific performance, money damages, and liquidated damages are all designed to aid the innocent party in the event of a breach of contract. However, as a practical matter, the time and cost of pursuing a remedy in a court of law may sometimes exceed the benefits to be derived. Moreover, there is the possibility that the judge for your case may not agree with your point of view. Therefore, even though you are the innocent party and you feel you have a legitimate case that can be pursued in the courts, you may find it more practical to agree with the other party (or parties) to simply rescind (i.e., cancel or annul) the contract. To properly protect everyone involved, the agreement to cancel must be in writing and signed by the parties to the original contract. Properly executed, *mutual rescission* relieves the parties to the contract from their obligations to each other.

An alternative to mutual rescission is novation. As noted earlier, this is the substitution of a new contract for an existing one. Novation provides a middle ground between suing and rescinding. Thus, the breaching party may be willing to complete the contract, provided the innocent party will voluntarily make certain changes to it. If this is acceptable, the changes should be put into writing (or the contract redrafted) and then signed by the parties involved.

STATUTE OF LIMITATIONS

The *statute of limitations* limits by law the amount of time a wronged party has to seek the aid of a court in obtaining justice. The aggrieved party must start legal proceedings within a certain period of time or the courts will not help. The amount of time varies from state to state and by type of legal action involved. However, time limits of three to seven years are typical for breach of contract.

IMPLIED OBLIGATIONS

As was pointed out at the beginning of this chapter, one can incur contractual obligations by implication as well as by oral or written contract. Home builders and real estate agents provide two timely examples. For many years, if a homeowner discovered poor design or workmanship after buying a new home, it was the homeowner's problem. The philosophy was *caveat emptor*—let the buyer beware—*before* buying. Today, courts of law find that in building a home and offering it for sale, the builder simultaneously implies that it is fit for living. Thus, if a builder installs a toilet in a bathroom, the implication is that it will work. In fact, Georgia has passed legislation that makes builders liable for their work for one year.

Similarly, real estate agent trade organizations, such as the National Association of REALTORS®, the Georgia Association of REALTORS®, and local REALTORS® associations, are constantly working to elevate the status of real estate brokers and salespersons to that of competent professionals in the public's mind. But as professional status is gained, there is an implied obligation to dispense professional-quality service. Thus, an individual agent is responsible not only for acting in accordance with written laws, but also for being competent and knowledgeable. Once recognized as a professional by the public, the real estate agent will not be able to plead ignorance.

In view of the current trend toward consumer protection, the concept of "Let the buyer beware" is being replaced with "Let the seller beware" and "Let the agent beware."

Review Questions

Answers to these questions can be found in Appendix D at the end of this book.

1. Which of the following would NOT be defined as an essential element of a contract?
   A. mutuality
   B. legal
   C. in writing
   D. competent parties

2. A contract based on a promise exchanged for a promise is a:
   A. semilateral contract
   B. dilateral contract
   C. binary contract
   D. bilateral contract

3. A contract based on one party's promise in exchange for an act from the other party is classified as:
   A. a bilateral contract
   B. an unenforceable contract
   C. an executed contract
   D. a unilateral contract

4. An option contract is enforceable against:
   A. either party
   B. the optionor
   C. the optionee
   D. neither party

5. A contract binding on one party but not the other is:
   A. unenforceable
   B. void
   C. voidable
   D. illegal

6. A person who has not reached the age of majority is also known as:
   A. a majoratee
   B. a majorator
   C. a minor
   D. an incompetent

7. As a rule, a contract between an adult and a minor is NOT:
   A. voidable by the minor
   B. enforceable against the adult
   C. enforceable against either party
   D. enforceable against the minor

8. An attorney-in-fact derives powers from:
   A. the state bar association
   B. a power of attorney
   C. judicial appointment
   D. popular election

9. A partnership may contract in the name of:
   A. the corporate officers
   B. the corporation
   C. the partnership
   D. the individual partners only

10. When an offeror makes a valid offer and communicates it to the offeree, which of the following is NOT an option of the offeree?
    A. Reject the offer.
    B. Accept the offer.
    C. Make a counteroffer.
    D. Bind the offeror to the counteroffer.

11. An offer may NOT be terminated by:
    A. withdrawal of the offer
    B. refusal from the offeree
    C. the lapse of time
    D. acceptance by the offeror

12. A contract with defect is considered to be:
    A. valid
    B. void
    C. invalid
    D. voidable

13. An act intended to deceive the other party in a contract is:
    A. duress
    B. menace
    C. mistake
    D. fraud

14. A contract made as a joke or in jest is precluded from becoming a valid contract because it lacks:
    A. legality
    B. competency
    C. contractual intent
    D. signatures

15. A contract that is in the process of being carried out is:
    A. executed
    B. executing
    C. executory
    D. executrix

16. When a lessee in a rented property assigns the lease to another party, the lessee assumes the role of:
    A. assignor
    B. assignee
    C. sublessee
    D. sublessor

17. Substitution of a new contract and a new party for a previous one is known as:
    A. innovation
    B. assignment
    C. subrogation
    D. novation

18. Legal action to force the breaching party to carry out the remainder of a contract is called a suit for:
    A. liquidated damages
    B. specific performance
    C. partial performance
    D. breach of contract

19. The law that limits the time in which a wronged party may file legal action for obtaining justice is the statute of:
    A. frauds
    B. limitations
    C. novation
    D. performance

20. In view of current trends toward consumer protection, the watchwords for real estate salespersons and brokers might well be:
    A. *caveat emptor*
    B. *caveat agent*
    C. *caveat fidelis*
    D. *caveat cervesa*

THE PRINCIPAL–BROKER RELATIONSHIP: EMPLOYMENT

CHAPTER 10

KEY TERMS

advance fee listing
broker
Buyer Brokerage Engagement Agreement
exclusive right-to-sell
multiple listing service (MLS)
net listing
ready, willing, and able buyer
real estate listing

OBJECTIVES

After successful completion of this chapter, you should be able to:

1. distinguish among the various kinds of listings;
2. explain the purpose behind the exclusive authority to purchase;
3. describe the multiple listing service, the employment period, and agent's authority;
4. explain the principle of earning commission;
5. define procuring cause;
6. explain how to terminate an employment contract; and
7. discuss "bargain" and "flat-fee" brokers.

OVERVIEW

This chapter covers the employment relationship between a broker and the principal. As has been previously pointed out, the term "broker," unless specifically referring to a person, is referring generically to the brokerage firm and any employees or licensees. The main topics of the chapter include the listing agreement, exclusive right-to-sell

listing, the exclusive agency listing, open listing, net listing, and the listing period. The chapter also covers the multiple listing service and broker compensation, and discusses procuring cause, employment contract termination, and bargain brokers. A broker may be hired by the seller/landlord, buyer/tenant, or both. While this chapter refers to the employment agreement as a listing, when between a seller and broker, it is best to think of ALL agreements of employment between a client and broker as a brokerage engagement agreement. This terminology is consistent with Georgia law and is likely what the future holds.

LISTING AGREEMENT

A **real estate listing** is an employment contract between a property owner and a real estate **broker**. Through it, the property owner appoints the broker as the owner's agent for the specific purpose of finding a buyer or tenant who is willing to meet the conditions set forth in the listing. It does not authorize the broker to sell or convey title to the property or to sign contracts.

real estate listing: a contract wherein a broker is employed to find a buyer or tenant

broker: one who acts as an agent for others in negotiating contracts or sales

Although persons licensed as real estate salespersons perform listing and sales functions, they are actually extensions of the broker. A seller may conduct all aspects of a listing and sale through a salesperson licensee, but it is the broker behind the salesperson with whom the seller has the listing contract and who is legally liable for its proper execution. If you plan to be a salesperson for a broker, be aware of what is legally and ethically required of a broker, because you are the broker's eyes, ears, hands, and mouth. If your interest is in listing your property with a broker, know that it is the broker with whom you have the listing contract even though your day-to-day contact is with the broker's sales associates. Sales associates are the licensed salespersons or brokers who work for a broker.

When a property owner signs a listing, all the essential elements of a valid contract must be present. The owner and broker must be legally capable of contracting, there must be mutual assent, and the agreement must be for a lawful purpose. Georgia requires that a brokerage engagement agreement be in writing and be signed by the parties. While the focus here will be primarily on the listing agreement between the seller and the brokerage company, the same principles apply to an engagement between the buyer–client and the brokerage company.

In Appendix E, you will find an example of an Exclusive Seller Listing Agreement (Form F1), which is part of the Georgia Association of Realtors® (GAR) packet of forms. In the field, licensees use this document or one very similar to it. Let's have a brief discussion of the key points of a typical Exclusive Seller Listing Agreement. The student is advised to study all of the forms presented in this text in detail to fully understand the provisions contained therein:

- *A description and identification of the property.* First is a provision for the description of the property, both legal and common. Remember that mutuality is a basic provision in contract law. If it is not clear between the parties what property is being listed, there can be no contract. This section may also provide for the term of the agreement with a beginning date and ending date. While filling out the blanks, put N/A in any unused areas.

- *Duties and responsibilities of the parties.* This portion of the listing agreement states the duties of the broker to the seller and the seller to the broker. Note that a broker does not have the duty to sell the property, but, rather, to use "best efforts to procure" a buyer for the property. This section also requires the seller to cooperate with the broker in the marketing of the property, provide accurate information on the property, and comply with state and federal laws.

- *Marketing.* This section of the listing agreement provides the broker with permission to advertise, put a "For Sale" sign on the property, cooperate with other brokers in the marketing of the property, and install a lockbox. This section also states what multiple listing services to which the broker belongs and provides authority and responsibility to the broker to submit the listing to the service(s).

- *Compensation.* This is the one we get up in the morning for—the commission! This obligates the seller to pay a commission if the property sells during the listing period, whether the buyer is procured by the broker, the seller, another party, or a cooperating broker. You will also find a "safety clause." This protects the broker under certain circumstances if the property sells after the expiration of the listing to a buyer introduced to the property during the listing period. This duty of the seller to pay the broker a commission is for a negotiated period of time between the seller and broker.

- *General protection language (legal boilerplate).* The typical listing agreements are full of preprinted language to disclose and protect all parties. In these sections, you will find that the seller must provide a seller disclosure statement. Also included are the broker's duties of confidentiality and a general statement of what the broker is not responsible for (to try to limit liabilities in a somewhat litigious society). There is also an important statement about disclosure of fraudulent activity. If the broker becomes aware of a potential illegal fraud involving the property, the broker is authorized to report the act. Obviously, this will probably sink a potential sale, and in the heat of negotiation, the seller may want to turn a blind eye. The time to take a strong stand is before you enter into the agreement with the client.

- *Agency disclosure.* Georgia law requires specific disclosure as to the agency relationship of the brokerage firm. In a later chapter, we will discuss Georgia's Brokerage Relationships in Real Estate Transactions Act (BRRETA). BRRETA requires that a broker disclose what agency relationships the brokerage company does and does not offer. Dual agency and designated agency are allowed by Georgia law but require written disclosure and informed consent.

- *Fax rights.* While online services such as DocuSign are becoming very common, faxing is still relevant, as we often communicate legal information in our business by fax. Thus, it becomes imperative that the fax number be accurate. Also included is an acknowledgment of the broker's rights to contact the seller by telephone and fax, which is required by federal laws.

- *Methods of communication (notification).* It is also very important that the listing agreement stipulates exactly how information may be communicated. This section commonly provides four distinctive methods of notification, and the licensee must follow these exactly to make sure the contracts are valid and enforceable. Many believe that the use of fax is the best way to communicate final acceptance because the notification is effective upon transmission so long as the sending fax produces a confirmation of transmission. All other methods typically require actual receipt, and the wise licensee would demand a written receipt from the receiving party to keep as part of the file.

Licensees must carefully read and understand any form contract they are using. What has been described here is generic and may be modified by specific forms.

EXCLUSIVE RIGHT-TO-SELL LISTING

The listing agreement mentioned earlier and printed in Appendix E is often referred to as an **exclusive right-to-sell** or *exclusive authorization-to-sell* listing. Its distinguishing characteristic is that no matter who sells the property during the listing period, the listing broker is entitled to a commission. This is the most widely used type of listing in the United States. Once signed by the owner and accepted by the broker, the primary advantage to the broker is that the money and effort the broker expends on advertising and showing the property will be to the broker's benefit. The advantage to the owner is that the broker will usually put more effort into selling a property if the broker holds an exclusive right rather than an exclusive agency or an open listing.

exclusive right-to-sell: a listing that gives the broker the right to collect a commission no matter who sells the property during the listing period

EXCLUSIVE AGENCY LISTING

The *exclusive agency listing* is similar to the exclusive right to sell, except that the owner may personally sell the property during the listing period and not owe a commission to the broker. The broker, however, is the only broker who may act as an agent during the listing period; hence, the term *exclusive agency*. For an owner, this type of listing may seem like the best of two worlds: The owner has a broker looking for a buyer, but if the owner finds a buyer first, the owner can save a commission fee. The broker is less enthusiastic, because the broker's efforts can too easily be undermined by the owner. Consequently, the broker may not expend as much effort on advertising and showing the property as with an exclusive right to sell.

OPEN LISTING

Open listings carry no exclusive rights. An owner can give an open listing to any number of brokers at the same time, and the owner can still find a buyer and avoid a commission. This gives the owner the greatest freedom of any listing form, but there is little incentive for the broker to expend time and money showing the property, as the broker has little control over who will be compensated if the property is sold. The broker's only protection is that if the broker does find a buyer at the listing price and terms, the broker is entitled to a commission. This reluctance to develop a sales effort usually means that few, if any, offers will be received, and the result may be no sale or a sale below market price. Yet, if a broker does find a buyer, the commission earned may be the same as with an exclusive right to sell.

NET LISTING

net listing: a listing agreement that pays the broker an uncertain amount of commission, generating the principal net proceeds from the sale

A **net listing** is created when an owner states the price wanted for the property and then agrees to pay the broker anything above that price as the commission. It can be written in the form of an exclusive right to sell, an exclusive agency, or an open listing. The problem is that there is no gross listed price between the seller and broker. If a homeowner asks for a "net $110,000" and the broker sells the home for $116,000, the commission would be $6,000. By using the net listing method, many owners feel that they are forcing the broker to look to the buyer for the commission by marking up the price of the property. In reality, though, would a buyer pay $116,000 for a home that is worth $110,000? Another problem with the net listing is that the broker may not want to disclose the true value of the property to the seller if the seller has an understated opinion of value. For instance, if the seller is not aware of proposed development nearby and tells the broker s/he wants to net $100,000 for the land, and the broker knows it to be worth $140,000, the broker may guarantee the seller his/her net of $100,000 and accept a commission of any amount above the guarantee. In this example, the broker would receive a commission potentially of $40,000, which most would consider excessive on a $140,000 property. Remember, above all else, that we have duties of fairness, integrity, honesty, and disclosure. Because of widespread misunderstanding regarding net listings, Georgia law prohibits them outright. When a seller says s/he has a net figure in mind, the broker may add his/her commission to the net and list the property at the gross price, and this would be neither a net listing nor illegal. There is no law that says a broker must accept a listing; a broker is free to accept only those listings for which the broker can perform a valuable service and earn an honest profit.

ADVANCE FEE AND ADVANCE COST LISTINGS

Traditionally, real estate brokers charge a fee for their services based on a percentage of the sales price. The fee is a *contingency fee* or performance fee, paid only if the broker performs. Out of this percentage, the broker: (1) pays all out-of-pocket costs of marketing the property, such as advertising and office overhead; (2) pays those who negotiate the transaction; and (3) earns a profit for the firm. If a buyer is not found, the broker receives no money. This means commissions earned from sold properties must also pay for costs incurred by nonsales. Sellers who have marketable property that is priced to sell subsidize sellers whose property is either unattractive or overpriced. As a solution to this inequity, attention is now being given by the real estate industry to the concept of advance fee listings and advance cost listings.

An **advance fee listing** is an agreement wherein the client pays a fee upfront when signing the brokerage engagement agreement. With this arrangement, the brokerage company is guaranteed to be paid for its services regardless of whether the property sells or the buyer finds the right property. Since the risk of being paid is eliminated and the seller shares the burden, the fee is generally lower than what would be competitive in the market. This fee may be a percentage of the listing price or a flat fee.

advance fee listing: listing in which a broker gets paid in advance and charges an hourly rate

An *advance cost listing* covers only out-of-pocket costs incurred by the broker, such as advertising, multiple listing fees, flyers, mailings, toll calls, survey, soil report, title report, travel expenses, and food served during open houses. With either the advance fee or advance cost arrangement, the broker can still charge a commission based on sales price. With the broker receiving payment for costs (and effort) upfront, the sales commission can be lowered.

With *flat fee listing*, there is an agreement between the broker and the seller that the commission will be an agreed-upon amount and not a percentage of the sales price. This fee may be paid upfront at the time of listing or it may be paid as a contingency only if the property sells. It also could be some combination of all of these concepts.

The mechanics of advance fee, advance cost, and flat fee listings must be very clearly explained to the seller before the listing is signed. There must be an accurate accounting of where the seller's money is being spent. (This is an ideal task for a computer.) Watch the advance fee trend. If it takes hold, it will be an important factor in changing real estate agents from commissioned salespeople to professionals who can command an hourly fee for their time.

BUYER BROKERAGE ENGAGEMENT AGREEMENT

Previous portions of this chapter have presumed the general rule that the real estate broker represents the seller. Historically, it has been the seller who has hired a broker to assist in marketing property. Consumers, though, are far more sophisticated and informed today. They are aware of the complexities of the market, property condition, and consumer protection laws. They want, and often need, advice from a real estate professional. The Real Estate Buyer's Agent Council (REBAC), a division of the National Association of REALTORS®, increased its membership from 5,000 to 15,000 in only one year, reflecting expanded interest in buyer's representation. Today, many home buyers retain the services of an agent to help them locate property, or to assist them in negotiating the acquisition of a specified property. In such cases, the broker's primary responsibility is

Buyer Brokerage Engagement Agreement: the agreement between a buyer and a brokerage firm hired to represent the interests of the buyer

to the purchaser rather than to the seller. In this circumstance, the purchaser can reveal confidential information to the broker and rely on the broker's expertise and competence. This may be particularly helpful in situations where a real estate transaction is complex or there are peculiar concerns unique to certain regions of the country (termites in Houston, radon in Maine, soil conditions in California) about which a buyer wants to be adequately advised before buying real estate in that area. In these situations, the principal (now the buyer) needs to be assured as to the scope of employment of the broker (i.e., locating the property), and, similar to a listing contract, the broker needs to be assured of being protected and that the buyer does not "go around" the broker and cut the broker out of a commission once the property has been identified. This is a major concern for buyer's brokers since the agent can aid and educate, only to have the buyer cut out the broker in hopes of a better sales price (with no commission or a lower commission paid). Buyers, then, need to be committed to their agent, and building that level of trust and confidence is not easy. A good employment contract, coupled with good service, develops this trust.

An example of an Exclusive Buyer Brokerage Agreement is provided in Appendix E. Much of the wording is similar to the Exclusive Listing Agreement, but it is the contract between the buyer and the broker when the buyer wants to be represented as a client. Care should be taken by the licensee not to use a "seller" mentality when representing a buyer. For instance, you would not commonly want to take a short-term listing and have the responsibility of marketing the property without a reasonable chance of being successful and being compensated. When dealing with a buyer who must buy in the next three days, holding out for a 90- or 180-day agreement would not make sense. Also, the liabilities in representing a buyer are considered much greater than those of representing a seller. When the transaction closes, if you are representing the seller, not much bad can happen. If you are representing the buyer, anything can happen after closing, such as discovery of defect.

MULTIPLE LISTING SERVICE

multiple listing service (MLS): organization of member brokers agreeing to share listing information and share commissions

Multiple listing service (MLS) organizations enable a broker with a listing to make a blanket offering of subagency and/or compensation to other member brokers, thus broadening the market exposure for a given property. Member brokers are authorized to show each other's properties to their prospects. If a sale results, the commission is divided between the broker who found the buyer and the broker who obtained the listing.

Market Exposure

A property listed with a broker who is a multiple listing service member receives the advantage of greater sales exposure, which in turn means a better price and a quicker sale. For the buyer, it means learning about what is for sale at many offices without having to visit each individually. For a broker or salesperson with a prospect but not a suitable property listed in that office, the opportunity to make a sale is not lost because the prospect can be shown the listings of other brokers.

To give a property the widest possible market exposure and to maintain fairness among their members, most multiple listing organizations obligate each member broker to provide information to the organization on each new listing within three to seven days after the listing is taken. To facilitate the exchange of information, multiple listing organizations have developed customized listing forms. The latest MLS systems are extremely high tech. The information on the property is fed into a computer at the local broker's office. A photograph of the home is scanned in with the data, and the listing is officially on MLS. Then, if Broker B has a prospect interested in a property listed by Broker A, Broker B telephones Broker A and arranges to show the property. If Broker B's prospect makes an offer on the property, Broker B contacts Broker A, and together they can present the offer.

In looking for a new property on behalf of the buyer, Broker B can scan the MLS website and sort elements to locate homes by zone area, square footage, number of bedrooms and baths, price range, and any number of other input data items that the buyer may be looking for. Obviously, this eliminates combing through the old MLS books of the past. Since the MLS data are updated as the information is posted, the system stays current.

MLS organizations have been taken to court for being open only to members of local real estate associations. Another idea that has been tested in courts is that an MLS be open to anyone who wants to list a property, that is, broker or owner. It is generally held, though, that the MLS membership criteria are valid and important to the system's function. Owners lacking real estate sophistication would place much inaccurate information in the MLS, and this would do considerable harm to MLS members who must rely on that information when describing and showing properties. It is important to note that the sharing of MLS information with nonmembers may violate federal copyright and/or trademark laws.

Computerized MLS

Not too many years ago, MLS information was available only by monthly or semimonthly distribution of books. These books were constantly outdated, heavy, and cumbersome to research. Today, almost all MLS information is available on the internet. All you need is access, provided by membership, and a computer. With current technology, this information can be accessed while in your car through laptop computers with a wireless internet connection or through a smartphone. Information is substantially more current and easier to search and access. Our business has changed more in the last 5 years than it did in the 15 years prior, and that trend is likely to continue.

Visual Tours

A prospective buyer can now take a visual tour through a neighborhood via video or the web without leaving the broker's office or even his/her home. Using computerized access to MLS files and other sites such as Google Earth and Google Street View, a person can see in specific detail a property before spending the time to visit. There are also virtual tours available on most MLS data systems. It is up to the listing broker whether these additional marketing tools will be utilized. Multiple photographs and virtual tours are both very effective marketing devices.

The internet now dominates the market for both practitioners and individual buyers and sellers. Not only can an individual seller post on many internet services (alternative sources are available for buyers and buyer's brokers), but the MLS is also on the internet in all locations. In addition, most real estate offices have their own websites (both buyer's and seller's brokers), and a few real estate companies have been developed to market solely to the internet customer and client. Some of these companies offer fewer services, and thus can offer lower fees or rebates to their principals.

These companies frequently take the position that they are providing fewer person hours for their services, so they can charge lower fees. Free enterprise and competition are a wonderful thing! In just a few short years, the internet has made a huge impact on the way real estate agents handle their business.

BROKER COMPENSATION

The listing broker earns a commission at whatever point in the transaction the broker and owner agree upon. In nearly all listing contracts, this point occurs when the broker produces a **ready, willing, and able buyer** at price and terms acceptable to the owner. "Ready and willing" refers to a buyer who is ready to buy at the seller's price and terms, with this being primary. I am "ready, willing, and able" to buy anything you have and I will let you name the price if I can name the terms. If you want $20 trillion for a half-acre lot on a dirt road with a 1962 Fleetwood single-wide mobile home, I will do it—if you let me name the terms. The deal will be 100% seller financing with no interest the first year, payments of $1 per week, and an agreement that after any four on-time payments, the seller will cancel any remaining debt without recourse. As this example shows, don't become so locked into *ready, willing, and able* without considering the price and terms. "Able" means financially capable of completing the transaction. An alternative arrangement is for the broker and owner to agree to a "no sale, no commission" arrangement whereby the broker is not entitled to a commission until the transaction is closed.

The difference between the two arrangements becomes important when a buyer is found at price and terms acceptable to the owner, but no sale results. The "ready, willing, and able" contract provides more protection for the broker since the commission does not depend on the deal reaching settlement. The "no sale, no commission" approach is to the owner's advantage, for commission payment

ready, willing, and able buyer: a buyer who is ready to buy at the seller's price and terms and who has the financial capability to do so

is not required unless there is a completed sale. Court decisions have tended to blur the clear-cut distinction between the two. For example, if the owner has a "no sale, no commission" agreement, it would appear that if the broker found a ready, willing, and able buyer at the listing price and terms and the owner refused to sell, the owner would owe no commission, for there was no sale. However, a court of law would find in favor of the broker for the full amount of the commission if the refusal to sell was arbitrary and without reasonable cause, or in bad faith.

In today's marketplace, buyers are usually prequalified for financial ability. Increased competition among lenders has made this quick, inexpensive, and easy. However, licensees should be careful only to pass on information and not to make representations about a buyer's financial ability.

Procuring Cause

A broker may have to prove that a sale of property is primarily due to his/her efforts. That is, s/he may have to be the *procuring cause,* the one whose efforts began an unbroken chain of events that ultimately led to the property being sold (purchased). Suppose the broker shows an open listed property to a prospect and, during the listing period or an extension, that prospect goes directly to the owner and concludes a deal. Even though the owner negotiated the transaction and prepared the sales contract, the broker is entitled to full commission for finding the buyer. This would also be true if the owner and the buyer used a "straw man" to purchase the property to avoid paying the commission. In general, the law protects a broker who has, in good faith, produced a buyer at the request of an owner.

When an open listing is given to two or more brokers, the first one who produces a buyer is entitled to the commission. For example, Broker 1 shows a property to Prospect B but no sale is made. Later, Prospect B goes to Broker 2 and makes an offer that is accepted by the owner. Although two brokers have attempted to sell the property, only one has succeeded, and that one is entitled to the commission. The fact that Broker 1 receives nothing, even though s/he may have expended considerable effort, is an important reason why brokers dislike open listings.

Buyer's brokers create a more complicated issue involving procuring cause, one that has caused considerable unrest in the real estate brokerage community. At times, the prospect may visit a property one or more times and spend a great deal of the listing broker's time asking questions and getting information. Before submitting an offer, however, the prospect may request the assistance and advice of a buyer's broker in preparing a contract for presentation to the owner's agent. Who was the procuring cause? While the listing agent might think that s/he was the procuring cause, the buyer is likely to support the buyer's broker position since the buyer chose to retain the services of that agent in presenting the offer.

In the age of email, the internet, and highly informed consumers, there is an argument that buyers want and need representation. Once a consumer has sought and obtained a buyer's broker's advice, technically the buyer's broker may become the procuring cause when the contract is signed and presented to the listing broker.

Much of this conflict will be eliminated by educating your buyers and maintaining some control over their activities. Educate them not to see property with other agents or contact other agents. Tell them that if they see a property they want information on, they should contact you. Explain to them that failure to do so may create a situation where they will have to pay a commission they were not planning on. Spending time counseling and educating our clients will not solve 100% of the problems, but it will go a long way.

TERMINATING THE EMPLOYMENT CONTRACT

The usual situation in an employment contract is that the broker produces a buyer acceptable to the owner. Thus, in most employment contracts, the obligations of the parties terminate because the objective of the contract has been completed. In the bulk of the transactions in which a buyer is not produced, the listing is terminated because the employment period expires. If no employment period is specified, the employment contract is considered to be effective for a "reasonable" length of time. A court might consider three to six months reasonable. Employment contracts without termination dates are revocable by the principal at any time, provided the purpose of the revocation is not to deprive the broker of an earned commission. A major disadvantage of employment contracts without termination dates is that, all too often, they evolve into expensive and time-consuming legal hassles.

Even when an employment contract has a specific termination date, it is still possible for the owner to revoke the agency. However, liability for breach of the employment aspect of the contract remains, and the broker may demand compensation for effort expended on behalf of the owner to that point. This can be as much as a full commission if the listing broker has already found a ready, willing, and able buyer at the owner's price and terms. Similarly, if a buyer's agent finds the product that meets the buyer's criteria and the buyer refuses to purchase, the broker is entitled to be compensated. In these situations, however, there is very little legal precedent for pursuing compensation through the courts.

Mutual Agreement

An employment agreement can be terminated by mutual agreement of both the principal and broker without money damages. Because employment agreements are the stock in trade of the brokerage business, brokers do not like to lose them, but sometimes this is the only logical alternative, since the time and effort in setting and collecting damages can be very expensive. Suppose, however, that a broker has an employment agreement and suspects that the owner or buyer wants to cancel to avoid paying a commission. The broker can stop working, but the principal is still obligated to pay a commission if the property is sold or acquired before the employment period expires. Whatever the broker and principal decide, they should put it in writing and sign it.

Abandonment

A listing can be terminated by improper performance or abandonment by the broker. Thus, if a broker acts counter to the principal's best financial interests, the employment is terminated, no commission is payable, and the broker may be subject to a lawsuit for any damages suffered by the principal. If a broker accepts an employment opportunity and then does nothing to promote it, the principal can assume that the broker abandoned it and thereby has grounds for revocation. The principal should keep written documentation in the event the matter ever goes to court. The agency is automatically terminated by the death of either the principal or the broker, or if either is judged legally incompetent by virtue of insanity; it might also be terminated if the principal becomes bankrupt. Understand, however, that termination of agency and termination of a listing are not the same. While a seller may terminate the agency without cause, that act does not necessarily terminate the obligations created under the listing agreement.

ALTERNATIVE BUSINESS MODELS

The historically traditional full-service real estate broker takes a listing and places it in the multiple listing service, places and pays for advertising, holds open houses, qualifies prospects, shows property, obtains offers, negotiates, opens escrow, and follows through until closing. Payment is typically a percentage of the selling price and is collected only if and when the sale closes. This payment at the end is a form of performance fee or contingency fee. This business model has been the mainstay of the real estate selling industry, and the vast majority of open-market sales are handled this way. The remainder are sold by owners, some handling everything themselves, and some using brokers with a business model that is something different than as defined at the beginning of this discussion. Let's look at a couple of variations, understanding that no particular business model is being promoted or suggested.

1. *Flat-fee brokerage*: In this model, a broker would charge a flat fee as a commission rather than a percentage of the sales price. The philosophy of this brokerage would be that it really doesn't take twice as much work to sell a $200,000 property as a $100,000 property, so how can a commission twice as high be justified? Another way of looking at it is that the brokerage does not work half as hard to sell a $100,000 property as a $200,000 property, so why is it charging half as much?
2. *Limited-service brokerage*: Just as we have evolved to self-service gas stations, some consumers want assistance but don't believe they need the whole package. This business model would fill that desire by offering fewer services, typically at a lower price. An example of this model would be where the broker gets paid a fee to enter the property into the Multiple Listing Service (MLS) but provides no further services.

3. *Upfront fee*: We identified earlier that historically, a brokerage firm is paid a contingency (or success) fee only if and when the sale closes. An upfront fee is the opposite. In this business model, the fee would be paid to the brokerage at the time of signing the contract. Typically, the client will pay a fee that is substantially less than a contingency fee, but it is paid regardless of whether the property sells. This philosophy may appeal to a seller who feels confident that the property will sell but needs some assistance in marketing.

4. *Menu of services*: Think about going to a car wash. It offers the basic wash, the bronze wash, the silver wash, the gold wash, the platinum wash, and the diamond wash. Each level contains all the services of the one underneath, plus more. Each also bears an increasing cost. This business model would allow the full-service broker to offer a product to compete with the limited-service brokerage.

Review Questions

Answers to these questions can be found in Appendix D at the end of this book.

1. Sales associate Lee secured a written listing on a property for sale, signed by the owner and the employing broker. Is this an enforceable listing contract?
   A. Yes, because the broker is a licensed agent.
   B. Yes, if all essential elements of a listing contract are present.
   C. No, because no contract exists until the property is sold.
   D. No, because no consideration will be paid until the property is sold.

2. A real estate listing:
   A. is an employment contract between a property owner and a real estate broker
   B. authorizes a real estate broker to sell and convey title to an owner's real property
   C. creates contractual obligations but not agency
   D. is an employment contract between the buyer and the broker

3. A listing to find a buyer for each of the following types of properties will usually be for a period of time ranging from six months to one year EXCEPT:
   A. farms
   B. commercial properties
   C. residential properties
   D. industrial properties

4. A typical exclusive right-to-sell listing requires the owner to:
   A. deliver title to any buyer who wishes to purchase
   B. pay a commission unless the owner finds the buyer
   C. pay a commission even if the owner finds the buyer
   D. reimburse marketing expenses to the broker if the property does not sell

5. The amount of commission to be paid the broker for selling a property is:
   A. set by state law
   B. negotiated at the time a buyer is found
   C. set forth in the rules of the state real estate commission
   D. stated in the listing contract

6. Under the terms of an exclusive agency listing, a commission is NOT due the listing broker if a buyer is found by:
   A. the listing broker
   B. a sales associate employed by the listing broker
   C. the owner's personal efforts
   D. another broker

7. Which of the following is NOT true of an exclusive right-to-sell listing?
   A. Brokers will usually exert their maximum sales effort under this type of listing.
   B. The broker will receive a commission regardless of whether the property is sold.
   C. The owner may not sell through personal efforts without liability for a commission to the broker.
   D. The property may not be listed with another broker during the listing period.

8. An exclusive agency listing:
   A. permits the owner to sell through personal efforts without liability to pay a commission to the listing broker
   B. allows the owner to list concurrently with other brokers
   C. is not allowed in Georgia
   D. will not allow dual agency since the agency is exclusive to the seller

9. All of the following are true of net listings EXCEPT:
   A. many states prohibit a broker from accepting a net listing
   B. most brokers are reluctant to accept them, even when permitted to do so
   C. all net listings are open listings
   D. the commission is the excess above the seller's net price

10. Which of the following is the LEAST likely form of compensation for a broker?
    A. an hourly fee for time spent in selling the property
    B. compensation for out-of-pocket expenses
    C. sales price minus the seller guarantee
    D. fixed fee paid upon closing

11. Which of the following is typically true of a buyer's broker?
    A. The commission is paid by the buyer.
    B. The commission will not be based on the sales price.
    C. The commission is paid by the seller or seller's agent.
    D. The commission is paid by both the buyer and the seller.

12. Which of the following is true under the terms of an exclusive right-to-sell listing agreement?
    A. The seller may be liable for two commissions on the sale if a cooperating broker procures a buyer.
    B. The seller may sell through personal efforts without any obligation to pay a commission.
    C. A cooperating broker may not be used since the listing broker has exclusive rights.
    D. The listing broker is due a commission if the property sells during the listing period.

13. The advantages of an exclusive right-to-sell listing arrangement do NOT include:
    A. greater market exposure of the property
    B. the possibility of a higher sales price
    C. quicker sale
    D. the ability for the seller to not pay a commission if s/he sells the property

14. Innovations for marketing properties through multiple listing services do NOT include:
    A. computerized listings
    B. video display of listings
    C. a requirement that a person be a licensee to search listings
    D. the ability to display listings other than those with the company hosting the website

15. When a property under an open listing is shown to a prospect by two different brokers and a sale results, the commission is:
    A. payable to the broker who first showed the property to the buyer
    B. divided between the two brokers
    C. payable to the broker who made the sale
    D. payable in full to each broker

16. An exclusive listing contract with a definite termination date is NOT terminable by:
    A. sale of the property
    B. death of the listing salesperson
    C. expiration
    D. mutual agreement

17. An open listing may NOT be terminated by which of the following means?
    A. sale of the property
    B. abandonment by the broker
    C. death of the owner
    D. revocation of the salesperson's license

18. If a purchaser arbitrarily defaults on a purchase contract, any earnest money previously paid, in the absence of an agreement to the contrary, will be:
    A. paid to the broker as compensation for efforts
    B. divided between the broker and the owner/seller
    C. returned to the purchaser
    D. paid to the owner/seller

19. Which of the following are most likely to accept only listings that they think will sell quickly?
    A. flat-fee brokers
    B. full-service brokers
    C. discount brokers
    D. self-help brokers

20. Which of the following statements is NOT true?
    A. The Statute of Frauds requires all agency agreements to be made in writing in order to be enforceable.
    B. A real estate listing is an agency contract.
    C. In a real estate listing, the property owner is the principal.
    D. A real estate broker is the agent under a real estate listing.

CHAPTER

11 REAL ESTATE SALES CONTRACTS

KEY TERMS

binder
default
earnest money deposit
equitable title
installment contract
lease-option
letter of intent
option contract
rider
right of first refusal
"time is of the essence"

OBJECTIVES

After successful completion of this chapter, you should be able to:

1. explain the provisions of a typical purchase contract;
2. describe the purpose and features of the property condition addendum;
3. explain the use of an installment contract and a lease with option to buy;
4. define and explain the right of first refusal; and
5. distinguish between practicing real estate and practicing law.

OVERVIEW

Chapter 11 focuses on real estate contracts, with in-depth explanation of the common provisions in a Georgia Purchase and Sale Agreement. Other contracts covered include the installment contract and a lease with option to buy. The right of first refusal is also discussed. The earnest money deposit will be covered in detail.

PURPOSE OF SALES CONTRACTS

What is the purpose of a real estate sales contract? If a buyer and a seller agree on a price, why can't the buyer hand the seller the necessary money and the seller

simultaneously hand the buyer a deed? The main reason is that the buyer needs time to ascertain that the seller is, in fact, legally capable of conveying title. For protection, the buyer enters into a written and signed contract with the seller, promising that the purchase price will be paid only after title has been searched and found to be in satisfactory condition. The seller, in turn, promises to deliver a deed to the buyer when the buyer has paid the money. This exchange of promises forms the legal consideration of the contract. A contract also gives the buyer time to arrange financing and to specify how such matters as taxes, existing debts, leases, and property inspections will be handled.

A properly prepared contract commits each party to its terms. Once a sales contract is in writing and signed, a seller cannot change his/her mind and sell to another person. The seller is obligated to convey title to the buyer when the buyer has performed as required by the contract. Likewise, the buyer must carry out the promises, including paying for the property, provided the seller has done everything required by the contract.

PURCHASE CONTRACTS

A purchase contract is sometimes known as deposit receipt, offer and acceptance, purchase offer, or purchase and sales agreement. No matter the name used, these prepared forms contain specific language that has been written or approved by attorneys and have often been court-tested. Extreme caution should be used when altering the forms from their original context.

The current GAR F201 Purchase and Sale Agreement is included in Appendix E for your review. While very detailed, this is the agreement that experts believe a licensee candidate/student should be exposed to as soon as possible since this is the form that will be used in over 90% of the residential real estate transactions in Georgia. If you are reading this book in preparation for taking the Georgia real estate licensing exam, you will not have to complete a form on the exam or be intimately familiar with what is contained in Section A.1 versus Section B.3, for example. You will, however, have to show a competence with the form during the course.

Following are common sections or provisions you will likely find in a typical purchase and sale agreement. It is not the intent of this section to follow the F201 exactly, but to be generic by nature.

Purchase and Sale

This paragraph would set forth the parties to the agreement (buyer and seller) and provide for the common legal description of the property. Blanks provided are typically consistent with a legal description referring to a recorded plat. In the event that another form of description (such as a metes and bounds) is used, it would be referenced here and an exhibit would be prepared and attached containing the complete legal description. This may be in the form of a warranty deed or security deed. Another acceptable method of legal description is to simply reference the deed book and page number at the county courthouse where the deed is recorded. Remember that any unused spaces that are part of the agreement should be nullified by placing "N/A" (not applicable) in the space.

Purchase Price

Simply put, this section would state the purchase price. The purchase price typically has to be paid by cash or cash equivalent, such as bank wire transfer or certified funds. Depending on the contract form, you may write it out like a check, with letters and numbers, or there may be only enough room for the numbers. In this event, it is EXTREMELY important that the typing be accurate. I know there are times when I am typing that my fingers mean to type $545,500 and instead they type something like $554,500, or some other nonsense. This is the kind of mistake that you will refer to as a "memory making moment," file it away in the "professional" rather than "personal" category, and never do it again!

Amount and Deposit of Earnest Money

The holder of the **earnest money** is designated here, which also states whether the deposit is cash, check, or wire transfer. Other common provisions of this paragraph would allow the broker to hold the earnest money in an interest-bearing account, require that the holder deposit the earnest money within five banking days after the binding agreement date, and make the contract voidable by the seller if the earnest money funds are dishonored. This section would also typically provide for the event that the buyer is tendering the earnest money *after* the offer date.

earnest money deposit: money that accompanies an offer to purchase as evidence of good faith; earnest money is NOT consideration or required by contract law

Date of Closing and Transfer of Possession

This section would stipulate the day of closing, but also allow for a different date if the parties were to agree. It also would commonly allow for a unilateral extension of the closing date under very specific circumstances (e.g., title problems, or the closing attorney or lender being unable to perform their obligations). It would also be stipulated here as to when the buyer will receive possession. The choices would be before closing, at closing, or after closing. At closing is the safest for all parties. Be aware that situations where a buyer receives possession before closing or a seller retains possession after closing often lead to problems.

Seller's Contributions at Closing

Most purchase and sale agreements state that the buyer will be responsible for all costs of closing the transaction. The seller, however, may make a contribution to be used by the buyer as s/he sees fit to offset these costs. The theory is that most of the costs are lender-created, and the buyer is the party that requires the lender.

With the buyer being responsible for the costs, it will make him/her more mindful when negotiating.

Method of Payment

This is one of the most complex and important sections of the contract form. Here, buyers warrant that they have sufficient cash to close and that they do not have to sell or lease another property to qualify for a loan or close. This section also states how the purchase price will be paid and allows for a *financing contingency period*.

This terminology places the responsibility on the buyer to apply for a loan and provide a letter of denial from a lender in the event that said loan is not approved. It also states certain criteria that are not acceptable as reasons for loan denial. If the buyer does not provide the denial letter within the time frame agreed upon, the financing contingency is removed and the buyer is obligated to close without regard to ability to obtain satisfactory financing.

The terminology used is *ability to obtain* the loan. It is very important in providing adequate protection for sellers from buyers who, without cause, decide they do not want to complete the transaction and try to circumvent their obligations by not making application, not providing reasonable documentation as required by the lender, or failing to accept a loan. Buyers are also required to obtain and provide any documentation required by the lender, including, but not limited to, a wood infestation report; well, septic, and flood plain certifications; and structural inspections.

Closing Attorney

One section will list which law firm will be appointed to close the transaction and discloses that the firm will be representing the interests of the lender. Under Georgia's Predatory Lending Act, the buyer has the right to choose the closing attorney, and this section would meet that requirement. In the event the buyer is paying cash and there is no lender, the closing attorney will typically represent the interests of the buyer.

Inspection

Buyers have the right to inspect the property and the duty to inspect the neighborhood for any conditions that they would find objectionable. Specifically, the website for the Georgia Violent Sex Offender Registry is commonly provided, and buyers are recommended to view this website if they have concerns.

Historically, the seller had provided for the termite inspection and had provided a clear wood infestation report. It is now believed that the buyer relying on a report the seller provided creates at least the perception of impropriety in the event that there are subsequent problems with wood infestation or damage, and ordering this inspection is now the responsibility of the buyer. It is always prudent to suggest that buyers order a termite inspection for themselves, even though lenders do not commonly require one. Remember, there are only two types of properties in Georgia—those with termites and those that will have termites!

Property Sold Subject to Due Diligence Period, or "As Is"

Although a buyer has the right to inspect the property in most purchase and sale agreements, that does not necessarily mean the buyer retains the right to terminate if the inspection identifies a problem. Most sales today are made subject to a *due diligence period,* commonly anywhere from seven to 21 days. The due diligence period is not mandated by law, is not required, and can be any period agreed to by the parties to the contract.

It is expected that the buyer will diligently pursue whatever knowledge the buyer deems important before the end of the due diligence period. That may include getting a structural inspection and a wood infestation inspection, pursuing financing, checking deed restrictions, and anything else the buyer feels is needed to make a firm decision to purchase the property. If the process makes the buyer aware of facts that are not acceptable, the buyer can terminate without penalty any time prior to the end of due diligence.

If there is not a due diligence period negotiated, the buyer is contracting to buy the property "as is," which is another way of saying no warranty, no guarantee, and "what I see is what I get." Even when buying property "as is," the seller has the legal duty to disclose knowledge of any latent defect. Remember, a latent defect is a defect that is concealed, or one that a buyer would have to possess certain training or knowledge to recognize. A patent defect is one that is open to observation and would take no special training to recognize. While a latent defect has to be disclosed and a patent defect does not, if there is any question of the category, the defect should be treated as latent and the necessary disclosure made. Once the due diligence period passes, the buyer is accepting the property as is.

Another item that some find confusing is the use of a seller disclosure form. Although a seller must disclose knowledge of any latent defect, there is no specific form required. There is a common form available that may or may not be completed by the seller. This form should never be completed by the real estate agent, nor should the agent assist in completing the form. The potential liability substantially outweighs any benefit.

Lead-Based Paint

On properties built before 1978, buyers have under federal law the right to inspect for lead-based paint. Buyers often waive this right because it is covered under their right to inspect in the contract.

Warranty

The seller will warrant the property to have a marketable title and allow the buyer to examine such. This section will also define *marketable title* and provide rights to the buyer in the event that the title is deemed not marketable.

Taxes and Prorations

Most purchase and sale agreements will have a provision for items that have been prepaid by the seller or are unpaid by the seller at closing. These could include property taxes, utilities, and community association fees. In the event the *ad valorem* property taxes were based on an estimated bill, the parties typically agree to immediately re-prorate when the bill comes out if it is substantially different from the estimate.

Risk of Damage to Property

The risk of damage section in the most commonly used purchase and sale contract requires that the property will be delivered to the buyer at closing in substantially the same condition as at the time of contract, free of trash and debris. It also states the requirements of the parties in the event that there is destruction or substantial damage to the property. Simply put, either party can cancel the agreement within 14 days of notification of damage. If neither party terminates, the seller shall have the responsibility to repair and restore the property, and the contract will extend for up to one year, as necessary.

Entitlement to and Disbursement of Earnest Money

This section entitles the buyer to the earnest money in the event that the seller defaults, there is no agreement entered into, a contingency cannot be met, or upon closing. The seller would be entitled to the earnest money in the event that the buyer defaults. If the seller accepts the earnest money upon **default** by the buyer, the earnest money is treated as liquidated damages and the seller relinquishes any legal right to make additional claims against the buyer. This section also stipulates under what circumstances the holder of the earnest money may disburse. These situations are consistent with Georgia license laws and rules, and include:

- withdrawal of an offer;
- rejection of an offer;
- closing of the contract;
- separate written agreement of all parties with an interest;
- court order;
- filing of an interpleader; or
- reasonable interpretation of the holder of the money.

default: failure to perform a legal duty, such as failure to carry out the terms of a contract

This section also protects the holders (usually brokers), in that they are indemnified from any and all suits, claims, or causes of action related to their performance of duties.

Agency and Brokerage

Agency has become a very important topic to the real estate licensee. Although there is an in-depth and comprehensive discussion of agency and disclosure requirements in other chapters, a brief explanation of this section will be provided now. This section defines the broker working with the buyer as the *selling broker* and the agent working with the seller as the *listing broker*. The wording goes on to state whether the broker is or is not representing the interests of the party. Working "with" a person is not the same as working "for" a person. Working "for" is agency and brings with it very specific and important responsibilities. This section also allows for the possibility of dual agency and designated agency choices. These options, while legal, are controversial and should only be chosen when in compliance with company policy and fully understood and explained. Furthermore, this section provides for compensation of the brokers, but does not stipulate exactly what that compensation will be. This is because the purchase and sale agreement is between the buyer and seller, and the compensation provisions are between the party responsible to pay and the brokers. This is typically negotiated in the brokerage engagement agreement. There is also a section for brokers to disclose any relationship they may have that could be perceived to be a conflict.

Disclaimer

This is a general catch-all statement to distance brokers from liability caused by their actions, statements, or claims. It essentially says that brokers and their affiliated licensees are robbing various small villages of their idiots, and that nobody should rely on anything the broker says or does. Although it obviously doesn't go quite that far, it is a pretty inclusive statement that attempts to shift the responsibility onto the buyer and seller to check items of importance for themselves, and reminds the parties that the brokers are not experts in many topics.

Notices

This is a very important section. A contract is not a contract unless it has been properly and effectively communicated between the parties. The notification section of the typical contract requires that all notices be in writing, and stipulates the five acceptable delivery methods:

1. in person
2. overnight delivery

3. fax
4. registered or certified U.S. mail, return receipt
5. email

Furthermore, notice is not effective until actual receipt, with the exception of a fax and email. If the fax being sent provides a written confirmation of transmission, the notice is effective upon transmission, regardless of receipt. If email is used, the notice is effective upon receiving notification of a "read receipt." Also provided here is imputed notice, which is the right of an agent to receive legal notice on behalf of a client, meaning, if the required notice is properly delivered to the agent, it is the same as delivery to the client.

Other Provisions

This section may include the following:

- The seller agrees to transfer any warranties, bonds, or contracts to the buyer at the buyer's expense.
- Any repairs will be made in a workmanlike manner.
- This agreement is the entire agreement between the parties. This makes it incumbent upon the buyer and seller to make sure that anything they deem important is included in the writing of the contract.
- The survival clause stipulates that obligations, such as title warranties and commission payments, shall continue after closing if not completed at closing.
- A statement that interpretation of agreement shall be based on Georgia law, and that all times included are Georgia times.
- **Time is of the essence** in this agreement. Simply put, times stipulated are obligations, not suggestions. If one party does not comply within the times stated in the contract, that party will be in breach.
- Legal terminology is addressed. Specifically, *plural* can mean *singular*, *singular* can mean *plural* (i.e., references to the word "buyer," for example, can refer to two people if the buyers are a married couple), etc.
- A provision clarifies that the binding agreement date (which is very important in this contract) is the date the acceptance is received by the offeror.
- A provision requires all parties to cooperate in doing all things reasonably necessary to fulfill the agreement.
- The contract includes a disclaimer for GAR to limit the use of the forms and the liability that GAR may have if there is any ensuing litigation (if a GAR contract is being used).

"time is of the essence": a phrase that means that the time limits of a contract must be faithfully observed or the contract is voidable

Exhibits and Addenda

Most purchase and sale agreements will provide for additional pages, called exhibits or addendums, to complete the agreement. For instance, many form contracts used in the field today are not automatically contingent on financing. If the buyer wants this kind of protection, a financing contingency exhibit would be added to the form and negotiated as part of the agreement. There also is typically room to add any special stipulations that would be required to complete the thoughts, understandings, and agreement between the parties.

FEDERAL CLAUSES

In two instances, the government requires that specific clauses be included in real estate sales contracts. First, an *amendatory language* clause must be included whenever a sales contract is signed by a purchaser prior to the receipt of an FHA Appraised Value or a VA Certificate of Reasonable Value on the property. The purpose is to ensure that the purchaser can terminate the contract without loss when it appears that the agreed-upon purchase price may be significantly above the appraised value. The specific clauses, which must be used verbatim, are available from FHA- and VA-approved lenders. Second, the Federal Trade Commission requires that builders and sellers of new homes include *insulation disclosures* in all purchase contracts. Disclosures, which may be based on manufacturer claims, must cite the type, thickness, and R-value of the insulation installed in the home. The exact clause will be provided by the builder or seller of the home based on model clauses provided by the National Association of Home Builders, as modified by local laws.

Federal law requires that, before a buyer or tenant becomes obligated under a contract for sale or lease, the sellers and landlords must disclose known *lead-based paint* and *lead-based paint hazards* and provide available reports to buyers or tenants. Sellers and landlords must give the buyer a pamphlet entitled, "Protect Your Family from Lead in Your Home." Unless otherwise agreed to, the home buyers are entitled to a 10-day period to conduct a lead-based paint inspection or risk assessment at their own expense.

Sales contracts and lease arrangements must include certain language to ensure that the disclosure notification actually takes place. This law places a special burden on real estate agents, who must ensure that sellers and landlords are aware of their obligations and that they disclose the proper information to buyers and tenants. The agent must comply with the law if the seller or landlord fails to do so.

Preprinted Clauses

In addition to the purchase and sale agreement, there are numerous special stipulations and prepared addendums available as part of the GAR form packet. These stipulations are organized by how they pertain to the sections of the contract form, as we have just discussed. Available stipulations include making the contract contingent upon appraisal, providing wording for a 1031 tax-deferred exchange, requiring the buyer to accept an interest rate up to 2% higher than that stipulated in the contract, and numerous others. When making additions or changes to the GAR contracts, it is prudent to engage the assistance of your broker, at the very least, and the assistance of legal counsel with your broker's approval and guidance, at the very best.

Riders

rider: any addition annexed to a document and made a part of the document by reference; also known as an addendum or attachment

A **rider** is any addition annexed to a document and made a part of the document by reference. A rider is usually written, typed, or printed on a separate piece of paper and stapled to the document. There will be a reference in the document that the rider is a part of the document, and a statement in the rider that it is a part of the document. It is good practice to have the parties to the document place their initials on the rider. Riders are also known as *addendums* or *attachments*.

NEGOTIATION

One of the most important principles of purchase contracts (and real estate contracts in general) is that nearly everything is negotiable and nearly everything has a price. In preparing or analyzing any contract, consider what the advantages and disadvantages of each condition are to each party to the contract. A solid contract results when the buyer and seller both feel that they have gained more than they have given up. The prime example is the sale price of the property itself. The seller prefers the money over the property, while the buyer prefers the property over the money. Each small, negotiable item in the purchase contract has its price, too. For example, the seller may agree to include the refrigerator for $200 more. Equally important in negotiating is the relative bargaining power of the buyer and seller. If the seller is confident of having plenty of buyers at the asking price, the seller can elect to refuse offers for less money and to reject those with numerous conditions or insufficient earnest money. However, if the owner is anxious to sell and has received only one offer in several months, the owner may be quite willing to accept a lower price and numerous conditions.

THE BINDER

Throughout most of the United States, the real estate agent prepares the purchase contract as soon as the agent is about to (or has) put a deal together. Using preprinted forms available from real estate trade associations (such as the GAR contracts introduced in this chapter), title companies, and stationery stores, the agent fills in the purchase price, down payment, and other details of the transaction, and has the buyer and seller sign it as soon as they reach agreement.

In a few communities, particularly in the northeastern United States, the practice is for the real estate agent to prepare a short-form contract called a **binder**. The purpose of a binder is to hold a deal together until a more formal purchase contract can be drawn up by an attorney and signed by the buyer and seller. In the binder, the buyer and seller agree on the purchase price, the down payment, and on how the balance will be financed. The brokerage commission (to whom and how much) is stated, along with an agreement to meet again to draw up a more formal contract that will contain all the remaining details of the sale. The agent then arranges a meeting at the office of the seller's attorney. In attendance are the seller and the seller's attorney, the buyer and the buyer's attorney, and the real estate agents responsible for bringing about the sale. Together, they prepare a written contract, which the buyer and seller sign. Note that when the seller's attorney writes the formal contract, the contract will favor the seller. This is because the seller's attorney is expected to protect the seller's best interests at all times. The purchaser, to protect personal interests, should not rely on the seller's attorney for advice, but should bring an attorney also. Licensees in Georgia are very fortunate to have the right to assist in the creation of contracts preserved. Most would agree that requiring an attorney to prepare the contract would be cumbersome and costly, with little, if any, added value. To keep this freedom, it is important that licensees understand what they may and may not do, and ensure that they never do anything that could be considered crossing the line and practicing law.

binder: a short purchase contract used to secure a real estate transaction until a more formal contract can be signed

LETTER OF INTENT

If two or more parties want to express their mutual intention to buy, sell, lease, develop, or invest, and wish to do so without creating any firm legal obligation, they may use a **letter of intent**. Generally, such a letter contains an outline of the proposal and concludes with language to the effect that the letter is only an expression of mutual intent, and that no liability or obligation is created by it. In other words, a letter of intent is neither a contract nor an agreement to enter into a contract. However, it is expected, and is usually stipulated in the letter, that the parties signing the letter will proceed promptly and in good faith to conclude the deal proposed in the letter. The letter of intent is usually found in connection with more complex transactions, such as commercial leases, real estate development, construction projects, and multimillion-dollar real estate sales.

letter of intent: an outline of the proposal with language to the effect that the letter is only an expression of mutual intent, and that no liability or obligation is created by it

PRACTICING LAW

Historically, the sale of real estate in the United States was primarily a legal service. Lawyers matched buyers with sellers, wrote the sales contract, and prepared the mortgage and deed. When persons other than lawyers began to specialize in real estate brokerage, the question of who should write the sales contract became important. The lawyer was more qualified in matters of contract law, but the broker wanted something that could be signed the moment the buyer and seller were in agreement. For many years, the solution was a compromise. The broker had the buyer and seller sign a binder, and they agreed to meet again in the presence of a lawyer to draw up and sign a more formal contract. The trend today, however, is for the real estate agent to prepare a complete purchase contract as soon as there is a meeting of the minds.

The preparation of contracts by real estate agents for their clients has not gone unnoticed by lawyers. The legal profession maintains that preparing contracts for clients is practicing law, and state laws restrict the practice of law to lawyers. This has been, and continues to be, a controversial issue between brokers and lawyers. Resolution of the matter has come in the form of accords between the real estate brokerage industry and the legal profession. In nearly all states, courts have ruled that a real estate agent is permitted to prepare purchase, installment, and rental contracts, provided the agent uses a preprinted form approved by a lawyer or the state's real estate department, and provided the agent is limited to filling in only the blank spaces on the form. Georgia law, specifically 43-40-25.1, allows a licensee to fill out this preprinted form agreement and requires that s/he include a method of payment, a legal description, and any special stipulations, as needed. If the preprinted form requires extensive cross-outs, changes, and riders, a lawyer should draft the contract. A real estate license is *not* a license to practice law.

INSTALLMENT CONTRACTS

installment contract: a method of selling and financing property whereby the seller retains title but the buyer takes possession while making the payments

An **installment contract** (also known as a *land contract, conditional sales contract, contract for deed,* or *agreement of sale*) combines features from a sales contract, a deed, and a mortgage. An installment contract contains most of the provisions of the purchase contract, plus wording similar to the warranty deed described in chapter 20, plus many of the provisions of the mortgage described in chapter 16.

The most important feature of an installment contract is that the seller does not deliver a deed to the buyer at the closing. Rather, the seller promises to deliver the deed at some future date. Meanwhile, the purchaser is given the right to occupy the property (the magic word is *possession*) and have, for all practical purposes, the rights, obligations, and privileges of ownership.

The widest use of the installment contract occurs when the buyer does not have the full purchase price in cash or is unable to borrow it from a lender. To sell under these conditions, the seller must accept a down payment plus monthly payments. To carry this out, the seller may choose to either: (1) deliver a deed to the buyer at the closing, and at the same moment take back from the buyer a promissory note and a mortgage secured by the property (a mortgage carryback; this would not be considered an installment contract but seller financing purchase money mortgage), or (2) enter into an installment contract wherein the buyer makes the required payments to the seller before the seller delivers a deed to the buyer.

Vendor, Vendee

Historically, installment contracts were most commonly used to sell vacant land where the buyer put only a modest amount of money down and the seller agreed to receive the balance as installment payments. When all the installments were made, the seller delivered a deed to the purchaser. The terms of these contracts were usually weighted in favor of the seller. For example, if the buyer (called the *vendee*) failed to make all the payments on time, the seller (called the *vendor*) could rescind the contract, retain payments already made as rent, and retake possession of the land. Additionally, the seller might insert a clause in the installment contract prohibiting the buyer from recording it. The public records would continue to show the seller as owner, and the seller could use the land as collateral for loans.

That such a one-sided contract would even exist may seem surprising. But if a buyer did not have all cash, or enough cash down to obtain financing from another source, the buyer was stuck with accepting what the seller offered or not buying the property. Sellers took the position that if they were selling to buyers who were unwilling or unable to find their own sources of financing, then sellers wanted a quick and easy way of recovering the property if the payments were not made. By selling on an installment contract and not allowing it to be recorded, the seller could save the time and expense of regular foreclosure proceedings. The seller would simply notify the buyer in writing that the contract was in default and thereby rescind it. Meanwhile, as far as the public records were concerned, title was still in the seller's name.

Public Criticism

Such strongly worded agreements received much public criticism, as did the possibility that even if the buyer made all the payments, the seller might not be capable of delivering good title. For example, the buyer could make all payments yet find that the seller had encumbered the property with debt, had gone bankrupt, had become legally incapacitated, or had died.

In the late 1970s, interest rates rose sharply. In order to sell their properties, sellers looked for ways of passing along the benefits of their fixed-rate, low-interest loans to buyers. The installment contract was rediscovered, and it moved from being used primarily to sell land to being used to sell houses and apartment buildings, and even office buildings and industrial property. Basically, the seller kept the property and mortgage in the seller's name and made the mortgage payments out of the buyer's monthly payments. This continued until the buyer found alternative financing, at which time the seller delivered the deed.

Protections

With the increased popularity of installment contracts, the need for more sophisticated and protective versions was created. Simultaneously, courts and legislatures in various states were listening to consumer complaints and finding existing installment contract provisions too harsh. One by one, states began requiring that a buyer be given a specified period to cure any default before the seller could rescind. Some states began requiring that installment contracts be foreclosed like regular mortgages. And most states now require that installment contracts be recorded and/or prohibit a seller from enforcing unrecorded clauses.

Buyers have become much more sophisticated, also. For example, it is common practice today to require the seller to place the deed (usually a warranty deed) in escrow at the time the installment contract is made. This relieves a number of the problems noted above regarding the unwillingness or inability of the seller to prepare and deliver the deed later. Additionally, the astute buyer will require that a collection account be used to collect the buyer's payments and make the payments on the underlying mortgage. This is done using a neutral third party, such as the escrow holder of the deed, a bank, or a trust company. The seller will probably insist that the buyer place one-twelfth of the annual property taxes and hazard insurance in the escrow account each month to pay for these items. The buyer will want to record the contract to establish the buyer's rights to the property. The buyer may also want to include provisions whereby the seller delivers a deed to the buyer and takes back a mortgage from the buyer once the buyer has paid, say, 30% or 40% of the purchase price.

If an installment contract is used for the purchase of real estate, it should be done with the help of legal counsel to make certain that it provides adequate safeguards for the buyer as well as the seller. In a future chapter, the installment contract is discussed as a tool to finance the sale of improved property when other sources of financing are not available.

EQUITABLE TITLE

Between the moment when a buyer and seller sign a valid purchase contract and the moment the seller delivers a deed to the buyer, who holds title to the property? Similarly, under an installment contract, until the seller delivers a deed to the buyer, who holds title to the property? The answer, in both cases, is the seller. But this is only technically true, because the buyer is entitled to receive a deed (and thereby title) once the buyer has completed the terms of the purchase or installment contract. During the period beginning with the buyer and seller signing the contract and the seller delivering the deed, the buyer is said to hold **equitable title** to the property. Equitable title is defined as "the assured future interest in the legal title." Legal title is simply the title held by the party with the deed. The concept of equitable title stems from the fact that a buyer has the exclusive right to purchase and can enforce specific performance of the contract to get title. Meanwhile, the seller holds bare or naked title (i.e., title in name only and without full ownership rights).

equitable title: the legally assured future interest in legal title

The equitable title that a purchaser holds under a purchase or installment contract is transferable by subcontract, assignment, or deed. Equitable title can be sold, given away, or mortgaged, and it passes to the purchaser's heirs and devisees upon the purchaser's death.

It is not unusual to see a property offered for sale wherein the vendee under an installment contract is offering those rights for sale. Barring any due-on-sale clause in the installment contract, this can be done. The buyer receives from the vendee an assignment of the contract, and with it, the vendee's equitable title. The buyer then takes possession and continues to make the payments called for by the contract. When the payments are completed, the deed and title transfer can be handled in one of two ways. One way is for the original seller to agree to deliver a deed to the new buyer. The other, more common, way is for the vendee to place a deed to the new buyer in escrow. When the last payment is made, the deed from the original seller to the vendee is recorded, and immediately after it, the deed from the vendee to the new buyer.

OPTION CONTRACTS

Recall that a purchase contract is a bilateral contract. In contrast, the **option contract** is a unilateral contract. Once the contract is executed, the buyer (optionee) then has a right to purchase the property, with no obligation to do so. Therefore, the remedy of specific performance against the buyer doesn't exist. The buyer has the right (not the obligation) to buy, but the seller does have the obligation to sell. In return for granting the option to purchase, the buyer must pay consideration to the seller (optionor) in order for the contract to be enforceable. In most cases, this is a cash payment directly to the seller in lieu of earnest money. In return for the cash payment, the seller takes the property off the market for the term of the option agreement. The buyer does not have to give the seller any reason for the termination, or give the seller copies of any reports, studies, or other investigated matters. Option contracts must be in writing. An oral option agreement would be not only unenforceable, but also void.

Exercising the option converts the option contract to a purchase and sale contract. At that point, the buyer has the duty to perform. Frequently, there are very short closing periods (e.g., five days), or the contract may simply convert to a bilateral executory contract where there is still an obligation for both parties to perform prior to closing. A prudent licensee (particularly a buyer's representative) should work closely with the buyer to ensure that the buyer doesn't default into a binding purchase contract because of a failure to give the required notice.

option contract: a person has a right, but not an obligation, to perform under agreed-upon terms, price, and time period

Option Contracts on Multiple Properties

In commercial real estate, it is quite common for large companies wanting to select sites in a given area to option five or 10 sites, knowing that they will never have the obligation to purchase any of them. This gives them the opportunity to investigate the sites in more detail, do whatever studies are required, and then purchase them if they choose to. Many feel that this makes the transaction much cleaner and eliminates disputes over repairs, inspections, and financing contingencies. The contract terminates at the end of the option period, if the option has not been exercised by the optionee. Note that some contracts require the buyer to send a notice of termination to the seller or the contract converts into a purchase and sales contract and the buyer becomes obligated to purchase. This is not true in all option contracts, however. Many option contracts simply have an option period (e.g., 60 days), and if the option is not exercised, the contract terminates by its own terms.

Lease with Option to Buy

Another popular option contract in real estate is the *lease with option to buy*. Often simply referred to as a **lease-option**, it allows the tenant to buy the property at a preset price and terms during the option period. For a residential property, the lease is typically for one year, and the option to buy must be exercised during that time. Let's look more closely.

In a lease-option contract, all the normal provisions of a lease are present, as will be discussed in a future chapter. All the normal provisions of a purchase contract are present, (as previously discussed). Additionally, there will be wording that states that the tenant has the option of exercising the purchase contract, provided the tenant notifies the landlord in writing of that intent during the option period. All terms of the purchase contract must be negotiated and in writing when the lease is signed. Both the tenant and the landlord must sign the lease. Only the landlord must sign the purchase contract and option agreement, although both parties often do so. If the tenant wants to buy during the option period, the tenant notifies the landlord in writing that the tenant wishes to exercise the purchase contract. Together, they proceed to carry out the purchase contract as in a normal sale.

If the tenant does not exercise the option within the option period, the option expires and the purchase contract is null and void. If the lease also expires at the end of the option period, the tenant must either arrange with the landlord to continue renting or move out. Alternatively, the tenant and landlord can negotiate a new purchase contract or a new lease-option contract.

Popularity of Lease-Options

Lease-options are particularly popular in soft real estate markets (when the home seller is having difficulty finding a buyer). One solution is to lower the asking price and/or make the financing terms more attractive. However, the seller may wish to hold out in the hope that prices will rise within a year. In the meantime, the seller needs someone to occupy the property and provide some income.

---

lease-option: allows the tenant to buy the property at a preset price and terms for a given period of time

The lease-option is attractive to a tenant because the tenant has a place to rent plus the option of buying any time during the option period for the price in the purchase contract. In other words, the tenant can wait a year and see if s/he likes the property and if values rise to or above the price in the purchase contract. If the tenant does not like the property and/or the property does not rise in value, the tenant is under no obligation to buy. Once the lease expires, the tenant is also under no obligation to continue renting.

Examples

To encourage a tenant to exercise the option to buy, the contract may allow the tenant to apply part or all of the rent paid to the purchase price. In fact, quite a bit of flexibility and negotiation can take place in creating a lease-option. For example, take a home that would rent for $1,500 per month and sell for $150,000 on the open market. Suppose the owner wants $165,000 and won't come down to the market price. Meanwhile, the home is vacant and there are mortgage payments to be made. The owner could offer a one-year lease-option with a rental charge of $1,500 each month and an exercise price of $165,000. Within a year, $165,000 might look good to the tenant, especially if the market value of the property has risen significantly above $165,000. The tenant can exercise the option or, if not prohibited by the contract, sell it to someone who intends to exercise it. The owner receives $15,000 more for the property than s/he could have gotten last year, and the tenant has the benefit of any value increase above that.

Continuing the previous example, what if the property rises to $155,000 in value? There is no economic incentive for the tenant to exercise the option at $165,000. The tenant can simply disregard the option and make an offer of $155,000 to the owner. The owner's choice is to sell at that price or continue renting the home, perhaps with another one-year lease-option.

Option Fee

The owner may also charge the tenant extra for the privilege of having the option, but it must make economic sense to the tenant. Suppose in the previous example that the purchase price is set equal to the current market value—that is, $150,000. This would be a valuable benefit to the tenant, and the owner could charge an upfront cash fee for the option and/or charge above-market rent. The amounts would depend on the market's expectations regarding the value of this home a year from now. There is nothing special about a one-year option period, although it is a very popular length of time. The owner and tenant may agree to a three-month, six-month, or nine-month option if it fits their needs, and the lease may run longer than the option period. Options for longer than one year are generally reserved for commercial properties—for example, a businessperson just starting out, or perhaps expanding, wants to buy a building but needs one or two years to see how successful the business will be and how much space it will need.

Caveats

Be aware that lease-options may create income tax consequences that require professional tax counseling. Legal advice is also very helpful in preparing and reviewing the lease-option papers. This is because the entire deal (lease, option, and purchase contract) must be watertight from the beginning. One cannot wait until the option is exercised to write the purchase contract or even a material part of it. If a real estate agent puts a lease-option together, the agent is entitled to a leasing commission at the time the lease is signed. If the option is exercised, the agent is due a sales commission on the purchase contract.

Evidence that the option to buy exists should be recorded to establish not only the tenant's rights to purchase the property, but also to establish those rights back to the date the option was recorded. An option is an example of a unilateral contract. When it is exercised, the option is executed and the ensuing purchase and sales agreement are bilateral. The lease portion of a lease-option is a bilateral contract. The party giving the option is called the *optionor* (owner in a lease-option). The party receiving the option is the *optionee* (tenant in a lease-option). Sometimes, an option to buy is referred to as a *call*.

RIGHT OF FIRST REFUSAL

Although a right of first refusal could be used in a purchase situation, it is more common to a lease. Sometimes, a tenant will agree to rent a property only if given an opportunity to purchase it before someone else does. In other words, the tenant is saying, "Owner, if you get a valid offer from someone else to purchase this property, show it to me and give me an opportunity to match the offer." This is called a **right of first refusal**. If someone presents the owner with a valid offer, the owner must show it to the tenant before accepting it. If the tenant decides not to match it, the owner is free to accept it.

A right of first refusal protects a tenant from having the rental property sold when, in fact, if the tenant knew about the offer, the tenant would have been willing to match the offer. The owner usually does not care who buys, as long as the price and terms are the same. Therefore, an owner may agree to include a right of first refusal clause in a rental contract for little or no additional charge if the tenant requests it. Another example of the use of the right of first refusal would be the right of a prospective purchaser or tenant. For example, a person leasing space in a shopping center to start a small restaurant may negotiate a right of first refusal for adjacent space in the event that it becomes available. Common sense dictates that if the business operator wants to expand his/her current operation, that expansion would be in adjoining space.

To briefly review what has been covered in this chapter:

- A sales contract has an obligation at a definite price for definite terms for a definite period.
- An option includes the right at a definite price for definite terms for a definite period.

right of first refusal: the right to match or better an offer before the property is sold to someone else

- A right of first refusal has a right at a price and terms to be determined, and, as opposed to a definite period, the parties don't even know if the opportunity will present itself.

THE E-SIGN ACT

The federal government has preempted all of the foregoing rules somewhat by authorizing electronic signatures and documents. The Electronic Signatures in Global and National Commerce Act became fully effective on March 1, 2001. This act, popularly referred to as "the E-Sign Act," has in fact as one of its primary purposes to repeal state law requirements for written instruments as they apply to electronic agreements. The operative language is quite clear and succinct:

> Notwithstanding any statute, regulation, or other rule of law [other than subsequent parts of this same statute], with respect to any transactions in or affecting interstate or foreign commerce
>
> 1. a signature, contract, or other record relating to such transaction may not be denied legal effect, validity or enforceability solely because it is in electronic form; and
> 2. a contract relating to such transaction may not be denied legal effect, validity, or enforceability solely because an electronic signature or electronic record was used in its formation.

The operative term, obviously, is *transaction*. The E-Sign legislation provides a very broad definition:

> The term "transaction" means an action or set of actions relating to the conduct of a business, consumer or commercial affairs between two or more persons, including any of the following types of conduct:
>
> **(A)** the sale, lease, exchange, or other disposition of personal property and intangibles; or
> **(B)** the sale, lease, exchange, or other disposition of any interest in real property, or any combination thereof.

Congress has provided that almost anything can be an electronic signature rendering a party bound to agreement. The statutory language states:

> The term "electronic signature" means an electronic sound, symbol, or process attached to or logically associated with a contract or other record and executed or adopted by a person with the intent to sign the record.

For instance, if you were sent an email that said: "I'll buy your property at 450 W. Meyer in Chicago for $50,000," and you typed at the top of this message "OK" and hit *Reply*, you might have a binding real estate contract. All I'd have to show is that the typing of the words "OK" indicated your intent to express agreement. The fact that you didn't even type your name would not matter, since you "attached" an "electronic symbol" to a contract. The parties must agree to an electronic transaction, but the use of email is arguably an implied consent. The contract would still have to meet standards of clarity and certainty. Perhaps an exchange this informal would not meet those standards in some jurisdictions, but the point is that a relatively simple and perhaps thoughtless act could result in the formation of a relatively serious contract.

Note that the act applies only to transactions in "interstate commerce." However, an email message, when it left my computer, could conceivably bounce to Detroit, then to Geneva, then to Mexico City, all on its way to your computer, even if your computer was located in the building next door. Further, it was carried via a variety of communications media commonly associated with interstate transactions. The likelihood is quite strong that even the current Supreme Court would have difficulty interpreting around the conclusion that email transactions are interstate commerce. There is a provision that allows states to supersede this legislation with their own version of the Uniform Electronic Transactions Act (UETA). Georgia has not created separate legislation but does allow use of the UETA, though it has not been formally adopted.

Review Questions

Answers to these questions can be found in Appendix D at the end of this book.

1. A formal real estate sales contract, prepared at the outset by an agent using prepared forms, may be identified as any of the following EXCEPT:
   A. a purchase contract
   B. an option contract
   C. an offer and acceptance
   D. a purchase offer

2. Martin purchased real estate from Steven under an agreement that called for Martin to pay for the property in installments and to receive a deed upon payment of the entire purchase price. This agreement could be properly described as any of the following EXCEPT a/an:
   A. land contract
   B. contract for deed
   C. installment contract
   D. option contract

3. In normal real estate brokerage practice, the amount of earnest money deposit paid by the purchaser is:
   A. determined by negotiation
   B. set by state law
   C. equal to the agent's commission
   D. the minimum required to make the contract valid

4. Property taxes, insurance, loan interest, etc., may be divided between the buyer and seller by the process of:
   A. allocation
   B. appropriation
   C. proration
   D. proportioning

5. Typically, physical possession of the property is given to the buyer:
   A. upon signing of the sale contract
   B. before close of escrow (settlement)
   C. the day of close of escrow (settlement)
   D. 30 days following close of escrow (settlement)

6. Martin is going to purchase a home from a seller. He will finance the purchase by means of a VA-guaranteed loan. The purchase contract must include:
   A. an amendatory clause
   B. insulation disclosures
   C. a due diligence clause
   D. a kick-out clause

7. Mr. and Mrs. Silver entered into a real estate contract with Mr. and Mrs. Gold. If Mr. Gold dies before settlement takes place, all of the following are true EXCEPT:
   A. Mr. and Mrs. Silver are obligated to carry out the contract.
   B. Mrs. Gold is obligated to carry out the contract.
   C. Mr. Gold's estate is obligated to carry out the contract.
   D. A new contract must be created between Silver and Gold.

8. The major weaknesses of a binder lie in:
   A. its unenforceability
   B. what it does not say
   C. both A and B
   D. the fact that it is not binding

9. A letter of intent is:
   A. one that creates no liability
   B. an agreement to enter into a contract
   C. binding on the seller
   D. binding on the buyer

10. When property is sold by means of an installment contract:
    A. the seller delivers a deed at closing
    B. the buyer is not given the right to occupy the property until the contract terms have been fulfilled
    C. the seller is the mortgagor
    D. the buyer is the vendee

11. In Georgia, closing costs in a real estate transaction are typically the responsibility of the:
    A. buyer and the seller equally
    B. buyer and the seller but prorated as of the date of closing
    C. buyer
    D. seller

12. Before receiving a VA or FHA appraisal, any purchase contract must contain a/an:
    A. right of first refusal
    B. lease option clause
    C. amendatory clause
    D. agreement that the buyer may cancel within 10 days if not satisfied with the outcome of the negotiation

13. Equitable title may be:
    A. transferred by sale
    B. inherited
    C. mortgaged
    D. all of the above

14. The option portion of a lease-option contract can be attached to the lease as a/an:
    A. rider
    B. accord
    C. binder
    D. purchase agreement

15. Lease-option contracts tend to increase in popularity during a/an:
    A. seller's market
    B. buyer's market
    C. hot market
    D. expanding market

16. An option to buy is an example of a/an:
    A. unenforceable contract
    B. executed contract
    C. unilateral contract
    D. bilateral contract

17. Under the terms of a right of first refusal, the tenant is given the right to:
    A. match an offer to purchase the property
    B. purchase the property at a previously agreed price
    C. sell the property to an investor
    D. terminate the lease if the property is sold to anyone else

18. The party with the least amount of flexibility in a lease-option agreement is the:
    A. optionor
    B. optionee
    C. lessor
    D. lessee

19. The phrase "time is of the essence" in a sales contract means that:
    A. the time limits set by the contract must be faithfully observed or the contract is voidable
    B. the parties are prohibited from giving each other an extension
    C. if either party fails to perform on time, the contract is void
    D. there are no stipulated times for performance agreed to beforehand

PART 4
FINANCE, TAXES, AND VALUATION

The structure that makes up our knowledge of the real estate business is now in place; our building is "dried in." It is now time to continue with a very important step. You will likely find most purchasers of real estate do not pay cash. Their ability to complete a purchase is dependent on their ability to secure financing. I learned early in my real estate career that a real estate agent who does not have a working knowledge of finance and does not engage with good lenders will not fare well in the business. Continuing with our construction analogy, this part will be the phase of completing all mechanicals, plumbing, electrical, and drywall. In this part, we will dig into the following chapters:

Chapter 12: Lending Practices

Chapter 13: The Loan and the Consumer

Chapter 14: Sources of Financing

Chapter 15: Types of Financing

Chapter 16: Notes and Security Documents

Chapter 17: Taxes and Assessments

Chapter 18: Real Estate Appraisal

CHAPTER

12 LENDING PRACTICES

KEY TERMS

amortized loan
balloon loan
conventional loans
equity
Federal Housing
　　Administration (FHA)
impound or reserve
　　account
loan origination fee
loan-to-value ratio
maturity
principal, interest, taxes,
　　insurance (PITI)
　　payment
private mortgage insurance
　　(PMI)
point
principal
upfront mortgage
　　insurance premium
　　(UFMIP)
U.S. Department of
　　Veterans Affairs (VA)

OBJECTIVES

After successful completion of this chapter, you should be able to:

1. explain the features of an amortized loan and its respective lending process;
2. describe a budget mortgage, a term loan, and a balloon loan;
3. explain the types of early payoff and the refinancing process;
4. describe loan-to-value ratio, equity, origination, and discount points;
5. describe the FHA and VA programs and lending procedures;
6. explain the function of the Rural Housing Service; and
7. understand the approval procedure for private mortgage insurance.

OVERVIEW

Chapter 12 explores some of the financial aspects within security deeds, mortgages, and trust deeds. We begin this chapter with term loans, amortized loans, balloon loans, partially amortized loans, loan-to-value ratio, equity, and points. These topics

are followed by a discussion of the functions and importance of the FHA and VA and private mortgage insurance. Chapter 13 discusses truth in lending and provides a helpful and informative description of the loan application and approval process that you (or your buyer) will experience when applying for a real estate loan. In Chapters 14 and 15, we look at sources and types of financing, including where to find mortgage loan money, where mortgage lenders obtain their money, and various types of financing instruments, such as the adjustable rate mortgage, equity mortgage, wraparound mortgage, seller financing, and so forth. As a reminder, from here on, whatever is said about mortgages applies equally to security deeds and deeds of trust.

One more thought before we start. The United States has had a long-standing commitment to individual homeownership. We have long had governmental assistance in the form of tax-deductible interest on mortgages and loans insured or guaranteed by the government. Other countries require significant down payments and have short-term loans. We have standardized appraisal systems, standardized secondary mortgage markets, and a proliferation of loan originators. For the next few chapters, we'll discuss how all these factors interrelate to produce this very profitable system and this unique way of life.

As we use calculations in explanation, you are encouraged to follow along with your own calculator. Any calculator that adds, subtracts, divides, and multiplies is sufficient. A financial calculator is not needed for the real estate licensing course or state exam, but is encouraged for the field. Also remember, as was stated in chapter 1, interest rates in the examples are not meant to reflect current market conditions. Interest rates can change daily. The purpose of providing an interest rate in the examples is so the student can practice the process of completing a computation. During that process, it is irrelevant whether 3% or 13% was used in the example. It is important only that you demonstrate the ability to manipulate the computation.

TERM LOANS

A loan that requires only interest payments until the last day of its life, at which time the full amount borrowed is due, is called a *term loan* (or straight loan). Until 1930, the term loan was the standard method of financing real estate in the United States. These loans typically were made for a period of three to five years. The borrower signed a note or bond agreeing to: (1) pay the lender interest on the loan every six months and (2) repay the entire amount of the loan upon **maturity**; that is, at the end of the life of the loan. As security, the borrower mortgaged the property to the lender.

maturity: the end of the life of a loan

Loan Renewal

In practice, most real estate term loans were not paid off when they matured. Instead, the borrower asked the lender, typically a bank, to renew the loan for another three to five years. The major flaw in this approach to lending was that the borrower might never own the property free and clear of debt. This left the borrower continuously at the mercy of the lender for renewals. As long as the lender was not pressed for funds, the borrower's renewal request was granted. However, if the lender was short of funds, no renewal was granted, and the borrower was expected to pay in full.

The inability to renew term loans caused hardship for hundreds of thousands of property owners during the Great Depression that began in 1929 and lasted the better part of a decade. Banks were unable to accommodate requests for loan renewals and at the same time satisfy unemployed depositors who needed to withdraw their savings to live. As a result, owners of homes, farms, office buildings, factories, and vacant land lost their property as foreclosures reached into the millions. The market was so glutted with properties being offered for sale to satisfy unpaid mortgage loans that real estate prices fell at a sickening pace.

AMORTIZED LOANS

In 1933, a congressionally legislated Home Owners' Loan Corporation (HOLC) was created to assist financially distressed homeowners by acquiring mortgages that were about to be foreclosed. The HOLC then offered monthly repayment plans tailored to fit the homeowner's budget that would repay the loan in full by its maturity date without the need for a balloon payment. The HOLC was terminated in 1951 after rescuing over a million mortgages in its 18-year life. However, the use of this stretched-out payment plan, known as an **amortized loan,** took hold in U.S. real estate; today, its is the widely accepted method of loan repayment. In the United States, 66% of all mortgages are 30-year, fixed-rate, long-term loans, which is a rarity in most other countries.

As a practical matter, there are a number of handheld computers that can help a student analyze loans in a variety of ways. Real estate agents are continually trained in the variety of loans to meet their clients' needs. As more loan products become available, it is always a new learning experience. Our purpose here is to discuss the fundamentals of how the amortization system works. As one becomes more experienced, one realizes that the high-tech approach to loan analysis changes from market to market, but the basics remain the same.

amortized loan: a loan requiring periodic payments that include both interest and partial repayment of principal

Repayment Methods

The amortized loan requires regular equal payments during the life of the loan. Payments must be of sufficient size and number to pay all interest due on the loan and reduce the amount owed to zero by the loan's maturity date. Figure 12-1 shows the contrast between an amortized and a term loan. Figure 12-1A shows a 6-year, $1,000 term loan with interest of $90 due each year of its life. At the end of the sixth year, the entire **principal** (the amount owed) is due in one lump sum payment along with the final interest payment. In Figure 12-1B, the same $1,000 loan is fully amortized by making six equal annual payments of $222.92.

principal: the balance owing on a loan

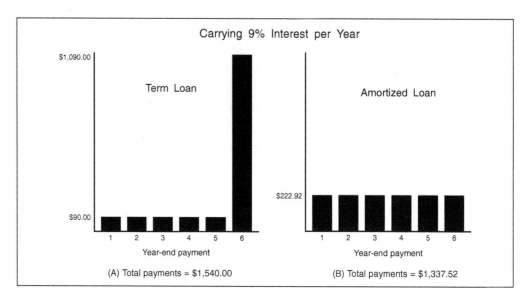

FIGURE 12-1 Repaying a 6-year, $1,000 loan
Source: © 2021 Mbition LLC

From the borrower's standpoint, $222.92 once each year is easier to budget than $90 for five years and $1,090 in the sixth year.

Furthermore, the amortized loan shown in Figure 12-1 actually costs the borrower less than the term loan. The total payments made under the term loan are $90 + $90 + $90 + $90 + $90 + $1,090 = $1,540. Amortizing the same loan requires total payments of 6 × $222.92 = $1,337.52. The difference is due to the fact that, under the amortized loan, the borrower begins to pay back part of the $1,000 principal with the first payment. In the first year, $90 of the $222.92 payment goes to interest and the remaining $132.92 reduces the principal owed. Thus, the borrower starts the second year owing only $867.08. At 9% interest per year, the interest on $867.08 is $78.04; therefore, when the borrower makes the second payment of $222.92, only $78.04 goes to interest. The remaining $144.88 is applied to reduce the loan balance, and the borrower starts the third year owing $722.20. Figure 12-2 charts this repayment program. Notice that the balance owed drops faster as the loan becomes older; that is, as it matures.

Monthly Payments

As you have just seen, calculating the payments on a term loan is relatively simple compared with calculating amortized loan payments. The widespread use of computers has greatly simplified the calculations, however. To illustrate how the amortization works, though, we should note that *amortization tables* are published and used throughout the real estate industry. Table 12-1 shows the monthly payments per $1,000 of loan for interest rates from 5% to 15% for periods ranging from five to 40 years. (Amortization tables are also published for quarterly, semiannual, and annual payments.) When you use an amortization table, notice that

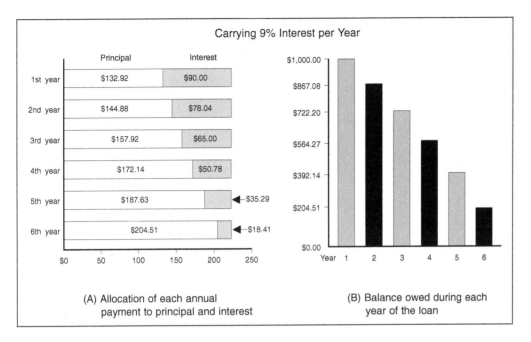

FIGURE 12-2 Repaying a 6-year, $1,000 amortized loan
Source: © 2021 Mbition LLC

there are five variables: (1) frequency of payment; (2) interest rate; (3) maturity; (4) amount of the loan; and (5) amount of the periodic payment. If you know any four of these, you can obtain the fifth variable from the tables. For example, suppose that you want to know the monthly payment necessary to amortize a $60,000 loan over 30 years at 9.5% interest. The first step is to look in Table 12-1 for the 9.5% line. Then locate the 30-year column. Where they cross, you will find the necessary monthly payment per $1,000: $8.41. Next, multiply $8.41 by 60 to get the monthly payment for a $60,000 loan: $504.60. If the loan is to be $67,500, then multiply $8.41 by 67.5 to get the monthly payment: $567.68.

Continuing the preceding example, suppose we reduce the repayment period to 15 years. First, look for the 9.5% line, then go over to the 15-year column. The number there is $10.45. Next, multiply $10.45 by 60 to get the monthly payment for a $60,000 loan: $627. If the loan is to be $67,500, then multiply $10.45 by 67.5 to get the monthly payment: $705.38.

Loan Size

Amortization tables are also used to determine the amount of loan a borrower can support given the amount the borrower has available to spend each month on loan payments. Suppose that a prospective home buyer can afford monthly principal and interest payments of $650 and lenders are making 30-year loans at 10%. How large a loan can this buyer afford? In Table 12-1, find where the 10% line and the 30-year column meet. You will see 8.78 there. This means that every $8.78 of monthly payment will support $1,000 of loan. To find how many

CHAPTER 12 Lending Practices

TABLE 12-1 Amortization table monthly payment per $1,000 of loan

Interest Rate per Year	Life of the Loan							
	5 years	10 years	15 years	20 years	25 years	30 years	35 years	40 years
5%	$18.88	$10.61	$7.91	$6.60	$5.85	$5.37	$5.05	$4.83
5.5	19.11	10.86	8.18	6.88	6.15	5.68	5.38	5.16
6	19.34	11.11	8.44	7.17	6.45	6.00	5.71	5.51
6.5	19.57	11.36	8.72	7.46	6.76	6.32	6.05	5.86
7	19.81	11.62	8.99	7.76	7.07	6.66	6.39	6.22
7.5	20.04	11.88	9.28	8.06	7.39	7.00	6.75	6.59
8	20.28	12.14	9.56	8.37	7.72	7.34	7.11	6.96
8.5	20.52	12.40	9.85	8.68	8.06	7.69	7.47	7.34
9	20.76	12.67	10.15	9.00	8.40	8.05	7.84	7.72
9.5	21.01	12.94	10.45	9.33	8.74	8.41	8.22	8.11
10	21.25	13.22	10.75	9.66	9.09	8.78	8.60	8.50
10.5	21.50	13.50	11.06	9.99	9.45	9.15	8.99	8.89
11	21.75	13.78	11.37	10.33	9.81	9.53	9.37	9.29
11.5	22.00	14.06	11.69	10.67	10.17	9.91	9.77	9.69
12	22.25	14.35	12.01	11.02	10.54	10.29	10.16	10.09
12.5	22.50	14.64	12.33	11.37	10.91	10.68	10.56	10.49
13	22.76	14.94	12.66	11.72	11.28	11.07	10.96	10.90
13.5	23.01	15.23	12.99	12.08	11.66	11.46	11.36	11.31
14	23.27	15.53	13.32	12.44	12.04	11.85	11.76	11.72
14.5	23.53	15.83	13.66	12.80	12.43	12.25	12.17	12.13
15	23.79	16.14	14.00	13.17	12.81	12.65	12.57	12.54

Source: © 2021 Mbition LLC

thousands of dollars $650 per month will support, just divide $650 by $8.78. The answer is 74.031 thousands or $74,031. By adding the buyer's down payment, you know what price property the buyer can afford to purchase. If interest rates are 7.5%, the number from the table is 7.00 and the loan amount is $92,857. (You can begin to see why the level of interest rates is so important to real estate prices.)

As you have noticed, everything in Table 12-1 is on a monthly payment per thousand basis. With a full book of amortization tables, rather than one page, it is possible to look up monthly payments for loans from $100 to $100,000 to determine loan maturities for each year from 1 to 40 years, and to calculate many more interest rates. Amortization books are available from most local bookstores.

Change in Maturity Date

An amortization table also shows the impact on the size of the monthly payment when the life of a loan is extended. For example, at 11% interest, a 10-year loan requires a monthly payment of $13.78 per $1,000 of loan. Increasing the life of the loan to 20 years drops the monthly payment to $10.33 per $1,000. Extending the loan payback to 30 years reduces the monthly payment to $9.53 per $1,000.

The smaller monthly payment is why 30 years is a popular loan term with borrowers. Note, however, that going beyond 30 years does not significantly reduce the monthly payment. Going from 30 to 35 years reduces the monthly payment by only 16 cents per $1,000, but adds 5 years of monthly payments. Extending the payback period from 35 to 40 years reduces the monthly payment by just 8 cents per $1,000 ($4 per month on a $50,000 loan) and adds another 60 months of payments at $464.50 per month. As a practical matter, amortized real estate loans are seldom made for more than 30 years.

BUDGET MORTGAGE

The *budget mortgage* takes the amortized loan one step further. In addition to collecting the monthly principal and interest payment (often called *P + I*), the lender collects one-twelfth of the estimated cost of the annual property taxes and hazard insurance on the mortgaged property. The money for tax and insurance payments is placed in an **impound account** (also called an *escrow* or **reserve account**). When taxes and insurance payments are due, the lender pays them. That way the lender makes certain that the value of the mortgaged property will not be undermined by unpaid taxes or uninsured damage. This form of mortgage also helps the borrower budget for property taxes and insurance on a monthly basis. To illustrate, if insurance is $240 per year and property taxes are $1,800 per year, the lender collects an additional $20 and $150, respectively, each month along with the regular principal and interest payments. This combined principal, interest, taxes, and insurance payment is often referred to as a **PITI payment**. All VA loans, all FHA loans, and most **conventional loans** (non-government) above 80% of the value of the property are budget mortgages.

impound or reserve account: an account into which the lender places monthly tax and insurance payments

PITI payment: a loan payment that combines principal, interest, taxes, and insurance

conventional loans: real estate loans that are not insured by the FHA or guaranteed by the VA

balloon loan: any loan in which the final payment is larger than the preceding payments

BALLOON LOAN

A **balloon loan** is any loan that has a final payment larger than any of the previous payments on the loan. The final payment is called a *balloon payment*. The term loan described at the beginning of this chapter is a type of balloon loan. Partially amortized loans, discussed next, are another type of balloon loan. In tight money markets, the use of balloon loans increases considerably. Balloon loans with maturities as short as three to five years are commonplace. This arrangement gives the buyer (borrower) three to five years to find cheaper and longer-term financing elsewhere. If such financing does not materialize and the loan is not repaid on time, the lender has the right to foreclose. The alternative is for the lender and borrower to agree to an extension of the loan, usually at prevailing interest rates.

PARTIALLY AMORTIZED LOAN

When the repayment schedule of a loan calls for a series of amortized payments followed by a balloon payment at maturity, it is called a *partially amortized loan.*

For example, a lender might agree to a 30-year amortization schedule with a provision that, at the end of the 10th year, all the remaining principal be paid in a single balloon payment. The advantage to the borrower is that for 10 years, the monthly payments will be smaller than if the loan was completely amortized in 10 years. (You can verify this in Table 12-1.) However, the disadvantage is that the balloon payment due at the end of the 10th year might be the borrower's financial downfall. Just how large that balloon payment will be can be determined in advance by using a *loan balance table* (also called a *remaining balance table*). Presuming an interest rate of 11.5% and a 30-year loan, at the end of 10 years, the loan balance table in Table 12-2 shows that for each $1,000 originally loaned, $929 would still be owed. If the original loan was for $100,000, at the end of 10 years, $92,900 (100 × $929) would be due as one payment. This qualifies it as a balloon loan.

As you can see from this example, when an amortized loan has a long maturity, relatively little of the debt is paid off during the initial years of the loan's life. Nearly all the early payments go for interest, so that little remains for principal reduction. For example, Table 12-2 shows that even after 16 years of payments on a 30-year, 11.5% loan, 82.5% of the loan is still unpaid. Not until this loan is about six years from maturity will half of it have been repaid.

TABLE 12-2 Balance owing on a $1,000 amortized loan

	9.5% Annual Interest						11.5% Annual Interest					
Age of Loan (yrs.)	Original life (years)					Age of loan (yrs.)	Original life (years)					
	10	15	20	25	30	35		10	15	20	25	30	35
2	$868	$934	$963	$978	$987	$992	2	$880	$944	$971	$984	$991	$995
4	708	853	918	952	971	983	4	729	873	935	965	981	989
6	515	756	864	921	953	971	6	539	784	889	940	967	982
8	282	639	799	883	930	957	8	300	672	831	909	950	972
10		497	720	837	902	940	10		531	759	870	929	960
12		326	625	781	869	920	12		354	667	821	902	945
14		119	510	714	828	896	14		132	553	759	868	926
16			371	633	780	866	16			409	682	825	903
18			203	535	721	830	18			228	585	772	873
20				416	650	787	20				462	704	836
22				273	564	735	22				308	620	789
24				100	460	671	24				115	513	729
26					335	595	26					380	655
28					183	503	28					211	561
30						391	30						444
32						256	32						296
34						94	34						110

Source: © 2021 Mbition LLC

EARLIER PAYOFF

During the late 1970s, when inflation rates exceeded interest rates, the popular philosophy was to borrow as much as possible for as long as possible. Then, in the early 1980s, inflation rates dropped below interest rates, and the opposite philosophy became attractive to many borrowers. This was especially true for those who had borrowed (or were contemplating borrowing) at double-digit interest rates. Let us use as an example an $80,000 loan at 11.5% interest. If the loan has a maturity of 30 years, from Table 12-1 we can determine the monthly payments to be $792.80. (Follow this example on your own.)

15-Year Loan

Suppose the maturity of the aforementioned loan is changed from 30 to 15 years. If you look at Table 12-1, you see that the monthly payments would now be $935.20. This is $142.40 more per month, but the loan is fully paid in 15 years, not 30 years. The total amount of interest paid on the 15-year loan is $(15 \times 12 \times \$935.20) - \$80,000 = \$88,336$. The total amount of interest paid on the 30-year loan is $(30 \times 12 \times \$792.80) - \$80,000 = \$205,408$. Thus, for an extra $142.40 per month for 180 months (which amounts to $25,632), the borrower saves the difference between $205,408 and $88,336 (which is $117,072). Many borrowers consider this a very good return on their money. (It is, in fact, an 11.5% compounded rate of return.) Lenders are also more receptive to making fixed-rate loans for 15 years than for 30 years. This is because the lender is locked into the loan for 15 years, not 30 years. As a result, a lender is usually willing to offer a 15-year loan at a lower rate of interest than a 30-year loan. In view of these benefits to borrower and lender alike, the 15-year loan is becoming a popular home financing tool.

Biweekly Payments

A growing number of lenders offer a biweekly repayment plan. The loan is amortized as if it were going to last 30 years. But instead of paying once a month, the borrower makes one-half of the monthly payment every two weeks. This may not sound like much of a difference, but the results are eye-opening. Assume you borrow $100,000 at 7% interest, paying (see Table 12-1) $666 per month. You will retire the loan in 30 years at a cost of $139,509 in interest. If you decide to pay half of $666 every two weeks, the loan will be fully paid in just 18 years and will have cost you only $105,046 in interest. This happens because biweekly payments result in 26 half-payments being made per year (the equivalent of 13 whole payments) versus 12 whole payments.

Existing Loans

Borrowers with existing loans who want to celebrate early mortgage repayment can simply add a few dollars each month to the required monthly payment.

This can be particularly beneficial for people who borrowed at rates of 11% or more. In effect, whatever extra amount is added to the monthly payment will "earn" interest at the loan's interest rate. Thus, if a loan has a 14% rate, early payments "earn" at 14%. If the borrower has no alternative places to invest that will yield 14%, then a few additional dollars each month will work miracles. For example, a 30-year, $100,000 loan at 14% interest requires monthly payments (see Table 12-1) of $1,185. Voluntarily adding an extra $19 per month reduces the maturity (payoff) date from 30 years to 25 years (see Table 12-1 again). If an extra $40 is added to the $19, the maturity date shrinks to 20 years. In other words, an extra $59 per month eliminates 10 years of payments.

You may be wondering why this has not been a popular idea with borrowers. When interest rates are around the 4% to 7% range (as they were in the 1960s and, more recently, in the 1990s and 2000s), the mathematics of early payoff are not nearly as impressive.

LOAN-TO-VALUE RATIO

loan-to-value ratio: a percentage reflecting what a lender will lend divided by the sale price or market value of the property, whichever is less

The relationship between the amount of money a lender is willing to lend and the lender's estimate of the market value of the property that will serve as security is called the **loan-to-value ratio** (often abbreviated as L/V or LTVR). For example, a prospective home buyer wants to purchase a house priced at $200,000. A local lender appraises the house, finds it has a market value of $200,000, and agrees to make an 80% L/V loan. This means that the lender will lend up to 80% of the $200,000, and the buyer must provide at least 20% in cash. In dollars, the lender will lend up to $160,000, and the buyer must make a cash down payment of at least $40,000. If the lender appraises the home for more than $200,000, the loan will still be $160,000. If the appraisal is for less than $200,000, the loan will be 80% of the appraised value, and the buyer must pay the balance in cash. The rule is that price or value, whichever is lower, is applied to the L/V ratio. This rule exists to prevent the lender from over-lending on a property. When you know the loan amount and the value of the property, the LTVR can be computed by dividing the loan amount by the value. For simplification's sake, if the resulting number is .90001 to .95, the LTVR is 95%. If the number is .80001 to .90, the LTVR is 90%, and if the number is .80 or below, the LTVR is 80%. For example, if the borrower needs a $125,000 loan on a $155,000 property, divide 125,000 by 155,000 for a result of .806452. This equates to a 90% LTVR.

EQUITY

equity: the market value of a property less the debt against it

The difference between the market value of a property and the debt owed against it is called the owner's **equity**. On a newly purchased $150,000 home with a $30,000 cash down payment, the buyer's equity is $30,000. As the value of the property rises or falls and as the mortgage loan is paid down, the equity changes.

For example, if the value of the home rises to $180,000 and the loan is paid down to $115,000, the owner's equity will be $65,000. If the owner completely repays the loan so that there is no debt against the home, the owner's equity is equal to the market value of the property.

LOAN POINTS

Probably no single term in real estate finance causes as much confusion and consternation as the word *points*. In finance, the word **point** means 1% of the loan amount. Thus, on a $100,000 loan, one point is $1,000. On an $80,000 loan, three points is $2,400. Let us take a closer look at how points can be used in a financial transaction.

point: 1% of the loan amount

Origination Fee

When a borrower asks for a mortgage loan, the lender incurs a number of expenses, including such things as the time its loan officer spends interviewing the borrower, office overhead, the purchase and review of credit reports on the borrower, an on-site appraisal of the property to be mortgaged, title searches and review, legal and recording fees, and so on. For these, some lenders make an itemized billing, charging so many dollars for the appraisal, credit report, title search, and so on. The total becomes the **loan origination fee**, which the borrower pays to get the loan. Other lenders do not make an itemized bill, but instead simply state the origination fee in terms of a percentage of the loan amount—for example, one point. Thus, a lender quoting a loan origination fee of one point is saying that, for a $95,000 loan, its fee to originate the loan will be $950.

loan origination fee: the expenses a lender incurs in processing a mortgage loan

Discount Points

Points charged to raise the lender's monetary return on a loan are known as *discount points*. A simplified example illustrates their use and effect. If you are a lender and agree to make a term loan of $100 to a borrower for one year at 10% interest, you would normally expect to give the borrower $100 now (disregard loan origination fees for a moment) and, one year later, the borrower would give you $110. In percentage terms, the *effective yield* on your loan is 10% per annum (year) because you received $10 for your one-year, $100 loan. Now suppose that instead of handing the borrower $100, you handed him/her $99 but still required him/her to repay $100 plus $10 in interest at the end of the year. This is a discount of one point ($1 in this case), and the borrower paid it out of the loan funds. The effect of this financial maneuver is to raise the effective yield (yield to maturity) to you without raising the interest rate itself. Therefore, if you loan out $99 and receive $110 at the end of the year, you effectively have a return of $11 for a $99 loan. This gives you an effective yield of $11 on a $99 investment or 11.1%, rather than 10%. Calculating the effective yield on a discounted 20- or 30-year mortgage loan is more difficult because the amount owed drops over the life of the loan and because the majority are paid in full ahead of schedule due to refinancing. Computers and calculators usually make these calculations; however, a useful rule of thumb states that on the typical home loan, each point of discount raises the effective yield by 1/8 of 1%. Thus, four discount points would raise the effective yield by approximately 0.5%, and eight points would raise it by 1%. Discount points are most often charged during periods of *tight money*—that is, when mortgage money is in short supply. During periods of *loose money,* when lenders have adequate funds to lend and are actively seeking borrowers, discount points disappear.

Real estate loans that are not insured by the Federal Housing Administration (FHA) or guaranteed by the Department of Veterans Affairs (VA) are termed conventional loans. The conventional loan market has a growing presence in the marketplace, as conventional lenders are very competitive with rates and loan processing procedures. FHA and VA loans now represent only a small fraction of the single-family loan origination market. The FHA handles a little more than 12%; the VA about 2%. Let's discuss the impact of the FHA and VA.

FHA INSURANCE PROGRAMS

FHA: Federal Housing Administration

The Great Depression caused a major change in the attitude of the federal government toward home financing in the United States. In 1934, one year after the Home Owner's Loan Corporation was established, Congress passed the National Housing Act. The act's most far-reaching provision was to establish the **Federal Housing Administration (FHA)** for the purpose of encouraging new construction as a means of creating jobs. To accomplish this goal, the FHA offered to insure lenders against losses due to non-repayment when they made loans on both new and existing homes. In turn, the lender had to grant 20-year, fully amortized loans with loan-to-value ratios of 80% rather than the three- to five-year, 50% to 60% term loans common up to that time.

The FHA did its best to keep from becoming a burden to the American taxpayer. When a prospective borrower approached a lender for an FHA-secured home loan, the FHA reviewed the borrower's income, expenses, assets, and debts. The objective was to determine whether there was adequate room in the borrower's budget for the proposed loan payments. The FHA also sent inspectors to the property to make certain that it was of acceptable construction quality and to determine its fair market value. To offset losses that would still inevitably occur, the FHA charged the borrower an annual insurance fee of approximately 0.5% of the balance owed on the loan. The FHA was immensely successful in its task. Not only did it create construction jobs, but it raised the level of housing quality in the nation and, in a pleasant surprise to taxpayers, actually returned annual profits to the U.S. Treasury. In response to its success, Congress changed its status from temporary to permanent in 1946.

Current FHA Coverage

The FHA has had a marked influence on lending policies in the real estate industry. Foremost among these is the widespread acceptance of the high loan-to-value, fully amortized loan. In the 1930s, lenders required FHA insurance before making 80% L/V loans. By the 1960s, lenders were readily making 80% L/V loans without FHA insurance. Meanwhile, the FHA insurance program was working so well that the FHA raised the portion it was willing to insure.

Down payment programs historically have been very complex. However, after a two-year pilot program, the FHA simplified the down payment calculation to streamline its program. Limits for the underwriting commitment now have only two categories for loans: (1) a 98.75% underwriting commitment for properties of $50,000 or less, and (2) a 97.75% commitment for properties of more than $50,000. The FHA requires some down payment; otherwise, it would be too easy for the borrower to walk away from the debt and leave the FHA to pay the lender's insurance claim.

The maximum amount the FHA will insure has varied from city to city and changes from time to time. As of 2020, the maximum loan amount in Georgia for single-family residential is $401,350. (This is in the Atlanta market; in Georgia, but outside of Atlanta, the maximum loan amount is currently $331,760. These amounts are fluid. Current limits can be researched at www.hud.gov.) The FHA has proposed eliminating loan limits by geographical area to simplify FHA loan underwriting, but this has not yet been implemented.

Assumability

Traditionally, FHA loans were popular because the 30-year fixed-rate loans could be assumed without any increase in interest. This led some borrowers to take advantage, and today any outstanding FHA loans may be assumed without an increase in the interest rate, but the buyer assuming the loan must qualify. The qualifying requirements are similar to those for approval for a new loan. If the borrower assumes a mortgage loan, the lender may not refuse to release the original borrower from liability on the loan.

Mortgage Insurance

The FHA charges a one-time **upfront mortgage insurance premium (UFMIP)** that is paid when the loan is made. Currently, the UFMIP is 1.75% of the loan amount. As this number is dynamic, do your own research at www.hud.gov or speak with a local lender who is actively involved in FHA-insured loans.

The FHA now also charges an annual premium amounting to 0.8% of the annual loan balance. One-twelfth of the annual premium is added to the monthly payment and must be included in the proposed monthly housing expense to qualify the borrower for the loan. The amount is calculated each year on the

UFMIP: upfront mortgage insurance premium; a one-time charge by the FHA for insuring a loan

unpaid principal balance without the UFMIP and excluding closing costs. On loans originated prior to April 1, 2013, the annual premium will be eliminated when homeowners build 22% equity in their homes as applied to the original value of the property. Depending on the interest rate and the down payment, a borrower could eliminate the annual premium by the 11th year of the loan. This keeps the FHA insurance program in line with the 1998 federal legislation that enables homeowners to eliminate private mortgage insurance once their homeowner equity reaches 78%. Unlike the Homeowners Protection Act (discussed later under Private Mortgage Insurance), the FHA continues to insure the mortgage. However, with the losses to the Mutual Mortgage Insurance Fund in the real estate market from 2006 to 2013, the annual MIP is now collected for the life of the loan on all loans originated after April 1, 2013.

Floating Interest Rates

At one time, the FHA set interest rate ceilings. Fixed-rate FHA loans are now negotiable and float with the market, and the seller also has a choice of how many points to contribute toward the borrower's loan. This can be none, some, or all of the points, and the seller can even pay the borrower's MIP. Typical purchase contract language is, "The seller will pay X points and the buyer will pay not more than Y points and the agreed-on interest rate is Z%." Thus, X is the contribution the seller will make, and the seller is protected from having to pay more. The buyer will pay any additional points, but not more than Y points. Beyond that, the buyer may cancel the purchase contract. That would happen if the market rates rose quickly while the rate at Z is fixed.

Loan Qualification

Before leaving the topic of the FHA, it is interesting to note that much of what we take for granted as standard loan practice today was the result of FHA innovation years ago. As already noted, before 1934, standard real estate loan practice called for short-term renewable loans. Then the FHA boldly offered 20-year amortized loans. Once these were shown to be successful investments for lenders, loans without FHA insurance were made for 20 years. Later, when the FHA successfully went to 30 years, non-FHA-insured loans followed. The FHA also established loan application review techniques that have been widely accepted and copied throughout the real estate industry. The biggest step in this direction was to analyze a borrower's loan application in terms of earning power.

HUD announced major revisions in its FHA single-family underwriting guidelines in January 1995, giving lenders more flexibility in considering an applicant's income and savings. The new regulations provide that the FHA may now participate in state housing finance agencies and programs to use alternative qualifying methods, such as: (1) the applicant's existing housing payments, (2) tax benefits of homeownership, and (3) non-housing debt history. In addition, the FHA now uses a three-year test for income stability instead of the previous five-year test. Only debts extending 10 or more months are included in debt-to-income calculations, and childcare costs are no longer counted as a recurring debt. FHA lenders can also use a three-repository merged credit report. HUD also gave the FHA limited approval for the use of automatic underwriting systems.

While it is important to understand the basics of the loan programs, the qualifying for the loan is typically left to a competent lender. It is recommended by most practitioners that the buyer should be encouraged to meet with a lender before they start seriously looking.

Construction Regulations

Since its inception, the FHA has imposed its own minimum construction requirements. Often, this was essential where local building codes did not exist or were weaker than the FHA wanted. Before issuing a loan, particularly on new construction, the FHA would impose minimum requirements as to the quantity and quality of building materials to be used. Lot size, street access, landscaping, siting, and general house design also were required to fit within broad FHA guidelines. During construction, an FHA inspector would visit the property several times to check whether work was being done correctly.

The reason for such care in building standards was that the FHA recognized that if a building is defective either from a design or construction standpoint, the borrower is more likely to default on the loan and create an insurance claim against the FHA. Furthermore, the same defects will lower the price the property will bring at its foreclosure sale, thus increasing losses to the FHA. Because building codes are now becoming stricter and more standardized in states, counties, and cities, the FHA anticipates eliminating its own minimum property standards. The FHA has also softened its standards for property defects. The FHA standards, which became effective January 1, 1995, advise underwriters to delete "conditions that have little or nothing to do with the safety and soundness of the property" from repair requirements stipulated by an appraiser.

As we leave our discussion of the FHA and go to the Department of Veterans Affairs, keep in mind that the FHA is not a lender; the FHA is an insurance agency. The loan itself is obtained from a savings and loan, bank, mortgage company, or similar lender. In addition to principal and interest payments, the lender collects an insurance premium from the borrower that is forwarded to the FHA. The FHA, in turn, guarantees repayment of the loan to the lender. This arrangement makes lenders much more willing to lend to buyers who are putting only 3% to 5% cash down. Thus, when you hear the phrase "FHA loan" in real estate circles, know that it is an *FHA-insured* loan, not a loan from the FHA.

DEPARTMENT OF VETERANS AFFAIRS

In 1944, to show its appreciation to servicemen returning from World War II, Congress passed far-reaching legislation to aid veterans in education, hospitalization, employment training, and housing. In housing, the popularly named G.I. Bill of Rights empowered the comptroller general of the United States to guarantee the repayment of a portion of first mortgage real estate loans made to veterans. For this guarantee, no fee would be charged to the veteran. Rather, the government itself would stand the losses. On March 15, 1989, the Veterans Administration was elevated to cabinet level and is now officially called the **Department of Veterans Affairs**, but it still uses its old initials, **VA**.

VA: Department of Veterans Affairs

No Down Payment

The original 1944 law provided that lenders would be guaranteed against losses of up to 50% of the amount of the loan, but in no case for more than $2,000. The objective was to make it possible for a veteran to buy a home with no cash down payment. Thus, on a house offered for sale at $5,000 (houses were much cheaper in 1944), this guarantee enabled a veteran to borrow the entire $5,000. From the lender's standpoint, having the top $2,000 of the loan guaranteed by the U.S. government offered the same asset protection as a $2,000 cash down payment. If the veteran defaulted and the property went into foreclosure, the lender had to net less than $3,000 before suffering a loss.

To keep up with the increased cost of homes, the guarantee has been increased several times. President George W. Bush signed the Veterans Benefits Act of 2003, which allows for a maximum guarantee amount of 25% of the Freddie Mac conforming loan limit. In 2020, the Freddie Mac conforming loan limit was raised to $510,400. Since lenders will typically lend up to four times the amount of the VA guarantee, the current loan limit with no money down is $510,400 ($510,400 × 25% = $127,600 loan guarantee; $127,600 × 4 = $510,400 maximum loan typically allowed by lenders with no down payment). This may sound confusing so, let's break it down. We started at $510,400, performed some mathematical calculations and got $510,400. It's important to understand, however, that these numbers can change frequently. For the most up-to-date figures, check the VA or Freddie Mac websites.

In the original G.I. Bill of 1944, eligibility was limited to World War II veterans. Subsequent legislation has broadened eligibility to include any veteran who served for at least 90 days in the armed forces of the United States or an ally between September 16, 1940, and July 25, 1947, or between June 27, 1950, and January 31, 1955. Any veteran of the United States who has served at least 181 days of continuous active duty from January 31, 1955, to September 7, 1980, is also eligible. If service was during the Vietnam conflict period (August 5, 1964, to May 7, 1975) or the Persian Gulf War, 90 days is sufficient to qualify.

The VA requires a length of service of at least two years for a veteran who enlisted after September 7, 1980, or was an officer and began service after October 16, 1981. These veterans must have completed one of the following: (1) at least 24 months in the service, or (2) the full period ordered active duty (not less than 90 days during wartime or 181 days during peacetime). The benefit is also available to those who served in the Select Reserves or National Guard at least six years with an honorable discharge.

The veteran's discharge must be on conditions other than dishonorable, and the guarantee entitlement is good until used. If not remarried, the spouse of a veteran who died as a result of service can also obtain a housing guarantee. Active duty personnel can also qualify. Shorter active duty periods are allowed for service-connected disabilities.

VA Certificates

To determine benefits, a veteran should apply to the Department of Veterans Affairs for a *certificate of eligibility*, which shows whether the veteran is qualified and the amount of guarantee available. This document (Form 26-1880), along with a copy of the veteran's discharge papers, are necessary to obtain a VA-guaranteed loan.

The VA works diligently to protect veterans and reduce foreclosure losses. When a veteran applies for a VA guarantee, the property is appraised and the VA issues a *certificate of reasonable value*. Often abbreviated *CRV*, it reflects the estimated value of the property as determined by the VA staff appraiser. Similarly, the VA establishes income guidelines to make certain that the veteran can comfortably meet the proposed loan payments. Also, the veteran must agree to occupy the property. Pursuant to the Safe Drinking Water Act and the Reduction of Lead in Drinking Water Act, if the building was constructed after June 19, 1988, the CRV must certify that any solders or fluxes used in construction do not contain more than 0.2% lead in any pipes, or that the pipe fittings do not contain more than 0.25% lead.

The VA guarantees fixed-rate loans for as long as 30 years on homes, and no prepayment penalty is charged if the borrower wishes to pay sooner. Moreover, there is no due-on-sale clause that requires the loan to be repaid if the property is sold. The VA guarantees loans for the purchase of townhouses and condominiums, to build or improve a home, and to buy a mobile home as a residence. A veteran wishing to refinance an existing home or farm can obtain a VA-guaranteed loan provided that there is existing debt that will be repaid. The VA also makes direct loans to veterans if there are no private lending institutions nearby.

Financial Liability

No matter what loan guarantee program is elected, the veteran should know that, in the event of default and subsequent foreclosure, s/he is required eventually to make good any losses suffered by the VA on the loan. (This is not the case with FHA-insured loans, for which the borrower pays for protection against foreclosure losses that may result from the loan.) Even if the veteran sells the property and the buyer assumes the VA loan, the veteran is still financially responsible if the buyer later defaults. To avoid this, the veteran must arrange with the VA to be released from liability. For VA loans underwritten after March 1, 1988, Congress created a new Guarantee and Indemnity Fund that allows a release from liability to the VA in the event of foreclosure, provided that the following requirements are met:

1. The loan payments must be current.
2. The prospective purchaser must meet creditworthiness standards as required by the VA.
3. The prospective purchaser must assume full liability for repayment of the loan, including indemnity liability to the VA.

In the event that borrowers are unable to make their mortgage payments, the VA offers an assistance procedure that may be helpful in declining markets. If the borrower can obtain a purchase offer that is insufficient to pay off the existing loan balance, a *compromise agreement* may allow the VA to pay the difference between the sales proceeds and the mortgage balance. To effect the compromise agreement, the borrower must be willing to find a purchaser who will pay the fair market value of the house, and the original borrower must agree to remain liable to the government for the amount that the VA pays to the noteholder.

A veteran is permitted a full new guarantee entitlement if complete repayment of a previous VA-guaranteed loan has been made. If a veteran has sold and let the buyer assume the VA loan, the balance of the entitlement is still available. For example, if a veteran has used $15,000 of his/her entitlement to date, the difference between $15,000 and the current VA guarantee amount is still available for use.

Funding Fee

From its inception until October 1, 1982, the VA made loan guarantees in behalf of veterans without a charge. Congress initially enacted a funding fee in 1982, increased it in 1991, and in 1993, established a funding fee with three categories of veterans, each with different fees depending on the veteran's status and down payment. Note the rates set out in Table 12-3. The most common VA loan is going to be one for a veteran with a 0% down payment. Referring to Table 12-3, you can see the funding fee as of January 1, 2020, is 2.3%. Funding fees can be added to the loan amount for calculating the loan-to-value ratio.

TABLE 12-3 VA funding fees

PURCHASE AND CONSTRUCTION LOANS

Loan Type	Required Down Payment	Active Duty Personnel and Veterans	
First-Time Use of VA Loan Guaranty Benefits			
Purchase/Construction	0% down	2.3%	
	5% down	1.65%	
	10% down	1.4%	
Second or Subsequent Use of VA Loan Guarantee Benefits			
Purchase/Construction	0%	3.6%	
	5%	1.65%	
	10%	1.4%	

OTHER LOANS

Loan Type		Active Duty Personnel and Veterans	National Guard and Reservists
All Interest Rate Reduction Refinance Loans		0.50%	0.50%
Native American Direct Loans		1.25%	1.25%
Manufactured (Mobile) Home Loans		1.00%	1.00%
Assumptions*		0.50%	0.50%
Vendee Loans		2.25%	2.25%

*This pertains to loans originally closed on or after March 1, 1988. There is no funding fee required for assumption of loans closed prior to March 1, 1988.

Source: © 2021 Mbition LLC

In the Field

A veteran who has a current, service-connected disability may be eligible to have the funding fee waived. If the disability is 10% or greater and the veteran is currently being paid disability benefits from the VA, there is no funding fee. At the current 2.3%, on a $200,000 loan, the funding fee would be $4,600. This type of knowledge saves the buyer substantial money and makes *your* knowledge and ability to educate him/her a value proposition.

Interest Rates

In 1992, Congress made a historic change that eliminated the interest rate ceilings on VA loans. The new program allows an interest rate and discount points agreed on by the veteran and the lender. Discount points may not be financed on any loan except interest-rate-reduction refinancing loans (IRRRLs). IRRRLs are limited to two discount points. The two-point limit does not include origination fees, which are limited to one point.

Assumption Requirements

On VA loans created before March 1, 1988, approval was not required prior to loan assumption. Therefore, sellers could sell their property on assumption without obtaining any approval from the VA, but sellers remained fully liable for repayment. As stated previously, they could be released from liability if the VA approved the creditworthiness of the new purchaser. After March 1, 1988, the VA required prior approval for transfer of the property. Federal law now requires that the mortgage or deed of trust and note for loans carry on the first page—in type 2-1/2 times larger than the regular type—the following statement:

> THIS LOAN IS NOT ASSUMABLE WITHOUT THE PRIOR APPROVAL OF THE DEPARTMENT OF VETERANS AFFAIRS OR AUTHORIZED AGENT.

Because Congress frequently changes eligibility and benefits, a person contemplating a VA or FHA loan should make inquiry to the field offices of these two agencies and to mortgage lenders to ascertain the current status and details of the law, as well as the availability of loan money. Field offices also have information on foreclosed properties that are for sale. Additionally, one should query lenders as to the availability of state veteran benefits. A number of states offer special advantages, including mortgage loan assistance, to residents who have served in the armed forces.

Adjustable-Rate Mortgages

The VA can also issue its guarantee for an adjustable-rate mortgage. The approved plan is structured the same as the plan for FHA adjustable-rate mortgages, underwritten at an interest rate 1% above the initial rate agreed on by the veteran and the lender. Increases in the interest rate are limited to an annual adjustment of 1% and capped at 5% over the life of the loan. The index for calculating interest-rate adjustments is the weekly average yield on Treasury securities to a constant maturity of one year as reported by the Federal Reserve Board. Additional information on the VA can be obtained from benefits.va.gov/homeloans.

PRIVATE MORTGAGE INSURANCE

In 1957, the Mortgage Guaranty Insurance Corporation (MGIC) was formed in Milwaukee, WI, as a privately owned business venture to insure home mortgage loans. Demand was slow but steady for the first 10 years and then grew rapidly; today, there are more than a dozen private mortgage insurance companies. As is the case with FHA insurance, the object of **private mortgage insurance (PMI)** is to insure lenders against foreclosure losses. But, unlike FHA insurance, PMI insures only the top 20% to 25% of a loan, not the whole loan. This allows a lender to make 90% and

PMI: private mortgage insurance source to insure lenders against foreclosure loss

95% L/V loans with about the same exposure to foreclosure losses as a 70% to 75% L/V loan. The borrower, meanwhile, can purchase a home with a cash down payment of either 5% or 10% rather than the 20% to 30% down required by lenders when mortgage insurance is not purchased. For this privilege, the borrower pays a fee to the insurer. This fee is typically less than 1% of the loan amount but may exceed 2% in situations where the borrower has poor credit and/or has difficulty in documenting income.

In 1998, Congress passed the Homeowners Protection Act (HPA), which became effective in 2000. The act requires servicers to automatically cancel PMI once principal on the loan falls to 78% of the property's original value. The act also requires notification to the borrower that s/he can request PMI cancellation when the loan principal falls to 80% of the property's original value. Lenders are allowed to require an appraisal to prove the value at that time, so some owners may choose to wait until the automatic cancellation is triggered. The act also allows lenders to refuse to cancel the insurance if the borrower does not have a good payment record. FHA and VA loans are exempted from this legislation.

Approval Procedure

Private mortgage insurers work to keep their losses to a minimum by first approving the lenders with whom they do business. Particular emphasis is placed on the lender's operating policy, appraisal procedure, and degree of government regulation. Once a loan is approved, a lender simply sends the borrower's application, credit report, and property appraisal to the insurer. Based on these documents, the insurer either agrees or refuses to issue a policy. Although the insurer relies on the appraisal prepared by the lender, the insurer sends, on a random basis, its own appraiser to verify the quality of the information being submitted. When an insured loan goes into default, the insurer has the option of either buying the property from the lender for the balance due or letting the lender foreclose and then paying the lender's losses up to the amount of the insurance. As a rule, insurers take the first option because it is more popular with lenders and it leaves the lender with immediate cash to relend. The insurer is then responsible for foreclosing.

RURAL HOUSING SERVICE

The Rural Housing Service (RHS) is a federal agency under the U.S. Department of Agriculture. Like the FHA, it came into existence due to the financial crises of the 1930s. The RHS offers programs to help purchase or operate farms. The RHS will either guarantee a portion of a loan made by a private lender or it will make the loan itself. RHS loans can also be used to help finance the purchase of homes in rural areas. RHS is a successor agency to the Farmers Home Administration (FmHA).

Review Questions

Answers to these questions can be found in Appendix D at the end of this book.

1. A loan wherein the principal is all repaid in one lump sum payment at the end of the loan's life is known as:
   A. a straight or term loan
   B. an amortized loan
   C. a budget mortgage
   D. an adjustable payment loan

2. The last day of a loan's life is known as the:
   A. settlement date
   B. maturity date
   C. sale date
   D. contract date

3. To determine the amount of loan payments by using an amortization table, you must know all the following EXCEPT:
   A. loan-to-value ratio
   B. frequency of payments
   C. interest rate
   D. amount of loan

4. Amortization tables would NOT be used by real estate agents to determine which of the following?
   A. frequency of payment
   B. interest rate
   C. income needed to qualify
   D. amount of loan

5. Which of the following is NOT true of VA and FHA financing programs?
   A. Interest rates are competitive.
   B. Low or no down payments are common.
   C. They are both government-insured.
   D. 30-year loan terms are available.

6. Kevin wants to know what portion of a 30-year, fully amortized loan would remain at the end of the fourth year of the loan's life. Kevin would consult:
   A. an amortization table
   B. a loan balance table
   C. a partial amortization table
   D. a loan-to-value ratio

7. By the 10th year of a 30-year amortization period, what percentage of a $1,000 loan with an interest rate of 11.5% will have been repaid under equal monthly installments? Use Table 12-2 in the text.
   A. 50%
   B. 33%
   C. 67%
   D. 7%

8. The primary purpose of the FHA is to:
   A. make loans to borrowers
   B. guarantee loans for lenders
   C. insure loans for lenders
   D. subsidize interest rates

9. Regarding mortgage insurance, which of the following statements is true?
   A. PMI insures only the top 20% or 25% of the loan.
   B. The FHA insures for the first 10 years only.
   C. FHA mortgage insurance is available on non-owner-occupied properties.
   D. PMI typically is about 2.5% of the loan amount.

10. Which of the following statements regarding the Rural Housing Services Administration is NOT correct?

    A. It guarantees loans on farms and rural homes.

    B. It makes loans on farms and rural homes.

    C. It has loan programs for farm operation.

    D. It is a private agency.

CHAPTER 13

THE LOAN AND THE CONSUMER

KEY TERMS

Annual Percentage Rate (APR)
credit report
Fair Credit Reporting Act
finance charge
liquid asset
redlining
Regulation Z
Truth in Lending Act

OBJECTIVES

After successful completion of this chapter, you should be able to:
1. explain the purpose and features of the Truth in Lending Act;
2. describe the loan application and approval process, and
3. define redlining, annual percentage rate, and trigger terms.

OVERVIEW

The previous chapter discussed lending practices applied to the types of payment arrangements that can be made in retiring debt. Consumer protection was enabled through the federal Consumer Credit Protection Act, and additional protections have been created through standardized loan procedures. This chapter will discuss the federal Truth in Lending Act and standard loan procedures that consumers need to use in order to apply for a loan.

Truth in Lending Act: a federal law that requires certain disclosures when extending or advertising credit

TRUTH IN LENDING ACT

The federal Consumer Credit Protection Act, popularly known as the **Truth in Lending Act**, went into effect in 1968. The act, implemented by Federal Reserve

Board **Regulation Z**, requires that a borrower be clearly shown, before committing to a loan, how much is being paid for credit in both dollar terms and percentage terms. The borrower is also given the right to rescind (cancel) the transaction in certain instances. The Act came into being because it was not uncommon to see loans advertised for rates lower than the borrower actually wound up paying. Once the Act took effect, several weaknesses and ambiguities of the Act and Regulation Z became apparent. Thus, the Truth in Lending Simplification and Reform Act (TILSRA) was passed by Congress and became effective October 1, 1982. Concurrently, the Federal Reserve Board issued a Revised Regulation Z (RRZ) that details rules and regulations for TILSRA. For purposes of discussion, we refer to all of this as the Truth in Lending Act (TILA or TIL). In 2010, the Wall Street Reform and Consumer Protection Act was passed into law. This Act is commonly referred to as Dodd–Frank. A part of this Act was the creation of the Consumer Financial Protection Bureau (CFPB), which received rulemaking authority in 2011. This will be covered more thoroughly in a later chapter when we study the Real Estate Settlement Procedures Act (RESPA).

Regulation Z: federal regulations that implement the Truth in Lending Act

Advertising

Whether you are a real estate practitioner or a property owner acting on your own behalf, TILA or TIL rules affect you when you advertise just about anything (including real estate) and include financing terms in the ad.

Trigger Terms

Five specific disclosures must be included in any ad that contains even one of the following trigger terms: (1) the amount of down payment (e.g., "only 5% down," "10% down," "$4,995 down," "95% financing"); (2) the amount of any payment (e.g., "monthly payments only $499," "buy for less than $650 a month," "payments only 1% per month"); (3) the number of payments (e.g., "only 36 monthly payments and you own it," "all paid up in 10 annual payments"); (4) the period of repayment (e.g., "30-year financing, owner will carry for 5 years," "10-year second available"); and (5) the dollar amount of any finance charge (e.g., "finance this for only $999") or the statement that there is no charge for credit ("pay no interest for 3 years"). A general rule of thumb is that if the advertisement includes a number referring to the credit, TILA has been triggered.

If any of the aforementioned trigger terms are used, then the following five disclosures must appear in the ad: (1) the cash price or the amount of the loan; (2) the amount of down payment or a statement that none is required; (3) the number, amount, and frequency of repayments; (4) the annual percentage rate; and (5) the deferred payment price or total payments. Item 5 is not a requirement in the case of the sale of a dwelling or a loan secured by a first lien on the dwelling that is being purchased.

> **In the Field**
>
> If an advertisement contains any item from the TILA list of financing terms, the ad must also include other required information. For example, an advertisement that reads: "Bargain! Bargain! Bargain! New 3-bedroom townhouses only $499 per month" may or may not be a bargain, depending on other financing information missing from the ad.

Annual Percentage Rate

APR: the annual percentage rate as calculated under the federal Truth in Lending Act by combining the interest rate with other costs of the loan

The **annual percentage rate (APR)** combines the interest rate with the other costs of the loan into a single figure that shows the true annual cost of borrowing. This is one of the most helpful features of the law, as it gives the prospective borrower a standardized yardstick by which to compare financing from different sources.

If the annual percentage rate being offered is subject to increase after the transaction takes place (such as with an adjustable rate mortgage), that fact must be stated—for example, "9% annual percentage rate subject to increase after settlement." Likewise, if the loan has interest rate changes that follow a predetermined schedule, those terms must be stated—for example, "7% first year, 9% second year, 11% third year, 13% remainder of loan, 12.5% annual percentage rate."

If you wish to say something about financing and avoid triggering full disclosure, you may use general statements. The following would be acceptable: "assumable loan," "financing available," "owner will carry," "terms to fit your budget," "easy monthly payments," or "FHA and VA financing available."

Lending Disclosures

If you are in the business of making loans, the Truth in Lending Act requires you to make 18 disclosures to your borrower. Of these, the 4 that must be most prominently displayed on the papers the borrower signs are: (1) the amount financed, (2) the finance charge, (3) the annual percentage rate, and (4) the total payments.

finance charge: the total amount the credit will cost over the life of the loan

The amount financed is the amount of credit provided to the borrower. The **finance charge** is the total dollar amount the credit will cost the borrower over the life of the loan. This includes interest plus such things as borrower-paid discount points, loan fees, loan finder's fees, loan service fees, required life insurance, and mortgage guarantee premiums. On a long-term mortgage loan, the total finance charge can easily exceed the amount of money being borrowed. For example, the total amount of interest on a 7%, 30-year, $160,000 loan is just over $223,000. The annual percentage rate was described earlier. The total payment is the amount in dollars the borrower will have paid after making all the payments as scheduled. In the aforementioned 7%, 30-year loan, it would be the interest of $223,000 plus the principal of $160,000, for a total of $383,000. The other 14 disclosures that a lender must make are as follows: (1) the identity of the lender; (2) the payment schedule; (3) prepayment penalties and rebates; (4) late payment charges; (5) any insurance required; (6) any filing fees; (7) any collateral required; (8) any required deposits; (9) whether the loan can be assumed; (10) the demand feature, if the note has one; (11) the total sales price of the item being purchased if the seller is also the creditor; (12) any adjustable-rate features of the loan; (13) an itemization of the amount financed; and (14) a reference to any terms not shown on the disclosure statement but that are shown on the loan contract. These disclosures must be delivered or mailed to the credit applicant within three business days after the creditor receives the applicant's written request for credit. The applicant must have this information before the transaction can take place—for example, before the closing.

Who Must Comply?

Any person or firm that regularly extends consumer credit subject to a finance charge (such as interest) or payable by written agreement in more than four installments must comply with the lending disclosures. This includes banks, savings and loans, credit unions, finance companies, and so on, as well as private individuals who extend credit more than five times a year.

Whoever is named on the note as the creditor must make the lending disclosures even if the note is to be resold. A key difference between the old and the new Truth in Lending Acts is that the new one does not include mortgage brokers or real estate practitioners as creditors just because they broker a deal containing financing. This is because they do not appear as creditors on the note. But if a broker takes back a note for part of the commission on a deal, that is considered an extension of credit, and the lending disclosures must be made.

Exempt Transactions

Certain transactions are exempt from the lending disclosure requirement. The first exemption is for credit extended primarily for business, commercial, or agricultural purposes. This exemption includes dwelling units purchased for rental purposes (unless the property contains four or fewer units and the owner occupies one of them, in which case special rules apply). The second exemption applies to credit for more than $50,000 secured by personal property, unless the property is the principal residence of the borrower. For example, a mobile home that secures a loan of more than $50,000 qualifies under this exemption if it is used as a vacation home, but is not exempt if it is used as a principal residence.

Failure to Disclose

If the Federal Trade Commission (FTC) determines that an advertiser has broken the law, it can order the advertiser to cease from further violations. Each violation of that order can result in a $10,000 civil penalty each day the violation continues. Failure to disclose properly when credit is extended can result in a penalty of twice the amount of the finance charge, with a minimum of $100 and a maximum of $1,000, plus court costs, attorney fees, and actual damages. In addition, the FTC can add a fine of up to $5,000 and/or a one-year imprisonment. If the required disclosures are not made or if the borrower is not given the required three days to cancel, the borrower can cancel the transaction at any time within three years after the date of the transaction. In that event, the creditor must return all money paid by the borrower, and the borrower returns the property to the creditor.

Right to Rescind

A borrower has a limited *right to rescission* (right to cancel) in a credit transaction. The borrower has three business days (which include Saturdays) to back out after signing the loan papers. This portion of the law was added primarily to protect a homeowner from unscrupulous sellers of home improvements and appliances when the credit to purchase is secured by a lien on the home. Vacant lots for sale on credit to buyers who expect to use them for principal residences are also subject to cancellation privileges. The right to rescind does not apply to credit used for the acquisition or initial construction of one's principal dwelling.

LOAN APPLICATION AND APPROVAL

When a mortgage lender reviews a real estate loan application, the primary concern for both applicant and lender is to approve loan requests that show a high probability of being repaid in full and on time, and to disapprove requests that are likely to result in default and eventual foreclosure. How is this decision made? Loan analysis varies. However, the five major federal agencies have recently combined their requirements for credit reports. All loans intended for underwriting by the Federal National Mortgage Association (Fannie Mae), the Federal Home Loan Mortgage Corporation (Freddie Mac), HUD, FHA, or the VA must comply with the new standards. Appendix E shows the Uniform Residential Loan Application (a requirement for standardized loan applications) and summarizes the key terms that a loan officer considers when making a decision regarding a loan request. Let's review these items and observe how they affect the acceptance of a loan by a lender. First, the borrower is requested to specify the type of mortgage and terms of the loan being sought. This greatly facilitates the lender's ability to determine the availability of the loan that the borrower may be seeking. Next, the lender will begin the loan analysis procedure by looking at the property and the proposed financing. Using the property address and legal description, an appraiser is assigned to prepare an appraisal of the property, and a title search is ordered. These steps are taken to determine the fair market value of the property and the condition of title. In the event of default, the property is the collateral the lender must fall back on to recover the loan. If the loan request is in connection with a purchase rather than the refinancing of an existing property, the lender will know the purchase price. As a rule, loans are made on the basis of the appraised value or purchase price, whichever is lower. If the appraised value is lower than the purchase price, the usual procedure is to require the buyer to make a larger cash down payment. The lender does not want to over-lend simply because the buyer overpaid for the property. Looking back at the subprime mortgage crisis of the late 2000s, one can see that the very protections put in place to protect lenders were violated as creative measures were employed to approve loans regardless of down payment, credit, appraisal or ability to pay. These measures led to record foreclosures and a collapse of the real estate market. Property owners found themselves with property that had debt far exceeding its value. When these owners had to sell, it was impossible to pay off their debt, and they were left with only foreclosure as an option. As the recession deepened, short sales became common lenders were gathering too much real estate inventory. All of this led to one of the longest real estate recessions this country has seen.

Settlement Funds

The lender wants to know whether the borrower has adequate funds for settlement. Are these funds in a checking or savings account, or are they coming from the sale of the borrower's property? In the latter case, the lender knows that the current loan is contingent on closing that escrow. If the down payment and settlement funds are to be borrowed, then the lender needs to be extra cautious, as experience has shown that the less money a borrower personally puts into a purchase, the higher the probability of default and foreclosure.

Purpose of Loan

The lender is also interested in the proposed use of the property. Lenders feel most comfortable when a loan is for the purchase or improvement of a property that the loan applicant will actually occupy. This is because owner-occupants usually have pride of ownership in maintaining their property and, even during bad economic conditions, will continue to make the monthly payments. An owner-occupant also realizes that losing the home still means paying for shelter elsewhere. It is standard practice for lenders to ask loan applicants to sign a statement declaring whether they intend to occupy the property.

If the loan applicant intends to purchase a dwelling to rent out as an investment, the lender will be more cautious because, during periods of high vacancy, the property may not generate enough income to meet the loan payments. At that point, a strapped-for-cash borrower is likely to default. Note, too, that lenders generally avoid loans secured by purely speculative real estate. If the value of the property drops below the amount owed, the borrower may see no further logic in making the loan payments.

Finally, the lender assesses the borrower's attitude toward the proposed loan. Someone with a casual attitude, such as, "I'm buying because real estate always goes up," or an applicant who does not appear to understand the obligation being undertaken, would bring a low rating here. Much more welcome is the applicant who shows a mature attitude and understanding of the loan obligation and who exhibits a strong and logical desire for ownership.

Borrower Analysis

In this section, the lender begins an analysis of the borrower and, if there is one, the co-borrower. At one time, age, sex, and marital status played an important role in the lender's decision to lend or not to lend. Often, the young and the elderly had trouble getting loans, as did women and persons who were single, divorced, or widowed. Today, the federal Equal Credit Opportunity Act prohibits discrimination based on age, sex, race, and marital status. Lenders are no longer permitted to discount income earned by women because a job is part-time or the woman is of childbearing age. If the applicant chooses to disclose it, alimony, separate maintenance, and child support must be counted in full. Young adults and single persons may not be turned down because the lender feels they have not "put down roots." Seniors may not be turned down as long as life expectancy exceeds the early risk period of the loan and collateral is adequate. In other words, the emphasis in borrower analysis is now on job stability, income adequacy, net worth, and credit rating.

Next in the loan application, we see questions directed at how long the applicant has held his/her current job and the stability of the job itself. An applicant who possesses marketable job skills and has been regularly employed with a stable employer is considered the ideal risk. Persons whose income can rise and fall erratically, such as commissioned salespersons, present greater risks. Persons whose skills (or lack thereof) or lack of job seniority result in frequent unemployment are more likely to have difficulty repaying a loan. In the application the lender also inquires as to the number of dependents the applicant must support from his/her income. This information provides some insight as to how much will be left over for monthly house payments.

Monthly Income

Next in the loan application, the lender considers the amount and sources of the applicant's income. Quantity alone is not enough for loan approval because the income sources must be stable, too. Thus, a lender will look carefully at overtime, bonus, and commission income to estimate the levels at which these may be expected to continue. Income from interest, dividends, and rentals is considered in light of the stability of its sources. Income from Social Security and retirement pensions is entered and added to the totals for the applicants. Alimony, child support, and separate maintenance payments received need not be revealed. However, such sums must be listed to be considered as a basis for repaying the loan.

Next in the loan application, the lender compares what the applicant has been paying for housing with what s/he will be paying if the loan is approved. Included in the proposed housing expense total are principal, interest, taxes, and insurance, along with any assessments or homeowner association dues (such as in a condominium). Some lenders add the monthly cost of utilities to this list.

Also, this portion of the loan application is where the lender will compare proposed monthly housing expense with gross monthly income. A general rule of thumb is that monthly housing expense (PITI) should not exceed 25% to 30% of gross monthly income. A second guideline is that total fixed monthly expenses should not exceed 33% to 38% of income. These include payments for housing, automobiles, installment loans, alimony, child support, and investments with negative cash flows. These are general guidelines, but lenders recognize that food, health care, clothing, transportation, entertainment, and income taxes must also come from the applicant's income. For instance, a location efficient mortgage (LEM) now being offered allows homeowners in urban areas to qualify for larger mortgages when they have significantly reduced transportation costs.

Assets and Liabilities

The lender is interested in the applicant's sources of funds for closing and whether, once the loan is granted, the applicant has assets to fall back on in the event of an income decrease (e.g., a job layoff) or unexpected expenses (e.g., hospital bills). Of particular interest is the portion of those assets in cash or readily convertible into cash in a few days. These are called **liquid assets**. If income drops, they are much more useful in meeting living expenses and loan payments than assets that may require months to sell and convert to cash—that is, assets that are *illiquid*.

liquid asset: an asset that is in cash or is readily convertible to cash

Note in this area of the loan application that two values are shown for life insurance. *Cash value* is the amount of money the policyholder would receive if the policy were surrendered to the insurance company, or, alternatively, the amount the policyholder could borrow against the policy. *Face amount* is the amount that would be paid in the event of the insured's death. Lenders feel most comfortable if the face amount of the policy equals or exceeds the amount of the proposed loan. Obviously, a borrower's death is not anticipated before the loan is repaid, but lenders recognize that its possibility increases the probability of default. The likelihood of foreclosure is lessened considerably if the survivors receive life insurance benefits.

The lender is interested in the applicant's existing debts and liabilities for two reasons. First, each month, these items compete with housing expenses for available monthly income. Thus, high monthly payments in this section of the application may lower the lender's estimate of what the applicant will be able to repay and, consequently, may influence the lender to reduce the size of the loan.

The presence of monthly liabilities is not all negative: It can also show the lender that the applicant is capable of repaying his/her debts. Second, the the applicant's total debts are subtracted from his/her total assets to obtain the applicant's *net worth*. If the result is negative (more owed than owned), the loan request will probably be turned down because it is too risky. In contrast, a substantial net worth can often offset weaknesses elsewhere in the application, such as too little monthly income in relation to monthly housing expense, or an income that can rise and fall erratically.

Declarations

The applicant will be asked to make a declaration concerning any situations that would reasonably call into question the applicant's ability to repay the loan, if approved. Applicants with a history of collections, adverse judgments, foreclosure, or bankruptcy will have to convince the lender that this loan will be repaid on time. Additionally, the applicant may be considered a poorer risk if s/he has guaranteed the repayment of someone else's debt by acting as a co-maker or endorser.

Redlining

redlining: a lender's refusal to make loans in certain neighborhoods

In the past, it was not uncommon for lenders to refuse to make loans in certain neighborhoods, regardless of the quality of the structure or the ability of the borrower to repay. This practice was known as **redlining**, and it effectively shut off mortgage loans in many older or so-called "bad-risk" neighborhoods across the country. Today, a lender may not refuse to make a loan simply because of the age or location of a property; the neighborhood income level; or the racial, ethnic, or religious composition of the neighborhood.

A lender *may* refuse to lend on a structure intended for demolition; a property in a known geological hazard area; a single-family dwelling in an area devoted to industrial or commercial use; or a property that is in violation of zoning laws, deed covenants, conditions or restrictions, or significant health, safety, or building codes.

Loan-to-Value Ratios

The lender next looks at the amount of down payment the borrower proposes to make, the size of the loan being requested, and the amount of other financing the borrower plans to use. This information is then converted into loan-to-value ratios. As a rule, the larger the down payment, the safer the loan for the lender. On an uninsured loan, the ideal loan-to-value (L/V) ratio for a lender on owner-occupied residential property is 70% or less. This means the value of the property would have to fall more than 30% before the debt owed would exceed the property's value, thus encouraging the borrower to stop making loan payments.

Loan-to-value ratios from 70% to 80% are considered acceptable but expose the lender to more risk. Lenders sometimes compensate by charging slightly higher interest rates. Loan-to-value ratios above 80% present even more risk of default to the lender, and the lender will either increase the interest rate charged on these loans or require insurance coverage from an outside insurer, such as the FHA or a private mortgage insurer.

Credit Report

As part of the loan application, the lender will order a **credit report** on the applicant(s). The applicant is asked to authorize this and to pay for the report. This provides the lender with an independent means of checking the applicant's credit history. A credit report that shows active use of credit with a good repayment record and no derogatory information is most desirable. The applicant will be asked by the lender to explain any negative information. Because it is possible for inaccurate or untrue information in a credit report to unfairly damage a person's credit reputation, Congress passed the **Fair Credit Reporting Act**. This Act gives individuals the right to inspect their file at a credit bureau, correct any errors, and make explanatory statements to supplement the file.

As previously discussed, the major federal agencies have combined their requirements for credit reports, and loans intended for underwriting by federal government agencies must comply with the new credit standards. Under these rules, the name of the consumer reporting agency must be clearly stated as well as the identities of those who ordered the report and those who are is paying for it. The information must be obtained from at least two national repositories for each area in which the borrower resided in the past two years, and must be verified for the previous two years. An explanation must be provided if the information is unavailable, and all questions must be responded to, even if the answer is "unable to verify." A history must be furnished, and all missing information must be verified by the lender. The history must have been checked within 90 days of the credit report, and the age of information that is not considered obsolete by the Fair Credit Reporting Act (7 years for general credit data or 10 years for bankruptcy) must be indicated. If any credit information is incomplete or if undisclosed information is discovered, the lender must have a personal interview with the borrower. The lender is additionally required to warrant that the credit report complies with all of the standards.

Real estate practitioners should be particularly aware of this law. If an applicant for rental of a property is rejected on the basis of a credit report, there are special disclosures (set out by federal law) that the owner, or the owner's agent, must make. If the applicant is rejected for reasons other than a credit report, the reasons must be disclosed. All disclosures must be made even if no request is made by the applicant.

credit report: a report reflecting the creditworthiness of a borrower by showing credit history

Fair Credit Reporting Act: federal law giving an individual the right to inspect his/her file with the credit bureau and correct any errors

Credit Scoring

A relatively new innovation, *credit scoring*, is being used as a method of evaluating credit risk. The scoring system is applied to a list of subjective factors that are considered relevant in evaluating credit risks. Credit scores are often shown on the credit report as additional information. It should be pointed out, however, that no standards exist for credit scoring. Most producers of credit scores are privately owned and maintain confidentiality regarding how the credit scores are calculated, stating that contractual arrangements between the producer and the credit reporting agencies prohibit disclosure of the factors that generated the score.

Fair Isaac Corporation (known as FICO) was the originator of the concept of credit scoring. While there are now other companies that have developed their own models, FICO is still considered to be the Granddaddy. For all practical purposes, all lenders use one or more of these models in the loan approval process. Lenders maintain that these scores provide a better assessment of how customers will perform on loan payments and allow them to better balance the credit risk they take into their loan portfolios. The scores generally run from about 500 to 850. A score of 720 or higher will get the borrower the most favorable interest rate on a mortgage. As the interest rate charged by the lender may vary depending on the applicant's credit score, bad credit can result in paying significantly higher interest rates, which, with the term of the loan, can be a huge differential in payments.

How can borrowers improve their credit scores? Fair Isaac uses five factors, each of which is weighted differently. They include type of credit use (10%), application for new credit (10%), length of credit history (15%), payment history (35%), and amounts owed (30%). The most important factors in evaluating credit are payment history and amounts owed. Most creditors suggest that you check your credit score frequently and correct any blatant errors that may show up (identity theft is a major problem). Other factors considered in creating the credit score include paying your bills on time, consistently reducing your credit card balances (and keeping them below 25% of your credit card limit), and not "moving debt around" by transferring debts to different credit cards or other sources of debt. Lots of information on how to improve your credit score is available through the FICO website at www.myfico.com.

FHA uses a credit scoring procedure called "TOTAL," an acronym for "Technology Open to Approved Lenders." The program assesses creditworthiness for FHA borrowers by evaluating certain mortgage applications and credit information to accurately predict the likelihood of a borrower default. It is intended to be used along with the FHA's automated underwriting system.

Subprime Loans

There continues to be a market for *subprime loans*. While the best borrowers with the best credit documentation and the best credit scores can negotiate the best interest rates and terms, there are lenders who cater to another market: borrowers with limited or blemished credit. These loans have risk-based pricing, which is reflected in higher interest rates. Subprime loan terms are not set in stone, and a borrower may find it beneficial to shop for credit. Lenders who work in this market have different criteria and profile the risk a borrower presents differently. Shopping this network may save tens of thousands of dollars over the life of a loan.

PREDATORY LENDING

In the next chapter, we are going to discuss sources of financing. There are many sources of financing readily available to most consumers, but a lot of consumers lack the knowledge to evaluate lending practices and are often preyed upon by unscrupulous lenders who are taking advantage of that lack of knowledge. In general terms, the industry refers to this as *predatory lending*.

The Mortgage Bankers Association has identified 12 practices considered to be predatory. These are: (1) steering borrowers/buyers to high-rate lenders; (2) engaging in the practice of intentionally structuring high-cost loans with payments the borrower cannot afford; (3) falsifying loan documents; (4) making loans to mentally incapacitated homeowners; (5) forging signatures on loan documents; (6) changing the loan terms at closing; (7) requiring credit insurance; (8) falsely identifying loans as lines of credit or open-end mortgages; (9) increasing interest charges for loan payments when loan payments are late; (10) charging excessive prepayment penalties or excessive charges for preparing releases; (11) failing to report good payment on borrowers' credit reports; and (12) failing to provide accurate loan balance and payoff amounts, a practice that includes not responding in a timely manner to credit inquiries for payoff information.

Coupled with the lending practices are shoddy appraisals made by unscrupulous appraisers to falsely inflate the value of the house. This behavior allows a borrower to: (1) make no down payment, or (2) resell property shortly after closing for large profits to a "straw man" who will not make any payments on the loan. A false appraisal dupes the lender into making too large a loan on the property. Most states are curbing this practice through legislation against predatory lending and mortgage fraud. In 2002, Georgia passed the Georgia Fair Lending Act, considered to be one of the toughest predatory lending laws in the nation—maybe too tough. It was substantially amended in 2003 because many lenders were choosing not to make their products available in Georgia due to the lack of definition of predatory lending and substantial penalties for violation. Whenever a real estate transaction is not "straight up," with an acceptable loan-to-value ratio and a defined down payment procedure, it is going to be suspect. If it doesn't "smell" right, or if information is being withheld from the lender during the closing, don't do it.

Review Questions

Answers to these questions can be found in Appendix D at the end of this book.

1. All of the following are exempt from the provisions of the federal Truth in Lending Act EXCEPT:
   A. commercial loans
   B. personal property loans in excess of $50,000
   C. financing extended to corporations
   D. consumer loans to natural persons

2. Which of the following loans would be exempt from the disclosure requirements of the Truth in Lending Act?
   A. an unsecured personal loan of $3,000
   B. an education loan from a commercial bank
   C. a second mortgage loan on a residence
   D. a $60,000 loan for the purchase of an $80,000 automobile

3. Penalties for violation of the Truth in Lending Act would not include:
   A. a fine of up to $5,000 and/or imprisonment for up to one year
   B. civil penalties of up to twice the amount of the finance charge up to a maximum of $1,000
   C. court costs, attorney fees, and actual damages
   D. $20,000-per-day civil penalty

4. Which of the following would violate the advertising requirements of the Truth in Lending Act?
   A. payments less than rent
   B. interest rates at historical lows
   C. down payments of less than $3,000
   D. long-term financing available

5. Which of the following is generally NOT a requirement of loan approval?
   A. having sufficient funds for the down payment
   B. signing a statement if the borrower intends to occupy the property
   C. having a job
   D. having sufficient income

6. Which of the following is given consideration in evaluation of a loan application?
   A. race
   B. marital status
   C. sex
   D. income adequacy

7. A lender may legally discriminate in loan terms based on the applicant's:
   A. religion
   B. marital status
   C. race or skin color
   D. intention to occupy (or not occupy) the mortgaged property

8. The right of individuals to inspect their files at a credit bureau is found in:
   A. the Truth in Lending Act
   B. the Fair Credit Reporting Act
   C. Regulation Z
   D. the Federal Consumer Credit Protection Act

9. The abbreviation APR stands for:
   A. average percentage rate
   B. allotted percentage rate
   C. approximate percentage rate
   D. annual percentage rate

10. The APR is:
    A. usually lower than the interest rate
    B. made up of the interest rate combined with the other costs of the loan
    C. the total dollar amount of the costs to borrow
    D. lowered when closing costs are paid by the borrower

CHAPTER 14
SOURCES OF FINANCING

KEY TERMS

alienation clause
automated underwriting systems
computerized loan origination
disintermediation
Fannie Mae
Freddie Mac
Ginnie Mae
mortgage broker
mortgage company
participation certificate
primary market
secondary mortgage market
usury

OBJECTIVES

After successful completion of this chapter, you should be able to:

1. describe the primary and secondary sources of mortgage money;
2. describe various loan programs and the roles of lenders and mortgage brokers;
3. explain the purpose and characteristics of FNMA and FHLMC; and
4. define mortgage terms and concepts such as usury, alienation clauses, and prepayment penalties.

OVERVIEW

After reading this chapter, you will be able to: (1) identify various mortgage lenders (the primary market), (2) describe where these lenders get much of their money (the secondary market), and (3) explain provisions of mortgage loan instruments that have an impact on the cost of funds. Many people feel that understanding the financing market is the most important of all real estate topics because, without financing, real estate profits and commissions would be difficult to achieve.

PRIMARY MARKET

The **primary market** (also called the *primary mortgage market*) is where lenders originate loans—that is, where lenders make funds available to borrowers. The primary market is what the borrower sees as the source of mortgage loan money, that is, the institution with which the borrower has direct and personal contact. It's the place where the loan application is taken, where the loan officer interviews the loan applicant, where the loan check comes from, and the place to which loan payments are sent by the borrower.

These sources of funds generally can be divided into two markets: (1) those markets regulated by the federal government, and (2) those markets that are not regulated by the government. The regulated lenders are commercial banks, savings and loan (S&L) associations, and savings banks. The unregulated lenders are commercial finance companies, investment bankers, life insurance companies, and finance companies. Unregulated sources of funds are not subject to the same restrictive regulations that are designed to protect the lender with deposits insured by the federal government. The regulated lenders are subject to examination by federal regulators, pay risk-based premiums on their deposit insurance, and are restricted to certain loan-to-value ratios. In today's markets, a purchaser is wise to contact both regulated and unregulated lenders to make an adequate comparison of available loan money. Markets differ widely within states and even within certain urban areas.

Most borrowers assume that the loan they receive comes from depositors who visit the same bank or S&L to leave their excess funds. This is partly true. But this, by itself, is an inadequate source of loan funds in today's market. Thus, primary lenders often sell their loans in what is called the *secondary market*. Insurance companies, pension funds, and individual investors, as well as other primary lenders with excess deposits, buy these loans for cash. This makes more money available to a primary lender who, in turn, can lend these additional funds to borrowers. The secondary market is so huge that it rivals the entire U.S. corporate bond market in the size of annual offerings. We discuss the secondary market later in this chapter. Meanwhile, let's discuss the various lenders a borrower will encounter when looking for a real estate loan.

primary market: the market in which lenders originate loans and make funds available to borrowers

SAVINGS AND LOAN ASSOCIATIONS

Historically, the origin of savings and loan associations can be traced to early building societies in England and Germany and to the first American building society, the Oxford Provident Building Association, started in 1831 in Pennsylvania. These early building societies were cooperatives whose savers were also borrowers. As times progressed, savings and loan associations became a primary source of residential real estate loans. To encourage residential lending, the federally chartered savings and loans were required by federal regulation to hold at least 80% of their assets in residential loans. In addition, they were subjected to special tax laws that permitted a savings and loan association to defer payment of income taxes on profits, as long as those profits were held in surplus accounts and not distributed to the savings and loan association's owners. During this same period, there were also limits on the interest rate that could be paid on savings accounts. This provided the savings and loan associations with a dependable source of funds at a fixed interest rate, which gave them the potential for making long-term loans at reasonable rates. For instance, if the passbook savings account was limited to 5.25% per annum, home loans in the vicinity of 7.5% to 8.5% would still allow for reasonable profit margins. Unfortunately, the nature of the finance markets began to change in the late 1970s when an inflationary economy caused interest rates to skyrocket. This change created problems that were unforeseen by the savings and loan industry. Many states had *usury* laws, which capped the rate a lender could charge. With the runaway inflation our nation was experiencing, these capped rates were lower than the market for lending. These usury laws in Georgia were repealed in the late 1970s.

Disintermediation

In addition to ordinary passbook accounts, savings and loans offer *certificates of deposit* (CDs) at rates higher than passbook rates in order to attract depositors. These rates are necessary to compete with higher yields offered by U.S. Treasury bills, notes, and bonds, and to prevent disintermediation. **Disintermediation** results when depositors take money out of their savings accounts and invest directly in government securities, corporate bonds, and money market funds. A major problem—and one that nearly brought the S&L industry to its knees in the late 1970s and early 1980s—was that S&Ls traditionally relied heavily on short-term deposits from savers and then lent that money on long-term (often 30-year) loans to borrowers. When interest rates rose sharply in the 1970s, S&Ls either had to raise the interest paid to their depositors or watch depositors withdraw their savings and take the money elsewhere for higher returns. Meanwhile, the S&Ls were holding long-term, fixed-rate mortgage loans and, with interest rates rising, borrowers were not eager to repay those loans early.

disintermediation: the process of individuals investing funds directly, often in government funds, instead of placing their money in banks and other such institutions, thus creating a scarcity of money available for traditional lending

Restructuring the System

Disintermediation was only the beginning of the problems. Loan demand at S&Ls was declining. In 1976, 57% of the residential mortgage loans were held by savings and loan institutions. By 2000, the percentage fell to 13%. There are many reasons for this flow of funds out of the S&L industry. One of the primary reasons, however, appears to be the deregulation of the lending industry. This, coupled with bad investments, inadequately trained executives, and loose government controls on S&L risks and investments, resulted in an industry that could not remain solvent.

In August 1989, President George H. W. Bush signed into law a sweeping revision of the regulatory authorities governing savings and loans. This law is referred to as the Financial Institutions Reform, Recovery, and Enforcement Act of 1989, commonly called FIRREA. The law redefined or created seven new regulatory authorities and initiated a system of federally designated real property appraisers, discussed in greater detail in Chapter 18. Because federal regulations of commercial banks and savings and loans are virtually the same, the difference between savings and loans and commercial banks as a primary source of funds is indistinguishable to the average borrower.

COMMERCIAL BANKS

The nation's 6,500 commercial banks store far more of the country's money than the S&Ls. However, only one bank dollar in six goes to real estate lending. Of the loans made by banks for real estate, the tendency is to emphasize short-term maturities and adjustable-rate mortgages because the bulk of a bank's deposit money comes from demand deposits (checking accounts), and a much smaller portion from savings and time deposits.

Oddly enough, the same factors that have plagued the S&Ls helped the commercial banks. During the Deregulation Acts of 1980 and 1982, banks began making more home loans, but they were short-term, with adjustable rates. These types of loans avoid the problem of disintermediation, as the loan rates can rise with the rates that are required by the source of funds. Commercial banks, too, have realized that first-lien residential loans are very secure, low-risk loans. Banks have also determined that maintaining all of a customer's loan accounts, including a home loan, in the bank's portfolio provides a market advantage. "One-stop banking" has become a very successful marketing tool. The merger of many banks into large, multistate national banks has created a larger source of funds to lend. To accommodate higher demand and facilitate the organization of sources of funds for the bank's lending purposes, many banks have organized their own mortgage departments to assist customers in making home loans, sometimes through sources other than bank deposits.

In 1999, Congress passed the Financial Services Modernization (FSM) Act, which lifted banking restrictions imposed by legislation dating back to 1933. The new legislation allows banks to become one-stop financial conglomerates marketing a range of financial products, such as annuities, certificates of deposit, stocks, and bonds, creating a tremendous potential for cross-marketing in very large banks. This diversification may have a far-reaching impact on future banking practices, including the availability of mortgage money and other financial services to homeowners.

During the 2007–2010 global financial crisis, the term "too big to fail" became almost a household term. The belief is that some institutions are so big and influential that if they were allowed to fail, they could bring the entire economy down with them. In 2008, the federal government implemented the Troubled Asset Relief Program (TARP). The TARP program was created to purchase assets and equities from financial institutions to strengthen the financial sector. Only time will tell if the short-term benefit of such programs will be ultimately beneficial.

Life Insurance Companies

As a group, the nation's life insurance companies have long been active investors in real estate as developers, owners, and long-term lenders. Although not federally regulated, life insurance companies are subject to state regulations. Their source of money is the premiums paid by policyholders. These premiums are invested and ultimately returned to the policyholders. Because premiums are collected in regular amounts on regular dates, and because policy payoffs can be calculated from actuarial tables, life insurers are in ideal positions to commit money to long-term investments. Life insurance companies channel their funds primarily into government and corporate bonds and real estate. The dollars allocated to real estate go to buy land and buildings, which are leased to users, and to make loans on commercial, industrial, and residential property. Generally, life insurers specialize in large-scale investments such as shopping centers, office and apartment buildings, and million-dollar blocks of home loans purchased in the *secondary mortgage market,* which is discussed later in this chapter. Repayment terms on loans made by insurance companies for shopping centers, office buildings, and apartment complexes sometimes call for interest and a percentage of any profits from rentals over a certain level. These *participation loans,* which provide a "piece of the action" for the insurance company, also provide the insurance company with more inflation protection than a fixed rate of interest.

MORTGAGE COMPANIES

mortgage company: a firm that makes mortgage loans and then sells them to investors

A **mortgage company** makes a mortgage loan and then sells it to a long-term investor. The process begins with locating borrowers, qualifying them, preparing the necessary loan papers, and, finally, making the loans. Once a loan is made, it is sold for cash on the secondary market. The mortgage company will usually continue to service the loan—that is, collect the monthly payments and handle such matters as insurance and property tax impounds, delinquencies, early payoffs, and mortgage releases.

Mortgage companies, also known as *mortgage bankers,* vary in size from one or two persons to several dozen. As a rule, they close loans in their own names and are locally oriented, finding and making loans within 25 or 50 miles of their offices. This gives them a feel for their market, greatly aids in identifying sound loans, and makes loan servicing much easier. For their efforts, mortgage bankers typically receive 1% to 3% of the amount of the loan when it is originated, and from 0.25% to 0.5% of the outstanding balance each year thereafter for servicing. Mortgage banking, as this business is called, is not limited to mortgage companies. Commercial banks, savings and loan associations, and mutual savings banks in active real estate areas often originate more real estate loans than they can hold themselves, and these are sold on the secondary market. As the shift in mortgage origination continues, it is important to note that the mortgage brokers' share of originations will probably continue to increase. Mortgage brokerage, discussed below, allows the originator to process loans without the long-term risk associated with borrower default, which came to the forefront during the financial crisis experienced in the late 2000s. Many of the traditional mortgage companies now also provide mortgage brokerage services.

MORTGAGE BROKERS

Mortgage brokers, in contrast to mortgage bankers, specialize in bringing together borrowers and lenders, just as real estate brokers bring together buyers and sellers. The mortgage broker does not lend money and usually does not service loans. The mortgage broker's fee is expressed in points and is usually paid by the borrower. Mortgage brokers are often small, locally oriented firms of fewer than 10 people. They seldom make loans in their own names as lenders.

mortgage broker: one who brings together borrowers and lenders

The mortgage brokering businesses actually felt an explosion during the late 1980s and early 1990s. The secondary market (discussed later in this chapter) has made investors' funds more readily available, and virtually anyone with some expertise in loan qualifications could originate loans and sell to secondary market purchasers. As a result, the federal government has required that states implement a licensing procedure for loan originators.

In the Field

The Real Estate Settlement Procedures Act (RESPA) has been strengthened over the years and requires a real service to be performed when receiving a fee. While some in the past saw this as a gray area, it has turned pretty much black and white. While the real estate practitioner may interact with some pretty aggressive and creative individuals, be cautious in crossing this line. You may be offered fees or compensation to refer your clients to particular lenders, attorneys, home warranty companies, etc. It is clear that RESPA will not allow this act. Some try to get creative in circumventing this legislation. I would simply ask you, "Is potentially having to defend yourself in federal court against the federal government using federal prosecutors being paid with YOUR tax money worth taking a chance on a questionable fee of maybe a few hundred dollars?"

COMPUTERIZED LOAN ORIGINATION

computerized loan origination: originating loans through the use of a networked computer system

The growth of computer networks has also enabled many independent loan processors to work under the guidance of large lending institutions and mortgage companies. Using a **computerized loan origination (CLO)**, real estate brokers, attorneys, insurance agents, or mortgage companies can arrange to have a computer link installed in their offices, which is connected to lenders' mainframe computers. By answering a series of questions, borrowers can obtain preliminary loan approval immediately from the loan originator and a firm acceptance or rejection from the lending institution within a few days.

A full-featured CLO has three basic functions: (1) It provides information on current market mortgage loan terms and types, (2) it conveys loan application information electronically, and (3) it monitors the loan approval process so that the practitioner can check on the progress of the loan application at any time. From the home buyer's perspective, the CLO provides the convenience of seeking home financing alternatives without calling and visiting a large number of local lenders, and, in many cases, it can increase the number of choices available. A broker should exercise caution, however, as conflicts can exist.

> **In the Field**
>
> RESPA regulations greatly limit the use of CLOs by real estate agents, so legal counsel should be consulted before a practitioner attempts to utilize a CLO as a second source of income.

MUNICIPAL BONDS

In some cities, *municipal bonds* provide a source of mortgage money for home buyers. The special advantage to borrowers is that municipal bonds pay interest that is free from federal income taxes. Knowing this, bond investors will accept a lower rate of interest than they would if the interest were taxable—as it normally is on mortgage loans. The savings are passed on to the buyer. Those who qualify will typically pay about 2% less than if they had borrowed through conventional channels. Municipal bonds have had limited use in Georgia to help stimulate the real estate market and economy in general. The most widely known of these is the Georgia Residential Finance Authority now known as the Georgia Housing and Finance Authority (GHFA).

The objective of such programs is to make homeownership more affordable for low- and middle-income households. A city may stipulate that loans be used in neighborhoods the city wants to revitalize. The loans are made by local lenders, who are paid a fee for originating and servicing these loans. Although they're popular with the real estate industry, the U.S. Treasury has been less than enthusiastic about the concept because it bears the cost in lost tax revenues. As a result, federal legislation has been passed to limit the future use of this source of money.

OTHER LENDERS

Pension funds and trust funds traditionally have channeled their money to high-grade government and corporate bonds and stocks. However, the trend now is to place more money into real estate loans. Already active buyers on the secondary market, pension funds and trust funds will likely become still larger sources of real estate financing in the future. In some localities, pension fund members can tap their own pension funds for home mortgages at very reasonable rates. Pension funds are an often-overlooked source of primary market financing.

Finance companies that specialize in making business and consumer loans also provide limited financing for real estate. As a rule, finance companies seek second mortgages at interest rates 2% to 5% higher than the rates prevailing on first mortgages. First mortgages are also taken as collateral; however, the lenders usually charge lower interest rates for these loans and thus are more competitive.

Credit unions normally specialize in consumer loans. However, real estate loans are becoming more and more important as many of the country's credit unions have branched out into first and second mortgage loans. Credit unions are an often-overlooked but excellent source of home loan money.

Individuals are sometimes a source of cash loans for real estate. The bulk of these loans are made between relatives or friends, often as investments with their IRAs or private pension plans that require a low-risk investment with attractive rates. Generally, loan maturities are shorter than those obtainable from the institutional lenders already described. In some cities, persons can be found who specialize in making or buying second and third mortgage loans of up to 10-year maturities. Individuals are also beginning to invest substantial amounts of money in secondary mortgage market securities. Ironically, these investments are often made with money that would have otherwise been deposited in a savings and loan.

SECONDARY MARKET

The *secondary market* (also called the **secondary mortgage market**) provides a way for a lender to sell a loan. It also permits investment in real estate loans without the need for loan origination and servicing facilities. Although not directly encountered by real estate buyers, sellers, and agents, the secondary market plays an important role in getting money from those who want to lend to those who want to borrow. In other words, think of the secondary market as a pipeline for loan money. Visualize that pipeline running via the Wall Street financial district in New York City. Wall Street (particularly Fannie Mae and Freddie Mac) is a major participant in residential mortgage lending. Figure 14-1 illustrates this pipeline and diagrams key differences between the traditional mortgage delivery system and the secondary market system.

secondary mortgage market: a market in which mortgage loans can be sold to investors

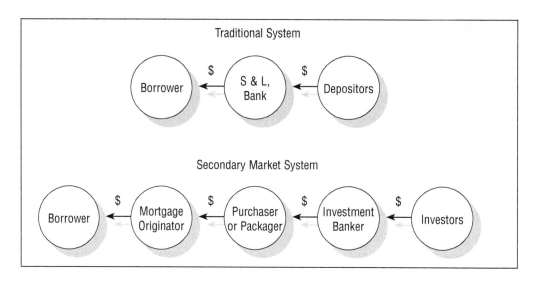

FIGURE 14-1 Mortgage loan delivery system
Source: © 2021 Mbition LLC

Traditional Delivery System

Notice in Figure 14-1 that, in the traditional system, the lender is a local institution gathering deposits from the community and then lending that money as real estate loans in the same community. Traditionally, each lender (S&L, bank, commercial bank, credit union) was an independent unit that developed its own appraisal technique, loan application form, loan approval criteria, note and mortgage forms, servicing method, and foreclosure policy. Nonetheless, three major problems needed solving. The first occurred when an institution had an imbalance of depositors and borrowers. Rapidly growing areas of the United States often needed more loan money than their savers were capable of depositing. Stable regions had more depositors than loan opportunities. Thus, it was common to see correspondent relationships between lenders. For example, a lender in Los Angeles would sell some of its mortgage loans to a savings bank in Brooklyn. This provided loans for borrowers and interest for savers. The system worked well, but it required individual correspondent relationships.

The second problem occurred when depositors wanted to withdraw their money from their accounts and invest it in other sources. Lenders, seeking to attract these depositors, raised their interest rates, which resulted in loan rates increasing.

The third problem was timing. Lenders must borrow "short" (from their deposit relationships) and lend "long" (30-year mortgages). Savers, then, were encouraged to leave their money on deposit for longer periods of time.

The answer to these three problems is relatively simple: Find a market where investors will pay cash for your loans, and reimburse the primary lender. The result is that the investor is willing to hold the loan long term for its guaranteed rate of return. The primary lender continues to make loans, gambling that it will find another investor in the secondary market to buy that loan for a long term. In effect, the primary lenders can make loans from the secondary market funds instead of their own deposits.

Secondary Market Delivery Systems

As shown in Figure 14-1, with the secondary market system, the borrower obtains a loan from a mortgage originator. These include mortgage companies, banks, CLOs, and thrifts that originate loans they intend to sell. The mortgage originator packages the loan with other loans and then either sells the package as a whole or keeps the package and sells securities that are backed by the loans in the package. If the originator is not large enough to package its own mortgages, it will sell the loans to someone who is.

There are now two sources for this secondary market. The first is private investors such as commercial banks, savings and loans, pension plans, trust funds, and other investors who are looking for low-risk, long-term returns on their investments. The second group of investors—relatively new in the investment business—is the investment *pools* or *poolers* who are looking for more security in their investments. This results in two primary investors in the secondary market: (1) the pure portfolio purchasers who are looking for the initial investments with an attractive return; and (2) the poolers who are looking for the longer-term, more stable return.

STANDARDIZED LOAN PROCEDURES

A major stumbling block to a highly organized and efficient secondary market has been the uniqueness of both lenders and loans. Traditionally, each primary lender developed its own special loan forms and procedures. Moreover, each loan is a unique combination of real estate and borrower. No two are exactly alike. How, then, do you combine such diversity into an attractive package for investors? A large part of the answer has come through standardized loan application forms; standardized appraisal forms; standardized credit report forms; standardized closing statements; standardized loan approval criteria; and standardized promissory notes, mortgages, and trust deeds. Loan terms have been standardized into categories such as fixed-rate 30-year loans, fixed-rate 15-year loans, and various adjustable-rate combinations. Additionally, nearly all loans must be insured. This can take the form of FHA or private mortgage insurance, or a VA guarantee on each loan in the package. Additionally, there will be some form of assurance of timely repayment of the mortgage package as a whole. The net result is a mortgage security that is attractive to investors who in the past have not been interested in investing in mortgages.

CHAPTER 14 Sources of Financing

Let's now look at some of the key secondary market participants, including the giants of the industry: the Federal National Mortgage Association, the Government National Mortgage Association, the Federal Home Loan Mortgage Corporation, and the Federal Agricultural Mortgage Corporation.

FEDERAL NATIONAL MORTGAGE ASSOCIATION (FNMA)

The *Federal National Mortgage Association (FNMA)* was organized by the federal government in 1938 to buy FHA mortgage loans from lenders. This made it possible for lenders to grant more loans to consumers. Ten years later, it began purchasing VA loans. FNMA (fondly known in the real estate business and to itself as **Fannie Mae**) was successful in its mission.

In 1968, Congress divided FNMA into two organizations: the Government National Mortgage Association (to be discussed in the next section) and FNMA as we know it today. As part of that division, FNMA changed from a government agency to a private profit-making corporation, chartered by Congress but owned by its shareholders and managed independently of the government. This changed in 2008. In light of substantial financial losses and charges of mismanagement, FNMA came under the conservatorship of the Federal Housing Finance Agency (FHFA) on September 7, 2008. Although Fannie Mae is still a major player in the secondary market, its stock was delisted from the New York Stock Exchange in 2010.

Fannie Mae buys FHA, VA, and conventional home loans from lenders across the United States. Money to buy these loans comes from the sale of FNMA stock plus the sale of FNMA bonds and notes. FNMA bond and note holders look to Fannie Mae for timely payment of principal and interest on these bonds and notes, and Fannie Mae looks to its mortgagors for principal and interest payments on the loans it owns. Thus, Fannie Mae stands in the middle and, although it is very careful to match interest rates and maturities between the loans it buys and the bonds and notes it sells, it still takes the risk of the middleman. In this respect, it is like a giant thrift institution.

Commitments

Fannie Mae's method of operation is to sell commitments to lenders pledging to buy specified dollar amounts of mortgage loans within a fixed period of time, usually at a specified yield. Lenders are not obligated to sell loans to Fannie Mae if they can find better terms elsewhere. However, Fannie Mae must purchase all loans delivered to it under the terms of the commitments. Loans must be made using FNMA-approved forms and loan approval criteria. As of 2020, the largest loan Fannie Mae would buy was $510,400 for a single-family unit. This limit is adjusted each year as housing prices change. Fannie Mae also buys loans on duplexes, triplexes, and fourplexes, all at larger loan limits. Although the FNMA loan limit may seem inadequate for some houses and neighborhoods, the intention of Congress is that Fannie Mae cater to the mid-range of housing prices and leave the upper end of the market to others.

Fannie Mae: a real estate industry nickname for the Federal National Mortgage Association

In addition to purchasing first mortgages, Fannie Mae also purchases second mortgages from lenders. The loan limit on second mortgages is typically 50% of the limit for first mortgages. FNMA forms and criteria must be used, and the loan-to-value ratio of the combined first and second mortgages may not exceed 80% if owner-occupied and 70% if not owner-occupied. This is a very helpful program for those who have watched the value of their homes increase and want to borrow against that increase without first having to repay the existing mortgage loan. Of course, if values have dropped, this program is likely not appropriate. Updates on these loan limits are available on the Frequently Asked Questions section of the Fannie Mae website: www.fanniemae.com.

FNMA Pooling

The demand for loans in the primary market could not match the demand that investors required in the secondary market, so Fannie Mae began purchasing large blocks of mortgage loans and assigning them to specified pools with an "agency guarantee" certificate that guaranteed long-term return to the pool investors. Fannie Mae guarantees to pass through to the certificate holders whatever principal, interest, and prepayments of principal are generated by the loans into the underlying pool of mortgage investors. Fannie Mae's pooling arrangements undertook the issuance of *mortgage-backed securities (MBS)*. Utilizing this system of issuing securities that are backed by mortgages, the securities markets could then be used as a source for investment funds. As late as 2008, the combination of FNMA and the smaller Federal Home Loan Mortgage Corporation (Freddie Mac for short) either owned or guaranteed almost one-half of the nation's $12 trillion mortgage market. In late 2008, FNMA was in financial trouble with burdensome foreclosures and nonperforming loans. What had once seemed like the cure for the financial markets became the disease. In June of 2010, with the stock price falling below $1, Fannie and Freddie were delisted from the New York Stock Exchange and, at the time of this writing, are still traded as over-the-counter stocks.

Revised Lending Practices

In 1992, as pressure increased from both Congress and the U.S. Department of Housing and Urban Development (HUD) to become more socially responsible in lending practices, Congress passed legislation requiring stricter supervision of Fannie Mae by a HUD-appointed oversight committee. Fannie Mae had also very aggressively adopted practices to provide affordable housing. Unfortunately, this very noble idea to help those in need was arguably a catalyst of the housing collapse. Not the only issue, but one issue.

GOVERNMENT NATIONAL MORTGAGE ASSOCIATION (GNMA)

The *Government National Mortgage Association (GNMA,* popularly known to the industry and to itself as **Ginnie Mae**) was created in 1968 when FNMA

Ginnie Mae: a federal agency that has some low-income housing functions but is best known for its mortgage-backed securities (MBS) program was partitioned into two separate corporations. Ginnie Mae is a federal agency entirely within HUD. Although Ginnie Mae has some low-income housing functions, it is best known for its mortgage-backed securities (MBS) program. As previously discussed, the MBS program attracts additional sources of credit to FHA, VA, and certain Rural Housing Service mortgages. Ginnie Mae does this by guaranteeing timely repayment of privately issued securities backed by pools of these mortgages. Remember that the FNMA MBS program offers "agency guarantees" for its investors. GNMA offers a government guarantee of repayment.

Ginnie Mae Procedures

Ginnie Mae is limited to underwriting only HUD/FHA, VA, and certain other loans. It is not possible to purchase loans as both FNMA and FHLMC (discussed next). Ginnie Mae sets its own requirements for loans that can be accepted into its mortgage pool, then it subsequently approves loan poolers who are committed to complying with those requirements. Ginnie Mae must examine the loans and the loan poolers before it can determine its ability to guarantee those loans into the loan pooler source of funds. The result is that Ginnie Mae issues guarantee certificates, popularly known as "Ginnie Maes." The sole purpose of Ginnie Mae today is to guarantee the timely payment of the principal and interest to the investor, with this guarantee backed by the full faith and credit of the U.S. government.

FEDERAL HOME LOAN MORTGAGE CORPORATION

Freddie Mac: a real estate industry nickname for the Federal Home Loan Mortgage Corporation

The *Federal Home Loan Mortgage Corporation (FHLMC,* also known to the industry and to itself as **Freddie Mac**) was created by Congress in 1970. Its goal, like that of FNMA and GNMA, is to increase the availability of financing for residential mortgages. FHLMC differs in that Freddie Mac deals primarily in conventional mortgages. Freddie Mac was initially established to serve as a secondary market for S&L members of the Federal Home Loan Bank System. More than 3,000 savings associations originally held the ownership of Freddie Mac. In 1988, the shares were released and sold publicly by the savings associations. Unlike Ginnie Mae, which guarantees securities issued by others, Freddie Mac issues its own securities against its own mortgage pools. These securities are its **participation certificates** and collateralized mortgage obligations. As is the case with Fannie Mae, Freddie Mac came under the conservatorship of the Federal Housing Finance Agency in September of 2008.

participation certificate: a certificate representing an undivided interest in a Freddie Mac pool

The Future of the Government Secondary Market

As we have discussed, the government secondary market was created in the 1930s as a way to guarantee liquidity for the primary mortgage market. This system seemed to work relatively well for some 70 years, but then the Achilles heel was bared from 2005 to 2010. You can do your own research and find there are fingers pointing in every direction. Some blame too much regulation, while others blame too little; some blame the investors, while others blame the consumers; some blame accounting errors, while others blame accounting fraud, while each political party seems to blame the other. It is not my intention, nor would it be appropriate for me, to use this space to promote my own beliefs, understandings, or agendas. If you are reading this, likely, you just want to pass your Georgia real estate exam, and we can leave the debate to others for another day. There is, however, one thing I believe all can agree on. The real estate meltdown that seemed to start around 2007 (I think we are yet to discover when it will truly end) exposed some weaknesses in our system. Prior to 1930, few thought the stock market could crash. Prior to 2007, few thought there could ever be an extended real estate recession. Will Fannie Mae and Freddie Mac survive? I certainly think so. Will they survive as managed up to 2008? Likely not. I believe the future will bring reorganization to the financial and mortgage markets and begin a new era of prosperity. As someone much smarter than I once said, "America has one of the worst political and financial systems in the world, with the exception of all the others." Just call me the eternal optimist.

Farmer Mac

The newest agency created by Congress to underwrite loan pools is the *Federal Agricultural Mortgage Corporation,* known as Farmer Mac. The Agricultural Credit Act of 1987 established Farmer Mac as a separate agency within the Farm Credit System to establish the secondary market needed for farm real estate loans. Farmer Mac started actual operations in 1989. Originally, Farmer Mac functioned similarly to Ginnie Mae in that it certified loan poolers rather than purchase loans. Farmer Mac guaranteed timely repayment of principal and interest in the loan but did not guarantee any individual loans within that pool. In 1996, Congress passed the Farm Credit System Reform Act allowing Farmer Mac to act as a pooler for qualified loans. Farmer Mac is now permitted to purchase loans directly from originators and to issue its own 100% guaranteed securities backed by the loans. For the first time, Farmer Mac became a true secondary market.

Loan Qualification

To qualify for a pool, a loan must be collateralized by agricultural real estate located in the United States. The real estate can include a home, which must cost no more than $100,000, and must be located in a rural community with a population of 2,500 or less. The maximum loan is $2.5 million or the amount secured by no more than 1,000 acres, whichever is larger. The loan-to-value ratio must be less than 80%, and the borrower must be a U.S. citizen engaged in agriculture who must demonstrate a capability to repay the loan.

Federal Housing Finance Agency (FHFA)

FHFA (NOT to be confused with the Federal Housing Administration or FHA) was created as several federal agencies were essentially merged into one in 2008. FHFA has the role of regulating Fannie Mae, Freddie Mac, and the Federal Home Loan Banks. It was under FHFA that Fannie Mae and Freddie Mac were put under conservatorship in September 2008. In 2011, FHFA filed suit against multiple financial institutions, accusing them of misrepresenting about $200 billion in mortgage-backed securities sold to Fannie Mae and Freddie Mac. These suits sought damages and penalties.

Private Conduits

The financial success of the three giants of the secondary mortgage market (FNMA, GNMA, and FHLMC) has brought private mortgage packagers into the marketplace. The 1990s saw substantial growth in commercial loan funding for the sale of mortgage bank securities, called *commercial mortgage-backed securities (CMBS)*. Organizations that handle CMBS are called *conduits,* and they originate commercial and multifamily housing loans for purposes of pooling them as collateral for the issuance of commercial mortgage-backed securities, rather than holding them in the lender's own portfolio. Conduits are often subsidiaries of commercial banks and security firms that lend money out to other banks or private investment sources. It is effectively a commercial secondary market without government support and has been very successful in generating fund availability for commercial projects. Conduits include organizations such as MGIC Investment Corporation (a subsidiary of Mortgage Guaranty Investment Corporation); Residential Funding Corporation (a subsidiary of Norwest Mortgage Corporation); financial subsidiaries of such household-name companies as General Electric, Lockheed Aircraft, and Sears, Roebuck; and mortgage-packaging subsidiaries of state REALTORS® associations. These organizations compete with the big three and specialize in markets not served by them, including commercial lending markets. For example, Residential Funding Corporation will package mortgage loans as large as $500,000, well above the limits imposed by FNMA and FHLMC and on FHA and VA loans. All of these organizations will buy from loan originators that are not large enough to create their own pools.

Computerization

Before leaving the topic of the secondary market, it is important to note that, without electronic data transmission and computers, the programs just described would be severely handicapped. There are currently thousands of mortgage pools, each containing $1 million to $500 million (or more) in mortgage loans. Each loan in a pool has its own monthly payment schedule, and each payment must be broken down into its principal and interest components and any property tax and insurance impounds. Computers do this work, as well as issue receipts and late notices. The pool, in turn, will be owned by several dozen to a hundred or more investors, each with a different fractional interest in the pool. Once a month, incoming mortgage payments are tallied, a small fee is deducted for the operation of the pool, and the balance is allotted among the investors—all by computer. A computer also prints and mails checks to investors and provides them with an accounting of the pool's asset level.

AUTOMATED UNDERWRITING SYSTEMS

The computer age has introduced a whole new system in underwriting procedures as they apply to the relationship between the loan originator and the investor (secondary market). In the past, underwriting guidelines would be published and circulated to the primary lenders weekly. As interest rates began to fluctuate wildly in the 1970s, the sheet was updated and circulated more often. In some real estate offices, one person was given the job of calling lenders daily for quotes on loan availability and interest rates.

The entire process was overhauled by a computerized mortgage loan underwriting system with the introduction of Freddie Mac's Loan Prospector program, which was made available on the internet in 1999. Fannie Mae also has introduced its version of automated underwriting, which is known as Desktop Underwriter/Desktop Originator. The idea of feeding the loan application information into a system streamlines the entire process. I don't want to keep revisiting the real estate crash, but inevitably it is necessary. Many lessons were learned from that period, and some, such as the fact that actions have consequences, were relearned. While automated underwriting should shorten the processing times, in reality, this is not always the case. Processors and underwriters, the human element for the lender, have become very cautious. They are careful, since an overabundance of loan files that ultimately default would quickly result in unemployment for lending staff. The process is much more complex than simply feeding information into a computer. Particularly for a well-qualified borrower making a substantial down payment, the process isn't as simple as pressing a button and setting a closing date after an instaneous loan approval. We are not there yet. At the end of the day, it comes down to customer service by humans.

automated underwriting systems: computerized systems for loan approval communication between a loan originator and the investor

Character Loans

Before we leave this subject, it should also be said that there continues to be availability of loans in the marketplace for certain individuals that do not "conform" to the typical underwriting standard. Recently, I spoke with a lender who had gotten a loan approval for a borrower yesterday with a 592 credit score at market rate. (A reminder: a 592 credit score is low; 720 is considered "A" credit.) The credit score was so low, not because of bad credit, but because of little credit. The person almost always paid cash, did not borrow money, and did not use credit cards. Other than the low score, which again was caused not by credit abuse but credit "under-use," the borrower was stellar. The lender considered them to be an excellent credit risk—a better credit risk than many with much higher scores. It is a relief to know there are still lenders who use their heads and don't fall into the trap of relying solely on statistical modeling done by a computer program.

AVAILABILITY AND PRICE OF MORTGAGE MONEY

Thus far, we have been concerned with the money pipelines between lenders and borrowers. Ultimately, though, money must have a source. These sources are savings generated by individuals and businesses as a result of their spending less than they earn *(real savings)* and government-created money, called *fiat money* or *printing press money*. This second source does not represent unconsumed labor and materials; instead, it competes for available goods and services alongside the savings of individuals and businesses.

In the arena of money and capital, real estate borrowers must compete with the needs of government, business, and consumers. Governments, particularly the federal government, compete the hardest when they borrow to finance a deficit. Not to borrow would mean bankruptcy and the inability to pay government employees and provide government programs and services. Strong competition also comes from business and consumer credit sectors. In the face of such strong competition for loan funds, home buyers must either pay higher interest or be outbid. One "solution" to this problem is for the federal government to create more money, thus making competition for funds easier and interest rates lower. Unfortunately, the net result is often too much money chasing too few goods, and prices are pulled upward by the demand caused by the newly created money. This is followed by rising interest rates, as savers demand higher returns to compensate for losses in purchasing power. Many economists feel that the higher price levels and interest rates of the 1970s resulted from applying too much of this "solution" to the economy starting in 1965. Fast-forward this thought to the 2007–2014 era. Interest rates were very stable, but at the same time, the federal government borrowed more than $17 trillion in national debt. Because of a sluggish economy, interest rates were held low by the Federal Reserve. Some see this as a ticking time bomb, like continuing to add fuel to smoldering embers trying to get them to ignite. The problem is, when they do ignite, what about all that fuel?

The alternative solution, from the standpoint of residential loans, is to increase real savings or decrease competing demands for available money. A number of plans and ideas have been put forth by civic, business, and political leaders. They include proposals to simplify income taxes and balance the federal budget, incentives to increase productive output, and incentives to save money in retirement accounts.

USURY

In the 1970s and 1980s, interest rates were very high. In an attempt to push down rates, legislators voted to impose interest rate ceilings. Known as **usury** laws and found in nearly all states, they were originally enacted to prohibit lenders from overcharging interest on loans to individuals. Most states raised usury limits in response to higher interest rates. Additionally, the U.S. Congress passed legislation in 1980 that exempted from state usury limits most first-lien home loans made by institutional lenders. These laws had little effect on interest rates, and since then, interest rates and the availability of funds for loans have been so competitive that usury is no longer much of an issue.

usury: charging an interest rate that is in excess of the legal rate

PRICE TO THE BORROWER

Ultimately, the rate of interest the borrower must pay to obtain a loan is dependent on the cost of money to the lender, reserves for default, loan servicing costs, and available investment alternatives. For example, go to a savings institution and see what it is paying depositors on various accounts. To this, add 2% for the cost of maintaining cash in the tills, office space, personnel, advertising, free gifts for depositors, deposit insurance, loan servicing, loan reserves for defaults, and a 0.5% profit margin. This gives you an idea of how much borrowers must be charged.

Life insurance companies, pension funds, and trust funds do not have to "pay" for their money as do thrift institutions. Nonetheless, they do want to safely earn the highest possible yields on the money in their custody. Thus, if a real estate buyer wants to borrow to buy a home, the buyer must compete successfully with the other investment opportunities available on the open market. To determine the rate for yourself, look at the yields on newly issued corporate bonds as shown in the financial section of your daily newspaper. Add 0.5% to this for the extra work in packaging and servicing mortgage loans, and you will have the interest rate home borrowers must pay to attract lenders.

DUE-ON-SALE

From an investment risk standpoint, when a lender makes a loan with a fixed interest rate, the lender recognizes that, during the life of the loan, interest rates may rise or fall. When they rise, the lender remains locked into a lower rate. Most loans contain a due-on-sale clause (also called an **alienation clause** or a *call clause*). In the past, lenders inserted the clause so that if a borrower sold the property to someone considered uncreditworthy by the lender, the lender could call the loan balance due. When interest rates increase, though, lenders can use these clauses to increase the rate of interest on the loan when the property changes hands by threatening to accelerate the balance of the loan unless the new owner accepts the higher interest rate.

alienation clause: requires immediate repayment of the loan if ownership transfers; also called a due-on-sale clause

PREPAYMENT

If loan rates drop, it becomes worthwhile for a borrower to shop for a new loan and repay the existing one in full. To compensate, loan contracts sometimes call for a *prepayment penalty* in return for giving the borrower the right to repay the loan early. A typical prepayment penalty amounts to six months' interest on the amount that is being paid early. However, the penalty varies from loan to loan and from state to state. Some loan contracts permit up to 20% of the unpaid balance to be paid in any one year without penalty. Other contracts make the penalty stiffest when the loan is young. In certain states, laws do not permit prepayment penalties on loans more than 5 years old. By federal law, prepayment penalties are not allowed on FHA and VA loans.

Review Questions

Answers to these questions can be found in Appendix D at the end of this book.

1. The place where a real estate borrower makes a loan application, receives a loan, and makes loan payments is the:
   A. primary mortgage market
   B. secondary mortgage market
   C. first loan market
   D. second loan market

2. Historically, the foremost single source of funds for residential mortgage loans in this country has been:
   A. commercial banks
   B. insurance companies
   C. mortgage companies
   D. savings and loan associations

3. When savings are removed from thrift institutions in large amounts for investment in Treasury securities:
   A. the real estate market enjoys an increase in activity
   B. disintermediation occurs
   C. money supply increases
   D. interest rates decline

4. Reasons for the decline in residential loans made by the S&Ls include all EXCEPT:
   A. deregulation of the lending industry
   B. proliferation of savings and loan organizations
   C. new laws that allowed higher-risk loans
   D. the success of the government support

5. A real estate loan that calls for the lender to receive interest plus a percentage of the rental income from a property is:
   A. designed to protect the lender from deflation
   B. known as a package loan
   C. a participation loan
   D. required if the loan is purchased by FNMA

6. Mortgage companies are NOT typically involved in:
   A. originating loans
   B. servicing loans that they have sold on the secondary mortgage market
   C. acting as a loan insurer
   D. lending their own money

7. The secondary mortgage market provides:
   A. a way to make loans available to consumers
   B. a source of funds for second mortgages
   C. a way for a lender to sell real estate loans
   D. regulatory oversight for FNMA

8. All of the following are true of the Federal National Mortgage Association EXCEPT that it is:
   A. an organization that does not make direct loans to consumers
   B. the same as Freddie Mac
   C. under the conservatorship of FHFA
   D. known as Fannie Mae

9. Which of the following is NOT an investor in the secondary market?
   A. Fannie Mae
   B. Freddie Mac
   C. Fannie Pac
   D. Ginnie Mae

10. The major difference between the primary and secondary markets is that the:
    A. primary market buys loans; secondary market makes loans
    B. primary market services loans; secondary market invests in loans
    C. primary market makes loans; secondary market buys loans
    D. primary market makes loans; secondary market services loans

CHAPTER 15

TYPES OF FINANCING

KEY TERMS

adjustable-rate mortgage (ARM)
affordable housing loan
blanket mortgage
construction loan
equity sharing
graduated payment mortgage
negative amortization
option
package mortgage
reverse-annuity mortgage (RAM)
seller financing
wraparound mortgage

OBJECTIVES

After successful completion of this chapter, you should be able to:

1. describe variable rate and adjustable rate;
2. explain the concepts of equity sharing and "rich uncle" financing;
3. describe other types of mortgages and loans;
4. distinguish between creative financing and overly creative financing; and
5. explain various activities such as investing in mortgages, renting property, and leasing land.

OVERVIEW

An "alphabet soup" of mortgaging alternatives is now available to a borrower. With computerized loan origination, the expanded secondary market, and the availability of mortgage funds from unregulated lending sources, a vast array of mortgaging techniques and types of financing has been created. Loan brokers are now using computer programs to customize mortgages for individual home buyers, usually on the internet. "Customized mortgages" are now part of an individualized pricing trend sweeping through the U.S. economy. What was once a "prime" or "subprime" generalized loan is now replaced by

an almost endless array of mortgage rates and accompanying fees. The documents and the sources of funds, already discussed, remain the same, but the number of alternative types of financing continues to expand. Only the most fundamental concepts will be discussed in this chapter, including types of financing, adjustable-rate mortgages, other generally accepted types of loans often encountered by a broker in real estate lending, and the newest concepts of the affordable housing programs.

ADJUSTABLE-RATE MORTGAGES

As we have already seen, a major problem for savings institutions is that they are locked into long-term loans while being dependent on short-term savings deposits. As a result, savings institutions now prefer to make mortgage loans that allow the interest rate to rise and fall during the life of the loan. To make this arrangement more attractive to borrowers, these loans are offered at a lower rate of interest than a fixed-rate loan of similar maturity.

The first step toward mortgage loans with adjustable interest rates came in the late 1970s. The loan was called a *variable-rate mortgage,* and the interest rate could be adjusted up or down by the lender during the 30-year life of the loan to reflect the rise and fall in interest rates paid to savers by the lender.

Current Format

The Office of Thrift Supervision (OTS) authorizes institutions to make the type of adjustable mortgage loan you are most likely to encounter in today's loan marketplace. This loan format is called an **adjustable-rate mortgage (ARM).** Other federal agencies followed but used differing guidelines. The main ARM requirement is that the interest rate on these loans be tied to some publicly available index that is mutually acceptable to the lender and the borrower. As interest rates rise and fall in the open market, the interest rate the lender is entitled to receive from the borrower rises and falls (see Figure 15-1). The purpose is to match more closely what the savings institution receives from borrowers to what it must pay savers to attract funds. The benefit of an ARM to a borrower is that it carries an initial interest rate that is lower than the rate on a fixed-rate mortgage of similar maturity. This often makes the difference between being able to qualify for a desired home and not qualifying for it. Other advantages to the borrower are that if market interest rates fall, the borrower's monthly payments fall. (This happens without incurring prepayment penalties or new loan origination costs, which could be the case with a fixed-rate loan.) Most ARMs allow assumption by a new buyer at the terms in the ARM, and most allow total prepayment without penalty, particularly if there has been an upward adjustment in the interest rate.

adjustable-rate mortgage (ARM): a mortgage on which the interest rate rises and falls with changes in prevailing interest rates

For the borrower, the disadvantage of an ARM is that if interest rates rise, the borrower is going to pay more. During periods of rising interest rates, property values and wages presumably will also rise. But the possibility of progressively larger

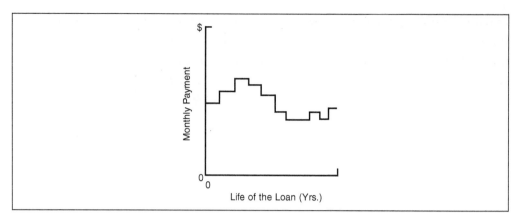

FIGURE 15-1 Adjustable rate mortgage
Source: © 2021 Mbition LLC

monthly payments for the family home is still not attractive. As a result, various compromises have been worked out between lenders and borrowers whereby rates can rise on loans, but not by too much. In view of the fact that about one-half of all mortgage loans originated by thrifts, banks, and mortgage companies are now adjustable, let's take a closer look at what a borrower gets with this loan format.

Interest Rate

The interest rate on an ARM is tied to an *index rate.* As the index rate moves up or down, so do the borrower's payments when adjustment time arrives. Lenders and borrowers alike want a rate that genuinely reflects current market conditions for interest rates. Two government requirements of this index rate are that it be readily verifiable by the borrower and that the rate not be controlled by the lender. The most popular index is based on an index that includes interest rates of all Treasuries and securities, from three-month bills to 30-year bonds. This index, called a one-year constant maturity Treasury, is published by the Federal Reserve based on daily calculations.

Margin

The *margin* is added to the index rate. The *combination of these two becomes the interest rate to the borrower.* Caution must be taken to compare loans and all terms. The margin by itself is not a true reflection of the quality of the loan. Also, the margin is not necessarily reflective of the lender's profit margin. Looking at history, the lender adds a margin to the index that would give it a competitive and safe investment if added to the ever-changing index. For example, a lender may consider an index, such as one-year Treasury bills. Looking over the last several years, if the lender could have received a rate of 2% over what the Treasury rate had been, this would have been considered a viable and safe investment. Periodically, as the rate is subject to change, the lender will add the margin, which is typically constant throughout the life of the loan, to the index rate; this will give the interest rate to the borrower for the next period.

Adjustment Period

The amount of time that elapses between adjustments is called the *adjustment period*. By far, the most common adjustment period is one year. Less commonly used are six-month, three-year, and five-year adjustment periods. When market rates are rising, the longer adjustment periods benefit the borrower. When market rates are falling, the shorter periods benefit the borrower because index decreases will show up sooner in the form of lower monthly payments.

Interest Rate Cap

Lenders are now required by federal law to disclose an *interest rate cap,* or a ceiling on how much the interest rate can increase for any one adjustment period during the life of the loan. If the cap is very low, say 0.5% per year, the lender does not have much more flexibility than if holding a fixed-rate loan. Thus, there would be little reduction of initial rate on the loan compared with a fixed-rate loan.

Compromises have prevailed, and the two most popular caps are 1% and 2% per year. In other words, the index rate may rise by 3%, but the cap limits the borrower's rate increase to 1% or 2%. Any unused difference may be added the next year, assuming the index rate has not fallen in the meantime. Federal law now requires a ceiling, consequently, many lenders simply impose a very high ceiling (e.g., 18%) if they choose not to negotiate with the borrower.

Payment Cap

What if a loan's index rate rises so fast that the annual rate cap is reached each year and the lifetime cap is reached soon in the life of the loan? A borrower might be able to handle a modest increase in payments each year, but not big jumps in quick succession. To counteract this possibility, a *payment cap* sets a limit on how much the borrower's monthly payment can increase in any one year. A popular figure historically in use was 7.5%. In other words, no matter how high a payment is called for by the index rate, the borrower's monthly payment can rise, at the most, 7.5% per year. For example, given an initial rate of 10% on a 30-year ARM for $100,000, the monthly payment of interest and principal is $878. If the index rate calls for a 2% upward adjustment at the end of one year, the payment on the loan would be $1,029. This is an increase of $151, or 17.2%. A 7.5% payment cap would limit the increase to 107.5% × $878 = $943.85.

Negative Amortization

Although the 7.5% payment cap in the foregoing example protects the borrower against a monthly payment that rises too fast, it does not make the difference

negative amortization: accrual of interest on a loan balance so that, as loan payments are made, the loan balance rises

between what's called for ($1,029) and what's paid ($943.85) go away. The difference ($85.15) is added to the balance owed on the loan and earns interest just as the original amount borrowed does. This is called **negative amortization**: Instead of the loan balance dropping each month as loan payments are made, the balance owed rises. This can bring concern to the lender who can visualize the day the loan balance exceeds the value of the property. A popular arrangement is to set a limit of 125% of the original loan balance. At that point, either the lender accrues no more negative amortization or the loan is reamortized depending on the wording of the loan contract. *Reamortized* in this situation means that the monthly payments will be adjusted upward by enough to stop the negative amortization.

Disclosures

In response to consumers' concern over adjustable-rate mortgages, Regulation Z requires creditors to provide consumers with more extensive information about the variable rate feature of ARMs. The amendments apply only to closed-end credit transactions secured by the consumer's principal dwelling. Transactions secured by the consumer's principal dwelling with a term of one year or less are exempt from the new disclosure. To comply with the amendment, lenders must provide consumers with a historical example that shows how actual changes in index values would have affected payments on a $10,000 loan as well as provide a statement of initial and maximum interest rates. Lenders must also provide prospective borrowers with an educational brochure about ARMs called *The Consumer Handbook on Adjustable Rate Mortgages,* or a suitable substitute. All the information must be given to the consumer at the time the loan application is provided or before a nonrefundable fee is paid, whichever is earlier. The maximum interest rate must be stated as a specified amount, or stated in a manner by which the consumer may easily ascertain the maximum interest rate at the time of undertaking the obligation.

Choosing Wisely

When a lender makes an ARM loan, the lender must explain to the borrower, in writing, the *worst-case scenario*. In other words, the lender must explain what will happen to the borrower's payments if the index raises the maximum amount each period up to the lifetime interest cap. If there is a payment cap, that and any possibility of negative amortization must also be explained. If the borrower is uneasy with these possibilities, then a fixed-rate loan should be considered. Most lenders offer fixed-rate loans as well as adjustable-rate loans. VA loans are fixed-rate loans, but the FHA now provides an adjustable-rate loan program.

Teaser rate ARMs have been offered from time to time by a few lenders, and these are best avoided. This type of loan is an ARM with an enticingly attractive, below-market initial rate. For example, the teaser rate may be offered at 2% below market.

A borrower who cannot qualify at the market rate might be able to do so at the teaser rate. However, in a year, the loan contract calls for a 2% jump followed by additional annual increases. This overwhelms the borrower who, unable to pay, allows foreclosure to take place.

GRADUATED PAYMENT MORTGAGE

The objective of a **graduated payment mortgage** is to help borrowers qualify for loans by basing repayment schedules on salary expectations. With this type of mortgage, the interest rate and maturity are fixed, but the monthly payment starts out artificially low and gradually rises. For example, a 10%, $60,000, 30-year loan normally requires monthly payments of $527 for complete amortization. Under the graduated payment mortgage, payments could start out as low as $437 per month the first year, gradually increase to $590 in the 11th year, and then remain at that level until the 30th year. Because the interest alone on this $60,000 loan is $500 per month in the first month, the amount owed on the loan actually increases (negative amortization) during its early years. Only when the monthly payment exceeds the monthly interest does the balance owed on the loan decrease. The most common example of the graduated payment mortgage is the FHA 245. With this loan program, the payments increase for either 5 or 10 years, depending on which of five programs is chosen by the borrower. These loans were very common during the periods of high inflation and increasing interest rates of the late 1970s and 1980s. They are seldom used now that inflation and interest rates remain moderate.

graduated payment mortgage: a mortgage with an interest rate and maturity that are fixed, but with a monthly payment that gradually rises because the initial monthly payments are insufficient to fully amortize the loan

EQUITY SHARING

Giving the party that provides the financing a piece of the action in the deal is not an innovation. Insurance companies that finance shopping centers and office buildings have long used the idea of requiring part of the rental income and/or part of the profits plus interest on the loan itself. In other words, in return for providing financing, the lender wants to share in some of the benefits normally reserved for the equity holder, called **equity sharing.** The equity holder would agree to this either to get a lower rate of interest or to get financing when financing was scarce, or when the equity holder was not big enough to handle the deal alone. For example, on a $5 million project, the lender might agree to make a loan of $4 million at a very attractive rate if it can buy a half-interest in the equity for $500,000.

equity sharing: an arrangement whereby a party providing financing gets a portion of the ownership

A variation of equity sharing is the *shared appreciation mortgage (SAM)*. While the format of SAMs varies considerably, the typical SAM offers an interest rate 1% to 2% below market rates, which makes buyer qualification easier. The lender earns about half the increase in appreciation over the term of the loan. At loan termination, the borrower is obligated to pay the loan balance plus the lender's share of the appreciated value of the home. For older homeowners, this may have more appeal than the reverse mortgage (discussed later) in that it preserves some equity in the home for the benefit of their heirs. Also, for it to be viable for the lender, there has to be the real expectation of value increase, which has not always been the case.

"RICH UNCLE" FINANCING

A second variation of equity sharing is often called "rich uncle" financing. The investor may be a parent helping a son or daughter buy a home, or a son or daughter buying a parent's current home while giving the parent the right to occupy it. A third variation is for an investor to provide most of the down payment for a home buyer, collect rent from the home buyer, pay the mortgage payments and property taxes, and claim depreciation. Each party has a right to a portion of any appreciation and the right to buy out the other. The FHLMC will buy mortgage loans on shared-equity properties. The FHLMC requires that the owner-occupant contribute at least 5% of the equity, that the owner-occupant and the owner-investor sign the mortgage and note, that both be individuals, and that there be no agreement requiring sale or buyout within seven years of the loan date. Equity sharing can provide attractive tax benefits; however, you must seek competent tax advice before involving yourself or someone else in such a plan.

PACKAGE MORTGAGE

package mortgage: a mortgage that secures personal property in addition to real property

Normally, we think of real estate mortgage loans as being secured solely by real estate. However, it is possible to include items classified as personal property in a real estate mortgage, thus creating a **package mortgage.** Probably the best example of this is the purchase of a condominium in a resort community. It is not uncommon for the lender to make a loan inclusive of the value of the real estate and furnishings. By doing this, there is some assurance that the owner will properly furnish the unit to become part of the rental pool. Once an item of personal property is included in a package mortgage, selling it without the prior consent of the lender is a violation of the mortgage.

BLANKET MORTGAGE

blanket mortgage: a mortgage secured by two or more properties

A mortgage secured by two or more properties is called a **blanket mortgage.** Suppose you want to buy a house plus the vacant lot next door, financing the purchase with a single mortgage that covers both properties. The cost of preparing one mortgage instead of two represents a savings. Also, by combining the house and the lot, you can finance the lot on better terms than if it were financed separately, as lenders more readily lend on a house and land than on land alone. Note, however, that if the vacant lot is later sold separately from the house before the mortgage loan is fully repaid, it will be necessary to have it released from the blanket mortgage. This is usually accomplished by including in the original mortgage agreement a partial release clause that specifies how much of the loan must be repaid before the lot may be released. Another common example is when a developer purchases raw land and develops it into multiple lots. Ultimately, there is one loan secured by multiple properties containing a partial release clause.

REVERSE MORTGAGE

With a regular mortgage, the lender makes a lump-sum payment to the borrower, who, in turn, repays it through monthly payments to the lender. With a *reverse mortgage,* also known as a *reverse-annuity mortgage* or **RAM**, the lender has two alternatives: (1) payment to the homeowner in a lump sum (sometimes referred to as a "line of credit" RAM), or (2) monthly payments to the homeowner as an annuity for the reverse term of the loan. The reverse mortgage can be particularly valuable for an elderly homeowner who does not want to sell, but whose retirement income is not quite enough for comfortable living. The homeowner receives a monthly check, has full use of the property, and is not required to repay until s/he sells or dies. If the home is sold, money from the sale is taken to repay the loan. If the borrower dies first, the property is sold through the estate and the loan repaid. In 1997, Fannie Mae introduced another type of reverse-annuity mortgage aimed at senior citizens that is activated at the time the house is purchased. It allows senior citizens (who must be 62 years or older) to obtain a mortgage against the equity in a house if a substantial down payment is made. Repayment of the mortgage is deferred until the borrower no longer occupies the principal residence. If the loan balance exceeds the value of the property, the borrower, or the estate, will never owe more than the value of the property. For instance, if a homeowner sells an existing home for $100,000 and chooses to purchase a retirement home, also costing $100,000, the homeowner would immediately qualify for a $52,000 loan, with a $48,000 down payment. There would be no monthly payments, and the homeowner would have $52,000 in cash!

reverse-annuity mortgage (RAM): a loan to the homeowner whereby periodic payments are made TO the borrower from the lender; typically for people 62 or older

CONSTRUCTION LOAN

Under a **construction loan**, also called an *interim loan,* money is advanced as construction takes place. For example, the owner of a vacant lot arranges to borrow $60,000 to build a house. The lender does not advance all $60,000 at once because the value of the collateral is insufficient to warrant that amount until the house is finished. Instead, the lender will parcel out the loan as the building is being constructed, always holding a portion until the property is ready for occupancy or, in some cases, actually occupied. Some lenders specialize only in construction loans and do not want to wait 20 or 30 years to be repaid. In this case, the buyer will have to obtain a permanent long-term mortgage from another source for the purpose of repaying the construction loan. This is known as a permanent

construction loan: short-term loan for new construction or remodeling of an existing structure; also called an interim loan

commitment or a takeout loan because it takes the construction lender out of the financial picture when construction is completed and allows the lender to recycle its money into new construction projects.

BLENDED-RATE LOAN

Many real estate lenders still hold long-term loans that were made at interest rates below the current market. One way of raising the return on these loans is to offer borrowers who have them a *blended-rate loan.* Suppose you owe $50,000 on your home loan and the interest rate on it is 7%. Suppose further that the current rate on home loans is 12%. Your lender might offer to refinance your home for $70,000 at 9%, presuming the property will appraise high enough and you have the income to qualify. The $70,000 refinance offer would put $20,000 in your pocket (less loan fees), but would increase the interest you pay from 7% to 9% on the original $50,000. This makes the cost of the $20,000 14% per year. The arithmetic is as follows: You will now be paying 9% × $70,000 = $6,300 in interest. Before, you paid 7% × $50,000 = $3,500 in interest. The difference, $2,800, is what you pay to borrow the additional $20,000. This equates to $2,800 ÷ $20,000 = 14% interest. This is the figure you should use in comparing other sources of financing (such as a second mortgage) or deciding whether you even want to borrow.

A blended-rate loan can be very attractive in a situation in which you want to sell your home and you do not want to help finance the buyer. Suppose your home is worth $87,500 and you have the aforementioned $50,000, 7% loan. A buyer would normally expect to make a down payment of $17,500 and pay 12% interest on a new $70,000 loan. But, with a blended loan, your lender could offer the buyer the needed $70,000 financing at 9%, a far more attractive rate and one that requires less income in order to qualify. Blended loans are available on FHA, VA, and conventional loans held by FNMA. Other lenders also offer them on fixed-rate, assumable loans they hold.

EQUITY MORTGAGE

An *equity mortgage* is a loan arrangement wherein the lender agrees to make a loan based on the amount of equity in a borrower's home. The maximum amount of the loan is generally 70% to 80% of the home value (although some lenders advertise 125%) minus any first mortgage or other liens against the property. It is typically a second mortgage that is used to tap the increase in equity resulting from rising home prices and first loan principal reductions. It's all done without having to refinance the first loan, and it uses the home as an asset against which the homeowner can borrow and repay as needed. While equity mortgages became popular as a source of money for cars, vacations, college bills, and the like, the 2017 tax law prohibited their use for expenses other than those for the home securing the loan.

AFFORDABLE HOUSING LOANS

An **affordable housing loan** is an umbrella term that covers many slightly different loans that target first-time home buyers and low- to moderate-income borrowers. Although there are no fixed standards for measurement, the generally accepted definition of a low-income borrower is a person or family with an income of not more than 80% of the median income for the local area. Moderate income is 115% of the median income for the area. *Median* means there is an equal number of people with incomes above the number and below the number. Funding for the programs is obtained through a commitment from an investor to buy the loans. Freddie Mac and Fannie Mae cooperate with local community, labor union, or trade associations by committing to buy a large block of mortgage loans, provided they meet the agreed-on standards. Affordable housing loans can be privately insured through the Mortgage Guaranty Insurance Company or GE Capital Mortgage Insurance Corporation.

Fannie Mae has also introduced its Construction-to-Permanent mortgage loan, which enables a borrower to cover the construction loan and a permanent mortgage with one loan. One interest rate can be locked in for both phases of the loan, which is sold to Fannie Mae as soon as it is closed.

The Department of Housing and Urban Development is also encouraging affordable housing loans. Its Good Neighbor Next Door Sales Program offers 50% discounts off the list price to law enforcement officers, teachers, firefighters, and emergency medical technicians buying homes if they agree to live in the property as their sole residence for three years. In addition, HUD has a program to sell foreclosed single-family homes to local governments for $1 each. The houses are FHA foreclosures that have remained unsold for six months. The program is designed to create housing for families in need and to revitalize neighborhoods. HUD also sets goals for FNMA and Freddie Mac for the purchase of mortgages made to low- and moderate-income persons, African Americans, Hispanics, and other minorities in underserved areas. More information about the programs can be found at www.hud.gov.

Fannie Mae also promotes its *Community Solutions Program* of flexible mortgages for school employees, police officers, firefighters, and healthcare workers. It provides greater flexibility with credit scores and credit histories, allows for a greater portion of income to go toward mortgage payment, and gives credit for overtime or part-time income. It offers 97% and 100% loan programs.

Fannie Mae also produces the HomeReady program, which provides mortgage options for borrowers of one- to four-family homes. It includes extra flexibilities for rural residents and may offer additional incentives for buyers of energy-efficient homes. It has a $300,700 loan limit on single-family homes and allows for a $500 or 1% down payment, greater flexibility on credit histories, and income limits up to 115% of the median in rural areas.

> **affordable housing loan:** an umbrella term that covers many slightly different loans that target first-time home buyers and low- to moderate-income borrowers

Another part of the MyCommunityMortgage program, *Fannie Neighbors* is a nationwide neighborhood-based mortgage program designed to increase home ownership and revitalization in areas underserved by HUD in low-to-moderate-income minority census tracts or in central cities. Lenders can use the Fannie Mae Property GeoCoder, a free online application, to determine whether a property qualifies for some of Fannie Mae's discount options.

Credit Criteria

Underwriting standards for affordable housing loans are modified to recognize different forms of credit responsibility. Many low- and moderate-income families do not have checking accounts. Recognizing the lack of payment records, most affordable housing programs accept timely payment of rent and utility bills as credit criteria. Initial cash down payments can be reduced if a lender permits borrowing or acceptance of grants from housing agencies or local communities, which sometimes offer cash assistance. Studies indicate that lower-income families pay a higher percentage of their income for housing than others, so an affordable housing program allows a higher ratio of income to be applied to housing (33% of gross income instead of 28% found in similar loans; the FHA housing guideline is 29%).

Consumer Education

One of the requirements to qualify for an affordable housing loan is for the borrower to take a pre-purchase home buyer education course. Many first-time buyers are unaware of real estate brokers, title insurance, or appraisals. These subjects, plus information on the care and maintenance of a home, are included in the variety of courses now available through community colleges, banks, and mortgage companies.

The four major supporting entities of these programs are Fannie Mae, Freddie Mac, MGIC, and GE Capital Mortgage Insurance Corporation. All of these entities provide videos and course outlines that are available for these educational purposes. Licensees should be aware that these programs are most effective if presented to a group of applicants. If there is no program in your area, one could be started. An agent may want to contact local lenders, as many are still not fully aware of the opportunities available, and some tend to overlook the lower-income market for economic reasons. Participation in the program, however, greatly benefits their Community Reinvestment Act rating. Effectively marketing these programs can be very profitable and can provide a great amount of personal satisfaction.

SELLER FINANCING

When a seller is willing to accept part of the property's purchase price in the form of the buyer's promissory note accompanied by a mortgage or deed of trust, it is called **seller financing**. This allows the buyer to substitute a promissory note for cash, and the seller is said to be "taking back paper." Seller financing is popular for land sales (where lenders rarely lend), on property where an existing mortgage is being assumed by the buyer, and on property where the seller prefers to receive the money spread out over a period of time with interest instead of lump-sum cash. For example, a retired couple sell a rental home that they own. The home is worth $120,000, and they owe $20,000. If they need only $60,000 in cash, they might be more than happy to take $60,000 down, let the buyer assume the existing mortgage, and accept the remaining $40,000 in monthly payments at current interest rates. Alternatively, the buyer and sellers can agree to structure the $40,000 as an adjustable, graduated, partially amortized, or interest-only loan.

If the sellers receive the sales price spread out over two or more years, income taxes are calculated using the installment reporting method discussed in Chapter 17. Being able to spread out the taxes on a gain may be an incentive to use seller financing. The seller should be aware, however, that the "paper" may not be convertible to cash without a long wait or without having to sell it at a substantial discount to an investor (although this can be remedied by a "balloon" provision). Additionally, the sellers are responsible for servicing the loan and subject to losses due to default and foreclosure. Note that some real estate agents and lenders refer to a loan that is carried back by a seller as a *purchase money mortgage* (PMM). Others define a purchase money loan as any loan (carryback or institutional) that is used to finance the purchase of real property. In Georgia, the term *purchase money mortgage* refers to seller financing.

seller financing: a note accepted by a seller instead of cash

Wraparound Mortgage

An alternative method of financing a real estate sale such as the one just reviewed is to use a **wraparound mortgage** or wraparound deed of trust. A wraparound encompasses existing mortgages and is subordinate (junior) to them. The existing mortgages stay on the property and the new mortgage wraps around them. Note Figure 15-2. To illustrate, assume the existing $20,000 loan in the previous example carries an interest rate of 7% and that there are 10 years remaining on the loan.

Assume, further, that current interest rates are 12%, and the current seller chooses to sell for $100,000. This is done by taking the buyer's $40,000 down payment and then creating a new junior mortgage (for $60,000) that includes not only the $20,000 owed on the existing first mortgage but also the $40,000 the buyer owes the seller. The seller continues to remain liable for payment of the first mortgage. If the interest rate on the wraparound is set at 10%, the buyer saves by not having to pay 12%, as s/he would on an entirely new loan. The advantage to the seller is that s/he is earning 10%, not only on his/her $40,000 equity, but also on the $20,000 loan for which s/he is paying 7% interest.

wraparound mortgage: a mortgage that encompasses any existing mortgages and is subordinate to them

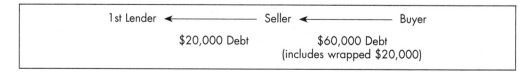

FIGURE 15-2 The wraparound mortgage
Source: © 2021 Mbition LLC

This gives the seller an actual yield of 11.5% on his/her $40,000. The calculation is as follows:

The seller receives 10% on $60,000, which amounts to $6,000. S/he pays 7% on $20,000, which is $1,400. The difference, $4,600, is divided by $40,000 to get the seller's actual yield of 11.5%.

There is an additional point of concern. If the monthly payment on the underlying $20,000 debt includes taxes and insurance (PITI payment), the wraparound mortgage payment amount should also include taxes and insurance so that the monthly payment is sufficient to meet *all* of the underlying debt.

Wraparounds are not limited to seller financing. If the seller in the foregoing example did not want to finance the sale, a third-party lender could provide the needed $40,000 and take a wraparound mortgage. The wraparound concept does not work when the underlying mortgage debt to be "wrapped" contains a due-on-sale clause. One other word of caution: If the seller defaults (and doesn't tell the buyer), the buyer may have an unwelcome surprise.

SUBORDINATION

Another financing technique is subordination. For example, a person owns a $200,000 vacant lot suitable for building, and a builder wants to build an $800,000 building on the lot. The builder has only $100,000 cash, and the largest construction loan available is $800,000. If the builder can persuade the lot owner to take $100,000 in cash and $100,000 later, the buyer would have the $1 million needed to pay for both the lot and construction.

However, the lender making the $800,000 loan will want to be the first mortgagee to protect its position in the event of foreclosure. The lot owner must be willing to take a subordinate position—in this case, a second mortgage. If the project is successful, the lot owner will receive $100,000 plus interest, either in cash after the building is built and sold, or as monthly payments. If the project goes into foreclosure, the lot owner can be paid only if the $800,000 first mortgage claim is satisfied in full from the sale proceeds. As you can surmise here, the lot owner must be very careful that the lender's loan actually goes into construction and that whatever is built is worth at least $800,000 in addition to the land.

CONTRACT FOR DEED

A contract for deed, also called an installment contract or land contract, enables the seller to finance a buyer by permitting him/her to make a down payment followed by monthly payments. However, title remains in the name of the seller. In addition to its wide use in financing land sales, contract for deed has been a very effective financing tool in several states as a means of selling homes. For example, a homeowner owes $25,000 on the home and wants to sell it for $85,000. A buyer is found but does not have the $60,000 down payment necessary to assume the existing loan. The buyer (vendee) does have $8,000, but for one reason or another, cannot or chooses not to borrow from an institutional lender. If the seller (vendor) is agreeable, the buyer can pay the seller $8,000 and enter into an installment contract with the seller for the remaining $77,000. The contract calls for monthly payments by the buyer to the seller that are large enough to allow the seller to meet the payments on the $25,000 loan plus allow the buyer to repay the $52,000 owed to the seller, with interest. Unless property taxes and insurance are billed to the buyer, the seller will also collect for these and pay them.

When the final payment is made to the seller (or the property refinanced through an institutional lender), title is conveyed to the buyer. Meanwhile, the seller continues to hold title and is responsible for paying the mortgage. In addition to wrapping around a mortgage, an installment contract can also be used to wrap around another installment contract, provided it does not contain an enforceable due-on-sale clause. (See Chapter 11 for more about the contractual side of installment contracts.)

OPTION

When viewed as a financing tool, an **option** provides a method by which the need to finance the full price of a property immediately can be postponed. For example, a developer is offered 100 acres of land for a house subdivision, but is not sure that the market will absorb that many houses. The solution is to buy 25 acres outright and take three 25-acre options at current prices on the remainder. If the houses on the first 25 acres sell promptly, the builder can exercise the options to buy the remaining land. If sales are not good, the builder can let the remaining options expire and avoid being stuck with unwanted acreage.

A popular variation on the option idea is the lease with option to buy combination. Under it, an owner leases to a tenant who, in addition to paying rent and using the property, also obtains the right to purchase it at a preset price for a fixed period of time. Homes are often sold this way, particularly when the resale market is sluggish. (See Chapter 9 for more about these topics.) Options can provide speculative opportunities to persons with limited amounts of capital. If prices do not rise, the optionee loses only the cost of the option; if prices do rise, the optionee exercises the option and realizes a profit.

option: a right, for a given period of time, to buy, sell, or lease property at a specified price and terms

OVERLY CREATIVE FINANCING?

One seller-financing arrangement that deserves special attention because of its traps for the unwary is the *over-encumbered property*. Institutional lenders are closely regulated regarding the amount of money they may lend against the appraised value of the property. Individuals are not regulated. The following illustrates the potential problem. Suppose a seller owns a house that is realistically worth $100,000 and the mortgage balance is $10,000. A buyer offers to purchase the property, with the condition that she be allowed to obtain an $80,000 loan on the property from a lender. The $80,000 is used to pay off the existing $10,000 loan and to pay the broker's commission, loan fees, and closing costs. The remaining $62,000 is split, $30,000 to the seller and $32,000 to the buyer. The buyer also gives the seller a note, secured by a second mortgage against the property, for $80,000. The seller may feel good about getting $30,000 in cash and an $80,000 mortgage, for this is more than the property is worth, or so it seems. But the $80,000 second mortgage stands junior to the $80,000 first mortgage. That's $160,000 of debt against a $100,000 property. The buyer might be trying to resell the property for $160,000 or more, but the chances of this are slim. More likely, the buyer will wind up walking away from the property. This leaves the seller the choice of taking over the payments on the first mortgage or losing the property completely to the holder of the first.

Although such a scheme sounds crazy when viewed from a distance, the reason it can be performed is that the seller wants more for the property than it's worth. Someone then offers a deal showing that price, and the seller looks the other way from the possible consequences. Real estate practitioners who participate in such transactions are likely to find their licenses suspended. State licensing authorities take the position that a real estate practitioner is a professional who should know enough not to take part in a deal that leaves the seller holding a junior lien on an over-encumbered property. This, too, seems logical when viewed from a distance. But when sales are slow and commissions thin, it is sometimes easy to put commission income ahead of fiduciary responsibility. When there is doubt about the propriety of a transaction, the Golden Rule of doing unto others as you would have them do unto you still applies. (Or, as some restate it: "What goes around, comes around.")

MORTGAGE FRAUD

No discussion of financing today would be complete without an exploration of the topic of mortgage fraud. Mortgage and real estate fraud, which includes identity theft, has become one of the fastest-growing crimes in the United States, and, sadly, Georgia seems to be one of the leaders. Not only does this crime lead to huge financial institution loss, but also to collateral damage to individuals and neighborhoods. Often, properties that were the target of mortgage fraud become a haven for drug dealers, prostitution, methamphetamine production, and other illegal activity. After the neighborhood has been infiltrated by such undesirables, values begin to decline. Adding insult to injury, one of the more popular methods of mortgage fraud (flipping) may actually make it look as if property values are increasing when, in fact, they are decreasing, with the perception causing property taxes to sometimes double on unsuspecting neighborhood victims.

Simply put, mortgage fraud involves obtaining loans with deceit or misrepresentation. In 2005, Georgia became the first state to enact a law specific to mortgage fraud. This law, the Georgia Residential Mortgage Fraud Act, puts teeth into prosecutors' ability to penalize and imprison fraudsters. Many states have since followed Georgia's lead. While the methods are too intricate and technical to explain in detail, following are some of the most common forms of fraud.

Illegal Flipping

Illegal flipping is purchasing a property and then selling it immediately at a fraudulent and increased price. The fraudster pockets the illegal gains. This often involves illegal appraisals, documentation fraud, identity theft, and/or the involvement of the lender, attorney, and real estate licensee.

Silent Second

Lenders typically want the borrower to be vested in the property by making a cash investment. The silent second involves increasing the sales price fraudulently and asking the seller to take a second loan with the increase in purchase price. The lender thinks the borrower has a cash commitment to the property when, in fact, the sales price was inflated and there existed an agreement between the borrower and seller that the second loan would be forgiven after the closing.

Chunking

Chunking is a scheme whereby the borrower makes multiple, simultaneous applications for a loan on one property. After closing multiple loans (one fraudster closed eight loans on one property on the same day!), the fraudster goes missing with the money.

Identity Theft

An unsuspecting victim has personal information stolen; it is then used to qualify for a loan on property. One of the most famous mortgage fraud felons is Matthew Cox. It was reported that, by the time he was arrested, he had either stolen the identity of or created an identity for more than 30 persons. He even created an identity and credit file for one of his favorite cartoon characters, C. Montgomery Burns from the Simpsons, and used the identity to purchase multiple properties with fraudulent loans.

Debt Cancellation/Deed Transfer

In this scheme, the security deed of a property is canceled and the property then fraudulently transferred into the name of the fraudster. With the title in the name of the fraudster and no outstanding debt, the property is then sold to an unsuspecting purchaser. To facilitate this scheme, one such fraudster would lease the property so s/he had possession to commit the fraud.

Red Flags of Mortgage Fraud

While none of the following are mortgage fraud by themselves, they are indications that there may be a problem and the situation should be given closer consideration:

- false information from parties involved in the transaction
- altered information on documents
- inflated appraisals
- unexpected costs
- higher payments than expected
- required credit insurance
- a request for deed or prepaid fees
- inability to communicate with the buyer or seller except via a third party
- multiple contracts
- request to sign blank documents
- closing statement that reflects a different price or seller than the contract
- approval by an unknown lender
- simultaneous closings
- inadequate identity documentation
- perpetual absence of seller from principal residence
- property in poor condition, but a higher price is offered
- loan involves money to make repairs
- missing documents
- payment or receipt of a kickback from sales proceeds

Reporting Mortgage Fraud

If you suspect mortgage fraud in a transaction, you are required to report it. If an attorney is involved, you may call the State Bar Association at 404-527-8700; if a mortgage banker/broker is involved, you may call the Georgia Department of Banking and Finance at 770-986-1633; if a real estate licensee or appraiser is involved, you may call the Georgia Real Estate Commission & Appraisers Board at 404-656-3916. Online resources include:

grefpac.org – Georgia Real Estate Fraud Prevention and Awareness Coalition, Inc.

gsccca.org – Georgia Superior Court Clerks' Cooperative Authority

mortgagefraudblog.com – great site for researching and reporting mortgage fraud

ustaxcourt.gov – website for retrieval of tax court records

mba.org – website of Mortgage Bankers Association; reports mortgage fraud activity

INVESTING IN MORTGAGES

Individuals can invest in mortgages in two ways. One is to invest in mortgage loan pools through certificates guaranteed by Ginnie Mae and Freddie Mac and available from stockbrokers. These yield about 0.5% below what FHA and VA borrowers are paying. Individuals can also buy junior mortgages at yields above Ginnie Mae and Freddie Mac certificates. These junior mortgages are seconds, thirds, and fourths offered by mortgage brokers. They yield more because they are riskier as to repayment and much more difficult to convert to cash before maturity. As many have said, "There is no such thing as a free lunch." Thus, it is important to recognize that when an investment of any kind promises above-market returns, there is some kind of added risk attached.

With junior mortgages, it is important to realize that when a borrower offers to pay a premium above the best loan rates available from banks and thrift institutions, it is because the borrower and/or the property do not qualify for the best rates. Before buying a mortgage as an investment, one should have the title to the property searched. This is the only way to know for certain what priority the mortgage will have in the event of foreclosure. There have been cases in which investors have purchased what they were told to be first and second mortgages, only to find in foreclosure that they were actually holding third and fourth mortgages and that the amount of debt exceeded the value of the property.

How does one find the value of a property? By having it appraised by a professional appraiser who is independent of the party making or selling the mortgage investment. This value is compared to the existing and proposed debt against the property. The investor should also run a credit check on the borrower. The investor's final protection, however, is making certain that the market value of the property is well in excess of the loans against it and that the property is well constructed, well located, and functional.

RENTAL

Even though tenants do not acquire fee ownership, rentals and *leases* are means of financing real estate. Whether the tenant is a bachelor receiving the use of a $30,000 apartment for which he pays $350 rent per month, or a large corporation leasing a warehouse for 20 years, leasing is an ideal method of financing when the tenant does not want to buy, cannot raise the funds to buy, or prefers to invest available funds elsewhere. Similarly, farming leases provide for the use of land without the need to purchase it. Some farm leases call for fixed rental payment. Other leases require the farmer to pay the landowner a share of the value of the crop that is actually produced—say, 25%—and the landowner shares with the farmer the risks of weather, crop output, and prices.

Under a *sale and leaseback* arrangement, an owner-occupant sells the property and then remains as a tenant. Thus, the buyer acquires an investment and the seller obtains capital for other purposes while retaining the use of the property. A variation is for the tenant to construct a building, sell it to a prearranged buyer, and immediately lease it back.

LAND LEASES

Although leased land arrangements are common throughout the United States for both commercial and industrial users and for farmers, anything other than fee ownership of residential land is unthinkable in many areas. Yet in some parts of the United States (e.g., Baltimore, Maryland; Orange County, California; throughout Hawaii; and parts of Florida), homes built on leased land are commonplace. Typically, these leases are at least 55 years in length and, barring an agreement to the contrary, the improvements to the land become the property of the fee owner at the end of the lease. Rents may be fixed in advance for the life of the lease, renegotiated at predetermined points during the life of the lease, or a combination of both. One example of this in Georgia is Jekyll Island, on the Atlantic coast near Brunswick and St. Simons Island. Jekyll is a state park, and all development on the island is with land leases, most of which are subject to expiration in the middle of this century. Potentially, all buildings and development will become state property at the end of the leases.

To hedge against inflation, when fixed rents are used in a long-term lease, it is common practice to use *step-up rentals*. For example, under a 55-year house-lot lease, the rent may be set at $400 per year for the first 15 years, $600 per year for the next 10 years, $800 for the next 10 years, and so forth. An alternative is to renegotiate the rent at various points during the life of a lease so that the effects of land value changes are more closely equalized between the lessor and the lessee. For example, a 60-year lease may contain renegotiation points at the 15th, 30th, and 45th years. At those points, the property would be reappraised and the rent adjusted to reflect any changes in the value of the property. Property taxes and any increases in property taxes are paid by the lessee.

FINANCING OVERVIEW

If people always paid cash for real estate, the last several chapters would not have been necessary. But 95% of the time, they don't; thus, means have been devised to finance their purchases. This has been true since the beginning of recorded history and will continue into the future. The financing methods that evolve will depend on the problems to be solved. For example, long-term, fixed-rate, amortized loans were the solution to foreclosures in the 1930s, and they worked well as long as interest rates did not fluctuate greatly. Graduated payment loans were devised when housing prices rose faster than buyers' incomes. Adjustable rate loans were developed so that lenders could more closely align the interest they receive from borrowers with the interest they pay their savers. Extensive use of loan assumptions, wraparounds, and seller financing became necessary in the early 1980s because borrowers could not qualify for 16% and 18% loans, and sellers were unwilling to drop prices.

With regard to the future, if mortgage money is expensive or in short supply, seller financing will play a large role. When interest rates are fluctuating, borrowers often gravitate toward adjustable rates, hoping to avoid the worst if rates go up, and to benefit from lower monthly payments if the rates come down. When interest rates are low (e.g., from 2009 to 2019, they were below 6% for a 30-year loan), fixed-rate loans are more popular. With the expanded role of the licensee in buyer representation, it is becoming even more important that licensees understand financing so that they may provide valuable, accurate, and timely counsel to their clients. The marketplace has become complex, and only by updating and studying daily can a person be well informed. The consumer depends on each of us to be that well-informed professional and demands value-added service.

Review Questions

Answers to these questions can be found in Appendix D at the end of this book.

1. In order to make adjustable-rate mortgage loans more attractive to borrowers, lenders offer:
   A. lower initial interest rates
   B. gifts such as appliances, trips, etc.
   C. lower insurance rates
   D. lower down payments

2. A loan that has a fixed interest rate and negative amortization is a:
   A. variable-rate mortgage
   B. renegotiable rate mortgage
   C. graduated payment mortgage
   D. balloon mortgage

3. When considering an ARM loan, the lender must explain to the borrower, in writing, the:
   A. worst-case scenario
   B. best-case scenario
   C. average-case scenario
   D. respective credit report

4. Equity sharing is based on the concept of someone who has assets sharing those assets in exchange for:
   A. cash
   B. tax benefits only
   C. tax benefits and ownership
   D. ownership only

5. When an existing loan at a low interest rate is refinanced by a new loan at an interest rate between the current market rate and the rate on the old loan, the result is a:
   A. combined loan
   B. blended loan
   C. wraparound loan
   D. merged loan

6. An individual who is contemplating the purchase of a mortgage as an investment would be LEAST concerned with having:
   A. the property appraised
   B. a credit check made on the borrower
   C. the title searched
   D. the power to evict a tenant

7. Under the terms of a shared appreciation mortgage, which is NOT true?
   A. The loan is made at a below-market interest rate.
   B. The lender receives a portion of the property's appreciation.
   C. The property is always sold after the agreed-upon period of time.
   D. The loan terms are favorable to the borrower.

8. Which of the following is NOT a common mortgage fraud term?
   A. chunking
   B. flipping
   C. flopping
   D. silent second

9. All of the following statements are true of seller financing EXCEPT:
   A. the seller of the property is the mortgagee under the mortgage
   B. mortgage terms and interest rates are negotiable between the seller and buyer
   C. if repayment is spread over two or more years, income taxes are calculated on the installment reporting method
   D. carryback mortgages are usually salable to investors without discount

10. Which of the following is NOT true of wraparound mortgages?
    A. They are junior mortgages, subordinate to an existing first mortgage.
    B. The interest rate on the buyer's note is usually the same as the market rate.
    C. They are useless when the first mortgage carries a due-on-sale clause.
    D. The yield to the seller (mortgagee) is usually greater than the interest rate specified on the note.

11. A sale may be made and financed under a contract for deed:
    A. only when the seller owns the property free and clear
    B. by combining wraparound financing with an existing mortgage loan on the property, provided the existing mortgage does not contain a due-on-sale clause
    C. to circumvent a due-on-sale clause
    D. for second mortgages, but not for firsts

CHAPTER 16
NOTES AND SECURITY DOCUMENTS

KEY TERMS

acceleration clause
alienation clause
beneficiary
deed of trust
defeasance clause
deficiency judgment
first mortgage
foreclosure
junior mortgage
mortgage
mortgagee
mortgagor
naked title
power of sale
promissory note
reconveyance deed
second mortgage
security deed
subordination
trustee
trustor

OBJECTIVES

After successful completion of this chapter, you should be able to:

1. distinguish between lien theory and title theory;
2. explain early mortgage application and the various pledge methods;
3. describe the parts of the promissory note and the mortgage instrument;
4. explain hypothecation, mortgage satisfaction, and the "subject to" clause;
5. list, in order, debt priorities;
6. explain the foreclosure process;
7. describe both judicial and nonjudicial foreclosure;
8. explain the purpose of a deed in lieu of foreclosure, and
9. distinguish between mortgages, trust deeds, and security deeds.

OVERVIEW

In this chapter, we will discuss the importance of a note as a financing document and how the security plays an important role in the financing of property. This chapter will

include an explanation of the alternative securities for the note: the mortgage, trust deed, and the deed to secure debt. Also included is a discussion on loan assumption, debt priority, and the foreclosure process.

There are two documents involved in a typical real estate loan. The first is the promissory note, and the second is the security document. Most states use a **mortgage** as the primary security instrument. However, in 16 states it is common to use a **deed of trust**, and Georgia has the unique position of using a third document known as a **security deed** or deed to secure debt. We begin by describing the promissory note because it is common to the mortgage, deed of trust, and security deed. We shall then discuss and differentiate among the mortgage, deed of trust, and security deed. This is followed by an explanation of **foreclosure**. Let's begin with the promissory note.

mortgage: a document that makes property security for the repayment of a debt

deed of trust: a document that conveys naked title to a neutral third party (a trustee) as security for a debt

security deed: a document used in Georgia to secure a note; replaces a mortgage or deed of trust

foreclosure: the procedure by which a person's property may be taken and sold to satisfy an unpaid debt

promissory note: a written promise to repay a debt; usually referred to simply as a note

PROMISSORY NOTE

The **promissory note** is a contract between a borrower and a lender. The note is the fundamental loan document and creates the *obligation* of the borrower to pay the lender. If there is no note, there is no debt. It establishes the amount of the debt, the terms of repayment, and the interest rate. A sample promissory note, usually referred to simply as a *note*, is shown in Figure 16-1. A note is considered to be a negotiable instrument in that it creates a debt, and the debt created may be conveyed to a third party.

To be valid as evidence of debt, a note must: (1) be in writing; (2) be between a borrower and lender, both of whom have contractual capacity; (3) state the borrower's promise to pay a certain sum of money; (4) show the terms of payment; (5) be signed by the borrower; and (6) be voluntarily delivered by the borrower and accepted by the lender. If the note is secured by a mortgage or trust deed, it must say so. Otherwise, it is solely a personal obligation of the borrower. Although interest is not required to make the note valid, most loans do carry an interest charge; when they do, the rate of interest must be stated in the note.

PROVISIONS AND TERMINOLOGY IN THE NOTE

Obligee and Obligor

The parties to a note are *obligee* and *obligor*. As has been stated before, the "-or" gives and the "-ee" receives. The obligor is the one giving the obligation or making the payments on the note. This is the borrower. The obligee, the lender, is receiving the payments.

Interest Conveyance

Think of interest on a loan as the rental charge for money. The lender provides the borrower with a loan and requires the borrower to make periodic payments of interest. The note will state when the payments are due, where the payments are to be made, the rate of interest, how the interest is to be computed, how the interest is to be applied, and the periodic payment obligation. Interest on real

Provisions and Terminology in the Note

PROMISSORY NOTE SECURED BY MORTGAGE

__City, State__ __March 31, 20xx__

For value received, I promise to pay to __Pennywise Mortgage Company__, or order, at __2242 National Blvd., [City, State]__, the sum of __Ninety-six thousand and no/100__ dollars, with interest from __March 31, 20xx__, on unpaid principal at the rate of __7__ percent per annum; principal and interest payable in installment of __six hundred thirty-nine and 36/100__ dollars on the __first__ day of each month beginning __May 1, 20xx__, and continuing until said principal and interest have been paid.

This note may be prepaid in whole or in part at any time without penalty.

There shall be a ten-day grace period for each monthly payment. A late fee of $25.00 will be added to each payment made after its grace period.

Each payment shall be credited first on interest then due and the remainder on principal. Unpaid interest shall bear interest like the principal.

Should default be made in payment of any installment when due, the entire principal plus accrued interest shall immediately become due at the option of the holder of the note.

If legal action is necessary to collect this note, I promise to pay such sum as the court may fix.

This note is secured by a mortgage bearing the same date as this note and made in favor of __Pennywise Mortgage Company__.

Mort Gage
__Borrower__

[this space for witnesses
and/or acknowledgment
if required by state law]

FIGURE 16-1 Promissory note
Source: © 2021 Mbition LLC

estate loans is almost always computed as *simple interest*. Simply put, the interest is computed against the current principal balance for each period. The amount of the payment required to retire the debt is referred to as the *debt service,* with the portion of the payment required for interest paid in arrears. For example, a $100,000 loan at an interest rate of 8% annually paid over 30 years would require a monthly debt service of $733.76. Don't worry about where the payment came from; just trust it is right. Of that payment, the interest is $666.67. If the due date of the payment was June 1, that payment would pay for the month of May (the 1st through the 31st). This would leave $67.09 available for debt reduction.

Prepayment Rights

The note may include a *prepayment privilege* or a *prepayment penalty.* Prepayment privilege is the right of the borrower to make additional and early payments against the loan balance without being penalized. All VA-guaranteed and FHA-insured loans feature prepayment privilege. Prepayment penalty provisions would require the borrower to pay a penalty if s/he pays off the loan early. While most conventional (nongovernment) loans do not have a prepayment penalty, they legally can. An example may be a penalty of 5% if the loan is paid off in the first year, 4% in the second, 3% in the third, 2% in the fourth, and 1% if the loan is paid off in the fifth year, with no penalty thereafter.

Default

The note will provide the lender with remedies in the event of a default. The default will be defined (e.g., not making payments within 15 days of the due date). In the event of a late payment, the note will provide for a penalty, usually a percentage of the overdue payment amount. In the event that the payments are not made, there will be a provision for acceleration. A common provision is that the lender may accelerate the note in the event that the borrower is more than 30 days late. If the lender has to take legal action against the borrower, the borrower will be responsible for all costs and expenses incurred by the lender.

Security

The note will state if there is supporting security such as a mortgage, trust deed, or security deed. In the event that the note is secured, which it virtually always will be in a real estate transaction, the note will tie defaults to the security as a default to the note. The common provisions of a security deed will be discussed next.

THE MORTGAGE INSTRUMENT

The mortgage is a separate agreement from the promissory note. Whereas the note is evidence of a debt and a promise to pay, the *mortgage* provides security (collateral) that the lender can sell if the note is not paid. The technical term for this is hypothecation. *Hypothecation* means the borrower retains the right to possess and use the property while it serves as collateral. In contrast, to pledge property means to give up possession to the lender while it serves as collateral. An example of pledging is the loan made by a pawn shop. The shop holds the collateral until the loan is repaid. The parties to the mortgage are the **mortgagor** and **mortgagee**. The mortgagor is the person giving the mortgage. Remembering that the mortgage is a security, it is the borrower who is giving security, so s/he would be the mortgagor. The lender is receiving the security, so it is the mortgagee. This terminology is often confused and misused. People merge "loan" and "mortgage" in their minds and treat them synonymously. The loan is given by the lender; the mortgage is given by the borrower.

mortgagor: the party giving a mortgage; the borrower

mortgagee: the party receiving a mortgage; the lender

DEED OF TRUST

In some states, debts are often secured by trust deeds. Whereas a mortgage is a two-party arrangement with a borrower and a lender, the *trust deed,* also known as a **deed of trust**, is a three-party arrangement consisting of the borrower (the **trustor**), the lender (the **beneficiary**), and a neutral third party (a **trustee**). The key aspect of this system is that the borrower executes a deed to the trustee rather than to the lender. If the borrower pays the debt in full and on time, the lender instructs the trustee to reconvey title back to the borrower. If the borrower defaults on the loan, the lender instructs the trustee to sell the property, at a nonjudicial foreclosure, to pay off the debt. The basic purpose of a trust deed is the same as a mortgage. Real property is used as security for a debt; if the debt is not repaid, the property is sold and the proceeds are applied to the balance owed.

trustor: one who creates a trust; the borrower in a deed of trust

beneficiary: one for whose benefit a trust is created; the lender in a deed of trust

trustee: one who holds property in trust for another; the third party in a deed of trust

PARTIES TO A DEED OF TRUST

When a debt is secured by a mortgage, the borrower delivers the promissory note and mortgage to the lender, who keeps them until the debt is paid. But when a note is secured by a deed of trust, three parties are involved: the borrower (the *trustor*), the lender (the *beneficiary*), and a neutral third party (the *trustee*). The lender makes a loan to the borrower, and the borrower gives the lender a promissory note and a deed of trust. In the deed of trust document, the borrower conveys title to the trustee, to be held in trust until the note is paid in full. (This is one of the distinguishing features of a deed of trust.)

The deed of trust is recorded in the county where the property is located and is then given to either the lender or the trustee for safekeeping. Anyone searching the title records would find the deed of trust conveying title to the trustee. This would alert the title searcher to the existence of a debt against the property. The title that the borrower grants to the trustee is sometimes referred to as a **naked title** or *bare title*. This is because the borrower still retains the usual rights of an owner, such as the right to occupy and use the property and the right to sell it. The title held by the trustee is limited to only what is necessary to carry out the terms of the trust. In fact, as long as the note is not in default, the trustee's title lies dormant. The lender does not receive title, but only a right that allows the lender to request the trustee to act. Before continuing, take a moment to reread this chapter thus far.

naked title: title that lacks the rights and privileges usually associated with ownership; also called a bare title

RECONVEYANCE

When the note is repaid in full under a regular mortgage, the lender cancels the note and returns it to the borrower, together with a mortgage satisfaction or release. Upon recordation, the mortgage satisfaction or release informs the world at large that the mortgage is nullified and no longer encumbers the property.

reconveyance deed: used to reconvey title to property back to the borrower once a debt has been paid on a deed of trust; also called a release deed

Under the deed of trust arrangement, the lender sends to the trustee the note, the deed of trust, and a request for reconveyance. The trustee cancels the note and issues to the borrower a **reconveyance deed**, also called a *release deed,* that releases the lien and/or reconveys title back to the borrower. The borrower records this document to inform the world that the trustee no longer has title. At the recorder's office, a marginal note may be made on the record copy of the original deed of trust to show that it has been discharged.

Default

If a borrower defaults under a deed of trust, the lender delivers the deed of trust to the trustee with instructions to sell the property and pay the balance due on the note. The trustee can do this because of two important features found in the deed of trust. First, by virtue of signing the deed of trust, the borrower has already conveyed title to the trustee. Second, the power of sale clause found in a deed of trust is designed to give the trustee the authority to sell the property without having to go through a court-ordered foreclosure proceeding.

Trustee

In nearly all states, a title, a trust, an escrow company, or the trust department of a bank may act as a trustee. An individual may be named as a trustee in most jurisdictions. However, this can present a problem if the person dies before reconveyance is made. Therefore, a corporate trustee is preferred because its life span is not limited by the human life span. In a few jurisdictions (Colorado, for example), the role of trustee is performed by a government official known as a *public trustee.*

Whether public or private, the trustee is expected to be neutral and fair to both the borrower and the lender. To accomplish this, the trustee carefully abides by the agreements found in the deed of trust. Because of the lack of title closings or escrow closings in Georgia, we lack the element of a natural third party to act as trustee. Because the use of a mortgage would require a judicial foreclosure (the lender would have to file formal suit and go to court if the borrower was in default; read into this time-consuming and expensive), mortgages, while legal, are not common in Georgia. An alternative to the judicial foreclosure when using a mortgage would be use of the trust deed as just explained. But also, as explained, we don't have a good, natural, neutral third party. By using the trust deed in Georgia, we have merely traded one problem for another and made no real improvement. Again, while legal, trust deeds are not commonly used in Georgia. What is used in Georgia, instead of a mortgage or trust deed, is the security deed.

SECURITY DEED (DEED TO SECURE DEBT)

A security deed in Georgia has the same basic purpose as a mortgage or trust deed: to provide security (collateral) for the note. Where the mortgage would simply convey lien rights to the lender and require judicial foreclosure, the security deed conveys legal title to the lender. With use of this document, the borrower is empowering the lender to act as attorney-in-fact and foreclose on the property in a nonjudicial process in the event of a default. Remember, a deed is a deed is a deed, and what a deed does is convey legal title.

As is the case with any deed, the parties are the grantor and grantee. Our rule is that the "-or" gives and the "-ee" receives. The grantor would be the party giving the deed; the borrower is giving the deed, transferring the interest in the property to the lender in the event of default. The grantee is the party receiving the deed; the lender is receiving the deed, accepting an interest in the property as security in the event of a borrower default.

Provisions of the Security Deed

The mortgage, trust deed, and security deed will have similar protection provisions—some for the lender and some for the borrower. In Appendix E, you will find a copy of a common security deed used in Georgia. Let us take a closer look to gain a better understanding of the provisions and clauses used in the Georgia security deed.

The first page of the security deed sets forth the parties to the document and defines the terms that will be used. The second page continues the definitions and then states that the security instrument grants from the borrower to the lender the rights in the property along with the power to sell the property. This is the "gotcha." The instrument then states, in detail, the covenants between the parties. Following is a simple explanation of some of the most important covenants.

Section 1 requires the borrower to make payments on time; if the payment is returned unpaid by the borrower's bank, the lender may require that all future payments be made in the form of cash, money order, or certified or cashier's check. This section also states that the lender has no responsibility to accept partial payments. Section 2 states that the payments received will be first applied to interest owed and then to principal. Unless there is a penalty for prepayment, this would allow the borrower to make extra payments of principal and pay off the loan early. The escrow account for budget loans is covered in section 3. The borrower is required to establish and maintain an account with the lender to cover future payments for items such as property taxes and insurance. Restrictions on how much may be collected by the lender and what will happen if there are excess funds or shortages are governed by RESPA. Section 4 is the *covenant to pay taxes*. Lenders are concerned about liens that have priority over their position and will require the borrower to discharge such debts. Section 5 is the *covenant to pay insurance*. The lender will require the borrower to maintain appropriate insurance to protect the lender from losses arising from fire, earthquake, flood, and any other hazard. The policy shall name the lender as a loss payee; the lender dictates the amount of insurance coverage. Usually, the lender will want insurance to cover the amount of the debt.

Section 6 requires the borrower to occupy the property within 60 days after closing and to occupy the property for at least one year as his/her primary residence. Funding of loans is typically more widely available and at favorable interest rates for owner-occupied dwellings than for investment properties. For this reason, it has become somewhat common for a borrower to "fudge" on the paperwork and state that the property is owner-occupied when it is not. This is loan fraud and subjects the parties to prosecution. The *covenant of good repair* is in section 7. The borrower agrees to maintain the property and not let it deteriorate. The lender's main concern is the property decreasing in value in the event that foreclosure is necessary. This section also allows the lender to make reasonable entries onto and into the property to make inspections. The borrower making false statements during a loan application is covered in section 8. In the event that the borrower makes a false statement, such as saying that the property is owner-occupied when it is not, the false statement shall constitute a default on the loan.

The lender's right to require the borrower to pay mortgage insurance is the subject of section 10. Unless waived by the lender, the mortgage insurance premiums shall be paid by the borrower to protect the lender against losses arising from the borrower's default. Also in this section is a reference to the rights the borrower shall have to cancel the insurance and/or receive unearned premiums under the Homeowners Protection Act of 1998. Section 18 is the **alienation clause**, which is alternatively known as the *due-on-sale clause*. If the borrower sells or conveys any interest in the property to another without the lender's prior written consent, such transfer is considered a default, and the lender has the right to call the entire loan balance due and payable. If the borrower does not pay, the lender may foreclose on the property. It is this clause that keeps most nongovernment loans (conventional) from being assumed. Section 19 refers to *equitable redemption*, which is the borrower's right to reinstate a defaulted loan after acceleration but before foreclosure under very specific circumstances. When a borrower has the right to reinstate ownership of the property after the foreclosure sale, the right is known as *statutory redemption*. Georgia does not recognize statutory redemption on a loan foreclosure.

The **acceleration clause** is covered in section 22. If the borrower defaults on any of the covenants contained in the security deed, the lender shall notify the borrower of such default and the borrower has 30 days to cure. In the event that the borrower does not cure the default, the lender may demand an immediate payment of the debt and invoke its power of sale. If the lender invokes the power of sale, it will provide the borrower with a copy of the sale notice, which is publicly advertised; the property is then sold on the courthouse steps on the first Tuesday of the month at public outcry. In this section, the borrower is appointing the lender to act as attorney-in-fact and convey indefeasible title to

---

alienation clause: clause that says if the borrower conveys any interest in the property to another without the lender's prior written consent, the lender has the right to call the entire loan balance due and payable; also called the due-on-sale clause

acceleration clause: allows the lender to demand immediate payment of the entire loan if the borrower defaults

the purchaser at the sale. The term "indefeasible" is in reference to the statutory redemption explained in the last paragraph. Section 23 requires the lender to cancel the security instrument upon full payment. This is sometimes referred to as the **defeasance clause**. The obligations of the borrower are terminated, and the lender must provide recorded proof that the debt has been paid.

defeasance clause: provides that the lender must cancel the security instrument upon full payment

Satisfaction of the Security Deed

When a borrower creates a debt against a property by signing a note and security deed, the security deed is recorded, and if a title search is completed, the security deed will show as an encumbrance on the property. Upon payoff of the note, the lender has the obligation to record a document showing that the debt is paid and the property is no longer encumbered. Often, the security deed has a provision printed on the document itself for the lender to sign showing that the property is being released as collateral; the security deed is then re-recorded at the county courthouse. When a title search is subsequently completed, the search will show the original security deed encumbering the property and then the release. This is similar to how a lien is released on an automobile. The lender holds the certificate of title while payments are being made, and upon the note being satisfied, the lender signs the document releasing its rights and sends the certificate to the owner of the vehicle. An alternative to having the security deed signed by the lender and re-recorded is to have the lender execute and record a separate document similar to a quitclaim deed. This document, which may be known as a "Cancellation of Deed to Secure Debt," is recorded at the office of the Clerk of the Superior Court in the county where the property is located.

Foreclosure on a Security Deed

The primary reason that a security deed is used in Georgia rather than a mortgage is the foreclosure process. Georgia is a lien theory state in relationship to the use of mortgages; that is, the lender simply receives lien rights to the property, and, in the event of default, the foreclosure process is judicial. This process of going to court to foreclose is expensive and time-consuming. An investor who is considering investing in mortgages secured by real estate would make funds available in a state that would provide for a nonjudicial process of foreclosure rather than judicial, with all other considerations being equal. Georgia has effectively circumvented the judicial foreclosure process by using the security deed, which transfers title to the lender (remember, a deed is a deed is a deed, and what a deed does is convey title). With the lender vested in legal title, the foreclosure process becomes nonjudicial. Although this directly benefits the lender, the borrowing public is benefited as a whole with lower interest rates, more available financing, and more programs from which to choose.

The security deed, like the mortgage and trust deed, contains an acceleration clause, which allows the lender to call the debt due upon the occurrence of an event.

This event could be a violation of any of the covenants in the security deed, but it is most commonly a default on the payments. The lender notifies the borrower of the default, and the borrower has a period of time to cure. If the default is not cured, the lender will send a demand letter to the borrower for payment.

At the time of making the demand, the lender (or lender's representative, such as a law firm) will begin advertising in the appropriate local newspaper. Every county has entered into a contract with a publisher, and its publication is deemed the "legal organ" for all legal notices. The property is advertised for four consecutive weeks and is then put up at public auction on the county courthouse steps on the first Tuesday of each month. Any party interested in the property may contact the lender or representative and receive information.

On the day of the sale, the lender's representative offers the property at public outcry and will typically bid the amount of debt and costs. Essentially, that's bidding on the note. Any other party wishing to bid must come with cash (typically, a letter of credit from a financial institution). The high bidder wins. If you have never attended a foreclosure sale, you should do so for the education and experience.

On a loan foreclosure in Georgia, the borrower has the legal right to pay off the loan any time before the sale and reclaim the property. This is known as equitable redemption. Once the sale is final, some states allow the borrower to reimburse the investor from the sale plus pay the investor an imputed rate of interest and reclaim the property. This is known as statutory redemption. Georgia does not recognize statutory redemption; the foreclosure against debt is final. Foreclosure is explained generically and in more depth later in this chapter.

"SUBJECT TO"

For the remainder of our discussion on financing, the term *mortgage* shall be used generically to refer to any security document. If the term *mortgage* shall mean specifically mortgage, exclusive of a security deed or trust deed, the text shall be specific and clear. If an existing mortgage on a property does not contain a due-on-sale clause, the seller may pass the benefits of that financing along to the buyer. (This can occur when the existing loan carries a lower rate of interest than currently available on new loans.) One method of doing this is for the buyer to purchase the property *subject to* the existing loan. In the purchase contract, the buyer states awareness of the existence of the loan and the mortgage that secures it, but takes no personal liability for it. Although the buyer pays the remaining loan payments as they come due, the seller continues to be personally liable to the lender for the loan. As long as the buyer faithfully continues to make the loan payments, which the buyer would normally do as long as the property is worth more than the debts against it, this arrangement presents no problem to the seller. However, if the buyer stops making payments before the loan is fully paid, the seller is totally liable. Even though it may be years later, the lender may require the seller to pay the balance due plus interest. This is true even though the seller was thought to be free of the loan because of selling the property. For obvious reasons, properties are seldom sold "subject to debt."

ASSUMPTION

The seller is on safer ground when requiring the buyer to assume the loan (*assumption*). Under this arrangement, the buyer promises in writing to the seller to pay the loan, thus becoming personally obligated to the seller. In the event of default on the loan, the lender will look to the seller because the seller's name is still on the original promissory note, but the seller has recourse against the buyer.

Assumption with a Release of Liability

The safest arrangement for the seller is to ask the lender to substitute the buyer's liability for his or her own. This is known as an assumption with a release of liability and is accomplished through a novation. This *novation* releases the seller from the personal obligation created by the promissory note, and the lender may now require only the buyer to repay the loan. The lender will require the buyer to prove financial capability to repay by having the buyer fill out a loan application and by running a credit check on the buyer. The lender may also adjust the rate of interest on the loan to reflect current market interest rates. The seller is also on safe ground against deficiency judgments, a topic that will be explained shortly.

ESTOPPEL

When a buyer is to continue making payments on an existing loan, the buyer will want to know exactly how much is still owed. A *certificate of reduction* is prepared by the lender to show how much of the loan remains to be paid. If a recorded mortgage states that it secures a loan for $135,000, but the borrower has reduced the amount owed to $50,000, the certificate of reduction will show that $50,000 remains to be paid. Roughly, the mirror image of a certificate of reduction is the *estoppel certificate*. In it, the borrower is asked to verify the amount still owed and the rate of interest. The most common application of an estoppel certificate is when the holder of a loan sells the loan to another investor. It avoids future confusion and litigation over misunderstandings as to how much is still owed on a loan. The word *estoppel* comes from Latin and literally means "to stop up." By signing an estoppel, a party is taking a position and is then legally prevented from taking a contrary position at a later date.

DEBT PRIORITIES

The same property can usually be used as collateral for more than one mortgage. This presents no problems to the lenders involved as long as the borrower makes the required payments on each note secured by the property. The difficulty arises when a default occurs on one or more of the loans and the price the property brings at its foreclosure sale does not cover all the loans against it. As a result, a priority system is necessary. The debt with the highest priority is satisfied first from the foreclosure sale proceeds, then the next highest priority debt is satisfied, then the next, and so on until either the foreclosure sale proceeds are exhausted or all debts secured by the property are satisfied.

First and Second Mortgages

In the vast majority of foreclosures, the sale proceeds are not sufficient to pay all the outstanding debt against the property; thus, it becomes extremely important that lenders know their priority position before making a loan. Unless there is a compelling reason otherwise, a lender will want to be in the most senior position possible. This is normally accomplished by being the first lender to record a mortgage against a property that is otherwise free and clear of mortgage debt; this lender is said to hold a **first mortgage** on the property. If the same property is later used to secure another note before the first is fully satisfied, the new mortgage is a **second mortgage**, and so on. The first mortgage is also known as the *senior mortgage*. Any mortgage with a lower priority is known as a **junior mortgage**. As time passes and higher-priority mortgages are satisfied, the lower-priority mortgages move up in priority. Thus, if a property is secured by a first and a second mortgage and the first is paid off, the second becomes a first mortgage. Note that nothing is stamped or written on a mortgage document to indicate if it is a first, second, or third mortgage. That can only be determined by searching the public records for mortgages recorded against the property that have not been released.

first mortgage: the mortgage loan with highest priority for repayment in the event of foreclosure; also called the senior mortgage

second mortgage: a mortgage in which property is used to secure another note before the first mortgage is fully satisfied

junior mortgage: any mortgage on a property that is subordinate to the first mortgage in priority

subordination: voluntary acceptance of a lower mortgage priority than one would otherwise be entitled to

Subordination

Sometimes, a lender will voluntarily take a lower-priority position than the lender would otherwise be entitled to by virtue of recording date. This is known as **subordination**, and it allows a junior loan to move up in priority. For example, the holder of a first mortgage may volunteer to become a second mortgagee and allow the second mortgage to move into the first position. Although it seems irrational that a lender would actually volunteer to accept a lower-priority position, it is sometimes done by landowners to encourage developers to buy their land. Another common example is refinancing. Many homeowners today have home equity loans that are seconds. If they wish to refinance the first to reduce the interest rate, this would push the second into a first position. Refinancing lenders would never allow themselves to be second to a home equity loan. To accomplish the needs of all, home equity lenders are asked to subordinate to the new loan, which they often and routinely do.

Chattel Liens

As discussed in the earlier topic of fixtures, an interesting situation regarding priority occurs when chattels are bought on credit and then affixed to land that is already mortgaged. If the chattels are not paid for, may the chattel lienholder come onto the land and remove them? If there is default on the mortgage loan against the land, are the chattels sold as fixtures? The solution is for the chattel lienholder to record a chattel mortgage or a financing statement. This protects the lienholder even though the chattel becomes a fixture when it is affixed to land. A *chattel mortgage* is a mortgage secured by personal property. If the borrower defaults, the lender is permitted to take possession and sell the mortgaged goods. A more streamlined approach is to file a *financing statement,* as provided by the Uniform Commercial Code, to establish lien priority regarding personal property.

THE FORECLOSURE PROCESS

With changing economic times, there have been periods of unprecedented incidents of foreclosure. In that Georgia has experienced all-time highs in distressed property transactions (and we can only hope those days are over and not to be repeated), it is important to have a basic understanding of what happens when foreclosure takes place. First, knowledge of what causes foreclosure can help in avoiding it; second, if foreclosure does occur, one should know the rights of the parties involved. As you read the following material, keep in mind that to *foreclose* simply means to cut off. What the lender is saying is, "Borrower, you are not keeping your end of the bargain. We want you out so the property can be put into the hands of someone who will keep the agreements." (What is often unsaid is that the lender has commitments to its savers that must be met. Can you imagine going to your bank and asking for the interest on your savings account and hearing the teller say the bank doesn't have it because its borrowers have not been making payments?)

Delinquent Loan

Although noncompliance with any part of the mortgage agreement by the borrower can result in the lender calling the entire balance immediately due, in most cases, foreclosure occurs because the note is not being repaid on time. When a borrower runs behind in payments, the loan is said to be a *delinquent loan.* At this stage, rather than presume that foreclosure is automatically next, the borrower and lender usually meet and attempt to work out an alternative payment program. Contrary to early motion picture plots in which lenders seemed anxious to foreclose their mortgages, today's lender considers foreclosure to be the last resort. This is because the foreclosure process is time-consuming, expensive, and unprofitable. The lender would much rather have the borrower make regular payments. Consequently, if a borrower is behind in loan payments, the lender prefers to arrange a new, stretched-out payment schedule rather than immediately declare the acceleration clause in effect and move toward foreclosing the borrower's rights to the property. If a borrower realizes that stretching out payments is not going to solve the financial problem, instead of presuming foreclosure to be inevitable, the borrower can seek a buyer for the property who can make the payments. It is only when the borrower cannot find a buyer and when the lender sees no further sense in stretching the payments that the acceleration clause is invoked and the path toward foreclosure taken.

Foreclosure Routes

Basically, there are two foreclosure routes: judicial and nonjudicial. *Judicial foreclosure* means taking the matter to a court of law in the form of a lawsuit that asks the judge to foreclose (cut off) the borrower. A *nonjudicial foreclosure* does not go to court and is not heard by a judge. It is conducted by the lender (or by a trustee) in accordance with provisions in the mortgage and in accordance with state law pertaining to nonjudicial foreclosures. Comparing the two, a judicial foreclosure is more costly and more time-consuming, but it does carry the approval of a court of law and may give the lender rights to collect the full amount of the loan if the property sells for less than the amount owed. It is also the preferred method when the foreclosure case is complicated and involves many parties and interests. The nonjudicial route is usually faster, simpler, and cheaper, and it is preferred by lenders when the case is simple and straightforward. Let us now look at the foreclosure process in the general sense.

JUDICIAL FORECLOSURE

The judicial foreclosure process begins with a title search. Next, the lender files a lawsuit naming as defendants the borrower and anyone who acquired a right or interest in the property after the lender recorded the mortgage. In the lawsuit, the lender identifies the debt and the mortgage securing it and states that it is in default. The lender then asks the court for a judgment directing that: (1) the defendants' interests in the property be cut off in order to return the condition of title to what it was when the loan was made, (2) the property be sold at a public auction, and (3) the lender's claim be paid from the sale proceeds.

Surplus Money Action

A copy of the complaint, along with a summons, is delivered to the defendants. This officially notifies them of the pending legal action against their interests. A junior mortgage holder that has been named as a defendant has basically two choices. One choice is to allow the foreclosure to proceed and file a *surplus money action*. By doing this, the junior mortgage holder hopes that the property will sell at the foreclosure sale for enough money to pay all senior claims as well as its own claim against the borrower. The other choice is to halt the foreclosure process by making the delinquent payments on behalf of the borrower and then adding them to the amount the borrower owes the junior mortgage holder. To do this, the junior mortgage holder must use cash out of pocket and decide whether this is a case of "good money chasing bad." In making this decision, the junior mortgage holder must consider whether its chances of being paid are better than those of the holder of the senior mortgage.

Notice of Lis Pendens

At the same time that the lawsuit to foreclose is filed with the court, a *notice of lis pendens* is filed with the county recorder's office where the property is located. This notice informs the public that a legal action is pending against the property. If the borrower attempts to sell the property at this time, the prospective buyer, upon making a title search, will learn of the pending litigation. The buyer may still proceed to purchase the property but is now informed of the unsettled lawsuit.

Public Auction

The borrower and any other defendants named in the lawsuit may now reply to the suit by presenting their side of the issue to the court judge. If no reply is made, or if the issues raised by the reply are found in favor of the lender, the judge will order that the interests of the borrower and other defendants in the property be foreclosed and the property sold. The sale is usually a *public auction*. The objective is to obtain the best possible price for the property by inviting competitive bidding and conducting the sale in full view of the public. To announce the sale, the judge orders a notice to be posted on the courthouse door and advertised in local newspapers.

Equity of Redemption

The sale is conducted by the county sheriff or by a referee or master appointed by the judge. At the sale, which is held either at the property or at the courthouse, the lender and all parties interested in purchasing the property are present. If the borrower should suddenly locate sufficient funds to pay the judgment, the borrower can, up to the minute the property goes on sale, step forward and redeem the property. This privilege to redeem property any time between the first sign of delinquency and the moment of foreclosure sale is the borrower's *equity of redemption*. If no redemption is made, the bidding begins. Anyone with adequate funds may bid. Typically, a cash deposit of 10% of the successful bid must be made at the sale, with the balance of the bid price due upon closing, usually 30 days later.

While the lender and borrower hope that someone at the auction will bid more than the amount owed on the defaulted loan, the probability is not high.

If the borrower was unable to find a buyer at a price equal to or higher than the loan balance, the best cash bid will probably be less than the balance owed. If this happens, the lender usually enters a bid. The lender is in the unique position of being able to *bid the loan*—that is, the lender can bid up to the amount owed without having to pay cash. All other bidders must pay cash, as the purpose of the sale is to obtain cash to pay the defaulted loan. In the event that the borrower bids at the sale and is successful in buying back the property, the junior liens against the property are not eliminated. Note, however, that no matter who the successful bidder is, the foreclosure does not cut off property tax liens against the property; they remain.

Deficiency Judgment

If the property sells for more than the claims against it, including any junior mortgage holders, the borrower receives the excess. For example, if a property with $150,000 in claims against it sells for $155,000, the borrower will receive the $5,000 difference, less unpaid property taxes and expenses of the sale. However, if the highest bid is only $40,000, how is the $110,000 deficiency treated? The laws of the various states differ on this question. Forty states (Georgia included) allow the lender to pursue a **deficiency judgment** for the $110,000, with which the lender can proceed against the borrower's other unsecured assets. In other words, the borrower is still personally obligated to the lender for $110,000, and the lender is entitled to collect it. This may require the borrower to sell other assets.

Only a judge can award a lender a deficiency judgment, and only after a confirmation of sale hearing. If the property sells for an obviously depressed price at its foreclosure sale, a deficiency judgment may be allowed only for the difference between the court's estimate of the property's fair market value and the amount still owing against it. Note that if a borrower is in a strong enough bargaining position, it is possible to add wording in the promissory note that the note is *without recourse*, or *no personal liability*. This prohibits the lender from seeking a deficiency judgment, but this must be negotiated before the note is signed.

The purchaser at the foreclosure sale receives either a *referee's deed in foreclosure* or a *sheriff's deed*. These are usually special warranty deeds that convey the title the borrower had at the time the foreclosed mortgage was originally made.

The purchaser may take immediate possession, and the court will assist in removing anyone in possession who was cut off in the foreclosure proceedings.

deficiency judgment: a judgment against a borrower if the foreclosure sale does not bring enough to pay the balance owed

Statutory Redemption

In states with *statutory redemption* laws, the foreclosed borrower has, depending on the state, from one month to one year or more after the foreclosure sale to pay in full the judgment and retake title. This leaves the high bidder at the foreclosure auction with the dilemma of not being certain of owning the property until the statutory redemption period has run out. Meanwhile, the high bidder receives a *certificate of sale* entitling that bidder to a referee's or sheriff's deed if no redemption is made. Depending on the state, the purchaser may or may not get possession until then. If not, the foreclosed borrower may allow the property to deteriorate and lose value. Knowing this, bidders tend to offer less than what the property would be worth if title and possession could be delivered immediately after the foreclosure sale. In this respect, statutory redemption works against the borrower as well as the lender. This problem can be made less severe if the court appoints a *receiver* (manager) to take charge of the property during the redemption period. Judicial foreclosure with public auction is the predominant method in 21 states, and 9 of them allow a statutory redemption period. As stated earlier, Georgia does not allow for a statutory redemption on a security deed foreclosure.

Strict Foreclosure

Strict foreclosure is a judicial foreclosure without a judicial sale, and usually without a statutory redemption period. Basically, the lender files a lawsuit requesting that the borrower be given a period of time to exercise the equitable right of redemption or lose all rights to the property, with title vesting irrevocably in the lender. Although this conjures up visions of a greedy lender foreclosing on a borrower who has nearly paid for the property and misses a payment or two, the court will give the borrower time to make up the back payments or sell the property on the open market. Much more likely is the situation in which the debt owed clearly exceeds the property's value. In this case, there is little to be gained by conducting a judicial sale. Strict foreclosure is the predominant method of foreclosure in two states and is occasionally used in others. Where the debt exceeds the property's value and the foreclosure prohibits a deficiency judgment, this method may be advantageous to the borrower.

NONJUDICIAL FORECLOSURE (POWER OF SALE)

In 27 states, the predominant method of foreclosure is by **power of sale**, also known as *sale by advertisement*. This clause, which must be placed in the mortgage before it is signed, gives the lender the power to conduct the foreclosure and sell the mortgaged property without taking the issue to court. The procedure begins when a lender files a *notice of default* with the public recorder. Next is a waiting period that is the borrower's equity of redemption. The property is then advertised at an auction held by the lender and open to the public. The precise procedures the lender must follow are set by state statutes. After the auction, the borrower may still redeem the property if that state offers statutory redemption. The deed the purchaser receives is prepared and signed by the lender or trustee.

Lenders foreclosing under power of sale may not award themselves a deficiency judgment. If there is a deficiency as a result of the sale, and lenders want a deficiency judgment, the lenders must go to court for it. Because power of sale foreclosures take place outside the jurisdiction of a courtroom, it is said that

power of sale: allows a mortgagee to conduct a foreclosure sale without first going to court

courts watch them with a careful eye. If a borrower feels mistreated by power of sale proceedings, the borrower can appeal the issue to a court. Wise lenders know this and keep scrupulous records and follow foreclosure rules carefully. The wise junior mortgage holder will have already filed a *request for notice of default* with the public records office when the junior mortgage was recorded. This requires anyone holding a more senior lien to notify the junior mortgagee if a default notice has been filed. (Usually, the junior mortgagee is aware of the problem, because if the borrower is not making payments to the holder of the first mortgage, the borrower probably is not making payments to any junior mortgage holders.) With the use of the security deed in Georgia, the foreclosure process is nonjudicial.

Entry and Possession

Used as the predominant method of foreclosure in one state and to a lesser degree in three others, *entry and possession* is based on the lender giving notice to the borrower that the lender wants possession of the property. The borrower moves out and the lender takes possession, and this is witnessed and recorded in the public records. If the borrower does not peacefully agree to relinquish possession, the lender will have to use a judicial method of foreclosure.

Deed in Lieu of Foreclosure

To avoid the hassle of foreclosure proceedings and possible deficiency judgment, a borrower may want to voluntarily deed the mortgaged property to the lender. In turn, the borrower should demand cancellation of the unpaid debt, as well as a letter to that effect from the lender. This method relieves the lender of foreclosing and waiting out any required redemption periods, but it also presents the lender with a sensitive situation. With the borrower in financial distress and about to be foreclosed, it is quite easy for the lender to take advantage of the borrower. As a result, a court of law will usually side with the borrower if the borrower complains of any unfair dealings. Therefore, the lender must be prepared to prove conclusively that the borrower received a fair deal by deeding the property voluntarily to the lender in return for cancellation of the debt. A word of caution, though. The debt cancellation may be taxable as income! If the property is worth more than the balance due on the debt, the lender must pay the borrower the difference in cash. A *deed in lieu of foreclosure* is a voluntary act by both borrower and lender and hence is sometimes called a "friendly foreclosure." Nonetheless, if either feels that regular foreclosure proceedings would be advantageous, no agreement is reached. Note also that, depending on state law, a deed in lieu of foreclosure may not cut off the rights of junior mortgage holders. This means the lender may have to make those payments or be foreclosed by the junior mortgage holder(s). Figure 16-2 summarizes through illustration the five methods of mortgage foreclosure that have just been discussed.

Nonjudicial Foreclosure (Power of Sale)

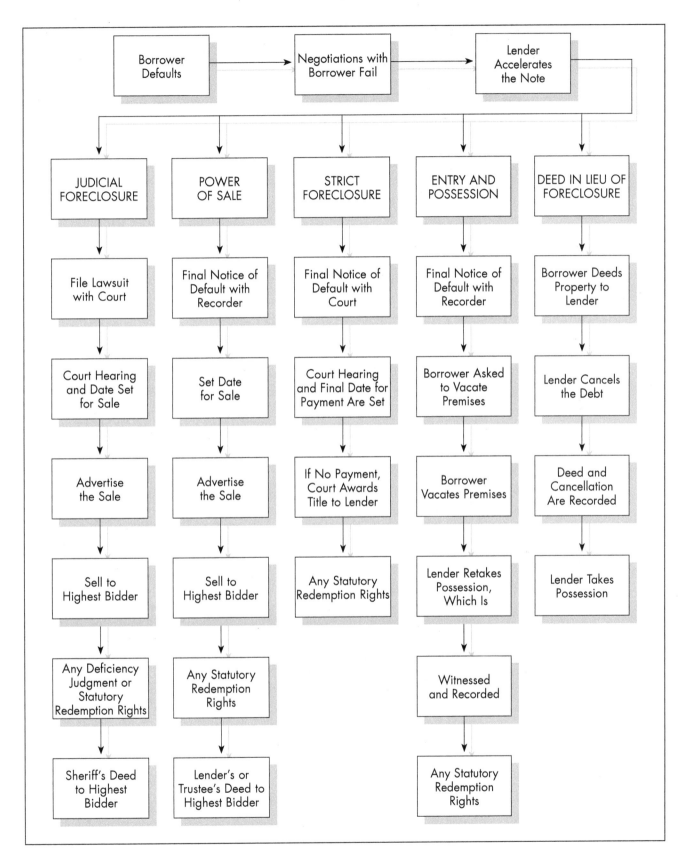

FIGURE 16-2 Mortgage foreclosure—simplified overview

Source: © 2021 Mbition LLC

EQUITABLE MORTGAGE

An *equitable mortgage* is a written agreement that, although it does not follow the form of a regular mortgage, is considered by the courts to be one. For example, Black sells his land to Green, with Green paying part of the price in cash now and promising to pay the balance later. Normally, Black would ask Green to execute a regular mortgage as security for the balance due. However, instead of doing this, Black makes a note of the balance due him on the deed before handing it to Green. The laws of most states would regard this notation as an equitable mortgage. For all intents and purposes, it is a mortgage, although not specifically called one. Another example of an equitable mortgage can arise from the deposit money accompanying an offer to purchase property. If the seller refuses the offer and refuses to return the deposit, the courts will hold that the purchaser has an equitable mortgage in the amount of the deposit against the seller's property.

CHOICE OF SECURITY INSTRUMENT

Generally speaking, a lender will choose, and ask the borrower to sign, whatever security instrument provides the smoothest foreclosure in that state. To illustrate, some states require a statutory redemption period for a mortgage foreclosure but not for a deed of trust foreclosure. Some will allow power of sale for a deed of trust but not for a mortgage. All states allow the use of a deed of trust, but some require that it be foreclosed like a mortgage. More and more states require installment contracts to be foreclosed like mortgages. An analogy for the development of security instrument law is that of a plant growing up through a pile of rocks. Its path up may be twisted and curved, but it reaches its goal: the sunlight. Security instruments follow many paths, but always with one goal in mind—to get money to the borrower, who uses it and then returns it to the lender.

Review Questions

Answers to these questions can be found in Appendix D at the end of this book.

1. Evidence of the amount and terms of a borrower's debt to a lender is provided by means of a:
   A. mortgage
   B. promissory note
   C. deed of trust
   D. first mortgage

2. A promissory note that fails to state that it is to be secured by a mortgage or deed of trust is:
   A. a professional obligation of the borrower
   B. a secured obligation of the borrower
   C. an unsecured obligation of the borrower
   D. not valid

3. Should a borrower fail to make payments when due, the lender may demand immediate payment of the entire balance under the terms of the:
   A. prepayment clause
   B. defeasance clause
   C. acceleration clause
   D. hypothecation clause

4. Which of the following statements is NOT correct?
   A. A promissory note is evidence of a borrower's debt to a lender.
   B. A mortgage hypothecates property as collateral for a loan.
   C. A note secures a mortgage.
   D. The lender in a mortgage is a mortgagee.

5. In Georgia, foreclosure on a mortgage is:
   A. judicial
   B. nonjudicial
   C. intermediate
   D. strict

6. Which of the following covenants will NOT appear in a mortgage?
   A. covenants to pay taxes and insurance
   B. covenant against removal
   C. covenant against encumbrances
   D. covenant of good repair

7. The clause that gives the lender the right to call in the note if the mortgaged property is sold or otherwise conveyed by the borrower is known as the:
   A. acceleration clause
   B. escalation clause
   C. alienation clause
   D. defeasance clause

8. Who may be held responsible for mortgage loan repayment when a property is sold subject to debt?
   A. the purchaser only
   B. the purchaser and seller
   C. the seller only
   D. the seller, purchaser, and lender

9. When a loan is assumed, the:
   A. seller cannot be relieved of liability
   B. buyer should verify the loan balance with the seller
   C. seller may be released of liability through novation
   D. interest rate will increase to market rates

10. For a security deed to be effective, it must be:
    A. signed by the lender
    B. witnessed by four witnesses
    C. recorded at the county courthouse
    D. prepared by legal counsel

11. The period of equitable redemption given to a borrower:
    A. is not recognized in Georgia
    B. extends from one month to one year after the foreclosure sale
    C. ends when the property is sold at foreclosure
    D. is not less than three months and not more than one year

12. When the amount received from a foreclosure sale is insufficient to pay off the mortgage loan and the other expenses of the sale, the lender may sometimes secure:
    A. a deficiency judgment
    B. a mechanic's lien
    C. an estoppel lien
    D. a statutory lien

13. The deed given to the purchaser at foreclosure by the sheriff or other officer of the court usually takes the form of a:
    A. general warranty deed
    B. quitclaim deed
    C. special warranty deed
    D. bargain and sale deed

14. The period of time set by state law after a foreclosure sale, during which the mortgagor may redeem the property, is known as the period of:
    A. equitable redemption
    B. legal redemption
    C. voluntary redemption
    D. statutory redemption

15. A borrower who feels mistreated by a power of sale foreclosure can:
    A. obtain a judicial foreclosure
    B. appeal the issue to the courts
    C. obtain a judgment
    D. obtain a lien

16. By voluntarily giving the lender a deed in lieu of foreclosure, a delinquent borrower does NOT avoid:
    A. foreclosure proceedings
    B. possible deficiency judgments
    C. a negative credit score
    D. increased expenses

17. Generally, lenders ask borrowers to sign whatever security instrument:
    A. is available
    B. is requested by the borrower
    C. permits the smoothest foreclosure proceedings in that state
    D. allows the highest interest rate

18. A document that for all intents and purposes is a mortgage, although not labeled one, would most likely be:
    A. an installment contract
    B. a deed of trust
    C. an equitable mortgage
    D. a deed as security

19. The borrower under a deed of trust is the:
    A. beneficiary
    B. trustee
    C. trustor
    D. assignor

20. The lender under a deed of trust is the:
    A. beneficiary
    B. trustee
    C. trustor
    D. assignee

CHAPTER

17 TAXES AND ASSESSMENTS

KEY TERMS

ad valorem taxes
amount realized
assessed value
assessment appeal board
basis
documentary tax
installment method
mill rate
tax certificate
tax lien

OBJECTIVES

After successful completion of this chapter, you should be able to:

1. explain the purpose of property taxes and how they are determined;
2. explain tax exemptions, variations, and limitation measures;
3. define special assessments and explain the process for confirmation and apportionment;
4. explain how to calculate income taxes on the sale of a residence;
5. calculate the amount realized, income tax exclusion, and capital gains on the sale of a residence;
6. describe property tax and interest deductions;
7. explain what the agent's liability is for tax advice; and
8. describe the applicability of conveyance taxes.

OVERVIEW

In this chapter, we are primarily concerned with *ad valorem* taxes and various types of property assessments. Determining how much tax the property owner must pay involves these basic steps: appropriation, assessment, and tax rate calculation. The chapter also covers unpaid property taxes, assessment appeal, property

tax exemptions and variations, tax limitation measures, and special assessments. In the latter half of the chapter, income taxes on the sale of a residence—including income tax exclusion, capital gains, and installment sales—are covered. The chapter concludes with coverage of property tax and interest deductions and the agent's liability for tax advice.

PROPERTY TAXES

The largest single source of income in the United States for local government programs and services is the property tax. Schools (from kindergartens through two-year colleges), fire and police departments, local welfare programs, public libraries, street maintenance, parks, and public hospital facilities are mainly supported by property taxes.

Some state governments also obtain a portion of their revenues from this source. Property taxes are *ad valorem* taxes. This means that they are levied according to the value of one's property; the more valuable the property, the higher the tax, and vice versa. The underlying theory of *ad valorem* taxation is that those owning the more valuable properties are wealthier and hence able to pay more taxes.

ad valorem taxes: taxes charged according to the value of a property

How does a local government determine the amount of tax to collect each year from each property owner? Step 1 is local budget preparation and appropriation. Step 2 is the appraisal of all taxable property within the taxation district. Step 3 is to allocate the amount to be collected among the taxable properties in the district. Let's look more closely at this process.

Budget and Appropriation

Each taxing body with the authority to tax prepares its budget for the coming year. Taxing bodies include counties, cities, boroughs, towns and villages, and, in some states, school boards, sanitation districts, and county road departments. Each budget, along with a list of sources from which the money will be derived, is enacted into law. This is the *appropriation process*. Then, estimated sales taxes, state and federal revenue sharing, business licenses, and city income taxes are subtracted from the budget. The balance must come from property taxes.

Appraisal and Assessment

Next, the valuation of the taxable property within each taxing body's district must be determined. A county or state assessor's office *appraises* each taxable parcel of land and the improvements thereon. In some states, this job is contracted out to private appraisal companies. Appraisal procedures vary from state to state. In some, the appraised value is the estimated fair market cash value of the property. This is the cash price one would expect a buyer and a seller to agree upon in a normal open market transaction. Other states start with the fair market value of the land and add to it the cost of replacing the buildings and other improvements on it, minus an allowance for depreciation due to wear and tear and obsolescence.

The appraised value is converted into an assessed value upon which taxes are based. In some states, the **assessed value** is set equal to the appraised value, but more commonly it is a percentage of the appraised value. Mathematically, the percentage selected makes no difference as long as each property in a taxing district is treated equally. Consider two houses with appraised values of $120,000 and $240,000, respectively. Whether the assessed values are set equal to appraised values or at a percentage of appraised values, the second house will still bear twice the property tax burden of the first.

assessed value: a value placed on a property for the purpose of taxation

Tax Rate Calculation

The assessed values of all properties subject to property taxation are added together in order to calculate the tax rate. Here's how the process works: Suppose that a building lies within the taxation districts of the Westside School District, the city of Rostin, and the county of Pearl River. The school district's budget for the coming year requires $8 million from property taxes, and the assessed value of taxable property within the district is $200 million. By dividing $8 million by $200 million, we see that the school district must collect a tax of 4% (.04) or $4 per thousand dollars of assessed valuation. This levy can be expressed three ways: (1) as a mill rate, (2) as dollars per hundred, or (3) as dollars per thousand. All three rating methods are found in the United States, but the mill rate is most common, and that is certainly true in Georgia. As a **mill rate**, this tax rate is usually expressed as dollars per thousand dollars of assessed valuation. Thus, a millage rate of 22 would be $22 per thousand dollars of assessed value; a millage rate of 17.25 would be $17.25 per thousand dollars of assessed value, and so on.

mill rate: property tax rate that is expressed in tenths of a cent per dollar of assessed valuation

The city of Rostin also calculates its tax rate by dividing its property tax requirements by the assessed value of the property within its boundaries. Suppose that its needs are $3 million and the city limits enclose property totaling $100 million in assessed valuation. (In this example, the city covers a smaller geographical area than the school district.) Thus, the city must collect $3 for each thousand dollars of assessed valuation in order to balance its budget. The county government's budget requires $20 million from property taxes, and the county contains $2 billion in assessed valuation. This makes the county tax rate $1 per thousand dollars of assessed valuation. Figure 17-1 shows the school district, city, and county tax rates expressed as mills, dollars per hundred, and dollars per thousand.

Applying the Rate

The final step is to apply the tax rate to each property. Applying the mill rate to a home with an assessed value of $200,000 is simply a matter of multiplying the 80 mills (the equivalent of $80 per thousand dollars of assessed value) by the

	Mill Rate	Dollars per Hundred	Dollars per Thousand
School district	40 mills	$4.00	$40.00
City	30	3.00	30.00
County	10	1.00	10.00
Total	**80 mills**	**$8.00**	**$80.00**

FIGURE 17-1 Expressing property tax rates
Source: © 2021 Mbition LLC

tax lien: a charge or hold by the government against property to ensure the payment of taxes

assessed valuation to arrive at property taxes of $16,000 per year. To calculate this number, multiply 200 (which represents the number of thousands) by 80 (which represents the tax rate per thousand). The result is $16,000. To ensure collection, a **tax lien** for this amount is placed against the property. It is removed when the tax is paid. Property tax liens are superior to other types of liens. A mortgage foreclosure does not clear property tax liens; they still must be paid.

To avoid duplicate tax bill mailings, all taxing bodies in a given county commonly have the county collect for them at the same time that the county collects on its own behalf. Property tax years are assessed and collected on a calendar year basis, January 1 through December 31.

Some counties require one payment per year; others collect in two installments. A few allow a small discount for early payment, and all charge penalties for late payments. Because of the monumental volume of numbers and calculations necessary to budget, appropriate, appraise, assess, and calculate property taxes, computers are widely used in property tax offices. Computers also prepare property tax bills, account for property tax receipts, and mail notices to those who have not paid.

UNPAID PROPERTY TAXES

If you own real estate and fail to pay the property taxes, you will lose the property. In some states, title to delinquent property is transferred to the county or state. A redemption period follows during which the owner, or any lienholder, can redeem the property by paying back taxes and penalties. If redemption does not occur, the property is sold at a publicly announced auction, and the highest bidder receives a *tax deed*. In Georgia, the sale is held soon after the delinquency occurs and the redemption period follows. At the sale, a **tax certificate** or *certificate of sale* in the amount of the unpaid taxes is sold. The purchaser is entitled to a deed to the property provided the delinquent taxpayer, or anyone holding a lien on the property, does not step forward and redeem it during the redemption period that follows. The redemption period for a tax sale in Georgia is one year. If it is redeemed, the purchaser receives the money back plus interest. A lienholder (such as a mortgage lender) is allowed to redeem a property because, if the property taxes are not paid, the lienholder's creditor rights in the property are cut off due to the superiority of the tax lien.

tax certificate: a document issued at a tax sale that entitles the purchaser to a deed at a later date if the property is not redeemed

The right of government to divorce property owners from their land for non-payment of property taxes is well established by law. However, if the sale procedure is not properly followed, the purchaser may later find the property's title successfully challenged in court. Thus, it behooves the purchaser to obtain a title search and title insurance and, if necessary, to conduct a quiet title suit.

ASSESSMENT APPEAL

By law, assessment procedures must be uniformly applied to all properties within a taxing jurisdiction. To this end, the assessed values of all lands and buildings are made available for public inspection. These are the *assessment rolls*. They permit property owners to compare the assessed valuation on their property with assessed valuations on similar properties. An owner who feels over-assessed may file an appeal before an **assessment appeal board** or before a board of review, board of equalization, or tribunal. Some states provide further appeal channels or permit appeal to a court of law if the property owner remains dissatisfied with the assessment. Note that the appeal process deals only with the methods of assessment and taxation, not with the tax rate or the amount of tax. In some states, the *board of equalization* performs another assessment-related task: that of equalizing assessment procedures among counties. This is particularly important where county-collected property taxes are shared with the state or other counties. Without equalization, it would be to a county's financial advantage to underassess so as to lessen its contribution. At present, two equalization methods are in common usage: One requires that all counties use the same appraisal procedure and assessed valuation ratio, and the other allows each county to choose its own method and then applies a correction as determined by the board. For example, a state may contain counties that assess at 20%, 24%, and 30% of fair market value. These could be equalized by multiplying assessed values in the 20% counties by 1.50, in the 24% counties by 1.25, and in the 30% counties by 1.00. These are known as equalization factors.

assessment appeal board: local governmental body that hears and rules on property owner complaints of over-assessment

PROPERTY TAX EXEMPTIONS

More than half the land in many cities and counties is exempt from real property taxation. This is because governments and their agencies do not tax themselves or each other. Thus, government-owned offices of all types, public roads and parks, schools, military bases, and government-owned utilities are exempt from property taxes. Also exempt are most properties owned by religious and charitable organizations (so long as they are used for religious or charitable purposes), hospitals, and cemeteries. In rural areas of many states, large tracts of land are owned by federal and state governments, and these, too, are exempt from taxation.

Property tax exemptions are used to attract industries. For example, a local government agency buys industrial land and buildings and leases them to industries at a price lower than would be possible if they were privately owned and, hence, taxed. Alternatively, outright property tax reductions may be granted for a certain length of time to newly established or relocating firms. The rationale is that the cost to the public is outweighed by the economic boost that the new industry brings to the community. Many states, Georgia included, grant an assessment reduction to homeowners that is known as a *homestead exemption.* This reduces the amount of taxes owed on property used as a primary residence.

California and several other states have enacted laws that allow elderly homeowners to postpone payment of their property taxes. The state delays collection of the taxes and puts a lien on the property. Interest is charged each year on the postponed taxes, and postponement can continue indefinitely. The amount due is not payable until the home is sold, or the owners die (in which case, the estate or heirs would pay), or the property, for some other reason, ceases to qualify. To qualify, all owners must live in the home and have reached a certain age—62 years, for example. Additionally, there may be a limitation on household income to qualify.

PROPERTY TAX VARIATIONS

Property taxes on similarly priced homes within a city or county can vary widely when prices change faster than the assessor's office can reappraise. As a result, a home worth $90,000 in one neighborhood may receive a tax bill of $1,800 per year, while a $90,000 home in another neighborhood will be billed $2,400. When the assessor's office conducts a reappraisal, taxes in the first neighborhood will suddenly rise 33%, undoubtedly provoking complaints from property owners who were unaware that previously they were being under-assessed. In times of slow-changing real estate prices, reappraisals were made only once every 10 years. Today, many assessors have computerized appraisal systems that can make adjustments annually.

As an aid to keeping current on property value changes, states are enacting laws that require a real estate buyer to advise the assessor's office of the price and terms of a purchase within 90 days after taking title. This information, coupled with building permit records and on-site visits by assessor's office employees, provides the data necessary to regularly update assessments. The amount of property taxes a property owner may expect to pay varies from one city to the next and from one state to the next. Why is this? The answer is found by looking at the level of services offered, other sources of revenue, taxable property, and government efficiency. Generally, cities with low property taxes offer fewer services to their residents. This may be by choice (such as smaller welfare payments, lower school expenditures per student, no subsidized public transportation, fewer parks and libraries), or because the city does not include the cost of some services in the property tax. For example, sewer fees may be added to the water bill, and trash may be hauled by private firms. Lower rates can also be due to location. Wage rates are lower in some regions of the country, and a city not subject to ice and snow will have lower street maintenance expenses. Finally, a city may have other sources of revenue, such as oil royalties from wells on city property.

Property tax levels are also influenced by the ability of local tax districts to obtain federal funds and state revenues (especially for schools) and to share in collections from sales taxes, license fees, liquor and tobacco taxes, and fines. The amount and type of taxable property in a community greatly affects local tax rates. Taxable property must bear the burden avoided by tax-exempt property, whereas privately owned vacant land, stores, factories, and high-priced homes generally produce more taxes than they consume in local government services and help to keep rates lower. Finally, one must look at the efficiency of the city. Has it managed its affairs in prior years so that the current budget is not burdened with large interest payments on debts caused by deficits in previous years? Is the city or county itself laid out in a compact and efficient manner, or does its sheer size make administration expensive? How many employees are required to perform a given service?

SPECIAL ASSESSMENTS

Often, the need arises to make local municipal improvements (such as the paving of a street; the installation of street lights, curbs, storm drains, and sanitary sewer lines; or the construction of irrigation and drainage ditches) that will benefit property owners within a limited area. Such improvements can be provided through *special assessments* on property. The theory underlying special assessments is that the improvements must benefit the land against which the cost will be charged, and the value of the benefits must exceed the cost. The area receiving the benefit of an improvement is the *improvement district* or *assessment district*, and the property within that district bears the cost of the improvement. This is different from a *public improvement*. A public improvement, such as reconstruction of the city's sewage plant, benefits the general public and is financed through the general (*ad valorem*) property tax. A local improvement, such as extending a sewer line into a street of homes currently using septic tanks or cesspools, does not benefit the public at large and should properly be charged only to those who directly benefit. Similarly, when streets are widened, owners of homes lining a 20-foot-wide street in a strictly residential neighborhood would be expected to bear the cost of widening it to 30 or 40 feet, and to donate the needed land from their front yards. But a street widening from two lanes to four to accommodate traffic not generated by the homes on the street is a different situation because the widening benefits the public at large. In this case, the street widening is funded from public monies, and the homeowners are paid for any land taken from them.

Forming an Improvement District

An improvement district can be formed by a group of concerned citizens who want and are willing to pay for an improvement. Property owners desiring the improvement take their proposal to the local board of assessors or similar public body in charge of levying assessments. A public notice showing the proposed improvements, the extent of the improvement district, and the anticipated costs is prepared by the board. This notice is mailed to landowners in the proposed improvement district, posted conspicuously in the district, and published in a local newspaper. The notice also contains the date and place of public hearings on the matter, at which property owners within the proposed district are invited to voice their comments and objections.

Confirmation

If the hearings result in a decision to proceed, then under the authority granted by state laws regarding special improvements, a local government adopts an ordinance that describes the project and its costs as well as the improvement district boundaries. An assessment roll is also prepared that shows the cost to each parcel in the district. Hearings are held regarding the assessment roll. When everything is in order, the roll is *confirmed* (approved). Then, the contract to construct the improvements is awarded, and work is started.

The proposal to create an improvement district can also come from a city council, board of trustees, or board of supervisors. When this happens, notices are distributed and hearings are held to hear objections from affected parties. Objections are ruled on by a court of law, and, if the objections are to have merit, the assessment plans must be revised or dropped. Once a proposal is approved, an assessment roll is prepared, more hearings are held, the roll is confirmed, and the contract is awarded.

Bond Issues

Upon completion of the improvement, landowners receive a bill for their portion of the cost. If the cost to a landowner is less than $100, the landowner pays the amount in full either to the contractor directly or to a designated public official who, in turn, pays the contractor. If the assessment is larger, the landowner can immediately pay it in full or let it *go to bond*. If s/he lets it go to bond, local government officials prepare a bond issue that totals all the unpaid assessments in the improvement district. These bonds are either given to the contractor as payment for the work or sold to the public through a securities dealer, and the proceeds are used to pay the contractor. The collateral for the bonds is the land in the district upon which assessments have not been paid.

The bonds spread the cost of the improvements over 5 to 10 years and are payable in equal annual (or semi-annual) installments plus accumulated interest. Thus, a $2,000 sewer and street-widening assessment on a 10-year bond would be charged to a property owner at the rate of $200 per year (or $100 each six months) plus interest. As the bond is gradually retired, the amount of interest added to the regular principal payment declines. Like property taxes, special assessments are a lien against the property. Consequently, if a property owner fails to pay the assessment, the assessed property can be sold in the same manner as when property taxes are delinquent.

Apportionment

Special assessments are apportioned according to benefits received rather than by the value of the land and buildings being assessed. In fact, the presence of buildings in an improvement district is not usually considered in preparing the assessment roll; the theory is that the land receives all the benefit of the improvement. Several illustrations can best explain how assessments are apportioned. In a residential neighborhood, the assessment for installation of storm drains, curbs, and gutters is made on a *front-foot basis*. A property owner is charged for each foot of the lot that abuts the street being improved.

In the case of a sanitary sewer line assessment, the charge per lot can be based either on front footage or on a simple count of the lots in the district. In the latter case, if there are 100 lots on the new sewer line, each would pay 1% of the cost. In the case of a park or playground, lots nearest the new facility are deemed to benefit more, and, thus, are assessed more than lots located farther away. This form of allocation is very subjective and usually results in spirited objections at public hearings from those who do not feel they will use the facility in proportion to the assessment that their lots will bear.

INCOME TAXES ON THE SALE OF ONE'S RESIDENCE

We now turn to the income taxes that are due if you sell your personal residence for more than you paid. Income taxes on investment income are levied by the federal government, by 43 states (the exceptions are Alaska, Florida, Nevada, South Dakota, Texas, Washington, and Wyoming), and by dozens of cities, including Baltimore, Cincinnati, Cleveland, Detroit, New York City, Philadelphia, and Pittsburgh. The discussion here centers on the federal income tax and includes key provisions of the Internal Revenue Code as it applies to owner-occupied residences. Aspects of this code that apply to real estate investments are discussed in a later chapter. State and city income tax laws generally follow the pattern of federal tax laws.

Calculating a Home's Basis

The first step in determining the amount of taxable gain upon the sale of an owner-occupied residence is to calculate the home's **basis**. This is the price originally paid for the home, plus any fees paid for closing services and legal counsel, and any fee or commission paid to help find the property. If the home was built rather than purchased, the basis is the cost of the land plus the cost of construction, including the cost of materials and construction labor, architect's fees, building permit fees, planning and zoning commission approval costs, utility connection charges, and legal fees. The value of labor contributed by the homeowner and free labor from friends and relatives cannot be added. If the home was received as compensation, as a gift, as an inheritance, or in a trade, or if a portion of the home was

basis: the price paid for property; used in calculating income taxes

depreciated for business purposes, special rules apply that will not be covered here; the seller should consult the Internal Revenue Service (IRS).

Assessments for local improvements and any improvements made by the seller are added to the original cost of the home. An improvement is a permanent betterment that materially adds to the value of a home, prolongs its life, or changes its use. For example, finishing an unfinished basement or upper floor, building a swimming pool, adding a bedroom or bathroom, installing new plumbing or wiring, installing a new roof, erecting a new fence, and paving a new driveway are classed as improvements and are added to the home's basis. Maintenance and repairs are not added, as they merely maintain the property in ordinary operating condition. Fixing gutters, mending leaks in plumbing, replacing broken window panes, and painting the inside or outside of the home are considered maintenance and repair items. However, repairs made as part of an extensive remodeling or restoration job may be added to the basis.

Calculating the Amount Realized

amount realized: the sales price of a property less commissions and closing costs; also called adjusted sales price

The next step in determining taxable gain is to calculate the **amount realized** (or *adjusted sales price*) from the sale. This is the selling price of the home minus selling expenses. Selling expenses include brokerage commissions, advertising, legal fees, title services, escrow or closing fees, and mortgage points paid by the seller. If the sale includes furnishings, the value of those furnishings is deducted from the selling price and reported separately as personal property. If the seller takes back a note and mortgage that are immediately sold at a discount, the discounted value of the note is used, not its face amount.

Calculating Gain on the Sale

The *gain on the sale* is the difference between the amount realized and the basis. Figure 17-2 describes this with an example. Unless the seller qualifies for tax postponement or tax exclusion (discussed next), this is the amount to be reported as gain on the seller's annual income tax forms. To increase compliance with this rule, effective January 1, 1987, reporting of real estate transactions on IRS Form

Buy home for $90,000; closing costs are $500	Basis is	$ 90,500
Add landscaping and fencing for $3,500	Basis is	94,000
Add bedroom and bathroom for $15,000	Basis is	109,000
Sell home for $125,000; sales commissions and closing costs are $8,000	Amount realized	$117,000
Calculation of gain	Amount realized	$117,000
	Less basis	−109,000
	Equals gain	$ 8,000

FIGURE 17-2 Calculation of gain on the sale of a home

Source: © 2021 Mbition LLC

1099 is required of persons in the following order: (1) the person responsible for the closing, (2) the mortgage lender, (3) the seller's broker, (4) the buyer's broker, and (5) any person designated by the IRS.

Income Tax Exclusion

IRS rules are constantly subject to change, but currently a taxpayer may exclude $250,000 of gain from the sale of the taxpayer's principal residence. If the taxpayer is married, there is a $500,000 exclusion for married individuals filing jointly, if: (1) either spouse meets the ownership test, (2) both spouses meet the use test (i.e., the taxpayer has resided there for two of the last five years), (3) a husband and wife file a joint return in the year of sale or exchange, and (4) neither spouse is ineligible for exclusion by virtue of sale or exchange of residence within the last two years. This rule eliminates taxable gain on the sale of your residence up to these limits. This exclusion is allowable each time the homeowner meets the eligibility requirement, but generally no more frequently than once every two years. The IRS does not receive notification of any home sales of $250,000 or under ($500,000 for married taxpayers), provided the home buyer provides to the escrow agent assurances that: (1) the home was a "principal residence," (2) there was no federally subsidized mortgage financing assistance, and (3) the final gain is excludable from gross income [*Internal Revenue Code* 6045(e)(5)].

There are a few exceptions to the two-year use rule. If a uniformed or foreign service personnel is called away to active duty, there's a change in the taxpayer's place of employment, the taxpayer is forced to move for health reasons, or there are other unforeseen circumstances recognized by the IRS, the taxpayer may prorate his/her tax exclusion. There is still a need to keep records for home improvements, however. The gain is calculated as the sales price, less the home's basis or adjusted basis, whichever is applicable. If you are in a house that will *never* exceed the allowable gain, then there is no need to keep a record of requirements.

Capital Gains

Capital gains tax is a tax levied on an investment. That investment could be stocks, bonds, precious metals, real estate, or anything else purchased with the hopes of making a profit. In general, investments held for less than one year are considered short-term investments, and taxes are paid at standard individual rates (short-term capital gains). Investments that are held for more than a year are treated as long-term capital gains and historically have had favorable tax rates.

There are interesting economic philosophies about capital gains tax. It is supposed to stimulate capital investments (good for a growing economy) by real estate transactions in which the proceeds of the sale are deferred beyond the year of sale providing tax breaks on profit when the capital asset is resold. Capital gains have a secondary effect, however. When the asset is sold, brokers, lawyers, title companies, and various service providers all make their fees. These fees are taxed at normal income rates.

The result is more total tax income to the government. If there are no tax incentives, the capital asset is not sold (because the investor prefers to keep the income), and no fees are generated. History has shown us that when the capital gains tax is reduced, the economy tends to strengthen. Capital gains taxation treatment has been somewhat of a political football, and the change of these tax rates often seems to depend on whose team is running the football. Since tax rules continue to change, creating many "window periods" involving sales dates and rate fluctuations, tax counsel should be consulted to determine the exact date and rate applicable for any given transaction.

INSTALLMENT METHOD

When a gain cannot be excluded, a popular method of deferring income taxes is to use the **installment method** of reporting the gain. This can be applied to homeowner gains that do not qualify for exclusion. Suppose that you have investment property, which is free and clear of debt, that is sold for $100,000. The real estate commission and closing costs are $7,500 and your basis is $40,000. As a result, the gain on this sale is $52,500. If you sell for all cash, you are required to pay all the income taxes due on that gain in the year of sale—a situation that may force you into a higher tax bracket. A solution is to sell to the buyer on terms rather than to send the buyer to a lender to obtain a loan.

For example, if the buyer pays you $20,000 down and gives you a promissory note calling for a principal payment of $5,000 plus interest this year, and a principal payment of $25,000 plus interest in each of the next three years, your gain is calculated and reported as follows. Of each dollar of sales price received, 52.5 cents is reported as gain. Thus, $10,500 is reported this year and in each of the next three years. The interest you earn on the promissory note is reported and taxed separately as interest income.

If there is a $30,000 mortgage on the property that the buyer agrees to assume, the $100,000 sales price is reduced by $30,000 to $70,000 for tax-calculating purposes. The portion of each dollar paid to you by the buyer that must be reported as gain is $52,500 divided by $70,000, or 75%. If the down payment is $20,000 followed by $10,000 per year for five years, you would report 75% of $20,000, or $15,000 this year, and $7,500 in each of the next five years. The gain is taxed at the income tax rates in effect at the time the installment is received.

If you sell by the installment method, that is, you sell property at a gain in one taxable year and receive one or more payments in later taxable years, the installment method of reporting is automatically applied. If this is not suitable, you may elect to pay all the taxes in the year of sale. The installment method is available only to those who are not "dealers" in real property. All dealers in real property are required to pay all the taxes in the year of sale.

---

installment method: sale of real estate in which the proceeds of the sale are deferred beyond the year of sale

PROPERTY TAX AND INTEREST DEDUCTIONS

The Internal Revenue Code provides for the deductibility of state and local real estate taxes. A homeowner may annually deduct up to $10,000 total in combined real and personal property taxes from other income when calculating income taxes. This applies to single-family residences, condominiums, and cooperatives. The deduction does not extend to special assessment taxes for improvement districts.

The Internal Revenue Code also provides for the deductibility of interest, but subject to two limitations that will be discussed separately. However, the basic rule is that interest paid to finance the purchase of a home is deductible against a homeowner's other income. Also deductible are the following: interest paid on improvement district bonds, loan prepayment penalties, and the deduction of points on new loans that are clearly distinguishable as interest and not service fees for making the loan.

Loan points paid by a seller to help a buyer obtain an FHA or VA loan are not deductible as interest (it is not the seller's debt), but can be deducted from the home's selling price in computing a gain or loss on the sale. FHA mortgage insurance premiums are not deductible, nor are those paid to private mortgage insurers. Research the current status of tax laws, and never give tax advice unless you are willing to accept the attendant responsibility.

INTEREST DEDUCTION LIMITATIONS

The Internal Revenue Code limits the interest deduction to the taxpayer's principal residence plus one other residence. All of the interest is deductible on a loan to purchase a first or second home, although the aggregate amount of acquisition indebtedness may not exceed $1 million. However, if a home is refinanced and the amount borrowed exceeds the home's basis (original cost plus improvements, etc.), the interest on the excess amount is not deductible. The aggregate amount of home equity indebtedness may not exceed $100,000. Thus, a homeowner will not only want to keep records of the home's basis for sale purposes but also as information for refinancing. In addition, if refinancing above basis is for medical or educational purposes, then careful records of those expenses must be kept in order to justify the deduction.

From an individual taxpayer's standpoint, the ability to deduct property taxes and mortgage interest on one's residence becomes more valuable in higher tax brackets. As viewed from a national standpoint, the deductibility of interest and property taxes encourages widespread ownership of the country's land and buildings.

IMPACT ON REAL ESTATE

Because tax rules for real estate are continually changing, only the major rules have been reported and discussed here (as well as briefly touched on in other chapters). As a real estate owner or agent, you need a source of more frequent and more detailed information, such as the annual income tax guide published by the Internal Revenue Service (free) or the privately published guides available in most bookstores. Additionally, you may wish to subscribe to a tax newsletter for up-to-the-minute tax information. Please be aware that tax law changes have an impact on real estate values. In the past, tax laws have been very generous to real estate—particularly deductions for depreciation and interest, as well as credits for the rehabilitation of old buildings. Many otherwise uneconomical real estate projects have become economically feasible because of tax laws. As tax laws change to reduce the incentive to buy real estate, this has a dramatic effect on real estate investors and, predictably, on the sales price of parcels of real estate.

AGENT'S LIABILITY FOR TAX ADVICE

The real estate industry's desire for professional recognition, coupled with the results of several key court cases, strongly suggest that a real estate agent be reasonably knowledgeable about taxes. This does not mean the agent must have knowledge of tax laws at the level of an accountant or tax attorney. Neither does it mean an agent can plead ignorance of tax laws. Rather, it means a real estate agent is now liable for tax advice (or lack of it) if the advice is material to the transaction, and to give such advice is common in the brokerage business.

An agent should have enough general knowledge of real estate tax laws to be able to answer basic questions accurately, and to warn clients and recommend tax counsel if the questions posed by the transaction are beyond the agent's knowledge. Note that the obligation to inform exists even when a client fails to ask about tax consequences. This is to avoid situations in which, after the deed is recorded, the client says, "Gee, I didn't know I'd have to pay all these taxes; my agent should have warned me," and then sues the agent. In addition, if the agent tries to fill the role of accountant or tax attorney for the client, then the agent will be held liable to the standards of an accountant or tax attorney.

To summarize, an agent must be aware of tax laws that affect the properties the agent is handling. An agent has a responsibility to alert clients to potential tax consequences, liabilities, and advantages whether they ask for the information or not. Lastly, an agent is responsible for the quality and accuracy of tax information s/he gives out. A prudent agent will recommend that a client contact a certified public accountant of the client's own choosing to confirm information given by the agent and for in-depth tax advice.

CONVEYANCE TAXES

documentary tax: a fee or tax on deeds and other documents payable at the time of recordation

Before 1968, the federal government required the purchase and placement of federal **documentary tax** stamps on deeds. The rate was $.55 for each $500 or fraction thereof, computed on the "new money" in the transaction. Thus, if a person bought a home for $75,000 and either paid cash or arranged for a new mortgage, the tax was based on the full $75,000. If the buyer assumed or took title subject to an existing $50,000 loan, then the tax was based on $25,000. Examples of federal documentary tax stamps, which look much like postage stamps, can still be seen on deeds recorded prior to 1968.

Effective January 1, 1968, the federal deed tax program ended, and many states took the opportunity to begin charging a deed tax, or *conveyance tax,* of their own. Some adopted fee schedules that are substantially the same as what the federal government previously charged. Others base the fee on the purchase price without regard to any existing indebtedness left on the property by the seller. Most states, the District of Columbia, and some counties and cities charge a transfer tax. The amount ranges from just a few dollars to as much as $4,500 on the sale of a $100,000 property. In Georgia, the rate is $0.10 per $100 (or any part of $100) on the adjusted sales price, or, simplified, $1 per $1,000 of sales price. The transfer tax on a $100,000 sale would be $100. The adjusted sales price is the sales price minus the loan assumed. These fees are paid to the county recorder prior to recording and are in addition to the charge for recording the document itself. Some states (Georgia included) also charge a separate tax on the value of any mortgage debt created by a transaction. In Georgia, that tax, known as an intangibles tax, is paid at the rate of $1.50 per $500 (or any part of $500) of any new loan recorded.

Review Questions

Answers to these questions can be found in Appendix D at the end of this book.

1. Local government programs and services are financed primarily through:
    A. property taxes
    B. federal income taxes
    C. state income taxes
    D. state sales taxes

2. Taxes on real property are levied:
    A. by the state and collected by the county
    B. on the value of the improvement only
    C. based on value
    D. in accordance with the value of the land

3. The assessment ratio of real property in a community:
    A. is typically a percentage of market value
    B. should be more than its fair market value
    C. should be more than its appraised value
    D. must be the appraised market value

4. Which of the following properties has the highest assessed value?
   A. market value $75,000, assessed at 75% of value
   B. market value $50,000, assessed at 100% of value
   C. market value $90,000, assessed at 50% of value
   D. market value $130,000, assessed at 35% of value

5. Tax rates are most commonly expressed as:
   A. a percentage of market value
   B. dollars of tax per hundred dollars of market value
   C. dollars of tax per thousand dollars of market value
   D. a millage rate

6. Which of the following would be the highest tax rate?
   A. 38 mills
   B. $3.80/$100
   C. $38/$1,000
   D. No difference

7. Jeff plans to bid on real estate being offered at a tax auction. Before bidding on a parcel, he would be wise to:
   A. conduct a title search
   B. purchase title insurance
   C. sign a contract
   D. obtain a tax receipt

8. Which of the following liens holds the highest degree of lien priority?
   A. federal income tax liens
   B. mechanic's liens
   C. *ad valorem* tax liens
   D. first mortgage liens

9. Records of the assessed valuations of all properties within a jurisdiction are known as:
   A. appraisal rolls
   B. allocation rolls
   C. appropriation rolls
   D. assessment rolls

10. Among the functions of the board of equalization is to:
    A. equalize assessments among counties
    B. equalize assessments among individual property owners
    C. equalize assessment procedures among counties
    D. equalize tax collections among counties

11. Which of the following is NOT an example of a property exempt from taxation?
    A. property used as a means of attracting industry to a community
    B. property used for religious or educational purposes
    C. property owned by currently serving elected officials
    D. property owned by the government

12. All of the following types of property are usually exempt from taxation EXCEPT:
    A. government-owned utilities
    B. residences owned by elderly homeowners
    C. property owned by charitable organizations
    D. hospitals

13. A property in Georgia sold for $125,000 with a $100,000 new loan. The transfer tax would be:
    A. $100
    B. $12.50
    C. $125
    D. $25

14. An improvement district is most commonly created as a result of action originated by:
    A. the federal government
    B. the state Department of Revenue
    C. a group of concerned citizens
    D. the local tax assessor's office

15. Which response to a question about taxes would create the greatest liability for an agent?
    A. "I am not sure, but I will find out for you."
    B. "You should consult with your accountant."
    C. "There would be no taxes on that sale."
    D. "I had a similar situation personally, and my accountant said there would be no taxes owed."

16. When persons sell land for more than they paid for it:
    A. there is no federal tax applicable to the gain
    B. the gain is taxed by all state governments
    C. there is always a tax owed
    D. there may be capital gains taxes owed

17. Which of the following would NOT be considered an improvement to a home in determining its cost basis?
    A. repairs to a leaky roof
    B. construction of a new fence
    C. repairs done as part of an extensive remodeling project
    D. conversion to central heating and air

18. Capital gains on a personal residence may be exempted if:
    A. the owner purchases another property of equal or greater value within two years
    B. the gains do not exceed $500,000 on a joint return
    C. the property was held for at least five years as the primary residence
    D. the property was held for at least two of the previous 10 years as a primary residence

19. A real estate agent should refer a client seeking information on income tax laws and rules to:
    A. tax guides published by the Internal Revenue Service
    B. privately published tax guides sold in bookstores
    C. privately published tax newsletters
    D. the client's CPA

20. Conveyance taxes on the transfer of title to real property are levied by:
    A. the federal government
    B. some state governments
    C. counties only
    D. the Federal Housing Administration

CHAPTER 18
REAL ESTATE APPRAISAL

KEY TERMS

appraisal
assemblage
capitalize
comparables
cost approach
depreciation
economic obsolescence
fictional depreciation
functional obsolesence
gross rent multiplier (GRM)
highest and best use
income approach
market (comparison) approach
market value
operating expenses
physical deterioration
plottage
plottage value
principles of value
scheduled gross (projected gross)
Uniform Standards of Professional Appraisal Practice (USPAP)

OBJECTIVES

After successful completion of this chapter, you should be able to:
1. estimate value based on the market comparison approach;
2. estimate the value of land and understand the need for competitive market analysis;
3. understand how to use gross rent multipliers;
4. apply the cost and income approaches to the determination of value;
5. explain how the three approaches are used to come up with the appraiser's best estimate;
6. describe the various types of appraiser reports;
7. explain the characteristics and principles of value;
8. understand the difference between a buyer's and a seller's market;
9. explain the many meanings of the word "value"; and
10. identify professional appraisal societies and describe their roles.

OVERVIEW

This chapter deals with the three approaches to estimating value: the market approach, the cost approach, and the income approach. The market approach is sometimes referred to as the market comparison approach, which provides an estimate of market or fair market value. The market approach is also used in estimating values of condominiums and townhouses. Other topics covered include competitive market analysis and gross rent multipliers. The cost and income approaches lead into a discussion of income forecasting, depreciation, construction costs, operating expense ratio, and capitalizing income. The chapter concludes with coverage of the appraisal report, principles of value, and the multiple meanings of the word *value*.

In this chapter, you will see demonstrations of the market, cost, and income approaches and how they are used in determining market value. **Market value**, also called *fair market value*, is the most probable price that a property should bring in a competitive and open market under all conditions requisite to a fair sale, including that both the buyer and seller are acting prudently and knowledgeably and that the price is not affected by undue stimulus. Simply put, market value is the most probable selling price in an arm's-length transaction.

This definition implies the consummation of a sale at a specified date and the passing of title from seller to buyer under conditions whereby: (1) buyer and seller are typically motivated; (2) both parties are well-informed or well-advised, and both are acting in what they consider their own best interests; (3) a reasonable time is allowed for exposure in the open market; (4) payment is made in terms of cash in U.S. dollars or in terms of financial arrangements comparable thereto; and (5) the price represents the normal consideration for the property sold, unaffected by special or creative financing or sales concessions granted by anyone associated with the sale. These conditions define an *arm's-length transaction*. Market value is at the heart of nearly all real estate transactions.

market value: the cash price that a willing buyer and a willing seller would agree upon, given reasonable exposure of the property to the marketplace, full information as to the potential uses of the property, and no undue compulsion to act; also called fair market value

PURPOSE AND USE OF APPRAISALS

An **appraisal** is a necessary part of most real estate transactions. Often, the decision to buy, sell, or grant a loan on real estate hinges on a real estate appraiser's estimate of property value. Appraisals are also used to set prices on property listed for sale and to set premiums on fire insurance policies; they are used by government to acquire and manage public property and to establish property tax levels for taxpayers. To *appraise* real estate means to estimate its value. Thus, an *informal appraisal* can be defined simply as an estimate of value based on intuition. But a *formal appraisal* is more accurately defined as "an independently and impartially prepared estimate expressing an opinion of a defined value of an adequately described property as of a specific date, which is supported by the presentation and analysis of relevant market information."

appraisal: an estimate of the value of something

THE REAL PROPERTY VALUATION PROCESS

The *valuation process* is the step-by-step procedure that appraisers use to conduct their work. The conventions for this process have been developed over a period of many years. However, this system has been refined and modified in recent years by **Uniform Standards of Professional Appraisal Practice (USPAP)**. Following the guidelines of USPAP, the valuation process involves the following steps: (1) define the appraisal problem; (2) conduct a preliminary analysis, formulate an appraisal plan, and collect the data; (3) estimate the highest and best use of the land as if vacant, and the property as improved; (4) estimate land value; (5) estimate the improved property value through the appropriate value approaches; (6) reconcile the results to arrive at a defined value estimate; and (7) report the conclusion of value.

USPAP: the Uniform Standards of Professional Appraisal Practice

CHARACTERISTICS OF VALUE

For a good or service to have value in the marketplace, it must possess four characteristics: demand, utility, scarcity, and transferability. This may be remembered using the acronym DUST. *Demand* is desire coupled with ability. For any product or service to have value, there must be a desire for that product or service. Fortunately for those in real estate sales, most people want what they have. The ability to purchase refers to money; in real estate, read that as borrowed money. *Utility* refers to the usefulness or function of the product or service. If consumers perceive great usefulness, they will perceive great value; if they perceive limited usefulness, they will perceive limited value. *Scarcity* means there must be a short supply relative to demand for there to be great value. Air, for example, has utility and is in demand, but it is not scarce. Finally, a good or service must have *transferability*—that is, it must have value to anyone other than the person possessing it. In real estate, transferability refers to marketable title. If the title has a defect, it will lower the value of the property.

PRINCIPLES OF VALUE

In real estate, value is determined by several key factors. These **principles of value** can be broken down as follows.

principles of value: the key factors that determine value in real estate

The *principle of anticipation* states that present value is influenced by the anticipation of future benefit. Thus, the buyer of a home anticipates receiving shelter plus the investment and psychological benefits of homeownership. The investor buys property in anticipation of future income.

The *principle of substitution* states that the present value of a property is influenced by what a person would have to pay for a reasonably desirable substitute. Thus, if there are two similar houses for sale, or two similar apartments for rent, the lower-priced one will generally be purchased or rented first. In the same manner, the cost of buying land and constructing a new building sets a limit on the value of existing buildings.

The *principle of competition* states that demand creates profits, profits create competition, and competition stabilizes prices. This principle is at the foundation of free enterprise. For example, if apartment rents increase to the point where owners of existing apartment buildings are making substantial profits, builders and investors will be encouraged to build more apartment buildings, creating competition and stabilizing prices.

The *principle of change* reminds us that real property uses are always in a state of change. Although it may be imperceptible on a day-to-day basis, change can easily be seen over longer periods of time. Because the present value of a property is related to its future uses, the more potential changes that can be identified, the more accurate the estimate of its present worth will be.

The *principle of conformity* holds that maximum value is realized when there is a reasonable degree of homogeneity in a neighborhood. This is the basis for zoning laws across the country; certain tracts in a community are zoned for single-family houses, others for apartment buildings, stores, and industry. Within a tract, there should also be a reasonable amount of homogeneity. For example, a $200,000 house would be out of place in a neighborhood of $90,000 houses.

The **highest and best use** of a property is the use that will give the property its greatest current value. This means that you must be alert to the possibility that the present use of a parcel of land may not be the one that makes the land the most valuable. Consider a 30-year-old house located at a busy intersection in a shopping area. To place a value on that property based on its continued use as a residence would be misleading if the property would be worth more with the house removed and shopping or commercial facilities built on the land instead.

highest and best use: that use of a parcel of land that will produce the greatest current value

Applied to real estate, the *principle of supply and demand* refers to the ability of people to pay for land coupled with the relative scarcity of land. This means that attention must be given to matters on the demand side such as population growth, personal income, and personal preferences. On the supply side, you must look at the available supply of land and its relative scarcity. When the supply of land is limited and demand is great, the result is rising land prices. Conversely, where land is abundant and there are relatively few buyers, supply and demand will be in balance at only a few cents per square foot.

The *principle of increasing returns* states that a dollar spent adds a dollar to cost but adds more than a dollar to value. For example, if remodeling a bathroom would cost $10,000 but increase the value of the overall property by $15,000, this would be an increasing return.

The *principle of decreasing returns* states that a dollar spent adds a dollar to cost but adds less than a dollar to value. The most common example is a swimming pool. While it may add $50,000 in cost, it would seldom add anywhere near that much in value.

The *principle of contribution* states that the worth of an improvement is measured by what it adds in overall value regardless of the cost. This principle ties together increasing and decreasing returns.

MULTIPLE MEANINGS OF THE WORD *VALUE*

When we hear the word *value*, we tend to think of *market value*. However, at any given moment in time, a single property can have other values, too. This is because value or worth is very much affected by the purpose for which the valuation was performed. For example, *assessed value* is the value given a property by the county tax assessor for purposes of property taxation. *Estate tax value* is the value that federal and state taxation authorities establish for a deceased person's property; it is used to calculate the amount of estate taxes that must be paid. *Insurance value* is concerned with the cost of replacing damaged property. It differs from market value in two major respects: (1) the value of the land is not included, as it is presumed that only the structures are destructible, and (2) the amount of coverage is based on the replacement cost of the structures. *Loan value* is the value set on a property for the purpose of making a loan.

Plottage Value

When two or more adjoining parcels are combined into one large parcel, it is called **assemblage**. If the assemblage causes an increase in value over the cost, the process is referred to as **plottage**. The increased value of the large parcel over and above the sum of the smaller parcels is called **plottage value**. For example, three small lots sit side by side and can be purchased for $10,000 each. Putting these three parcels under one ownership is assemblage. If the value of the whole is increased because of added benefit and the value of the whole is $40,000, this is plottage, with the plottage value being $10,000.

Rental Value

Rental value is the value of a property expressed in terms of the right to its use for a specific period of time. The fee simple interest in a house may have a market value of $120,000, whereas the market value of one month's occupancy might be $900.

Replacement Value

Replacement value is value as measured by the current cost of building a structure of equivalent utility. *Salvage value* is what a structure is worth if it has to be removed and taken elsewhere, either as a whole or dismantled for parts. Because salvage operations require much labor, the salvage value of most buildings is usually very low.

---

assemblage: combining two or more adjacent properties into one larger parcel

plottage: assemblage with a value increase greater than the cost

plottage value: the amount of the value increase due to plottage

This list of values is not exhaustive, but it points out that there are many different types of value. When reading an appraisal report, always read the first paragraph to see why the appraisal was prepared. Before preparing an appraisal, make certain you know its purpose, and then state it at the beginning of your report.

BUYER'S AND SELLER'S MARKETS

Whenever supply and demand are unbalanced because of excess supply, a *buyer's market* exists. This means buyers can negotiate prices and terms more to their liking, and a seller who wants to sell must accept them. When the imbalance occurs because demand exceeds supply, it is a *seller's market;* sellers are able to negotiate prices and terms more to their liking as buyers compete for the available merchandise.

A *broad market* means that many buyers and sellers are in the market at the same time. This makes it relatively easy to establish the price of a property and for a seller to find a buyer quickly, and vice versa. A *thin market* is said to exist when there are only a few buyers and a few sellers in the market at the same time. It is often difficult to appraise property in a thin market because there are so few sales to use as comparables.

VALUE APPROACHES

There are three approaches to making this estimate. The first is to locate similar properties that have sold recently and use them as benchmarks in estimating the value of the property you are appraising. This is the *market approach,* also called the *market data approach* or **market comparison approach**. The second approach is to add together the cost of the individual components that make up the property being appraised. This is the **cost approach**; it begins with an estimate of the current cost of the improvement, including labor and materials. Depreciation (because the improvement is not new) is estimated and subtracted from the cost to obtain the current depreciated cost of the building. The land value is then estimated and added to the depreciated building cost to arrive at the estimate of value supported by the cost approach. The third approach is to consider only the amount of net income that the property can reasonably be expected to produce for its owner, plus or minus any anticipated price increase or decrease. This is the **income approach**. For the person who owns or plans to own real estate, knowing how much a property is worth is a crucial part of the buying or selling decision. For the real estate agent, being able to estimate the value of a property is an essential part of taking a listing and conducting negotiations.

market comparison approach: a method of valuing property based on recent sales of similar properties

cost approach: a method of valuing property based on adding together the cost of the property's components

income approach: a method of valuing a property based on the monetary returns it can be expected to produce

MARKET COMPARISON APPROACH

Let's begin by demonstrating the application of the *market comparison approach* to a single-family residence. The residence to be appraised is called the *subject property* and is described as follows:

The subject property is a one-story, wood-frame house of 1,520 square feet containing three bedrooms, two bathrooms, living room, dining room, kitchen, and utility room. There is a two-car garage with concrete driveway to the street, a 300-square-foot concrete patio in the backyard, and an average amount of landscaping. The house is located on a 10,200-square-foot level lot that measures 85 by 120 feet. The house is 12 years old, in good repair, and located in a well-maintained neighborhood of houses of similar construction and age.

Comparables

After one becomes familiar with the physical features and amenities of the subject property, the next step in the market approach is to locate houses with similar physical features and amenities that have sold recently under market value conditions. These are known as **comparables**, or "comps." The more similar they are to the subject property, the fewer and smaller the adjustments that must be made in the comparison process, and, hence, the less room for error. As a rule, it is best to use comparable sales no more than 6 months old. During periods of relatively stable prices, this can be extended to 1 year. However, during periods of rapidly changing prices, even a sale 6 months old may be out of date.

comparables: properties similar to the subject property that have sold recently

Sales Records

The market comparison approach requires that the following information be collected for each comparable sale: date of sale, sales price, financing terms, location of the property, and a description of its physical characteristics and amenities. Recorded deeds at public records offices can provide dates and locations of recent sales. Although a deed seldom states the purchase price, Georgia levies a deed transfer tax, the amount of which is shown on the recorded deed. This tax provides a clue as to the purchase price. Basically, transfer tax is paid at the rate of $1 per $1,000 of sales price, so if the transfer tax paid on the deed was $175, you could safely assume that the purchase price was $175,000. The exception to this is if the sale involved a loan assumption. In those cases, it is pretty obvious that the sales price indicated by the transfer tax is not the full sales price.

Records of sales can often be obtained from title and abstract companies. Property tax assessors keep records on changes in ownership as well as property values. Where these records are kept up to date and are available to the public, they can provide information on what has sold recently and for how much. Assessors also keep detailed records of improvements made to land. This can be quite helpful in making adjustments between the subject property and the comparables. For real estate salespeople, locally operated multiple listing services provide asking prices and descriptions of properties currently offered for sale by member brokers, along with descriptions, sales prices, and dates for properties that have been sold. In some cities, commercially operated financial services publish information on local real estate transactions and sell it on a subscription basis.

Verification

Production of the most accurate appraisal possible requires inspection of each sale used as a comparable and verification of the price and terms. An agent who specializes in a given neighborhood will have already visited the comparables when they were still for sale. The agent can verify price and terms with the selling broker or from multiple listing service sales records.

Number of Comparables

Three to five comparables usually provide enough basis for reliable comparison. To use more than five, the additional accuracy must be weighed against the extra effort involved. When the supply of comparable sales is more than adequate, one should choose the sales that require the fewest adjustments. It is also important that the comparables selected represent current market conditions. Sales among relatives or close friends may result in an advantageous price to the buyer or seller; sales prices that for some other reason appear to be out of line with the general market should not be used. Listings and offers to buy should not be used in place of actual sales. They do not represent a meeting of minds between a buyer and a seller. Listing prices do indicate the upper limit of prices, whereas offers to buy indicate lower limits. Thus, if a property is listed for sale at $180,000 and there have been offers as high as $170,000, it is reasonable to presume the market price lies somewhere between $170,000 and $180,000.

Adjustment Process

Let's now work through the example shown in Table 18.1 to demonstrate the application of the market comparison approach to a house. We begin at lines 1 and 2 by entering the address and sales price of each comparable property. For convenience, we shall refer to these as comparables A, B, and C. On lines 3 through 10, we make adjustments to the sales price of each comparable to make it equivalent to the subject property today. Adjustments are made for price changes since each comparable was sold as well as for differences in physical features, amenities, and financial terms. The result indicates the market value of the subject property. In making adjustments there are two simple rules to remember. Number one, ALWAYS adjust the comparable, never the subject. The second rule helps us add and subtract properly. Remember it by using the abbreviations CIA and CBS. These stand for Comparable Inferior Add; Comparable Better Subtract. When beginning, if one does not use this process, the most natural thing to do is make the adjustments backward, which can be disastrous.

TABLE 18.1 Sales comparison approach

Line	Item	Comparable Sale A		Comparable Sale B		Comparable Sale C	
1	Address	1702 Brookside Ave.		1912 Brookside Ave.		1501 18th Street	
2	Sales price		$191,800		$188,000		$188,300
3	Time adjustment	sold 6 mos. ago, add 5%	+4,590	sold 3 mos. ago, add 2.5%	+2,200	just sold	0
4	House size	160 sq. ft. larger at $60 per sq. ft.	−9,600	20 sq. ft. smaller at $60 per sq. ft.	+1,200	same size	0
5	Garage/carport	carport	+4,000	3-car garage	−2,000	2-car garage	0
6	Other	larger patio	−300	no patio	+900		
7	Age, upkeep, and overall quality of house	superior	−3,000	inferior	+800	equal	0
8	Landscaping	inferior	+2,000	equal	0	superior	−900
9	Lot size, features, & location	superior	−3,890	inferior	+900	equal	0
10	Terms & conditions of sale	equal	0	special financing	−1,500	equal	0
11	Total adjustments		−6,200		+2,500		−900
12	Adjusted Market Price		$185,600		$190,500		$187,400
13	Correlation process:						
	Comparable A $185,600 × 20% =		$37,120				
	Comparable B $190,500 × 30% =		57,150				
	Comparable C $187,400 × 50% =		93,700				
14	Indicated Value		$187,970				
		Round to	$188,000				

Source: © 2021 Mbition LLC

Time Adjustments

Returning to line 3 in Table 18.1, let us assume that house prices in the neighborhood where the subject property and comparables are located have risen 5% during the six months that have elapsed since comparable A was sold. If it were for sale today, comparable A would bring 5%, or $4,590, more. Therefore, we must add $4,590 to bring it up to the present. Comparable B was sold three months ago, and to bring it up to the present, we need to add 2.5%, or $2,200, to its sales price. Comparable C was just sold and needs no time correction since its price reflects today's market.

House Size

Because house A is 160 square feet larger than the subject house, it is logical to expect that the subject property would sell for less money. Hence, a deduction is made from the sales price of comparable A on line 4 (CBS). The amount of this deduction is based on the difference in floor area and the current cost of similar construction, minus an allowance for depreciation. If we value the extra 160 square feet at $60 per square foot, we must subtract $9,600. For comparable B, the house is 20 square feet smaller than the subject house. At $60 per square foot, we add $1,200 (CIA) to comparable B, since it is reasonable to expect that the subject property would sell for that much more because it is that much larger. Comparable C is the same size as the subject property, so no adjustment is needed.

Garage and Patio

Next, the parking facilities (line 5) are adjusted. We first look at the current cost of garage and carport construction and the condition of these structures. Assume that the value of a carport is $3,000; a one-car garage, $5,000; a two-car garage, $7,000; and a three-car garage, $9,000. Adjustments would be made as follows. The subject property has a two-car garage worth $7,000 and comparable A has a carport worth $3,000. Therefore, based on the difference in garage facilities, we can reasonably expect the subject property to command $4,000 more than comparable A. By adding $4,000 to comparable A, we effectively equalize this difference. Comparable B has a garage worth $2,000 more than the subject property's garage. Therefore, $2,000 must be subtracted from comparable B to equalize it with the subject property. For comparable C, no adjustment is required, as comparable C and the subject property have similar garage facilities. On line 6, the subject property has a 300-square-foot patio in the backyard worth $900. Comparable A has a patio worth $1,200; therefore, $300 is deducted from comparable A's selling price. Comparable B has no patio. As it would have sold for $900 more if it had one, a $900 addition is required. The patio at comparable C is the same as the subject property's. Any other differences between the comparables and the subject property, such as swimming pools, fireplaces, carpeting, drapes, roofing materials, and kitchen appliances, would be adjusted in a similar manner.

Building Age, Condition, and Quality

On line 7, we recognize differences in building age, wear and tear, construction quality, and design usefulness. Where the difference between the subject property and a comparable can be measured in terms of material and labor, the adjustment is the cost of that material and labor. For example, the $800 adjustment for comparable B reflects the cost of needed roof repair at the time B was sold. The adjustment of $3,000 for comparable A reflects the fact that it has better-quality plumbing and electrical fixtures than the subject property. Differences that cannot be quantified in terms of labor and materials are usually dealt with as lump-sum judgments. Thus, one might allow $1,500 for each year of age difference between the subject and a comparable, or make a lump sum adjustment of $3,000 for an inconvenient kitchen design. Keep in mind that adjustments are made on the basis of what each comparable property was like on the day it was sold. Thus, if an extra bedroom was added or the house was painted after its sale date, these items are not included in the adjustment process.

Landscaping

Line 8 shows the landscaping of comparable A to be inferior to the subject property. A positive correction is necessary here to equalize it with the subject. The landscaping of comparable B is similar and requires no correction; that of comparable C is better and thus requires a negative adjustment. The dollar amount of each adjustment is based on the market value of lawn, bushes, trees, and the like.

Lot Features and Location

Line 9 deals with any differences in lot size, slope, view, and neighborhood. In this example, all comparables are in the same neighborhood as the subject property, thus eliminating the need to judge, in dollar terms, the relative merit of one neighborhood over another. However, comparable A has a slightly larger lot and a better view than the subject property. Based on recent lot sales in the area, the difference is judged to be $890 for the larger lot and $3,000 for the better view. Comparable B has a slightly smaller lot judged to be worth $900 less, and comparable C is similar in all respects.

Terms and Conditions of Sale

Line 10 in Table 18.1 accounts for differences in financing. As a rule, the more accommodating the terms of the sale to the buyer, the higher the sales price, and vice versa. We are looking for the highest cash price the subject property may reasonably be expected to bring, given adequate exposure to the marketplace and a knowledgeable buyer and seller not under undue pressure. If the comparables were sold under these conditions, no corrections would be needed in this category. However, if it can be determined that a comparable was sold under different conditions, an adjustment is necessary. For example, if the going rate of interest on home mortgages is 12% per year and the seller offers to finance the buyer at 9% interest, it is reasonable to expect that the seller can charge a higher selling price. Similarly, the seller can get a higher price if the seller has a low-interest loan that can be assumed by the buyer. Favorable financing terms offered by the seller of comparable B enabled the seller to obtain an extra $1,500 in selling price. Therefore, we must subtract $1,500 from comparable B. Another situation that requires an adjustment on line 10 is if a comparable was sold on a rush basis. If a seller is in a hurry to sell, a lower selling price usually must be accepted than if the property can be given more time in the marketplace.

Adjusted Market Price

Adjustments for each comparable are totaled and either added or subtracted from its sales price. The result is the *adjusted market price*, shown on line 12. This is the dollar value of each comparable sale after it has gone through an adjustment process to make it the same as the subject property. If it were possible to precisely evaluate every adjustment, and if the buyers of comparables A, B, and C had paid exactly what their properties were worth at the time they purchased them, the three prices shown on line 12 would be the same. However, buyers are not that precise, particularly in purchasing a home, where amenity value influences price and varies considerably from one person to the next.

Correlation Process

A comparison of properties usually makes it apparent that some comparables are more like the subject property than others. The *correlation process* gives the appraiser the opportunity to assign more weight to the more similar comparables and less to the others. A mathematical weighting is one available technique.

On line 13, comparable C is given a weight of 50% since it is more like the subject and required fewer adjustments. Moreover, this sameness is in areas where adjustments tend to be the hardest to estimate accurately: time, age, quality, location, view, and financial conditions. Of the remaining two comparables, comparable B is weighted slightly higher than comparable A because it is a more recent sale and required fewer adjustments overall. In the correlation process, the adjusted market price of each comparable is multiplied by its weighting factor and totaled on line 14. The result is the indicated value of the subject property. It is customary to round off to the nearest $50 or $100 for properties under $10,000; to the nearest $250 or $500 for properties between $10,000 and $100,000; to the nearest $1,000 or $2,500 for properties between $100,000 and $250,000; and to the nearest $2,500 or $5,000 above that.

Unique Issues

Condominium, Townhouse, and Cooperative Appraisal

The process for estimating the market value of a condominium, townhouse, or cooperative living unit by the market approach is similar to the process for houses, except that fewer steps are involved. For example, in a condominium complex with a large number of two-bedroom units of identical floor plan, data on a sufficient number of comparable sales may be available within the building. This would eliminate adjustments for differences in unit floor plan, neighborhood, lot size and features, age and upkeep of the building, and landscaping. The only corrections needed would be those that make one unit different from another. This would include the location of the individual unit within the building (end units and units with better views sell for more), the upkeep and interior decoration of the unit, a time adjustment, and an adjustment for terms and conditions of the sale. When there are not enough comparable sales of the same floor plan within the same building and it is necessary to use different-sized units, an adjustment must be made for floor area. If the number of comparables is still inadequate and units in different condominium buildings must be used, adjustments will be necessary for neighborhood, lot features, management, upkeep, age, and overall condition of the building.

Vacant Land Valuation

Subdivided lots zoned for commercial, industrial, or apartment buildings are usually appraised and sold on a square-foot basis. Thus, if apartment land is currently selling for $30 per square foot, a 100,000-square-foot parcel of comparable zoning and usefulness would be appraised at $3 million. Another method is to value on a front-foot basis. For example, if a lot has 70 feet of street frontage and if similar lots are selling for $1,000 per front foot, that lot would be appraised at $70,000. Storefront land is often sold this way. House lots can be valued either by the square-foot, front-foot, or lot method. The lot method is useful when one is comparing lots of similar size and zoning in the same neighborhood.

For example, recent sales of 100-by-100-foot house lots in the $180,000 to $200,000 range would establish the value of similar lots in the same neighborhood. Rural land and large parcels that have not been subdivided are usually valued and sold by the acre. For example, how would you value 21 acres of vacant land when the only comparables available are 16-acre and 25-acre sales? The method is to establish a per-acre value from comparables and apply it to the subject land. Thus, if 16- and 25-acre parcels sold for $32,000 and $50,000, respectively, and are similar in all other respects to the 21-acre subject property, it would be reasonable to conclude that land is selling for $2,000 per acre. Therefore, the subject property is worth $42,000.

Competitive Market Analysis

A variation of the market comparison approach, and one that is very popular with agents who list and sell residential property, is the *competitive market analysis (CMA)*. This method is based on the principle that value can be estimated not only by looking at similar homes that have sold recently but also by taking into account homes currently on the market plus homes that were listed for sale but did not sell. The CMA is a listing tool that a sales agent prepares to show a seller what the home is likely to sell for, and the CMA helps the agent decide whether to accept the listing. Figure 18-1 shows a competitive market analysis form previously published by the National Association of REALTORS®. There are many similar forms utilized by relocation companies today, so we will use this one as an example. The procedure in preparing a CMA is to select homes that are comparable to the subject property.

The greater the similarity, the more accurate the CMA will be, and the more likely it is that the client will accept the agent's counsel. It is usually best to use only properties in the same neighborhood; this is easier for the seller to relate to

COMPETITIVE MARKET ANALYSIS

Property Address _____ Date _____

For Sale Now: [1] | Bedrms. | Baths | Den | Sq. Ft. | 1st Loan | List Price | Days on Market | Terms

Sold Past 12 Mos. [2] | Bedrms. | Baths | Den | Sq. Ft. | 1st Loan | List Price | Days on Market | Date Sold | Sale Price | Terms

Expired Past 12 Mos. [3] | Bedrms. | Baths | Den | Sq. Ft. | 1st Loan | List Price | Days on Market | Terms

[4] F.H.A. — V.A. Appraisals

Address | Appraisal | Address | Appraisal

[5] **Buyer Appeal**　　　　　　　　　　　[6] **Marketing Position**

(Grade each item 0 to 20% on the basis of desirability or urgency)

1 Fine Location _____ %　　　　　1 Why Are They Selling _____ %
2 Exciting Extras _____ %　　　　　2 How Soon Must They Sell _____ %
3 Extra Special Financing _____ %　　3 Will They Help Finance .... Yes ___ No ___ %
4 Exceptional Appeal _____ %　　　4 Will They List at Competitive Market Value .... Yes ___ No ___ %
5 Under Market Price _____ Yes ___ No ___ %　5 Will They Pay for Appraisal .... Yes ___ No ___ %

　　　　Rating Total _____ %　　　　　　　Rating Total _____ %

[7]
Assets _____
Drawbacks _____
Area Market Conditions _____

Recommended Terms _____

[8] **Selling Costs**

Brokerage	$
Loan Payoff	$
Prepayment Privilege	$
FHA — VA Points	$
Title and Escrow Fees: IRS Stamps Recons Recording	$
Termite Clearance	$
Misc. Payoffs: 2nd T.D., Pool, Patio, Water Softener, Fence, Improvement Bond.	$
	$
	$
Total	$

Top Competitive Market Value $ _____

[9]
Probable Final Sales Price $ _____

Total Selling Costs $ _____

Net Proceeds $ _____　Plus or Minus $ _____

Copyright © REALTORS® NATIONAL MARKETING INSTITUTE of the NATIONAL ASSOCIATION OF REALTORS® 1975. All rights reserved.
10-75-F606
BY PERMISSION

The statements and figures presented herein, while not guaranteed, are secured from sources we believe authoritative

Prepared by _____

FIGURE 18-1 Competitive market analysis
Source: © 2021 Mbition LLC

and removes the need to compensate for neighborhood differences. The comparables should also be similar in size, age, and quality. Although a CMA does not require that individual adjustments be shown as in Table 18.1, it does depend on the agent's understanding of the process that takes place in that table. That is why Table 18.1 and its explanation are important. A residential agent may not be called upon to make a presentation as is done in Figure 18-1; nonetheless, all those steps should be considered and consolidated in the agent's mind before entering a probable final sales price on the CMA.

Homes for Sale

In section [1] of the CMA shown in Figure 18-1, similar homes currently offered for sale are listed. This information is usually taken directly from the agent's multiple listing service (MLS) book, and ideally the agent will already have toured these properties and have firsthand knowledge of their condition. These are the homes the seller's property will compete against in the marketplace. In section [2], the agent lists similar properties that have sold in the past several months. Ideally, the agent will have toured the properties when they were for sale. Sales prices are usually available through MLS sales records. Section [3] is for listing homes that were offered for sale but did not sell. In other words, buyers were unwilling to take these homes at the prices offered.

In section [4], recent FHA and VA appraisals of comparable homes can be included if it is felt that they will be useful in determining the price at which to list. Two words of caution are in order here. First, using someone else's opinion of value is risky. It is better to determine your own opinion based on actual facts. Second, FHA and VA appraisals often tend to lag behind the market. This means that in a rising market, they will be too low; in a declining market, they will be too high.

Buyer Appeal

In section [5], Buyer Appeal, and in section [6], Marketing Position, the agent evaluates the subject property from the standpoint of whether it will sell if placed on the market. It is important to make the right decision to take or not to take a listing. Once a listing is taken, the agent knows that valuable time and money must be committed to sell a property. Factors that make a property more appealing to a buyer include good location, extra features, small down payment, low interest, meticulous maintenance, and a price below market. Similarly, a property is more salable if the sellers are motivated to sell, want to sell soon, will help with financing, and will list at or below market. A busy agent will want to avoid spending time on overpriced listings, listings for which no financing is available, and listings where the sellers have no motivation to sell. Under the rating systems in sections [5] and [6], the closer the total is to zero, the less desirable the listing, and the closer to 100%, the more desirable the listing. Section [7] provides space to list the property's high and low points, current market conditions, and recommended terms of sale. Section [8] shows the seller how much to expect in selling costs. Section [9] shows the seller what to expect in the way of a sales price and the amount of cash that can be expected from the sale.

The emphasis in the CMA is on a visual inspection of the data on the form in order to arrive at market value directly. No pencil-and-paper adjustments are made. Instead, adjustments are made in a generalized fashion in the minds of the agent and the seller. In addition to its application to single-family houses, the CMA can also be used on condominiums, cooperative apartments, townhouses, and vacant lots—provided sufficient comparables are available.

Gross Rent Multipliers

A popular market comparison method that is used when a property produces income is the **gross rent multiplier**, (**GRM**). The GRM is an economic comparison factor that relates the gross rent a property can produce to its purchase price. For apartment buildings and commercial and industrial properties, the GRM is computed by dividing the sales price of the property by its gross annual rent. For example, if an apartment building grosses $100,000 per year in rents and has just sold for $700,000, it is said to have a GRM of 7. The use of a GRM to value single-family houses is questionable since they are usually sold as owner-occupied residences rather than as income properties. Note that if you do work a GRM for a house, it is customary to use the monthly (not yearly) rent.

Where comparable properties have been sold at a fairly consistent gross rent multiplier, the GRM technique presumes that the subject property can be valued by multiplying its gross rent by that multiplier. To illustrate, suppose that apartment buildings were recently sold in your community, as shown in Table 18.2. These sales indicate that the market is currently paying seven times gross. Therefore, to find the value of a similar apartment building grossing $24,000 per year, multiply by 7 to get an indicated value of $168,000.

The GRM method is popular because it is simple to apply. Having once established what multiplier the market is paying, one need only know the gross rents of a building to set a value. However, this simplicity is also the weakness of the GRM method because the GRM takes into account only the gross rent a property

gross rent multiplier: a number that is multiplied by a property's gross rents to produce an estimate of the property's worth

TABLE 18.2 Calculating gross rent multipliers

Building	Sales Price		Gross Annual Rents		Gross Rent Multiplier
No. 1	$245,000	÷	$ 34,900	=	7.02
No. 2	160,000	÷	22,988	=	6.96
No. 3	204,000	÷	29,352	=	6.95
No. 4	196,000	÷	27,762	=	7.06
As a group:	$805,000	÷	$ 115,002	=	7.00

Source: © 2021 Mbition LLC

produces. Gross rent does not allow for variations in vacancies, uncollectible rents, property taxes, maintenance, management, insurance, utilities, or reserves for replacements.

To illustrate the problem, suppose that two apartment buildings both gross $100,000 per year. However, the first has expenses amounting to $40,000 per year, and the second has expenses of $50,000 per year. Using the same GRM, the buildings would be valued the same, yet the first produces $10,000 more in net income for its owner. The GRM also overlooks the expected economic life span of a property. For example, a building with an expected remaining life span of 30 years would be valued exactly the same as one expected to last 20 years, if both currently produce the same rents. One method of partially offsetting these errors is to use different GRMs under different circumstances. Thus, a property with low operating expenses and a long expected economic life span might call for a GRM of 7 or more, whereas a property with high operating expenses or a shorter expected life span would be valued using a GRM of 6 or 5 or even less.

COST APPROACH

There are times when the market approach is an inappropriate valuation tool. The market approach is of limited usefulness in valuing a fire station, school building, courthouse, or highway bridge. These properties are rarely placed on the market, and comparables are rarely found. Even with properties that are well suited to the market approach, there may be times when it is preferable to apply another valuation approach. For example, a real estate agent may find that comparables indicate that a certain style and size of house is selling in a particular neighborhood for $150,000. Yet, the astute agent discovers through the cost approach that the same house can be built from scratch, including land, for $125,000. The agent builds and sells 10 of these and concludes that, yes, there really is money to be made in real estate. Let us take a closer look at the cost approach.

Table 18.3 demonstrates the cost approach. Step 1 is to estimate the value of the land upon which the building is located. The land is valued as though vacant, using the market comparison approach described earlier. In Step 2, the cost of

TABLE 18.3 Cost approach to value

Step 1:	Estimate land as vacant		$ 30,000
Step 2:	Estimate new construction cost of similar building	$120,000	
Step 3:	Less estimated depreciation	–12,000	
Step 4:	Indicated value of building		108,000
Step 5:	Appraised property value by the cost approach		$138,000

Source: © 2021 Mbition LLC

constructing a similar building at today's costs is estimated. These costs include the current prices of building materials, construction wages, architect's fees, contractor's services, building permits, utility hookups, and so on, plus the cost of financing during the construction stage and the cost of construction equipment used at the project site. Step 3 is the calculation of the amount of money that represents the subject building's wear and tear, lack of usefulness, and obsolescence when compared to the new building of Step 2. In Step 4, depreciation is subtracted from today's construction cost to give the current value of the subject building on a used basis. Step 5 is to add this amount to the land value. Let us work through these steps.

Estimating New Construction Costs

To choose a method of estimating construction costs, one must decide whether cost will be approached on a reproduction or on a replacement basis. *Reproduction cost* is the cost at today's prices of constructing an *exact replica* of the subject improvements using the same or very similar materials. *Replacement cost* is the cost, at today's prices and using today's methods of construction, for an improvement having the same or *equivalent usefulness* as the subject property. Replacement cost is the more practical choice of the two as it eliminates nonessential or obsolete features and takes full advantage of current construction materials and techniques. It is the approach that will be described here.

Square-Foot Method

The most widely used approach for estimating construction costs is the *square-foot method*. It provides reasonably accurate estimates that are fast and simple to prepare. The square-foot method is based on finding a newly constructed building that is similar to the subject building in size, type of occupancy, design, materials, and construction quality. The cost of this building is converted to cost per square foot by dividing its current construction cost by the number of square feet in the building.

Quantity Survey Method

The most accurate but also most time-consuming and difficult method to estimate construction cost is the *quantity survey method*. This procedure estimates the cost of the building brick by brick, board by board; it is inclusive of all direct and indirect costs of construction including material, labor, and administrative. Appraisers would seldom use this method in that they would not typically have the information or motivation.

Unit in Place

This method is a combination of the first two. The *unit in place method* would take into consideration the cost of a unit of construction inclusive of labor and materials and then estimate how many units would be needed. For example, an appraiser may say that basic and simple construction of a single-family home would be $65 per square foot. In addition, if the home has two fireplaces, the estimate for a fireplace may be $4,000 inclusive of the firebox, mantel, hearth, flue, fire starter, and labor to build and install. Since there are two fireplaces, $8,000 would be added to include the cost of the fireplaces in places that were not included in the $65-per-square-foot cost.

Cost Handbooks

Cost information is also available from construction cost handbooks. Using a *cost handbook* starts with selecting a handbook appropriate to the type of building being appraised. From photographs of houses included in the handbook, along with brief descriptions of the buildings' features, the appraiser finds a house that most nearly fits the description of the subject house. Next to pictures of the house is the current cost per square foot to construct it. If the subject house has a better-quality roof, floor covering, or heating system; more or fewer built-in appliances or plumbing fixtures; or a garage, basement, porch, or swimming pool, the handbook provides costs for each of these. Figure 18-2 shows the calculations involved in the square-foot method.

Estimating Depreciation

Once the appraiser estimates the current cost of constructing the subject improvements, the next step in the cost approach is to estimate the loss in value due to depreciation since they were built. In making this estimate, we look for three kinds of **depreciation**: physical deterioration, functional obsolescence, and economic obsolescence.

Types of Depreciation

depreciation: loss in value due to deterioration and obsolescence

physical deterioration: a loss in value due to wear and tear, such as rotted wood, age, worn carpet, and peeling paint

functional obsolescense: a loss in value due to a change in consumer demand, such as outdated kitchens and baths

Physical deterioration (or **physical depreciation**) results from wear and tear through use, such as wall-to-wall carpet that has been worn thin or a dishwasher, garbage disposal, or water heater that must be replaced. Physical deterioration also results from the action of nature in the form of sun, rain, heat, cold, and wind, and from damage due to plants and animal life, such as tree roots breaking sidewalks and termites eating wood. Physical deterioration can also result from neglect (such as an overflowing bathtub) and from vandalism.

Functional obsolescence (or **functional depreciation**) results from outmoded equipment (old-fashioned plumbing fixtures in the bathrooms and kitchen), faulty or outdated design (a single bathroom in a three- or four-bedroom house or an illogical room layout), inadequate structural facilities (inadequate wiring to handle today's household appliance loads), and over-adequate structural facilities (high ceilings in a home). Functional and physical depreciation can be separated

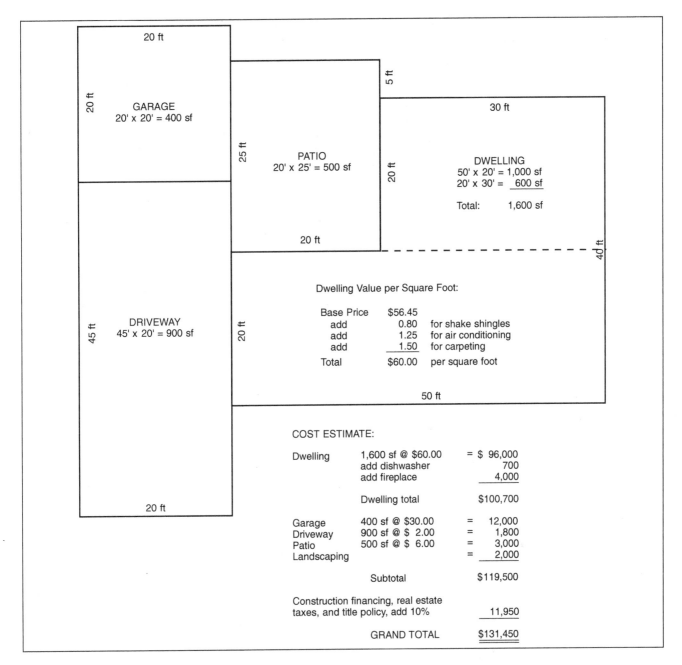

FIGURE 18-2 Square-foot method of cost estimating
Source: © 2021 Mbition LLC

into curable and incurable components. *Curable depreciation* is when the benefit to cure equals or exceeds the cost to cure. Examples may repairing or replacing worn carpeting, a leaky roof, or outdated faucets in bathrooms. *Incurable depreciation* occurs when the cost to cure exceeds the economic benefit, such redoing an illogical room layout.

Economic obsolescence, also known as *external obsolescence,* is the loss of value due to external forces or events. Economic obsolescence is always

economic obsolescense: a loss in value that comes from factors outside the subject property, such as noise pollution

considered to be incurable. For example, a once-popular neighborhood becomes undesirable because of air or noise pollution or because surrounding property owners fail to maintain their properties. Or a city that is dependent on a military base finds the base closed and, with it, a big drop in demand for real estate. Or the motel district in town loses customers because a new interstate highway has been built several miles away. An estimate of economic obsolescence is an important part of the cost approach to value. However, in the long run, most properties experience economic appreciation, not economic obsolescence. The appreciation can come from new industries moving to town, city growth in a new direction, a shortage of land in beach or waterfront areas, and so on. Thus, it is quite possible for the economic appreciation of a property to more than offset the depreciation it experiences. The result is a building that is physically and functionally depreciating and at the same time appreciating in value. Consequently, while the chronological age of a building is important to value, what is more important is the remaining economic life of the building and whether it is functionally adequate for use in the future. This is what real estate investors look for.

Computing Depreciation

The most common method of computing depreciation is the *straight-line method*. To apply this method, we must first define and understand some terminology. Actual age is the age of a property measured in years. If a house was built in 1990 and this is 2020, the house has a 30-year actual age. Effective age is the apparent age: the age the building appears to be, considering quality of construction, maintenance, and remodeling. While the building may be 30 years old, it may appear older or newer. Physical life is the number of years a building will be physically sound. Economic life is how long the building can continue to be productive. Economic life is almost always shorter than physical life; buildings get torn down because they can no longer be productive; typically they don't *fall* down. To compute straight-line depreciation (also known as the age/life method), divide cost of the building by the economic life. The resulting depreciation per year is multiplied by the effective age. For example, if a 2,000-square-foot building would cost $68 per square foot to build, and the building has an economic life of 60 years with an effective age of 10 years, what is the amount of depreciation? The computation will be:

$$2{,}000 \times 68 = \$136{,}000 \text{ current cost to build}$$
$$(\$136{,}000 \div 60) \times 10 = \$22{,}666.67 \text{ in accrued depreciation}$$

A number like this would be rounded to something like $22,700 by an appraiser so as not to indicate an accuracy that is beyond ability.

Final Steps in the Cost Approach

After calculating the current construction cost of the subject improvements and estimating the amount of depreciation, the next step is to subtract the amount of depreciation from the current construction cost to get the depreciated value of the improvements. This is added to the value of the land upon which the subject improvements rest. The total is the value of the property by the cost approach.

INCOME APPROACH

The income approach considers the monetary returns a property can be expected to produce and converts that into a value the property should sell for if placed on the market today. This is called capitalizing the income stream. To **capitalize** means to convert future income to current value. To illustrate, suppose that an available apartment building is expected to return, after expenses, $18,000 per year. How much would you, as an investor, pay for the building? The answer depends on the return you require on each dollar you invest. Suppose you will accept a return of 9% per year. In that case, you will pay $200,000 for this building. The calculation is as follows:

capitalize: to convert future income to current value

$$\frac{\text{Income}}{\text{Rate}} = \text{Value} \qquad \frac{\$18,000}{0.09} = \$200,000$$

This is the basic principle of capitalization. The appraisal work comes in estimating the net income a property will produce and looking at recent sales of similar properties to see what capitalization rates are currently acceptable to investors. Let us look at the techniques one would use in estimating a property's income. Pay close attention, because each $1 error in projected annual income or expenses can make a difference of from $8 to $15 in the market value of the property.

Income and Expense Forecasting

The best starting point is to look at the actual record of income and expenses for the subject property over the past three to five years. Although the future will not be an exact repetition of the past, the record of a property is usually the best guide to future performance. These historical data are blended with the current operating experience of similar buildings in order to estimate what the future will bring. The result is a projected operating statement, such as the one shown in Table 18.4, which begins with the estimated rents that the property can be expected to produce on an annual basis. This is the **projected gross**, or **scheduled gross**, and represents expected rentals from the subject property on a fully occupied basis. From this, *vacancy and collection losses* are subtracted. These are based

scheduled (or projected) gross: the estimated rent a fully occupied property can be expected to produce on an annual basis

TABLE 18.4 Projected annual operating statement (also called a pro forma statement)

Scheduled gross annual income	$84,000	
Vacancy allowance and collection losses	4,200	
Effective gross income		$79,800
Operating expenses		
Property taxes	$ 9,600	
Hazard and liability insurance	1,240	
Property management	5,040	
Janitorial services	1,500	
Gardener	1,200	
Utilities	3,940	
Trash pickup	600	
Repairs and maintenance	5,000	
Other	1,330	
Reserves for replacement		
Furniture and furnishings	1,200	
Stoves and refrigerators	600	
Furnace and/or air conditioning	700	
Plumbing and electrical	800	
Roof	750	
Exterior painting	900	
Total operating expenses		34,400
Net operating income		$ 45,400
Operating expense ratio: $34,400 ÷ $79,800 = 43.1%		

Source: © 2021 Mbition LLC

partly on the building's experience and partly on the operating experience of similar buildings.

Operating Expenses

operating expenses: expenditures necessary to maintain the production of income

The next step is to itemize anticipated **operating expenses** for the subject property. These are expenses necessary to maintain the production of income. For an apartment building without recreational facilities or an elevator, the list in Table 18.4 is typical. Again, we must consider both the property's past operating expenses and what we expect those expenses to be in the future. For example, even though a property is currently being managed by its owner and no management fee is being paid, a typical management fee, say 5% of the gross rents, is included. Not included as operating expenses are outlays for capital improvements, such as the construction of a new swimming pool, the expansion of parking facilities, and assessments for street improvements. Improvements are not classified as expenses because they increase the usefulness of the property, which increases the rent the property will generate and therefore the property's value.

Reserves

Reserves for replacement are established for items that do not require an expenditure of cash each year. For example, lobby furniture (and furniture in apartments rented as "furnished") wears out a little each year, eventually requiring replacement. Suppose that these items cost $7,200 and are expected to last six years, at which time they must be replaced. An annual $1,200 reserve for replacement not only reflects wear and tear of the furniture during the year but also reminds us that to avoid having to meet the entire furniture and furnishings replacement cost out of one year's income, money should be set aside for this purpose each year. In a similar manner, reserves are established for other items that must be replaced or repaired more than once during the life of the building, but not yearly.

Net Operating Income

The operating expense total is then subtracted from the effective gross income. The balance that remains is the *net operating income*. From the net operating income, the property owner receives both a return *on* and a return *of* investment. The return *on* investment is the interest received for investing money in the property. The return *of* investment is compensation for the fact that the building is wearing out.

Operating Expense Ratio

At this point, the *operating expense ratio* can be calculated. It is obtained by dividing the total operating expenses by the effective gross income. The resulting ratio provides a handy yardstick against which similar properties can be compared. If the operating expense ratio is out of step compared to similar properties, it signals the need for further investigation. A range of 25% to 45% is typical for apartment buildings. The Institute of Real Estate Management of the National Association of REALTORS® publishes books and articles that give typical operating ratios for various types of income properties across the United States. Local inquiry to appraisers and brokers who specialize in income properties will also provide typical ratios for buildings in a community.

Capitalizing Income

The final step in the income approach is to capitalize the net operating income. In other words, what price should an investor offer to pay for a property that produces a given net income per year? The solution is: Income divided by rate equals value. If the annual net operating income is $45,400 and if the investor intends to pay all cash, expects to receive a 10% return on his investment, and anticipates no change in the value of the property while owning it, the solution is to divide $45,400 by 10%. However, most investors today borrow much of the purchase price and usually expect an increase in property value. Under these conditions, how much should the investor pay?

The best-known method for solving this type of investment question involves using the Ellwood Tables, published in 1959 by L.W. Ellwood, a member of the Appraisal Institute. A simpler and more usable method was subsequently developed by Charles Akerson. These concepts and calculations go well beyond what most users of this textbook are looking for, but there is an article you may read at ccim.com/cire-magazine/articles/cap-rate-calculations, should you be so motivated. This article appears in a magazine published by CCIM (Certified Commercial Investment Member), an arm of the National Association of REALTORS®. However, for the person who does not use these tables regularly, the arithmetic involved can prove confusing. As a result, mortgage equity tables are now available from bookstores and online. These allow the user to look up a single number, called an *overall rate,* and divide it into the net operating income to find a value for the property. For example, suppose an investor who is interested in buying the above property can obtain a 9%, fully amortized, 25-year mortgage loan for 75% of the purchase price. The investor wants a 10% return on equity in the property, plans to hold it 10 years, and expects it will increase 50% in value (after selling costs) during that time. How much should the investor offer to pay the seller? In Table 18.5, we look for an interest rate of 9% and for appreciation of 50%. This gives an overall rate of 0.09376, and the solution is:

$$\frac{\text{Income}}{\text{Overall Rate}} = \text{Value} \qquad \frac{\$45,400}{0.9376} = \$484,215$$

Further exploration of the numbers in Table 18.5 shows that as loan money becomes more costly, the overall rate rises, and as interest rates fall, so does the overall rate. If the investor can anticipate appreciation in value, the overall rate drops; if not, the overall rate climbs. You can experiment by dividing some of the other overall rates in this table into $45,400 to see how the value of this property changes under different circumstances.

Depreciation

The pro forma in Table 18.4 provides reserves for replacement of such items as the roof, furnace, air conditioning, plumbing, electrical, and exterior paint. Nonetheless, as the building ages, the style of the building will become dated, the neighborhood will change, and the structure will experience physical deterioration. Allowance for this is usually accounted for in the selection of the capitalization rate: The less functional, economic, and physical obsolescence expected to take place, the lower the acceptable "cap" rate, and vice versa.

In contrast to actual depreciation, there is the **fictional depreciation** that the U.S. Treasury allows property owners to deduct as an expense when calculating

fictional depreciation: an accounting device allowed by governments as an incentive to invest in property; for tax purposes, the property is considered to be depreciating, even if it is actually going up in value

TABLE 18.5 Overall rates: 10-year holding period, 25-year loan for 75% of the purchase price, 18% investor return

Appreciation, Depreciation	Loan Interest Rate			
	9%	10%	11%	12%
+100%	0.07251	0.07935	0.08631	0.09338
+50%	0.09376	0.10060	0.10756	0.11463
+25%	0.10439	0.11123	0.11819	0.12526
+15%	0.10864	0.11548	0.12244	0.12951
+10%	0.11077	0.11761	0.12457	0.13164
+5%	0.11289	0.11973	0.12669	0.13376
0	0.11502	0.12186	0.12882	0.13589
−5%	0.11715	0.12399	0.13095	0.13802
−10%	0.11927	0.12611	0.13307	0.14014
−15%	0.12140	0.12824	0.13520	0.14227
−25%	0.12565	0.13249	0.13945	0.14652
−50%	0.13628	0.14312	0.15008	0.15715
−100%	0.15753	0.16437	0.17133	0.17840

Source: © 2021 Mbition LLC

income taxes. The Internal Revenue Service allows a purchaser of an apartment building to completely depreciate the structure over 27-1/2 years regardless of the age or condition of the structure. This figure may be an understatement of the remaining life of the structure, but it was chosen by Congress to create an incentive to invest in real estate, not as an accurate gauge of a property's life. Thus, it is quite common to see depreciation claimed on buildings that are, in reality, appreciating because of rising income from rents and/or falling capitalization rates.

CHOICE OF APPROACHES

Whenever possible, all three appraisal methods discussed in this chapter should be used to provide an indication, as well as a cross-check, of a property's value. If the marketplace is acting rationally and is not restricted in any way, all three approaches will produce the same value. If one approach is out of line with the others, it may indicate an error in the appraiser's work or a problem in the market itself. It is not unusual to find individual sales that seem out of line with prevailing market prices. Similarly, there are times when buyers will temporarily bid the market price of a property above its replacement cost.

For certain types of real property, some approaches are more suitable than others. This is especially true for single-family residences. Here you must rely almost entirely on the market and cost approaches, as very few houses are sold on their ability to generate cash rent. Unless you can develop a measure of the "psychic income" in homeownership, relying heavily on rental value will lead to a property value below the market and cost approaches. Applying all three approaches to special-purpose buildings may also prove to be impractical. For example, in valuing a college or university campus or a state capital building, the income and market approaches have only limited applicability.

When appraising a property that is bought for investment purposes, such as an apartment building, shopping center, office building, or warehouse, the income approach is the primary method of valuation. As a cross-check on the income approach, an apartment building should be compared to other apartment buildings on a price-per-apartment-unit basis or price-per-square-foot basis. Similarly, an office, store, or warehouse can be compared to other recent office, store, or warehouse sales on a price-per-square-foot basis. Additionally, the cost approach can be used to determine whether it would be cheaper to buy land and build rather than to buy an existing building.

RECONCILIATION

After applying the market, cost, and income approaches to the subject property, the appraiser must reconcile the differences found in the results. One method is to assign each approach a weighting factor, based on a judgment of its relevance and reliability in the appraisal of this property. To demonstrate, the results of a 20-year-old single-family house appraisal might be reconciled as follows:

Market Approach	$180,000 × 75%	=	$135,000
Cost Approach	$200,000 × 20%	=	40,000
Income Approach	$160,000 × 5%	=	8,000
Final Indicated Value			$183,000

What the appraiser is suggesting here is that recent sales of comparable properties have the most influence on current sales prices. Thus, the market approach is given the most weight. The cost approach is given much less weight because it required a difficult judgment of accrued depreciation for the subject improvements. By weighting the income approach at only 5%, the appraiser is recognizing that houses in this neighborhood are mostly owner-occupied and are rarely bought for rental purposes. In the reconciliation process, it is never considered appropriate to average.

APPRAISER'S BEST ESTIMATE

It is important to realize that the appraised value is the appraiser's best *estimate* of the subject property's worth. No matter how painstakingly it is done, property valuation requires the appraiser to make many subjective judgments. Because of this, it is not unusual for three highly qualified appraisers to look at the same property and produce three different appraised values. It is also important to recognize that an appraisal is made as of a specific date. It is not a certificate of value, good forever until used. If a property was valued at $115,000 on January 5 of this year, the more time that has elapsed since that date, the less accurate that value is as an indication of the property's current worth.

An appraisal does not take into consideration the financial condition of the owner, the owner's health, sentimental attachment, or any other personal matter. An appraisal does not guarantee that the property will sell for the appraised market value. (The buyer and the seller determine the actual selling price.) Nor does buying at the appraised market value guarantee a future profit for the purchaser. (The real estate market can change.) An appraisal is not a guarantee that the roof will not leak, that there are no termites, or that everything in the building works. An appraisal is not an offer to buy, although a buyer can order one made so as to know how much to offer. An appraisal is not a loan commitment, although a lender can order one made so as to apply a loan-to-value ratio when making a loan.

Review Questions

Answers to these questions can be found in Appendix D at the end of this book.

1. Which of the following is NOT one of the three standard approaches to the appraisal of real property?
   A. income approach
   B. cost approach
   C. assessment approach
   D. market approach

2. To apply the market data approach, a real estate appraiser must collect all the following data on each comparable sale EXCEPT:
   A. date of sale
   B. marketability of title
   C. financing terms
   D. sale price

3. Adjustments for advantageous financing would be made in the:
   A. market comparison approach to appraisal
   B. cost approach to appraisal
   C. income approach to appraisal
   D. capitalization approach to appraisal

4. After all adjustments are made to a comparable property, its comparative value for appraisal purposes is known as its:
   A. adjusted market price
   B. indicated market value
   C. amended market price
   D. revised market price

5. The value of vacant land is commonly stated in any of the following terms EXCEPT value per:
   A. square foot
   B. acre
   C. front foot
   D. square yard

6. To evaluate a home in order to list it for sale, a real estate agent would NOT use the:
   A. standard market comparison method
   B. competitive market analysis method
   C. assessed value method
   D. amount of depreciation

7. Seller motivation is considered most in the:
   A. income approach
   B. cost approach
   C. gross rent multiplier method
   D. competitive market analysis method

8. Which of the following approaches is most likely to provide only a rough estimate of the value of a rental property?
   A. cost approach
   B. income approach
   C. market comparison approach
   D. gross rent multiplier

9. In appraising a historically significant residence built in the Victorian era using the cost approach, an appraiser will probably appraise it on the basis of its:
   A. reproduction cost
   B. restoration cost
   C. replacement cost
   D. reconstruction cost

10. Which of the following results from factors outside the property?
    A. functional obsolescence
    B. physical deterioration
    C. economic obsolescence
    D. legal obsolescence

11. The conversion of future income into present value is known as:
    A. capitalization
    B. amortization
    C. hypothecation
    D. appreciation

12. The rents that a property can be expected to produce on an annual basis may be referred to as the:
    A. effective gross
    B. statistical gross
    C. projected gross
    D. operating gross

13. The operating expense ratio of a building is determined by dividing the total operating expenses by the:
    A. effective net income
    B. net operating income
    C. effective gross income
    D. actual gross income

14. From the viewpoint of a qualified real estate appraiser, the value of the subject property is NOT affected by:
    A. demand
    B. scarcity
    C. highest and best use
    D. transferability

15. The use of a property that will give it its greatest current value is its:
    A. highest use
    B. best use
    C. highest and best use
    D. maximum use

16. The relationship between added cost and the value it returns is known as the principle of:
    A. anticipation
    B. substitution
    C. contribution
    D. conformity

17. The principle that holds that maximum value is realized when a reasonable degree of homogeneity is present in a neighborhood is known as the principle of:
    A. harmony
    B. homogeneity
    C. similarity
    D. conformity

18. The process of combining two or more parcels of land into one larger parcel is called:
    A. assemblage
    B. plottage
    C. salvage
    D. reproduction

19. A market where there is an excess of supply over demand is known as a:
    A. buyer's market
    B. broad market
    C. seller's market
    D. thin market

20. A CMA is most similar to the:
    A. cost approach
    B. income approach
    C. market comparison approach
    D. GRM approach

PART 5
CLOSING, TRANSFER, AND LEASES

We're now in the home stretch! As we learned in the last part, there is very little value if an item cannot be transferred to another person. The ability to close the transaction and transfer the rights to the property is what our career is building toward. It is a systematic process from start to finish. Part 5 is where we substantially complete the construction of our knowledge. In our building analogy, this is where we install the trim, install the cabinets, paint, and complete the flooring. At this point, we are almost finished, and what we are building is really taking shape! In this part we will look at the following chapters:

Chapter 19:   Closing the Transaction

Chapter 20:   Transferring Title

Chapter 21:   Recordation, Abstracts, and Title Insurance

Chapter 22:   Real Estate Leases

CHAPTER 19
CLOSING THE TRANSACTION

KEY TERMS

closing
closing agent
prorating
Real Estate Settlement Procedures Act (RESPA)
settlement statement
walk-through

OBJECTIVES

After successful completion of this chapter, you should be able to:

1. describe the buyer's walk-through and title closing;
2. explain the buyer's and seller's responsibilities at the closing;
3. describe the transaction, and relate the roles of the real estate agent and closing attorney;
4. determine insurance, tax, interest, and other prorations at closing;
5. explain what happens when there are delays or a failure to close;
6. describe the residential and/or HUD closing or settlement statement(s); and
7. explain the restrictions and benefits of the Real Estate Settlement Procedures Act.

OVERVIEW

Numerous details must be handled between the time a sales contract is signed and the day title is conveyed to the buyer. Title must be searched, a decision made as to how to take title, a deed prepared, loan arrangements made, property tax records checked, and so forth. In this chapter, we will look at the final steps in the process; in particular, the buyer's walk-through, the closing, prorations, and the settlement statement.

BUYER'S WALK-THROUGH

walk-through: a final inspection of the property just prior to settlement

To protect both the buyer and the seller, it is good practice for a buyer to make a **walk-through**. This is a final inspection of the property just prior to the settlement date. It is quite possible the buyer has not been on the parcel or inside the structure since the initial offer and acceptance. Now, several weeks later, the buyer wants to make certain that the premises have been vacated, that no damage has occurred, that the seller has left behind personal property agreed on, and that the seller has not removed and taken any real property. If the sales contract requires all mechanical items to be in normal working order, then the seller will want to test the heating and air conditioning systems, dishwasher, disposal, stove, and garage door opener, as well as the refrigerator, washer, and dryer, if included. The buyer will also want to test all of the plumbing to be certain that the water heater works, faucets and showers run, toilets flush, and sinks drain. A final inspection of the structure is made, including walls, roof, gutters, driveway, decks, and patios, as well as the land and landscaping.

Note that a walk-through is not the time for the buyer to make the initial inspection of the property; that is done before the contract is signed. If there are questions in the buyer's mind regarding the structural soundness of the property, a thorough inspection (possibly with the aid of a professional house inspector) should be conducted after signing the purchase contract, making the satisfactory inspection a condition to the buyer's obligation to purchase. The walk-through is for the purpose of giving the buyer the opportunity to make certain that agreements regarding the condition of the premises have been kept. If, during the walkthrough, the buyer notes that the walls were damaged when the seller moved out, or the furnace does not function, the buyer (or the buyer's agent) notes these items and asks that funds be withheld at the closing to pay for repairs.

CLOSING

closing: a meeting at which the buyer pays for the property and receives a deed, and at which all other matters pertaining to the sale are concluded

Closing refers to the completion of a real estate transaction. This is when the buyer pays for the property and the seller delivers the deed. The day on which this occurs is called the *closing date*. Depending on where one resides in the United States, the title closing process is referred to as a *closing, settlement,* or *escrow*. All accomplish the same basic goal, but the method of reaching that goal can follow one of two paths. In Georgia, we simply use the term *closing*.

In some parts of the United States, the closing process is concluded at a meeting of all parties to the transaction, or their representatives. Elsewhere, closing is conducted by an escrow agent who is a neutral third party mutually selected by the buyer and seller to carry out the closing. With an escrow, there is no closing meeting; in fact, most of the closing process is conducted by mail. In Georgia, the closing must be conducted by a licensed, practicing attorney. The law firm will typically represent the interest of the lender in the transaction. If there is no lender, the law firm will represent whoever is indicated in the contract.

The Georgia Bar Association has rendered an opinion that the closing firm cannot be transactional but must represent someone.

CLOSING OR SETTLEMENT MEETING

When a meeting is used to close a real estate transaction, the seller meets in person with the buyer and delivers the deed. At the same time, the buyer pays the seller for the property. To ascertain that everything promised in the sales contract has been properly carried out, the buyer and seller may each have an attorney present, though this is not common in a Georgia residential transaction. The real estate agents who brought the buyer and seller together are typically present. A representative of the lender may also be present.

The location of the meeting and the selection of the person responsible for conducting the closing will depend on local custom and the nature of the closing. If there is a new loan involved, an attorney representing the lender will be conducting the closing. If the seller is unable to attend the closing meeting, the seller appoints someone (typically the lawyer or real estate agent) as his/her representative. Similarly, a buyer who is unable to attend can appoint a representative to be present at the meeting. Appointment of a representative is accomplished by preparing and signing a power of attorney.

In The Field

It is never a good idea for a representative of the brokerage firm to act as an attorney-in-fact on behalf of a client. Imagine the situation where, at the closing table, an issue comes up and a decision must be made as to whether to proceed. To not proceed may put the brokerage compensation at risk. If the client disagrees with the decision made, it will be perceived that the decision was tainted because of the monetary compensation. Suggest the client appoint a friend, neighbor, or relative to be the attorney-in-fact.

Seller's Responsibilities at Closing

To ensure a smooth closing, each person attending is responsible for bringing certain documents. The seller and attorney are responsible for preparing and bringing the deed along with the most recent property tax bill (and receipt if it has been paid). An *offset statement* is a statement by an owner or lienholder as to the balance due on an existing lien against the property. A *beneficiary statement* is a statement of the unpaid balance on a note secured by a trust deed.

The loan payment booklet, keys to the property, garage door opener, and the like are also brought to the meeting. If the property is a condominium, cooperative, or planned unit development, the seller will bring to the closing such items as the articles of incorporation; bylaws; conditions, covenants, and restrictions (CC&Rs); annual budget; reserve fund status report; and the management company's name. If the property produces income, then existing leases, rent schedules, current expenditures, and letters advising the tenants of the new owner must also be furnished.

Buyer's Responsibilities at Closing

The buyer's responsibilities include having adequate settlement funds ready, having an attorney present if desired, and, if borrowing, obtaining the loan commitment, and advising the lender of the meeting's time and place. The real estate agent is present primarily to observe on behalf of the broker, receive the commission check, and make sure all goes smoothly.

If a new loan is involved, the lender provides proceeds for the amount of the loan (usually in the form of a wire transfer to the closing agent), along with a note and mortgage for the borrower to sign. If an existing loan is to be paid off as part of the transaction, the lender is present to receive a check and release the mortgage held on the property. If a lender elects not to attend, the check and/or loan papers are given to the person in charge of the closing, along with instructions for their distribution and signing. A title insurance representative is also present to provide the latest status of title and the title insurance policy. The closing attorney is usually an agent for the title insurance company. The buyer should be made aware early on that the law firm conducting the closing will require a wire transfer of funds prior to the actual closing.

In The Field

Beware of Cyber Fraud. Fraudulent email attempting to induce the buyer to wire money to criminal computer hackers is increasingly common in real estate transactions. Under this scam, computer hackers fraudulently assume the online identity of the actual mortgage lender, closing attorney, and/or real estate broker with whom the buyer is working in the real estate transaction. Posing as a legitimate company, they then direct the buyer to wire money to them. In many cases, the fraudulent email is sent from what appears to be the authentic webpage of the legitimate company responsible for sending the wiring instructions. Buyers should be made abundantly aware of this potential activity and instructed to verify all emails so that they don't fall prey to these tactics.

Real Estate Agent's Duties

The sellers may be unaware of all the things expected of them at the closing. It is the duty of the agent who listed the property to make certain that they are prepared for the meeting. Similarly, it is the duty of the agent who found the buyer to make certain that the buyer is prepared. If the agent both lists and sells the property, the agent assists both the buyer and seller. If more than one real estate agent is involved in the transaction, each should keep the other(s) fully informed so the transaction will go as smoothly as possible. At all times, the buyer and seller are to be kept informed as to the status of the closing. A real estate agent should give them a preview of what will take place, explain each payment or receipt, and, in general, prepare the parties for informed participation at the closing.

The Transaction

Once everyone has arrived and the closing attorney is ready, all parties are called into the closing room. The attorney will introduce everybody and explain the proceedings. This is a culmination of one of the most important financial transactions the parties will ever be involved in, so they must feel comfortable and secure with what transpires. You can reasonably expect a smooth residential transaction to take approximately one hour to close.

A **settlement statement** (also called a *closing statement*), while not required by law, is typically given to the buyer and seller to summarize the financial aspects of their transaction. It is prepared by the person in charge of the closing, either just prior to or at the meeting. It provides a clear picture of where the buyer's and seller's money is going at the closing by identifying each party to whom money is being paid. If everyone involved in the closing has done his/her homework and comes to the meeting prepared, the closing usually goes smoothly. The closing attorney explains each document, which is then signed by the appropriate party. Some paperwork is signed only by the buyer, some only by the seller, and some by both buyer and seller. Some paperwork needs to be witnessed and notarized so it can be recorded. The buyer will provide funds for any balance owed, usually in the form of a wire transfer prior to closing unless it is an amount less than $1,000, and the attorney will provide a check to the seller. At the end, everyone stands, shakes hands, and departs. The deed, new security deed, and release of the old security deed are recorded, and the transaction is complete.

settlement statement: an accounting of funds given to the buyer and the seller at the completion of a real estate transaction

Dry Closing

Occasionally, an unavoidable circumstance can cause delays in a closing. Perhaps an important document, known to be in the mail, has not arrived—yet it will be difficult to reschedule the meeting. In such a situation, the parties concerned may agree to a *dry closing,* or *close into escrow.* In a dry closing, all parties sign their documents and entrust them to the person in charge of the closing for safekeeping. No money is disbursed, and the deed is not delivered until the missing paperwork arrives. When it does, the closing attorney completes the transaction and delivers the money and documents by mail or messenger.

DELAYS AND FAILURE TO CLOSE

When a real estate purchase contract is written, a closing date is also negotiated and placed in the contract. The choice of closing date will depend on when the buyer wants possession; when the seller wants to move out; and how long it will take to obtain a loan, title search, and termite report and otherwise fulfill the contract requirements. In a typical residential sale, this is 30 to 60 days, with 45 days being a popular choice when new financing is involved. Delays along the way are sometimes encountered and may cause a delay in the closing. This is usually not a problem as long as the buyer still intends to buy, the seller still intends to sell, and the delay is for a reasonable cause and a justifiable length of time. Many preprinted real estate purchase contracts include a statement that the closing date may be extended under specific circumstances. Even if the contract contains a "time is of the essence" clause, unless there is supporting evidence in the contract that time really is of the essence, reasonable delays for reasonable causes are usually permitted by law.

Suppose, however, that the delay will be quite lengthy. For example, there may be a previously undisclosed title defect that will take months to clear, or perhaps there are unusual problems in financing, or there may have been major damage to the premises. In such cases, relieving all parties from further obligations may be the wisest choice for all involved. If so, it is essential that the buyer and seller sign termination and release papers. These are necessary to rescind the purchase contract and cancel the transaction. The buyer's deposit is also returned. Without release papers, the buyer still has a vaguely defined liability to buy, and the seller can still be required to convey the property. A mutual release gives the buyer the freedom to choose another property and the seller the chance to fix the problem and remarket the property later.

A stickier problem occurs when one party wants out of the contract and attempts to use any delay in closing as grounds for contract termination. The buyer may have found a preferable property for less money and better terms. The seller may have received a higher offer since signing the purchase contract. Although the party wishing to cancel may threaten with a lawsuit, courts will rarely enforce cancellation of valuable contract rights because of reasonable delays that are not the fault of the other party. Moreover, courts will not go along with a reluctant buyer or seller who manufactures delays so as to delay the closing and then claim default and cancellation of the contract. If the reluctance continues and negotiations to end it fail, the performing party may choose to complete its requirements and then ask the courts to force the reluctant party to the closing table.

REPORTING REQUIREMENTS

The Internal Revenue Code now requires that the seller's proceeds from all sales of real estate be reported to the Internal Revenue Service on Form 1099-S.

The responsibility for filing Form 1099-S goes in the following order: the person responsible for the closing, the mortgage lender, the seller's broker, the buyer's broker, and any person designated by the U.S. Treasury. It is important to determine at the closing who needs to file Form 1099-S. This form must be filed at no charge to the taxpayer.

The Taxpayer Relief Act of 1997 provides that real estate reporting persons generally do not need to file Form 1099-S for sales or exchanges of a principal residence with a sales price at or below $250,000 for a single individual or $500,000 for a married couple, as long as the reporting person obtains a certification from the seller in a form that is satisfactory to the secretary of the Treasury. The form must be in writing and signed by the seller, and it must confirm that: (1) the seller has owned and used the principal residence for two of the last five years; (2) the seller has not owned or exchanged another principal residence during this two-year period; (3) no portion of the residence has been used for business or rental purposes; and (4) the sales price, capital gains, and marital status filing requirements are met.

The form must be sworn to, under penalty of perjury. It must be obtained any time on or before January 31 of the year after the sale or exchange, and it must be retained in the title company's files for four years.

PRORATING AT THE CLOSING

If items such as property taxes, hazard insurance, and interest on debt were paid every day, there would be no reason to prorate. Fortunately (or unfortunately), those items are not paid on a daily basis, and so **prorating** is required. When an item is prepaid by the seller and then not completely used, the unused portion must be calculated and refunded to the seller. If an item is to be paid by the seller once used (arrears), then the used portion must be computed and the seller charged for that period. When you calculate the prorations, several assumptions should be made unless otherwise indicated:

prorating: the division of ongoing expenses and income items between the buyer and the seller

1. The day of closing is the responsibility of the seller, with the exception of interest on a new loan. On a new loan, interest paid to the lender is the responsibility of the borrower.
2. Annual bills should be prorated on a 365-day year with the exception of interest. For interest, use a 360-day banker's year.
3. When you calculate new loan amounts, the loan should be in $100 units and you should round the amount *down* in $100 increments as necessary.
4. Loan payments are made on the first day of the month and are current.
5. When computing prorations or percentages, use a calculator displaying at least four digits past the decimal to get accurate answers. All answers on prorations will be to the nearest penny.

With every proration, draw a line graph like the one below. This will help give a visual representation of the computation and crystallize your thinking.

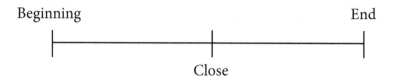

In this line graph, everything before the closing is the responsibility of the seller; everything after the closing is the responsibility of the buyer.

Property Taxes

Prorated property taxes are common to nearly all real estate transactions. The amount of proration depends on when the property taxes are due, what portion has already been paid, and what period of time they cover. For our purposes, you will be told the amount of the tax bill (or given the information needed to compute it), what has or has not been paid, and that the taxes will be paid for a calendar year (January 1 through December 31). In the field, you will have to verify the information with the local government.

Let's look at an example. If the closing is to take place on March 15 with an unpaid annual tax bill of $2,070, what is the number of days of proration, and who will be credited and debited?

The formula for property tax proration is:

(Annual tax bill ÷ 365) × Days owed = Tax proration

The seller will owe from January 1 through March 15. That is 31 + 28 + 15 = 74 days. To compute the amount of the seller's responsibility and buyer credit, divide the annual tax bill by 365 and multiply by the 74 days:

($2,070 ÷ 365) × 74 = $419.67

Another example: If the closing is to take place on September 10 and the $1,756 tax bill has been paid for the year, what is the number of days of proration, and who will be credited and debited?

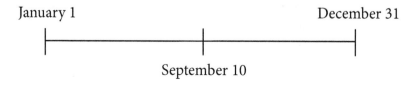

In this case, the seller will be refunded from the day after closing (remember, the seller owes for the day of closing) through December 31. There are 30 days in September minus the 10 days that the seller used, for a 20-day refund in September. The calculation is 20 + 31 + 30 + 31 = 112 days; refund for the seller, debit for the buyer. To compute the amount, divide $1,756 by 365 and multiply by 112 to get a proration of $538.83. Try the next six on your own. The answers can be found in Appendix A.

Annual Taxes	Closing Date	Taxes Paid?	Who Is Credited?	Days	Amount
$2,598	March 3	No			
$865	October 13	Yes			
$1,398	June 9	No			
$4,876	April 7	No			
$2,723	August 20	Yes			
$1,250	November 3	Yes			

Hazard Insurance

Hazard insurance policies for such things as fire, wind, storm, and flood damage are paid for in advance for an insurance year. If a policy begins on January 1, think of it as beginning on that day at 12:01 a.m. and ending one year later, December 31, at midnight. The next policy would begin again at 12:01 a.m. on January 1. Most insurance policies, however, do not run for a nice, neat calendar year. The policy begins the day of closing and is prepaid for one year. A policy that begins on April 3 would end the next year on April 2. A policy that begins on November 11 would end the next year on November 10, and so on. Since the policy is always prepaid, the seller will always be refunded from the day after closing through the end of the paid policy. For example, if the $425 annual policy began on June 15 and closing occurred on January 27, for how many days would the seller be refunded?

The formula for insurance proration is:

(Annual insurance bill ÷ 365) × Days owed = Insurance proration

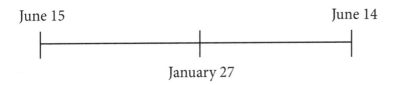

The seller will be refunded from and including January 28 through June 14: 4 (days remaining in January) + 28 + 31 + 30 + 31 + 14 = 138 days.

The annual bill of ($425 ÷ 365) × 138 = $160.68 is refunded to the seller.

Another example: If closing occurs on December 11 and the $672 policy was paid on April 23, what are the days of proration and the amount of refund for the seller?

The seller will be refunded from and including December 12 through April 22. There are 31 days in December minus the 11 days the seller used equals 20 + 31 + 28 + 31 + 22 = 132 days. The annual insurance bill of $672 ÷ 365 × 132 means that $243.02 will be refunded to the seller. Try the next six on your own. The answers can be found in Appendix A.

Begin Date	Closing Date	Annual Bill	Days	Amount
October 4	January 17	$317		
March 22	August 4	$815		
January 10	April 16	$713		
July 24	February 7	$476		
August 7	July 28	$957		
May 16	September 16	$593		

Accrued Interest

When a seller has an existing loan on the property the day of closing, that loan will either be paid off or the buyer will assume the debt. Either way, the seller will be responsible for the interest on that loan from the last payment date through the closing date. When a payment is made on a real estate loan, the interest is paid in arrears and that payment satisfies the interest on the debt from the previous payment through the day prior to the due date, but it does not pay for the due date. To illustrate, a June 1 payment would pay the loan interest from May 1 through May 31, but would not pay for June 1. The July 1 payment would pay the loan interest from June 1 through June 30, but would not pay for July 1. If a payment were due on the 15th of the month, it would pay from the 15th of the previous month through the 14th of the current month. If a payment were due on the 20th of the month, it would pay from the 20th of the previous month through the 19th of the current month.

Let's look at an example: If the closing took place on March 23 and the seller had a loan balance of $79,265 at 7% interest as of the March 1 payment, what is the amount of accrued interest?

The formula for an accrued interest proration is:

Existing loan amount × Annual interest rate ÷ 360 × Days owed = Accrued interest

Remember, interest uses a 360-day banker's year.

The seller will be responsible for the interest from March 1 through March 23, which is 23 days.

$$\$79{,}265 \times 7\% \div 360 \times 23 = \$354.49$$

Let's look at another example. The closing is to take place on August 8 and the payments were due on the 20th of the month, with the last payment made July 20. The current loan balance is $248,937 at an annual interest rate of 6.5%. What is the accrued interest?

The accrued interest will be from July 20 through August 8. The seller is responsible for the entire 31 days in July, but paid for 19 with their payment. 31 − 19 = 12 days owed in July + 8 days in August is 20 days accrued interest. $248,937 × 6.5% ÷ 360 × 20 = $898.94 accrued interest.

Complete the following six examples. The answers can be found in Appendix A.

Loan Amount	Rate	Due Date	Closing Date	Days	Accrued interest
$274,934	8%	July 1	July 22		
$264,735	5.25%	April 10	April 27		
$73,586	5.75%	October 3	November 1		
$86,524	6.625%	February 1	February 17		
$95,476	11.125%	October 1	October 8		
$194,573	9.25%	May 20	June 7		

CHAPTER 19 Closing the Transaction

New Loans and Down Payments

New loans are typically represented as a percentage of the sales price, known as the loan-to-value ratio (L/V ratio). The higher the L/V ratio, the higher the potential risk to the lender in the event the borrower defaults. The L/V ratio is computed by dividing the loan amount by the value of the property, with the value being the lower of the sales price or appraisal, if both are given. For our purposes, we will assume loans are in the traditional increments of 80%, 90%, and 95%. Any L/V ratio at 80% or below will be treated as an 80% loan; any L/V ratio above 80% to 90% will be treated as a 90% loan; and an L/V ratio above 90% to 95% will be treated as a 95% loan.

Down payments are the difference between the sales price and loan amount. *Always* compute the loan amount first; round down in $100 increments if necessary and then subtract the loan amount from the sales price and you will get the down payment *every* time. If you try to take a shortcut and don't fully understand the principle, you will get the correct answer *sometimes*. On a test—and when you have money on the line in the field—*every* time is better.

Let's look at an example: Sales price of $157,000 with an L/V ratio of 90%. What is the down payment and loan amount?

$$\$157,000 \times 90\% = \$141,300 \text{ new loan amount}$$
$$\$157,000 - \$141,300 = \$15,700 \text{ down payment}$$

Let's try another example: If Sally was applying for a 95% loan on a purchase of $172,400, what is the down payment?

$$\$172,400 \times 95\% = \$163,780 \text{ (round down to } \$163,700\text{)}$$
$$\$172,400 - \$163,700 = \$8,700 \text{ down payment}$$

Complete the following six examples. The answers can be found in Appendix A.

Sales Price	L/V Ratio	Loan Amount	Down Payment
$267,000	90%		
$173,200	95%		
$135,600		$123,000	
$385,000		$327,600	
$87,500	95%		
$172,450		$157,900	

Many lenders make loans in exact amounts and do not round down in $100 increments. If the contract form calls for an exact loan amount, we recommended that you do round down. If a contract were to be contingent on the "purchaser's ability to obtain a loan of not less than $87,775" and the lender made loans only in $50 or $100 increments, the letter of the contract could not be met and the buyer might opt to void the agreement and demand that the earnest money be refunded. While the GAR contracts that are commonly used in the field simply state a percentage and not a loan amount, there is no guarantee that these contracts will be used in every situation. When dealing with national builders and corporations, you may be forced to use a contract that is not as user-friendly. Rounding down in $100 increments is just a good habit to be in; a loan available for $75 more than expected is not a problem, whereas one for $75 less than expected might be.

Interest Adjustment

When buyers receive a new loan at closing, they will always have at least a calendar month between the closing date and the date of the first payment. If the closing is on the first of the month, the first payment will be the first day of the following month. That payment will pay the interest for the previous month, which is exactly how long the borrower had the money, so there is no adjustment necessary. If the closing is any day of the month except the first, the borrower's first payment will not be due the following month, but rather, the month after that. To illustrate, if the closing occurred on May 1, the borrower's first payment would be due June 1, which would pay for the month of May, and there will be no interest adjustment required. But if the closing were on May 2, the borrower's first payment would be July 1. This payment would satisfy the interest required for the month of June, but the borrower had the benefit of the loan from May 2 through May 31 and has not paid for the use of the money. These 30 days (31 − 1 = 30) would represent the interest adjustment.

Let's look at an example: John and Mary purchased a property for $225,000 contingent on their ability to obtain a 90% conventional loan with an interest rate of 6%. The closing is to take place on March 7. What is the interest adjustment?

The formula for interest adjustment is:

Sales price × Loan to value ratio = Loan amount
(Loan amount × Interest rate = Annual interest) ÷ 360 ×
Number of days = Interest adjustment

The buyer will owe the interest on the new loan from and including March 7 through March 31, which is 25 days (31 − 6 days the borrower did not have the money in March = 25 days' interest adjustment):

$225,000 × 90% = $202,500, the new loan amount
($202,500 × 6%) ÷ 360 × 25 = $843.75
interest adjustment the buyer will pay on the new loan

Let's look at another example: Bocephus and Glory contract to purchase a property for $176,900 contingent on their ability to obtain a 90% loan with an interest rate of 6.625%. Closing will take place on July 3. What is the amount of interest adjustment? Bocephus and Glory will owe the interest from July 3 through July 31, which is 29 days (31 − 2 = 29):

$$\$176{,}900 \times 90\% = \$159{,}210 \text{ (remember our rule that new loans}$$
$$\text{are in \$100 increments; round down to \$159,200)}$$
$$(\$159{,}200 \times 6.625\%) \div 360 \times 29 = \$849.62$$

Complete the following examples. The answers can be found in Appendix A.

Sales Price	L/V Ratio	Rate	Closing Date	1st Pymt. Date	Loan Amount	Days	Amount
$295,000	80%	6.5%	March 13				
$172,500	95%	6.75%	October 27				
$223,500	90%	6.75%	May 6				
$88,700	95%	7%	June 1				
$675,800	75%	7.25%	November 17				
$108,000	90%	5.75%	January 11				

Rent Proration

Rent is paid in advance and is usually due on the first of the month. When closing on a tenant-occupied property, prorate prepaid rent between the seller and buyer. Remember, the seller is responsible for the day of closing, so the seller will credit the buyer from the day after closing through the end of the month. For example: Closing is on March 20 and the $850-per-month rent will be prorated. What are the days and amount debited to the seller and credited to the buyer?

The formula for rent proration is:

**Monthly rent ÷ Days in the month × Days from
the day after closing through the end of the month = Rent proration**

March has 31 days. 31 − 20 (which is the number of days that the seller was responsible) = 11 days proration.

$$\$850 \div 31 \times 11 = \$301.61$$

Let's try another one: Margaret purchases a tenant-occupied property from Frank. The closing is expected to be September 4 and the rent of $1,250 is to be prorated. What are the number of days and the amount of the proration?

$$30 - 4 = 26 \text{ days' proration}$$
$$\$1{,}250 \div 30 \times 26 = \$1{,}083.33$$

Complete the following six examples. The answers can be found in Appendix A.

Closing Date	Monthly Rent	Days	Amount
October 10	$1,480		
May 3	$825		
June 28	$1,450		
February 17	$725		
July 20	$1,800		
September 9	$900		

Mortgage Insurance

Mortgage insurance is to be expected on conventional loans above 80% L/V ratio and FHA loans. Private mortgage insurance (PMI) is typically paid with an upfront amount at closing (usually in the range of 0.5% to 1% of the loan amount) and then an annual premium (usually in the range of 0.3% to 1% of the loan amount) until the loan is below 80% L/V ratio. With the FHA, the upfront amount is typically 1.75% of the loan amount and an annual premium of 1.35%. (These percentages are provided as examples. The percentages are somewhat dynamic, particularly in the current real estate market. These numbers should not be relied on in the field. Do your own research online, or ask a local lender.)

For example: Ted is purchasing a property for $175,000 with a 90% L/V ratio. The lender requires 0.8% upfront and annual premiums of 0.65%. What are Ted's PMI requirements? The formula is:

Loan amount × Required percentages = Amount due up front and annual PMI premium

$175,000 × 90% = $157,500 loan amount
$157,500 × 0.8% = $1,260 PMI upfront
$157,500 × 0.65% = $1,023.75 annual premium

Let's take a look at another example: Ethel contracts to purchase a property for $122,000 with an FHA loan. The loan amount will be $116,400. What are the upfront and annual mortgage insurance requirements?

$116,400 × 1.75% = $2,037 upfront
$116,400 × 1.35% = $1,571.40 annual premium

Complete the following six examples. The answers can be found in Appendix A.

CHAPTER 19 Closing the Transaction

Sales Price	Type	Loan Amount	Upfront %	Annual %	Upfront Amount	Annual Amount
$225,000	90%		.75%	.5%		
$420,000	95%		.9%	.75%		
$142,000	FHA	$135,400				
$284,500	95%		.85%	.65%		
$94,300	FHA	$90,000				
$88,250	90%		.6%	.45%		

Tax Escrows

Many loans will require the borrower to escrow an amount with the lender to pay future payments of such things as property taxes, homeowners insurance, and mortgage insurance. The account is then maintained by the borrower paying one-twelfth of the annual amount to the lender each month, along with the payment. These loans are referred to as budget loans and the payments as budget payments. For our purposes, all FHA loans, all VA loans, and conventional loans above 80% will be budget loans. The Real Estate Settlement Procedures Act (RESPA) places requirements on lenders as to how much they can require a borrower to deposit into the escrow account as a prerequisite of being approved for a loan. The formula for the number of months a lender will require a borrower to deposit for tax escrow is somewhat complex and will be different from county to county, depending on when the taxes are collected. For our exercises, you will be told how many months to escrow; all you will have to do is compute the amount. For example: If the annual taxes were $2,275 and the lender required a seven-month escrow, what is the amount of the tax escrow? The formula is:

Annual tax bill ÷ 12 × Number of months required = Tax escrow

$2,275 ÷ 12 × 7 = $1,327.08 tax escrow

Complete the following six examples. The answers can be found in Appendix A.

Annual Taxes	Number of Months	Tax Escrow
$2,750	3	
$1,635	9	
$1,397	13	
$4,286	5	
$3,264	8	
$982	10	

Insurance

Insurance proration, whether for hazard (homeowners) insurance or mortgage insurance, will require either a two- or three-month escrow requirement from the lender. We will use a worst-case scenario of three months unless otherwise indicated. For example: If the annual insurance is $450, what is the escrow requirement? The formula is:

Annual insurance bill ÷ 12 × Months of escrow required = Insurance escrow requirement

$450 ÷ 12 × 3 = $112.50

Complete the following six examples. The answers can be found in Appendix A.

Annual Insurance Bill	Insurance Escrow
$865	
$504	
$1,649	
$973	
$2,974	
$776	

Transfer Tax

Transfer tax is a state tax paid when recording a deed transfer. There is always a transfer tax, and it can be paid by the seller or the buyer. The transfer tax is paid on the adjusted sales price, which is the sales price minus the loan assumed. The tax is paid at the rate of $0.10 per $100 increment or any portion thereof. Transfer tax will always end in "0." It could be $37.30 or $37.40, but it could not possibly be $37.38. For example, if the sales price is $126,700 and there is no loan assumed, how much is the transfer tax? The formula is:

Sales price − Loan assumed ÷ 100 = Transfer tax

If this is not a whole number, round up to the next whole number. That number times $0.10 equals the transfer tax.

$126,700 ÷ 100 = 1,267 × $0.10 = $126.70 in transfer tax

Let's try another: Sales price of $98,700 with an existing loan of $73,214 being assumed. What is the transfer tax?

$98,700 − $73,214 = $25,486 adjusted sales price
$25,486 ÷ 100 = 254.86, which is rounded up to 255
255 × $0.10 = $25.50 transfer tax

Complete the following six examples. The answers can be found in Appendix A.

Sales Price	Existing Loan	Assumed?	Transfer Tax
$265,800	$174,473	No	
$163,700	$149,576	Yes	
$125,000	$95,674	Yes	
$374,700	$202,395	No	
$254,600	$201,578	Yes	
$96,500	$79,746	No	

Intangibles Tax

Whenever there is a recorded new loan, there will be an intangibles tax, with very few exceptions. Intangibles tax is paid at the rate of $1.50 per $500 increment, or any part thereof on the new loan. If there is no new loan, there is no intangibles tax. Since intangibles tax is paid in $1.50 increments, the tax could be $411.00 or $412.50, but it could not be $411.75. For example, if the sales price was $225,000 and the buyer was getting a new 90% loan, what is the intangibles tax? The formula for intangibles tax is:

New loan ÷ 500 (rounding up to the next whole number) × $1.50 = Intangibles tax

$225,000 × 90% = $202,500 new loan amount
$202,500 ÷ 500 = 405 increments × $1.50 = $607.50 intangibles tax

Let's try another: Sales price of $167,400 with a 90% loan. What is the intangibles tax?

$167,400 × 90% = $150,660 (rounded down to $150,600 new loan amount)
$150,600 ÷ 500 = 301.2 increments (rounded up to 302)
302 × $1.50 = $453.00 intangibles tax

Complete the following six examples. The answers can be found in Appendix A.

Sales Price	New Loan Type	Loan Amount	Intangibles Tax
$88,500	90%		
$165,000	80%		
$126,200	95%		
$458,500	80%		
$217,200	100%		
$95,500	90%		

BUYER AND SELLER WORKSHEETS

Figures 19-1 and 19-2 are the ESTIMATED PURCHASER COST and ESTIMATED NET TO SELLER worksheets. There are many versions of these documents in the field, and the one preferred by your brokerage company will probably be similar to these. There are also software programs through MLS services and other providers that may do these computations and worksheets for you. A word of caution: If you rely on the software to do the work and do not have a working understanding of how to manipulate the calculations and worksheets, you are at the mercy of technology. It will be difficult to convincingly explain the information to customers and clients unless you are intimately familiar with it. Having a solid understanding of this work will be considered a value-added service to your clients and will help differentiate you. Take advantage of it!

REAL ESTATE SETTLEMENT PROCEDURES ACT

In response to consumer complaints regarding real estate closing costs and procedures, Congress passed the **Real Estate Settlement Procedures Act (RESPA)**. The Act took effect on June 20, 1975, throughout the United States. The purpose of RESPA, which is administered by the U.S. Department of Housing and Urban Development (HUD), is to regulate and standardize real estate settlement practices when federally related first mortgage loans are made on one- to four-family residences, condominiums, and cooperatives. *Federally related* is defined to include FHA, VA, or other government-backed or government-assisted loans; loans from lenders with federally insured deposits; loans that are to be purchased by FNMA, GNMA, FHLMC, or other federally controlled secondary mortgage market institutions; and loans made by lenders that make or invest more than $1 million per year in residential loans. As the bulk of all home loans now made fall into one of these categories, the impact of this law is far-reaching.

Real Estate Settlement Procedures Act (RESPA): a federal law that deals with procedures to be followed in certain types of real estate closings

Restrictions

RESPA prohibits kickbacks and fees for services not performed during the closing process. For example, in some regions of the United States prior to this Act, it was common practice for attorneys and **closing agents** to channel title business to certain title companies in return for a fee. This increased settlement costs without adding services. Now there must be a justifiable service rendered for each closing fee charge. The Act also prohibits the seller from requiring that the buyer purchase title insurance from a particular title company. RESPA underwent major revisions in 1996. Recall the discussion in a previous chapter as to how disclosures must now be made for business referrals and origination fees.

closing agent: the person placed in charge of closing a real estate transaction

ESTIMATED PURCHASER COST

Purchaser _____ Date of estimate _____
Property address _____
Estimated closing date _____ Prepared by _____
Type of loan _____

DOWN PAYMENT
1. Purchase price _____
2. New first mortgage _____
3. New second mortgage _____
4. Amount of existing loan assumed _____
5. Down payment (Line 1 minus lines 2, 3 and 4) _____

FINANCING EXPENSES
6. Closing costs (____% of the loan amount if applicable) _____
7. Discount points (____% of the loan amount) _____
8. Mortgage insurance _____
9. Transfer fee on loan assumption _____
10. Intangibles tax _____
11. Other financing expenses _____
12. Total financing expenses _____

PREPAID ITEMS
13. Purchaser's share of prepaid property taxes _____
14. Homeowner's insurance _____
15. Interest adjustment on new loan _____
16. Next payment due on loan assumed, if required _____
17. Other prepaid items _____
18. Total prepaid items _____

ESCROW ITEMS
19. Purchase of seller's escrow account (L/A only) _____
20. Property tax escrow _____
21. Homeowner's insurance escrow _____
22. Mortgage insurance escrow _____
23. Other escrow item _____
24. Total escrow items _____

MISCELLANEOUS EXPENSES
25. Purchase of personal property _____
26. Wood infestation report _____
27. Survey _____
28. Home inspection _____
29. Other miscellaneous expenses _____
30. Total miscellaneous expenses _____

CREDITS
31. Earnest money deposited _____
32. Seller's share of unpaid property taxes _____
33. Seller's contribution to closing costs _____
34. Accrued interest on seller's loan (L/A only) _____
35. Other credits _____
36. Total credits _____

SUMMARY LINE
37. **Estimated funds needed to close (Line 5 plus 12, 18, 24 and 30 minus line 36)** _____

ESTIMATED MONTHLY PAYMENT
A. Principal and interest _____
B. Property tax escrow _____
C. Homeowner's insurance escrow _____
D. Mortgage insurance escrow _____
E. Other _____
F. **Total estimated monthly payment** _____

FIGURE 19-1 Estimate of cost to buyer

Source: © 2021 Mbition LLC

ESTIMATED NET TO SELLER

Seller _____ Date _____
Property address _____
Purchaser _____ Closing date _____
Purchaser's estimated loan amount _____

1. Purchase price _____

SELLER'S PRESENT LOAN EXPENSES

2. First loan balance _____
3. Accrued interest on first _____
4. Second loan balance _____
5. Accrued interest on second _____
6. Failure to give notice of payoff _____
7. Prepayment penalty _____
8. Other loan expenses _____
9. Total present loan expenses (_____)

MARKETING COSTS

10. Georgia transfer tax _____
11. Seller's share of prorated property taxes _____
12. Wood infestation report _____
13. Broker's fee _____
14. Other marketing expenses _____
15. Total marketing expenses (_____)

FINANCING COSTS

16. Closing costs (____% of the loan amount if applicable) _____
17. Discount points (____% of the loan amount) _____
18. Mortgage insurance _____
19. Transfer fee on loan assumption _____
20. Intangible tax (if not included in closing costs) _____
21. Survey _____
22. Other financing expenses _____
23. Total financing expenses (_____)

MISCELLANEOUS EXPENSES

24. Purchase money mortgage _____
25. Rent proration _____
26. Transfer of security deposit _____
27. Other miscellaneous expenses _____
28. Total miscellaneous expenses (_____)

CREDITS

29. Escrow refund _____
30. Purchaser's share of prorated property taxes _____
31. Homeowners insurance refund _____
32. Sale of personal property _____
33. Other credits _____
34. Total credits _____

SUMMARY LINE
35. Estimated net to seller (Line 1 minus line 9, 15, 23 and 28 plus line 34) _____

FIGURE 19-2 Estimate of net to seller
Source: © 2021 Mbition LLC

The Real Estate Settlement Procedures Act also contains restrictions on the amount of advance property tax and insurance payments a lender may collect and place in an impound or reserve account. The amount is limited to the property owner's share of taxes and insurance accrued prior to settlement, plus one-sixth of the estimated amount that will come due for these items in the 12-month period beginning at settlement. This requirement ensures that the lender has an adequate but not excessive amount of money impounded when taxes and insurance payments fall due. If the amount in the reserve account is not sufficient to pay an item when it comes due, the lender must temporarily use its own funds to make up the difference. Then the lender bills the borrower or increases the monthly reserve payment. If there is a drop in the amount the lender must pay out, then the monthly reserve requirement can be reduced.

Revisions made in 1997 also allow a voluntary increased payment into escrow for newly constructed homes. The homes are often taxed at the vacant lot rate, then the tax rate increases dramatically after construction. This results in escrow shortages and huge increases in monthly payments to cover those shortages. The new rule is intended to prevent "payment shock" by increasing the monthly payment.

Considerable criticism and debate have raged over the topic of reserves. Traditionally, lenders have not paid interest to borrowers on money held as reserves, effectively creating an interest-free loan to themselves. This has tempted many lenders to require overly adequate reserves. RESPA sets a reasonable limit on reserve requirements, and some states now require that interest be paid on reserves. Although not always required to do so, some lenders now voluntarily pay interest on reserves.

Consumer Financial Protection Bureau (CFPB)

In 2010, the Wall Street Reform and Consumer Protection Act was signed into law. This act is commonly referred to as Dodd-Frank, recognizing Senator Christopher Dodd and Representative Barney Frank, who worked tirelessly and whose influence was essential in the passing of this Act. The Act is far-reaching into regulation of the banking, investment, and finance industries, but as far as the real estate industry is concerned, the most direct impact of this Act was the creation of the Consumer Financial Protection Bureau (CFPB). With the empowerment of CFPB in 2011, most rule-making, implementation and enforcement of RESPA have been transferred to the CFPB. This is also true of the Truth in Lending Act (TILA), which was studied in a previous chapter.

TILA-RESPA Integrated Disclosures (TRID)

For the last 40 years RESPA has mandated, with few exceptions, that a HUD-1 Settlement Statement be used in the closing of a residential real estate transaction. With TRID and the focus on education of the borrower, there is no longer a document or form required to show all the financial credits and debits between the parties. While the closing document (CD) does that, the CD is a confidential document provided just for the consumer. That has caused some angst for real estate professionals, the seller, and others. The American Land Title Association has developed a form known as the ALTA Settlement Statement-Combined. This appears to be the form being adopted by most closing attorneys to provide to all parties the information traditionally supplied in the CD. A copy of this form is found in Appendix E.

TRID brought with it more than just a new disclosure form. It also comes with more regulation and controls. An obvious goal of TRID is to slow down the transaction and make sure the borrower fully understands his/her responsibilities before they become obligations. In fact, the slogan of TRID is "Know before you owe." Under TRID, there are six specific pieces of information, which once collected, compose a formal loan application:

1. name
2. income information
3. Social Security number for credit report
4. property address
5. estimated value of property used for security
6. amount of loan being sought

Once the prospective borrower (formally known as the consumer) has provided these six pieces of information, TRID considers this a formal application and the liabilities begin. The lender must provide to the consumer a Loan Estimate within three business days and no less than seven business days prior to consummation of the transaction, which is the date that the borrower becomes contractually liable for the loan. It may or may not be same day as closing or settlement, which is when the buyer becomes contractually obligated to the seller. TRID considers any day but Sunday or a federal holiday to be a business day. If circumstances change, a revised loan estimate must be provided within three business days.

No later than three business days prior to consummation, the lender must provide to the consumer a Closing Disclosure. A sample CD is provided in Appendix E. This shows all charges, debits, and credits for the transaction and is confidential between the lender and borrower. The seller and real estate agents will have no access to this document or information unless it is released to them by the buyer. Once the three days have passed, the parties may have a settlement, or what we more commonly in Georgia refer to as a closing. Under TRID, this is called consummation. This is typically going to be at the same time, same day. In the event there are certain changes in the CD, a new CD must be provided. If mailed, a three-day delivery period is assumed. The consumer must have three days to review the new CD, and the parties may close on the seventh day.

Remember, Sunday is not a day under TRID, so it will be at least eight calendar days. The changes in the CD that could cause a delay are:

- APR becomes inaccurate;
- loan product is changed; or
- a pre-payment penalty is added.

Penalties

The penalties that may be imposed under TRID are substantial and potentially could rise into the millions of dollars. For that reason, implementation of TRID was delayed for several months in 2015. The CFPB agreed to tread softly on the implementation of penalties except for the most egregious violations until all parties could experience the new regulations and have a full understanding of how to comply. The penalties are:

- $5,000 per day for routine violations;
- $25,000 per day for knowing violations; and
- $1 million for reckless violations.

Review Questions

Answers to these questions can be found in Appendix D at the end of this book.

1. Which of the following is NOT a detail that is typically handled between the time a purchase contract is signed and the closing?
   A. title search
   B. deed preparation
   C. buyer qualification
   D. checking the property taxes

2. A buyer's walk-through is conducted for the purpose of:
   A. appraising the property in order to get a loan on it
   B. inspecting the property for major structural defects
   C. meeting the seller and obtaining the keys to the property
   D. making a final inspection just prior to closing

3. If a closing is to take place on June 25 and the annual taxes of $1,800 have not been paid, which of the following is true of the proration?
   A. The seller is credited with $867.95
   B. The buyer is credited with $867.95
   C. The seller is debited with $932.05
   D. The buyer is debited with $932.05

4. How much is the transfer tax on a $225,000 sale with a 90% new loan and an existing loan payoff of $154,500?
   A. $154.50
   B. $202.50
   C. $70.50
   D. $225

5. In Georgia, the closing may legally be conducted by:
   A. a real estate broker only
   B. a salesperson, if under the supervision of a licensed attorney
   C. a licensed attorney only
   D. a licensed attorney or real estate broker

6. Which of the following must be provided to the consumer within three business days of the application?
   A. a CD
   B. a HUD-1 Settlement Statement
   C. a LE
   D. a Good Faith Estimate

7. Figures used on the settlement statement may be important:
   A. only if there is a new loan.
   B. but should never be represented by a real estate agent
   C. if the broker (not an attorney) is closing the transaction
   D. as early as listing the property

8. Which of the following transactions would NOT typically require a lender escrow account?
   A. 100% VA
   B. FHA
   C. 90% conventional
   D. 80% conventional

9. Barnes sold his home to Hyatt through broker Quinn. The lender is Dorsey. The closing attorney will represent:
   A. Barnes
   B. Hyatt
   C. Quinn
   D. Dorsey

10. In a $210,000 sale with a 95% conventional loan, how much is the intangible tax?
    A. $630
    B. $210
    C. $598.50
    D. $199.50

11. How much is the interest adjustment on a $175,400 loan at 6.25% with a May 13 closing date?
    A. $395.87
    B. $913.54
    C. $578.58
    D. $772.56

12. If a property sold for $185,000, the seller had an existing loan with a balance of $127,587 at 7%, and the buyer was getting a 90% conventional loan at 8%, what is the accrued interest if the closing takes place on February 24?
    A. $863.33
    B. $124.04
    C. $595.41
    D. $185

13. If the annual homeowner's insurance was paid on September 15 and the closing takes place on June 3, which of the following is true of the insurance proration?
    A. The seller is credited.
    B. The buyer is credited.
    C. Both the buyer and seller are credited.
    D. Both the buyer and seller are debited.

14. If a lender has a policy of charging a PMI of 1.0% on 95% L/V ratio and 0.6% on 90% L/V ratio, what is the PMI if the sales price is $265,700 and the loan is $240,500?
    A. $1,202.50
    B. $2,675.00
    C. $1,337.50
    D. $2,405.00

15. TRID replaces which documents?
    A. Truth In Lending Disclosure Statement and HUD-1
    B. Good Faith Estimate and HUD-1
    C. Truth in Lending Disclosure Statement and Good Faith Estimate
    D. Good Faith Estimate and Loan Application

16. When a home is sold and a new loan by an institutional lender is required to complete the transaction, the typical time between purchase contract signing and settlement will most likely be:
    A. 0–29 days
    B. 30–60 days
    C. 61–120 days
    D. over 120 days

17. Among the items NOT to be prorated at a settlement is (are):
    A. taxes
    B. rents from income-producing properties
    C. title insurance
    D. interest on existing debt

18. Prorations of items in a real estate closing are made usually as of the date of the:
    A. signing of the sales contract
    B. title transfer
    C. buyer's walk-through
    D. mortgage payment

19. In a typical closing, insurance prorations will usually be:
    A. a credit to the seller and an expense to the buyer
    B. a credit to the buyer and an expense to the seller
    C. a credit to the seller and a credit to the buyer
    D. an expense to the buyer and an expense to the seller

20. What document is provided to the borrower by the lender at least three days prior to the closing and is considered confidential?
    A. a CD
    B. a HUD-1 Settlement Statement
    C. a LE
    D. a Good Faith Estimate

CHAPTER 20
TRANSFERRING TITLE

KEY TERMS

accretion
adverse possession
alluvion
avulsion
bargain and sale deed
cloud on the title
codicil
color of title
consideration
covenant
deed
general warranty deed
grantee
grantor
holographic will
intestate succession
nuncupative will
quitclaim deed
reliction
special warranty deed
testate
warranty

OBJECTIVES

After successful completion of this chapter, you should be able to:
1. understand the essential elements of a deed;
2. describe the various covenants and warranties;
3. explain the different types of deeds, such as the general warranty deed, the special warranty deed, the bargain and sale deed, and the quitclaim deed;
4. explain how real estate is conveyed after death;
5. define codicil, adverse possession, tacking on, easement by prescription, and ownership by accession;
6. explain how property is transferred by public grant, dedication, and alienation, and
7. define a gift deed, guardian deed, and other types of deeds.

OVERVIEW

In this chapter, you will learn how the ownership of real estate is conveyed from one owner to another. Voluntary conveyance of real estate by deed, conveyance after

death, conveyance by occupancy, accession, public grant, dedication, and forfeiture are covered. An important part of this chapter, and a part that you should review very carefully, is the coverage of the essential elements of a deed. Likewise, the various covenants and warranties should be reviewed.

DEEDS

deed: a written document that, when properly executed and delivered, conveys title to land

A **deed**, when properly executed and delivered, is a written legal document by which ownership of real property is conveyed from one party to another. Deeds were not always used to transfer real estate. In early England, when land was sold, its title was conveyed by inviting the purchaser onto the land. In the presence of witnesses, the seller picked up a clod of earth and handed it to the purchaser. Simultaneously, the seller stated that he was delivering ownership of the land to the purchaser. In times when land sales were rare because ownership usually passed from generation to generation, and when witnesses seldom moved from the towns or farms where they were born, this method worked well. However, as transactions became more common and people more mobile, this method of title transfer became less reliable. Furthermore, it was susceptible to fraud if enough people could be bribed or forced to make false statements. In 1677, England passed a law known as the *Statute of Frauds*. This law, subsequently adopted by each of the American states, requires that transfers of real estate ownership be in writing and signed in order to be enforceable in a court of law. Thus, the need for a deed was created.

Essential Elements of a Deed

What makes a written document a deed? What special phrases, statements, and actions are necessary to convey the ownership rights one has in land and buildings?

grantor: the person named in a deed who conveys ownership

Name of grantor—The **grantor** (the "giver" of the deed) is typically the seller. It could be an executor, administrator, or sheriff, or the transfer could involve a gift rather than sale. The grantor must have legal capacity to contract and convey. This means s/he must be of legal age and of sound mind. Although a minor may have the ability to enter into some contracts, a minor may not function as the grantor on a deed.

grantee: the person named in a deed who acquires ownership

Name of the grantee—The **grantee** (the "receiver" of the deed) is typically the buyer. The grantee could be receiving the transfer through a gift deed, and thus not truly be a buyer. The grantee must be clearly identified, but it is not required that s/he have full legal capacity. There is a story about a tree that owns itself. The property was conveyed to the tree and the legal guardian is a major university. The original grantor funded a substantial endowment to the university, which is dependent on the life of the tree. The university is VERY motivated to take care of the tree and make sure it survives!

Legal description—The property must be identified geographically, exclusive of any other property on the face of the earth. In Georgia, this is typically satisfied with either a metes and bounds description or a reference to a recorded document, such as a plat.

Granting clause—The deed must clearly state the intention to convey the property from the grantor to the grantee. You can see the wording in the deed in Figure 20-1: "...grant, bargain, sell, alien, convey and confirm...."

Consideration—A deed is a contract between the grantor and grantee, and, as such, requires consideration. Most deeds will state a nominal consideration, as does Figure 20-1. Notice the wording: "TEN AND 00/100 DOLLARS ($10.00) and other good and valuable consideration...." The consideration in a gift deed is typically "good" rather than "valuable." Instead of stating a monetary consideration, the deed will use words such as "love and affection." While most deeds will state only nominal consideration, if the transfer is involuntary, a full recitation of consideration is required. An example would be a foreclosure sale; you would expect to see the full sale price stated rather than a nominal payment. This is to erase any doubt of what was paid for the property in order to avoid the perception of impropriety, as would occur with a sale to a friend at less than market value, for example.

consideration: anything given, good or valuable, to induce another to enter into a contract

Restriction and exceptions—The deed illustrated in Figure 20-1 contains the wording "Subject to all easements and restrictions of record." This is common boilerplate language, but there may be other exceptions or restrictions, as well. The grantor may be reserving an easement for himself/herself to access adjoining property; the transfer may place conditions on the use of the property, such as that it must be used only as a city park; and/or the transfer may be reserving certain rights that are typically treated as appurtenant, such as water rights, mineral rights, or air rights.

Signature of the grantor—The grantor is required to sign the deed; however, the grantee is not. If there were any question about the grantee accepting the transfer or if there were a condition or obligation in the deed that the grantee may object to, prudent parties may require the grantee to sign to eliminate any question of acceptance. An example of this may be a person purchasing a property at a discount because of a toxic spill. The grantor may want to ensure the buyer's knowledge of this problem and the buyer's acceptance of responsibility by having him/her sign the deed. The grantee may also sign the deed in the case of a loan assumption where the buyer was going to contractually become responsible for the payment of debt.

Delivery and acceptance—For a deed to be valid, the deed must be delivered by the grantor and accepted by the grantee (or a person empowered to accept on behalf of the grantee). This delivery and acceptance must take place during the lifetime of the parties. For example, if a grantor executed a deed and put it in a safe deposit box in an envelope with instructions to deliver in the event the grantor were to die, the deed would die along with the grantor. However, if the grantor were to execute a deed and deliver it to a third party with instructions to deliver

> **WARRANTY DEED**
>
> State of
> County of
>
> THIS INDENTURE made this day, _____, between (name of grantor) as party or parties of the first part, hereinafter called Grantor, and (name of grantee) as Joint Tenants with Rights of Survivorship and not as Tenants in Common as party or parties of the second part, hereinafter called Grantee (the words "Grantor" and "Grantee" to include their respective heirs, successors and assigns where the context requires or permits).
>
> WITNESSETH that: Grantor, for and in consideration of the sum of TEN AND 00/100 DOLLARS ($10.00) and other good and valuable consideration in hand paid at and before the sealing and delivery of these presents, the receipt whereof is hereby acknowledged, has granted, bargained, sold, aliened, conveyed and confirmed, and by these presents does grant, bargain, sell, alien, convey and confirm unto the said Grantee, the following described property:
>
> [legal description of land]
>
> Subject to all easements and restrictions of record.
>
> TO HAVE AND TO HOLD the said tract or parcel of land, with all and singular the rights, members and appurtenances thereof, the same being, belonging, or in anywise appertaining, to the only proper use, benefit and behoof of the said Grantee, forever in FEE SIMPLE.
>
> AND THE SAID Grantor will warrant and forever defend the right and title to the above described property unto the said Grantee against the claims of all persons whomsoever.
>
> IN WITNESS WHEREOF, Grantor has hereunto set grantor's hand and seal this day and year first above written.
>
> Signed, sealed and delivered in the presence of:
>
> _____   _____(Seal)
> Witness
>
> _____   _____(Seal)
> Notary Public
> My Commission Expires:

FIGURE 20-1 Sample warranty deed

Source: © 2021 Mbition LLC

the deed to the grantee when the grantor dies, the transfer is effective when given to the agent for the grantee because there was an intention to deliver. Delivery does not require physical passing of the document, just intention.

Figure 20-2 demonstrates the essential elements that combine to form a deed. Notice that the example includes an identification of the grantor and grantee, fulfills the requirement for consideration, has words of conveyance, gives a legal

> Witnesseth, __John Stanley__, grantor, for valuable consideration given by __Robert Brenner__, grantee, does hereby grant and release unto the grantee, his heirs and assigns to have and to hold forever, the following described land: [insert legal description here].
>
> _John Stanley_
> Grantor's signature

FIGURE 20-2 Essential elements of a deed
Source: © 2021 Mbition LLC

description of the land involved, and has the grantor's signature. The words of conveyance are *grant and release*, and the phrase *to have and to hold forever* says that the grantor is conveying all future benefits, not just a life estate or a tenancy for years. Ordinarily, the grantee does not sign the deed.

Covenants and Warranties

Although legally adequate, a deed meeting the preceding requirements can still leave a very important question unanswered in the grantee's mind: "Does the grantor possess all the rights, title, and interest purported by conveying this deed?" As a protective measure, the grantee may ask the grantor to include certain **covenants** and **warranties** in the deed. These are written promises by the grantor that the condition of title is as stated in the deed together with the grantor's guarantee that if title is not as stated, the grantor will compensate the grantee for any loss suffered. Five covenants and warranties have evolved over the centuries for use in deeds, and a deed may contain none, some, or all of them, in addition to the essential elements already discussed. They are seizin, quiet enjoyment, against encumbrances, further assurance, and warranty forever.

Under the *covenant of seizin* (sometimes spelled *seisin*), the grantor warrants (guarantees) to be the owner and possessor of the property being conveyed and to have the right to convey it. Under the *covenant of quiet enjoyment*, the grantor warrants to the grantee that the grantee will not be disturbed, after taking possession, by someone else claiming an interest in the property. The term *quiet enjoyment* is also used in a leasing situation. A tenant has, by implication if not expression, the right to use and enjoy a leased property for the purposes for which it was leased. In the *covenant against encumbrances*, the grantor guarantees to the grantee that the title is not encumbered with any easements, restrictions, unpaid property taxes, assessments, mortgages, judgments, and so on, except as stated in the deed. If the grantee later discovers an undisclosed encumbrance, the grantee may sue the grantor for the cost of removing it. The *covenant of further assurance*

covenant: a written agreement or promise

warranty: an assurance or guarantee that something is true as stated

requires the grantor to procure and deliver to the grantee any subsequent documents that might be necessary to make good the grantee's title. *Warranty forever* is a guarantee to the grantee that the grantor will bear the expense of defending the grantee's title. If at any time in the future someone else can prove to be the rightful owner, the grantee may sue the grantor for damages up to the value of the property at the time of the sale. This warranty forever essentially creates a money-back guarantee from the seller to the buyer. Because these warranties and covenants are a formidable set of promises, grantors often back them up with title insurance (discussed in the next chapter). The grantee is also more comfortable if the deed is backed by title insurance.

Habendum clause—This is commonly referred to as the "to have and to hold" clause. Is the property to be held by the grantees as tenants in common, or joint tenants coupled with the rights of survivorship? Notice that in Figure 20-1, the wording "as Joint Tenants with Rights of Survivorship and not as Tenants in Common" has been included. Because joint tenancy has the rights of survivorship of the tenancy, not the family, this must be clearly stated, as has been done here. The wording further clarifies matters by stating that it is ". . . not as Tenants in Common."

Date—While a date is common in the deed, it is not required. The date in the deed is commonly the date it was executed and delivered. The date that is important, however, is the date of recording. The date of recording is the date the world is constructively notified of the grantee's interest in the property.

Witnesses—Witnesses are not required for the deed to be valid, but they are required to record the deed. In Georgia, two witnesses are required to record, with one of them being an official witness—typically a notary public, but possibly another official witness such as a judge. This signing in front of witnesses, with one of them being an official witness, creates an acknowledgment, which is a requirement for recording. An acknowledgment is the witnessed declaration made by a person signing a document that his action was voluntary. While acknowledgment is not a requirement of a valid deed, acknowledgment is a requirement to record at the county courthouse into public record.

Recording—Recording a deed is not required for it to be valid between the parties, but it is the most effective way to provide constructive notice to the world of the owner's interest in the property. If constructive notice is not given, an innocent subsequent buyer could enter into a purchase of the property from the previous owner. If there was no reasonable way to know that the person claiming to be the owner did not own the property, the sale would be valid and the first buyer would have to take legal action against the seller/fraudster. The moral of the story is, record the deed as soon as possible, even if not required for validity.

Deed preparation—The exact style or form of a deed is not critical as long as it contains all the essentials clearly stated and is in conformity with state law. For example, one commonly used warranty deed format begins with the words *Know all men by these presents*, is written in the first person, and has the date at the end. Although a person may prepare a personal deed, the writing of deeds should be left to experts in the field. In fact, some states permit only attorneys to write deeds for other persons. Even the preparation of preprinted deeds from stationery stores and title companies should be left to knowledgeable persons. Preprinted deeds contain several pitfalls for the unwary. First, the form may have been prepared and printed in another state and, as a result, may not meet the laws of your state. Second, if the blanks are incorrectly filled in, the deed may not accomplish its intended purpose. This is a particularly difficult problem when neither the grantor nor grantee realizes it until several years after the deed's delivery. Third, the use of a form deed presumes that the grantor's situation can be fitted to the form and that the grantor will be knowledgeable enough to select the correct form. Meanwhile, let us turn our attention to examples of the most commonly used deeds in the United States.

General Warranty Deed

The **general warranty deed**, also known as the *full covenant and warranty deed* or *warranty deed*, contains all five covenants and warranties. It is thus considered to be the best deed a grantee can receive and is used extensively in most states, Georgia included. Figure 20-1 is a copy of the warranty deed that parties would typically see at a closing of a sale. Because this deed conveys with all warranties from the grantor to the grantee, it is essentially a money-back guarantee if there is ever a problem with the title, even if the problem originated prior to the ownership of the grantor and the grantor had no knowledge.

general warranty deed: grantor makes full guarantee to buyer against defects of title

Special Warranty Deed

In a **special warranty deed**, also known as the *limited warranty deed*, the grantor warrants the property's title only against defects occurring during the grantor's ownership and not against defects existing before that time. The special warranty deed is commonly used by executors and trustees who convey on behalf of an estate or principal because the executor or trustee has no authority to warrant and defend the acts of previous holders of title. This form of deed has also become very common in typical property transfers in Georgia. The grantee can protect against this gap in warranty by purchasing title insurance. The special warranty deed is also known in some states as a bargain and sale deed with a covenant against only the grantor's acts.

special warranty deed: grantor warrants title only against defects occurring during the grantor's ownership

```
                    BARGAIN AND SALE DEED
     THIS DEED made    (date)    , between      (name of grantor)      re-
siding at           (city, town, etc.)          , herein called the Grantor,
and         (name of grantee)        residing at    (city, town,
     etc.)    , herein called the Grantee.
     WITNESSETH, that the Grantor, in consideration of _____, does
hereby grant and release unto the Grantee, the Grantee's heirs, successors, and as-
signs forever, all that parcel of land described as
                      [legal description of land]
     TOGETHER WITH the appurtenances and all the estate and rights of the
Grantor in and to said property.
     TO HAVE AND TO HOLD the premises herein granted together with the ap-
purtenances unto the Grantee. This conveyance is made however, without any war-
ranties, express, implied, or statutory.
     IN WITNESS WHEREOF, the Grantor sets his hand and seal the day and year
first written above.
                                              (Grantor's signature)   L.S.
     [location of the acknowledgment]
```

FIGURE 20-3 Sample bargain and sale deed
Source: © 2021 Mbition LLC

Bargain and Sale Deed

bargain and sale deed: a deed that contains no covenants but does imply that the grantor owns the property being conveyed

The basic **bargain and sale deed** contains no covenants and only the minimum essentials of a deed (see Figure 20-3). It has a date, identifies the grantor and grantee, recites consideration, describes the property, contains words of conveyance, and has the grantor's signature. But lacking covenants, what assurance does the grantee have of acquiring title to anything? Actually, none. In this deed, the grantor only implies ownership of the property described in the deed and a granting of it to the grantee. Logically, then, a grantee will much prefer a warranty deed over a bargain and sale deed, or require title insurance.

Quitclaim Deed

quitclaim deed: a legal instrument used to convey whatever title the grantor has; it contains no covenants, warranties, or implication of the grantor's ownership

A **quitclaim deed** has no covenants or warranties (see Figure 20-4). Moreover, the grantor makes no statement or even implies ownership of the property being quitclaimed to the grantee. Whatever rights the grantor possesses at the time the deed is delivered are conveyed to the grantee. If the grantor has no interest, right, or title to the property described in the deed, none is conveyed to the grantee. However, if the grantor possesses fee simple title, fee simple title will be conveyed to the grantee.

The critical wording in a quitclaim deed is the grantor's statement to *hereby remise, release, and quitclaim forever*. Quitclaim means to renounce all possession,

> **QUITCLAIM DEED**
>
> THIS DEED, made the (date) day of ___(city)___, 20 xx,
> BETWEEN (city, town, etc.) of (name of grantor), party of the first part, and (name of grantor) of (city, town, etc.), party of the second part.
>
> WITNESSETH, that the party of the first part, in consideration of ten dollars ($10.00) and other valuable consideration, paid by the party of the second part, does hereby remise, release, and quitclaim unto the party of the second part, the heirs, successors, and assigns of the party of the second part forever.
>
> ALL that certain parcel of land, with the buildings and improvements thereon, described as follows:
>
>   [legal description of land]
>
> TOGETHER WITH the appurtenances and all the estate and rights of the Grantor in and to said property.
>
> TO HAVE AND TO HOLD the premises herein granted unto the party of the second part, the heirs or successors and assigns of the party of the second part, forever.
>
> IN WITNESS WHEREOF, the party of the first part has duly executed this deed the day and year first above written.
>
>   (Grantor's signature)
>
> [location of the acknowledgment]

FIGURE 20-4 Sample quitclaim deed
Source: © 2021 Mbition LLC

right, or interest. Remise means to give up any existing claim one may have, as does the word release. If the grantor subsequently acquires any right or interest in the property, the grantor is not obligated to convey it to the grantee. At first glance, it may seem strange that such a deed should even exist, but it does serve a very useful purpose. Situations often arise in real estate transactions when a person claims to have a partial or incomplete right or interest in a parcel of land. Such a right or interest, known as a *title defect* or **cloud on the title**, may have been due to an inheritance, dower, curtesy, or community property right, or to a mortgage or right of redemption because of a court-ordered foreclosure sale. Through use of the quitclaim deed to release that claim to the fee simple owner, the cloud on the fee owner's title is removed. A quitclaim deed may also be used to create an easement, as well as release (extinguish) an easement. It may also be used to release remainder and reversion interests. It may not be used to perpetrate a fraud, however.

cloud on the title: any claim, lien, or encumbrance that impairs title to property

Other Types of Deeds

A *gift deed* is created by simply replacing the recitation of money and other valuable consideration with the statement *in consideration of his [her, their] natural love and affection*. This phrase may be used in a warranty, special warranty, or grant deed. However, it is most often used in quitclaim or bargain and sale deeds, as these permit the grantor to avoid being committed to any warranties regarding the property. A guardian's deed is used to convey a minor's interest in real property. It contains only one covenant: that the guardian and minor have not encumbered the property. The deed must state the legal authority (usually a court order) that permits the guardian to convey the minor's property.

Sheriff's deeds and *referee's deeds in foreclosure* are issued to the new buyer when a person's real estate is sold as the result of a mortgage or other court-ordered foreclosure sale. The deed should state the source of the sheriff's or referee's authority and the amount of consideration paid. Such a deed conveys only the foreclosed party's title and, at most, carries only one covenant: that the sheriff or referee has not damaged the property's title. A *correction deed*, also called a deed of confirmation, is used to correct an error in a previously executed and delivered deed. For example, a name may have been misspelled or an error found in the property description. A quitclaim deed containing a statement regarding the error is used for this purpose. A *cession deed* is a form of quitclaim deed wherein a property owner conveys street rights to a county or municipality. An *interspousal deed* is used in some states to transfer real property between spouses. A tax deed is used to convey title to real estate that has been sold by the government because of the nonpayment of taxes. A *deed of trust or security deed* (also known as a *deed to secure debt*) may be used to convey real estate to a third party as security for a loan, and is discussed later.

CONVEYANCE AFTER DEATH

Intestate

If a person dies without leaving a last will and testament (or leaves one that is subsequently ruled void by the courts because it was improperly prepared), that person is said to have died intestate, which means without a testament. When this happens, state law directs how the deceased's assets shall be distributed. This is known as a *title by descent* or **intestate succession**. The surviving spouse and children are the dominant recipients of the deceased's assets. The deceased's grandchildren receive the next largest share, followed by the deceased's parents, brothers and sisters, and brothers' and sisters' children. These are known as the deceased's heirs or, in some states, *distributees*. The amount each heir receives, if anything, depends on individual state law and on how many persons with superior positions in the succession are alive. If no heirs can be found, the deceased's property escheats (reverts) to the state.

intestate succession: when a person dies without a last will and testament, it directs how the deceased's assets will be distributed; also called title by descent

Testate

A person who dies and leaves a valid will is said to have died **testate**, which means that a testament with instructions for property disposal was left behind. The person who made the will is the *testator* (masculine) or *testatrix* (feminine).

testate: when a person dies leaving a last will and testament

In the will, the testator names the persons or organizations that are to receive the testator's real and personal property. Real property that is willed is known as a *devise,* and the recipient, the *devisee.* Personal property that is willed is known as a *bequest* or *legacy,* and the recipient, a *legatee.* In the will, the testator usually names an *executor* (masculine) or *executrix* (feminine) to carry out the instructions. If one is not named, the court appoints an *administrator* or *administratrix.* In some states, the person named in the will or appointed by the court to settle the estate is called a *personal representative.*

Notice an important difference between the transfer of real estate ownership by deed and by will: Once a deed is made and delivered, the ownership transfer is permanent; the grantor may not have a change of mind and take back the property. With respect to a will, the devisees, although named, have no rights to the testator's property until the testator dies. Until that time, the testator is free to have a change of mind, revoke the old will, and write a new one.

Probate or Surrogate Court

Upon death, the deceased's will must be filed with a court having power to admit and certify wills, usually called a *probate court* or *surrogate court.* This court determines whether the will meets all the requirements of law: in particular, that it is genuine, properly signed and witnessed, and that the testator was of sound mind when the will was made. At this time, anyone may step forward and contest the validity of the will. If the court finds the will to be valid, the executor is permitted to carry out its terms. If the testator owned real property, its ownership is conveyed using an *executor's deed* prepared and signed by the executor. The executor's deed is used both to transfer title to a devisee and to sell real property to raise cash. It contains only one covenant: that the executor has not encumbered the property. An executor's deed is a special warranty deed.

Protecting the Deceased's Intentions

Because the deceased is not present, state laws attempt to ensure that fair market value is received for the deceased's real estate by requiring court approval of proposed sales and, in some cases, by sponsoring open bidding in the courtroom. As protection, a purchaser should ascertain that the executor has the authority to convey title.

For a will to be valid, it must meet specific legal requirements. All states recognize the *formal* or *witnessed* will, a written document prepared in most cases by an attorney. The testator must declare it to be his/her will and sign it in the presence of two to four witnesses (depending on the state), who, at the testator's request and in the presence of each other, sign the will as witnesses. A formal will prepared by an attorney is the preferred method, as the will then conforms explicitly to the law. This greatly reduces the likelihood of it being contested after the testator's death. Additionally, an attorney may offer valuable advice on how to word the will to reduce estate and inheritance taxes.

Holographic Will

holographic will: a handwritten will with no witnesses

A **holographic will** is a will that is entirely handwritten, with no typed or pre-printed words. The will is dated and signed by the testator, but the real key is that there are no witnesses. Nineteen states recognize holographic wills as legally binding. Persons selecting this form of will generally do so because it saves the time and expense of seeking professional legal aid and because it is entirely private. Besides the fact that holographic wills are considered to have no effect in Georgia or 30 other states, they often result in much legal argument in states that do accept them. This can occur when the testator is not fully aware of the law as it pertains to the making of wills. Many otherwise happy families have been torn apart by dissension when a relative dies and they read the will, only to find that there is a question as to whether it was properly prepared and, hence, valid. Unfortunately, what follows is not what the deceased intended; those who would receive more from intestate succession will request that the will be declared void and of no effect. Those with more to gain if the will stands as written will muster legal forces to argue for its acceptance by the probate court.

Oral Will

nuncupative will: oral or spoken will made in anticipation of death

An *oral will*, more properly known as a **nuncupative will**, is a will spoken by a person who is very near death. This will, sometimes referred to as a *soldier and sailor will*, is recognized in Georgia. The will must be heard by two parties with no interest in the estate, and they must put what they heard into writing within 30 days. Most states that recognize the nuncupative will allow only the transfer of personal property, but Georgia has the somewhat unique distinction that it will also allow the transfer of real property.

Codicil

codicil: an amendment or change to a will rather than a complete re-creation

A **codicil** is a written supplement or amendment made to a previously existing will. It is used to change some aspect of the will or to add a new instruction without the work of rewriting the entire will. The codicil must be dated, signed, and witnessed in the same manner as the original will. The only way to change a will is by adding a codicil or by writing a completely new will. The law will not recognize cross-outs, notations, or other alterations made on the will itself.

ADVERSE POSSESSION

Through the unauthorized occupation of another person's land for a long enough period of time, it is possible under certain conditions to acquire ownership by

adverse possession. The roots of adverse possession go back many centuries to a time before written deeds were used as evidence of ownership. At that time, in the absence of any claims to the contrary, a person who occupied a parcel of land was presumed to be its owner. Today, adverse possession is, in effect, a statute of limitations that bars legal owners from claiming title to land when they have done nothing to oust an adverse occupant during the statutory period. From the adverse occupant's standpoint, adverse possession is a method of acquiring title by possessing land for a specified period of time under certain conditions. Courts of law are quite demanding of proof before they will issue a decree in favor of a person claiming title by virtue of adverse possession. The claimant must have maintained actual, visible, continuous, hostile, exclusive, and notorious possession and be publicly claiming ownership to the property. These requirements mean that the claimant's use must have been visible and obvious to the legal owner, continuous and not just occasional, and exclusive enough to give notice of the claimant's individual claim. Furthermore, the use must have been without permission (hostile), and the claimant must have acted as the owner, even in the presence of the actual owner. Finally, the adverse claimant must be able to prove that s/he has met these requirements for a period ranging from 3 to 30 years (20 years in Georgia, unless the claimant has color of title, and then the period is reduced to 7 years), as shown in Table 20.1.

adverse possession: acquisition of land through prolonged and unauthorized occupation

Color of Title

The required occupancy period is shortened and the claimant's chances of obtaining legal ownership are enhanced in many states if the claimant has been paying the property taxes and the possession has been under "color of title." **Color of title** suggests some plausible appearance of ownership interest, such as an improperly prepared deed that purports to transfer title to the claimant, or a claim of ownership by inheritance. In accumulating the required number of years, adverse claimants may tack on their period of possession to that of a prior adverse occupant, commonly called *tacking*. This may be done through the purchase of that right. The current adverse occupant could, in turn, sell that claim to a still later adverse occupant until enough years were accumulated to present a claim in court. Although the concept of adverse possession often creates the mental picture of a trespasser moving onto someone else's land and living there long enough to acquire title in fee, this is not the usual application. More often, adverse possession is used to extinguish weak or questionable claims to title—for example, if a man sold property to a person and 10 years later, when the new owner was to resell this property, it was discovered that the previous owner had a wife. Prior to selling the property, there was a divorce, and it was decreed that the wife would convey her interest to the husband. Unfortunately, this never happened, and the wife is still on the title. If the wife could not be found to issue the required deed, a *quiet title suit* would be an alternative solution.

color of title: some plausible but not completely clear-cut indication of ownership rights

TABLE 20.1 Adverse possession: Number of years of occupancy required to claim title*

	Adverse occupant lacks color of title and does not pay the property taxes	Adverse occupant has color of title and/or pays the property taxes		Adverse occupant lacks color of title and does not pay the property taxes	Adverse occupant has color of title and/or pays the property taxes
Alabama	20	3-10	Montana		5
Alaska	10	7	Nebraska	10	10
Arizona	10	3	Nevada		5
Arkansas	15	2-7	New Hampshire	20	20
California		5	New Jersey	30-60	20-30
Colorado	18	7	New Mexico	10	10
Connecticut	15	15	New York	10	10
Delaware	20	20	North Carolina	20-30	7-21
District of Columbia	15	15	North Dakota	20	10
Florida		7	Ohio	21	21
Georgia	20	7	Oklahoma	15	15
Hawaii	20	20	Oregon	10	10
Idaho	5	5	Pennsylvania	21	21
Illinois	20	7	Rhode Island	10	10
Indiana		10	South Carolina	10-20	10
Iowa	10	10	South Dakota	20	10
Kansas	15	15	Tennessee	20	7
Kentucky	15	7	Texas		3-5
Louisiana	30	10	Utah		7
Maine	20	20	Vermont	15	15
Maryland	20	20	Virginia	15	15
Massachusetts	20	20	Washington	10	7
Michigan	15	5-10	West Virginia	10	10
Minnesota	15	15	Wisconsin	20	10
Mississippi	10	10	Wyoming	20	10
Missouri	10	10			

*As may be seen, in a substantial number of states, the waiting period for title by adverse possession is shortened if the adverse occupant has color of title and/or pays the property taxes. In California, Florida, Indiana, Montana, Nevada, and Utah, the property taxes must be paid to obtain the title. Generally speaking, adverse possession does not work against minors and other legal incompetents. However, when the owner becomes legally competent, the adverse possession must be broken within the time limit set by each state's law (the range is 1 to 10 years). In the states of Louisiana, Oklahoma, and Tennessee, adverse possession is referred to as *title by prescription*.

Source: © 2021 Mbition LLC

Another source of successful adverse possession claims arises from encroachments. If a building extends over a property line and nothing is said about it for a long enough period of time, the building will be permitted to stay.

EASEMENT BY PRESCRIPTION

An easement may also be acquired by prolonged adverse use. This is known as acquiring an *easement by prescription*. As with adverse possession, the laws are strict: The usage must be openly visible, continuous, and exclusive, as well as hostile and adverse to the owner. Additionally, in Georgia, the use must have occurred over a period of 7 years for private property and 20 years for public property. All these facts must be proved in a court of law before the court will issue the claimant a document legally recognizing ownership of the easement. As an easement is a right to use land for a specific purpose and not ownership of the land itself, courts rarely require the payment of property taxes to acquire a prescriptive easement.

As may be seen from the foregoing discussion, landowners must be given obvious notification at the location of their land that someone is attempting to claim ownership or an easement. Since an adverse claim must be continuous and hostile, an owner can break it by ejecting the trespassers, by preventing them from trespassing, or by simply giving them permission to be there. Any of these actions would demonstrate the landowner's superior title. Owners of stores and office buildings with private sidewalks or streets used by the public can take action to break claims to a public easement by either periodically barricading the sidewalk or street or by posting signs giving permission to pass. These signs are often seen in the form of brass plaques embedded in the sidewalk or street. Federal, state, and local governments protect themselves against adverse claims to their lands by passing laws making themselves immune.

OWNERSHIP BY ACCESSION

The extent of one's ownership of land can be altered by **accession**. This can result from natural or manmade causes. With regard to natural causes, the owner of land fronting on a lake, river, or ocean may acquire additional land because of the gradual accumulation of rock, sand, and soil. This process is called **accretion**, and the results are referred to as *alluvion* and *reliction*. **Alluvion** is the increase of land that results when waterborne soil is gradually deposited to produce firm, dry ground. **Reliction** (or dereliction) results when a lake, sea, or river permanently recedes, exposing dry land. When land gradually wears away because of the action of wind or water, the process is known as *erosion*. Accretion, erosion, and reliction may result in changing property lines. When land is rapidly washed away by the action of water, it is known as *avulsion*. **Avulsion** does not typically alter the property line. Manmade accession occurs through *annexation* of personal property to real estate. For example, when lumber, nails, and cement are used to build a house, they alter the extent of one's landownership.

accretion: a gradual addition to land

alluvion: the increase of land caused by the gradual depositing of waterborne soil

reliction: the permanent receding of water, exposing dry land

avulsion: a sudden washing away of land that does not typically alter the property lines

PUBLIC GRANT

A transfer of land by a government body to a private party is called a *public grant*. Since 1776, the federal government has granted millions of acres of land to settlers, land companies, railroads, state colleges, mining and logging promoters, and any war veteran from the American Revolution through the Mexican War. Most famous was the *Homestead Act* passed by the U.S. Congress in 1862. That act permitted persons wishing to settle on otherwise unappropriated federal land to acquire fee simple ownership by paying a small filing charge and occupying and cultivating the land for five years. Similarly, for only a few dollars, a person may file a mining claim to public land for the purpose of extracting whatever valuable minerals can be found. To retain the claim, a certain amount of work must be performed on the land each year. Otherwise, the government will consider the claim abandoned, and another person may claim it. If the claim is worked long enough, a public grant may be sought and fee simple title obtained. In the case of both the homestead settler and the mining claim, the conveyance document that passes fee title from the government to the grantee is known as a *land patent*. In 1976, the U.S. government ended the homesteading program in all states except Alaska.

DEDICATION

When an owner makes a voluntary gift for the use of land to the public, it is known as *dedication*. Dedication is not a transfer of title, but, rather, a dedication of use for the benefit of the public. To illustrate, a land developer buys a large parcel of vacant land and develops it into streets and lots. The lots are sold to private buyers, but what about the streets? In all probability, they will be dedicated to the town, city, or county. By doing this, the developer, and later the lot buyers, will not have to pay taxes on the streets, and the public will be responsible for maintaining them. The fastest way to accomplish the dedication is by either statutory dedication or dedication by deed. In *statutory dedication*, the developer prepares a map showing the streets, has the map approved by local government officials, and then records it as a public document. In dedication by deed, the developer prepares a deed that identifies the streets and grants them to the city.

Common law dedication takes place when landowners, by their acts or words, show that they intend part of their land to be dedicated, even though they have never officially made a written dedication. For example, landowners may encourage the public to travel on their roads in an attempt to persuade a local road department to take over maintenance.

FORFEITURE OF TITLE

Forfeiture of title can occur when a deed contains a condition or limitation. For example, a grantor states in the deed that the land conveyed may be used for residential purposes only. If the grantee constructs commercial buildings, the grantor can reacquire title on the grounds that the grantee did not use the land for the required purpose.

ALIENATION OF TITLE

A change in ownership of any kind is known as an *alienation of title*. The word *alienation* in this context simply means "to transfer." In addition to the forms of alienation discussed in this chapter, alienation can result from court action in connection with escheat, eminent domain, partition, foreclosure, execution sales, quiet title suits, and marriage. These topics are discussed in other chapters.

Review Questions

Answers to these questions can be found in Appendix D at the end of this book.

1. A written legal document by which ownership of real property is transferred from one party to another is a:
   A. bill of sale
   B. lease
   C. contract of sale
   D. deed

2. Which of the following is essential to the validity of a deed?
   A. The grantee must be of legal age.
   B. The grantee must be of sound mind.
   C. The grantor must sign.
   D. The grantor must receive valuable consideration.

3. Which of the following may NOT be conveyed by deed?
   A. fee simple estate
   B. life estate
   C. easements
   D. leasehold estate

4. With the words *conveyance in a deed*, grantors:
   A. state that they are receiving a grant of the property from the grantee
   B. warrant that they have the right to receive title to the property
   C. warrant that they have the ability to convey title to the property
   D. provide essentially a money-back guarantee.

5. To convey title to real property, a deed must be signed by the:
   A. grantee
   B. grantor
   C. agent
   D. buyer

6. To convey title, a deed must be:
   A. delivered by the grantee to the grantor
   B. accepted by the grantor
   C. delivered by the grantor to the grantee
   D. delivered and accepted by the grantor

7. Grantees are assured that they will not be disturbed by someone else claiming an interest in the property by the covenant of:
   A. seizin
   B. quiet enjoyment
   C. further assurance
   D. warranty forever

8. Should additional documents be necessary to perfect the grantee's title, this would be required by the:
   A. covenant of seizin
   B. covenant of further assurance
   C. covenant against encumbrances
   D. covenant of warranty forever

9. The deed considered to be the best deed a grantee can receive is a:
   A. general warranty deed
   B. special warranty deed
   C. bargain and sale deed
   D. quitclaim deed

10. Which of the following are the same?
    A. Grantor—party acquiring title
    B. Grantee—party conveying title
    C. Grantor—party alienating title
    D. Grantee—party transferring title

11. The phrase "the grantee's heirs and assigns forever" indicates the conveyance of a:
    A. fee simple estate
    B. life estate
    C. leasehold estate
    D. less-than-freehold estate

12. The description of the land in a deed in Georgia may NOT be by:
    A. metes and bounds
    B. reference to recorded document
    C. recorded plat
    D. rectangular survey

13. Which of the following is NOT a common use of a quitclaim deed?
    A. Remove a cloud from the title.
    B. Convey the grantor's interest without imposing any future obligations to defend the title upon the grantor.
    C. Convey title with limited warranties.
    D. Transfer title when the grantor is unsure of his/her interest.

14. You would expect to find the words *remise* and *release* in a:
    A. warranty deed
    B. special warranty deed
    C. grant deed
    D. quitclaim deed

15. A court of law with the power to admit and certify wills is called a:
    A. superior court
    B. recorder's court
    C. probate court
    D. civil court

16. Title acquired as the result of inheritance from a person who dies intestate is known as:
    A. title by ascent
    B. a devise
    C. title by testate succession
    D. title by intestate succession

17. A handwritten will signed by the testator but not witnessed is known as:
    A. a nuncupative will
    B. a holographic will
    C. an oral will
    D. a formal will

18. An easement acquired by prolonged adverse use is acquired by:
    A. implied grant
    B. necessity
    C. prescription
    D. condemnation

19. Which of the following would NOT break a claim of adverse possession?
    A. ejecting the trespasser
    B. giving the trespasser permission
    C. posting "No Trespassing" signs
    D. abandoning of property by the claimant

20. The process of increasing land due to the gradual deposition of waterborne soil is known as:
    A. reliction
    B. avulsion
    C. accretion
    D. alluvion

CHAPTER 21
RECORDATION, ABSTRACTS, AND TITLE INSURANCE

KEY TERMS

abstract of title
acknowledgment
actual notice
chain of title
constructive notice
inquiry notice
marketable title
public recorder's office
quiet title suit
title insurance
Torrens system

OBJECTIVES

After successful completion of this chapter, you should be able to:

1. understand the need for public records;
2. delineate and explain the requirements for recording;
3. describe the typical public records organization;
4. define an abstract and a chain of title;
5. explain the purpose and application of title insurance;
6. describe a quiet title suit;
7. describe the Torrens system; and
8. explain the purpose and application of marketable title acts.

OVERVIEW

This chapter focuses on: (1) the need for a method of determining real property ownership; (2) the process by which current and past ownership are determined from public records; (3) the availability of insurance against errors made in determining ownership; (4) the Torrens system of land title registration; and (5) uniform marketable title acts.

415

NEED FOR PUBLIC RECORDS

Until the enactment of the Statute of Frauds in England in 1677, determining who owned a parcel of land was primarily a matter of observing who was in physical possession. A landowner gave notice to the world of a claim to ownership by visibly occupying the land. When land changed hands, the old owner moved off the land and the new owner moved onto the land. After 1677, written deeds were required to show transfers of ownership. The problem then became one of finding the person holding the most current deed to the land. This was easy if the deed holder also occupied the land, but more difficult if that was not the case. The solution was to create a government-sponsored public recording service where a person could record a deed. These records would then be open, free of charge, to anyone. In this fashion, owners could post notice to all that they claimed ownership of certain land.

Constructive Notice

There are two ways a person can give notice of a claim or right to land. One is by recording documents in the public records that give written notice to that effect. The other is by visibly occupying or otherwise visibly making use of the land. At the same time, the law holds interested parties responsible for examining the public records and looking at the land for this notice of right or claim. **Constructive notice** (also sometimes referred to as *legal notice*) is knowledge that a person may not readily possess but knowledge that is available by making a diligent search. By recording documents at the county courthouse, a person with rights to the property provides constructive notice to the world of his/her interest. The fact is, the world in general may not care. Until and unless circumstances change and a person has a reason to search for the knowledge, this knowledge is simply constructive.

constructive notice: notice given by the public records and by visible possession, coupled with the legal presumption that all persons are thereby notified

Inquiry Notice

A person interested in a property is also held by law to be responsible for making further inquiry of anyone giving visible or recorded notice. This is referred to as **inquiry notice** and is notice that the law presumes a reasonably diligent person would obtain by making further inquiry. Another way to put this is that ignorance is not a legal defense. For example, suppose you are considering the purchase of vacant acreage and, upon inspecting it, see a dirt road cutting across the land that is not mentioned in the public records. The fact that the dirt road is there is constructive knowledge to all but since you are considering obtaining an interest in the property, the law expects you to make further inquiry. The road may be a legal easement across the property. Another example is the fact that any time you buy rental property, you are expected to make inquiry as to the rights of the occupants. They may hold substantial rights (such as an option to purchase) that

inquiry notice: information the law presumes a reasonably diligent person would obtain by making further inquiry

you would not know about without asking. Essentially, circumstances are what differentiate constructive notice (knowledge) from inquiry notice (knowledge). Constructive notice has no circumstances for the law to expect one to investigate; inquiry notice does.

Actual Notice

Actual notice is knowledge that one has actually gained based on what one has seen, heard, read, or observed. For example, if you read a deed from Jones to Smith, you have actual notice of the deed and Smith's claim to the property. If you go to the property and you see someone in possession, you have actual notice of that person's claim to be there.

Remember that anyone claiming an interest or right is expected to make it known either by recorded claim or visible use of the property. Anyone acquiring a right or interest is expected to look in the public records and go to the property to make a visual inspection for claims and inquire as to the extent of those claims.

actual notice: knowledge gained from what one has actually seen, heard, read, or observed

Recording Acts

All states have passed *recording acts* to provide for the recording of every instrument (i.e., document) by which an estate, interest, or right in land is created, transferred, or encumbered. Within each state, each county has a **public recorder's office**, known variously as the county recorder's office, county clerk's office, circuit court clerk's office, county registrar's office, or bureau of conveyances. The person in charge is called the recorder, clerk, or registrar. Located at the seat of county government, each public recorder's office will record documents submitted to it that pertain to real property in that county. Thus, a deed to property in XYZ County is recorded with the public recorder in XYZ County. Similarly, anyone seeking information regarding ownership of land in XYZ County would go to the recorder's office in XYZ County. Some cities also maintain record rooms where deeds are recorded. The recording process itself involves photocopying the documents and filing them for future reference.

public recorder's office: a government-operated facility wherein documents are entered in the public records

To encourage people to use public recording facilities, laws in each state decree that: (1) a deed, mortgage, or other instrument affecting real estate is not effective as far as subsequent purchasers and lenders (without actual notice) are concerned if it is not recorded; and (2) prospective purchasers, mortgage lenders, and the public at large are presumed notified when a document is recorded. Figure 21-1 demonstrates the concept of public recording.

Mortgage Electronic Registration System

The mortgage electronic registration system, commonly known as MERS, is a computerized book registration system of tracking the beneficial interests or

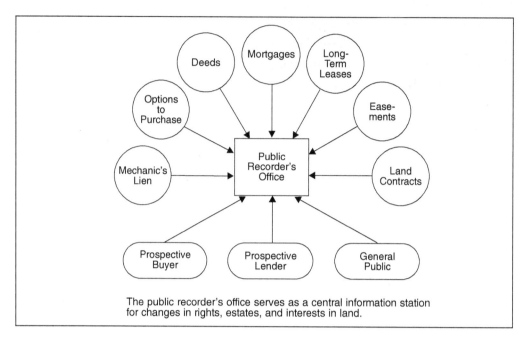

FIGURE 21-1 Public recording
Source: © 2021 Mbition LLC

"bundle of rights" connected with both residential and commercial real estate loans. Formally known as the "MERS® System," it records all of the beneficial interests connected to a mortgage electronically. The 20 largest mortgage banking organizations in the United States, as well as the secondary market (discussed elsewhere and all Wall Street rating agencies, automatically register notes and security interests in accordance with the Uniform Electronic Transactions Act (UETA). The federal Electronic Signatures in Global and National Commerce Act (E-Sign) system also provides payoff information to title industry members. Theoretically, MERS will be the mortgagee of record for all security instruments registered, whether in the form of the original mortgage, deed of trust, or recorded assignment. Regardless of the number of times a beneficial interest or a mortgage is bought or sold among MERS members, no transfer or assignment need be recorded in the real property records. In a lending market that drowns in a sea of paper, MERS is an efficient method of keeping track of loan data on a national basis.

Unrecorded Interests

Although recording acts permit the recording of any estate, right, or interest in land, many lesser rights are rarely recorded. Month-to-month rentals and leases for a year or less fall into this category. Consequently, only an on-site inspection would reveal their existence, or the existence of any developing adverse possession or prescriptive easement claim.

Summary

To summarize, if you are a prospective purchaser (or lessee or lender), you are presumed by law to have inspected both the land itself and the public records to determine the present rights and interests of others. If you receive a deed, mortgage, or other document relating to an estate, right, or interest in land, have it recorded *immediately* in the county in which the land is located. If you hold an unrecorded rental or lease, you should visibly occupy the property.

REQUIREMENTS FOR RECORDING

Nearly all states require that a document be *acknowledged* before it is eligible to be recorded. A few states will permit proper witnessing as a substitute. Some states require both. The objective of these requirements is to make certain that the person who signs the document is the same person named in the document, and that the signing was a free and voluntary act. This is done to reduce the possibility that forged or fraudulently induced documents will enter the public records.

Witnesses

In states that accept witnesses, the person executing the document signs in the presence of at least two witnesses, who, in turn, sign the document indicating that they are witnesses. To protect themselves, witnesses should not sign unless they know that the person named in the document is the person signing. In the event that the witnessed signature is contested, the witnesses would be summoned to a court of law to testify, under oath, to the authenticity of the signature. An example of a witness statement is shown in Figure 21-2.

Acknowledgment

An **acknowledgment** is a formal declaration by a person signing a document that s/he did, in fact, sign the document. Persons authorized to take acknowledgments include *notaries public,* recording office clerks, commissioners of deeds, judges of courts of record, justices of the peace, and certain others as authorized

acknowledgment: a formal declaration by a person signing a document that s/he did, in fact, sign the document

---

IN WITNESS whereof, the grantor has duly executed this deed in the presence of:

_____   _____
        Witness   Grantor

_____
        Witness

FIGURE 21-2 Witness statement

Source: © 2021 Mbition LLC

by state law. Commissioned military officers are authorized to take the acknowledgments of persons in the military; foreign ministers, foreign notaries public, and consular agents may take acknowledgments abroad. If an acknowledgment is taken outside the state where the document will be recorded, either the recording county must already recognize the out-of-state official's authority or the out-of-state official must provide certification that s/he is qualified to take acknowledgments. The official seal or stamp of the notary on the acknowledgment normally fulfills this requirement.

An acknowledgment is shown in Figure 21-3. Notice the words used: The person signing the document must personally appear before the notary, and the notary must state that s/he knows that person to be the person described in the document. If they are strangers, the notary will require proof of identity. The person acknowledging the document does so by acknowledging to the notary that s/he signed it. Note that it is the signer who does the acknowledging. not the notary. The notary takes the acknowledgment. At the completion of the signing, a notation of the event is made in a permanent record book kept by the notary. This record is later given to the state government for safekeeping.

PUBLIC RECORDS ORGANIZATION

Each document brought to a public recorder's office for recordation is photocopied and then returned to its owner. The photocopy is placed in chronological order with photocopies of other documents. These are stamped with consecutive page numbers and bound into a book. These books are placed in chronological order on shelves that are open to the public for inspection. Before modern-day photocopy machines, public recorder's offices used large cameras with light-sensitive paper (from roughly 1920 to 1955). Before that, documents were copied by hand using typewriters (from roughly 1900 to 1920), and before that, copying was done in longhand. One current trend is toward entirely paperless systems wherein documents are recorded directly onto microfilm and then returned to their owners. Each document is assigned a book and page number or a reel and frame number. Microfilm readers are made available to anyone wanting to read the microfilms.

In Georgia we have the Georgia Superior Court Clerks' Cooperative Authority (gsccca.org). Through this portal, most interactions with the county clerk's office that were historically completed by going to the county courthouse can now be accomplished using a personal computer and internet connection.

Filing incoming documents in chronological order is necessary to establish the chronological priority of documents; however, it does not provide an easy means for a person to locate all the documents relevant to a given parcel of land. Suppose that you are planning to purchase a parcel of land and want to make certain that the person selling it is the legally recognized owner. Without an index

```
┌─────────────────────────────────────────────────────────────────────┐
│                  ACKNOWLEDGMENT FOR AN INDIVIDUAL                   │
│  STATE OF _____                                           │
│  COUNTY OF _____                                            │
│                                                                     │
│  On this _____ day of _____, 20 _____, before me, the un-
│  dersigned, a Notary Public in and for said State, personally appeared [name of
│  person executing document] known to me to be the person whose name is
│  subscribed to the within instrument and acknowledged that he (she) executed the
│  same [in some states, the words "by his (her) free act and deed" are added here].
│  Witness my hand and official seal.                                 │
│                                                                     │
│                                              _____    │
│   [space for seal or stamp              Signature of notary public  │
│    of the notary public]                                            │
│                                         My commission expires _____│
│                                                              Date   │
└─────────────────────────────────────────────────────────────────────┘
```

FIGURE 21-3 Acknowledgment
Source: © 2021 Mbition LLC

to guide you, you might have to inspect every document in every volume. Consequently, recording offices have developed systems of indexing. The two most commonly used are the grantor and grantee indexes, used by all states, and the tract index, used by nine states.

Tract Indexes

Of the two indexing systems, the *tract index* is the simplest to use. In it, one page is allocated either to a single parcel of land or to a group of parcels, called a *tract*. On that page, you will find listed all the recorded deeds, mortgages, and other documents at the recorder's office that relate to that parcel. A few words describing each document are given, together with the book and page where a photocopy of the document can be found.

Grantor and Grantee Indexes

Grantor and grantee indexes are alphabetical indexes and are usually bound in book form. There are several variations in use in the United States, but the basic principle is the same. For each calendar year, the *grantor index* lists in alphabetical order all grantors named in the documents recorded that year. Next to each grantor's name is the name of the grantee named in the document, the book and page where a photocopy of the document can be found, and a few words describing the document. The *grantee index* is arranged by grantee name and gives the name of the grantor and the location and description of the document.

Example of Title Search

As an example of the application of the grantor and grantee indexes to a title search, suppose Robert T. Davis states that he is the owner of Lot 2, Block 2, in the Hilldale Tract in your county, and you would like to verify that statement in the public records. You begin by looking in the grantee index for his name, starting with this year's index and working backward in time. The purpose of this first step is to determine whether the property was ever granted to Davis. If it was, you will find his name in the grantee index and, next to his name, a book and page reference to a photocopy of his deed to that parcel.

The Next Step

The next step is to look through the grantor index for the period of time starting from the moment he received his deed up to the present. If he has granted the property to someone else, Davis's name will be noted in the grantor index with a reference to the book and page where you can see a copy of the deed. (Davis could have reduced your efforts by showing you the actual deed conveying the lot to him. However, you would still have to inspect the grantor index for all dates subsequent to his taking title to see if he has conveyed title to a new grantee. If you do not have the name of the property owner, you would first have to go to the property tax office.)

Suppose your search shows that on July 1, 2007, in Book 2324, page 335, a warranty deed from John S. Miller to Davis, for Lot 2, Block 2, of the Hilldale Tract was recorded. Furthermore, you find that no subsequent deed showing Davis as grantor of this land has been recorded. Based on this, it would appear that Davis is the fee owner. However, you must inquire further to determine if Miller was the legally recognized owner of the property when he conveyed it to Davis. In other words, on what basis did Miller claim his right of ownership and, subsequently, the right to convey that ownership to Davis? The answer is that Miller based his claim to ownership on the deed he received from the previous owner.

CHAIN OF TITLE

By looking for Miller's name in the 2007 grantee index and then working backward in time through the yearly indexes, you will eventually find his name and a reference to Lot 2, Block 2, in the Hilldale Tract. Next to Miller's name, you will find the name of the grantor and a reference to the book and page where the deed was recorded.

By looking for that name in the grantee index, you will locate the next previous deed. By continuing this process you can construct a chain of title. A **chain of title** shows the linkage of property ownership that connects the present owner to the original source of title. In most cases, the chain starts with the original sale or grant of the land from the government to a private citizen. It is used to prove

chain of title: the linkage of property ownership that connects the present owner to the original source of title how title came to be *vested* in (i.e., possessed by) the current owner. In Georgia, a 50-year title search is considered sufficient. Figure 21-4 demonstrates the chain-of-title concept.

Sometimes, while tracing (running) a chain of title back through time, one will see that an apparent break or dead end has occurred. This can happen because the grantor is an administrator, executor, sheriff, or judge; because the owner died; or because a mortgage against the land was foreclosed. To regain the title sequence, one must search outside the recorder's office by checking probate court records in the case of a death, or by checking civil court actions in the case of a foreclosure. The chain must be complete from the original source of title to the present owner. If there is a missing link, the current "owner" does not have valid title to the property.

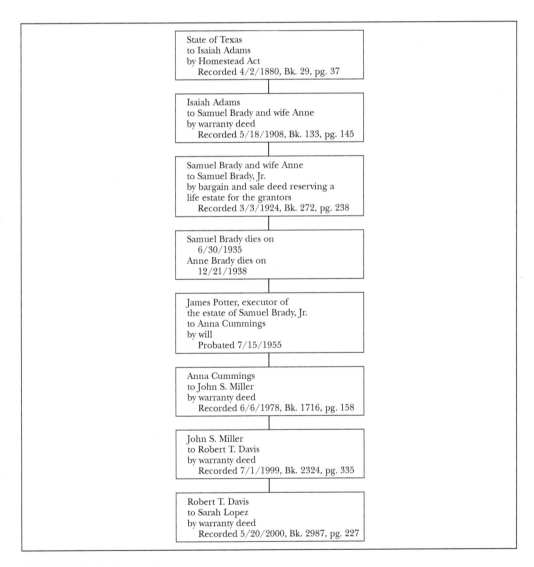

FIGURE 21-4 Chain of title

Source: © 2021 Mbition LLC

In addition to looking for grantors and grantees, one must search for any outstanding mortgages, judgments, actions pending, liens, and unpaid taxes that may affect the title. With regard to searching for mortgages, states again differ slightly. Some place mortgages in the general grantor and grantee indexes, listing the borrower (mortgagor) as the grantor and the lender (mortgagee) as the grantee. Other states have separate index books for mortgagors and mortgagees. The process involves looking for the name of each owner in each annual *mortgagor index* published while that owner owned the land. If a mortgage is found, a further check will reveal whether it has been satisfied and released. If it has been released, the recorder's office will have noted in the margin of the recorded mortgage the book and page where the release is located. When one knows the lender's name, the mortgage location and its subsequent release can also be found by searching the *mortgagee index.*

Title may be clouded by judgments against recent owners, or there may be lawsuits pending that might later affect title. This information is found, respectively, on the *judgment rolls* and in the *lis pendens index* at the office of the county clerk. The term *lis pendens* is Latin for "pending lawsuits." A separate search is made for mechanic's liens against the property by workmen and material suppliers. This step includes both a search of the public records and an on-site inspection of the land for any recent construction activity or material deliveries. A visit is made to the local tax assessor's office to check the tax rolls for unpaid property taxes and to county map records to determine changes in deed restriction or subdivision plats. This does not exhaust all possible places that must be visited to do a thorough title search. A title searcher may also be found researching birth, marriage, divorce, and adoption records; probate records; military files; and federal tax liens in an effort to identify all the parties with an interest or potential interest in a given parcel of land and its improvements.

ABSTRACT OF TITLE

Although it is useful for the real estate practitioner to be able to find a name or document in the public records, full-scale title searching should be left to professionals. In a sparsely populated county, title searching is usually done on a part-time basis by an attorney. In more heavily populated counties, a full-time abstracter will search the records. These persons are experts in the field of title search and, for a fee, will prepare an abstract of title for a parcel of land.

abstract of title: a summary of all recorded documents affecting title to a given parcel of land

An **abstract of title** is a complete historical summary of all recorded documents affecting the title of a property. It recites in chronological order all recorded grants, conveyances, recorded easements, mortgages, wills, tax liens, judgments, pending lawsuits, marriages, divorces, and any other action that might affect title. The abstracter will summarize each document, note the book and page (or other source) where it was found, and give the date it was recorded or entered. In the case of a deed, for example, the abstracter identifies the grantor, grantee, and type of deed, provides a brief description of the property and any conditions or restrictions found in the deed, and lists the date on the deed, the recording date, and the book and page. For a mortgage, the abstracter identifies the borrower and lender, gives a brief description of the mortgage contents, and, if repaid, lists the book and page location of the mortgage release document and its date of recordation. The abstract also includes a list of the public records searched, and not searched, in preparing the abstract.

The abstract is next sent to an attorney. On the basis of the attorney's knowledge of law and the legal history presented in the abstract, s/he renders an *opinion of title* as to who the fee owner is, and names anyone else with a legitimate right or interest in the property. This opinion, when written, signed by the attorney, and attached to the abstract, is known in many states as a *certificate of title*. In some parts of the United States, this certified abstract is so valuable that it is brought up to date each time the property is sold and passed from seller to buyer. Generally speaking, the seller pays the cost of updating the abstract and getting a current attorney's opinion and certificate.

"What Ifs"

Despite the diligent efforts of abstracters and attorneys to give as accurate a picture of landownership as possible, there is no guarantee that the finished abstract, or its certification, is completely accurate. Persons preparing abstracts and opinions are liable for mistakes due to their own negligence, and they can be sued if that negligence results in a loss to a client. But what if a recorded deed in the title chain is a forgery? What if a married person represented himself on a deed as a single person, thus resulting in unextinguished dower rights? What if a deed was executed by a minor or an otherwise legally incompetent person? What if a deed contained an erroneous land description? What if a document was misfiled, or there were undisclosed heirs, or a missing will later came to light, or there was confusion because of similar names on documents? These situations can result in substantial losses to a property owner, yet the fault may not lie with the abstracter or attorney. The recorder's office is not responsible for verifying the contents of a deed; the recorder's office is responsible only for verifying that it shows an acceptable acknowledgment. Private companies have been established to sell insurance against losses arising from title defects, as well as from errors in title examination.

TITLE INSURANCE

Efforts to insure titles date back to the 1800s and were primarily organized by and for the benefit of attorneys who wanted protection from errors that they might make in the interpretation of abstracts. As time passed, **title insurance** became available to anyone wishing to purchase it. The basic principle of title insurance is similar to any form of insurance: Many persons pay a small amount into an insurance pool that is then available if any one of them should suffer a loss. In

title insurance: an insurance policy against defects in title not listed in the title report or abstract

some parts of the United States, it is customary to purchase the title insurance policy through the attorney who reads and certifies the abstract. Elsewhere, it is the custom to purchase it from a title company that combines the search and policy in one fee.

Title Commitment

When a title company receives a request for a title insurance policy, the first step is an examination of the public records. An abstracter or title searcher employed by the title company usually takes care of this. A company attorney then reviews the findings and renders an opinion as to who the fee owner is and lists anyone else with a legitimate right or interest in the property, such as a mortgage lender or easement holder. This information is typed up and becomes the title commitment. An example of a title commitment is shown in plain language in Figure 21-5. Note that it commits to the proposed insured that the title company will issue a policy in the future, provided certain conditions are met. Most of these conditions are predictable (i.e., required payoff of certain liens or other defects so the title will be clear).

Notice how a title commitment differs from an abstract. Whereas an abstract is a chronologically arranged summary of all recorded events that have affected the title to a given parcel of land, a title commitment is more like a snapshot that shows the condition of title at a specific moment in time. A title commitment does not tell who the previous owners were; it only tells who the current owner is. A title commitment does not list all mortgage loans ever made against the land, but only those that have not been removed. The title commitment in Figure 21-5 states that a search of the public records shows Barbara Baker to be the fee owner of Lot 17, Block M, at the time the search was conducted.

In Schedule C, the report lists all recorded objections that could be found to Baker's fee estate—in this case, county property taxes, a mortgage, and two easements. In Schedule B, the title company states that there may be certain unrecorded matters that either could not be or were not researched in preparing the report. Note, in particular, that the title company does not make a visual inspection of the land, nor does it make a boundary survey. The buyer is responsible for making the on-site inspection and for hiring a surveyor if uncertain as to the land's boundaries. It is also the buyer's responsibility to check the zoning of the land and any other governmental restrictions on it.

Although owners may purchase a title insurance policy on their property at any time, it is most often purchased when real estate is originally bought. In connection with a sale, the title commitment is used to verify that the seller is indeed the owner. Additionally, the title commitment alerts the buyer and seller as to what needs to be done to bring title to the condition called for in the sales contract. For example, in Figure 21-5, the present owner (Barbara Baker) may have agreed to remove the existing mortgage so that the buyer can get a new and larger loan. Once this is done and the seller has delivered her deed to the

> **TITLE COMMITMENT**
>
> The title insurance company agrees to issue to you our title insurance policy when the provisions of Schedule B and C have been complied with.
>
> **SCHEDULE A**
>
> LAND DESCRIPTION: Lot 17, Block M, Atwater's Addition, Jefferson County, State of _____.
> PROPOSED INSURED: George W. Bush
> DATE AND TIME OF SEARCH: March 3, 20xx at 9:00 A.M.
> TITLE APPEARS TO BE VESTED IN: Barbara Baker, a single woman
> ESTATE OR INTEREST: Fee simple
> EXCEPTIONS:
>
> **SCHEDULE B**
>
> 1. Taxes or assessments not shown by the records of any taxing authority or by the public records.
> 2. Any facts, rights, interests, or claims that, although not shown by the public records, could be determined by inspection of the land and inquiry of persons in possession.
> 3. Discrepancies or conflicts in boundary lines or area or encroachments that would be shown by a survey, but which are not shown by the public records.
> 4. Easements, liens, or encumbrances not shown by the public records.
> 5. Zoning and governmental restrictions.
> 6. Unpatented mining claims and water rights or claims.
>
> **SCHEDULE C**
>
> 1. A lien in favor of Jefferson County for property taxes, in the amount of $645.00, due on or before April 30, 20xx.
> 2. A mortgage in favor of the First National Bank in the amount of $30,000.00, recorded June 2, 1974, in Book 2975, Page 245, of the Official County Records.
> 3. An easement in favor of the Southern Telephone Company along the eastern five feet of said land for telephone poles and conduits. Recorded on June 15, 1946, in Book 1210, Page 113, of the Official County Records.
> 4. An easement in favor of Coastal States Gas and Electric Company along the north ten feet of said land for underground pipes. Recorded on June 16, 1946, in Book 1210, Page 137, of the Official County Records.

FIGURE 21-5 Title commitment
Source: © 2021 Mbition LLC

buyer, the title company issues a title policy that deletes the old mortgage, adds the new mortgage, and shows the buyer as the owner. Note that long-term leases (10 years or more) often require title policies. Tenants also want to know who has property rights superior to theirs.

Policy Premium

It is customary in Georgia that the cost of title insurance to protect the lender be included in the lender's quoted closing costs. In addition, title insurance to protect the interests of the buyer is available. Customarily, when a property is sold, the buyer will obtain an insurance policy protecting his/her interest in an amount equal to the purchase price. This insurance remains effective as long as the buyer (owner) or heirs have an interest in the property.

The insurance premium consists of a single payment. On the average-priced home, the combined charge for a title report and title insurance amounts to about $3 to $5 per $1,000 (0.3% to 0.5%) of the amount of insurance purchased. Each time the property is sold, a new policy must be purchased. The old policy may not be assigned to the new owner. Some title insurance companies offer reduced *reissue rates* if the previous owner's policy is available for updating.

Lender's Policy

Thus far, our discussion of title insurance has centered on what is called an *owner's title policy*. In addition, title insurance companies also offer what is called a *lender's title policy*. This gives title protection to a lender who has taken real estate as collateral for a loan. There are three significant differences between an owner's title policy and a lender's title policy. First, the owner's policy is good for the full amount of coverage stated on the policy for as long as the insured or the insured's heirs have an interest in the property. In contrast, the lender's policy protects only for the amount owed on the mortgage loan. Thus, the coverage on a lender's policy declines and finally terminates when the loan is fully repaid. The second difference is that the lender's policy does not make exceptions for claims to ownership that could have been determined by physically inspecting the property. The third difference is that the lender's policy is assignable to subsequent holders of that same loan; an owner's policy is not.

The cost of a lender's policy (also known as a mortgagee's title policy or a loan policy) is similar to an owner's policy. Although the insurance company takes added risks by eliminating some exceptions found in the owner's policy, this is balanced by the fact that the liability decreases as the loan is repaid. When an owner's and a lender's policy are purchased at the same time, as in the case of a sale with new financing, the combined cost is only a few dollars more than the cost of a single policy. Note that the lender's policy covers only title problems; it does not insure that the loan will be repaid by the borrower.

Claims for Losses

The last item in a title policy is a statement as to how the company will handle claims. Although this "Conditions and Stipulations Section" is too lengthy to reproduce here, its key aspects can be summarized as follows: When an insured defect arises, the title insurance company reserves the right to either pay the loss or fight the claim in court. If it elects to fight, any legal costs the company incurs are in addition to the amount of coverage stated in the policy. If a loss is paid, the amount of coverage is reduced by that amount, and any unused coverage is still in effect. If the company pays a loss, it acquires the right to collect from the party who caused the loss.

In comparing title insurance to other forms of insurance (e.g., life, fire, automobile), note that title insurance protects against something that has already happened but has not been discovered. A forged deed may result in a disagreement over ownership: The forgery is a fact of history; the insurance is in the event of its discovery. But in some cases, the problem will never be discovered. For example, a married couple may be totally unaware of dower and curtesy rights and fail to extinguish them when they sell their property. If neither later claims them, when they die, the rights extinguish themselves, and the intervening property owners will have been unaffected.

Only a small part of the premiums collected by title insurance companies are used to pay claims. This is largely because title companies take great pains to maintain on their own premises complete photographic copies (often computer-indexed) of the public records for each county in which they do business. These are called *title plants*. In many cases, they are actually more complete and better organized than those available at the public recorder's office. The philosophy is that the better the quality of the title search, the fewer the claims that must be paid.

The Growth of Title Insurance

Four important factors have caused the title insurance business to mushroom. First, in a warranty deed, the grantor makes several strongly worded covenants. As you will recall, the grantor covenants that s/he is the owner, that the grantee will not be disturbed in his/her possession, that there are no encumbrances except as stated in the deed, that the grantor will procure any necessary further assurance of title for the grantee, and that the grantor will bear the expense of defending the grantee's title and possession. Thus, signing a warranty deed places a great obligation on the grantor. By purchasing title insurance, the grantor can transfer that obligation to an insurance company.

Second, a grantee is also motivated to have title insurance. Even with a warranty deed, there is always the lingering question of whether the seller would be financially capable of making good on his/her covenants and warranties. They are useless if one cannot enforce them. Moreover, title insurance typically provides a grantee broader assurance than a warranty deed. For example, an outsider's claim must produce physical dispossession of the grantee before the covenant of quiet enjoyment is considered broken. Yet the same claim would be covered by title insurance before dispossession took place.

Third, the broad use of title insurance has made mortgage lending more attractive, and borrowing a little easier and cheaper for real property owners. This is because title insurance has removed the risk of loss due to defective titles. As a result, lenders can charge a lower rate of interest. Secondary market purchasers of loans, such as the Federal National Mortgage Association (FNMA) and the Federal Home Loan Mortgage Corporation (FHLMC), both discussed elsewhere, require title insurance on every loan they buy.

marketable title: title that is reasonably free from litigation

Fourth, title insurance has made titles to land much more marketable. In nearly all real estate transactions, the seller agrees to deliver marketable title to the buyer. **Marketable title** is title that is reasonably free of litigation. Even when the seller makes no mention of the quality of the title, courts ordinarily require that marketable title be conveyed. To illustrate, a seller orders an abstract prepared, and the seller's attorney reads the abstract and certifies it as showing marketable title. The buyer's attorney thinks that certain technical defects in the title chain contradict certification as marketable and advises the buyer to refuse to complete the sale.

The line between what is and what is not marketable title can be exceedingly thin, and differences of legal opinion are quite possible. One means of breaking the stalemate is to locate a title insurance company that will insure the title as being marketable. If the defect is not serious, the insurance company will accept the risk. If it is a serious risk, the company may either accept the risk and increase the insurance fee or recommend a quiet title suit.

Quiet Title Suit

When a title defect (also called a *cloud on the title* or a *title cloud*) must be removed, it is logical to remove it by using the path of least resistance. For example, if an abstract or title report shows unpaid property taxes, the buyer may require the seller to pay the taxes in full before the deal is completed. A cloud on the title as a result of pending foreclosure proceedings can be halted by either bringing the loan payments up to date or negotiating with the lender for a new loan repayment schedule. Similarly, a distant relative with ownership rights might be willing, upon negotiation, to quitclaim them for a price.

Sometimes, a stronger means is necessary to remove title defects. For example, the distant relative may refuse to negotiate, or the lender may refuse to remove a mortgage lien despite pleas from the borrower that it has been paid, or there is a missing link in a chain of title. The solution is a **quiet title suit** (also called a *quiet title action*). Forty-seven states have enacted legislation that permits a property owner to ask the courts to hold hearings on the ownership of land. At these hearings, anyone claiming to have an interest or right in the land in question may present oral or written evidence of that claim. A judge, acting on the evidence presented and the laws of that state, rules on the validity of each claim. The result is to recognize legally those with a genuine right or interest and to "quiet" those without a genuine interest.

quiet title suit: court-ordered hearings held to determine landownership

THE TORRENS SYSTEM

Over a century ago, Sir Robert Torrens, a British administrator in Australia, devised an improved system of identifying landownership. He was impressed by the relative simplicity of the British system of sailing-ship registration.

The government maintained an official ships' registry that listed on a single page a ship's name, its owner, and any liens or encumbrances against it. Torrens felt land titles might be registered in a similar manner. The system he designed, known as the **Torrens system** of land title registration, starts with a landowner's application for registration and the preparation of an abstract. This is followed by a quiet title suit, which all parties named in the abstract and anyone else claiming a right or interest to the land in question may attend and be heard.

Torrens system: a state-sponsored method of registering land titles

Torrens Certificate of Title

Based on the outcome of the suit, a government-appointed *registrar of titles* prepares a *certificate of title*. This certificate names the legally recognized fee owner and lists any legally recognized exceptions to that ownership, such as mortgages, easements, long-term leases, or life estates. The registrar keeps the original certificate of title and issues a duplicate to the fee owner. (Although they sound similar, a Torrens certificate of title is not the same as an attorney's certificate of title. The former shows ownership and claims against that ownership as established by a court of law. The latter is strictly an opinion of the condition of title.)

Once a title is registered, any subsequent liens or encumbrances against it must be entered on the registrar's copy of the certificate of title in order to give constructive notice. When a lien or encumbrance is removed, its notation on the certificate is canceled. In this manner, the entire concept of constructive notice for a given parcel of land is reduced to a single-page document open to public view at the registrar's office. This, Torrens argued, would make the whole process of title transfer much simpler and cheaper.

When registered land is conveyed, the grantor gives the grantee a deed. The grantee takes the deed to the registrar of titles, who transfers the title by canceling the grantor's certificate and issuing a new certificate in the name of the grantee. With a Torrens property, this is the point in time when title is conveyed, not when the deed is delivered by the grantor to the grantee. Any liens or other encumbrances not removed at the same time are carried over from the old to the new certificate. The registrar keeps the deed and certificate; the grantee receives a duplicate of the certificate. If the conveyance is accompanied by a new mortgage, it is noted on the new certificate, and the registrar retains a copy of the mortgage. Except for the quiet title suit aspect, the concept of land title registration is quite similar to that used in the United States for registering ownership of motor vehicles.

Adoption

The first state to have a land registration act was Illinois in 1895. Other states slowly followed, but often their laws were vague and cumbersome to the point of being useless. At one point, 19 states had land title registration acts, but since then 9 states have repealed their acts and only 10 remain: Colorado, Georgia,

Hawaii, Massachusetts, Minnesota, New York, North Carolina, Ohio, Virginia, and Washington.

In all 10 states, Torrens coexists with the regular recording procedures described earlier in this chapter. Thus, it is possible for a house on one side of the street to be Torrens-registered and a house on the other side of the street to be recorded the regular way. Also, it may be customary to use Torrens only in certain areas of the state. In Minnesota, it's used in the Minneapolis area; in Massachusetts, the Boston area; and in New York, Suffolk County (eastern Long Island). In Hawaii, Torrens is used statewide, but primarily by large landowners and subdivision developers who want to clear up complex title problems. In the remaining six states, including Georgia, the public has made relatively little use of land title registration. This limited adoption of Torrens is because of, among other things, the promotion, widespread availability, and lower short-run cost of title insurance. (The quiet title suit can be costly.) Note, too, that although a state-run insurance fund is usually available to cover registration errors, some lenders feel this is not adequate protection and require title insurance.

MARKETABLE TITLE ACTS

At least 10 states have a *marketable title act*. This is *not* a system of title registration. Rather, it is legislation aimed at making abstracts easier to prepare and less prone to error. This is done by cutting off claims to rights or interests in land that have been inactive for longer than the act's statutory period. In Connecticut, Michigan, Utah, Vermont, and Wisconsin, this is 40 years. Thus, in these states, the law regards a person who has an unbroken chain of title with no defects for at least 40 years as having marketable title. Any defects more than 40 years old are outlawed. The result is to concentrate the title search process on the immediate past 40 years. Thus, abstracts can be produced with less effort and expense, and the chance for an error either by the abstracter or in the documents themselves is greatly reduced. This is particularly true in view of the fact that record keeping procedures in the past were not as sophisticated as they are today.

The philosophy of a marketable title act is that persons have 40 years to come forward and make their claim known; if they do not, then they apparently do not consider it worth pursuing. As protection for a person actively pursuing a claim that is about to become more than 40 years old, the claim can be renewed for another 40 years by again recording notice of the claim in the public records. In certain situations, a title must be searched back more than 40 years (e.g., when there is a lease of more than a 40-year duration or when no document affecting ownership has been recorded in more than 40 years). In Nebraska, the statutory period is 22 years; in Florida, North Carolina, and Oklahoma, it is 30 years; in Indiana, 50 years. As mentioned earlier, a full title search in Georgia is considered to be 50 years.

Marketable title acts do not eliminate the need for legal notice, nor do they eliminate the role of adverse possession.

Review Questions

Answers to these questions can be found in Appendix D at the end of this book.

1. Once a person is aware of another's rights or interest in property, that person is said to have:
   A. constructive notice
   B. legal notice
   C. inquiry notice
   D. actual notice

2. Constructive notice requires that:
   A. a person interested in property be willing to search federal records
   B. documents be recorded
   C. information be readily available
   D. a search of property be conducted

3. The public recorder's office:
   A. serves as a central information station for documents pertaining to interests in land
   B. is an agency of the federal government
   C. requires annual membership fees
   D. does not require that a fee be paid to record, as it is a public service

4. Farmer Sorensen leases 320 acres adjacent to his ranch. Sorensen can give notice to the world at large by:
   A. plowing the land
   B. storing his equipment on it
   C. putting a fence around it
   D. doing all of the above

5. Priority of a recorded instrument is determined by the date of:
   A. acknowledgment
   B. delivery to the grantee
   C. the instrument
   D. recordation

6. Deeds and other instruments that affect land titles should be recorded:
   A. within one year after delivery or execution
   B. in order to provide actual notice
   C. in order to provide constructive notice
   D. only if required by law

7. The purpose of having a person's signature acknowledged is:
   A. to provide constructive notice
   B. to make the document admissible as evidence in court
   C. to make certain the person signing the document is the same person named in the document, and that the signing was voluntary
   D. nonexistent, since signatures are not acknowledged; people are

8. In a jurisdiction that indexes recorded instruments by grantee and grantor, if one knew the name of the current owner of a property and wished to search the records to verify the chain of title, one would look in the:
   A. grantor index only
   B. grantee index only
   C. grantee and grantor index
   D. Torrens index

9. Instruments are recorded in the public records in what order?
   A. alphabetical order, based on the grantee's last name
   B. chronological order, as received for recordation
   C. according to the date of the instrument
   D. alphabetical order, based on the grantor's last name

10. The name of the buyer would be filed alphabetically in the:
    A. mortgagee index
    B. grantee index
    C. *lis pendens* index
    D. lender's index

11. Which of the following would NOT ordinarily be checked in searching a title to a parcel of land?
    A. judgment records
    B. lien records
    C. chattel mortgage records
    D. *lis pendens* index

12. A *lis pendens* index is:
    A. an index of existing leases on property
    B. an index of pending lawsuits
    C. a tract index
    D. a chain of title

13. It is conceivable that, in some circumstances, a title searcher may find it necessary to check:
    A. birth, death, and marriage records only
    B. divorce, adoption, military, and tax records only
    C. birth, death, and divorce records
    D. Bee Gees, Beatles, and Iron Butterfly records

14. A summary of all recorded documents affecting title to a given parcel of land is called:
    A. a chain of title
    B. an abstract of title
    C. a title report
    D. title insurance

15. Protection against a loss occasioned by which of the following would NOT be covered by title insurance?
    A. forged deed, or deeds by incompetents
    B. unextinguished dower or curtesy rights
    C. claims by undisclosed or missing heirs
    D. destruction of improvements by a tornado

16. Should a title insurance company elect to fight a claim in court, the legal expenses incurred will be:
    A. deducted from the coverage under the policy
    B. assumed by the title insurance company without affecting the policy coverage
    C. shared by the insured and the insurance company
    D. paid by the insured

17. The purchase of title insurance eliminates the need for:
    A. casualty insurance
    B. a survey of the property
    C. constructive notice
    D. seller warranties

18. All of the following are true of a quiet title suit EXCEPT that it:
    A. is a judicial proceeding
    B. removes all claims to title other than the owner's
    C. quiets those without a genuine interest in the property
    D. can be used to clear up a disputed title

19. In Georgia, a full title search is considered to be:
    A. 22 years
    B. 40 years
    C. 50 years
    D. 75 years

20. The linkage of ownership, claims, and releases through the years is most properly known as:
    A. insurance
    B. abstract of title
    C. marketable title
    D. chain of title

CHAPTER 22

REAL ESTATE LEASES

KEY TERMS

actual eviction
assignment
constructive eviction
gross lease
index lease
leasehold estate

lessee
lessor
net lease
nondisturbance clause
option clause
percentage lease

quiet enjoyment
retaliatory eviction
reversion
sublessee
sublessor
sublet

OBJECTIVES

After successful completion of this chapter, you should be able to:
1. define leasehold estate and explain how to create a valid lease;
2. describe a lease document;
3. explain landlord–tenant laws;
4. define assignment, option clause, gross lease, economic rent, and contract rent;
5. describe the eviction process;
6. distinguish between subletting and assignment;
7. explain the processes of setting rents and terminating leases; and
8. discuss the functions of on-site management, including collection of rents and property maintenance.

OVERVIEW

In this chapter, you will look at leases from the standpoint of the tenant, owner, and property manager. First, we will cover some of the important terminology and explain common elements of a lease agreement. Landlord–tenant laws, setting

rents, gross leases, and lease termination are also covered in this chapter. Specific terminology and concepts covered include assignment and subletting.

Earlier chapters of this book discussed leases as estates in land and as a means of financing. This chapter will look at leases from the standpoint of the tenant, the property owner, and the property manager. (During your lifetime, you will be in one of these roles, and perhaps all three.) Our study will include a discussion of the common provisions of a lease agreement. Emphasis will be on residential property, although a number of key points regarding commercial property leases will also be included.

THE LEASEHOLD ESTATE

A lease conveys to the **lessee** (tenant) the right to possess and use another's property for a period of time. During this time, the **lessor** (the landlord or fee owner) possesses a **reversion** that entitles the lessor to retake possession at the end of the lease period. Notice that a lease separates the right to use property from the property's ownership. The tenant gets the use of the property during the lease period and pays rent. The property owner is denied use of the property but receives rent in return. At the end of the lease, the property owner gets the use of the property back, but no more rent. The tenant no longer has the use of the property and no longer pays rent. This chapter describes how this very simple idea is carried out in practice.

lessee: the tenant

lessor: the landlord

reversion: the right to retake possession at a future date

A tenant's right to occupy land and/or buildings thereon is called a **leasehold estate**. The two most commonly found leasehold estates are the periodic estate and the estate for years. The *periodic estate* is one for a definite period of time with an automatic renewal if not terminated. A month-to-month lease is an example of this. As each period comes to an end, either the landlord or the tenant may give notice to terminate. An *estate for years* is a lease with a specific starting and ending date. It can be for any length of time, does not automatically renew itself, and does not require notice to terminate. A lease for one year is an example. There are two other leasehold categories: estate at will and tenancy at sufferance. An *estate at will* is for an indefinite period of time and can be terminated by either the landlord or the tenant giving notice. In Georgia, the notice requirement for the tenant is 30 days and the requirement for the landlord is 60 days. For example, the owner of a rental house decides to sell it upon expiration of the current lease. The owner and tenant agree that the tenant will be able to continue to rent until the house is sold. A *tenancy at sufferance* occurs when a tenant stays beyond the legal tenancy without the consent of the landlord. The tenant is commonly called a *holdover tenant,* and no advance notice is required for eviction. A holdover tenant differs from a trespasser in that the original entry onto the property was legal.

leasehold estate: a tenant's right to occupy land and/or buildings thereon

CREATING A VALID LEASE

A lease is both a conveyance and a contract. As a conveyance, it conveys rights of possession to the tenant in the form of a leasehold estate. As a contract, it contains provisions for the payment of rent and any other obligations the landlord and tenant have to each other. For a valid lease to exist, it must meet the usual requirements of a contract. That is to say, the parties involved must be legally competent, and there must be mutual agreement, lawful objective, and sufficient consideration.

The main elements of a lease are: (1) the names of the lessee and lessor, (2) a description of the premises, (3) an agreement to convey (let) the premises by the lessor and to accept possession by the lessee, (4) provisions for the payment of rent, (5) the starting date and duration of the lease, and (6) signatures of the parties to the lease, if and as required. While most written leases will require the signatures of the tenant and landlord, legally only the landlord must sign a written lease. Taking possession of the property and paying rent is considered the tenant's agreement to the terms of the lease.

In Georgia, a lease for a term longer than one year must be in writing to be enforceable in court. A lease for one year or less, or a month-to-month lease, can be oral and still be valid and enforceable, but as a matter of good business practice, any lease should be put in writing and signed. This gives all parties involved a written reminder of their obligations under the lease and reduces the chance for dispute.

THE LEASE DOCUMENT

A training copy of a standard residential lease is included in Appendix E. This lease is produced by the Georgia Association of REALTORS® (GAR) and is used here with permission. Reproducing all or in part, or use without permission from GAR, is a violation of their copyright.

Provisions of the Lease

The lease sets forth the agreement between the tenant (lessee) and landlord (lessor) and should be written in simple and easy-to-understand language. Assistance from an attorney familiar with landlord/tenant laws is crucial if you do not have available a form lease such as the one just mentioned. This lease is specifically for residential property; more complex situations, such as commercial and industrial properties, will require legal counsel. Common provisions of the lease will include:

Term—The beginning and ending of the lease should be clearly stated along with rights and methods of termination.

Use restrictions—Are there any restrictions on the use of the property, such as the number of occupants, the right to have pets, the number or size limitation of pets, operation of a business from a leased home, types of vehicles that can be parked on the property, performance of maintenance on vehicles on the property, the storage of disabled vehicles, and so on?

Maintenance—The lease should clearly state who is responsible for the maintenance of the property. Although this responsibility often is that of the landlord in a residential lease, the tenant may agree to take care of the maintenance for a reduced rent.

Security deposit—The security deposit is paid by the tenant as security for breach of the lease or damage to the property. The amount of the deposit, where it is held, by whom it is held, whether it is in an escrow or non-escrow account, whether it is interest-bearing and who will get the interest, under what circumstances the tenant will receive a refund, and what rights the landlord has to keep all or part of the deposit should be detailed.

Quiet enjoyment—The tenant has the right to use the property for the purposes for which s/he leased it. If that reasonable right to use is destroyed by the landlord, the tenant may claim a constructive eviction, leave the property, and have no further responsibility to pay rent. The tenant may also claim damages because of the breach. For instance, in a residential lease, it would be assumed, if not expressed, that the tenant should have the right to be able to sleep in relative peace and quiet at night. If other tenants are having loud parties during the week and the landlord does not control the situation, the tenant may not be able to continue to use the property for the purposes for which s/he has leased it and can claim a breach of quiet enjoyment.

quiet enjoyment: the right of possession and use of property without undue disturbance by others

Disrepair—The tenant may not cause undue harm to the property. Normal wear and tear is typically excluded.

Destruction of the premises—Substantial damage to the property should be anticipated, along with the responsibilities of the parties. If the roof is ripped off by a tornado, obviously the tenant would not be expected to continue to pay rent if s/he cannot use the property. The destruction of property would probably terminate the obligations. The question, however, is whether the landlord would have any liability to the tenant for the loss in wages, damage to personal property, or additional moving expenses. While common sense may dictate an answer of "No," the tenant may look at this differently when faced with unexpected costs. A good lease would recommend that the tenant have renter's insurance and stipulate that the landlord has no liability for damages out of his/her control.

LANDLORD–TENANT LAWS

Traditionally, courts have been strict interpreters of lease agreements. This philosophy still prevails for leases on commercial property. However, with regard to residential rental property, the trend today is for state legislatures to establish special landlord–tenant laws. The intent is to strike a reasonable balance between the responsibilities of landlords to tenants, and vice versa. Typically, these laws limit the amount of security deposit a landlord may require, tell the tenant how many days' notice must be given before vacating a periodic tenancy, and require the landlord to deliver possession on the date agreed. The landlord must maintain the premises in a fit condition for living, and the tenant is to keep the unit clean and not damage it. The tenant is to obey the house rules, and the landlord must give advance notice before entering an apartment, except in legitimate emergencies. Additionally, the laws set forth such things as the procedure for accounting for any deposit money not returned, the right of the tenant to make needed repairs and bill the landlord, the right of the landlord to file court actions for unpaid rent, and the proper procedure for evicting a tenant. The Georgia Landlord Tenant Act can be found in Title 44, Chapter 7, of the Official Code of Georgia Annotated (O.C.G.A.).

SETTING RENTS

gross lease: tenant pays a fixed rent and the landlord pays all property expenses

There are several methods for setting rents. The most common is the gross lease. Under a **gross lease**, the tenant pays a fixed rent, and the landlord pays all the operating expenses of the property. A tenant paying $600 per month on a month-to-month apartment lease and a person paying $13,000 per year for a one-year house lease are both examples of fixed rents. A landlord will usually agree to a level rent for one year, but what if the tenant wants a longer lease term, such as 2 years, 5 years, 10 years, 25 years, or 99 years? For these situations, the following rent-setting methods are used in the real estate industry. The simplest is to have a *step-up,* or graduated, rent. For example, a five-year office lease might call for monthly rents of $2 per square foot of floor space the first year, $2.25 the second year, $12.50 the third year, $2.75 the fourth year, and $3.25 the fifth. A residential tenant wishing a two-year lease might find the landlord more receptive if the monthly rent is stepped up the second year.

net lease: tenant pays a base rent plus maintenance, property taxes, and insurance

Office and industrial leases of five or more years often include an *escalator* or *participation clause.* This allows the landlord to pass along to the tenant increases in such items as property taxes, utility charges, and maintenance. A variation is to have the tenant pay for all property taxes, insurance, repairs, utilities, and so on, in addition to the base rent. This arrangement is called a **net lease** or a *triple net lease.* It is commonly used when an entire building is being leased, as well as for long-term ground leases.

percentage lease: tenant pays a percentage of sales as all or a portion of the rent owed to the landlord

Another type is the **percentage lease**, wherein the owner receives a percentage of the tenant's gross receipts as rent. For example, a farmer who leases land may give the landowner 20% of the value of the crop when it is sold. The monthly rent for a small hardware store might be $600 plus 6% of gross sales above $10,000. A gasoline station may pay $1,000 plus 2 cents per gallon pumped. A supermarket may pay $7,500 plus 1.5% of gross above $50,000 per month.

index lease: rent payments are adjusted periodically according to an index, such as the Consumer Price Index (CPI)

Still another way of setting rents on long-term leases is to create an **index lease** to index the rent to some economic indicator, such as an inflation index. If there is inflation, rents increase; if there is deflation, rents decrease. Arrangements such as step-ups, escalators, percentages, indexes, and net leases are all efforts by landlords to protect against rising costs of property operation and declining purchasing power, yet meet tenants' needs to have property committed to them for more than a year.

OPTION CLAUSES

Option clauses give the tenant the right at some future time to purchase or lease the property at a predetermined price. This gives a tenant flexibility. For example, suppose that a prospective tenant is starting a new business and is not certain how successful it will be. Therefore, in looking for space to rent, the prospective tenant desires a lease that allows an "out" if the new venture does not succeed but permits continued occupancy if the venture is successful. The solution is a lease with options. The landlord could offer a one-year lease, plus an option to stay for two more years at a higher rent, plus a second option for an additional five years at a still higher rent. If the venture is not successful, the tenant is obligated for only one year. But if successful, the tenant has the option of staying two more years, and if still successful, for five years after that. Another option possibility is to offer the tenant a lease that also contains an option to buy the property for a fixed period of time at a preset price. This is called a *lease with option to buy.*

option clause: gives the right at some future time to purchase or lease a property at a predetermined price

ASSIGNMENT AND SUBLETTING

Unless otherwise provided in the lease contract, a lessee may assign the lease or sublet. An **assignment** is the total transfer of the lessee's rights to another person. These parties are referred to as the *assignor* and the *assignee,* respectively. The assignee acquires all the right, title, and interest of the assignor—no more and no less. However, the assignor remains liable for the performance of the contract, unless released in writing by the landlord. To **sublet** means to transfer only a portion of the rights held under a lease. The *sublease* thereby created may be for a portion of the premises, or part of the lease term. The party acquiring those rights is called the **sublessee**. The original lessee is the **sublessor** with respect to the sublessee. The sublessee pays rent to the lessee, who, in turn, remains liable to the landlord for rent on the entire premises.

assignment: the total transfer of the lessee's rights to another party

sublet: to transfer only a portion of one's lease rights

sublessee: a lessee who rents from another lessee

sublessor: a lessee who rents to another lessee

LEASE TERMINATION

Most leases terminate because of the expiration of the term of the lease. The tenant has received the use of the premises, and the landlord has received rent in return. However, a lease can be terminated if the landlord and the tenant mutually agree. The tenant surrenders the premises, and the landlord releases him/her from the contract. This should, of course, be done in writing.

Eviction

If a tenant fails to live up to the terms of the lease agreement, the landlord has grounds for eviction. Usually, this is for nonpayment of rent, but it can also be for violation of some other aspect of the agreement, such as holding over past the term of the lease, bringing animals into a "no pets" apartment, occupancy by more than the number of persons specified in the agreement, or operating in an illegal manner on the premises. Called **actual eviction**, the process usually begins with the landlord having a notice served on the tenant requiring the tenant to comply with the lease agreement or move out. If the tenant neither complies nor vacates, the landlord takes the matter to court. If the landlord wins the case, either by a preponderance of evidence or because the tenant does not appear to contest the eviction, then the court will terminate the tenant's lease rights and authorize a marshal or sheriff to go on the premises and force the tenant out. This process of actual eviction is straightforward in theory. In practice, many would argue, the laws favor the tenant over the landlord, particularly in Georgia. There are many stories of nonpaying tenants staying in a property for months before the landlord could have them legally dispossessed.

A lease agreement may also be terminated through **constructive eviction**. This occurs when the landlord does not keep the premises fit for occupancy, and the tenant is forced to move. For example, the landlord may continually fail to repair broken plumbing lines or a leaking roof. The tenant's legal remedies are to claim wrongful eviction, move out, stop paying rent, and sue the landlord for breach of contract, thereby forcing the landlord either to make repairs or to terminate the lease, possibly with money damages.

A **retaliatory eviction** is one whereby a landlord evicts a tenant because of a complaint made by the tenant. For example, a tenant may have complained to public health officials or building and safety authorities about conditions on the premises that are in violation of health laws or building codes. The landlord may retaliate or threaten to retaliate with an eviction (or a rent increase or a decrease in services); however, this is illegal.

actual eviction: the removal of a defaulting tenant through legal proceedings

constructive eviction: for all intents and purposes, typically because of an action or inaction of the landlord, the tenant cannot use the property for the intended purpose

retalitory eviction: the illegal removal of a tenant by a landlord because of complaints or actions against the landlord by the tenant

Eminent Domain

The government, under its *right of eminent domain*, may also terminate a lease, but it must provide just compensation. An example of this would be construction of a new highway that requires the demolition of a building rented to tenants. Both the property owner and the tenants would be entitled to compensation. Eminent domain may be for a portion of a property rather than the entire parcel. This is known as a *partial take*. In a partial take, the condemnation may terminate the obligations under the lease if the take was sufficient to the extent that the tenant can no longer use the property for the purposes for which s/he leased it. This would be another example of termination of quiet enjoyment.

Foreclosure

A mortgage foreclosure can also bring about lease termination; it all depends on priority. If the mortgage was recorded before the lease was signed, then foreclosure of the mortgage also forecloses the lease, unless the mortgage contained a **nondisturbance clause**. The nondisturbance clause is an agreement by a lender to not disturb a performing tenant on a valid lease in the event the lender has to foreclose. While uncommon in residential mortgages, this type of clause may be seen on mortgages for commercial properties. There are laws for protecting tenants in residential situations. As an alternative, if the mortgage does not have a nondisturbance clause, the tenant should be successful in inducing the lender into one before signing the lease. If the lease was recorded first, then the lease still stands. Because a lease can cloud a lender's title, wording is sometimes inserted in the lease that makes it subordinate to any future financing of the property. This is highly technical, but nonetheless a very significant matter in long-term shopping center, office building, and industrial leases.

nondisturbance clause: an agreement found in a mortgage where a lender forgoes the right to terminate a valid lease of a performing tenant

JOB OPPORTUNITIES

In reading this chapter, you may have become interested in a career in real property management. The most successful apartment managers seem to be those who have had previous experience in managing people and money and who are handy with tools. Those with prior military experience or experience as owners or managers of small businesses are eagerly sought after. Least successful as on-site property managers are those who see it as a quiet, peaceful retirement job, those who are unable to work with and understand people, those who are disorganized or cannot make decisions, those without a few handyman skills, and those strictly looking for an 8-to-5, Monday-to-Friday job. Commercial and industrial property management positions tend to be filled by persons who have had prior property management experience and who have a good understanding of how business and industry make use of real estate. In a medium-to-large property management firm, there will be job opportunities for building service personnel, purchasing agents, bookkeepers, clerks, secretaries, office managers, field supervisors, and executive managers. In a small office, one person plus a secretary will be responsible for all the off-site duties.

TRAINING PROGRAMS

Finding experienced and capable property managers is not an easy task. Formal education in property management is not widely available in the United States. Instead, most managers learn their profession almost entirely by experience. An individual property owner can place an advertisement in a newspaper and attract a manager from another project, but most professional management firms have found it necessary to develop their own internal training programs. With such a program, a management firm can start a person with no previous property management experience as an assistant manager on a large project. If the person learns the job and enjoys the work, there is a promotion to manager of a 50- or 60-unit building and an increase in salary. If this works well, there is a move to a larger complex with an assistant and another increase in salary. Each step brings more responsibility and more pay. This system provides a steady stream of qualified managers for the management firm. It is also a source of executive-level personnel for the off-site management office. In larger cities, executive-level positions pay upwards of $100,000 per year. The dominant professional organization in the property management field is the *Institute of Real Estate Management (IREM)*. Established in 1933, the institute is a division within the National Association of REALTORS®. Its primary purposes are to serve as an exchange medium for management ideas and to recognize specialists in the field. The institute awards the designation *certified property manager (CPM)* to members who successfully complete required educational courses in property management. The institute also offers an educational program for resident managers of apartment buildings. The designation *accredited resident manager (ARM)* is awarded upon successful completion.

Second in size to IREM is the BOMI International. Incorporated in 1970 as Building Owners & Managers Institute International, BOMI provides educational programs aimed primarily at the commercial property management industry. Several courses are offered, ranging from design, operation, and maintenance of buildings to accounting, insurance, law, investments, and administration. Successful completion of the courses leads to the designation of *real property administrator (RPA)*. BOMI also offers courses in heating, plumbing, refrigeration, air handling, electrical systems, control systems maintenance, energy management, and supervision as they apply to commercial buildings. Those who complete these courses receive the systems maintenance administrator *(SMA)* designation.

Review Questions

Answers to these questions can be found in Appendix D at the end of this book.

1. A lease for a definite period of time that terminates when that time has expired is:
   A. an estate for years
   B. a periodic estate
   C. an estate at will
   D. an estate at sufferance

2. A lease of fixed length that continually renews itself for like periods of time until the lessor or lessee acts to terminate it is:
   A. a holdover estate
   B. a periodic estate
   C. an estate at will
   D. an estate at sufferance

3. A lease is NOT a(n):
   A. conveyance
   B. contract
   C. security
   D. agreement

4. To be valid and enforceable, which of the following must be in writing and signed?
   A. a month-to-month lease
   B. a lease for more than a year
   C. a three-month lease
   D. all of the above

5. The right of the lessee to uninterrupted use of the leased premises is called:
   A. quiet possession
   B. quiet enjoyment
   C. quiet rights
   D. tenant rights

6. A written lease agreement is still legal even though it fails to include:
   A. the terms of the lease
   B. a property description
   C. consideration
   D. signature of the tenant

7. One thing that distinguishes a periodic lease from a lease for years is that it:
   A. may be for less than a year
   B. must be for less than a year
   C. automatically renews
   D. does not require notice to terminate

8. Bob Short and Bill Tall rent an apartment unit from owner Haf High. Bill dies during the lease term. Would the lease be binding on the parties after the death of Bill?
   A. No, death would terminate the responsibilities of the parties to a lease.
   B. No, not unless the lease contained a survival clause.
   C. Yes, but only on the landlord, who is still living.
   D. Yes, death does not terminate the responsibilities of the parties to a lease.

9. The word *waive* means to:
   A. say goodbye
   B. demand
   C. relinquish
   D. die naturally

10. A lease that calls for specified rental increases at predetermined intervals is known as a:
    A. net lease
    B. gross lease
    C. graduated lease
    D. percentage lease

11. The clause in a lease that allows the landlord to pass along to the tenant certain increases in operating expenses is called:
    A. an acceleration clause
    B. an alienation clause
    C. an escalator clause
    D. a nondisturbance clause

12. When the tenant pays a base rent plus some or all of the operating expenses of a property, the result is a:
    A. gross lease
    B. net lease
    C. percentage lease
    D. graduated lease

13. A lease in which the tenant pays a rent based upon the gross sales made from the rented premises is known as a:
    A. percentage lease
    B. participation lease
    C. net lease
    D. gross lease

14. Which of the following is NOT specifically designed to protect against rising operating costs?
    A. a net lease
    B. an escalator clause
    C. an index clause
    D. a gross lease

15. A lease for years is NOT terminated by:
    A. constructive eviction
    B. death of the party
    C. mutual agreement
    D. actual eviction

16. A written lease agreement is still legal even though it fails to include:
    A. the amount of rent to be paid
    B. a security deposit
    C. a legal description
    D. the signature of the landlord

17. Flint leased a building to Newton under an agreement that gave Newton the right to occupy the premises for two years, with an option to renew for an additional one-year period. In order to be enforceable, must this lease be in writing and signed by both Flint and Newton?
    A. Yes, because all contracts dealing with real property must be in writing in order to be enforceable.
    B. Yes, because the lease is for a period of time in excess of one year.
    C. No, because oral leases for five years or less are enforceable.
    D. No, because a two-year oral lease is enforceable.

18. Generally, today's laws regarding eviction of a tenant for nonpayment of rents, as compared to those in the past, favor the:
    A. tenant
    B. landlord
    C. property manager
    D. real estate broker

19. The best defense against losses from uncollected rent is:
    A. a threat of legal action against the delinquent tenant
    B. careful tenant selection, good service, and a businesslike policy on rent collections
    C. to accept partial payments when available
    D. to ask for, but don't follow up on, references

20. The Institute of Real Estate Management awards the designation:
    A. REM
    B. CPM
    C. MAI
    D. SREA

PART 6

GEORGIA-SPECIFIC LICENSE LAW, RULES AND REGULATIONS, AND GEORGIA PRACTICE

This is where we bring it all together and complete what we began! You should be tired, maybe a little overwhelmed, but feeling like you have accomplished an important task. In our construction analogy, this is where we put on the finishing touches. The final grade and landscaping are installed; all the systems are checked; the final cleanup is completed; and the Certificate of Occupancy is issued by the local government. It is an exciting time! In this final and last part, we will complete our course of study with that which is specific to Georgia. We will study the following chapters:

Chapter 23: Georgia License Law

Chapter 24: Georgia Rules and Regulations

Chapter 25: Georgia Practice

CHAPTER 23
GEORGIA LICENSE LAW

KEY TERMS

associate broker
broker
brokerage agreement
commission
commissioner
licensee
real estate
Real Estate Education, Research, and Recovery Fund
salesperson

OBJECTIVES

After successful completion of this chapter, you should be able to:

1. define key terms used in Georgia license law;
2. describe the requirements of licensure;
3. discuss the various violations of license law;
4. discuss the makeup of the Georgia Real Estate Commission;
5. explain the difference between a commission member and the commissioner;
6. discuss the use and limitations of the recovery fund; and
7. describe the exceptions to licensure.

OVERVIEW

This chapter will discuss Title 43, Chapter 40, of Georgia Statutes and Codes, which relates specifically to real estate licensing. Having a thorough understanding and working knowledge of license law is important to every licensee, as it is this law that the state uses to protect the interests of its citizens from the unscrupulous and improper practice of real estate licensees.

Real estate license law is just that—law. The state legislature has passed these laws, and the governor has signed them. To change, repeal, or add to these laws

broker: a person who provides acts of licensure for another for compensation

associate broker: any person who meets the requirements of a broker but chooses to work for a broker

salesperson: any person, other than an associate broker, who may perform acts of real estate on behalf of a broker

brokerage agreement: the written contract between a broker and a client; also called a brokerage engagement

commission: the Georgia Real Estate Commission, which is made up of six members

commissioner: full-time employee of the commission who supervises the department

licensee: any person with a real estate license

real estate: any interest in real property, freehold or non-freehold; tangible or intangible

requires the same process: passage by the state legislature and signature by the governor. This process is, by design, contentious and difficult. When government limits or restricts the rights of its citizens in a free country, it SHOULD be difficult. To paraphrase a familiar quote attributed to Otto von Bismarck, "There are two things the American people would reject outright if they ever intimately saw how they were made: law and sausage."

In this chapter, we will review, section by section, the Georgia license law covered in Title 43, Chapter 40, "Real Estate Brokers and Salespersons." It is not important that you remember the code or section numbers. They are provided for you here simply for reference. You should download the current license law at the Georgia Real Estate Commission website, which is www.grec.state.ga.us, under the tab "Obtaining a License." While every effort will be made to keep this textbook updated, please understand that the law can change without much notice. Always check with an instructor or refer to the actual law for updates. Also realize that, by reading this chapter, you are receiving an overview of the law put into what we hope is easier-to-understand language. To see the words as written by the state legislature in context, again, refer to the actual law.

43-40-1 DEFINITIONS

The first section of the law defines many of the words that are used in this code. We will paraphrase some, but not all, of the definitions. A **broker** is a person who, for compensation, performs an act of real estate for another. An act of real estate could be defined as negotiating contracts or procuring prospects for a real estate transaction. An associate broker is a person, other than a salesperson, who acts on behalf of a real estate broker in performing acts of real estate. An **associate broker** meets the age, education, experience, and examination requirements to be a broker but chooses to work for another broker. A **salesperson** is any person, other than an associate broker, who is licensed to perform acts of real estate on behalf of a broker. A **brokerage agreement** is a written contract between a broker and a client whereby the broker is hired to represent the interests of the client in a transaction and be compensated for doing so. The **commission** refers to the Georgia Real Estate Commission, and **commissioner** refers to the real estate commissioner, who is the administrative head of the commission. A **licensee** is any person with a real estate license, active or inactive; a *person* could be an individual or firm, and a firm is any business entity such as a corporation, partnership, or limited liability company. Under this provision of law, **real estate** is defined as any interest in real property, whether that interest be corporeal (tangible) or incorporeal (intangible), freehold or non-freehold, and would also include a mobile home if permanently attached to the land.

43-40-2 CREATION OF THE COMMISSION

The commission is composed of six members who are appointed by the governor for a five-year term, with their appointment approved by the state senate. Five of the six members must be licensed in real estate for five years and residents of Georgia for five years. The sixth member is a consumer member who may not have any connection with the real estate industry and who has a recognized interest in consumer affairs and concerns. This is to provide the perception of balance and to avoid having a "good ol' boy network" listening to consumer complaints against licensees. In the event a vacancy occurs, the governor shall appoint a person to fill the unexpired term; such appointment is not confirmed by the senate. The commission shall each year select from the membership a chairperson. The commission is required to meet at least one day per month, with a quorum of four members present being required to conduct official business. As compensation, the members are paid $25 per meeting day plus expenses; obviously, this very important job is being done by people with a desire to serve—not for the money. Also provided in this section is the governor's ability to remove members for their inability to perform, negligence to perform, incompetence, dishonest conduct, or for having disciplinary sanctions imposed upon them by any licensing agency. This section of law also empowers the commission to pass rules and regulations relating to professional conduct or licensees. Also required is a written report to be filed by the chairperson with the governor each year.

43-40-3 DETERMINATION OF FEES

While the commission is an agency of the state of Georgia, it does not receive tax dollar support. It is required to collect fees and operate from those fees. This section empowers the commission to establish and collect fees that approximate its cost of operation.

43-40-4 OFFICE OF COMMISSIONER

While the commission is made up of six members who are appointed by the governor, there is also a separate commissioner, who is a full-time employee of the commission. The commission appoints this person and sets the salary. Essentially, it is the commissioner's job to run the department on a daily basis. This person hires and is responsible for the staff that shall assist him in his/her duties.

43-40-5 STATUS OF THE LICENSE OF COMMISSION EMPLOYEES

While an employee of the commission, no licensee is allowed to maintain an active real estate license. Anyone who becomes employed by the commission who is licensed shall place that license on inactive status during employment. There is no fee to be charged to such persons while employed by the commission.

43-40-6 SEAL AND RECORDS

The commission has an official seal, which, when affixed to a document with the signature of the commissioner, shall have the same bearing and effect as an original document. In the maintaining of records, the commission shall be able to certify the license history of a licensee for five years.

43-40-7 APPLICATION FOR LICENSES AND CONFIDENTIALITY

A person who wishes to become licensed by the commission must file an application approved by the commission. This application may require a request for any information that the commission deems necessary. Supporting documents and other such personal information shall be kept confidential; however, such information as the licensee's name, license number, license status, and any disciplinary information shall be available to the general public. This information is now available at the commission's website, www.grec.state.ga.us.

43-40-8 QUALIFICATIONS OF LICENSEES; COURSES; CONTINUING EDUCATION; REINSTATEMENT AND RENEWAL

To qualify to be an applicant for a **community association manager's license**, an individual must:

1. be at least 18 years old;
2. be a resident of the state, unless qualifying under nonresident licensure;
3. be a high school graduate or hold a certificate of equivalency;
4. complete a community association manager's course of at least 25 in-class hours; and
5. pass a state examination after completing all above requirements.

To qualify to be an applicant for a **salesperson's license**, an individual must:

1. be at least 18 years old;
2. be a resident of the state, unless qualifying under nonresident licensure;
3. be a high school graduate or hold a certificate of equivalency;
4. complete a salesperson's course of at least 75 in-class hours; and
5. pass a state examination after completing all above requirements.

In addition to the requirements to become licensed as a salesperson, each licensee must also complete a post-license course of study consisting of at least 25 hours of education within one year of issuance of his/her license. It is expected that a licensee will take a course specific to the discipline of real estate that the licensee will practice. This course completion shall require an examination approved by the commission. In the event that the course is not completed by the licensee within the time limits stipulated here, the license shall lapse. If the licensee properly enrolls in the post-license course but fails to complete it in a timely manner, though the license lapses, the licensee may reinstate the license by completing the course within six months of lapse of license. If the licensee fails to reinstate in this manner, the licensee shall be required to complete the course and pay penalty fees as imposed by the commission in the rules and regulations to reinstate.

To qualify to be an applicant for a **broker's license**, an individual must:

1. be at least 21 years old;
2. be a resident of the state, unless qualifying under nonresident licensure;
3. be a high school graduate or hold a certificate of equivalency;
4. have been actively licensed for at least three of the previous five years prior to the application;
5. complete a broker's course of at least 60 in-class hours (If the applicant was licensed as a community association manager, the applicant must provide proof of an additional 75 in-class hours approved by the commission. This is typically the salesperson's pre-license course.); and
6. pass a state examination after completing all above requirements.

In addition to the requirements for licensure and the post-license education required of salespeople, Georgia law requires that all individuals licensed after December 31, 1979, complete continuing education. The individual must provide proof, at the time of renewing the license, of completing a minimum of six hours of education per year of the renewal period. The power to set the license period is passed to the commission; currently, that period is four years. An exemption from meeting the continuing education requirements exists for licensees serving on active duty in the armed forces or in the general assembly. It is their choice whether to meet the continuing education requirements while serving. If they choose to not maintain the continuing education while serving and they serve for more than two years, they shall be required to complete a 25-hour course within six months of conclusion of service. Remember, this information, like all of the law discussed here, is dynamic and subject to change at the legislative level. Check the commission website periodically for updates.

43-40-9 NONRESIDENT LICENSEES

Licensure in Georgia does not necessarily require residency in Georgia. With Georgia sharing state lines with Alabama, Tennessee, South Carolina, North Carolina, and Florida, it is not surprising that persons living in these states, particularly those living in close proximity to Georgia, often want to gain the right and ability to legally practice real estate in Georgia. This section of law allows for that to happen in one of two ways.

The first scenario involves a person who is not licensed in his/her state but wants to obtain a real estate license to practice in Georgia. For example, an individual who lives in Chattanooga, Tennessee, has an opportunity to work with a real estate company in the north Georgia mountains but must first have a license. S/he may obtain the license by meeting the same age, education, and examination requirements of a resident licensee as stipulated in 43-40-8.

The second scenario would involve a person who is licensed in his/her state but also wants to be licensed in Georgia. For example, a person licensed in South Carolina practices primarily in lake properties, specializing in Lake Hartwell. If s/he also had a Georgia license, s/he could assist buyers and sellers in the purchase and sale of properties on both sides of the lake. There are several requirements that the commission MAY stipulate before issuing a license. These requirements could include:

1. providing proof of licensure in his/her state;
2. paying fees;
3. stating in writing that s/he has read the law, rules, and regulations and agrees to abide by them;
4. affiliating with a broker (resident or nonresident), if s/he is licensed as anything other than a broker;
5. providing documentation with copies of disciplinary actions;
6. appointing the real estate commissioner as agent to receive legal notices on behalf of the licensee; and
7. providing a written agreement that the licensee will cooperate with investigations by the commission.

This section also allows a licensee from another state to enter into a written agreement with a Georgia broker, which would allow the out-of-state licensee to practice in Georgia without a license. The Georgia broker would be responsible for the verification of licensure of the person and also be required to maintain a copy of the written agreement for a minimum of three years. The written agreement shall include, in part, provisions for:

1. how any commissions will be split between the Georgia broker and the out-of-state licensee;
2. any listings or management agreements to be in the name of the Georgia broker;
3. the out-of-state licensee to conduct negotiations only with the express permission of the Georgia broker;
4. any advertising to identify the Georgia broker;
5. any contracts to identify the Georgia broker; and
6. any trust funds to be held in the Georgia broker's trust account unless all parties agree in writing to the contrary.

In the event that the out-of-state licensee violates Georgia law, the commission is limited to suspending or revoking the Georgia broker's rights to enter into further agreements with out-of-state brokers unless the Georgia broker participated in or ratified the violation, or if the Georgia broker failed to have a written agreement with the out-of-state licensee that includes all the provisions of this section.

43-40-10 GRANTING OF A BROKER'S LICENSE

If a broker's license is to be issued to a firm, the firm is required to designate an individual licensed as a broker to be its qualifying broker, and the qualifying broker shall have the authority to bind the firm in cases before the commission. This qualifying broker will be responsible for making sure that the firm and all licensees comply with the law and rules. The qualifying broker is responsible for making sure that all persons acting as licensees for the firm are properly licensed, and that if the firm or its licensees engage in any activities that violate the law or rules the qualifying broker is subject to being sanctioned. In a nutshell, qualifying brokers are on the hot seat for actions by the firm or the firm's licensees.

Until July 1, 2006, the commission, through this section, was authorized to issue licenses to salespeople and associate broker corporations under limited circumstances. The reason for this provision was to allow these licensees the protections available from legal and tax liability. The only reason for the corporation license was to allow the earnings to flow through a corporation since a broker could pay licensees only for performing acts of licensure. In 2006, the law was amended to allow the broker to pay nonlicensed corporation fees earned by licensees so long as there is written instruction and at least 20% of the corporate stock is owned by the licensee. At this time, the licenses of salesperson and associate broker corporations were terminated, as their need had expired.

43-40-11 FORM OF LICENSE

This simple section empowers the commission to prescribe the form of the license. Each license shall be delivered or mailed to the broker, and the broker shall maintain custody and control. In addition, the commission shall provide a pocket card certifying the licensure of the person.

43-40-12 FEES; INACTIVE STATUS; PENALTY FEES

The commission is empowered to establish nonrefundable fees that licensees shall be required to pay to fund the maintenance and operation of the office of the commission, with all fees deposited into the state treasury. Fees shall include:

- *an examination fee*—In the event that the candidate fails the examination, s/he may take another by filing another application for examination and paying another fee;

- *an activation fee*—Any person applying for a real estate license must first pay an activation fee; and
- *renewal fees*—Real estate licenses must be periodically renewed, and the period of renewal is at the discretion of the commission as stated in the rules and regulations. The rules require that all licenses of individuals be renewed by the last day of the birth month every four years.

In the event that a license lapses due to failure to pay fees, the licensee may reinstate the license within two years of the lapse by paying all renewal fees, late charges, and a reinstatement fee. If the lapse period is greater than two years but less than five years, the licensee may reinstate the license by paying all renewal fees, late charges, and a reinstatement fee, plus completing any education course required by the commission. Currently, the commission requires in its rules and regulations that, in this circumstance, the licensee must complete the prelicense course for the license being reinstated. For example, if the licensee is reinstating a salesperson's license, the licensee must pay all fees and complete the salesperson's pre-license educational course of study. If the lapse period is more than five years, the licensee may not reinstate the license but must requalify as an original applicant, including education and examination. If the license of a licensee is lapsed for more than than one year and the license was not subject to continuing education, upon reinstatement, the licensee shall be subject to continuing education requirements.

In the event that a person does not wish to continue to be actively licensed, s/he may make a written request to the commission to have have/her license placed in an inactive status. Such a request must be made within 30 days of ceasing work for a broker. While inactive, the licensee may not be engaged in any brokerage activity except for property the licensee owns, and if the licensee wishes to reinstate to an active status, s/he must obtain the signature of a broker who agrees to be responsible for the license and activities. While inactive, the license must be renewed each period, with the renewal fees being paid to the commission. If the licensee wishes to reactivate, the licensee must complete continuing education courses equal to what would have been required if the licensee had maintained an active license. For example, if the licensee was inactive for six years, s/he must show completion of 36 hours of continuing education approved by the commission prior to activation.

Penalty fees, not to exceed the renewal fee charged to brokers, may be imposed on a licensee who submits a check to the commission for which there is insufficient funds, or who fails to do any of the following:

- notify the commission in writing of a change of address, the opening or closing of a trust account, transfer to a new company, or departure from a firm to go inactive (These notifications must be made within 30 days.);
- affiliate with a new company or go inactive within 30 days of being notified by a broker that the broker no longer wishes to hold the license; or
- respond within 30 days to a commission inquiry.

43-40-13 DISPOSITION OF FEES

The fees collected by the commission shall be deposited in the state treasury, and the expenses of the commission shall be paid from these funds. It is further required that the expenses of the commission be kept within the monies collected and that the expense of the commission shall not be supported by state tax dollars.

The commission must be self-supporting and not impose a burden on the taxpayers of the state to fund its operation.

43-40-14 POWER OF THE COMMISSION TO ISSUE, REVOKE, SUSPEND, AND CENSURE

Remembering that what is being discussed here is law as created by the state legislature, the commission is empowered to regulate the issuance of licenses, revoke or suspend licenses, and censure licensees. In addition, the commission is empowered to enter into contracts with others, such as certified public accountants or forensic accountants, to assist in the examination of brokers' trust accounts.

43-40-15 GRANTING, REVOKING, AND SUSPENDING LICENSES

For the commission to grant a license to a person, the individual shall have a reputation for honesty, trustworthiness, integrity, and competence to do business in such a manner as to safeguard the interest of the public. The commission may also deny a license to a company if any stockholder, member, or partner with more than 20% of the ownership of the company does not have a good reputation for honesty, trustworthiness, and integrity, or if such person or persons have been convicted of any crimes stated in this section. Crimes that can be sufficient cause for refusal of license include forgery, embezzlement, obtaining money under false pretenses, theft, extortion, conspiracy to defraud, and other like offenses, or if the person has been convicted of a crime involving a moral turpitude.

This code section has recently been strengthened with language that defines a conviction to be a felony or crime involving a moral turpitude. Further, no person who has a conviction may be eligible to apply for a license until all terms of a sentence have been completed and at least two years have passed since satisfaction of all terms of sentencing for a single conviction; five years must have passed since satisfaction of all terms of sentencing for multiple convictions. The reason for this stiffening of the law is that the commission was receiving applications that had no chance of being approved because of recent felonies. Providing for investigations and hearings simply consumed time and money with consistent results: application denied. This change in law should free up those resources. Additionally, an applicant for licensure as an associate broker or broker who has been convicted of any of these offenses may not be licensed by the commission until three conditions are met:

1. at least 10 years have passed since the conviction or release, whichever is later;
2. there are no criminal charges pending; and

3. the applicant provides satisfactory proof that s/he now has a reputation for honesty, trustworthiness, integrity, and competence, and will do business in such a manner as to safeguard the interest of the public.

Another serious matter is making false statements on the application. Such false statements are grounds for refusal to issue, suspension, or revocation. It is recommended that if you are going to miss, miss on the side of disclosure. If you are not sure whether information is pertinent, disclose and let the commission decide if it considers the information pertinent. A person who is perceived to have falsified the application would not be considered to have a reputation for honesty, trustworthiness, and integrity or to demonstrate a competency to safeguard the interest of the public.

In addition to other infractions, any sanction by an occupational body of this or any other state can also be sufficient grounds for refusal to issue. This could include a medical license, nursing license, cosmetology license, law license, engineer's license, and others. Upon the conviction of any crimes named in this section, the licensee must immediately notify the commission of the conviction. The license shall be automatically revoked in 60 days unless the licensee makes a written request for a hearing.

Two other offenses that may be cause for the refusal to issue a license or the suspension of a license are not being in compliance with a child support order or being in default on a student loan guaranteed by the Georgia Higher Education Loan Program. If you go to the commission website and check the disciplinary actions, you will see that a substantial number of the suspensions are for violations of one of these two matters. If you are behind in child support or student loan payments, get current.

43-40-16 REFUSAL TO ISSUE

If the commission refuses to issue a license after proper application, the commission must provide for a hearing in accordance with the Georgia Administrative Procedure Act. In the event that the applicant is not satisfied with the final decision after the hearing, the applicant shall be entitled to a judicial review in the superior court of the county where the commission is located, in accordance with the act.

43-40-18 MANAGEMENT OF FIRMS AND LICENSED AFFILIATES

Every brokerage firm must have a broker or qualifying broker. This person shall be responsible for the acts of the firm and its licensees and is responsible for violations unless the broker can demonstrate that s/he had procedures for supervision, did not participate in any violation, and did not ratify the violation.

If the firm is a sole proprietorship, it must be owned entirely by the broker. If the firm is a partnership or limited partnership, the qualifying broker must be a general partner. If the firm is a limited liability company, the qualifying broker must be a member, and if the firm is a corporation, the qualifying broker must be an officer. In any instance, the broker or qualifying broker must have the ability to sign on all trust accounts maintained by the firm.

This code section requires that the activities of the firm be under the direct supervision of the broker or qualifying broker and that the firm establish the following procedures:

- ensure that all advertising complies with law and rules;
- provide training to licensees on the law and rules;
- provide for a review of all offers and contracts within 30 days of the date of offer or contract;
- conduct an ongoing review of the firm's trust account procedures;
- provide assurance that all personnel performing acts of a licensee be properly licensed;
- make sure that trust account disbursements are properly made;
- provide for a reasonable safekeeping of all transaction records. The commission does not require that these records be kept as paper and ink. They may be kept electronically as long as they can be retrieved upon request of the commission;
- provide a written policy and procedures manual to all licensees;
- establish a written agreement with all licensees that states how the licensee will be compensated for work while with the broker and how the licensee will be compensated for work not completed before leaving the broker. The commission does not care what the agreement is between brokers and licensees, and it will not arbitrate compensation disputes; and
- ensure that a person with management authority for the firm is reasonably available.

43-40-19 CHANGE OF PLACE OF BUSINESS AND TRANSFERRING LICENSEES

In the event that a brokerage firm changes its address of place of business, it must notify the commission of that change, in writing, within 30 days of the change. Note that most of the administrative notifications required in the law are 30 days. When a licensee leaves a broker, the broker is required to forward the license of that person to the commission. As an alternative, the transferring broker may forward the license to the new broker and notify the commission in writing of that action. A licensed individual is not authorized to conduct the acts of a licensee for the new broker until the licensee personally delivers the application to the commission or has the U.S. Postal Service postmark the envelope with the application. In the event that an individual is applying to become a broker or qualifying broker for a firm, the licensee is not authorized to practice for that firm until the license has been received.

Salespersons and community association managers may practice real estate only for the broker holding their license, with one exception. If a licensee leaves a broker and has transactions that have begun but are not yet completed, the licensee may continue to act for the former broker under these conditions:

- The brokers agree in writing.
- The transactions are specifically identified.
- The former broker accepts full responsibility for the licensees' activities on the transactions.
- The agreement states the form of compensation.

43-40-20 TRUST ACCOUNTS

A source of anxiety and scrutiny for the commission is escrow or trust accounts. It is required that each broker who at any time takes money belonging to others (such as earnest money, security deposits, and rents) maintain an escrow account (which is not subject to garnishment or attachment) and deposit those funds into this account. Once the money is deposited, the broker may not use it for fees or commissions until the transaction is consummated or terminated. If brokers do not accept monies belonging to others, they are not required to maintain an escrow account, but if they find themselves in a situation where they do take money belonging to others, they must open a trust account within one day of receiving the funds. Brokers may maintain as many trust accounts as they wish so long as they notify the commission of the proper information. Any time a broker opens an account, s/he must notify the commission of the name of the bank and the account number.

Any broker with an escrow account must allow the commission to audit the account any time the commission has reasonable cause. The commission is required to audit each broker's escrow account at least one time each renewal period. As an alternative to an audit, the commission may accept a report from a certified public accountant that the account is maintained in accordance with the law. In lieu of examination each renewal period, the commission may accept a summary of the data and records from the broker on a form provided by the commission at the time of renewal.

This code section also allows a nonresident broker to maintain a trust account in his/her resident state so long as the commission has the authority to audit. In the event that a licensee is selling property that the licensee owns and is receiving money that is concurrently due, those parts of any payments that will be due on any existing obligations must be placed into a trust account. An example of this would be a wraparound mortgage. Note the following information:

- Sale price: $150,000
- Down payment: $10,000
- Current seller debt: $80,000 at 6% annual interest; $600 monthly payment

Seller-financed wraparound mortgage of $140,000 at 9% annual interest; $1,100 monthly payment.

The purchaser will make payments to the licensee seller of $1,100 per month, and the seller is required to make payments of $600 per month on the underlying note and can keep the $500 difference. If the seller takes the purchaser's money and does not make the payment, it will ultimately be the purchaser who will lose. Since the $600 is being taken for the benefit of the purchaser, the licensed seller must make deposits of $600 from the purchaser's payment into a trust account and then make the payment on the underlying first note from escrow.

This code section also stipulates that if a licensee other than a broker receives security deposits or other trust funds on his/her own property, those funds must be placed into a trust account. This may be the broker's trust account or a trust account owned by the salesperson, community association manager, or associate broker. If the licensee elects to have his/her own trust account, the account must be approved by the broker, the broker must properly notify the commission of the existence of the account, and the licensee must provide, on at least a quarterly basis, a reconciliation of the trust account.

43-40-21 VIOLATIONS INVOLVING TRUST ACCOUNTS

In the event that a broker fails to maintain his/her trust accounts in accordance with 43-40-20, or if the broker refuses to submit his/her books or other account information to the commission, the commission may conclude that the account is in an unsafe or unsound condition and shall immediately submit a report to the attorney general. In such an event, action may be brought against the broker. S/he may be enjoined from continuing the violation, and the court shall have the power to impound the account and appoint a receiver.

43-40-22 REAL ESTATE EDUCATION, RESEARCH, AND RECOVERY FUND

Prior to 1973, an individual wishing to be a broker had to be eligible to purchase a $1,000 insurance bond, which would provide protection to the public in the event that someone was harmed because of the unlawful actions of the broker. At that time, the bond would typically cost about $40 per year. In July of 1973, a recovery fund was created to protect the public against the illegal practices of brokers. Later, monies from this fund also became available for education and

Real Estate Education, Research and Recovery Fund: a fund that provides an avenue of protection to members of the public harmed by the illegal acts of a licensee

research, thus, the name **Real Estate Education, Research, and Recovery Fund.** Today, many of the disbursals from the fund are used for the development and presentation of education for licensees in the state.

Following are highlights of this code section:

- The fund is created and maintained by all new licensees paying into the fund, at the time of initial application for licensure, an amount as designated by the commission. Currently, that amount is $20.
- The fund must always maintain a minimum balance of $1 million. If the fund falls below $1 million, each licensee, at the time of renewal, may be assessed up to $30 for each year in the renewal period.
- The fund may not be obligated for more than $25,000 on any one transaction. So if $29,000 was misappropriated by a licensee, the fund could not be responsible for more than $25,000.
- The fund may not be obligated for more than $75,000 total for the acts of any one licensee, regardless of the number of transactions, the number of claimants, or the amount of damage.
- No one person shall ever obtain more than $25,000 from the fund. If a person does receive $25,000 from the fund in one or more claims, that person will never have access again.
- The following do not have a right to a claim against the fund:
    o a bonding company acting as a bonding company, not as a principal in the transaction
    o a licensee acting as an agent or principal
    o a spouse, parent, sibling, child, or personal representative of the violating licensee
- Actions for which the fund may be liable must be started within two years of the accrual of the cause of action, and the commission must be notified at the time of filing. The commission shall then have the right to intervene in and defend any such action.
- The fund is not an avenue of first recourse. In the event that a person feels that s/he has been harmed by a licensee, that person must take appropriate action against that licensee and receive a judgment. The person must do everything reasonably possible to receive payment from the licensee on the judgment. Only upon failure to recover may the person go back to court and ask the court to issue an order to the commission to pay from the recovery fund. It is only on that court order that the commission will pay.
- Should the commission be required to pay from the fund, the license of the licensee shall be automatically revoked and the licensee may not be eligible for a new license unless the licensee first makes full restitution to the fund, including interest.

- Monies received by the commission under this code section shall be deposited into the state treasury and then may be invested anywhere it is legal for a domestic insurance company to invest, with interest on the investments being deposited back into the fund.

In addition to the Research, Education, and Recovery Fund of this code section, the law also provides for requiring community association managers to have their funds protected by a fidelity bond or fidelity insurance. The requirements for the bond or insurance are established by the commission in the rules.

43-40-23 COUNTY OR MUNICIPALITY OCCUPATIONAL TAX

This code section references 48-13-17 of the law, which states that a county or city may not require a real estate broker or affiliated licensees to pay a fixed-amount tax unless the broker maintains a physical office in the jurisdiction. It does, however, allow the taxing jurisdiction to charge a gross receipts tax on brokers for commissions earned on sales in that jurisdiction. Essentially, this is saying that if a broker has an office in Cobb County but sells property in Fulton County, Cobb County can require the broker to obtain a business license, but Fulton County cannot. Fulton County could assess a gross receipts tax on the broker for commissions earned in Fulton County.

43-40-24 REQUIREMENTS TO BRING ACTION UNDER THIS CHAPTER

Any person who is bringing an action against someone else for the payment of a commission must first prove that s/he was properly licensed at the time of the cause of action. For a broker to bring action against another for payment of a commission, s/he must also prove that any licensees who worked on his/her behalf were also properly licensed. This code section also empowers the commission to bring actions for any violations of this chapter.

In the Field

The Georgia Real Estate Commission conducts in excess of 2,000 investigations per year. When a violation is found, the investigation almost always finds the respondent in violation of one or more of the following 36 Unfair Trade Practices. A Georgia real estate licensee would be prudent in studying this list, understanding how the violations occur, and developing a business practice to avoid these activities.

43-40-25 UNFAIR TRADE PRACTICES AND VIOLATIONS

This is possibly the most important section of the law, not only for the person preparing to take a Georgia licensing exam, but also for the practitioner. This section sets forth an expected code of conduct for licensees in the protection of the public and fair business practices. Adherence to these practices is not only mandatory by law, but just good business. Any person violating this section could be sanctioned in one or more of the following ways:

- refusal to grant or renew a license;
- a formal reprimand, which, while it may not seem like much, can be taken into consideration in any future hearings or investigations;
- suspension of license, which is considered temporary;
- revocation of license, which is permanent. While a person may be able to requalify for another license at a later date, this one is gone and will never be reinstated;
- revocation of license of a broker or associate broker with simultaneous issuance of a salesperson's license;
- a charge to the licensee to reimburse for expenses incurred in an investigation and hearing;
- imposition of a fine of not more than $1,000 per violation and not more than $5,000 per hearing;
- requirement that the licensee complete education;
- requirement of the filing of periodic reports by an accountant on the broker's trust account limit; or
- restriction of the licensee as deemed necessary to protect the public.

Violations of this code section are defined as follows:

1. Licensees must not treat people differently because of race, color, religion, sex, disability, familial status, or national origin. It would be hoped that by this time, this is no surprise. These are violations not only of license law, but also violations of state and federal fair housing laws.
2. It is wrong to advertise in such a way that is intentionally misleading or inaccurate. Although it is okay to make the truth sound fascinating, it must still be the truth. It is recommended that you set for yourself a standard that exceeds minimum requirements.
3. Failure to account for money that belongs to others is a violation. This is another one that should need no explanation or be a surprise. If someone gives an agent $5,000 in earnest money and the agent loses the money, the commission will have a problem with the conduct of the licensee and the concept of him/her having the ability to protect the public.

4. To commingle a licensee's money with that of a principal is never acceptable. Monies of others must be kept separate from our own funds, and the funds of others must not be used to pay our bills.

5. Failure to deposit funds held for another is also a violation. When a licensee accepts money from another, it is expected that the funds will be deposited into an escrow account as soon as reasonably possible. The exception to this is if the parties having an interest in the funds direct the broker in writing to hold the funds for a period of time before depositing. It is common in a sales contract that the broker is directed to deposit the money five days after the binding agreement date.

6. It is wrong to accept, give or charge undisclosed commissions, rebates, or profits on expenditures by a principal. The operative word is undisclosed. Referring a principal to an insurance company, inspector, lender, or contractor and then receiving a profit or rebate without disclosure is illegal. The moral is, if you're not sure, disclose. If you are going to miss, miss on the side of disclosure.

7. It is a violation to represent a broker who does not hold the license of the licensee without the express consent of the licensee's broker. A licensee may represent another broker on transactions that have not been completed when that licensee leaves the broker for another firm. This still requires express consent in the form of a written agreement between brokers.

8. To accept commissions from anyone other than the broker without the broker's consent is a violation. If a salesperson refers a buyer to his/her friend in another area of the state and there is a referral fee agreed upon, the fee must flow through the broker.

9. Undisclosed dual capacity is another violation. When a licensee enters into a contract as a principal, s/he must disclose both that s/he is licensed and is the principal; no straw purchasers. The question often comes up: "If I am an officer in a corporation and the corporation is the principal, do I have to disclose my involvement and licensure?" A good rule of thumb is, if you have to ask whether you have to disclose, the answer is yes.

10. Licensees cannot guarantee profits. You can say, "It may increase in value," "We hope it increases in value," or "Others have experienced an increase in value," but you must not say, "It will increase in value."

11. Placing a sign on property without written consent is a violation. This written consent is usually found in the listing agreement. This subsection also requires that the sign be removed within 10 days from the expiration of the permission.

12. Unauthorized offerings are another violation. A licensee must not offer property for sale or lease without consent of the owner, and must not offer the property except under terms authorized by the owner. For example, to

say the seller will take back financing from a purchaser without the owner consenting to the financing would be a violation.

13. Inducing a person to break a contract for the purposes of entering into another contract is also a violation. For example, if a licensee knows a broker offers a termination without penalty in his/her listing agreements and then proceeds to induce the seller to break the agreement with that broker so the licensee can list the property, that action will and should get that licensee in the jackpot.

14. It is a violation to negotiate directly with the client of another broker when possessing knowledge that an exclusive brokerage engagement agreement exists. For example, salesperson Sally with ABC Realty, representing a buyer-client, may not directly contact and negotiate with the seller-client of XYZ Realty. The exception to this would be if the brokerage engagement agreement states that the agent will not provide negotiation services to the client. If a seller wishes to purchase limited services from a broker that include marketing but not negotiating, the agent working with the buyer may negotiate directly with the seller. It is recommended that an agent in this circumstance working with the buyer receive written permission from the listing broker (either by remarks in the MLS or fax) and make a pointed and written agency disclosure to the seller.

15. Representing that work a licensee has completed or expressing that an opinion is an appraisal without first obtaining classification as an appraiser is a violation of this chapter. What a licensee does in the course of his/her work is sometimes very close to what an appraiser would do, but a real estate licensee may not indicate that the licensee is an appraiser without first gaining the education and certification through the Georgia Real Estate Appraisers Board.

16. If a Georgia licensee wishes to perform an act of real estate in another state, s/he must comply with that state's laws and rules. Failure to do so would not only be a violation of the laws of that state, but also a violation of this code section, and would subject the licensee to sanction by the commission.

17. Compensating a person for performing services of a real estate licensee without that person first becoming licensed is a violation. Think of the services of a real estate licensee as negotiating contracts or procuring prospects for a real estate transaction. If a friend or former client refers a prospect to a licensee, that licensee cannot pay a referral fee unless the friend or client is licensed. To do so would be paying a nonlicensee for procuring prospects. It is allowed, however, for a broker to pay a nonlicensed corporation that is at least 20% owned by one of the brokerage's licensees a commission on the behalf of that licensee as long as the unlicensed corporation does not conduct the acts of a licensee and there is a written agreement between the brokerage and the licensee. This allows a licensee of a brokerage to benefit from being treated as a corporation for tax and liability purposes.

18. All written listing agreements must have a definite expiration date. Also, failure to provide a copy of the agreement to the principal is a violation.
19. Failure to deliver within a reasonable period of time to all parties a copy of any offers or completed contracts to purchase is a violation. All offers on property must be presented to a client until such time that the transaction is closed. Even an oral offer must be presented as a material fact.
20. A broker must provide a closing statement to all parties in a transaction showing disbursement of all monies handled by the broker. Until 2005, a broker could conduct a closing. Currently, a closing in Georgia may be conducted only by practicing attorneys. This section was primarily applicable when the broker conducted the closing; however, because it survived the removal of the section allowing real estate licensees to conduct closings, the law is interpreted to mean that brokers are expected to ensure that all parties receive a copy of the closing statement, even if an attorney is conducting the closing.
21. It is a violation for a licensee to make a substantial misrepresentation. "Substantial" is not defined within this law; thus, this is somewhat of a catch-all.
22. Representing more than one party in a transaction (dual agency) is a violation if all parties have not provided written consent. Though not specifically stated in this section, the consent should be informed, meaning the situation has been explained and the parties understand the conflict.
23. Failure by a licensee to turn over to the broker as soon as practicably possible any funds s/he has accepted is a violation. There is no provision of this law or its accompanying rules that would allow a community association manager, salesperson, or associate broker to hold funds accepted on the broker's behalf for any period of time.
24. Filing a document for the purposes of clouding the title to property without a valid claim is a violation. For instance, a broker may not arbitrarily record a listing contract essentially creating a lien unless there was a valid claim. Georgia has a lien law in place for commercial properties, which is discussed in another chapter of this textbook.
25. Another catch-all violation is conduct that demonstrates dishonest dealing or incompetence to deal in a manner to safeguard the public. This violation could involve conduct specific or nonspecific to real estate. For instance, if a licensee has multiple driving infractions, which would demonstrate an inability to safely control a vehicle while showing property, the commission sees that as a violation of this code section.
26. Entering into a brokerage engagement, sales contract, or lease with a person while knowing that another broker has an exclusive brokerage engagement agreement with that person is a violation. For example, agent Bob is working in a subdivision selling new homes, and buyer Sally comes into the model home to request information. During conversation, Sally discloses to Bob that she has a buyer's agency agreement with Mark. Bob cannot induce Sally

to enter into a brokerage engagement or sales agreement with him, because to do so may make Sally liable for compensating two brokers. An exception to this would exist if the second broker (Bob) has written permission from the first broker (Mark).

27. A broker must maintain for not less than three years copies of all documentation related to any real estate transaction or closing. These include, but are not limited to, purchase agreements, listing agreements, closing statements, lease contracts, option contracts, and any records related to the maintenance of trust accounts.

28. Any falsification of contracts or other documents used in a real estate transaction is a violation. This could include creating second contracts to take to a lender to increase the loan amount (kiting); falsifying employment records to assist a buyer in qualifying; or creating the illusion of seller financing when the financing is going to be canceled after closing but failing to share this information with the lender (a silent second).

29. Prior to depositing money into an interest-bearing escrow account, the broker must obtain a written agreement from all parties indicating who shall receive the interest earned on the deposits. Failure to do so is a violation.

30. Any agency relationship that a licensee has with a party in a transaction must be disclosed in a timely fashion, which is typically considered to be as soon as reasonably possible. Timely is not necessarily at first meeting or contact. If a prospective buyer calls to inquire about a sign on a property, it might not be reasonable to disclose agency with the seller-client during that first contact. If the potential buyer hangs up as soon as s/he hears the price, there was no reasonable opportunity to make the disclosure at first contact.

31. Being licensed as a community association manager is kind of like being "licensed lite." This person is restricted to performing only acts within the limited constraints of that license.

32. This section requires a licensee who is performing community association management services to receive written permission of the association to enter into agreements with any of its members to sell, lease, or exchange the members' property.

33. This section makes it a violation for the community association manager to fail to provide to the association, within 30 days of termination of the community association management agreement or such time period as provided for in the management agreement, an accounting of all records used in the handling of trust funds and failing to return within the 30 days any documents provided by the owner.

34. This section makes it a violation for a property manager to fail to provide to the owner, within 30 days of termination of the management agreement or such time period as provided for in the management agreement, an

accounting of all records used in the handling of trust funds and failing to return within the 30 days any documents given to him/her by the owner.

35. A licensee changing the compensation of another licensee without prior written consent is a violation. It is common in the real estate business that a broker who lists a property for sale would offer to share the commission with another broker who can bring a buyer to the table. This is commonly referred to as a co-op, which is short for cooperation; two brokers work together to assist a buyer and seller in a real estate transaction. If ABC Realty has a listing and is offering to split its $10,000 commission with a cooperating broker 50/50, XYZ Realty could not arbitrarily change the commission to $14,000 so it could receive a larger compensation.

36. In the real estate business, it is not uncommon that a client/customer will have needs that cannot be fulfilled by a licensee due to knowledge, experience, or geography. If a licensee refers that client/customer to another licensee, the referring licensee must inform the client/customer of the referral and must also inform the client/customer if there will or will not be a referral fee paid for the referral. Failure to do so is a violation. For example, ABC Realty has the Valdosta property of Mr. and Mrs. Brown listed for sale. This is the Browns' personal residence, and they are selling to move to Augusta. ABC Realty can refer the Browns to a company in Augusta and receive a fee for doing so, but only after making proper disclosure.

If a licensee is brought before the commission for a violation of this code section, the commission may consider previous sanctions imposed on the licensee by the commission or other licensing authorities in determining the severity of the new sanction. For instance, if a licensee's violation is relatively minor and would typically cause the commission to reprimand, but the commission has already reprimanded the licensee twice in the previous 18 months, it might believe that a reprimand for minor violations is obviously not the answer and that it is time to crack down on the licensee.

A subset to this code section of particular importance is 43-40-25.1. This section allows licensees to complete listing contracts, sales contracts, and lease contracts so long as the form was prepared by legal counsel. The section states that this shall not constitute the practice of law. This obviously had been questioned in terms of whether a licensee should be allowed to negotiate contracts without being an attorney. As an industry, we want to protect this right and make sure that we do not cross the line and give what could be construed as legal advice. We want to make sure that this practice truly constitutes work incidental to our brokerage business. It would indeed be a sad day if real estate licensees no longer had the legal ability to negotiate contracts for clients and customers. This section also states that, when completing a lease or offer to buy, sell, lease, rent, or exchange real estate, a licensee is required to include a method of payment, a legal description, special stipulations as required by the situation, and dates as necessary to make sure the parties to the agreement meet their responsibilities.

Another subset to this section is 43-40-25.2. This section allows the commission to issue a citation without a hearing if, after investigation, it is apparent there has been a violation of this code. The licensee shall have 30 days to request a hearing, or the citation will stand. This gives the commission the ability to discipline without a hearing when both the commission and licensee agree there has been a violation.

43-40-26 HEARINGS

The commission shall provide a licensee with the opportunity of a hearing in accordance with the Georgia Administrative Procedure Act before censuring the licensee or suspending or revoking the license. If the licensee fails to appear for the hearing after proper notice, the hearing shall proceed as if the licensee were present. If a person disagrees with the findings of the commission, s/he is entitled to a judicial review in the superior court of the county where the commission is located.

43-40-27 INVESTIGATION OF COMPLAINTS

This code section states that the commission MAY investigate upon its own motion, but SHALL investigate upon a sworn written request of any person the actions of any licensee, instructor, or applicant for license. Unless the actions of the licensee involve serious violations of law, such as mishandling of funds or fraudulent conduct, or if the investigation involves activities that have been litigated in court, the commission shall not investigate unless the act or acts occurred within three years of the investigation. If the commission revokes or suspends a license, it may publish the name on the commission website.

43-40-28 INJUNCTIVE ACTIONS

The office of the attorney general for Georgia essentially acts as legal counsel for state agencies. In this code section, the attorney general may bring an injunctive action to stop acts and practices that the commission deems violate or will violate this chapter. For instance, if a person practices real estate without a license, the attorney general could bring action for that person to cease the activity and/or qualify for a real estate license.

43-40-29 EXCEPTIONS

The chapter has dealt primarily with the licensing of persons who perform acts of real estate in Georgia. Acts of real estate include negotiating contracts or procuring prospects for the listing, sale, lease exchange, or option of real estate. This code section outlines the exceptions to this chapter, the instances where a person can do acts of real estate for another without first obtaining a license. Currently, there are 14 such exceptions:

1. An owner, spouse of an owner, general partner of a limited partnership, or a person who manages apartments under a contract approved by a federal agency with an organization that is tax-exempt is exempt from licensure. For instance, Mary has inherited 150 acres of land with a farmhouse. Mary's husband, John, could negotiate the sale of the property on Mary's behalf without being licensed.

2. An attorney-in-fact under a properly executed power of attorney is exempt. If Mark was closing a sale of his property on Friday but was called out of town on an emergency, Mark could appoint his friend Sue as his attorney-in-fact to execute any necessary documents at closing, and Mark could compensate Sue for her time.

3. A practicing attorney acting solely incidental to his/her practice of law is exempt. An example would be an attorney who is contacted by a client to look over an offer to have a contractor construct a new home. If subsequently the attorney contacted the builder and negotiated some of the terms, the act of negotiating the contract is incidental to his/her practice of law and would not be in violation of this code.

4. A person acting as an officer of the court, such as an administrator, executor, or guardian, would be exempt if his/her acts were in the context of his/her authority. An example would be a trustee of the bankruptcy court carrying out the order of the court and disposing of real estate.

5. An employee of a government agency would be exempt. A person working for the Government Services Agency (GSA), whose job it is to locate office space for federal agencies, is an example of a person who would be exempt.

6. An employee of a public or private utility company would be exempt when doing acts of real estate for the utility company. An example would be an employee of Georgia Power whose job is to negotiate power line easements for the company.

7. An owner or a person who is a full-time employee of a person engaged by the owner of property is exempt from licensure. For example, ABC Development Inc. could engage Bob as a full-time employee to provide property management services for its office building on Peachtree Street in Atlanta. Bob could subsequently hire Martha as a full-time employee to help Bob in the management of the Peachtree Street property.

8. A full-time employee of the owner of property is another example. For instance, a person who is employed by a builder to sell only his/her properties would be exempt from licensure. This exception also includes a person

employed fulltime by a community association to provide community association management services.

9. A person may act as a referral agent and not be required to have a real estate license. The referral agent must not be involved in the contract negotiations or management of property; the activity must involve no more than the mere referral of one person to another; any fee paid may not be paid by the person being referred; there must be no advance fee charged; and the exempt party must not a referral agent in more than three transactions per year. An example would be a tenant living in an apartment complex. The unlicensed property manager could pay a referral fee to the tenant for referring a friend who enters into a valid lease.

10. Another person exempt from being licensed when providing the services of a licensee is a person employed by a broker when the broker has a written management agreement with an owner of property. This exemption comes with some restrictions, but this employee of the broker may provide many services if s/he is under the supervision and authority of the broker.

11. A person who is providing property management services for property not meant for permanent occupancy is exempt under very strict circumstances. The property must be available for less than 90 days; the agreement must not be a lease or rental; zoning laws must be complied with; the guest must pay any required state or local taxes and the manager must have obtained any applicable business licenses; there must be no separate charge for utilities; notice must not be required to terminate occupancy; and the space must not be the permanent occupancy of the guest. This exemption is primarily for people who work in extended-stay hotels.

12. Providing community association services to an association of which the person is a member is an exemption. For example, Karen is an owner in Pine Woods Subdivision. As its owner's association president, she provides what could be deemed community association management services; she may do so unlicensed so long as she is a member of the association.

13. A person who performs only physical maintenance on property is exempt. A person can mow your lawn, trim your hedges, and unstop your toilet and not have a real estate license.

14. A licensed certified public accountant acting solely incidental to his/her duties as an accountant is exempt from real estate licensure. An example would be an accountant explaining terms of a contract to a person on behalf of a client who is trying to effect a 1031 tax-deferred exchange of property.

The exemptions to licensure as provided in this code section do not apply to timeshare properties as defined in Title 44 of Chapter 44, to persons who have a license, or to persons who are using the code section to evade licensure. An individual who has a license and wishes to perform acts of real estate as an employee of the owner, such as a developer or builder, must surrender the license before providing brokerage services for the owner.

43-40-30 ACTING WITHOUT A LICENSE

A person providing acts as defined in 43-40-1 must first obtain a real estate license unless the person is exempt from licensure as stipulated in 43-40-29. Providing the services of a licensee without first obtaining a license is a violation of this code section, and the commission is empowered to issue a cease-and-desist order against such a person and impose a fine not to exceed $1,000 per violation, with each day of practice without a license being a separate violation. If one plans to operate as a licensee without first obtaining proper licensure, then s/he should bring a checkbook. Also under this section is the statement that the relationship between a broker and his/her affiliated licensees is at the discretion of the licensees involved. Nothing in this chapter shall be construed to establish the relationship as employer–employee or broker–independent contractor.

43-40-31 PENALTY

Any person found guilty of violating the provisions of this chapter shall be guilty of a misdemeanor.

Review Questions

Answers to these questions can be found in Appendix D at the end of this book

1. Which of the following most completely meets the requirements to become licensed as a broker in Georgia?
   A. Be 21 years old; have three years of active licensure; complete 60 hours of pre-license education; pass a state exam.
   B. Be 21 years old; have two years of active licensure; complete 75 hours of pre-license education; pass a state exam.
   C. Be 18 years old; have three years of active licensure; complete 45 hours of pre-license education; pass a state exam.
   D. Be 18 years old; no licensure requirement; have 75 hours of pre-license education; pass a state exam.

2. Which of the following is NOT true about members of the commission?
   A. They are all appointed by the governor.
   B. They all must be licensed for five years.
   C. Five of the six must be residents of Georgia for five years.
   D. Initial appointments are approved by the state senate.

3. Of the following choices, which is a violation of the license law?
   A. requiring a review of all offers within 30 days of creation
   B. requiring agents to attend training on license law and rules
   C. providing a written policy and procedure manual to all licensed affiliates
   D. allowing affiliated licensees to advertise without reviewing such ads, so long as the broker agrees to be responsible for any violation

4. The fees that a licensee must pay are:
   A. set by the commission and approved by the governor
   B. deposited into the state treasury
   C. set by the legislature and paid to the commission
   D. different for brokers and salespeople

5. Seller Miller has refused to pay broker Johnson a commission that Johnson feels has been earned. Which of the following best describes what Johnson must do to be successful in a lawsuit against Miller for the commission?
   A. Johnson must prove that s/he was properly licensed at the time of earning the commission.
   B. Johnson must prove that s/he had an exclusive brokerage engagement agreement with Miller.
   C. Johnson must prove that s/he was the procuring cause of the sale.
   D. Johnson must prove that s/he and any licensees who worked on Johnson's behalf were properly licensed at the time of earning the commission.

6. Smith has been damaged by the illegal acts of licensee Brown. The maximum amount that could be obtained from the recovery fund for the acts of Brown is:
   A. $10,000
   B. $25,000
   C. $75,000
   D. $60,000

7. Which of the following statements is TRUE concerning a broker's trust account?
   A. The account must be non-interest bearing.
   B. If interest-bearing, the buyer will receive the interest.
   C. The bank may be in or out of state.
   D. A broker must have one account and may have more, if approved by the commission.

8. If a licensee is found to be in violation of the license law, sanctions could include which of the following?
   A. a fine of not less than $1,000 per violation with a maximum of $5,000 per hearing
   B. a revocation of license for not greater than three years
   C. a reprimand, but only for first offenses
   D. revocation of the broker's license and simultaneous issuance of a sales license

9. A Texas broker wishes to do the acts of a licensee in Georgia but does not have a Georgia real estate license. Under what circumstances may the Texas broker come to Georgia to practice real estate and not be considered in violation of Georgia law?
   A. The Texas broker enters into a written agreement with a Georgia broker.
   B. The Texas broker receives a written "Agreement of Reciprocity" from the Texas Real Estate Commission.
   C. The Texas broker must receive written permission from the Georgia governor's office.
   D. The Texas broker must receive written permission from the commission.

10. Amy, a lifelong resident of Georgia, wishes to receive a real estate salesperson's license. To do so, Amy must:
    A. successfully take a state examination
    B. be at least 21 years old
    C. be a high school graduate
    D. complete a pre-license course of at least 60 in-class hours

11. According to the license law, the commission has the power to:
    A. modify the license law with rules and regulations
    B. set commission rates within usury limits
    C. impose and collect fees from licensees
    D. revoke the license of a person for doing acts of real estate without a license

12. A person providing community association management (CAM) services:
    A. must have at least a CAM license, unless the association has 50 or fewer properties
    B. must have at least a CAM license, unless exempt
    C. may also list and sell property in the community with a CAM license, if this is agreed to in the management agreement
    D. must provide an accounting of all records and funds within 15 days of termination of the management agreement

13. Which of the following would NOT be exempt from licensing under Georgia real estate license law?
    A. the spouse of an owner negotiating a lease
    B. a full-time employee of an owner working only for that owner in the sale of real estate
    C. a government employee who is procuring office space for governmental agencies
    D. tenants in an apartment complex who receive $50 from each person they refer to the complex, so long as they do not make more than three referrals per year

14. The commission receives a sworn written complaint against broker Dole for violations involving aggressive advertising. Which of the following is TRUE?
    A. The commission must investigate the complaint.
    B. Aggressive advertising is not a violation of law.
    C. Broker Dole may be fined but may not have his/her license revoked unless this is a recurring violation.
    D. Aggressive advertising is a clear violation of the law.

15. At a commission meeting, a vote ends up in a tie. What role does the commissioner have in this instance?
    A. The commissioner is empowered to cast a deciding vote.
    B. The commissioner, not being a member, may not attend commission meetings.
    C. The commissioner has no voting power.
    D. The commissioner has voting power, but only in procedural matters.

16. Of the following, which is a violation of Georgia license law?
    A. refusing to answer a client's question regarding the ethnic makeup of a neighborhood
    B. telling a prospect that values in a neighborhood may increase in the future
    C. entering into a listing with a seller with a five-year expiration
    D. placing a sign on property after receiving oral permission from the owner

17. Violations of license law are:
    A. felonies
    B. misdemeanors
    C. punishable by the commission, but not crimes
    D. always involving moral turpitude

18. A licensee may place his/her license on an inactive status:
    A. for no more than 10 years
    B. forever, so long as the licensee continues paying the renewal fees
    C. forever, but the licensee must pay all back fees if s/he reactivates
    D. only with the broker's permission

19. Phil, a salesperson with XYZ Realty, has begun a program of inducing past clients to refer their friends by agreeing to pay $250 for each referral that results in a sale. This program:
    A. is a common business practice and not a violation of license law
    B. is not a violation of license law so long as the fee is $500 or less
    C. is a violation of license law and would subject both Phil and XYZ Realty to sanctions
    D. is a violation of license law and would subject only Phil to sanctions

20. Carol receives a real estate salesperson's license in June 2007. What are Carol's obligations regarding post-license education?
    A. She must complete a course of study of at least 24 hours within two years.
    B. She must complete a course of study of at least 24 hours within one year.
    C. She must complete a course of study of at least 25 hours within two years.
    D. She must complete a course of study of at least 25 hours within one year.

21. Broker Sara sells a property that she personally owns to Mark. Sara's current loan requires payments of $600 per month for principal and interest, plus $175 per month for tax and insurance escrow. Sara agrees to finance the transaction for Mark using a wraparound mortgage, with Mark making monthly payments of $1,200 to Sara, inclusive of the escrow requirements. What obligations does Sara have in regard to the $1,200 monthly payment?
    A. Sara must place $775 of the payment into a trust account and make the first mortgage payment from that trust account.
    B. Sara must place the $1,200 payment into a trust account and pay the $775 first mortgage payment from that trust account.
    C. Sara has no obligation to place any money in a trust account because this is a personal transaction.
    D. Sara has no obligation to place any money in a trust account because she is a broker, not a salesperson.

22. Broker Jerry, who is not a nice person, steals client money from multiple people in multiple transactions: $22,000 from Sid, $18,000 from Mary, $25,000 from Sue, another $7,000 from Sid in another transaction, and, finally, $5,000 from Dick. What is the maximum potential liability of the Education, Research, and Recovery Fund?
    A. $25,000
    B. $73,000
    C. $75,000
    D. $77,000

23. Salesperson Fred, licensed with PDQ Realty, has an opportunity to go to work for Built Better Builders as an onsite agent. Built Better Builders does not use a real estate company to market its properties but, rather, employees. Which of the following is most true of how Fred must proceed?
    A. Fred must surrender his license if he wishes to work as an employee of Built Better Builders, and will have to requalify as an original licensee if he ever wants to become licensed again.
    B. Fred must surrender his license if he wishes to work as an employee of Built Better Builders, but may reinstate his license at any time in the future by paying the proper fees.
    C. Fred may place his license on an inactive status while working with Built Better Builders and then reactivate at a later date if he wishes.
    D. With written permission of the broker of PDQ Realty, Fred may continue to be actively licensed with PDQ Realty and work as an onsite agent employee of Built Better Builders.

24. The real estate license that most limits the actions of the licensee is:
    A. the community association manager's license
    B. the salesperson's license
    C. the associate broker's license
    D. none of the above; each license allows the licensee the same basic abilities

25. Under what circumstances could a broker file a contract to create a lien?
    A. if the closing date has passed
    B. only if the filing does not cloud the title of the owner
    C. if a valid claim exists
    D. under no circumstances

GEORGIA RULES AND REGULATIONS

CHAPTER 24

KEY TERMS

agency
citation
client
customer
firm
hearing
ministerial acts
post-license education
preliminary decision

OBJECTIVES

After successful completion of this chapter, you should be able to:

1. differentiate between a customer and a client;
2. discuss the requirements to maintain a real estate license;
3. explain how to reinstate a lapsed license;
4. define the management responsibilities of a real estate firm;
5. explain the use of unlicensed support personnel;
6. discuss the requirement for the maintenance of a trust account; and
7. describe the requirements of licensee advertising.

OVERVIEW

Rules and regulations differ from license law in that the rules are created by the Georgia Real Estate Commission, and the law is created by legislative action. The commission was created by law and then empowered to draft these rules, which sometimes repeat the law and sometimes amplify the law, but cannot change or conflict with the law. There are rules and regulations for schools, instructors, educational grants, and the investigation and hearing process. Our focus will be on the substantive regulations, which are found in 520-1.

The substantive regulations of the rules are primary in the business of a Georgia licensee. While other rules stipulate requirements for schools and instructors, outline the investigation and **hearing** process, set forth requirements for courses, and regulate the procedures for educational grants, substantive regulations oversee the daily life of the licensee. On the next few pages, we will study the rules section by section. We will take what can seem to be very technical language and explain in simple terms what is significant and what it means. We will also explain why the rules exist. As with the license law, the rules are dynamic and subject to change. While every reasonable effort will be made to keep the text updated, the publishing process of textbooks does not allow that to happen instantaneously. The student is always encouraged to look for up-to-date information on the commission's website at www.grec.state.ga.us. You also may subscribe to the commission's free newsletter on its website.

hearing: the formal process that must be offered to a person prior to imposing a sanction

We will look at the substantive rules by outlining information in each section. Remember, this is an overview of what is considered to be most significant. If you have further questions, or if anything seems out of context or incomplete, refer to the actual rules available on the website.

520-1-.01 ORGANIZATION OF THE COMMISSION

At the first scheduled meeting of the calendar year, the commission shall select from its members a chair and a vice-chair. In the absence of the chair at a monthly meeting, the vice-chair shall perform the duties of chair. At one time, there was a requirement that the chair have served at least one year with the commission; that requirement is no longer in effect.

In the event that a person would like to make an appearance before the commission at one of its monthly scheduled meetings, that person should make a written request. The first three persons or groups making such a request shall be heard. The presentation to the commission is limited to 15 minutes. At the discretion of the commission, others not scheduled may also be heard, with their presentation limited to five minutes. People or groups may wish to speak to the commission personally rather than write a letter because they have an issue that they feel can be best represented in person. If you think about it, people are never more influential than when they are face to face with other people.

If a person feels the need for a new rule or for an existing rule to be amended or repealed, s/he may provide a written statement to the commission; the statement must be signed and notarized. The commission then shall, within 30 days of receipt, provide a written denial with its reasoning or instigate procedures to adopt such a rule or revision. In the event that a person needs a clarification or insight into a rule, s/he may make a written request for a declaratory ruling from the commission. The request must be signed and notarized. Unless the commission feels the need to seek counsel from the attorney general, it will respond within 60 days of receipt of the request. Contrary to popular belief, it may be better to get permission before you act rather than hope for forgiveness afterward.

520-1-.02 DEFINITIONS

This section contains definitions for words used throughout the rules. Many terms are the same as are used in the law, such as broker, associate broker, commission, commissioner, licensee, person, and so on. The definitions become very important to all concerned when interpreting the meaning of the rules and the spirit in which they were created. Following are some of the definitions used in the rules.

Agency—A relationship created by express contract whereby a broker represents another person in a real property transaction. This is in reference to the relationship with a client rather than a customer.

Bank—A federally regulated financial institution that provides federally insured checking accounts. This will be important in the context of brokers' trust accounts.

Brokerage engagement—A written contract between a person and a broker whereby the person becomes a client of the broker. It is said, repeatedly and consistently, that brokerage engagements in Georgia must be in writing. The only way to become a client and legally receive client-level service is to sign a brokerage engagement. The definition in the rules is consistent with the definition in the law, but goes further in giving examples.

Client—A person who has entered into a brokerage engagement with a broker.

Customer—A person who has not entered into a brokerage engagement with a broker. The broker is limited to performing only ministerial acts for the customer. Everybody a licensee works with in a real estate transaction is either a client or a customer; the only way to become a client is by entering into a written brokerage engagement agreement. No written brokerage engagement, no client. It is amazing how many practitioners in the field still do not get it.

Dual agent—A broker who has a brokerage engagement with both parties in the same transaction. Regarded by many in the business as a recipe for disaster.

Firm—Any person licensed as a broker, whether it be a sole proprietorship, partnership, limited liability company, or corporation.

Franchise name—A name that requires the permission of another who has a right to the trade name. The firm that has the right to use the name is the franchisee, and the business entity that owns the trade name is the franchisor. This terminology becomes important in the advertising rules.

Ministerial acts—Acts that do not require discretion (confidentiality) or adjudication (the exercise of judgment, the provision of advice).

---

agency: the relationship between a broker and a client

client: a person who has entered into a brokerage engagement

customer: a person who has not entered into a brokerage engagement

firm: any individual or entity licensed by the commission as a broker

ministerial acts: acts that do not required discretion or adjudication

Timely—A reasonable time under the circumstances. Each situation will be different, and communication will be the key. What may be reasonable to one may not be reasonable to another; it is best to communicate so all are singing from the same page of the same hymnal. If the commission or court has to determine whether the time limits were reasonable, everybody loses.

520-1-.03 COMMISSION OPERATIONS

Upon written request, the commission will provide a certification of history of a licensee's records for only the immediately preceding five years, unless there is disciplinary action, in which case the commission will provide that history regardless of the date of occurrence. In the event that the commission investigates the actions of a licensee, the investigative files shall be maintained by the commission for 40 years if there was any disciplinary action or payment from the recovery fund, and 15 years for all other investigative files. In the event that a licensee surrenders his/her license or the license is suspended or revoked, the licensee shall immediately forward his/her wall license and pocket card to the commission. If the license is a broker's license, the broker shall also forward any wall licenses and pocket cards in the broker's possession. Upon license surrender, suspension, or revocation, the commission does not prorate or refund any fees paid by the licensee. Any person whose license has been revoked or surrendered must qualify as an original applicant to receive another license.

520-1-.04 OBTAINING A LICENSE

Since the primary purpose of the commission is to protect the public through the licensure of those involved in the defined acts of real estate, this rule section is pretty involved. As with the entire discussion on the laws and rules, it is the intent here to simplify and minimize.

To activate a license, an applicant shall pay an activation fee of $45, which includes the $20 fee for the Real Estate Education, Research, and Recovery Fund. Once activated, the license of an individual is good until the last day of the licensee's birth month four years later, and it can be renewed in like four-year periods with payment of a $125 renewal fee. The renewal fee is reduced to $100 if the renewal is submitted online. This code section also allows for the assessment of additional fees, from $25 for failure to notify the commission of a change of address within 30 days to $100 for submitting a bad check to the commission. For a complete list of fees, see rule section 520-1-.04(1).

As was discussed in the law, a candidate for a broker's license must have at least three years of licensed experience within the previous five years to qualify. But what if the candidate was licensed in another state? Would that time count toward the three-year requirement, or does the commission require that the licensed experience occur in Georgia? The answer is, the experience from another licensing jurisdiction does apply so long as the candidate can provide certification from the licensing authority. (The commission uses the term *licensing jurisdiction* rather than *state* to allow the possibility of using experience while licensed in another country.) There are alternative forms of certification available to the candidate, such as copies of transaction files or an affidavit from a broker for whom the candidate had worked.

In addition to age, education, and experience requirements needed for licensure, one must also pass a state examination. There is a credit available for candidates for licensure who have served in the armed forces of the United States and were honorably discharged. Licensure candidates who have served at least one year, of which at least 90 days came during a period of wartime, are eligible to receive a 5-point credit on their examination to become licensed. If candidates have a service-connected disability of at least 10%, they shall be eligible to receive a 10-point credit. For example, if a qualifying veteran scores a 72 on an examination requiring a minimum score of 75, 5 points can be added to the score to obtain a passing grade. Candidates seeking the preference points must present proper documentation, which is the DD214 if service was after 1949.

A candidate for licensure who moves to Georgia from another state may be exempt from examination and education requirements if the candidate can supply the commission with certification from a licensing body proving that s/he passed an examination for licensure equivalent to the license for which the candidate is applying; has met all education requirements of that state; is licensed in good standing; and has not had any formal disciplinary actions. In addition, this section of the rules states that the supplying of information from the examination is grounds for denial of license or any other sanctions permitted under the law. A school or instructor is also prohibited from obtaining test information from examinees, accepting it, or using it. In addition, a person may not take the examination to obtain information from the exam.

Application for licensure must be on forms approved by the commission and may be filed with the commission by personal delivery, U.S. Postal Service, private courier, or facsimile transmission. The effective date shall be the date postmarked or the date received by the commission if not mailed. In accordance with the Americans with Disabilities Act, the commission shall provide reasonable accommodations to candidates for licensure. In addition, the commission shall maintain all paper applications for licensure for 15 years and maintain all other paper records for a minimum of one year. All electronic records shall be maintained for 15 years.

Any person who has successfully taken a licensing examination shall have 12 months from the date of examination to activate the license. Candidates for the community association manager's license or salesperson's license must activate within three months of successfully taking the examination or the license fee doubles. When applying for the license, the candidate must also provide a Georgia Crime Information Center (GCIC) report that has been issued in the previous 60 days. This report can be obtained for a small fee from most police stations, sheriff's offices, or probate courts. Whenever an applicant for licensure has had a criminal conviction or has been disciplined by a licensing agency, the applicant shall supply the commission a certified copy of the citation or allegations and a copy of the sentence or final order of the licensing agency.

Also included in this section about obtaining a license is the requirement that a firm operate under the name in which the license is issued. If a firm wishes to use a trade name, it must certify the trade name with the clerk of the county and submit the certification with its application for licensure. If the trade name of a franchise is being used, in addition to the name of the franchise, there must also be the firm's name or trade name, which clearly distinguishes the company from any other.

An individual with a past that includes criminal convictions, disciplinary proceedings, or other behavior that s/he feels may make him/her ineligible for licensure may make a request for a **preliminary decision** from the commission before spending the time and money to become eligible for a license. The preliminary decision is not binding, but it is a good indication as to whether the commission will approve an applicant. If the commission denies a license based on prior convictions or disciplinary action, it must provide the applicant with an opportunity for a hearing before the commission. The request must be made within 60 days of the commission's mailing of the notice of denial to the applicant. If, after the hearing, the denial of license is affirmed, the applicant may not apply for licensure again without first passing the state examination and paying any fees. It is recommended that whatever kept this person from being licensed the first time be fixed, or the person should expect the same results the next time.

preliminary decision: issued by the commission after proper request of a licensure candidate to help determine the candidate's eligibility to receive a license

520-1-.05 MAINTAINING A LICENSE

While the last rule section dealt with getting a license, this section deals primarily with keeping it. The first thing required to keep a salesperson's license is completion of **post-license education**. This course must be approved by the commission and contain a minimum of 25 hours of education. The course must be taken no earlier than one year prior to licensure and no later than one year after licensure. While this may seem odd, the reason is to enable individuals who have limited opportunities to complete the post-licensure education first if it is available. In the event that the license lapses due to failure to complete the post-license course within one year of licensure, the licensee may reinstate according to 43-40-8.

post-license education: the 25-hour course of study that must be completed within one year by all original salesperson licensees

As was stated in the law {O.C.G.A. 43-40-8(e)}, all Georgia licensees who become initially licensed after December 31, 1979, prior to renewal, must complete at least six hours of continuing education per year of licensure. All licensees subject to the continuing education requirement who have renewed their license since June 30, 2015, have been required to complete a minimum of 36 hours of continuing education. In addition, since July 1, 2016, licensees subject to the requirement have had to show that they have completed at least three hours of continuing education in license law.

Licensees other than a broker may be licensed under only one Georgia broker at any time. If licensees wish to affiliate with a nonresident broker, they may do so, provided that state allows affiliation in both states and they receive written permission from the Georgia broker. Upon original application for licensure, licensees may not begin work until their broker has received their wall license. Licensees who have their license released by a broker may not engage in activities of real estate until they affiliate with a new broker and mail the application to the commission or, if they wish to serve in a broker capacity, receive the wall license from the commission. Licensees wishing to activate an inactive license must have satisfactorily completed the continuing education requirements that would have been required if such licensee had been on active status or requalify as an original applicant.

Active licensees who wish to perform brokerage activities for another must do so as a broker or on behalf of a broker. In the event that a licensee wishes to use the exemptions allowed by 43-40-29, the licensee must first surrender his/her license, and if the licensee wishes to become licensed again, s/he must requalify as an original applicant. All licenses of individuals lapse on the last day of the birth month every four years, and licenses of a firm lapse on the last day of the anniversary month every four years.

A license can lapse for nonrenewal or failure to complete education. If a license that is exempt from continuing education lapses for more than one year, upon reinstatement, that license shall thereafter be subject to the continuing education requirements. If a license lapses for two years or less, the licensee may reinstate by paying all back fees, late fees, and reinstatement fees and by taking any required continuing education. If the license lapses for more than two years, but less than five years, the license may be reinstated by paying all back fees, late fees, and reinstatement fees and by completing the pre-license education required for the license being reinstated. A licensee may also opt to complete any required education and pass the state examination rather than pay all the back fees, which can be substantial. Any person whose license has lapsed for more than five years must requalify as an original applicant to receive another license. In the event that a licensee wishes to reinstate a lapsed license or activate an inactive license, the licensee may not engage in real estate activity until the wall license is received by the affiliated broker.

Any time a licensee is involved in an administrative, civil, or criminal action outlined in the law, the licensee shall notify the commission in writing of the final disposition within 10 days of the conclusion. The notice shall include the indictment, accusation, and conviction. A licensee who becomes a resident of another state may place his/her license on inactive status or apply for nonresident status. If the license is that of a broker, that broker may be the qualifying broker of any firm licensed by the commission. If a Georgia licensee wishes to perform any acts of real estate in another state, the licensee must first become licensed in that state or comply with that state's laws.

In the event that a licensee who retires after 20 years of active licensure or the family of a deceased licensee wishes to retain a copy of the wall license and pocket card, a written request may be made to the commission.

520-1-.06 BROKERAGE RELATIONSHIPS

All exclusive brokerage engagement agreements must have a definite expiration date, and each person who signs shall receive a true copy. A true copy is generally considered to be one created by the same stroke of the pen: a photocopy or a carbon copy. For instance, if a salesperson took two forms and filled both out and had the seller sign each and gave the seller one, that would not be a true copy; something could be different in the copy given to the seller, even if it was a mistake.

Also, net brokerage engagements are prohibited. A net engagement is one that does not have a gross listed price. For example, if a seller wanted to net $160,000, a broker could not list the property guaranteeing the seller the $160,000 and taking as commission anything generated above that amount. What the broker could do is add the commission to the net and list the property at the gross price. If the broker's commission on this type of property is $10,000, the property could be listed for $170,000, with the broker receiving $10,000 in commission and the seller receiving the remaining $160,000.

The rules require certain provisions in a written property management agreement. Those provisions include:

- identification of the property;
- inclusion of all terms and conditions of the management agreement;
- a statement of the terms and conditions under which the broker will remit income to the owner and provide periodic written statements of income and expenses. The periodic statements must be provided at least annually;
- a specification of what property expenses will be paid by the broker;
- the amount of compensation for the broker;
- the person who will hold any prepaid rent or security deposits;

- the effective and termination date of the agreement;
- terms and conditions for termination; and
- signatures of the parties.

When a broker is providing community association management services and s/he collects or has access to more than $60,000, the broker shall be covered by a fidelity bond or fidelity insurance. This bond or insurance shall:

- be written by a company authorized to write in Georgia;
- cover the maximum amount that the broker shall have access to at any one time but shall not be less than three months' assessments of all members plus reserve amounts;
- name the association as an additional insured;
- cover any person or persons who have access to the money; and
- not be terminated without a 30-day notice unless it is for nonpayment, in which case, it can be a 10-day notice.

A separate bond or insurance shall be maintained for each association, a copy shall be maintained by the broker, and a copy shall be provided to the association.

Another sensitive issue for the commission in protecting the public is disclosure of brokerage relationships. If a licensee buys, sells, or leases property for himself/herself, the licensee must clearly disclose his/her position as principal in the transaction and insert a clause in the contract stating that position and that s/he is licensed.

A licensee must also make a written disclosure that reveals for whom the firm is acting as agent and from whom the licensee will receive compensation. This written disclosure must be made in a timely manner, but no later than the time of an offer. This rule section also requires that if a licensee is going to pay a fee to another licensee who represents another party, this must be done with full knowledge and written consent of all parties. For example, if a listing broker is going to share commissions funded by the seller, all parties must be notified and agree in writing. This is usually preprinted in the listing agreement.

520-1-.07 MANAGEMENT RESPONSIBILITIES OF FIRMS

This rule section governs the duties of brokers, qualifying brokers, and firms. First, the rule requires that brokers conduct their business in the name under which the license was issued. That might seem pretty simple, but it could become critical. The use of cute names or names that limit the firm or identify it specifically with particular areas or property types should be well thought out. For instance, naming the firm "ABC Residential Properties" may be a hindrance if the company wishes to expand into commercial real estate.

A broker is responsible for the acts of any licensees affiliated with the firm and for training licensees on the license law and rules. The broker shall also notify the commission of any violations. In addition, the broker is responsible for making sure that each licensee with the firm enters into a written agreement that states how the licensees will be compensated while with the firm, and also how they will be compensated for work that has begun but is not yet completed when they leave the firm. The commission does not dictate what the compensation should be, but it is requiring the written agreement so that it does not get pulled into compensation disputes between brokers and their licensees. It is funny how just a few thousand dollars can make some people do things you did not think possible.

In the event that a qualifying broker leaves a firm, the firm must obtain a new qualifying broker within 60 days. The qualifying broker is the person ultimately responsible for the actions of the firm and its licensees, and this person may serve as the qualifying broker for multiple firms. A licensee who is serving as an associate broker may serve as the qualifying broker for one or more other firms so long as s/he informs his/her broker in writing of his/her intention. So if Sally, who is an associate broker with ABC Realty in Macon, wants to serve as the qualifying broker of XYZ Realty in Blairsville, where she has a mountain cabin and spends many weekends, she may do so after making written notification to the broker of ABC Realty.

There are also rules that must be followed when a licensee leaves a broker. There is no provision in the law or rules for a broker to refuse to transfer a licensee upon request. If the licensee owes the broker money, the broker must transfer the license upon request and then may sue if s/he wishes; if the licensee has done something illegal, the broker must transfer the license upon request and may file a sworn, written complaint with the commission; if the licensee has done something unethical, the broker must transfer the license upon request and then may file a grievance with the Board of REALTORS®, if the parties are members. Upon transfer, the release shall be signed by the qualifying broker or by an associate broker who has the written permission of the broker. After signing the release, the broker may send the wall license and release to the commission or notify the commission in writing that the license has been forwarded to the new broker. If the transferring broker sends the wall license to the commission, the licensee may request that the license be transferred to a new broker or request that the license be placed on inactive status. Either decision must be made within one month of the license being released from the firm. If a broker wishes to release the license of an affiliated licensee and that licensee cannot be located, or for any reason the licensee cannot or will not sign the transfer, the broker shall mail a letter to the licensee's last known address informing the licensee that the license is being sent back to the commission. The letter must state that the licensee has one month to transfer the license to another broker or go inactive, and a copy of the letter must accompany the release sent to the commission.

Also contained in this rule section are requirements about handling items provided to the licensee by the broker when s/he leaves the broker. The rule requires that any written brokerage engagements entered into while with the broker belong to the broker, and that the transferring licensee may not have any contact with clients of the firm without written permission from the former broker.

This portion of the rule also requires the licensee to account for the names of any clients or customers provided to him/her by the firm and return in person any ". . . plats of property, keys, and other property which the releasing broker owns or for which the releasing broker is responsible, 'for sale' signs, notebooks, listing cards, or records of any kind that have been used in connection with the listing or selling of property. . . ." The written agreement mentioned earlier must also provide how this obligation will be fulfilled.

If a licensee of a broker wishes to hire a support person, s/he may do so, but both the broker and the licensee will be responsible for the actions of this person. If a broker decides to allow a licensee to hire a support person, then there shall be a contract between the broker and licensee authorizing the use of the support person, stating the duties of the support person, and approving the compensation agreement. There also must be a written agreement between the broker and the support person and one between the licensee and the support person specifying what duties the support person may engage in. Unless licensed, the support person may not perform any duties of licensure; s/he may perform only ministerial acts. There is a noninclusive list in the rule that identifies some of the duties the support person may and may not perform.

Duties s/he *may* perform include:

- answering the phone;
- assembling closing documents;
- having keys made and installing and removing lockboxes;
- writing advertisements (which must be approved);
- typing contract forms;
- computing commission checks (one of the things I enjoy doing myself);
- placing and removing signs;
- acting as a courier;
- scheduling appointments
- scheduling open houses;
- accompanying a licensee to an open house or a showing only for security purposes; and
- physically maintaining the property (my personal favorite).

Duties the unlicensed support person *may not* perform include:

- making cold calls;
- hosting open houses;
- showing property;
- discussing or explaining contracts with anyone outside the firm;
- negotiating commissions or fees;
- discussing the attributes or amenities of a property with a prospect;
- collecting or holding deposit monies or rents; and
- providing advice, recommendations, or suggestions to clients or customers concerning the sale or lease of property.

520-1-.08 MANAGING TRUST ACCOUNTS AND TRUST FUNDS

Another area of concern for the commission is the handling of other people's money. Licensees can expect particular scrutiny in this area when audited by the commission. Neither the law nor rules require a broker to maintain a trust account unless s/he has on deposit the money of others. There are some brokers, such as exclusive tenant representatives, whose practice would not include holding security deposits or earnest money. If a broker decides to maintain a trust account (or is required to), s/he may have multiple accounts so long as the commission is notified of the name of the bank and the account's name or number within one month of opening.

Licensees who work for a broker are required to turn all valuables received over to the broker as soon as practicably possible after receipt. There is no provision in the law or rules that would allow a community association manager, salesperson, or associate broker to maintain custody of the money for any period of time. There are some licensees who want to hold the earnest money that has been deposited with an offer until final acceptance and binding agreement. This is a violation if the licensee is not a broker. The broker must deposit the money as soon as practicably possible after receipt unless all parties having an interest in the money have agreed otherwise in writing. It is common for a provision to be contained in an offer authorizing the broker to deposit the earnest money several days after the binding agreement date. This is so the broker can give any earnest money back to the potential buyer immediately if the negotiations fail. In the event that a licensee receives money belonging to others on the sale or lease of properties owned by the licensee, including security deposits on rental properties, these monies must be deposited into the trust account of the broker or a trust account approved by the broker.

In the event that a broker wishes to maintain an interest-bearing trust account, prior to depositing funds into the account, the broker shall obtain a written agreement of all parties stating to whom any interest earned on the deposit shall be disbursed. The trust account is for the deposit of money that belongs to others, but there are specific and strict circumstances under which the broker may have his/her own money in the account, in addition to the interest earned. There are three specifically:

1. to maintain a minimum deposit required by the bank;
2. to cover service charges required by the bank; or
3. to be converted to a commission if agreed to by the parties.

Every month, the broker must remove money from the trust account if it exceeds the amount required to maintain the minimum balance or to cover service charges. The commission has detailed requirements on the accounting system used for trust accounts. It requires that the broker maintain precise records, which include:

- the name of parties with an interest in the deposit;
- the amount and date of deposit;
- an identification of the property involved; and
- the amount, payee, and date of each check drawn.

Once a transaction closes, the total of all checks written against deposits must reflect a zero balance. In addition, the broker is required to produce a written reconciliation statement at least monthly, and if the reconciliation does not balance with the bank statement, the reconciliation must explain any discrepancies and actions taken. When brokers renew their licenses, along with the renewal application, they shall submit a summary of data on the trust account(s) and a report from a certified public accountant, both of these on forms required by the commission. If brokers wish to claim any portion of money paid to them in trust as commission, the transaction must have been closed. If it is a lease, possession must have been delivered. If it is a lease/purchase, the specified date of closing or extensions must have passed, or the broker must have a written agreement signed by all parties with an interest in the money that the broker is entitled to the commission. In the event that a licensee who owns a trust account files for bankruptcy, the licensee shall immediately notify the commission in writing of the bankruptcy petition. Copies of all documents related to the trust account must be made available to the commission upon reasonable request and at reasonable cost to the commission.

When a broker manages properties for owners or holds funds as a community association manager, there are additional restrictions. One is that if the broker is paying bills on behalf of an owner, there must be enough money credited to the owner's account to pay the bills. Also, if security deposits are being kept, there must always be a balance at least equal to the amount of security deposits being held. A final thought on this subject: there is no specific rule or law that requires separate trust accounts for earnest money held in sales and security deposits held on rental property. If a broker provides services in both sales and leasing of real estate, the broker may keep earnest money and security deposits in the same account so long as there is proper accounting.

The final portion of this rule section regulates when funds from the trust account may be disbursed. In the event that a broker disburses funds in a manner contrary to the contract, the broker shall be deemed to have demonstrated an incompetence to interact with the public in a manner that safeguards the public.

In the Field

If one were to read the disbursement section of 521-1-.08 carefully and properly interpret it, while a broker will have fulfilled his/her obligations as far as the commission is concerned, the broker will not be getting a free pass with the civil courts. If a broker disburses money in accordance with this rule, while the commission may say the broker properly complied with the rule, the courts could still find the broker responsible if the court thinks the money was disbursed to the wrong person. It is always prudent to get the opinion of legal counsel before disbursing funds if they are in any way being contested and and if not all parties have agreed in writing.

There are seven specific circumstances under which the broker may disburse funds from a trust account and be deemed by the commission to have fulfilled his/her duties:

1. *upon rejection of the offer*—It is suggested that the licensee receive a written rejection from the seller before disbursal. The seller could simply write REJECTED across the face of the form and sign and date it;
2. *upon withdrawal of the offer*—Again, it would be before any funds are disbursed to have this withdrawal in writing and verify that it has been communicated before any acceptance of the offer;
3. *at closing*—The buyer offers, the seller accepts, and there is a closing of the agreement. This is when we prefer to disburse earnest money;
4. *upon the separate written agreement of all parties with an interest in the trust funds*—If this transaction doesn't close, this should occur before disbursal;
5. *upon the filing of an interpleader*—Essentially, this is a lawsuit against both parties (buyer/seller; landlord/tenant). This might be used if there is no agreement as to disbursal, the contract is not going to close, and there are legal technicalities that make the broker uncomfortable about making a

decision. The money and contract are sent to the court; the court, it is hoped, makes the decision;

6. *upon court order*—If one of the parties files suit and the court orders the broker to disburse, the broker has no choice but to follow the court order; and

7. *upon reasonable interpretation of the contract*—For instance, if the contract is contingent upon the buyer's ability to obtain financing, if s/he has lost his/her job, if s/he has complied with all provisions of the financing contingency, and if s/he has been denied by a lender, the broker may feel comfortable under the circumstances simply returning the earnest money. A broker must not disburse funds without reasonable assurance that the bank has credited those funds to the account, and if the broker makes a disbursal to which all parties have not expressly agreed, the broker must notify all parties in writing of the disbursal.

In the Field

While a broker is required to supervise a licensee and approve all advertising, that does not always occur. A common violation in this unsupervised environment is advertising. ALL advertising by a licensee is subject to this rule, including website, social media, emails, etc. Advertising by licensees is being scrutinized by the GREC, and the prudent agent will make sure all advertising complies.

520-1-.09 ADVERTISING

This is a rule section that has been subject to change over the last few years and will probably see more changes in coming years. The rule regulates any type of advertising done by or for a licensee and includes any form of media that is a promotion to the public. An area that has been somewhat of a challenge for the commission is internet and social media marketing. As the internet and social media have become a routine part of our daily lives—and that is unlikely to change—a licensee must be ultra-careful to disclose in all communications to the public the fact that the communication is from a real estate licensee. As has been my position in other circumstances, if you have to even ask yourself whether you must disclose, the answer is yes. If you are going miss, miss on the side of disclosure. Although not currently required by law or rule, providing the real estate license number in any advertising when possible and reasonable is a step toward greater transparency.

It should be obvious that any misleading advertising is prohibited. While puffing is not misrepresentation, a licensee should be careful to make sure his/her statements are not and cannot be misunderstood by the public. While it is all right to make the truth sound fascinating, the statement must be the truth. Advertising also must not be in reference to or directed toward a person or persons of any particular race, color, religion, national origin, sex, handicap, or familial status. Be careful in making any references about classifications of fair housing, but, when deemed appropriate and needed, talk about the property, not about the person. For instance, advertise the property as being "handicapped-accessible" or "wheelchair ramps installed," NOT "perfect for the handicapped" or "easily accessible for those in a wheelchair." Remember, all advertising by salespersons, associate brokers, and community association managers must be done in the name of the licensed broker and under that broker's direct supervision.

The advertising of property by a licensee requires written permission of the owner or the owner's agent. Within our industry, specifically through the National Association of REALTORS®, licensees enjoy an agreement called Internet Data Exchange (IDX). With this agreement, ABC Realty can make available to the public information about properties listed not only with ABC Realty, but also with any broker who allows the exchange of data. When this information is made available on a website, there must be permission from the listing agency as well as a conspicuous disclosure that the information is being provided through a reciprocal agreement with another broker, and a disclosure of the identity of that broker, unless the listing broker has waived the disclosure. With this agreement, consumers can enter the website of a broker and have available literally all properties in the market in which they are interested, regardless of who the listing broker may be. This allows the consumers to truly be served and provides value-added service by the industry. When placing advertising of properties on the internet, a licensee must update outdated information or remove the advertising within 30 days of that advertising becoming outdated. Recognizing that aggregators of internet information have become common, this rule releases the licensee from liability if outdated information is present that was not placed by the licensee, but, rather, gathered by the aggregator. When advertising specific properties, licensees must observe additional regulations from this rule section. On all advertising of specific properties, the name and telephone number of the firm must appear in at least equal size, prominence, and frequency as the name or telephone number of an individual licensee or group of licensees. If the name of the firm includes a trade name or franchise name, the name of the broker as registered with the commission must be included. When a trade or franchise name is used, there must be a unique identifier. For example, if the franchise name is 3rd Millennium, brokers could advertise as 3rd Millennium ABC Realty and 3rd Millennium XYZ Realty, but not simply as 3rd Millennium. This rule was created because some licensees were advertising in a way that confused the public and the public was unable to figure out the identify of the listing firm or how to communicate with management of the firm, if needed.

Any advertising by a licensee must be under the supervision of the broker and in the name of the broker. No advertising can be executed in such a way that the members of the public do not reasonably know that they are calling a licensee when responding to the advertisement. An advertisement without proper disclosure is known as a *blind ad*. Any property listed with a broker may only be advertised in the name of the broker. However, when licensees advertise properties in their own name, which is not listed with a broker, they must:

- notify the broker in writing, if they are actively licensed with a broker, of their intent to advertise the property;
- disclose in the advertisement that they own the property and also include the statement, "seller, buyer, landlord, tenant (select appropriate title) holds a real estate license" or, as an alternative, include the disclosure, "Georgia Real Estate License #000000." As an alternative to "Georgia Real Estate License #," "GA R.E. Lic" may be substituted; and
- receive written permission from the broker for the advertisement, if the licensee is affiliated with a broker.

520-1-.10 HANDLING REAL ESTATE TRANSACTIONS

As has been stated before and is confirmed here, offers must be presented as soon as reasonably possible. What this rule section actually states is, "... promptly tender to any customer or client any signed offer ... ," but in other parts of the law, this concept is expanded, and any offer, whether written or not, must be presented until closing. Even if a seller has accepted an offer on the property and it is scheduled to close in the next week, if another offer is received, it must be presented to the seller. This would provide the opportunity to the seller to negotiate a backup contract with the second purchaser. It is also required that any offers provide the license numbers of any participating firms and licensees and that any individual signing receives a copy of the document that has been signed. Once the document has been fully signed and accepted, a copy must be provided to each person and each firm.

Copies of all documents used in a transaction must be maintained by the broker for at least three years. Brokers may use whatever storage system they deem appropriate so long as they can produce a true and correct copy for the commission upon reasonable request and at reasonable cost. This storage system might be maintaining paper copies of all documents or scanning the documents and maintaining them on film, tape, or other electronic media.

Any representation made in a transaction that is false or has the intent to deceive is a violation. This may involve stating a false sales price or lease payment; a false down payment, amount of earnest money, or form of down payment or earnest money; or any other false statement. For example, providing a fraudulent contract to a lender that represents a sales price in excess of the actual sales price is known as kiting and is illegal. Assisting a purchaser in any way to falsely represent to a lender that a property the buyer owns is leased and that s/he is receiving lease payments to help him/her qualify for a loan to purchase a property is a violation. To know a purchaser is representing to a lender that an investment property is going to be owner-occupied to qualify for favorable financing is a violation. In short, do not falsify, mislead, or misrepresent with any artifice, contrivance, or machination.

520-1-.11 LICENSEES ACTING AS PRINCIPALS

In the event that a licensee working for a broker wishes to buy, sell, or lease a property in his/her own name or in the name of an entity such as a corporation in which s/he has an interest, s/he must first notify his/her broker in writing. As was stated in 520-1-.09, the licensee must receive written permission from the broker for any advertising that is used.

If a licensee offers to buy or lease a property as an inducement to enter into a brokerage engagement agreement or to enable a person to buy or lease another property, the licensee must first enter into an agreement with the party that expresses all terms and conditions of the purchase or lease. A common example of this is a "guaranteed sale." If a licensee is inducing an owner of property to enter into a listing agreement with him/her by offering to purchase the property at the end of the listing if it does not sell, the licensee must enter into the purchase agreement with the seller first, showing the price and terms of the purchase. If John, the broker of ABC Realty, has made a presentation to owner Pam on her property on Elm Street, and to entice Pam to list, John offers to buy her property at the end of the 120-day listing if it does not sell, John must first enter into the purchase agreement with Pam, showing her the terms and the price that he would be willing to pay. This would allow Pam to make a decision based on fact rather than perception if John is not going to pay full price and cash for the property.

520-1-.12 BUSINESS BROKERAGE

There are people and companies that specialize in selling business interests rather than real estate. Oftentimes, however, the sale involves ownership of real estate or leases to real estate. Unless s/he is otherwise exempt by 43-40-29, when a business broker negotiates the sale of a business that involves the transfer of real property, the business broker and any of the broker's associates involved in the negotiations must be properly licensed by the Georgia Real Estate Commission.

520-1-.13 FAIR HOUSING

This rule section is consistent with federal fair housing law, Georgia fair housing law, and real estate license law. It is a violation to treat a person or persons differently based on race, color, religion, national origin, sex, handicap, or familial status. Violations would include:

- making statements that the makeup of a neighborhood is changing based on a protected class or that the presence of a protected class would cause lower

property values, an increase in criminal or antisocial behavior, or a decline in the quality of area schools;
- denying housing based on protected classifications;
- discriminating against a person based on a protected classification in the facilities or services in connection with a property;
- refusing to accept or transmit offers based on a protected classification;
- refusing to negotiate based on a protected classification; and
- representing that housing is not available or refusing to permit a person to inspect housing accommodations based on a protected classification.

520-1-.14 CITATIONS

When the commission determines by investigation that the law or rules have been violated, it may impose a sanction after completing the hearing process, or it may issue a **citation**. Think of a citation as a plea bargain in the criminal court system before a trial. This process saves time and money and often results in a lesser penalty than would be imposed by sanction after a hearing. A citation may require the completion of education, the filing of periodic reports by an independent accountant, or the paying of fines not to exceed $1,000 per violation with a maximum fine of $5,000 per citation in the event that there are multiple violations. This rule section also stipulates maximum penalties for specific violations. These maximum penalties range from $100 (for failure to turn over trust funds as soon as possible, failure to include financing terms in a sales contract, or failure to provide a copy of a document used in a transaction to any individual signing) to $500 (for failure to reconcile a trust account at least monthly, failure to handle trust funds as required by the law and rules, or failure by a school to have a student complete the required number of hours or to complete all exercises or examinations required).

A citation issued by the commission becomes final when 30 days have passed since the date of service of the citation, unless the parties reach an alternative agreement or the licensee requests a hearing. Unless the order prescribes a different timetable, the licensee must meet any requirements in the citation within 30 days of the effective date. In the event that the commission initiates a hearing, the parties may continue to negotiate and agree to the issuance of a citation and have the hearing dismissed. In the event that a licensee is sanctioned by the commission in a contested case, the commission may not consider any prior citations if the licensee has fully complied with the terms of the citation. For example, if a licensee was being sanctioned in 2019 for violations of 43-40-25, the commission could not consider a citation issued in 2014 in imposing the current sanction, so long as the licensee fully complied with the 2014 citation.

---

citation: issued by the commission as a penalty instead of imposing a sanction

Review Questions

Answers to these questions can be found in Appendix D at the end of this book.

1. Which of the following is NOT an acceptable way to notify the commission of a name or address change?
   A. by personal delivery to the commission's office
   B. by email to the commission's office
   C. by letter postmarked by the U.S. Postal Service
   D. by private courier

2. How long does a candidate for a broker's license have to activate the license after passing the examination without retaking the examination?
   A. 3 months
   B. 6 months
   C. 12 months
   D. 24 months

3. What is the post-license education requirement for salespersons?
   A. 25 hours within the first year of licensing
   B. 25 hours within the first year after passing the examination
   C. 24 hours within the first year of licensing
   D. 24 hours within the first year after passing the examination

4. Under what circumstances must a broker who provides community association management services maintain a fidelity bond or fidelity insurance?
   A. A broker must always maintain a fidelity bond or fidelity insurance to protect the public.
   B. Only if the broker has access to more than $60,000.
   C. Only if the broker has access to less than $60,000.
   D. A broker never has to maintain a fidelity bond or fidelity insurance.

5. A broker must conduct business under what name?
   A. the name as registered with the secretary of state
   B. the name as shown on the birth certificate
   C. the name shown on the certificate of trade name
   D. the name on the license as issued by the commission

6. Which of the following acts may NOT be performed by an unlicensed support person?
   A. collecting rent money
   B. placing and removing signs
   C. ordering repairs as directed by the licensee
   D. writing advertisements for the approval of the licensee and supervising broker

7. A broker who deposits funds into a trust account may disburse those funds:
   A. only upon the closing of the transaction
   B. upon acceptance of the offer
   C. upon reasonable interpretation of the contract
   D. upon demand by either party with an interest

8. Which of the following must be included when a firm is advertising a specific property?
   A. the name of the firm, the name of the qualifying broker, and the firm's telephone number in equal or greater prominence than that of any salesperson
   B. the name of the firm, the name of the salesperson, and the salesperson's telephone number in equal or greater prominence than that of any salesperson
   C. the name of the firm, the firm's telephone number, and the firm's mailing address in equal or greater prominence than that of any salesperson
   D. the name of the firm and the firm's telephone number in equal or greater prominence than that of any salesperson

9. If a licensee is instructed by a seller-client not to present any offers below $150,000 and an offer for $135,000 for the property is presented from another firm, what is the best course of action for the licensee?
   A. Follow the instructions of the client and reject the offer.
   B. Disregard the seller's instructions and present the offer.
   C. Tell the other company to go back to its buyer and get an offer for $150,000 or greater.
   D. Tell the other firm that you do not have the authority to reject the offer but that you cannot present the offer, either.

10. Which of the following is true of a declaratory ruling?
    A. Once issued, a declaratory ruling has the same effect as law.
    B. Declaratory rulings are issued by the commission and approved by the attorney general.
    C. A request for a declaratory ruling may be made verbally, but it is recommended that it be made in writing.
    D. The signature of the petitioner for a declaratory ruling must be notarized.

11. A brokerage engagement:
    A. must be in writing and witnessed
    B. is between a broker and a client
    C. is between a broker and a customer
    D. may be oral or in writing

12. The commission will provide a certification of license history only for the previous:
    A. 5 years
    B. 7 years
    C. 10 years
    D. 15 years

13. If a candidate for licensure has his/her application denied by the commission and s/he disagrees with that decision, s/he must make written request for a formal hearing within:
    A. 30 days
    B. 60 days
    C. 90 days
    D. 180 days

14. How long does a candidate for a salesperson's license have to activate the license after passing the examination without retaking the examination?
    A. 3 months
    B. 6 months
    C. 12 months
    D. 24 months

15. Sue is issued an original license from the commission on November 15, 2014. Unless renewed, that license will expire on:
    A. November 15, 2018
    B. Sue's birthday in 2018
    C. December 31, 2018
    D. The last day of Sue's birth month in 2018

16. After making an original application for licensure, a salesperson may not begin work for a broker until:
    A. the commission has mailed the license to the broker
    B. the broker has received the wall license
    C. the salesperson has received the wall license
    D. the salesperson has completed the post-license course of study

17. Randy, who is a legal resident of Tennessee, could become a licensed salesperson in Georgia:
    A. only by becoming a legal resident of Georgia
    B. by meeting the age, education, and examination requirements
    C. only if he is currently licensed in Tennessee
    D. by entering into an agreement with a Georgia broker

18. Alice, a Georgia licensee, moves to Chicago. What options are available to Alice?
    A. Alice must surrender her license or go inactive.
    B. Alice may place her license on inactive status or maintain licensure as is.
    C. Alice may place her license on inactive status or apply for a nonresident licensure.
    D. If Alice does not surrender her license, she must place it on nonresident status.

19. Of the following, which is NOT a requirement of a written management agreement?
    A. The agreement must state the compensation to be paid to the broker.
    B. The agreement must contain the effective date and termination date.
    C. The agreement must provide that the broker will provide written statements of property income and expenses not less than annually.
    D. The agreement must be signed by either the broker or the owner.

20. Laura is the qualifying broker of XYZ Realty and Associates, Inc. Laura has three offices and 68 salespeople in the company. Which of the following is a true statement?
    A. Laura can be the qualifying broker for ABC Realty at the same time as she is the qualifying broker for XYZ Realty and Associates, Inc.
    B. Laura must have a qualifying broker for each branch office.
    C. Laura is responsible for the actions of the agents within her firm if they are employees, but not if they are independent contractors.
    D. Laura cannot require the salespeople to attend training on license law and rules if they are independent contractors.

CHAPTER

25

GEORGIA PRACTICE

KEY TERMS

boycotting
Brokerage Relationships in Real Estate Transactions Act (BRRETA)
community association manager (CAM)
closing disclosure
Commercial Real Estate Broker Lien Act
Georgia Property Owners' Association Act
Georgia Time-Share Act
listing presentation
loan estimate
monopoly
price fixing
Real Estate Settlement Procedures Act
tie-in (or tying) agreement

OBJECTIVES

After successful completion of this chapter, you should be able to:

1. describe the requirements of BRRETA;
2. define brokerage engagement, subagency, dual agency, and designated agency;
3. describe the information needed to make a listing presentation;
4. explain Georgia's Commercial Real Estate Broker Lien Act;
5. define the buyers an agent must, should, and should not represent;
6. explain the functions of property management; and
7. define and explain antitrust violations.

OVERVIEW

While practicing real estate in Georgia shares many similarities with practicing across the nation, differences do exist. In this chapter, we will take an in-depth look at the law in Georgia that regulates the agency relationship between the broker and the client. We will then discuss the working relationship with sellers and buyers,

including marketing property and writing and negotiating contracts. There will be a discussion on property management and then the nuances of financing in Georgia. The specifics of community association management will be explained, and then we will describe and explain antitrust laws. Finally, we will have a brief discussion of timeshare properties and the impact of the Georgia Time-Share Act.

It is anticipated that the primary use of this work will be in preparation to successfully take a state examination and ultimately be licensed to practice the profession of real estate in Georgia. A portion of that examination is a section titled "Georgia Practice." The focus of this segment of the examination is how a licensee in Georgia would properly act and react in certain circumstances. Much of the information we will present is a review of content previously covered; remember, repetition is the mother of learning. Also included is a more in-depth look at agency, as well as a discussion of Georgia's agency law. Finally, some of the content reveals the day-to-day responsibilities of a licensee, such as the duties of a licensee from contract to closing.

WORKING WITH CLIENTS; WORKING WITH CUSTOMERS

The heart of any real estate transaction is the way we interact with the parties involved. Historically, the real estate industry as a whole has been confused about the concept of agency. This confusion became evident in the 1970s when the Federal Trade Commission conducted a study and found that well more than half of all buyers in a real estate transaction thought the agent they were working with represented the interest of the buyer. A similar number of sellers in these transactions also misunderstood and thought the selling company represented the interest of the buyer. Sadly, this was almost never the case. Legally, it was the duty of the selling company to represent the interest of the seller through subagency. This confusion continued, and in the late 1980s and early 1990s, there was a multitude of lawsuits for misrepresentation, breach of agency duty, and undisclosed dual agency. This culminated with a suit out of Minnesota, which changed our industry. It also changed how the real estate business is practiced in Georgia. In 1994, the state legislature passed a law that governs and codifies agency in Georgia. This law, the **Brokerage Relationships in Real Estate Transactions Act (BRRETA),** was revised in 2000 and today provides guidelines and protections for the consumer and the licensee. Let's take a closer look at this law.

BRRETA: Brokerage Relationships in Real Estate Transactions Act; governs real estate agency in Georgia

BROKERAGE RELATIONSHIPS IN REAL ESTATE TRANSACTIONS ACT (BRRETA) 10-6A

The core of this Act is the definitions. BRRETA defines a *client* as "a person who is being represented by a broker . . . pursuant to a brokerage engagement." A *customer* is "a person who is not represented by a real estate broker . . . for whom a broker may perform ministerial acts . . . ." A *brokerage engagement* "means a written contract wherein the seller, buyer . . . becomes the client of the broker...." *Ministerial acts* refer to "acts which do not require the exercise of the broker's... professional judgment or skill."

To put these terms in useful context, every person a licensee comes into contact with in a real estate transaction is a customer until such time as that person becomes a client. The only way to become a client is to enter into a written brokerage engagement agreement. Put simply, no brokerage engagement, no client. It is amazing how many licensees still do not seem to understand this. Giving the buyer a client level of service without a signed brokerage engagement agreement would be considered a violation of BRRETA. To a customer, a licensee can provide only ministerial acts that do not involve providing advice or exercising knowledge or skills to his/her benefit. The client we work *for*; the customer we work *with*. It is appropriate to provide the client with advice and adjudication of information; to a customer, the licensee will give information without advice. A client has the right to expect confidentiality; a customer does not. Working within the confines of law is required and creates value-added service for the client.

BRRETA also defines *material facts* as "those facts that a party does not know, could not reasonably discover, and would reasonably want to know." When working with a client, we are required to disclose all material facts, which is just about everything. If you are not sure whether to disclose, miss on the side of disclosure. If you are going to be accused of anything by a client, be accused of giving too much information, not failing to disclose. For example, Georgia rules and regulations require a licensee to present all signed offers. What if a buyer will make only an oral offer because the buyer does not want to waste his/her time if an unmotivated seller will not be reasonable? Must the offer be presented? The short answer is yes. The existence of an oral offer would meet the requirements of a material fact: The seller-client does not know about the offer, could not reasonably discover the existence of an oral offer on his/her own, and would want to know. Sellers typically want to know everything. The rule is, present all offers until closing and give the seller-client the opportunity to negotiate a backup contract.

An interesting nuance of BRRETA is in 10-6A-4. The relationship between the broker and the client is not deemed to be a fiduciary relationship unless the parties agree to such in writing. The reason for this is that Georgia defines a fiduciary relationship as one that requires extraordinary skill, knowledge, and ability. If an agent does not meet the requirements as created by law or contract, that agent is negligent in the discharge of duties. The burden of meeting a requirement of extraordinary knowledge and skill is almost impossible. Theoretically, an agent under this requirement would be guilty of negligence in almost every transaction. BRRETA protects the broker from this unreasonable standard by stating that the broker is "only responsible for exercising reasonable care in the discharge of its specified duties...." If a broker provides advice to the client and the client feels harmed by that advice, the client would have to show that the advice given was not up to a standard that is reasonable and ordinary of a licensed real estate broker.

BRRETA sets forth requirements of a broker representing a client in a transaction in code sections 10-6A-5, 10-6A-6, 10-6A-7, and 10-6A-8. These code sections are specifically for sellers, landlords, buyers, and tenants, respectively. As the basic requirements of how to treat clients are the same, there is a great deal of similarity in these sections, so we will explain them as one. When engaged by a client, a broker shall do the following:

1. perform the duties set forth in the brokerage engagement;
2. seek a buyer, tenant, or property suitable for the client at a price and terms that are acceptable;
3. present all offers in a timely manner;
4. disclose material facts;
5. advise the client to seek out expert advice in matters beyond the expertise of the broker;
6. account for all money in a timely manner;
7. exercise reasonable skill and care; and
8. keep information confidential that is made confidential by express request.

Beyond the generic requirements of representing a client, whether that client is a seller, buyer, landlord, or tenant, there are additional considerations when that client is a buyer or tenant. If the client is a buyer and the seller is being asked to provide the financing, or if the transaction is financed through a loan assumption, the broker must disclose to the seller all material facts concerning the buyer's financial ability to perform the terms of the sale. In these circumstances, a buyer's inability to make payments would be similar to a defect in the property and has to be disclosed, even if the disclosure proves harmful to the client. Also in these circumstances, and in the case of a residential property, the broker must disclose the buyer's intent to occupy the property as a principal residence. If the client is a tenant, the broker must disclose to a landlord any adverse material facts concerning the tenant's financial ability to perform the terms of the lease or intent to occupy.

A broker is required to disclose to all parties in a transaction:

1. *Adverse material facts pertaining to the physical condition of the property.* The broker is liable to disclose only if the broker possesses actual knowledge of defect and if such defect could not be discovered by diligent inspection. This provides substantial protection to the broker and puts some responsibilities on consumers to inspect and familiarize themselves with a property, neighborhood, and market.
2. *The existence of adverse physical conditions in a neighborhood.* The disclosure requirement is limited to within one mile of the property, and the broker is

liable to disclose only if the broker possesses actual knowledge of neighborhood defect, and if such defect could not be discovered by diligent inspection of the neighborhood and available government information such as land use maps, zoning ordinances, tax maps, floodplain maps, and school district boundary maps. This code section provides additional protection to the broker if s/he provides false information to a consumer.

Brokers are not liable for false information if they did not know the information was false at the time of providing it and they supply the source of the information. For example, if a broker told a person that, according to the tax records, the property taxes for the previous year were $2,400, the broker would not be liable for misrepresentation if the records were in error and the taxes were actually $4,200, since the broker had given the source of the information.

In addition to requiring that brokerage engagements be in writing, code section 10-6A-9 states that the engagement continues until performance, expiration, or agreement to terminate. In the event that the engagement does not have a set date of expiration, the agreement shall terminate in one year. According to Rule 520-1-.06(1)(a), exclusive brokerage engagements must have definite expiration dates so the one-year requirement would apply only to a nonexclusive (open) engagement. This code section also states that if a broker is in conflict between his/her duty to maintain confidentiality and his/her duty not to give false information or misrepresent, the duty not to give false information is the greater duty. For example, if a buyer-client tells the broker not to disclose his/her poor financial position when negotiating a contract where the seller is being asked to finance a portion of the purchase price, the broker would be in conflict between the duty of confidentiality and the duty to disclose this material fact. The duty to disclose is the greater duty, so the broker would have to share the financial information with the seller.

Code section 10-6A-10 requires that all brokerage engagement agreements contain an office brokerage policy. This policy will include:

1. advising the prospective client of the types of agency relationships available through the broker;
2. advising the prospective client of any brokerage relationship that would conflict with the interests of the prospective client. For instance, if the prospective client is a buyer and is looking for investment property, and the broker is also looking for similar investment property for his/her own portfolio, this should be disclosed so there is no perception of a conflict of interest;
3. advising the prospective client of compensation and whether the broker will share any compensation paid by the client to another broker who represents another party in the transaction. For example, if the listing broker intends to share any commission paid with a selling broker who is representing the buyer, this disclosure must be made in the brokerage engagement; and

4. advising the prospective client of the broker's obligation to keep information confidential when such information is made confidential.

10-6A-11 reminds us that the payment of a commission has nothing to do with the creation of an agency relationship. The misunderstanding of this concept is what caused the fiasco of subagency some years ago. Many people felt that since the selling broker was sharing a commission paid by the seller, then the selling broker must represent the seller. This concept proved to be a disaster.

Code section 10-6A-12 sets forth the duties of a broker in dual agency. If a broker seeks to act as an agent for both parties in a transaction, there must be an informed, written consent of the clients. Informed consent can only be provided after all relevant information needed to make a conscious choice has been divulged. Dual agency obviously brings with it conflict. What does the broker do about the duty of full disclosure and confidentiality? To maintain confidentiality, one cannot make full disclosure. To maintain full disclosure, one must breach confidentiality. This conflict must be disclosed and the broker relieved of his/her duty of full disclosure as it relates to confidential information. The principals to the dual agency must also sign stating that they do not have to consent to the dual agency and that they are doing so voluntarily. Many brokerage firms today discourage dual agency, and this code section requires that the broker develop, enforce, and disclose the firm's dual agency practice. It is my guess that dual agency as we know it will one day be a memory.

As an alternative to dual agency, 10-6A-13 allows for designated agency. In designated agency, there is one broker and two clients, but the broker designates different associates to represent the individual position of each client. While this code section stipulates that this is not a dual agency for the broker or affiliated licensees, a prudent broker will be very careful with policies and practices if this is allowed. Imagine a broker who has a policy of sharing information at sales meetings to help motivate the staff. Vick, one of the firm's agents, with the inducement and blessings of the broker, relates the story at a sales meeting of a difficult negotiation on her listing on Elm Street. She tells all, including intimate details about the negotiation and how the seller finally agreed to a sales price of $275,000 even though the property was listed at $299,000. Five days later, the prospective purchaser loses his job and cannot qualify. The property is put back on the market at $299,000. Ten days later, Jack, a fellow agent (who was at the sales meeting and heard how the seller on Elm Street had accepted an offer of $275,000), has a buyer-client who would be interested in the Elm Street property. Jack is required to make full disclosure to the buyer-client, including the prior negotiation since this is actual knowledge possessed by Jack. The disclosure of this information will be harmful to the seller, but that is not Jack's concern, as the seller is not his client. A broker who has a policy of offering designated agency should never allow such a conversation among the affiliated licensees. The broker must anticipate this type of scenario and protect the firm's clients from having their negotiating position compromised.

There are also times when it is appropriate for the firm to represent no one in the transaction. This is known as a transaction broker and is allowed by 10-6A-14. As a transaction broker, the licensee owes to the parties only ministerial acts and the disclosure of adverse material facts. This may come as the result of a licensee wanting to help an acquaintance. For example, Fred contacts Mary, who is a salesperson with ABC Realty, asking for help in completing a transaction. On a whim, Fred advertised his property for sale and now has an interested party. Fred is like a dog chasing cars: If it catches one, it doesn't know what to do. Mary could offer Fred and the buyer guidance and charge a fee for her time in shepherding the transaction to closing, but may not feel comfortable taking on an agency role for either party. In this situation, ABC Realty would be a transaction broker.

Now that we understand BRRETA, we can apply this to practice in the field. Within the confines of this law, a brokerage firm can implement an agency policy that would include any or all of the following seven choices.

SINGLE AGENCY SELLER AGENCY

In this case, the firm would exclusively represent the seller and not have a brokerage engagement with the buyer. In pure seller agency, a firm would never enter into a brokerage engagement agreement with a buyer, thereby almost eliminating the possibility of dual agency. For example, ABC Realty has a business model and mission statement that allows the agents of the firm to represent sellers only. The firm will enter into listing agreements with sellers and then market that property to consumers interested in purchasing property, as well as to other firms that have a relationship with buyers. In either case, the exclusive client for ABC Realty is the seller, and the buyer or the cooperating broker would be treated as a customer.

SINGLE AGENCY BUYER AGENCY

This is essentially the opposite of seller agency. The firm enters into a brokerage engagement with the buyer, and in pure buyer agency, would never list properties and represent the seller in the marketing of the property. Again, this would virtually eliminate dual agency. For example, XYZ Realty has a business model and mission statement to be the best company in its market area representing the interests of consumers wishing to purchase residential real estate. According to policy, XYZ Realty would never enter into a brokerage engagement with a seller, and will pursue properties for the buyer-client and treat sellers and sellers' agents as customers.

SINGLE AGENCY CO-OP

Many firms today would view pure seller agency or pure buyer agency as being too restrictive. These firms do not want to potentially give up half of the business in their market, so they have a policy that the firm will represent both buyers and sellers, but not both in the same transaction. In this scenario, there would be two firms, each representing a single client. For example, if ABC Realty has entered into a brokerage engagement with seller Sara and XYZ Realty has entered into a brokerage engagement with buyer Bob, the two firms could engage in a negotiation on behalf of their respective clients. While the commission is typically split between brokers, the loyalty is always owed to the client, and the client is always the person who entered into the brokerage engagement with the firm. Most licensees would agree that this method of practice is the most comfortable and most fair, and it leads to the least amount of conflict.

DUAL AGENCY

While most firms would agree that single agency co-op is the most comfortable agency situation, that does not mean it is without potential conflict. Consider this scenario: Suzi is an agent with ABC Realty and has a listing of property on Elm Street owned by the Millers. The list price is $200,000. Through a referral from a former client, Suzi begins to work with prospective buyers, Mr. and Mrs. Stanton. After a consulting session, Suzi learns that the Stantons do not want to spend more than $150,000 on their new home. Suzi has no listings that would meet the Stantons' needs, so she agrees, through ABC Realty, to represent them as a buyer. After Suzi shows the Stantons almost 20 properties, the Stantons realize that they will be very unhappy with what $150,000 will buy in this market and agree to spend more money, up to $220,000. Suzi thinks the Elm Street property would be perfect for them but she did not consider it earlier because of the Stantons' expressed financial limit. If Suzi shows the Elm Street property to the Stantons, would this create a dual agency? The answer is a resounding yes! Licensees must always be mindful of situations that could cause a dual agency and have policies and procedures to handle the conflict. One suggestion may be to explain to both parties and receive permission to show the property. If the Stantons are not interested, no harm, no foul. If the Stantons do want to pursue the Elm Street property, offer to refer both the Millers and the Stantons to other agents who do not have loyalty and confidentiality conflicts. Suzi can still take a substantial referral fee, and the agents to whom she refers the clients can be within ABC Realty, if the company allows designated agency. This policy would cost Suzi a little money in the short term, but she gets to keep her integrity in the long term. That is a good thing!

DESIGNATED AGENCY

BRETTA says that designated agency is not a dual agency, but prudent brokers will treat it as such to protect themselves. In the above dual agency scenario, if Suzi's broker designated Mark to represent the interest of the Millers, and Carol to represent the interest of the Stantons (both Mark and Carol are licensed affiliates with ABC Realty), this would constitute a designated agency. But to whom do Mark and Carol go with questions if they need help in this negotiation? Of course, they go to their broker, who is one and the same. This can tend to put the broker in the jackpot! Again, understanding this, brokers and agents need to be experienced and be able to think ahead to see where their decisions may land them. The law of laws is cause and effect: Each decision made causes something else to happen. We must be able to predict the effect of our actions and understand the impact, not just in the short term, but in the long term, as well.

SUBAGENCY CO-OP

In subagency co-op, there are two brokers representing the seller. The listing broker is the primary agent for the seller, and the selling broker is an agent of the listing broker, and, as such, has a subordinate relationship to the seller. This subordinate relationship makes the selling broker a subagent for the seller. The scenario could look like this: Tom, a salesperson for ABC Realty, is servicing the listing of Mr. and Mrs. Jones on Maple Street. Nicole, a salesperson for XYZ Realty, is helping Mr. and Mrs. Miller find a property to purchase but does not have a signed brokerage engagement agreement with the Millers. Through a multiple listing service (MLS) search, Nicole locates the Joneses' property, in which she thinks the Millers would be interested. ABC Realty has a policy of offering subagency, and XYZ Realty has a policy of accepting subagency, which would make XYZ Realty an agent of ABC Realty and a subagent of the Joneses. This creates a situation that may be best described as emotionally confrontational. Intellectually, Nicole knows that her loyalty is to the seller, but emotionally, she feels that she should be assisting the Millers, as they have become all but her new best friends. This leads to inappropriate behavior, bad decisions on the part of the subagent, and, ultimately, to unintentional, unrecognized, undisclosed, and illegal dual agency. While subagency is legal, it is all but extinct in the field.

TRANSACTION BROKERAGE

As a transaction broker, the firm has no client. The choice here is to treat everyone as a customer. For example, Barbara is a salesperson for ABC Realty and has been talking to Mark, who is an investor. Mark will not enter into an exclusive brokerage engagement with any firm, and ABC Realty has a policy of representing clients exclusively. According to company policy, Barbara can work with Mark as a customer but not enter into an agency relationship. Bill, an acquaintance of Barbara's, calls and tells her he is contemplating selling a property and will protect her if she has a buyer who would be interested. Barbara immediately thinks of Mark and how this property would perfectly fit his needs. She enters into a commission agreement with Bill and, with permission, shows the property to Mark, who agrees that it is ideal and wants to make a full-price offer immediately.

Barbara can help the parties from contract to closing and have only a customer relationship with both. The only thing that is different is the disclosures and level of service the parties will receive.

WORKING WITH SELLERS

It has often been said that property listings are the lifeblood of the real estate industry; you list to last! While buyer representation has taken hold and created a new business model, it cannot be denied that a broker must have properties available to sell for any real estate transaction to take place. Somebody must be serving sellers and marketing property for this business to work. The process of listing property begins with prospecting for property owner who desire to sell their properties and need the services of a real estate broker. This prospecting can take many avenues, such as contacting for sale by owners (FSBO), telephone solicitation (be aware of and honor Do Not Call registries), email solicitation (before starting this, research the CAN-SPAM Act regulating commercial email), working a sphere-of-influence list containing the names of people you know and/or have done business with in the past, and simply meeting and greeting people as you go about your daily activities. There are many courses and seminars available to help you learn effective prospecting techniques.

Listing Presentations

Once a lead has been obtained, the agent should make an appointment with the property owner to conduct a **listing presentation**. This can be done as a one-step or two-step presentation. In a two-step process, an appointment is made with the property owner to meet and gather information needed to give an informative and impressive presentation in a second meeting. Information gathered may include such things as:

listing presentation: the organized presentation of information to a seller organized in five sections

1. loan information (This will assist in completing a seller's net sheet. Also available is a loan information form, which, once signed by the seller, can be sent to the lender, authorizing the lender to supply the broker with such loan information as balance, interest rate, term, and any penalties.);
2. age of improvements;
3. condition of improvements;
4. a survey of the property showing size, shape, and boundary lines;
5. a warranty deed giving the names of the owners, the form of ownership, proper spelling of the owners' names, and a sufficient legal description (Typically, the best place to get a legal description is from the seller's warranty deed or seller's security deed. Caution must be taken, however, as there are circumstances under which the legal description in the seller's deed is not appropriate, such as when the seller is not selling the entire parcel or the seller has previously sold a portion of the property. In situations such as

these, the licensee should consult with his/her broker to receive guidance on how to proceed.);

6. the seller's motivation; and
7. the seller's expectations of the listing agent and company.

Whether this information is gathered in a face-to-face meeting with the owner or completed through telephone questions and online research, the next step is to prepare an informative and unique package of information to present to the owner. The listing presentation may be divided into five sections:

1. Why have the property marketed professionally?
2. The benefit of having the property marketed by our company
3. The benefit of having the property marketed by me
4. The marketing plan
5. The paperwork

In the first section of the presentation, "Why have the property marketed professionally?," the goal is to build rapport and share with the owner the benefits of having his/her property marketed by a real estate company. The agent should ask questions of the owner to discover the level of experience, motivation, primary needs, and objections. If the owner indicates an immediate desire to list the property, this will be a short phase.

The second section of the presentation, "the benefit of having the property marketed by our company," begins to tell the story of the company and matches company assets and programs with the needs discovered in the first section. As in step one, if the owner is predisposed to listing the property with you, this phase can be short. Do not, however, shortchange yourself by making assumptions. Unless the owner has made an undeniable commitment to you and your company, make sure the owner knows the benefits.

In the third section, "the benefit of having the property marketed by me," the presentation becomes more specific regarding your strengths. Again, match your strengths with the needs discovered during the first section, and sell the benefits. Providing testimonials from previous satisfied clients, statistics to show a pattern of success, and a resume (as if you are applying for a job, which is exactly what you are doing) are good ways to sell the potential client on your value. As in the previous sections, if this is a past client, someone you know, or a strong referral, this phase may be minimized.

As we move to the fourth section, "the marketing plan," you must take your time and be sure that there is effective communication between you and the owner. Many of the problems in the field attributable to marketing property and interacting with sellers can be traced back to a lack of communication at the time of listing. Left to their own interpretation, sellers create expectations well beyond the intent or ability of the agent or company. The agent should explain to the seller the plan of exposing the property through advertising in local publications, internet presence, fax broadcast, MLS, signage, and any other method offered. This is also a good time to present a competitive market analysis to assist the owner in properly pricing the property. In this analysis, focus should be given on properties that have sold and closed in the last year and are similar to the subject, as well as properties that are currently for sale in the market area and are similar to the subject. The sold properties indicate what the subject may sell for, and the listings tend to set an upper limit of value. Because of the principle of substitution, it should not be expected that buyers would pay more for a property than what they would have to pay for an equally desirable substitute. If not done earlier in the presentation, this also would be the time to have a discussion about agency and educate the owner about issues that will directly affect them, such as the showing of the property by agents of cooperating brokers.

The last section of the presentation, "the paperwork," is also critical to getting the relationship off to a good start. This final phase may include a seller's net worksheet so the seller will understand how much money to expect to receive at closing after any loan payoffs and expenses; a profile sheet to submit to the MLS that details the property information; a loan information letter to be sent to the lender to get specific information about the loan; and the brokerage engagement agreement. The brokerage engagement (listing) agreement should be explained thoroughly and signed by all parties, and a copy must be left with the seller. In explaining the brokerage engagement, take care to explain the company agency policy, which is required by BRRETA.

While having documents signed by the parties may seem simple enough, there are challenges. If the property is owned by a husband and wife, a man has no automatic authority to sign for his wife, nor does a woman have automatic authority to sign for her husband. If a person is signing for a spouse, a power of attorney must be executed first, transferring the authority to sign and make decisions to the attorney-in-fact. The power of attorney should then be attached to the document and made part of the file. If the seller is a corporation, the agent should ask for a copy of the corporate resolution and maintain a copy for the file. The corporate resolution will authorize the corporation to sell property and indicate who can sign for the corporation. If the seller is a partnership, the agent should ask for a copy of the partnership agreement and retain it in the file. Typically, any general partner can sign for and bind a partnership.

Seller's Property Disclosure Form

Another document that is often completed at this time, but is not required by Georgia law, is a Seller's Property Disclosure form. This document informs the potential buyer of the history of the property and makes a written disclosure of any known latent defect. The agent should NEVER assist the seller by completing the form or even acting as a scribe. When property is sold "as is," that simply means there is no warranty or guarantee of the condition of the property being made by the owner. "As is" has no effect on the seller or seller's agent's duty to disclose defect; any known latent defect has to be disclosed, period.

Defect can sometimes be challenging to define. BRRETA provides guidance on the requirements to disclose defect within a neighborhood, but what about a property on which a murder, suicide, or heinous crime has occurred? Or how about a property that has been occupied by a person with a communicable disease such as AIDS? Properties such as these are generally considered to be *psychologically impacted,* and the answer to disclosure of defects of an emotional nature varies.

Georgia has passed a Stigmatized Property Act, which can be found and read in its entirety in O.C.G.A. 44-1-16. This Act was originally adopted in 1989 and protects the owner, broker, and affiliated licensees from responsibility to disclose such psychological defects. The Act does indicate that, if asked, the licensee should answer such questions truthfully to the best of his/her knowledge. This situation becomes more complex if the issue is a disease such as AIDS. Subsequent to this Act being adopted, federal law has made class may not be answered. In this situation, if a buyer were to ask if the seller was infected with AIDS, a proper response would be, "While I appreciate that you feel so comfortable with me that you could ask a question that obviously is of a sensitive nature, I could not legally answer that question, even if I knew the answer." That is about as close to a legal, politically correct, nonanswer as one can get. Seriously, though, laws exist for a reason, and it is the job of the licensee to know those laws and apply them as appropriate.

Commercial Real Estate Broker Lien Act

Before leaving this section on working with sellers, mention should be made of Georgia's **Commercial Real Estate Broker Lien Act** (O.C.G.A. 44-1-600, et seq.). As we have previously learned, a broker's commission is typically earned when the broker produces a person who is ready, willing, and able to perform at the contract price and terms or at such price and terms that would be acceptable to the party agreeing to pay the commission. So if a seller listed a property with a broker and the broker brought a ready, willing, and able buyer at the seller's requested contract price and terms, the commission is earned even if the seller decides not to sell.

Historically, if the seller refused to pay the earned commission, the broker could not file a mechanic's lien on the property, as the broker has not improved the property through his/her labor or materials. The broker could file suit against the owner with no guarantee that there would be any property to lien. With the amount of compensation involved in some commercial transactions, the problem of the seller refusing to pay earned commissions intensified, and, unfortunately, too many sellers had the mindset of: "I may owe you but I am not going to pay you. Catch me if you can." The Commercial Real Estate Broker Liens act allows

Commercial Real Estate Broker Lien Act: a Georgia Act that allows a broker to lien a property to protect a commission right

a broker to file a lien on a commercial property in this situation. It is allowed only on nonresidential properties and is very similar to a mechanic's lien. To that end, the affidavit of lien must be filed within 90 days of the due date of the commission, and legal proceedings must be initiated within one year of the date of recording the lien affidavit.

WORKING WITH BUYERS

Another side of the real estate business is working with the buyer. Historically, the buyer has been treated as a customer, but since the early 1990s, it has become common that the buyer is offered client-level service. Most licensees would agree that client-level service is most comfortable and satisfying. It allows for open communication without concern about what can be disclosed and what cannot. When one represents the buyer as a client, the duty is to advocate for the buyer, make full disclosure, and maintain confidentiality. This does not mean that buyer representation is without challenges. It should be pointed out that there is more potential liability associated with representing buyers than there has ever been with representing sellers.

When one represents a seller in a transaction, when the transaction closes and the seller receives their money, there is not much that can go wrong. But if the licensee has a duty to represent the buyer and a closing occurs, the liability has just begun. Imagine if, after closing, the buyer found a defect in the foundation, became aware of a registered sex offender living in the neighborhood, discovered s/he paid too much money for the property, was told about a public landfill that was recently approved by the county, or learned that boundary lines or square footage of the property were not as represented. It is this kind of potential liability that should make licensees take their role in working with a buyer seriously.

The selection of the buyer's role as customer or client begins with company policy. A broker should create and implement a policy that allows agents of the company to provide valuable services and at the same time manage risk. This will start by understanding that there are four categories of buyers: those you must represent, those you should represent, those who need representation, and those you should not represent. Let us look at each of these.

Must represent:

- Yourself—Licensees cannot work with and treat themselves as customers. A classic example of dual agency would be if Bob has a listing on a property and wants to buy the property for himself. That is about the only situation in which this author would accept a dual agency.
- Buyers requiring anonymity—If buyers do not want others to know their identity, the agent must represent them to provide confidentiality. An example of this might be a celebrity or developer.

- Current clients—If a seller-client wants his/her agent to assist in the purchase of a replacement property, how could the agent represent the person in one transaction but not the other when the transactions are running concurrently?

Should represent:

- Former clients—Former clients received client-level service in the past and would expect the same this time around.
- Referrals from a former client—The person referred would expect the same level of service received by the person who was so impressed that s/he referred the agent.
- Friends and relatives—While an argument can be made that a licensee should not mix business with family or friends, if a licensee is going to work with these people, they expect and should receive client-level service.
- Business associates—These are people you have come to know through business, either yours or theirs. A client-level service is most comfortable for all involved.

Need representation:

- First-time home buyers—When home buyers do not possess experience in a business transaction as important as making a real estate investment, they really need the experience and counsel of an ethical and knowledgeable licensee.
- Buyers who are relocating—Local market knowledge is very important in a real estate transaction. Regardless of experience, a person who does not possess that knowledge needs the advocacy of someone who does.

Should not represent:

- Unmotivated buyers—The buyer's need and desire to complete a purchase should be measured by asking probing questions as soon as reasonably possible.
- Unrealistic buyers—Unrealistic expectations can often be controlled by a good agent, but, unfortunately, the agent too often becomes part of the problem by making promises that cannot be kept, such as negotiating a price 10% below the listing price. Make a commitment to be part of the solution, not part of the problem.
- Unqualified buyers—If you could arrange with your favorite airline to purchase an around-the-world flight for a dollar and the prospective buyers could not afford to take the flight, forget about representing them. The bigger question is, "How did they even get in your car?"
- Buyers that present a conflict to represent the seller-client—If an agent is holding open the property of a seller-client and a potential buyer shows interest, representing the buyer would create dual agency conflict. This buyer should be offered a customer level of service.

- Buyers who expect something unethical or illegal—An example would be a buyer who wants the agent to commit mortgage fraud to get a loan. Why we would not represent this person should require no explanation.

The first step in working with a buyer is setting up an interview. If at all possible, schedule the interview to take place before showing property and as a separate appointment. During this interview/consultation, the agent will ask questions to determine the experience, knowledge, needs, and motivation of the buyer. There are several schools of thought as to where this interview is best conducted. Some believe the initial meeting should take place in the office of the broker to create and maintain a professional atmosphere and also control the environment. Being in the office also makes available any necessary resources. As an alternative, some like to conduct the first interview in the home of the buyer. With the buyers in their own environment, they may feel less threatened, drop any defensive barriers, and, as a bonus, the agent gets to see how the buyers live. A third option is to meet the buyers in a neutral place such as a coffeehouse, bookstore, or restaurant. Many commercial establishments today provide access to wifi and cater to the business meeting crowd.

Once the licensee determines what level of service is appropriate for the buyer, the real presentation begins. The track is similar to the listing presentation in that the basic stages are to build rapport, identify dominant needs, relate benefits to those needs, and, finally, to ask for the buyer's business. Early on in the presentation, proper agency disclosure must be made. The type of disclosure will depend on whether the agent has identified the buyer as a potential client or customer. If a client-level relationship is desired, the presentation will finalize with the brokerage engagement agreement. As with all agreements, careful explanation of all terms must be provided, and, once the agreement is signed, copies are given to all parties.

Most important at this juncture is to clearly identify the buyer as a client or customer and to proceed in a manner consistent with that choice. *Clients* we advocate for, and we provide them loyalty, obedience, confidentiality, and full disclosure. If the choice is *customer*, it is appropriate that we only provide information, treat them with basic fairness, and make limited disclosure. It is not the duty of the licensee to advocate for or to diligently protect the position of the customer. Keep in mind the four Ds:

Decide—the level of service.

Disclose—all pertinent and legally required information.

Document—everything that is said and done.

Do—what you said you would do. Be consistent with your service decision.

Once a property is found, the negotiations begin. The formal negotiations typically begin with the writing of the offer from the buyer to the seller. In the writing, presenting, and negotiating of the offer, let us review a number of points:

1. *Real estate licensees are not attorneys and may not draft legal forms.* In Georgia law (O.C.G.A. 43-40-25.1), licensees are permitted to use forms that have been approved by legal counsel and essentially fill in the blanks. An exhaustive bank of forms and stipulations is available through the Georgia Association of REALTORS®, which covers most day-to-day contracts and situations. The licensee should be very judicious about redacting the form and writing stipulations. This should be done with the guidance of legal counsel. When it is deemed appropriate to redact the form, the change should be initialed by all parties, dated, and timed.

2. *Sales contracts and leases require a sufficient legal description.* A street address is not enough. While the description is often available as a short form from the listing broker (remember, s/he should have obtained it from the seller's warranty deed or security deed), the description may be a more complex metes-and-bounds description. In this case, the legal description will have to be included as an attachment. However it is done, without a proper description, the contract will lack mutuality and, therefore, be void. As always, if there are any questions, contact your broker.

3. *License law requires that the offer contain a sufficient method of payment.* The method of payment must be clear, and the purchase price must be definite. Statements such as "Purchase price to be determined at a later date" or "Purchase price to be determined by a VA or FHA appraisal" are not sufficient. A statement such as "Purchase price to be $25,000 plus the outstanding loan balance assumed by the purchaser at closing" would be better. "The purchase price shall be $150,000 paid in cash at closing" would be best. The good news is that the forms used in the field are user-friendly and usually simply require filling in the blanks.

4. *Earnest money, while common, is not the consideration in a contract and is not required to have a valid agreement.* The consideration in a sales contract is the promise by the buyer to pay the price and the promise by the seller to convey the property.

5. *Avoid conflicting information in the contract.* What takes precedence if there is conflicting information in the contract? Which will control? The most important rule is, "Do not have conflicting information in the agreement." Be intimately familiar with the wording of the preprinted form and do not create conflict. But when there is conflict, one rule is that handwritten language controls typewritten language, and typewritten language controls preprinted language. Another rule is that the last statement is the controlling statement. For example, if on page one of the agreement, it is stipulated that the seller will contribute $4,000 to assist the buyer in getting a loan, and then a page is later added that stipulates that the seller will contribute $5,000, the last statement controls, and the seller's obligation is to contribute $5,000. Another consideration is that if there is conflict between a

written agreement and oral agreement, the written agreement controls. This is sometimes known as the *best evidence rule*. For instance, if the buyer and seller orally agreed that the wooden deck will be pressure-washed and sealed before closing, but when the agreement was put in writing there was no mention of the deck, the seller would not be obligated to do the work. The last consideration is that if the wording in the agreement is vague, courts will often construe the words most harshly or literally against the party responsible for the words. For example, if the agent representing the buyer wrote into the offer, "$2,000 will be paid to sand and finish the hardwood floors," while the agent may have meant that the seller would contribute the $2,000, since it was unclear and written by the buyer's agent, a court may construe that the $2,000 must be paid by the purchaser.

6. *When filling out the lines of a preprinted form, leave no lines blank.* If the line does not apply, the simplest solution is to insert "N/A," meaning not applicable.

7. *When adding additional pages to the agreement such as a metes-and-bounds description, reference the additional pages in the agreement as an exhibit, addendum, or rider.* The additional pages should cross-reference the original document and then be signed or initialed by all parties and attached to the primary contract form.

8. *Most contracts can be assigned to someone else unless there is a stipulation prohibiting such assignment.* This prohibitive statement is common and would have to be removed to make the contract assignable. In the event that a buyer asks for permission to assign, the seller and licensee should proceed cautiously, as assignment of contracts is often the first step in mortgage fraud, and, as such, should be viewed as a red flag.

9. *The presentation of the offer to the seller is controlled by the agent representing the seller.* While it is not inappropriate for the buyer's agent to ask to assist on behalf of his/her client in the presentation, it is typically a law violation for the buyer's agent to negotiate with the seller without the listing agent present. The exception to that is if the seller has not purchased negotiation services from the listing agent, in which case the selling agent may negotiate directly with the seller on behalf of the buyer-client.

10. *A seller who is not satisfied with the buyer's offer may counteroffer.* In doing so, the seller may execute the counteroffer by striking out that which is not acceptable in the original offer; write what would be acceptable; date, time, and initial the change; and sign the form. If the counteroffer is acceptable to the buyers, they would then initial the changes and communicate that acceptance back to the seller. An alternative method of executing a counteroffer is by using a counteroffer form. The form would be completed, referencing the original offer and stating an acceptance of all portions with the exception of those items stipulated in the counteroffer form. If the counteroffer is

acceptable to the buyers, they would sign and communicate their acceptance back to the seller.

11. *An offer does not become a contractual obligation until the acceptance has been properly communicated back to the offeror.* A good contract form will state how notifications must be made. Be sure to follow the letter of the contract.

CONTRACT TO CLOSING

While listing and marketing a property, working with buyers, showing property, and negotiating a contract are all exciting, the job is not yet completed. There is much detail to be attended to until the parties go to closing. Some duties are legal requirements, some are customary, and some are created to provide "mint on the pillow" service to build a business into the future. The primary duty of the agent is to write a good contract, explain the obligations to the parties completely, and then maintain an open line of communication with all parties until closing. Once the contract is signed by all parties, a true and correct copy must be provided to the buyer, the seller, the listing broker, and the selling broker. The lender and the attorney conducting the closing also need copies of the contract.

Most contracts today contain multiple contingencies for such things as financing and inspections. With time being of the essence in most contracts, the time limits must be faithfully followed. Consumers do not always understand the importance of timely compliance with contractual obligations and rights. Most protective contingencies are written in such a way that nonperformance means obligation. For example, a buyer may have 15 days in a contract to diligently pursue financing and notify the seller if the application has been denied. If the application is denied and the buyer makes proper notification, the obligation to purchase is terminated. If the buyer fails to notify within the 15 days, the transaction by default becomes a cash transaction and the buyer may not claim that lack of financial ability is a reason not to close. Failure to close would be a breach of contract and subject the buyer to forfeiture of earnest money and/or a specific performance or damage suit.

Another important and common contingency is the right to inspect. Most contracts today obligate the purchaser to inspect for structural defect and wood infestation. The period of time to conduct these inspections is called the due diligence period. If the inspections expose conditions that are not acceptable, the purchaser has the right to notify the seller of termination and demand a refund of earnest money, or, as an alternative, the purchaser may amend the contract and negotiate with the seller to correct deficiencies. Either way, if the purchaser does not exercise the right to terminate, the default position is the purchaser's obligation to close the transaction, with failure being breach of contract.

When repairs are required, the salesperson may assist in getting contractor estimates but should not execute contracts personally. The contracts should be between the person desiring the repair and the contractor. Do not obligate yourself to pay for others' improvements. Making this mistake one time and paying for someone else's roof is a real memory-making moment.

Another job of the salesperson is to follow up on loan applications and make sure all is going smoothly. There are many loan products available, and having access to good loan officers with competent staff to support them is crucial to the success of the real estate agent. It is recommended that the agent encourage the purchaser to use local lenders who have a commitment to the community and are vested in the success of the loan application. While there are many lenders available on the internet, you must accept that valuable control and input are lost. Coordination of the closing is often a job that falls on the shoulders of the agent. To ensure a smooth transaction, the closing attorney must receive appropriate and accurate information to prepare and conduct the closing. The attorney's office must have a copy of the contract, and seller loan information is also helpful to the attorney in obtaining loan payoffs. If taxes have been recently paid, a receipt should be supplied to the attorney. If the buyer has paid for the homeowner's insurance, a paid receipt should be supplied. The schedules of all involved must be considered before setting the date, time, and location for the closing. The buyer and seller should be further prepared for what is going to happen at the closing table. If the buyers or sellers wish to read all documents prior to signing, they have that right, but they will not have the time at closing. The attorney's office can supply blank documents prior to closing for the parties to read the preprinted language if they wish. The agents should further prepare the buyers and sellers by providing them with cost and net worksheets, which should approximate the closing statement if completed properly. The parties should also be informed of how long to expect the closing to take and be prepared for the procedure of document signing.

The closing itself is usually governed by the **Real Estate Settlement Procedures Act (RESPA).** RESPA sets the ground rules and requires that disclosure be made to the borrower in such a way that s/he can make informed decisions. Among other things, the Act requires that a **Loan Estimate** be provided to the consumer (borrower) no later than three business days after the consumer submits a loan application. The loan estimate promotes comparison shopping by providing a summary of applicable loan terms and estimates of loan and closing costs consumers can expect to pay (or not pay) at closing. The **Closing Disclosure** form integrates and replaces the Housing and Urban Development Settlement Statement (HUD-1) and the final Truth in Lending disclosure statement. The creditor must provide the closing disclosure to the consumer no later than three business days prior to consummation of the loan.

While the agent or broker is not required to attend the closing, one or the other usually does as a courtesy to the client. The salesperson is usually the one attending, and it is his/her job to observe on behalf of the broker and represent the interests of the firm's client. In Georgia, only a licensed attorney may conduct the closing.

RESPA: Real Estate Settlement Procedures Act; an Act that sets the ground rules for a closing

Loan Estimate: gives a summary of applicable loan terms and estimates of loan and closing costs consumers can expect to pay at closing

Closing Disclosure: includes a detailed accounting of the final terms of the mortgage transaction

PROPERTY MANAGEMENT

The concept of property management extends well past simply negotiating a lease for space. Property management services the needs of the owner, the needs of the asset, and the needs of the tenants. A competent property manager will be able to demonstrate skills and knowledge in communication, maintenance, financing, property law, insurance, sales, accounting, security, and negotiations, among others. The relationship between the broker and the owner begins with the property management agreement. Georgia Rule 520-1-.06(2) outlines the basic requirements of every written agreement. It must:

1. identify the property;
2. contain all terms and conditions under which the property will be managed;
3. specify how the broker will remit income to the owner and how the broker will provide written statements to the owner of income and expenses. (These statements must be submitted at least annually.);
4. specify what expenses are to be paid by the broker and how the payments are to be funded;
5. state the terms and amount of compensation to the broker;
6. specify whether security deposits and prepaid rents are to be held by the owner or broker;
7. contain a beginning and ending date;
8. provide for terms and conditions of termination by either party; and
9. contain the signatures of both parties.

As with all signed documents, the signing party must receive a copy for his/her files. It also should be noted that, as a personal service agreement, a management contract does not survive the sale of a property unless the agreement stipulates that it will and the purchaser of the property is notified of the management contract and the survival provision. The most effective way to provide this notification to a potential purchaser is to record the management contract.

Functions of a Property Manager

As has been mentioned, the roles of the property manager are numerous and diverse. Let us take a short look at some of the duties and expectations of the manager.

Property Maintenance

It is typically the duty of the manager to maintain the property to maximize the income and economic life. Maintenance falls into three categories:

1. *Custodial maintenance*—the day-to-day cleaning and maintenance of the property. This would include vacuuming, emptying trash, cleaning bathrooms, sweeping sidewalks, caring for breezeways, and landscaping.

2. *Preventive maintenance*—the periodic care for items to extend the economic and useful life. This could include changing of furnace filters on a monthly basis, semiannual cleaning, adjusting the climate control systems, and annual pressure washing of painted surfaces.
3. *Corrective maintenance*—the as-needed repair or replacement of items. Included in this list could be repairing leaking faucets, replacing burst plumbing pipe, repairing or replacing failed climate control units, and repainting when needed.

Marketing

The goal of marketing is to expose the property to the right people, at the right time, in a manner that is both effective and efficient. With this in mind, the manager must consider the following:

- Where will my next tenants come from, and where are they now?
- Who is the person that would be most likely to lease the property?
- What do they read?
- Where do they drive?
- What radio and television stations do they tune in to?
- What does that tenant need?
- What are the features of the subject property, and how can they become a benefit to a prospective tenant?
- When will I have space available?
- Who is the competition?

Market Analysis

The ultimate challenge for the property manager is to maximize the net income and economic life of the property. Maximizing the income is accomplished through keeping the property as fully occupied as possible, with tenants paying the highest rent possible. That can be a fine balance. If the rents are too high, excessive vacancies occur. If rents are too low, the building may have very low vacancy and low turnover, but the property is not producing what it should. The property manager should constantly be measuring the market and analyzing movement.

What incentives are the competition using to entice prospective tenants? What are the lease rates for competing properties with similar location and amenities? If it is a residential property, are there incentive programs for families to buy their own home rather than rent that will drain the supply of tenants? What new buildings are coming on the market? How are the demographics changing in the area? A person who seeks property management as a career may consider earning the *Certified Property Manager (CPM)* or *Accredited Residential Manager (ARM)* designation awarded through the *Institute of Real Estate Management (IREM)*. IREM is an arm of the National Association of REALTORS®, and there is a massive amount of information available to its members at its website: www.realtor.org.

Budgeting

Any budget has two main categories: income and expenses. The estimated projected income for a property is documented by analyzing the past performance of the subject property and the performance of competing properties in the area. As was just stated in the market analysis section, high rents do not necessarily equate to high income. The property must be competitive.

On the income side of the ledger, the manager would compute the total amount of rents that could be generated in one year if every unit of every building were rented every day of every month and every tenant paid his/her rent. This number is referred to as *gross rent income (GRI)*. Added to GRI is income generated from other sources, such as laundry facilities, parking, vending, and, on tall buildings, income from renting access to the roof for antennas. Adding the other income to the GRI results in *gross potential income (GPI)*. It is not reasonable to predict in most circumstances that the property will actually produce the GPI over one year. The GPI is reduced due to *vacancy and collection losses (V&C)*. Vacancy losses are those reductions to GPI caused by the unit being vacant over a period during the year. Collection losses are reductions from GPI, not because there is no tenant to pay, but because the tenant will not pay. While it is possible to have vacancy losses but no collection losses, and it is possible to have collection losses but no vacancy losses, and it is even possible to have no vacancy or collection losses, in most situations, a property will experience both vacancy and collection losses over one year. If a property truly is experiencing no V&C, this is typically an indication that the rents are too low, so the property is not actually producing to its potential. By subtracting the V&C from the GPI, the result is the gross effective income (GEI). The GEI is the amount of money that is expected to be collected and deposited in behalf of the property in one year.

The other side of the ledger is expenses. There are commonly three expense categories: fixed expenses, variable expenses, and reserves for replacements. Fixed expenses are costs that are predictable in both amount and time. This category would typically include items such as debt service (which is not an expense for appraisal but would be considered in property management), property taxes, insurance, landscape maintenance, and employee salaries. Variable expenses are costs that are not as predictable in amount or time. This category would include, for example, management fees (if they are a percentage of rent collection), repairs, electric bills, and water and sewer bills. The last category is reserves for replacement. These are items that are replaced one or more times over the life of the building but less often than once a year. Examples in this category are roof, appliances, carpet, heating systems, and air conditioning units. Charging off a $20,000 roof once every 20 years would skew the bottom line of measuring performance for the property in every year. The proper method of handling the $20,000 roof is to expense $1,000 per year for the 20 years. Members of the Building Owners and Managers Association (BOMA) can access data to help estimate the operating expenses of specific property types in an area.

Tenant Selection

Having vacant space is not good, but having tenants who do not pay rent, are damaging the property, are a nuisance to other valuable tenants, and have to be evicted is worse. Tenant qualification should include procuring a credit report, checking personal references, checking with former landlords or mortgage companies, and verifying employment and banking information. While the property manager does not have to lease to every prospective tenant, classifications protected by fair housing laws can never be the consideration for denial.

Negotiating the Lease

Basic contract law applies to leases. Leases for more than one year must be in writing to be enforceable, according to the Statute of Frauds. The use of preprinted forms is common in residential properties, but the more unique the property, the more unique the form. An attorney will have to be retained to draft more complex lease agreements.

Rent Collection

The lease will stipulate the amount of the lease payments, the form they are to take, and to whom, when, and where they are to be made. It is usually a function of the property manager to collect rents, pay bills, and remit remaining income to the owner. The stipulations in the lease must be adhered to, including the timely collection of rents and the enforcement of late fees, if applicable. If a manager allows a tenant to pay late, this could create a new standard and a ratification of the agreement.

To protect everyone's interest, if there are rules, they should be followed. If the rules are not going to be followed, do not have the rules. This includes the provisions of the contract. Again, one caveat is to be mindful of fair housing laws. In one case before HUD, a tenant requested that he be allowed to make his payments late because he had become disabled and was depending on a disability check. The check came on the 20th of the month and the tenant wanted the rent to be due on that date. The landlord refused to modify the lease and charged a late fee. The tenant complained to HUD, and HUD agreed that a modification of the lease would be a reasonable accommodation for the handicap. The landlord was assessed a penalty and had to pay costs. When the tenant's lease came up for renewal, the landlord refused to renew the lease. Again, the tenant filed a complaint with HUD, claiming a retaliatory eviction. HUD agreed, and the landlord had to pay more than $11,000 in penalties. The moral of the story is, a property manager, above all, must use logic and common sense.

Retaining Tenants

The primary statistic used to assess the effectiveness of a property manager is probably the turnover rate. There is always going to be turnover, but limiting that is a huge positive. When a tenant leaves, there will be lost rents due to the vacancy and additional costs to prepare the space for a new tenant. It is less expensive to keep what you have. If tenants are treated fairly, the manager is responsive to complaints, the property is well-maintained, and the rent is competitive for the product, tenants will not usually be induced to move. We are better to stay with what we know unless there is reason to change.

GEORGIA REAL ESTATE FINANCE

Borrowing money and then paying it back over time is not really different in Georgia from what it is in Vermont, Florida, Colorado, New Hampshire, or anywhere else. Georgia does have a unique method of securing the loan. As has been discussed earlier, when consumers borrow money on time, they will be required to execute a promissory note creating an obligation to pay the loan back, typically in monthly installments with the loan accruing interest. (The interest serves as the *rental charge* for the money.) The interest on a real estate loan is computed as simple interest; the interest charge is computed against the loan balance each period. As the loan balance reduces, the amount of interest owed also reduces. Without any document executed other than the note, the note is unsecured. If the borrower defaults on his/her promise to pay, the lender will have to file suit, obtain a judgment, and attach the judgment lien against assets. The lender would then attempt to seize the assets, have them sold at a public sale, and ask that the proceeds of the sale be used to satisfy the judgment. As you can imagine, this is a time-consuming and costly process. Lenders of money would much prefer to make secured loans. When one borrows to purchase a car, this loan is typically secured with the certificate of title to the automobile. In many states, a loan for real estate is secured by a mortgage document; in others, a deed of trust. Georgia is unique in that we use a security deed or deed to secure debt. In Georgia, the use of a mortgage would only create a lien on the property and require a judicial foreclosure. In the 1800s, Georgia required the borrower to issue a warranty deed to the lender conveying legal title; the lender would then execute a bond for title, which would convey the title back to the borrower upon satisfaction of the debt. Later the warranty deed and bond for title became one in the form of the deed to secure debt. The deed to secure debt effectively conveys a legal title to the lender, which is defeasible upon satisfaction of the underlying debt.

The borrower in return retains equitable title coupled with the right of redemption. The borrower may redeem the legal title that s/he possessed prior to execution of the security deed by simply fulfilling the obligation and paying off the debt. Upon satisfaction of debt, the lender may either sign the satisfaction portion of the original security deed and re-record or execute and record a cancellation of security deed.

The financing of real estate changes almost daily based on national and international influences. In that real estate in general is a huge portion of the U.S. economy, the government has a vested interest in making sure the real estate market is stable. When the real estate market sours, it drags the entire economy down with it. In times of recession or a weakening economy, the government will induce lower interest rates and programs to make homeownership possible for more people by providing financing. Remember, money in an economy is like gasoline for an automobile. Your car can be mechanically perfect, but if there is no fuel, you have nothing more than a driveway ornament. For an economy to have energy and grow, there must be money flowing through it. Providing easy financing is one way for the economy to continue to have fuel running through the engine.

With the federal government's role in the secondary market, specifically the Federal National Mortgage Association (Fannie Mae or FNMA), the Government National Mortgage Association (Ginnie Mae or GNMA), and the Federal Home Loan Mortgage Corporation (Freddie Mac or FHLMC), loan availability can be influenced, thus energizing the economy. Loans of up to 100% may even be available by allowing borrowers to acquire secondary financing rather than make a down payment. Historically, lenders would require a borrower to have at least as much cash in the transaction as any secondary financing. For example, if a borrower wanted a lender to make a loan at 80% of the value of the property, the lender would allow the borrower to obtain secondary financing of up to 10% of the value and make a 10% down payment. The motivation for this is elimination of mortgage insurance. A borrower might find a lender who would allow an 80% loan, coupled with a 20% second mortgage with no down payment. Below is a comparison of these two concepts.

	80/10/10	80/20
Sales price	$150,000	$150,000
1st loan	120,000	120,000
2nd loan	15,000	30,000
Down payment	15,000	0

In this example, obviously the borrower in the 80/10/10 loan is more motivated to keep the loan out of default than the 80/20 borrower. This type of aggressive financing is good in the shortterm since it makes it easy to sell property and keep the money flowing through the economy. The question that will have to be asked is, "Is the pain worth the gain?" This type of aggressive financing has helped create historically high foreclosure rates, a scenario that is costly not only to the lenders, but also to the consumer, as the losses by the lenders are passed on to their customers in the form of higher ATM charges, increased interest rates, and bank charges.

The primary reason for the use of the security deed in Georgia is to allow a nonjudicial foreclosure. If a lender in Georgia allowed the use of a mortgage, which is legal, the mortgage would simply create a lien interest on behalf of the lender, and, upon default, the foreclosure process would be judicial. With the use of the security deed, the lender obtains title and can foreclose in a nonjudicial action called the power of sale. If a borrower defaults, the lender notifies the borrower and demands that the loan be paid; if it is not, the lender will begin foreclosure procedures.

In a foreclosure, the property must be advertised in the local legal organ for four consecutive weeks prior to the public sale. With the authority gained by the security deed, a representative of the lender will offer the property for sale at a public auction at the county courthouse on the first Tuesday of each month. The lender's representative will commonly bid the amount of the debt and hope someone outbids. If there are no bids from the public, the lender's interest is cleared, and the lender owns the property. The next step is to gain possession of the property, secure it, rehabilitate it as needed, and market it. If the borrower is still in possession, the lender may have to initiate an eviction action to obtain control of the property. Some lenders offer the borrower cash to leave the property "broom clean" in a reasonable period of time. Some lenders have found that this is more economical in the long run because they avoid the expense of eviction and having the occupant apply a "scorched earth" policy on the way out, causing damage.

Another result of the increased foreclosures has been the short sale. With the overfinancing of so many properties, there is little doubt the lender will lose money in a foreclosure. Some investors have negotiated with lenders to buy properties at a discount if the lender will accept less than the amount of the debt to get the property off the books. Remember, lenders are in the money business, not the real estate business. They have no desire to manage a real estate portfolio. For example, a loan balance may be $150,000, and the lender would be fortunate to sell the property for $145,000. The lender also has to consider the costs involved in holding, maintaining, and marketing the property. If those estimated costs are $15,000, the lender's net from a sale would be $130,000. An investor may induce the lender to "short sale" the property upfront for the $130,000, thus controlling the amount of loss and eliminating the property from the portfolio. If a lender loses money in a foreclosure, it can attempt to obtain a deficiency judgment against the borrower. To do so, the lender must first obtain a confirmation of sale, which is a stipulation of the court that the sale was a market sale. If the lender allowed a short sale, this may impair the chances of obtaining a deficiency judgment.

COMMUNITY ASSOCIATION MANAGEMENT

Georgia license law defines a community association as "an owner organization of a residential or mixed use common interest realty association in which membership is mandatory as an incident to ownership . . ." [O.C.G.A. 43-40-1(4.1)]. The law then defines community association management services as "collecting, controlling, or disbursing the funds; obtaining insurance, arranging for and coordinating maintenance to the association property; and otherwise overseeing the day-to-day operations of the association" [O.C.G.A. 43-40-1 (4.2)]. In essence, a community association is a homeowners association. Many subdivisions have been developed in Georgia, some of them with formal owners' associations, some of them without. Some of the associations have mandatory membership; others are voluntary.

The concept of suburban development with subdivisions dates back to the 1940s with the development of Levittown on Long Island, New York. Most subdivisions through the 1960s did not have owners' associations. That began to change in the 1970s, when some communities had amenities such as swimming pools and tennis courts and the owners found that having a homeowners association was a good way to regulate themselves and maintain the common elements. Most associations of this day were not mandatory, as it was thought that owners would want to be members so they could use the amenities. The associations did not think ahead enough to realize that lifestyle changes and the age of the amenities would cause some members to opt out of membership, leaving fewer and fewer dues-paying members to maintain the common elements. All around suburban Georgia, you can find subdivisions with swimming and tennis facilities that have been abandoned, are in disrepair, and are eyesores and safety hazards. Since the middle to late 1980s, developments with amenities have mostly been mandatory. This has created a new business model for community association management.

Owners' associations are created as not-for-profit corporations and are not dissimilar in structure to any other corporation. Property owners make up the membership of the association and elect a board of directors by which they manage themselves. In accordance with the bylaws of the association, officers are elected, typically including a president, vice president, secretary, and treasurer. Some communities will also elect a fifth officer, sometimes known as an agent, to eliminate the chances of tie voting. The board then manages the community assets and may elect to hire a community association manager to assist in the day-to-day operations. The functions of association management include preparing budgets and keeping records, collecting assessments and paying bills, interacting with accountants and attorneys on behalf of the association, notifying the membership and conducting meetings, hiring contractors and overseeing the repair and maintenance of association property, maintaining insurance and security as needed for the community, enforcing rules and regulations, administering architectural control procedures, and keeping detailed minutes of association meetings. All of these are duties that may be performed by a community association manager. Unless the manager is a member of the association, the community association manager must be licensed by the Georgia Real Estate Commission.

A status of licensing is recognized by the commission for **community association management (CAM)**. As outlined in O.C.G.A. 43-40-8(a), to obtain the CAM license, one must be at least 18 years old, be a Georgia resident unless qualifying under nonresident licensure, be a high school graduate or have a certificate of equivalency, complete a course of at least 25 instructional hours, and stand and pass a state examination. With a CAM license, the affiliated licensee is limited to providing community association management services and may not be involved in the sale, lease, listing, optioning, or exchanging of real estate. All management contracts must be with a broker, and the CAM licensee must be affiliated with a broker. Community association management services can be provided by any licensee or broker, not just those with a CAM license.

In 1994, the state legislature passed the **Georgia Property Owners' Association Act** (O.C.G.A. 44-3-22, et seq.). It is not mandatory that an association be subject to this Act, but if it voluntarily submits the property, there are benefits. The Act provides a specific framework for the enforcement of liens, penalties, and late fees for nonpaying property owners. If a community subjects itself to the Act, liens for dues are automatic and the association does not need to record at the courthouse. By being subject to the Act, any title researcher is put on notice of the possibility of a lien, and the title attorney must contact the association to receive a statement showing all assessments past due, plus late charges and interest. The statement must be provided by the association within five days of receipt of the request or the lien becomes invalid. Property owners are jointly and severally liable for the assessments, meaning that if a property is purchased with back assessments, the past and present owner is liable for the debt. In the event that the assessments are not paid, the association has the power to foreclose on the property.

ANTITRUST LAWS

For a free enterprise, capitalistic society to survive, it is of utmost importance that competition exist. Without competition, any business holding a **monopoly** could charge whatever it desires and the consumer would have no choice but to pay the price. With no competition, there is no motivation to develop new products or methods of manufacture and delivery. In place to promote competition are antitrust and fair business practice laws.

Sherman Antitrust Act

The Sherman Antitrust Act was created in 1890 to control interstate monopolistic activities. The Act made illegal any activity that endangers business competition. Real estate comes under the Act because real estate activity routinely

---

community association manager (CAM): one who manages owners' associations rather than property.

Georgia Property Owners' Association Act: the Georgia law that may be used to govern a homeowners association

monopoly: created when one business has no competition

involves interstate funds, interstate insurance, consumers who travel between states, companies that have national ties through affiliations with franchise and referral networks, and residential closings that fall under the Real Estate Settlement Procedures Act (RESPA). Sherman considers real estate business as a trade since it is carried out for profit. Claims by brokers that their business is not subject to Sherman because it is a personal service, or that it is a profession rather than a trade, have been consistently denied by the courts. There have been many lawsuits against the real estate community for violation of Sherman, and there are multiple major suits currently being conducted, one by the Department of Justice, which will likely have lasting impact on the industry. As the business evolves and changes and the boundaries become almost limitless because of technology, licensees must become more aware of the laws within which we all must work. The primary violations of Sherman include price fixing, boycotting, monopolies, and tie-in agreements, which are discussed below.

Price Fixing

When two or more brokers work in concert to raise prices, it is known as **price fixing** and is a violation of antitrust laws. A broker can set pricing policies for his/her firm, and those prices can be firm without violating antitrust laws; however, the pricing should never be discussed with other brokers. Violations of antitrust laws do not require formal agreements or even intent. Two agents of competing firms having a casual conversation that alludes to price structure could be considered price fixing.

price fixing: the setting of prices or fees in concert with other business owners to the detriment of the consumer

Boycotting

Boycotting is the act of eliminating competition by refusing the competition access to materials or information needed to compete. Some years ago, there was a lawsuit against a multiple listing service that denied membership with no apparent cause. The plaintiff claimed that the company needed access to the MLS information to compete and was being unduly denied that access. The plaintiff won, and MLS membership and information have been more accessible since. As business models expand and are created to include things such as discount brokerage, limited service companies, and fee-based companies, understanding boycotting is of premium importance. Failure to engage these hybrid business models could be perceived to be a group boycott.

boycotting: the elimination of competition by refusal to allow membership or access

Monopolies

When a company becomes so big that no one can compete, it is called a monopoly. There are examples in marketplaces past and present that have come awfully close to being monopolies. There are such things as government-sponsored monopolies, which occur when the government feels that a monopoly is in the best interest of the public. Historically, public utility companies that provide electricity, gas, water, and sewage treatment have been protected by the government and regulated by public service commissions as state-sponsored monopolies.

Tie-in (or Tying) Agreements

tie-in (or tying) agreements: tying one contract to another and forcing a business relationship

When a business requires that a customer enter into a second contract as a requirement of entering into a first contract, that "tying in" of the second contract to the first may be illegal if there is no competition and substantial commerce is affected. In the real estate industry, an example would be a developer offering lots for sale. A builder is interested in purchasing 10 lots from the developer to build homes. As an inducement to enter into the contract to sell the 10 lots to the builder, the developer requires the builder to enter into a listing agreement for the 10 homes with a real estate company owned by the developer. If the builder has no choice but to purchase the lots from the developer because there are no other developed lots available, this *tie-in requirement* could be a violation of antitrust laws. Violation of Sherman is a felony and punishable with a fine of up to $350,000 and up to three years in prison for an individual. The penalty for a corporation is a fine of up to $10 million.

Fair Business Practices Act of 1975 (FBPA) O.C.G.A. 10-1-390, et seq.

The FBPA is administered by the Governor's Office of Consumer Affairs and is the primary consumer protection law in Georgia. The Act regulates unfair or deceptive practices in consumer transactions and applies primarily to advertising, whether that advertising is in the media or some other form of communication. For prosecution under the FBPA, an actual transaction must have taken place and the alleged practice must have affected more than an individual consumer. For example, if a salesperson told an individual that a lakefront property from a developer would include a sea wall when the salesperson knew that it would not, the misrepresentation may be a fraud, but it is not a violation of the FBPA since only one person was affected by the statement.

Uniform Deceptive Trade Practices Act (UDTPA)

The UDTPA is another avenue that can be taken by a consumer damaged by antitrust activity that occurs within the boundaries of the state. The UDTPA is easier to apply than the FBPA because the same strict standards do not apply. The claimant is not required to show that there was more than one person affected, nor does s/he have to prove there was an actual consumer transaction. Simply making deceptive statements or engaging in unfair practices could be enough to be a violation of the UDTPA. The penalties for violation of the FBPA and the UDTPA are similar, with fines of up to $25,000, the filing of an injunction, up to treble damages, loss of licensure for a real estate licensee, and the possibility of being sued in civil court.

TIMESHARES

A timeshare is an arrangement where the use and possession of the property is divided into predetermined and recurring time periods. This right may be developed through an actual fee ownership or a long-term lease. The most common use and example of a timeshare is vacation ownership in which a person buys the right in one-week intervals. In addition to the purchase price for the timeshare, there is an annual assessment, which is the obligation of the owner. The timeshare industry has had some challenges due to a reputation earned at the hands of some developers who exhibited less-than-ethical business practices. In recent years, entry into the timeshare market by well-known and trusted companies such as Marriott and Ritz-Carlton has helped the industry gain credibility.

In 1983, Georgia adopted the **Georgia Time-Share Act**, which was then amended in 1995 (O.C.G.A. 44-3-160, et seq.). This Act governs the sale of all timeshare properties located within Georgia as well as out-of-state properties that are marketed in Georgia. By definition, the sale of a timeshare interest is real estate and a person engaged by another to sell real estate must be licensed unless that person is exempt under very strict guidelines in the license law (O.C.G.A. 43-40-29).

Georgia Time-Share Act: the Georgia law that regulates the sale of properties in time increments

The Act requires that timeshare developers:

1. make disclosures through a public offering statement, which is a written document containing essential information to prospective buyers, such as details of management, program operation, and the buyer's right to rescind the contract within seven days;
2. deposit trust funds into escrow;
3. use only licensed brokers and agents if required by license law;
4. provide for a seven-day right to rescind the contract; and
5. ensure that all advertising and promotions comply with the FBPA.

The Act also requires that detailed information about exchange programs be disclosed to the buyer. This information includes the name and address of the exchange company; whether the buyer's participation in the exchange program is voluntary, mandatory, or dependent on the project's continued affiliation with the exchange program; a complete description of the exchange procedure and limitations of the program; and fees charged for the exchange program.

Review Questions

Answers to these questions can be found in Appendix D at the end of this book.

1. When both the buyer and the seller hire the same broker to represent their interest in a single transaction, and the broker appoints separate agents to represent the individual interests of the clients, this is most likely:
   A. single agency
   B. appointed agency
   C. designated agency
   D. dual agency

2. When a company controls all business in an area and there is no competition, this is known as:
   A. a monopoly
   B. a dream come true
   C. boycotting
   D. price fixing

3. Which of the following would be a typical property management function?
   A. providing maintenance on behalf of the tenant
   B. appraising the property for resale
   C. managing the construction of a new building on the property
   D. providing the owner with a market analysis

4. What federal law restricts the growth and practices of monopolies?
   A. Sherman
   B. FBPA
   C. UDTPA
   D. HUD

5. Under what circumstances must a salesperson involved with timeshare property be licensed?
   A. only if the property is located in Georgia
   B. only if the salesperson is a full-time employee of the owner
   C. under no circumstances, since it is actually short-term rental rather than sales
   D. always, unless exempt

6. Which of the following is NOT a requirement of the office brokerage policy disclosure?
   A. advising of the types of agencies offered
   B. advising that information is not confidential
   C. advising of compensation issues
   D. advising of potential conflict

7. In Georgia, who can conduct a closing of a real estate transaction?
   A. an attorney or a broker
   B. an attorney only
   C. an attorney or a paralegal
   D. an attorney, a broker, or a salesperson, with supervision

8. To file a lien under the Commercial Real Estate Broker Lien Act, which of the following is true?
   A. The lien must be filed within one year of listing the property.
   B. The lien attaches to real and personal property.
   C. The commission must be earned to file the lien.
   D. The property cannot be used for residential occupancy.

9. Which of the following is NOT a person who must be represented?
   A. yourself
   B. a buyer who wants to remain anonymous
   C. a current client
   D. a former client

10. Which is least important when working with clients and customers?
    A. deciding the level of service
    B. disclosing required information
    C. demanding to be paid
    D. doing what you said you would do

11. Which of the following is true in writing contracts?
    A. All contracts for real estate must be in writing to be enforceable.
    B. Earnest money is not required, as it is not the consideration in a sales contract.
    C. Preprinted controls typewritten when there is conflict.
    D. Blanks that do not apply must be stricken, dated, timed, and initialed.

12. Which of the following would be a circumstance where a Closing Disclosure is NOT required?
    A. The seller is paying all costs to close.
    B. The loan is government-related.
    C. The closing costs are divided between the buyer and seller.
    D. The loan is for a non-owner-occupied duplex.

13. Which of the following does NOT represent an expense category for a property?
    A. vacancy and collection losses
    B. fixed
    C. variable
    D. reserve for replacement

14. Which of the following is the best example of a short sale?
    A. John negotiates a purchase that must close in 10 days.
    B. Mark negotiates a purchase with a seller of a property at 80% of appraised value.
    C. Sue negotiates a purchase with a lender who accepts 90% of the present loan amount.
    D. Larry negotiates a purchase with a lender who agrees to finance 100% of the purchase price.

15. Which of the following is a violation of the Sherman Antitrust Act?
    A. Broker Bob requires a minimum commission of $6,000, regardless of the sales price.
    B. Salesperson Betty tells a prospective seller that the commission is 7% of the list price and refuses to negotiate.
    C. Broker Ken shares a listing commission paid by the seller with buyer's broker Mary without the seller's permission.
    D. Broker Ann instructs her staff not to show ABC Realty's listings because it is a discount broker.

16. "That which does not require the exercise of professional judgment or skill" best defines:
    A. brokerage
    B. ministerial acts
    C. client-level service
    D. material facts

17. When a broker offers dual agency to clients, the broker must:
    A. receive informed consent
    B. provide at least an oral disclosure
    C. designate different salespeople to represent the separate clients' interests
    D. do nothing, as dual agency is illegal in Georgia and cannot be offered

18. Broker Jeff does not feel comfortable providing client-level services to either the buyer or seller. Broker Jeff may:
    A. continue as a designated agent
    B. not assist either the buyer or seller if he will not accept agency duty
    C. continue as a transaction broker
    D. not continue until he makes a decision about whom to represent

19. Of the following, which best defines when an offer becomes a binding contract?
    A. when the offer is accepted
    B. at closing
    C. when a call is made telling the offeror of the acceptance
    D. upon communication of the acceptance

20. The purpose of a brokerage engagement agreement is to:
    A. act as a contract of employment between the client and the broker
    B. define the relationship between a broker and his/her customers
    C. notify the closing attorney of the amount of commission to be paid to the broker
    D. list the amenities and features of a property

APPENDIX A

SOLUTIONS TO STUDENT CALCULATIONS FROM CHAPTER 19

Annual Taxes	Closing Date	Taxes Paid?	Who Is Credited?	Days	Amount
$2,598	March 3	No	Buyer	62	$441.30
$865	October 13	Yes	Seller	79	$187.22
$1,398	June 9	No	Buyer	160	$612.82
$4,876	April 7	No	Buyer	97	$1,295.81
$2,723	August 20	Yes	Seller	133	$992.22
$1,250	November 3	Yes	Seller	58	$198.63

Begin Date	Closing Date	Annual Bill	Days	Amount
October 4	January 17	$317	259	$224.94
March 22	August 4	$815	229	$511.33
January 10	April 16	$713	268	$523.52
July 24	February 7	$476	166	$216.48
August 7	July 28	$957	9	$23.60
May 16	September 16	$593	241	$391.54

Loan Amount	Rate	Due Date	Closing Date	Days	Accrued interest
$274,934	8%	July 1	July 22	22	$1,344.12
$264,735	5.25%	April 10	April 27	18	$694.93
$73,586	5.75%	October 3	November 1	30	$352.60
$86,524	6.625%	February 1	February 17	17	$270.69
$95,476	11.125%	October 1	October 8	8	$236.04
$194,573	9.25%	May 20	June 7	19	$949.89

Sales Price	L/V Ratio	Loan Amount	Down Payment
$267,000	90%	$240,300	$26,700
$173,200	95%	$164,500	$8,700
$135,600	95%	$128,820	$6,780
$385,000	90%	$346,500	$38,500
$87,500	95%	$83,125	$4,375
$172,450	95%	$163,828	$8622

APPENDIX A Solutions to Student Calculations from Chapter 19

Sales Price	L/V Ratio	Rate	Closing Date	1st Pymt. Date	Loan Amount	Days	Amount
$295,000	80%	6.5%	March 13	May 1	$236,000	19	$809.61
$172,500	95%	6.75%	October 27	December 1	$163,800	5	$153.56
$223,500	90%	6.75%	May 6	July 1	$201,100	26	$980.36
$88,700	95%	7%	June 1	July 1	$84,200	0	0
$675,800	75%	7.25%	November 17	January 1	$506,800	14	$1,428.89
$108,000	90%	5.75%	January 11	March 1	$97,200	21	$326.03

Closing Date	Monthly Rent	Days	Amount
October 10	$1,480	21	$1,002.58
May 3	$825	28	$745.16
June 28	$1,450	2	$96.67
February 17	$725	11	$284.82
July 20	$1,800	11	$638.71
September 9	$900	21	$630.00

Sales Price	Type	Loan Amount	Upfront %	Annual %	Upfront Amount	Annual Amount
$225,000	90%	$202,500	.75%	.5%	$1,518.75	$1,012.50
$420,000	95%	$399,000	.9%	.75%	$3,591.00	$2,992.50
$142,000	FHA	$135,400	1.75%	1.35%	$2,369.50	$1,827.90
$284,500	95%	$270,200	.85%	.65%	$2,296.70	$1,756.30
$94,300	FHA	$90,000	1.75%	1.35%	$1,575.00	$1,215.00
$88,250	90%	$79,400	.6%	.45%	$476.40	$357.30

Annual Taxes	Number of Months	Tax Escrow
$2,750	3	$687.50
$1,635	9	$1,226.25
$1,397	13	$1,513.42
$4,286	5	$1,785.83
$3,264	8	$2,176.00
$982	10	$818.33

Annual Insurance Bill	Insurance Escrow
$865	$216.25
$504	$126.00
$1,649	$412.25
$973	$243.25
$2,974	$743.50
$776	$194.00

APPENDIX A Solutions to Student Calculations from Chapter 19

Sales Price	Existing Loan	Assumed?	Transfer Tax
$265,800	$174,473	No	$265.80
$163,700	$149,576	Yes	$14.20
$125,000	$95,674	Yes	$29.40
$374,700	$202,395	No	$374.70
$254,600	$201,578	Yes	$53.10
$96,500	$79,746	No	$96.50

Sales Price	New Loan Type	Loan Amount	Intangibles Tax
$88,500	90%	$79,600	$240.00
$165,000	80%	$132,000	$396.00
$126,200	95%	$119,800	$360.00
$458,500	80%	$366,800	$1,101.00
$217,200	100%	$217,200	$652.50
$95,500	90%	$85,900	$258.00

APPENDIX B

REAL ESTATE MATH REVIEW

Percent

Percent (%) means parts per hundred. For example, 25% means 25 parts per hundred; 10% means 10 parts per hundred. Percentages are related to common and decimal fractions as follows:

5%	=	0.05	=	1/20
10%	=	0.10	=	1/10
25%	=	0.25	=	1/4
75%	=	0.75	=	3/4
99%	=	0.99	=	99/100

A percentage greater than 100% is greater than 1. For example:

110%	=	1.10	=	1 1/10
150%	=	1.50	=	1 1/2
200%	=	2.00	=	2
1,100%	=	11.00	=	11

To change a decimal fraction to a percentage, move the decimal point two places to the right and add the % sign. For example:

0.001	=	0.1%
0.01	=	1%
0.06	=	6%
0.356	=	35.6%
1.15	=	115%

A percentage can be changed to a common fraction by writing it as hundredths and then reducing it to its lowest common denominator. For example:

20%	=	20/100	=	1/5
90%	=	90/100	=	9/10
225%	=	225/100	=	2 1/4

Adding and Subtracting Decimals

To add decimals, place the decimal points directly over one another. Then place the decimal point for the solutions in the same column and add. For example:

```
  6.25
  1.10
 10.277
 17.627
```

If you are working with percentages, there is no need to convert to decimal fractions; just line up the decimal points and add. For example:

```
  68.8%
   6.0%
  25.2%
 100.0%
```

When subtracting, the same methods apply. For example:

```
  1.00      100%
 -0.80      -80%
  0.20       20%
```

When there is a mixture of decimal fractions and percentages, first convert them all either to percentages or to decimal fractions.

Multiplying and Dividing Decimals

Multiplying decimals is like multiplying whole numbers except that the decimal point must be correctly placed. This is done by counting the total number of places to the right of the decimal point in the numbers to be multiplied. Then round off the same number of places in the answer. The following examples illustrate this:

```
  0.6      0.2     1.01     0.1     0.11     0.03
× 0.3    × 0.2     × 2     × 6     × 6     × 0.02
  0.18     0.04    2.02     0.6     0.66    0.0006
```

When dividing, the process starts with properly placing the decimal point. A normal division then follows. When a decimal number is divided by a whole number, place the decimal point in the answer directly above the decimal point in the problem. For example:

```
    1.03           0.033
 3)3.09         3)0.099
```

To divide by a decimal number, you must first change the divisor to a whole number. Then you must make a corresponding change in the dividend. This is done by simply moving both decimal points the same number of places to the right. For example, to divide 0.06 by 0.02, move the decimal point of each to the right two places:

$$0.02 \overline{)0.06} \quad \text{becomes} \quad 2\overline{)6}$$

$$0.5\overline{)3} \quad \text{becomes} \quad 5\overline{)30}$$

$$0.05\overline{)30} \quad \text{becomes} \quad 5\overline{)3{,}000}$$

When multiplying or dividing with percentages, first convert them to decimal form. Thus, 6% of 200 is:

$$\begin{array}{r} 200 \\ \times\, 0.06 \\ \hline 12.00 \end{array}$$

Problems Involving Rates

A simple way to solve rate problems is to think of:

The word *is* as = (an equal sign).
The word *of* as × (a multiplication sign).
The word *per* as ÷ (a division sign).

For example:

"7% of $50,000 is $3,500"

translates to:

"7% × $50,000 = $3,500"

Another formula for solving rate problems is "the Whole times the percentage Rate equals a Part," or:

W × R = P

What do you do if they give you the whole and the part and ask for the rate? Just use the simple circle formula:

Insert the values that you are given in the circle. The position of the numbers will tell you whether to multiply or divide.

For example, you start with $4,000 (the Whole) and you end up with some percent of that number, like $360 (the Part). When you put $4,000 in for W and $360 for P, you will notice that $360 is on top of $4,000, which means $360 is being divided by $4,000:

$$\frac{360}{4,000} = 0.09$$

So 360 is 9% of $4,000.

PROBLEM 1

Beverly Broker sells a house for $60,000. Her share of the commission is to be 2.5% of the sales price. How much does she earn?

Her commission is 2.5% of $60,000
Her commission = 0.025 × $60,000
Her commission = $1,500

PROBLEM 2

Sam Salesman works in an office that will pay him 70% of the commission on each home he lists and sells. With a 6% commission, how much would he earn on a $50,000 sale?

His commission is 70% of 6% of $50,000
His commission = 0.70 × 0.06 × $50,000
His commission = $2,100

PROBLEM 3

Newt Newcomer wants to earn $21,000 during his first 12 months as a salesperson. He feels he can average 3% on each sale. How much property must he sell?

3% of sales is $21,000
0.03 × sales = $21,000
sales = $21,000 ÷ 0.03
sales = $700,000

Note: An equation will remain an equation as long as you make the same change on both sides of the equal sign. If you add the same number to both sides, it is still an equation. If you subtract the same amount from each side, it is still equal.

If you multiply both sides by the same thing, it remains equal. If you divide both sides by the same thing, it remains equal.

PROBLEM 4

An apartment building nets the owners $12,000 per year on their investment of $100,000. What percent return are they receiving on their investment?

$12,000 is _____ % of $100,000

$12,000 = _____ % × $100,000

$$\frac{\$12,000}{\$100,000} = 12\%$$

PROBLEM 5

Smith wants to sell his property and have $47,000 after paying a 6% brokerage commission on the sales price. What price must Smith get?

$47,000 is 94% of selling price

$47,000 = 0.94 × selling price

$$\frac{\$47,000}{0.94} = \text{selling price}$$

$50,000 = selling price

PROBLEM 6

Miller sold his home for $75,000, paid off an existing loan of $35,000, and paid closing costs of $500. The brokerage commission was 6% of the sales price. How much money did Miller receive?

Amount = $75,000
Less $4,500 (0.06 × $75,000)
Less $35,000 (payoff)
Less $500 (closing costs)
Yields $35,000 to receive

PROBLEM 7

The assessed valuation of the Kelly home is $100,000. If the property tax rate is $6.00 per $100 of assessed valuation, what is the tax?

$$\text{The tax is } \frac{\$6.00}{\$100} \text{ of } \$100,000$$

$$\text{tax} = \frac{\$6.00}{\$100} \times \$100,000$$

tax = $6,000

PROBLEM 8

Property in Clark County is assessed at 75% of market value. What should the assessed valuation of a $40,000 property be?

Assessed valuation is 75% of market value
Assessed valuation = 0.75 × $40,000
Assessed valuation = $30,000

PROBLEM 9

An insurance company charges $0.24 per $100 of coverage for a one-year fire insurance policy. How much would a $40,000 policy cost?

Cost is $\frac{\$0.24}{\$100}$ of $40,000

Cost = $\frac{\$0.24}{\$100}$ × $40,000

Cost = $96

Area Measurement

The measurement of the distance from one point to another is called "linear" measurement. Usually, this is along a straight line, but it can also be along a curved line. Distance is measured in inches, feet, yards, and miles; less commonly used are chains (66 feet) and rods (16½ feet). Surface areas are measured in square feet, square yards, acres (43,560 square feet), and square miles. In the metric system, the standard unit of linear measurement is the meter (39.37 inches). Land area is measured in square meters and hectares. A hectare contains 10,000 square meters or 2.471 acres.

To determine the area of a square or rectangle, multiply its length times its width. The formula is:

Area = Length × Width
A = L × W

PROBLEM 10

A parcel of land measures 660 feet by 330 feet. How many square feet is this?

Area = 660 feet × 330 feet
Area = 217,800 square feet

How many acres does this parcel contain?

Acres = 217,800 ÷ 43,560
Acres = 5

If a buyer offers $42,500 for this parcel, how much is the offering per acre?

$42,500 ÷ 5 = $8,500 per acre

To determine the area of a right triangle, multiply one-half of the base times the height:

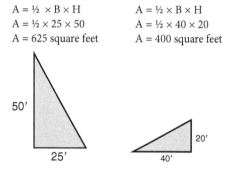

$A = ½ \times B \times H$
$A = ½ \times 25 \times 50$
$A = 625$ square feet

$A = ½ \times B \times H$
$A = ½ \times 40 \times 20$
$A = 400$ square feet

To determine the area of a circle, multiply 3.14 (π) times the square of the radius:

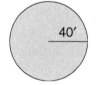

$A = \pi \times r^2$
$A = 3.14 \times 40^2$
$A = 3.14 \times 1,600$
$A = 5,024$ sq. ft.

Note: Where the diameter of a circle is given, divide by 2 to get the radius.

To determine the area of composite figures, separate them into their various components. Thus:

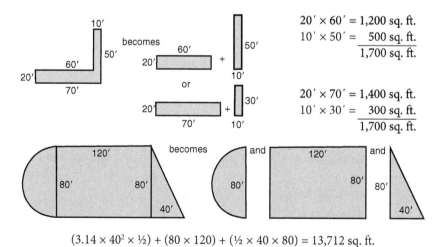

20' × 60' = 1,200 sq. ft.
10' × 50' = 500 sq. ft.
         1,700 sq. ft.

20' × 70' = 1,400 sq. ft.
10' × 30' = 300 sq. ft.
         1,700 sq. ft.

$(3.14 \times 40^2 \times ½) + (80 \times 120) + (½ \times 40 \times 80) = 13,712$ sq. ft.

Volume Measurement

Volume is measured in cubic units. The formula is:

Volume = Length × Width × Height
V = L × W × H

For example, what is the volume of a room that is 10 ft. by 15 ft. with an 8 ft. ceiling?

V = 10′ × 15′ × 8′
V = 1,200 cu. ft.

Caution: When solving area and volume problems, make certain that all the units are the same. For example, if a parcel of land is 1 mile long and 200 feet wide, convert one measurement so that both are expressed in the same unit; thus, the answer will be either in square feet or in square miles. There is no such area measurement as a mile-foot. If a building is 100 yards long by 100 feet wide by 16′6″ high, convert to 300 feet by 100 feet by 16.5 feet before multiplying.

Ratios and Proportions

If the label on a five-gallon can of paint says it will cover 2,000 square feet, how many gallons are necessary to cover 3,600 sq. ft.?

A problem like this can be solved two ways. One way is to find out what area one gallon will cover. In this case, 2,000 sq. ft. ÷ 5 gallons = 400 sq. ft. per gallon. Then divide 400 sq. ft./gal into 3,600 sq. ft. and the result is 9 gallons.

The other method is to set up a proportion:

$$\frac{5 \text{ gal}}{2,000 \text{ sq. ft.}} = \frac{Y \text{ gal}}{3,600 \text{ sq. ft.}}$$

This reads, "5 gallons is to 2,000 sq. ft. as 'Y' gallons is to 3,600 sq. ft." To solve for "Y," multiply both sides of the proportion by 3,600 sq. ft. Thus:

$$\frac{5 \text{ gal} \times 3,600 \text{ sq. ft.}}{2,000 \text{ sq. ft.}} = Y \text{ gal}$$

Divide 2,000 sq. ft. into 3,600 sq. ft. and multiply the result by 5 gallons to get the answer.

5 gal × 1.6 = 8 gal

Front-Foot Calculations

When land is sold on a front-foot basis, the price is the number of feet fronting on the street times the price per front foot.

Price = Front footage × Rate per front foot

Thus, a 50 ft. by 150 ft. lot priced at $1,000 per front foot would sell for $50,000. Note that in giving the dimensions of a lot, the first dimension given is the side facing the street.

APPENDIX

C MEASUREMENT CONVERSION TABLE

MILE =
5,280 feet
1,760 yards
320 rods
80 chains
= **1.609 kilometers**

SQUARE MILE =
640 acres
= **2.590 sq. kilometers**

ACRE =
43,560 sq. feet
4,840 sq. yards
160 sq. rods
= **4,047 sq. meters**

ROD =
16.5 feet
= **5.029 meters**

CHAIN =
66 feet
4 rods
100 links
= **20.117 meters**

METER =
39.37 inches
= **1,000 millimeters**
3.281 feet
= **100 centimeters**
1.094 yards
= **10 decimeters**

KILOMETER =
0.6214 mile
3,281 feet
1,094 yards
= **1,000 meters**

SQUARE METER =
10,765 sq. feet
1.196 sq. yards
= **10,000 sq. centimeters**

HECTARE =
2.47 acres
107,600 sq. feet
11,960 sq. yards
= **10,000 sq. meters**

SQUARE KILOMETER =
0.3861 sq. miles
247 acres
= **1,000,000 sq. meters**

KILOGRAM =
2.205 pounds
= **1,000 grams**

LITER =
1.052 quarts
0.263 gallon
= **1,000 milliliters**

METRIC TON =
2,205 pounds
1.102 tons
= **1,000 kilograms**

APPENDIX

ANSWERS TO CHAPTER REVIEW QUESTIONS

Chapter 1

1. D
2. A
3. D
4. C
5. A
6. B
7. B
8. D
9. B
10. C

Chapter 2

1. B
2. D
3. D
4. A
5. B
6. B
7. A
8. D
9. B
10. C
11. D
12. A
13. A
14. A
15. A
16. B
17. D

Chapter 3

1. B
2. A
3. B
4. D
5. C
6. D
7. B
8. A
9. C
10. C
11. B
12. D
13. C
14. B
15. D
16. D
17. C
18. C
19. B
20. A

APPENDIX D Answers to Chapter Review Questions

Chapter 4

1. B
2. C
3. A
4. B
5. D
6. C
7. A
8. A
9. C
10. D

Chapter 5

1. C
2. A
3. B
4. C
5. A
6. D
7. A
8. A
9. B
10. C
11. A
12. D
13. A
14. B
15. C

Chapter 6

1. B
2. D
3. C
4. A
5. B
6. C
7. C
8. A
9. C
10. A
11. B
12. C
13. A
14. A
15. D
16. C
17. D
18. B
19. D
20. B

Chapter 7

1. D
2. D
3. C
4. D
5. A
6. D
7. C
8. D
9. A
10. B
11. A
12. B
13. D
14. C
15. D
16. B
17. C

Chapter 8

1. C	8. A	15. D
2. B	9. D	16. D
3. D	10. C	17. B
4. C	11. B	18. A
5. A	12. B	19. D
6. C	13. C	20. B
7. B	14. C	

Chapter 9

1. C	8. B	15. C
2. D	9. C	16. A
3. D	10. D	17. D
4. B	11. D	18. B
5. C	12. D	19. B
6. C	13. D	20. B
7. D	14. C	

Chapter 10

1. B	8. A	15. C
2. A	9. C	16. B
3. C	10. C	17. D
4. C	11. C	18. D
5. D	12. D	19. C
6. C	13. D	20. A
7. B	14. C	

Chapter 11

1. B	3. A	5. C
2. D	4. C	6. C

APPENDIX D Answers to Chapter Review Questions

7. D
8. B
9. A
10. D
11. C

12. C
13. D
14. A
15. B
16. C

17. A
18. A
19. A

Chapter 12
1. A
2. B
3. A
4. C

5. C
6. B
7. D
8. C

9. A
10. D

Chapter 13
1. D
2. D
3. D
4. C

5. C
6. D
7. D
8. B

9. D
10. B

Chapter 14
1. A
2. D
3. B
4. D

5. C
6. C
7. C
8. B

9. C
10. C

Chapter 15
1. A
2. C
3. A
4. C

5. B
6. D
7. C
8. C

9. D
10. B
11. B

APPENDIX D Answers to Chapter Review Questions

Chapter 16

1. B	8. C	15. B
2. C	9. C	16. C
3. C	10. C	17. C
4. C	11. C	18. C
5. A	12. A	19. C
6. C	13. C	20. A
7. C	14. D	

Chapter 17

1. A	8. C	15. C
2. C	9. D	16. D
3. A	10. C	17. A
4. A	11. C	18. B
5. D	12. B	19. D
6. D	13. C	20. B
7. A	14. C	

Chapter 18

1. C	8. D	15. C
2. B	9. A	16. C
3. A	10. C	17. D
4. A	11. A	18. A
5. D	12. C	19. A
6. C	13. C	20. C
7. D	14. C	

Chapter 19

1. C	3. B	5. C
2. D	4. D	6. C

7. D
8. D
9. D
10. C
11. C
12. C
13. A
14. D
15. C
16. B
17. C
18. B
19. A
20. A

Chapter 20

1. D
2. C
3. D
4. C
5. B
6. C
7. B
8. B
9. A
10. C
11. A
12. D
13. C
14. D
15. C
16. D
17. B
18. C
19. C
20. C

Chapter 21

1. D
2. C
3. A
4. D
5. D
6. C
7. C
8. C
9. B
10. B
11. C
12. B
13. C
14. B
15. D
16. B
17. D
18. B
19. C
20. D

Chapter 22

1. A
2. B
3. C
4. B
5. B
6. D
7. C
8. D
9. C
10. C
11. C
12. B
13. A
14. D
15. B

16. B
17. B
18. A
19. B
20. B

Chapter 23

1. A
2. B
3. D
4. B
5. D
6. B
7. C
8. D
9. A
10. A
11. C
12. B
13. D
14. A
15. C
16. D
17. B
18. B
19. C
20. D
21. A
22. B
23. A
24. A
25. C

Chapter 24

1. B
2. C
3. A
4. B
5. D
6. A
7. C
8. D
9. B
10. D
11. B
12. A
13. B
14. C
15. D
16. B
17. B
18. C
19. D
20. A

Chapter 25

1. C
2. A
3. D
4. A
5. D
6. B
7. B
8. C
9. D
10. C
11. B
12. A
13. A
14. C
15. D
16. B
17. A
18. C
19. D
20. A

APPENDIX

 DOCUMENTS FOR REVIEW

TABLE OF CONTENTS

2021 NAR Code of Ethics	556
Exclusive Buyer Brokerage Engagement Agreement	564
Exclusive Seller Brokerage Engagement Agreement	571
Loan Estimate	579
Closing Disclosure	582
ALTA Settlement Statement – Combined	587
Lease for Residential Property	590
Purchase and Sale Agreement	602
Uniform Residential Loan Application	610
Security Deed	620

CODE OF ETHICS AND STANDARDS OF PRACTICE
OF THE NATIONAL ASSOCIATION OF REALTORS®
Effective January 1, 2021

Where the word REALTORS® is used in this Code and Preamble, it shall be deemed to include REALTOR ASSOCIATE®s.

While the Code of Ethics establishes obligations that may be higher than those mandated by law, in any instance where the Code of Ethics and the law conflict, the obligations of the law must take precedence.

Preamble

Under all is the land. Upon its wise utilization and widely allocated ownership depend the survival and growth of free institutions and of our civilization. REALTORS® should recognize that the interests of the nation and its citizens require the highest and best use of the land and the widest distribution of land ownership. They require the creation of adequate housing, the building of functioning cities, the development of productive industries and farms, and the preservation of a healthful environment.

Such interests impose obligations beyond those of ordinary commerce. They impose grave social responsibility and a patriotic duty to which REALTORS® should dedicate themselves, and for which they should be diligent in preparing themselves. REALTORS®, therefore, are zealous to maintain and improve the standards of their calling and share with their fellow REALTORS® a common responsibility for its integrity and honor.

In recognition and appreciation of their obligations to clients, customers, the public, and each other, REALTORS® continuously strive to become and remain informed on issues affecting real estate and, as knowledgeable professionals, they willingly share the fruit of their experience and study with others. They identify and take steps, through enforcement of this Code of Ethics and by assisting appropriate regulatory bodies, to eliminate practices which may damage the public or which might discredit or bring dishonor to the real estate profession. REALTORS® having direct personal knowledge of conduct that may violate the Code of Ethics involving misappropriation of client or customer funds or property, discrimination against the protected classes under the Code of Ethics, or fraud, bring such matters to the attention of the appropriate Board or Association of REALTORS®. (Amended 1/21)

Realizing that cooperation with other real estate professionals promotes the best interests of those who utilize their services, REALTORS® urge exclusive representation of clients; do not attempt to gain any unfair advantage over their competitors; and they refrain from making unsolicited comments about other practitioners. In instances where their opinion is sought, or where REALTORS® believe that comment is necessary, their opinion is offered in an objective, professional manner, uninfluenced by any personal motivation or potential advantage or gain.

The term REALTOR® has come to connote competency, fairness, and high integrity resulting from adherence to a lofty ideal of moral conduct in business relations. No inducement of profit and no instruction from clients ever can justify departure from this ideal.

In the interpretation of this obligation, REALTORS® can take no safer guide than that which has been handed down through the centuries, embodied in the Golden Rule, "Whatsoever ye would that others should do to you, do ye even so to them."

Accepting this standard as their own, REALTORS® pledge to observe its spirit in all of their activities whether conducted personally, through associates or others, or via technological means, and to conduct their business in accordance with the tenets set forth below. (Amended 1/07)

Duties to Clients and Customers

Article 1

When representing a buyer, seller, landlord, tenant, or other client as an agent, REALTORS® pledge themselves to protect and promote the interests of their client. This obligation to the client is primary, but it does not relieve REALTORS® of their obligation to treat all parties honestly. When serving a buyer, seller, landlord, tenant or other party in a non-agency capacity, REALTORS® remain obligated to treat all parties honestly. (Amended 1/01)

- **Standard of Practice 1-1**
  REALTORS®, when acting as principals in a real estate transaction, remain obligated by the duties imposed by the Code of Ethics. (Amended 1/93)

- **Standard of Practice 1-2**
  The duties imposed by the Code of Ethics encompass all real estate-related activities and transactions whether conducted in person, electronically, or through any other means.

  The duties the Code of Ethics imposes are applicable whether REALTORS® are acting as agents or in legally recognized non-agency capacities except that any duty imposed exclusively on agents by law or regulation shall not be imposed by this Code of Ethics on REALTORS® acting in non-agency capacities.

  As used in this Code of Ethics, "client" means the person(s) or entity(ies) with whom a REALTOR® or a REALTOR®'s firm has an agency or legally recognized non-agency relationship; "customer" means a party to a real estate transaction who receives information, services, or benefits but has no contractual relationship with the REALTOR® or the REALTOR®'s firm; "prospect" means a purchaser, seller, tenant, or landlord who is not subject to a representation relationship with the REALTOR® or REALTOR®'s firm; "agent" means a real estate licensee (including brokers and sales associates) acting in an agency relationship as defined by state law or regulation; and "broker" means a real estate licensee (including brokers and sales associates) acting as an agent or in a legally recognized non-agency capacity. (Adopted 1/95, Amended 1/07)

- **Standard of Practice 1-3**
  REALTORS®, in attempting to secure a listing, shall not deliberately mislead the owner as to market value.

- **Standard of Practice 1-4**
  REALTORS®, when seeking to become a buyer/tenant representative, shall not mislead buyers or tenants as to savings or other benefits that might be realized through use of the REALTOR®'s services. (Amended 1/93)

- **Standard of Practice 1-5**
  REALTORS® may represent the seller/landlord and buyer/tenant in the same transaction only after full disclosure to and with informed consent of both parties. (Adopted 1/93)

- **Standard of Practice 1-6**
  REALTORS® shall submit offers and counter-offers objectively and as quickly as possible. (Adopted 1/93, Amended 1/95)

- **Standard of Practice 1-7**
  When acting as listing brokers, REALTORS® shall continue to submit to the seller/landlord all offers and counter-offers until closing or execution of a lease unless the seller/landlord has waived this obligation in writing. Upon the written request of a cooperating broker who submits an offer to the listing broker, the listing broker shall provide, as soon as practical, a written affirmation to the cooperating broker stating that the offer has been submitted to the seller/landlord, or a written notification that the seller/landlord has waived the obligation to have the offer presented. REALTORS® shall not be obligated to continue to market the property after an offer has been accepted by the seller/landlord. REALTORS® shall recommend that sellers/landlords obtain the advice of legal counsel prior to acceptance of a subsequent offer except where the acceptance is contingent on the termination of the pre-existing purchase contract or lease. (Amended 1/20)

- **Standard of Practice 1-8**
  REALTORS®, acting as agents or brokers of buyers/tenants, shall submit to buyers/tenants all offers and counter-offers until acceptance but have no obligation to continue to show properties to their clients after an offer has been accepted unless otherwise agreed in writing. REALTORS®, acting as agents or brokers of buyers/tenants, shall recommend that buyers/tenants obtain the advice of legal counsel if there is a question as to whether a pre-existing contract has been terminated. (Adopted 1/93, Amended 1/99)

- **Standard of Practice 1-9**
  The obligation of REALTORS® to preserve confidential information (as defined by state law) provided by their clients in the course of any agency relationship or non-agency relationship recognized by law continues after termination of agency relationships or any non-agency relationships recognized by law. REALTORS® shall not knowingly, during or following the termination of professional relationships with their clients:
  1) reveal confidential information of clients; or
  2) use confidential information of clients to the disadvantage of clients; or
  3) use confidential information of clients for the REALTOR®'s advantage or the advantage of third parties unless:
     a) clients consent after full disclosure; or
     b) REALTORS® are required by court order; or
     c) it is the intention of a client to commit a crime and the information is necessary to prevent the crime; or
     d) it is necessary to defend a REALTOR® or the REALTOR®'s employees or associates against an accusation of wrongful conduct.

  Information concerning latent material defects is not considered confidential information under this Code of Ethics. (Adopted 1/93, Amended 1/01)

- **Standard of Practice 1-10**
  REALTORS® shall, consistent with the terms and conditions of their real estate licensure and their property management agreement, competently manage the property of clients with due regard for the rights, safety and health of tenants and others lawfully on the premises. (Adopted 1/95, Amended 1/00)

- **Standard of Practice 1-11**
  REALTORS® who are employed to maintain or manage a client's property shall exercise due diligence and make reasonable efforts to protect it against reasonably foreseeable contingencies and losses. (Adopted 1/95)

- **Standard of Practice 1-12**
  When entering into listing contracts, REALTORS® must advise sellers/landlords of:
  1) the REALTOR®'s company policies regarding cooperation and the amount(s) of any compensation that will be offered to subagents, buyer/tenant agents, and/or brokers acting in legally recognized non-agency capacities;
  2) the fact that buyer/tenant agents or brokers, even if compensated by listing brokers, or by sellers/landlords may represent the interests of buyers/tenants; and
  3) any potential for listing brokers to act as disclosed dual agents, e.g., buyer/tenant agents. (Adopted 1/93, Renumbered 1/98, Amended 1/03)

- **Standard of Practice 1-13**
  When entering into buyer/tenant agreements, REALTORS® must advise potential clients of:
  1) the REALTOR®'s company policies regarding cooperation;
  2) the amount of compensation to be paid by the client;
  3) the potential for additional or offsetting compensation from other brokers, from the seller or landlord, or from other parties;
  4) any potential for the buyer/tenant representative to act as a disclosed dual agent, e.g., listing broker, subagent, landlord's agent, etc.; and
  5) the possibility that sellers or sellers' representatives may not treat the existence, terms, or conditions of offers as confidential unless confidentiality is required by law, regulation, or by any confidentiality agreement between the parties. (Adopted 1/93, Renumbered 1/98, Amended 1/06)

- **Standard of Practice 1-14**
  Fees for preparing appraisals or other valuations shall not be contingent upon the amount of the appraisal or valuation. (Adopted 1/02)

- **Standard of Practice 1-15**
  REALTORS®, in response to inquiries from buyers or cooperating brokers shall, with the sellers' approval, disclose the existence of offers on the property. Where disclosure is authorized, REALTORS® shall also disclose, if asked, whether offers were obtained by the listing licensee, another licensee in the listing firm, or by a cooperating broker. (Adopted 1/03, Amended 1/09)

- **Standard of Practice 1-16**
  REALTORS® shall not access or use, or permit or enable others to access or use, listed or managed property on terms or conditions other than those authorized by the owner or seller. (Adopted 1/12)

Article 2

REALTORS® shall avoid exaggeration, misrepresentation, or concealment of pertinent facts relating to the property or the transaction. REALTORS® shall not, however, be obligated to discover latent defects in the property, to advise on matters outside the scope of their real estate license, or to disclose facts which are confidential under the scope of agency or non-agency relationships as defined by state law. (Amended 1/00)

- **Standard of Practice 2-1**
  REALTORS® shall only be obligated to discover and disclose adverse factors reasonably apparent to someone with expertise in those areas required by their real estate licensing authority. Article 2 does not impose upon the REALTOR® the obligation of expertise in other professional or technical disciplines. (Amended 1/96)

- **Standard of Practice 2-2**
  (Renumbered as Standard of Practice 1-12 1/98)

- **Standard of Practice 2-3**
  (Renumbered as Standard of Practice 1-13 1/98)

- **Standard of Practice 2-4**
  REALTORS® shall not be parties to the naming of a false consideration in any document, unless it be the naming of an obviously nominal consideration.

- **Standard of Practice 2-5**
  Factors defined as "non-material" by law or regulation or which are expressly referenced in law or regulation as not being subject to disclosure are considered not "pertinent" for purposes of Article 2. (Adopted 1/93)

Article 3

REALTORS® shall cooperate with other brokers except when cooperation is not in the client's best interest. The obligation to cooperate does not include the obligation to share commissions, fees, or to otherwise compensate another broker. (Amended 1/95)

- **Standard of Practice 3-1**
  REALTORS®, acting as exclusive agents or brokers of sellers/landlords, establish the terms and conditions of offers to cooperate. Unless expressly indicated in offers to cooperate, cooperating brokers may not assume that the offer of cooperation includes an offer of compensation. Terms of compensation, if any, shall be ascertained by cooperating brokers before beginning efforts to accept the offer of cooperation. (Amended 1/99)

- **Standard of Practice 3-2**
  Any change in compensation offered for cooperative services must be communicated to the other REALTOR® prior to the time that REALTOR® submits an offer to purchase/lease the property. After a REALTOR® has submitted an offer to purchase or lease property, the listing broker may not attempt to unilaterally modify the offered compensation with respect to that cooperative transaction. (Amended 1/14)

- **Standard of Practice 3-3**
  Standard of Practice 3-2 does not preclude the listing broker and cooperating broker from entering into an agreement to change cooperative compensation. (Adopted 1/94)

- **Standard of Practice 3-4**
  REALTORS®, acting as listing brokers, have an affirmative obligation to disclose the existence of dual or variable rate commission arrangements (i.e., listings where one amount of commission is payable if the listing broker's firm is the procuring cause of sale/lease and a different amount of commission is payable if the sale/lease results through the efforts of the seller/landlord or a cooperating broker). The listing broker shall, as soon as practical, disclose the existence of such arrangements to potential cooperating brokers and shall, in response to inquiries from cooperating brokers, disclose the differential that would result in a cooperative transaction or in a sale/lease that results through the efforts of the seller/landlord. If the cooperating broker is a buyer/tenant representative, the buyer/tenant representative must disclose such information to their client before the client makes an offer to purchase or lease. (Amended 1/02)

- **Standard of Practice 3-5**
  It is the obligation of subagents to promptly disclose all pertinent facts to the principal's agent prior to as well as after a purchase or lease agreement is executed. (Amended 1/93)

- **Standard of Practice 3-6**
  REALTORS® shall disclose the existence of accepted offers, including offers with unresolved contingencies, to any broker seeking cooperation. (Adopted 5/86, Amended 1/04)

- **Standard of Practice 3-7**
  When seeking information from another REALTOR® concerning property under a management or listing agreement, REALTORS® shall disclose their REALTOR® status and whether their interest is personal or on behalf of a client and, if on behalf of a client, their relationship with the client. (Amended 1/11)

- **Standard of Practice 3-8**
  REALTORS® shall not misrepresent the availability of access to show or inspect a listed property. (Amended 11/87)

- **Standard of Practice 3-9**
  REALTORS® shall not provide access to listed property on terms other than those established by the owner or the listing broker. (Adopted 1/10)

- **Standard of Practice 3-10**
  The duty to cooperate established in Article 3 relates to the obligation to share information on listed property, and to make property available to other brokers for showing to prospective purchasers/tenants when it is in the best interests of sellers/landlords. (Adopted 1/11)

- **Standard of Practice 3-11**
  REALTORS® may not refuse to cooperate on the basis of a broker's race, color, religion, sex, handicap, familial status, national origin, sexual orientation, or gender identity. (Adopted 1/20)

Article 4

REALTORS® shall not acquire an interest in or buy or present offers from themselves, any member of their immediate families, their firms or any member thereof, or any entities in which they have any ownership interest, any real property without making their true position known to the owner or the owner's agent or broker. In selling property they own, or in which they have any interest, REALTORS® shall reveal their ownership or interest in writing to the purchaser or the purchaser's representative. (Amended 1/00)

- **Standard of Practice 4-1**
  For the protection of all parties, the disclosures required by Article 4 shall be in writing and provided by REALTORS® prior to the signing of any contract. (Adopted 2/86)

Article 5

REALTORS® shall not undertake to provide professional services concerning a property or its value where they have a present or contemplated interest unless such interest is specifically disclosed to all affected parties.

Article 6

REALTORS® shall not accept any commission, rebate, or profit on expenditures made for their client, without the client's knowledge and consent.

When recommending real estate products or services (e.g., homeowner's insurance, warranty programs, mortgage financing, title insurance, etc.), REALTORS® shall disclose to the client or customer to whom the recommendation is made any financial benefits or fees, other than real estate referral fees, the REALTOR® or REALTOR®'s firm may receive as a direct result of such recommendation. (Amended 1/99)

- **Standard of Practice 6-1**
  REALTORS® shall not recommend or suggest to a client or a customer the use of services of another organization or business entity in which they have a direct interest without disclosing such interest at the time of the recommendation or suggestion. (Amended 5/88)

Article 7

In a transaction, REALTORS® shall not accept compensation from more than one party, even if permitted by law, without disclosure to all parties and the informed consent of the REALTOR®'s client or clients. (Amended 1/93)

Article 8

REALTORS® shall keep in a special account in an appropriate financial institution, separated from their own funds, monies coming into their possession in trust for other persons, such as escrows, trust funds, clients' monies, and other like items.

Article 9

REALTORS®, for the protection of all parties, shall assure whenever possible that all agreements related to real estate transactions including, but not limited to, listing and representation agreements, purchase contracts, and leases are in writing in clear and understandable language expressing the specific terms, conditions, obligations and commitments of the parties. A copy of each agreement shall be furnished to each party to such agreements upon their signing or initialing. (Amended 1/04)

- **Standard of Practice 9-1**
  For the protection of all parties, REALTORS® shall use reasonable care to ensure that documents pertaining to the purchase, sale, or lease of real estate are kept current through the use of written extensions or amendments. (Amended 1/93)

- **Standard of Practice 9-2**
  When assisting or enabling a client or customer in establishing a contractual relationship (e.g., listing and representation agreements, purchase agreements, leases, etc.) electronically, REALTORS® shall make reasonable efforts to explain the nature and disclose the specific terms of the contractual relationship being established prior to it being agreed to by a contracting party. (Adopted 1/07)

Duties to the Public

Article 10

REALTORS® shall not deny equal professional services to any person for reasons of race, color, religion, sex, handicap, familial status, national origin, sexual orientation, or gender identity. REALTORS® shall not be parties to any plan or agreement to discriminate against a person or persons on the basis of race, color, religion, sex, handicap, familial status, national origin, sexual orientation, or gender identity. (Amended 1/14)

REALTORS®, in their real estate employment practices, shall not discriminate against any person or persons on the basis of race, color, religion, sex, handicap, familial status, national origin, sexual orientation, or gender identity. (Amended 1/14)

- **Standard of Practice 10-1**
  When involved in the sale or lease of a residence, REALTORS® shall not volunteer information regarding the racial, religious or ethnic composition of any neighborhood nor shall they engage in any activity which may result in panic selling, however, REALTORS® may provide other demographic information. (Adopted 1/94, Amended 1/06)

- **Standard of Practice 10-2**
  When not involved in the sale or lease of a residence, REALTORS® may provide demographic information related to a property, transaction or professional assignment to a party if such demographic information is (a) deemed by the REALTOR® to be needed to assist with or complete, in a manner consistent with Article 10, a real estate transaction or professional assignment and (b) is obtained or derived from a recognized, reliable, independent, and impartial source. The source of such information and any additions, deletions, modifications, interpretations, or other changes shall be disclosed in reasonable detail. (Adopted 1/05, Renumbered 1/06)

- **Standard of Practice 10-3**
  REALTORS® shall not print, display or circulate any statement or advertisement with respect to selling or renting of a property that indicates any preference, limitations or discrimination based on race, color, religion, sex, handicap, familial status, national origin, sexual orientation, or gender identity. (Adopted 1/94, Renumbered 1/05 and 1/06, Amended 1/14)

- **Standard of Practice 10-4**
  As used in Article 10 "real estate employment practices" relates to employees and independent contractors providing real estate-related services and the administrative and clerical staff directly supporting those individuals. (Adopted 1/00, Renumbered 1/05 and 1/06)

- **Standard of Practice 10-5**
  REALTORS® must not use harassing speech, hate speech, epithets, or slurs based on race, color, religion, sex, handicap, familial status, national origin, sexual orientation, or gender identity. (Adopted and effective November 13, 2020)

Article 11

The services which REALTORS® provide to their clients and customers shall conform to the standards of practice and competence which are reasonably expected in the specific real estate disciplines in which they engage; specifically, residential real estate brokerage, real property management, commercial and industrial real estate brokerage, land brokerage, real estate appraisal, real estate counseling, real estate syndication, real estate auction, and international real estate.

REALTORS® shall not undertake to provide specialized professional services concerning a type of property or service that is outside their field of competence unless they engage the assistance of one who is competent on such types of property or service, or unless the facts are fully disclosed to the client. Any persons engaged to provide such assistance shall be so identified to the client and their contribution to the assignment should be set forth. (Amended 1/10)

- **Standard of Practice 11-1**
  When REALTORS® prepare opinions of real property value or price they must:
  1) be knowledgeable about the type of property being valued,
  2) have access to the information and resources necessary to formulate an accurate opinion, and
  3) be familiar with the area where the subject property is located

  unless lack of any of these is disclosed to the party requesting the opinion in advance.

  When an opinion of value or price is prepared other than in pursuit of a listing or to assist a potential purchaser in formulating a purchase offer, the opinion shall include the following unless the party requesting the opinion requires a specific type of report or different data set:
  1) identification of the subject property
  2) date prepared
  3) defined value or price
  4) limiting conditions, including statements of purpose(s) and intended user(s)
  5) any present or contemplated interest, including the possibility of representing the seller/landlord or buyers/tenants
  6) basis for the opinion, including applicable market data
  7) if the opinion is not an appraisal, a statement to that effect
  8) disclosure of whether and when a physical inspection of the property's exterior was conducted
  9) disclosure of whether and when a physical inspection of the property's interior was conducted
  10) disclosure of whether the REALTOR® has any conflicts of interest (Amended 1/14)

- **Standard of Practice 11-2**
  The obligations of the Code of Ethics in respect of real estate disciplines other than appraisal shall be interpreted and applied in accordance with the standards of competence and practice which clients and the public reasonably require to protect their rights and interests considering the complexity of the transaction, the availability of expert assistance, and, where the REALTOR® is an agent or subagent, the obligations of a fiduciary. (Adopted 1/95)

- **Standard of Practice 11-3**
  When REALTORS® provide consultive services to clients which involve advice or counsel for a fee (not a commission), such advice shall be rendered in an objective manner and the fee shall not be contingent on the substance of the advice or counsel given. If

brokerage or transaction services are to be provided in addition to consultive services, a separate compensation may be paid with prior agreement between the client and REALTOR®. (Adopted 1/96)

- **Standard of Practice 11-4**
The competency required by Article 11 relates to services contracted for between REALTORS® and their clients or customers; the duties expressly imposed by the Code of Ethics; and the duties imposed by law or regulation. (Adopted 1/02)

Article 12

REALTORS® shall be honest and truthful in their real estate communications and shall present a true picture in their advertising, marketing, and other representations. REALTORS® shall ensure that their status as real estate professionals is readily apparent in their advertising, marketing, and other representations, and that the recipients of all real estate communications are, or have been, notified that those communications are from a real estate professional. (Amended 1/08)

- **Standard of Practice 12-1**
Unless they are receiving no compensation from any source for their time and services, REALTORS® may use the term "free" and similar terms in their advertising and in other representations only if they clearly and conspicuously disclose:

    1) by whom they are being, or expect to be, paid;
    2) the amount of the payment or anticipated payment;
    3) any conditions associated with the payment, offered product or service, and;
    4) any other terms relating to their compensation. (Amended 1/20)

- **Standard of Practice 12-2**
(Deleted 1/20)

- **Standard of Practice 12-3**
The offering of premiums, prizes, merchandise discounts or other inducements to list, sell, purchase, or lease is not, in itself, unethical even if receipt of the benefit is contingent on listing, selling, purchasing, or leasing through the REALTOR® making the offer. However, REALTORS® must exercise care and candor in any such advertising or other public or private representations so that any party interested in receiving or otherwise benefiting from the REALTOR®'s offer will have clear, thorough, advance understanding of all the terms and conditions of the offer. The offering of any inducements to do business is subject to the limitations and restrictions of state law and the ethical obligations established by any applicable Standard of Practice. (Amended 1/95)

- **Standard of Practice 12-4**
REALTORS® shall not offer for sale/lease or advertise property without authority. When acting as listing brokers or as subagents, REALTORS® shall not quote a price different from that agreed upon with the seller/landlord. (Amended 1/93)

- **Standard of Practice 12-5**
REALTORS® shall not advertise nor permit any person employed by or affiliated with them to advertise real estate services or listed property in any medium (e.g., electronically, print, radio, television, etc.) without disclosing the name of that REALTOR®'s firm in a reasonable and readily apparent manner either in the advertisement or in electronic advertising via a link to a display with all required disclosures. (Adopted 11/86, Amended 1/16)

- **Standard of Practice 12-6**
REALTORS®, when advertising unlisted real property for sale/lease in which they have an ownership interest, shall disclose their status as both owners/landlords and as REALTORS® or real estate licensees. (Amended 1/93)

- **Standard of Practice 12-7**
Only REALTORS® who participated in the transaction as the listing broker or cooperating broker (selling broker) may claim to have "sold" the property. Prior to closing, a cooperating broker may post a "sold" sign only with the consent of the listing broker. (Amended 1/96)

- **Standard of Practice 12-8**
The obligation to present a true picture in representations to the public includes information presented, provided, or displayed on REALTORS®' websites. REALTORS® shall use reasonable efforts to ensure that information on their websites is current. When it becomes apparent that information on a REALTOR®'s website is no longer current or accurate, REALTORS® shall promptly take corrective action. (Adopted 1/07)

- **Standard of Practice 12-9**
REALTOR® firm websites shall disclose the firm's name and state(s) of licensure in a reasonable and readily apparent manner.

    Websites of REALTORS® and non-member licensees affiliated with a REALTOR® firm shall disclose the firm's name and that REALTOR®'s or non-member licensee's state(s) of licensure in a reasonable and readily apparent manner. (Adopted 1/07)

- **Standard of Practice 12-10**
REALTORS®' obligation to present a true picture in their advertising and representations to the public includes Internet content, images, and the URLs and domain names they use, and prohibits REALTORS® from:

    1) engaging in deceptive or unauthorized framing of real estate brokerage websites;
    2) manipulating (e.g., presenting content developed by others) listing and other content in any way that produces a deceptive or misleading result;
    3) deceptively using metatags, keywords or other devices/methods to direct, drive, or divert Internet traffic; or
    4) presenting content developed by others without either attribution or without permission; or
    5) otherwise misleading consumers, including use of misleading images. (Adopted 1/07, Amended 1/18)

- **Standard of Practice 12-11**
REALTORS® intending to share or sell consumer information gathered via the Internet shall disclose that possibility in a reasonable and readily apparent manner. (Adopted 1/07)

- **Standard of Practice 12-12**
REALTORS® shall not:

    1) use URLs or domain names that present less than a true picture, or
    2) register URLs or domain names which, if used, would present less than a true picture. (Adopted 1/08)

- **Standard of Practice 12-13**
The obligation to present a true picture in advertising, marketing, and representations allows REALTORS® to use and display only professional designations, certifications, and other credentials to which they are legitimately entitled. (Adopted 1/08)

Article 13

REALTORS® shall not engage in activities that constitute the unauthorized practice of law and shall recommend that legal counsel be obtained when the interest of any party to the transaction requires it.

Article 14

If charged with unethical practice or asked to present evidence or to cooperate in any other way, in any professional standards proceeding or investigation, REALTORS® shall place all pertinent facts before the proper tribunals of the Member Board or affiliated institute, society, or council in which membership is held and shall take no action to disrupt or obstruct such processes. (Amended 1/99)

- **Standard of Practice 14-1**
REALTORS® shall not be subject to disciplinary proceedings in more than one Board of REALTORS® or affiliated institute, society,

or council in which they hold membership with respect to alleged violations of the Code of Ethics relating to the same transaction or event. (Amended 1/95)

- **Standard of Practice 14-2**
  REALTORS® shall not make any unauthorized disclosure or dissemination of the allegations, findings, or decision developed in connection with an ethics hearing or appeal or in connection with an arbitration hearing or procedural review. (Amended 1/92)

- **Standard of Practice 14-3**
  REALTORS® shall not obstruct the Board's investigative or professional standards proceedings by instituting or threatening to institute actions for libel, slander, or defamation against any party to a professional standards proceeding or their witnesses based on the filing of an arbitration request, an ethics complaint, or testimony given before any tribunal. (Adopted 11/87, Amended 1/99)

- **Standard of Practice 14-4**
  REALTORS® shall not intentionally impede the Board's investigative or disciplinary proceedings by filing multiple ethics complaints based on the same event or transaction. (Adopted 11/88)

Duties to REALTORS®

Article 15

REALTORS® shall not knowingly or recklessly make false or misleading statements about other real estate professionals, their businesses, or their business practices. (Amended 1/12)

- **Standard of Practice 15-1**
  REALTORS® shall not knowingly or recklessly file false or unfounded ethics complaints. (Adopted 1/00)

- **Standard of Practice 15-2**
  The obligation to refrain from making false or misleading statements about other real estate professionals, their businesses, and their business practices includes the duty to not knowingly or recklessly publish, repeat, retransmit, or republish false or misleading statements made by others. This duty applies whether false or misleading statements are repeated in person, in writing, by technological means (e.g., the Internet), or by any other means. (Adopted 1/07, Amended 1/12)

- **Standard of Practice 15-3**
  The obligation to refrain from making false or misleading statements about other real estate professionals, their businesses, and their business practices includes the duty to publish a clarification about or to remove statements made by others on electronic media the REALTOR® controls once the REALTOR® knows the statement is false or misleading. (Adopted 1/10, Amended 1/12)

Article 16

REALTORS® shall not engage in any practice or take any action inconsistent with exclusive representation or exclusive brokerage relationship agreements that other REALTORS® have with clients. (Amended 1/04)

- **Standard of Practice 16-1**
  Article 16 is not intended to prohibit aggressive or innovative business practices which are otherwise ethical and does not prohibit disagreements with other REALTORS® involving commission, fees, compensation or other forms of payment or expenses. (Adopted 1/93, Amended 1/95)

- **Standard of Practice 16-2**
  Article 16 does not preclude REALTORS® from making general announcements to prospects describing their services and the terms of their availability even though some recipients may have entered into agency agreements or other exclusive relationships with another REALTOR®. A general telephone canvass, general mailing or distribution addressed to all prospects in a given geographical area or in a given profession, business, club, or organization, or other classification or group is deemed "general" for purposes of this standard. (Amended 1/04)

Article 16 is intended to recognize as unethical two basic types of solicitations:

First, telephone or personal solicitations of property owners who have been identified by a real estate sign, multiple listing compilation, or other information service as having exclusively listed their property with another REALTOR® and

Second, mail or other forms of written solicitations of prospects whose properties are exclusively listed with another REALTOR® when such solicitations are not part of a general mailing but are directed specifically to property owners identified through compilations of current listings, "for sale" or "for rent" signs, or other sources of information required by Article 3 and Multiple Listing Service rules to be made available to other REALTORS® under offers of subagency or cooperation. (Amended 1/04)

- **Standard of Practice 16-3**
  Article 16 does not preclude REALTORS® from contacting the client of another broker for the purpose of offering to provide, or entering into a contract to provide, a different type of real estate service unrelated to the type of service currently being provided (e.g., property management as opposed to brokerage) or from offering the same type of service for property not subject to other brokers' exclusive agreements. However, information received through a Multiple Listing Service or any other offer of cooperation may not be used to target clients of other REALTORS® to whom such offers to provide services may be made. (Amended 1/04)

- **Standard of Practice 16-4**
  REALTORS® shall not solicit a listing which is currently listed exclusively with another broker. However, if the listing broker, when asked by the REALTOR®, refuses to disclose the expiration date and nature of such listing, i.e., an exclusive right to sell, an exclusive agency, open listing, or other form of contractual agreement between the listing broker and the client, the REALTOR® may contact the owner to secure such information and may discuss the terms upon which the REALTOR® might take a future listing or, alternatively, may take a listing to become effective upon expiration of any existing exclusive listing. (Amended 1/94)

- **Standard of Practice 16-5**
  REALTORS® shall not solicit buyer/tenant agreements from buyers/tenants who are subject to exclusive buyer/tenant agreements. However, if asked by a REALTOR®, the broker refuses to disclose the expiration date of the exclusive buyer/tenant agreement, the REALTOR® may contact the buyer/tenant to secure such information and may discuss the terms upon which the REALTOR® might enter into a future buyer/tenant agreement or, alternatively, may enter into a buyer/tenant agreement to become effective upon the expiration of any existing exclusive buyer/tenant agreement. (Adopted 1/94, Amended 1/98)

- **Standard of Practice 16-6**
  When REALTORS® are contacted by the client of another REALTOR® regarding the creation of an exclusive relationship to provide the same type of service, and REALTORS® have not directly or indirectly initiated such discussions, they may discuss the terms upon which they might enter into a future agreement or, alternatively, may enter into an agreement which becomes effective upon expiration of any existing exclusive agreement. (Amended 1/98)

- **Standard of Practice 16-7**
  The fact that a prospect has retained a REALTOR® as an exclusive representative or exclusive broker in one or more past transactions does not preclude other REALTORS® from seeking such prospect's future business. (Amended 1/04)

- **Standard of Practice 16-8**
  The fact that an exclusive agreement has been entered into with a REALTOR® shall not preclude or inhibit any other REALTOR® from

- **Standard of Practice 16-9**
  REALTORS®, prior to entering into a representation agreement, have an affirmative obligation to make reasonable efforts to determine whether the prospect is subject to a current, valid exclusive agreement to provide the same type of real estate service. (Amended 1/04)

- **Standard of Practice 16-10**
  REALTORS®, acting as buyer or tenant representatives or brokers, shall disclose that relationship to the seller/landlord's representative or broker at first contact and shall provide written confirmation of that disclosure to the seller/landlord's representative or broker not later than execution of a purchase agreement or lease. (Amended 1/04)

- **Standard of Practice 16-11**
  On unlisted property, REALTORS® acting as buyer/tenant representatives or brokers shall disclose that relationship to the seller/landlord at first contact for that buyer/tenant and shall provide written confirmation of such disclosure to the seller/landlord not later than execution of any purchase or lease agreement. (Amended 1/04)

  REALTORS® shall make any request for anticipated compensation from the seller/landlord at first contact. (Amended 1/98)

- **Standard of Practice 16-12**
  REALTORS®, acting as representatives or brokers of sellers/landlords or as subagents of listing brokers, shall disclose that relationship to buyers/tenants as soon as practicable and shall provide written confirmation of such disclosure to buyers/tenants not later than execution of any purchase or lease agreement. (Amended 1/04)

- **Standard of Practice 16-13**
  All dealings concerning property exclusively listed, or with buyer/tenants who are subject to an exclusive agreement shall be carried on with the client's representative or broker, and not with the client, except with the consent of the client's representative or broker or except where such dealings are initiated by the client.

  Before providing substantive services (such as writing a purchase offer or presenting a CMA) to prospects, REALTORS® shall ask prospects whether they are a party to any exclusive representation agreement. REALTORS® shall not knowingly provide substantive services concerning a prospective transaction to prospects who are parties to exclusive representation agreements, except with the consent of the prospects' exclusive representatives or at the direction of prospects. (Adopted 1/93, Amended 1/04)

- **Standard of Practice 16-14**
  REALTORS® are free to enter into contractual relationships or to negotiate with sellers/landlords, buyers/tenants or others who are not subject to an exclusive agreement but shall not knowingly obligate them to pay more than one commission except with their informed consent. (Amended 1/98)

- **Standard of Practice 16-15**
  In cooperative transactions REALTORS® shall compensate cooperating REALTORS® (principal brokers) and shall not compensate nor offer to compensate, directly or indirectly, any of the sales licensees employed by or affiliated with other REALTORS® without the prior express knowledge and consent of the cooperating broker.

- **Standard of Practice 16-16**
  REALTORS®, acting as subagents or buyer/tenant representatives or brokers, shall not use the terms of an offer to purchase/lease to attempt to modify the listing broker's offer of compensation to subagents or buyer/tenant representatives or brokers nor make the submission of an executed offer to purchase/lease contingent on the listing broker's agreement to modify the offer of compensation. (Amended 1/04)

- **Standard of Practice 16-17**
  REALTORS®, acting as subagents or as buyer/tenant representatives or brokers, shall not attempt to extend a listing broker's offer of cooperation and/or compensation to other brokers without the consent of the listing broker. (Amended 1/04)

- **Standard of Practice 16-18**
  REALTORS® shall not use information obtained from listing brokers through offers to cooperate made through multiple listing services or through other offers of cooperation to refer listing brokers' clients to other brokers or to create buyer/tenant relationships with listing brokers' clients, unless such use is authorized by listing brokers. (Amended 1/02)

- **Standard of Practice 16-19**
  Signs giving notice of property for sale, rent, lease, or exchange shall not be placed on property without consent of the seller/landlord. (Amended 1/93)

- **Standard of Practice 16-20**
  REALTORS®, prior to or after their relationship with their current firm is terminated, shall not induce clients of their current firm to cancel exclusive contractual agreements between the client and that firm. This does not preclude REALTORS® (principals) from establishing agreements with their associated licensees governing assignability of exclusive agreements. (Adopted 1/98, Amended 1/10)

Article 17

In the event of contractual disputes or specific non-contractual disputes as defined in Standard of Practice 17-4 between REALTORS® (principals) associated with different firms, arising out of their relationship as REALTORS®, the REALTORS® shall mediate the dispute if the Board requires its members to mediate. If the dispute is not resolved through mediation, or if mediation is not required, REALTORS® shall submit the dispute to arbitration in accordance with the policies of the Board rather than litigate the matter.

In the event clients of REALTORS® wish to mediate or arbitrate contractual disputes arising out of real estate transactions, REALTORS® shall mediate or arbitrate those disputes in accordance with the policies of the Board, provided the clients agree to be bound by any resulting agreement or award.

The obligation to participate in mediation and arbitration contemplated by this Article includes the obligation of REALTORS® (principals) to cause their firms to mediate and arbitrate and be bound by any resulting agreement or award. (Amended 1/12)

- **Standard of Practice 17-1**
  The filing of litigation and refusal to withdraw from it by REALTORS® in an arbitrable matter constitutes a refusal to arbitrate. (Adopted 2/86)

- **Standard of Practice 17-2**
  Article 17 does not require REALTORS® to mediate in those circumstances when all parties to the dispute advise the Board in writing that they choose not to mediate through the Board's facilities. The fact that all parties decline to participate in mediation does not relieve REALTORS® of the duty to arbitrate.

  Article 17 does not require REALTORS® to arbitrate in those circumstances when all parties to the dispute advise the Board in writing that they choose not to arbitrate before the Board. (Amended 1/12)

- **Standard of Practice 17-3**
  REALTORS®, when acting solely as principals in a real estate transaction, are not obligated to arbitrate disputes with other REALTORS® absent a specific written agreement to the contrary. (Adopted 1/96)

- **Standard of Practice 17-4**
  Specific non-contractual disputes that are subject to arbitration pursuant to Article 17 are:

  1) Where a listing broker has compensated a cooperating broker and another cooperating broker subsequently claims to be the procuring cause of the sale or lease. In such cases

the complainant may name the first cooperating broker as respondent and arbitration may proceed without the listing broker being named as a respondent. When arbitration occurs between two (or more) cooperating brokers and where the listing broker is not a party, the amount in dispute and the amount of any potential resulting award is limited to the amount paid to the respondent by the listing broker and any amount credited or paid to a party to the transaction at the direction of the respondent. Alternatively, if the complaint is brought against the listing broker, the listing broker may name the first cooperating broker as a third-party respondent. In either instance the decision of the hearing panel as to procuring cause shall be conclusive with respect to all current or subsequent claims of the parties for compensation arising out of the underlying cooperative transaction. (Adopted 1/97, Amended 1/07)

2) Where a buyer or tenant representative is compensated by the seller or landlord, and not by the listing broker, and the listing broker, as a result, reduces the commission owed by the seller or landlord and, subsequent to such actions, another cooperating broker claims to be the procuring cause of sale or lease. In such cases the complainant may name the first cooperating broker as respondent and arbitration may proceed without the listing broker being named as a respondent. When arbitration occurs between two (or more) cooperating brokers and where the listing broker is not a party, the amount in dispute and the amount of any potential resulting award is limited to the amount paid to the respondent by the seller or landlord and any amount credited or paid to a party to the transaction at the direction of the respondent. Alternatively, if the complaint is brought against the listing broker, the listing broker may name the first cooperating broker as a third-party respondent. In either instance the decision of the hearing panel as to procuring cause shall be conclusive with respect to all current or subsequent claims of the parties for compensation arising out of the underlying cooperative transaction. (Adopted 1/97, Amended 1/07)

3) Where a buyer or tenant representative is compensated by the buyer or tenant and, as a result, the listing broker reduces the commission owed by the seller or landlord and, subsequent to such actions, another cooperating broker claims to be the procuring cause of sale or lease. In such cases the complainant may name the first cooperating broker as respondent and arbitration may proceed without the listing broker being named as a respondent. Alternatively, if the complaint is brought against the listing broker, the listing broker may name the first cooperating broker as a third-party respondent. In either instance the decision of the hearing panel as to procuring cause shall be conclusive with respect to all current or subsequent claims of the parties for compensation arising out of the underlying cooperative transaction. (Adopted 1/97)

4) Where two or more listing brokers claim entitlement to compensation pursuant to open listings with a seller or landlord who agrees to participate in arbitration (or who requests arbitration) and who agrees to be bound by the decision. In cases where one of the listing brokers has been compensated by the seller or landlord, the other listing broker, as complainant, may name the first listing broker as respondent and arbitration may proceed between the brokers. (Adopted 1/97)

5) Where a buyer or tenant representative is compensated by the seller or landlord, and not by the listing broker, and the listing broker, as a result, reduces the commission owed by the seller or landlord and, subsequent to such actions, claims to be the procuring cause of sale or lease. In such cases arbitration shall be between the listing broker and the buyer or tenant representative and the amount in dispute is limited to the amount of the reduction of commission to which the listing broker agreed. (Adopted 1/05)

- **Standard of Practice 17-5**
  The obligation to arbitrate established in Article 17 includes disputes between REALTORS® (principals) in different states in instances where, absent an established inter-association arbitration agreement, the REALTOR® (principal) requesting arbitration agrees to submit to the jurisdiction of, travel to, participate in, and be bound by any resulting award rendered in arbitration conducted by the respondent(s) REALTOR®'s association, in instances where the respondent(s) REALTOR®'s association determines that an arbitrable issue exists. (Adopted 1/07)

Explanatory Notes

The reader should be aware of the following policies which have been approved by the Board of Directors of the National Association:

In filing a charge of an alleged violation of the Code of Ethics by a REALTOR®, the charge must read as an alleged violation of one or more Articles of the Code. Standards of Practice may be cited in support of the charge.

The Standards of Practice serve to clarify the ethical obligations imposed by the various Articles and supplement, and do not substitute for, the Case Interpretations in Interpretations of the Code of Ethics.

Modifications to existing Standards of Practice and additional new Standards of Practice are approved from time to time. Readers are cautioned to ensure that the most recent publications are utilized.

430 North Michigan Avenue | Chicago, IL 60611-4087
800.874.6500 | www.nar.realtor

©2021 NATIONAL ASSOCIATION OF REALTORS®

166-288-21 (01/21 BFC)

EXCLUSIVE BUYER BROKERAGE ENGAGEMENT AGREEMENT

2021 Printing

State law prohibits Broker from representing Buyer as a client without first entering into a written agreement with Buyer under O.C.G.A. § 10-6A-1 et. seq.

A. KEY TERMS AND CONDITIONS

1. **Exclusive Buyer Brokerage Engagement Agreement.** For and in consideration of the mutual promises contained herein and other good and valuable consideration, the undersigned buyer(s) ("Buyer") and the undersigned broker ("Broker") do hereby enter into this Exclusive Buyer Brokerage Engagement Agreement ("Agreement") on the terms and conditions set forth herein.

2. **Term.** The term of this Agreement shall begin on the date of _____ ("Starting Date") and shall continue through the date of _____, as the same may be extended by written agreement of the parties or as provided for herein ("Ending Date").

3. **Agency and Brokerage.** The following are types of agency relationship(s) **NOT** offered by Broker:
   ☐ seller agency   ☐ buyer agency   ☐ designated agency   ☐ dual agency
   ☐ sub-agency   ☐ tenant agency ☐ landlord agency

   Buyer ☐ does or ☐ does not consent to Broker acting in a dual agency capacity, as that agency relationship is explained in Section B.3(b) below and in the CB01 ABCs of Agency. Buyer expressly consents to Broker acting in any other agency relationship offered by Broker.

4. **Commission.**

   A. Buyer agrees that Broker shall be entitled to the following commission ("Commission") at the closing of a Contract to Purchase (as that term is hereinafter defined) as follows: *[Select one or more of the following sections below. The sections not marked shall not be part of this Agreement]*

   ☐ _____ percent (%) of the sales price;
   ☐ $_____;
   ☐ (other) _____

   B. In the event Seller does not pay the Broker the full amount of the Commission, Buyer ☐ shall **OR** ☐ shall not pay Broker the difference at closing between Broker's Commission and the commission actually paid to Broker at the closing of a Contract to Purchase (as that term is hereinafter defined).

5. **Separate Commission on Lease.** If Buyer leases property or enters into a lease/purchase contract or a lease with an option to purchase agreement during this Agreement, Buyer shall also pay Broker a separate leasing commission (except where the commission is paid by the Landlord) in the amount of $_____ and as follows: _____. Notwithstanding any provision to the contrary contained herein, the payment of a leasing Commission (including in lease/purchase transactions or lease with an option to purchase transactions) shall not relieve Buyer from paying the Commission at the closing of a Contract to Purchase, as provided elsewhere in this Agreement.

6. **Protected Period:** The length of the Protected Period, as that term is hereinafter defined, shall be _____ days ("Protected Period").

B. CORRESPONDING PARAGRAPHS FOR SECTION A.

1. **Exclusive Buyer Brokerage Engagement Agreement.** Buyer hereby agrees to hire Broker to act Buyer's exclusive real estate broker in locating, and to the extent requested by Buyer, negotiating the purchase or exchange of real property on behalf of Buyer and filing out a pre-printed form contract for Buyer's review and approval. Buyer is not a party to any other current exclusive buyer brokerage engagement agreement and all such previous agreements, if any, have expired and not been renewed. Buyer acknowledges that Buyer may have to pay previous broker a real estate commission if Buyer is: a) subject to a current buyer brokerage engagement agreement; b) terminated a previous buyer brokerage agreement without the consent of the previous broker and enters into a Contract to Purchase, as that term is defined herein, or lease during what would have been the term of a previous exclusive brokerage engagement agreement had it not been terminated by buyer; or c) enters into a Contract to Purchase or lease on a Protected Properties during the Protected Period.

THIS FORM IS COPYRIGHTED AND MAY ONLY BE USED IN REAL ESTATE TRANSACTIONS IN WHICH _____ IS INVOLVED AS A REAL ESTATE LICENSEE. UNAUTHORIZED USE OF THE FORM MAY RESULT IN LEGAL SANCTIONS BEING BROUGHT AGAINST THE USER AND SHOULD BE REPORTED TO THE GEORGIA ASSOCIATION OF REALTORS® AT (770) 451-1831.

Copyright© 2021 by Georgia Association of REALTORS®, Inc.   F110, Exclusive Buyer Brokerage Engagement Agreement, Page 1 of 7, 01/01/21

2. **Term.**
   a. The term of this Agreement shall begin on the Starting Date and shall continue through the Ending Date as the same may be extended upon the written agreement of the parties or as provided for herein. If Buyer is a party to a Contract to Purchase, as that term is hereinafter defined, but the term expires prior to the closing, then the term of this Agreement shall be automatically extended through the closing of the Contract to Purchase.
   b. **Extension:** If during the term of this Agreement, Buyer and a prospective seller enter into a real estate purchase and sale agreement, option to purchase real property, agreement to exchange real property or contract to purchase the shares, partnership or membership interests in a legal entity owning real property (hereinafter, collectively, "Contract to Purchase") which is not closed or consummated for any reason whatsoever, then the original expiration date of this Agreement may be extended for the number of days that Buyer was under contract ("Extension Period") by Broker providing written notice of the same to Buyer within five (5) days of the date the Contract to Purchase not being consummated but in no event later than prior to the expiration of this Agreement (hereinafter "Notification Period"). If such written notice is not given before the end of the Notification Period, then the Extension Period for that transaction shall be deemed to have been waived by Broker.

3. **Agency and Brokerage.**
   a. **Broker's Policy on Agency:** Unless Broker has indicated elsewhere herein that Broker is not offering a specific agency relationship, the types of agency relationships offered by Broker are: seller agency, buyer agency, designated agency, dual agency, sub-agency, landlord agency, and tenant agency.
   b. **Dual Agency Disclosure:** *[Applicable only if Broker's agency policy is to practice dual agency and Buyer has consented to Broker acting in a dual agency capacity.]* If Buyer and a prospective seller are both being represented by the same Broker and the Broker is not acting in a designated agency capacity, Buyer is aware that Broker is acting as a dual agent in this transaction and hereby consents to the same. Buyer has been advised that:
      (1) In serving as a dual agent, Broker is representing two parties, Buyer and the seller, as clients whose interests are or at times could be different or even adverse;
      (2) Broker will disclose all adverse, material facts relevant to the transaction and actually known to the dual agent to all parties in the transaction except for information made confidential by request or instructions from either party which is not otherwise required to be disclosed by law;
      (3) Buyer does not have to consent to dual agency. The consent of the Buyer to dual agency has been given voluntarily in Section A and the Buyer has read and understands this Agreement.
      (4) Notwithstanding any provision to the contrary contained herein, Buyer hereby directs Broker, while acting as a dual agent, to keep confidential and not reveal to the other party any information which could materially and adversely affect their negotiating position except as required by law.
      (5) Broker or Broker's affiliated licensees will timely disclose to each party the nature of any material relationship with other party other than that incidental to the transaction. A material relationship shall mean any actually known personal, familial, or business relationship between Broker and a party which would impair the ability of Broker to exercise fair and independent judgment relative to another client. The other party whom Broker may represent in the event of dual agency may not be identified at the time Buyer enters into this Agreement. If any party is identified after the Agreement and has a material relationship with Broker, then Broker shall timely provide to Buyer a disclosure of the nature of such relationship.
      (6) Upon signing this brokerage engagement with the dual agency disclosures contained herein, Buyer's consent to dual agency is conclusively deemed to have been given and informed in accordance with state law, provided that Buyer has consented to Broker acting in a dual agency capacity in Section A(3) above.
   c. **Designated Agency Disclosure:** *[Applicable only if Broker's agency policy is to practice designated agency.]* Buyer does hereby consent to Broker acting in a designated agency capacity in transactions in which Broker is representing Buyer and a prospective seller, but where Broker assigns one or more of its affiliated licensees exclusively to represent the Buyer and one or more of its other affiliated licensees exclusively to represent the prospective seller.
   d. **No Other Adverse Agency Relationships:** Unless specified herein, Broker has no other known agency relationships with other parties which would conflict with any interests of Buyer (except that Broker may represent other buyers, sellers, landlords, and tenants in buying, selling or leasing property).

4. **Commission.**
   a. **Broker's Entitlement to Commission:** If during the term of this Agreement (as the same may be extended by the written agreement of the parties or as provided for herein) Buyer enters a Contract to Purchase or a lease, Buyer agrees that Broker shall be entitled to the Commission set forth herein at the closing of the transaction (regardless of whether the closing is during or after the Ending Date) or to a Leasing Commission, if buyer leases, leases to purchase or a leases with an option to purchase real property (regardless of ether the commencement of the lease is before or after the expiration of this Agreement). There may be properties shown to Buyer by Broker where a bonus is being offered to Broker in addition to the Commission or by Broker to an affiliated licensee for finding a buyer to purchase the property listed by Broker. Buyer consents to Broker and Broker's affiliated licensees receiving such bonuses.
   b. **Seller Normally Pays Commission:** In the event Seller does not pay the Broker the full amount of the Commission, the difference in Commission will be paid by Buyer as agreed in Section A.4(a).
   c. **Commission on Property Sold For Sale By Owner ("FSBO"):** In the event Buyer purchases, leases, leases to purchase or leases with an option to purchase property that is being sold or leased by owner ("FSBO") without a broker and the owner is unwilling to pay Broker its Commission at or before the closing, Buyer agrees to pay Broker the Commission set forth herein at or before the closing or the Leasing Commission, if applicable, prior to the commencement of the lease.

5. **Separate Commission on Lease.** Notwithstanding the above, if Buyer leases property or enters into a lease/purchase or lease with an option to purchase contract during this Agreement, Buyer shall also pay Broker a separate Leasing Commission (except where the commission is paid by the Landlord) in the amount as indicated elsewhere in this Agreement. Notwithstanding any provision to the contrary contained herein, the payment of a leasing commission (including in lease purchase and lease with an option to purchase transactions) shall not relieve either Buyer from paying the Commission at the closing of a Contract to Purchase, as provided elsewhere in this Agreement.

6. **Protected Period.** The Protected Period shall be the period of time set forth in this Agreement commencing upon the expiration of this Agreement or what would have the expiration of this Agreement had it not been unilaterally terminated by Buyer during which Broker shall be protected for its Commission and/or Leasing Commission, as applicable. There shall be no Protected Period if Buyer and Broker mutually terminate this Agreement. In the event Buyer enters into a Contract to Purchase or lease, lease to purchase or lease with an option to purchase of real property which, during the term of this Agreement or what would have been the term of this Agreement had it not been unilaterally terminated by Buyer, was shown to Buyer by Broker, either virtually or in person, or which Buyer otherwise visited ("Protected Properties"), then Buyer shall pay Broker at closing or prior to the commencement of the lease the Commission and/or Leasing Commission, as applicable, set forth above.

   For the purposes of this section, the term "Buyer" shall include Buyer, all members of the Buyer's immediate family, any legal entity in which buyer or any member of Buyer's immediate family owns or controls, directly or indirectly, more than ten percent (10%) of the shares or interests therein, and any third party who is acting under the direction or control of any of the above parties. For the purposes of this Agreement, the term "seller" shall include seller, all member of the seller's immediate family, any legal entity in which seller or any member of seller's immediately family owns or controls, directly or indirectly, more than ten percent (10%) of the shares or interests therein, and any third party who is acting under the direction or control of any of the above parties.

C. OTHER TERMS AND CONDITIONS

1. **Broker's Duties to Buyer.** Broker's sole duties to Buyer shall be to:
   a. make all disclosures required by law;
   b. attempt to locate property suitable to Buyer for purchase;
   c. comply with all applicable laws in performing its duties hereunder including the Brokerage Relationships in Real Estate Transactions Act, O.C.G.A. § 10-6A-1 et. seq; and
   d. assist, to the extent requested by Buyer, in negotiating the terms of and filling out a pre-printed real estate purchase and sale agreement.

2. **Buyer's Duties.** Buyer agrees to:
   a. be reasonably available to see property with Broker or property for which Broker has arranged Buyer to see;
   b. timely respond to communications from Broker;
   c. provide Broker with accurate and complete information;
   d. inspect and become familiar with any property that Buyer Contracts to Purchase, including, but not limited to, potentially adverse conditions and conditions of special concern to Buyer relating to the physical condition of any property in which Buyer becomes interested, any improvements located thereon and the neighborhood surrounding such property;
   e. carefully read the terms of all disclosures, reports and Contracts to Purchase and comply with the duties and deadlines contained therein;
   f. work exclusively with Broker (and not with any other real estate broker or licensee) in identifying, previewing and seeing property for purchase by Buyer since if Buyer identifies, previews or sees property with another broker or fails to disclose to the seller's broker that Buyer is working with Broker a Commission will likely not be paid to Broker by the seller's broker and Buyer shall be responsible for the same;
   g. disclose to Broker at the commencement of this Agreement whether Buyer previously worked with any other real estate broker and the addresses of the properties, if any, Buyer made an offer to purchase or for which Buyer may owe a commission to another broker if Buyer now purchases; and
   h. not contact or see a property listed For Sale By Owner ("FSBO") without first giving Broker a reasonable opportunity to contact the owner thereof and attempt to enter into an agreement with the owner to pay Broker a commission should Buyer purchase the owner's property.

3. **Limits on Broker's Authority and Responsibility.** Buyer acknowledges and agrees that Broker:
   a. may show property in which Buyer is interested to other prospective buyers;
   b. shall have no duty to inspect the Property or advise Buyer or seller on any matter relating to the Property which could have been revealed through a survey, appraisal, title search, Official Georgia Wood Infestation Report, utility bill review, septic system inspection, well water test, tests for radon, asbestos, mold, and lead-based paint; inspection of the Property by a licensed home inspector, construction expert, structural engineer, or environmental engineer; review of this Agreement and transaction by an attorney, financial planner, mortgage consultant, or tax consultant; and consulting appropriate governmental officials to determine, among other things and without limitation, the zoning of the Property, the propensity of the Property to flood, flood zone certifications, whether any condemnation action is pending or has been filed or other nearby governmental improvements are planned. Buyer acknowledges that Broker does not perform or have expertise in any of the above tests, inspections, and reviews or in any of the matters handled by the professionals referenced above. Buyer should seek independent expert advice regarding any matter of concern to Buyer relative to the Property and this Agreement. Buyer acknowledges that Broker shall not be responsible to monitor or supervise or inspect any portion of any construction or repairs to Property and that such tasks fall outside the scope of real estate brokerages services;

    c. shall owe no duties to Buyer nor have any authority on behalf of Buyer other than what is set forth in this Agreement;
    d. shall not be responsible for ensuring that Buyer complies with the duties and deadlines contained in any purchase agreement entered into by Buyer and that Buyer shall be solely responsible for the same; and
    e. shall be held harmless by Buyer from any and all claims, causes of action, or damages arising out of or relating to:
        (1) inaccurate and/or incomplete information provided by Buyer to Broker;
        (2) earnest money handled by anyone other than Broker; or
        (3) any injury to persons and/or loss of or damage to property.
    f. shall have no authority to bind Buyer to any contract or agreement or to give notices on behalf of Buyer other than to forward, if requested by Buyer, a notice signed by Buyer pertaining to a real estate transaction. Under the standard GAR Purchase and Sale Agreement Forms, notice received by the Broker is deemed to be notice received by the Buyer.

4. **LIMIT ON BROKER'S LIABILITY. BUYER ACKNOWLEDGES THAT BROKER:**
    a. SHALL, UNDER NO CIRCUMSTANCES, HAVE ANY LIABILITY GREATER THAN THE AMOUNT OF THE REAL ESTATE COMMISSION PAID HEREUNDER TO BROKER (EXCLUDING ANY COMMISSION AMOUNT PAID TO A COOPERATING REAL ESTATE BROKER, IF ANY) OR, IF NO REAL ESTATE COMMISSION IS PAID TO BROKER, THAN A SUM NOT TO EXCEED $100; AND
    b. NOTWITHSTANDING THE ABOVE, SHALL HAVE NO LIABILITY IN EXCESS OF $100 FOR ANY LOSS OF FUNDS AS THE RESULT OF WIRE OR CYBER FRAUD.

5. **Disclosures.**
    a. Broker agrees to keep confidential all information which Buyer asks to be kept confidential by express request or instruction unless the Buyer permits such disclosure by subsequent word or conduct or such disclosure is required by law. Buyer acknowledges, however, that Seller and Seller's broker may possibly not treat any offer made by Buyer (including its existence, terms and conditions) as confidential unless those parties have entered into a Confidentiality Agreement with Buyer.
    b. Broker may not knowingly give false information.
    c. In the event of a conflict between Broker's duty not to give false information and the duty to keep the confidences of Buyer, the duty not to give false information shall prevail.
    d. Unless specified below, Broker has no other known agency relationships with other parties that would conflict with any interests of Buyer (except that Broker may represent other buyers, sellers, tenants and landlords in buying, selling or leasing property.)

6. **Disclosure of Potentially Fraudulent Activities** as required by the Georgia Residential Mortgage Fraud Act (O.C.G.A. § 16-8-100 et seq.)
    a. To help prevent fraud in real estate transactions, Buyer does hereby give Broker permission to report any suspicious, unusual and/or potentially illegal or fraudulent activity (including but not limited to mortgage fraud) to:
        (1) Governmental officials, agencies and/or authorities and/or
        (2) Any mortgage lender, mortgage insurer, mortgage investor and/or title insurance company (and/or their agents and representatives) could potentially be harmed if the activity was in fact fraudulent or illegal.
    b. Buyer acknowledges that Broker does not have special expertise with respect to detecting fraud in real estate transactions. Therefore, Buyer acknowledges that:
        (1) Activities which are fraudulent or illegal may be undetected by Broker; and
        (2) Activities which are lawful and/or routine may be reported by Broker as being suspicious, unusual or potentially illegal or fraudulent.

7. **Miscellaneous.**
    a. **Arbitration.** All claims arising out of or relating to this Agreement and the alleged acts or omissions of any or all the parties hereunder shall be resolved by arbitration in accordance with the Federal Arbitration Act 9 U.S.C. § 1 et. seq. and the rules and procedures of the arbitration company selected to administer the arbitration. Upon making or receiving a demand for arbitration, the parties shall work together in good faith to select a mutually acceptable arbitration company with offices in Georgia to administer and conduct the arbitration. If the parties cannot mutually agree on an arbitration company, the company shall be selected as follows. Each party shall simultaneously exchange with the other party a list of three arbitration companies with offices in Georgia acceptable to that party to administer and conduct the arbitration. If there is only one (1) arbitration company that is common to both lists, that company shall administer and conduct the arbitration. If there is more than one arbitration company that is common to both lists, the parties shall either mutually agree on which arbitration company shall be selected or flip a coin to select the arbitration company. If there is not initially a common arbitration company on the lists, the parties shall repeat the process by expanding their lists by two each time until there is a common name on the lists selected by the parties. The decision of the arbitrator shall be final and the arbitrator shall have authority to award attorneys' fees and allocate the costs of arbitration as part of any final award. All claims shall be brought by a party in his or her individual capacity and not as a plaintiff or class member in any purported class or representative proceeding. The arbitrator may not consolidate more than one person's claims, and may not otherwise preside over any form of a representative or class proceeding. Notwithstanding anything to the contrary contained herein, this agreement to arbitrate shall not apply to: (1) any claim regarding the handling and disbursement of earnest money; and (2) any claim of Broker regarding the entitlement to or the non-payment of a real estate commission hereunder.
    b. **Assignability.** As part of a sale of all or substantially all of the assets of Broker to another firm, Buyer consents to this Agreement being assigned by Broker to the other brokerage firm. In such event, the assignee, upon consenting to the assignment, shall: 1) thereafter be responsible for performing all of the duties of the assignor under this Agreement; and 2) have all the rights of the assignor including the right to receive the commission under this Agreement.
    c. **Attorney's Fees:** In the event this Agreement, or any provision therein, is enforced through or is the subject of a dispute resulting in litigation or arbitration, the prevailing party shall be entitled to recover its actual attorney's fees, reasonably incurred.

d. **Broker:** Where the context indicates the term "Broker" shall include Broker's affiliated licensees.
e. **Entire Agreement:** This Agreement represents the entire agreement of the parties. No representation, promise, or inducement not included in this Agreement shall be binding upon any party hereto. This Agreement and the terms and conditions herein may not be amended or waived except by the written agreement of Buyer and Broker. The failure of the parties to adhere strictly to the terms and conditions of this Agreement shall not constitute a waiver of the right of the parties later to insist on such strict adherence.
f. **Fair Housing Disclosure:** Buyer acknowledges that Broker is committed to providing equal housing opportunities to all persons. While Broker may show Buyer properties of a type or in any specific geographical area requested by Buyer, Broker may not steer buyers to or away from particular areas based upon race, color, religion, national origin, sex, familial status, disability, sexual orientation or gender identity and may not answer questions based upon the demographics of different neighborhoods.
g. **GAR Forms:** The Georgia Association of REALTORS®, Inc. ("GAR") issues certain standard real estate forms. These GAR forms are frequently provided to the parties in real estate transactions. No party is required to use any GAR form. Since these forms are generic and written with the interests of multiple parties in mind, they may need to be modified to meet the specific needs of the parties using them. If any party has any questions about his or her rights and obligations under any GAR form, he or she should consult an attorney. Provisions in the GAR Forms are subject to differing interpretations by our courts other than what the parties may have intended. At times, our courts may strike down or not enforce provisions in our GAR Forms, as written. No representation is made that the GAR Forms will protect the interests of any particular party or will be fit for any specific purpose. The parties hereto agree that the GAR forms may only be used in accordance with the licensing agreement of GAR. While GAR forms may be modified by the parties, no GAR form may be reproduced with sections removed, altered or modified unless the changes are visible on the form itself or in a stipulation, addendum, exhibit or amendment thereto.
h. **Governing Law and Interpretation:** This Agreement may be signed in multiple counterparts each of which shall be deemed to be an original and shall be interpreted in accordance with the laws of Georgia. No provision herein, by virtue of the party who drafted it, shall be interpreted less favorably against one party than another. All references to time shall mean the time in Georgia. If any provision herein is to be unenforceable, it shall be severed from this Agreement while the remainder of the Agreement shall, to the fullest extent permitted by law, continue to have full force and effect as a binding contract.
i. **Independent Contractor Relationship:** This Agreement shall create an independent contractor relationship between Broker and Buyer. Broker shall at no time be considered an employee of Buyer. Unless otherwise stipulated, all affiliated licensees of Broker are independent contractors of Broker.
j. **No Imputed Knowledge:** Buyer acknowledges and agrees that with regard to any property in which Buyer develops an interest, there shall be no knowledge imputed between Broker and Broker's licensees or between the different licensees of Broker. Broker and each of Broker's licensees shall be deemed to have only actual knowledge of such properties.
k. **Notices between Buyer and Broker:**
    (1) Communications Regarding Real Estate Transactions: Buyer acknowledges that many communications and notices in real estate transactions are of a time sensitive nature and that the failure to be available to receive such notices and communications can have adverse legal, business and financial consequences. During the term of this Agreement, Buyer agrees to remain reasonably available to receive communications from Broker.
    (2) Notices between Broker and Buyer Regarding this Agreement: Buyer and Broker agree that communications and notices between them regarding the terms of this Agreement shall be in writing, signed by the party giving the notice, and may be delivered in person or to any address, e-mail address and/or facsimile number to the person to whom the communication or notice is being given specifically set forth in this Agreement. It is the intent of the parties that those means of transmitting notices for which a party has not provided an address or number shall not be used for receiving notices and communications. For example, if a party has not provided an e-mail address in this Agreement, it shall mean that the party is not accepting notices or communications sent by this means.
l. **Referrals:** Should Buyer seek to purchase real property in an area with which Broker is unfamiliar or for the sale of Buyer's property, Buyer hereby authorizes Broker to refer Buyer to another broker or licensee for brokerage or relocation services. Buyer acknowledges and agrees that Broker may receive a valuable consideration for the referral.
m. **Statute of Limitations:** All claims of any nature whatsoever against Broker and/or their affiliated licensees, whether asserted in litigation or arbitration and sounding in breach of contract and/or tort, must be brought within two (2) years from the date any claim or cause of action arises. Such actions shall thereafter be time-barred.
n. **Survival:** The rights and obligations of Broker to a commission subsequent to the termination or expiration of this Agreement as set forth herein, the limitation of liability, the obligation to arbitrate and indemnify Broker and other similar provisions that by their terms are meant to protect Broker shall survive the termination of this Agreement.
o. **Third Party Vendors:** Broker may provide Buyer with the names of vendors to perform services on behalf of Buyer relative to real estate transactions involving Buyer. Broker does not warrant or endorse the performance of any such vendor and the names of vendors are provided solely as a courtesy and starting point for Buyer to identify possible vendors to perform services on behalf of Buyer. Buyer agrees to do his or her own due diligence regarding the skills, expertise and reputation of all such vendors performing services for Buyer and the terms of all contracts with vendors (including whether there is a limitation of liability in such contracts). All decisions regarding which vendor to hire shall be solely that of Buyer.
p. **Time of Essence:** Time is of the essence of this Agreement.

8. **Buyer Default.** Notwithstanding any provision to the contrary herein, Buyer agrees to immediately pay Broker its Commission in the event any of the following occur:
    a. Buyer defaults under a Contract to Purchase real estate under which Broker would have been paid a commission had the transaction closed;
    b. Buyer agrees with a seller to mutually terminate a Contract to Purchase under which Broker would have been paid a commission had the transaction closed without the prior consent of Broker; or

c. Buyer unilaterally terminates this Agreement and then enters into a Contract to Purchase property, lease, lease to purchase, or lease with an option to purchase of property, as applicable, either during what would have been the remaining term of this Agreement had the Agreement not been unilaterally terminated, or during the Protected Period, as provided for in the Protected Period section of this Agreement.

9. **WARNING TO BUYERS AND SELLERS: BEWARE OF CYBER-FRAUD.** Fraudulent e-mails attempting to get the buyer and/or seller to wire money to criminal computer hackers are increasingly common in real estate transactions. Specifically, criminals are impersonating the online identity of the actual mortgage lender, closing attorney, real estate broker or other person or companies involved in the real estate transaction. In that role, the criminals send fake wiring instructions attempting to trick buyers and/or sellers into wiring them money related to the real estate transaction, including, for example, the buyer's earnest money, the cash needed for the buyer to close, and/or the seller's proceeds from the closing. These instructions, if followed, will result in the money being wired to the criminals. In many cases, the fraudulent email is believable because it is sent from what appears to be the email address/domain of the legitimate company or person responsible for sending the buyer or seller wiring instructions. The buyer and/or seller should verify wiring instructions sent by email by independently looking up and calling the telephone number of the company or person purporting to have sent them. Buyers and sellers should never call the telephone number provided with wiring instructions sent by email since they may end up receiving a fake verification from the criminals. Buyer and sellers should be on special alert for: 1) emails directing the buyer and/or seller to wire money to a bank or bank account in a state other than Georgia; and 2) emails from a person or company involved in the real estate transaction that are slightly different (often by one letter, number, or character) from the actual email address of the person or company.

10. **Brochures.** Brochures referenced herein are prepared courtesy of GAR. The recommendations are general in nature and may not be applicable to the transaction reflected in this Agreement, and are not intended to either be exhaustive or specific advice that Buyer should rely on without Buyer first consulting with independent experts and professionals of Buyer's own choosing to ensure that Buyer is protected.

    The following Brochures and/or Exhibits have been received by the Buyer(s):
    - ☐ GAR CB01 – The ABC's of Agency
    - ☐ GAR CB04 – Lead Based Paint Pamphlet
    - ☐ GAR CB07 – Mold Pamphlet
    - ☐ GAR CB08 – EPA Home Buyer's and Seller's Guide to Radon Pamphlet
    - ☐ GAR CB13 – Protect Yourself When Buying Real Property
    - ☐ GAR CB16 – What to Consider When Buying a Home in a Community with a Homeowners Association (HOA)
    - ☐ GAR CB19 – What to Consider When Buying a Home in a Condominium
    - ☐ GAR CB22 – Protect Yourself When Buying a Home to be Constructed
    - ☐ GAR CB25 – What Buyers Should Know About Flood Hazard Areas and Flood Insurance
    - ☐ GAR CB28 – What Buyers and Sellers Should Know About Short Sales and Distressed Properties
    - ☐ GAR F149 – Retainer Fee Exhibit

SPECIAL STIPULATIONS: The following Special Stipulations, if conflicting with any exhibit, addendum, or preceding paragraph, shall control:

☐ Additional Special Stipulations are attached.

BY SIGNING THIS AGREEMENT, BUYER ACKNOWLEDGES THAT: (1) BUYER HAS READ ALL PROVISIONS AND DISCLOSURES MADE HEREIN; (2) BUYER UNDERSTANDS ALL SUCH PROVISIONS AND DISCLOSURES AND HAS ENTERED INTO THIS AGREEMENT VOLUNTARILY; AND (3) BUYER IS NOT SUBJECT TO A CURRENT BUYER BROKERAGE ENGAGEMENT AGREEMENT WITH ANY OTHER BROKER.

BUYER'S ACCEPTANCE AND CONTACT INFORMATION

1 Buyer's Signature

_____
Print or Type Name   Date

_____
Buyer's Address for Receiving Notice

_____
Buyer's Phone Number: ☐ Cell ☐ Home ☐ Work

_____
Buyer's E-mail Address

2 Buyer's Signature

_____
Print or Type Name   Date

_____
Buyer's Address for Receiving Notice

_____
Buyer's Phone Number: ☐ Cell ☐ Home ☐ Work

_____
Buyer's E-mail Address

☐ Additional Signature Page (F146) is attached.

BROKER / BROKER'S AFFILIATED LICENSEE CONTACT INFORMATION

_____
Brokerage Firm

_____
Broker/Affiliated Licensee Signature

_____
Print or Type Name   Date

_____
Licensee's Phone Number   Fax Number

_____
Licensee's E-mail Address

_____
GA Real Estate License Number

_____
REALTOR® Membership

_____
MLS Office Code   Brokerage Firm License Number

_____
Broker's Phone Number   Fax Number

_____
Broker's Address

RECEIPT OF A COPY OF THIS AGREEMENT IS HEREBY ACKNOWLEDGED BY BUYER.
The above Agreement is hereby accepted, _____ o'clock _____ .m., on the date of _____.

EXCLUSIVE SELLER BROKERAGE ENGAGEMENT AGREEMENT

2021 Printing

State law prohibits Broker from representing Seller as a client without first entering into a written agreement with Seller under O.C.G.A. § 10-6A-1 et. seq.

A. KEY TERMS AND CONDITIONS

1. **Exclusive Seller Brokerage Engagement Agreement.** For and in consideration of the mutual promises contained herein and other good and valuable consideration, the undersigned seller(s) ("Seller") and the undersigned broker ("Broker") do hereby enter into this Exclusive Seller Brokerage Engagement Agreement ("Agreement") for Broker to exclusively list the property described below ("Property") for sale on the terms and conditions set forth herein.

   a. **Property Identification:** Address: _____
      City _____, County _____, Georgia, Zip Code _____
      Tax Parcel I.D. Number: _____

   b. **Legal Description:** The legal description of the Property is *[select one of the following below]*:

      ☐ (1) attached as an exhibit hereto;

      ☐ (2) the same as described in Deed Book _____, Page _____, et. seq., of the land records of the above county; **OR**

      ☐ (3) Land Lot(s) _____ of the _____ District, _____ Section/ GMD, Lot _____, Block _____, Unit _____, Phase/Section _____ of _____ Subdivision/Development, according to the plat recorded in Plat Book _____, Page _____, et. seq., of the land records of the above county; **OR**

      ☐ (4) described below if Property is a condominium unit and a full unit legal description is to be used

      [NOT TO BE USED IF PROPERTY IS A FEE SIMPLE TOWNHOME]:
      Unit _____ of _____ Condominium ("Condominium"), located in Land Lot _____ of the _____ District of _____ County, Georgia, together with its percentage of undivided interest in the common elements of the Condominium, and its interest in the limited common elements assigned to the unit ("Unit"). The Condominium was created pursuant to the Declaration of Condominium for any Condominium ("Declaration"), recorded in Deed Book _____, Page _____, et seq., _____ County, Georgia records ("Declaration"), and shown and delineated on the plat of survey filed in Condominium Plat Book _____, Page _____, _____ County, Georgia records, and on the floor plans filed in Condominium Floor Plan Book _____, Page _____, _____ County, Georgia records.

2. **List Price and Listing Period.** The price at which the Property shall be listed for sale is $_____ ("List Price"). The term of this Agreement shall begin on the date of _____ ("Starting Date") and made available to the public on the date of _____ ("Marketing Commencement Date") and shall continue through the date of _____ ("Ending Date"), as the same may be extended by written agreement of the parties or as provided for herein (hereinafter, "Listing Period").

3. **Marketing.** Broker agrees to file this listing with the following Multiple Listing Service(s): _____ _____

4. **Commission.** *[Select one or more of the following below.]*

   a. Seller agrees to pay Broker the following commission ("Commission") at the closing of any Contract to Sell (as that term is hereinafter defined) of the Property as follows:
      ☐ _____ percent (%) of the sales price;
      ☐ $_____;
      ☐ (other) _____.

   b. Broker agrees to pay cooperating broker, if any,
      ☐ _____% of the sales price;
      ☐ $_____;
      ☐ (other) _____.

c. **Commission Adjustment to Cooperating Broker:** There may be circumstances where Seller's Broker shall not pay the cooperating broker the Commission referenced in Section A.4(b) above. These circumstances and the Commission that shall be paid in such circumstances are as follows: _____
_____

☐ Check if an additional page(s) is attached (in which event, the same are incorporated herein).

d. **Separate Commission on Lease.** If Seller leases the Property or enters into a lease/purchase agreement or a lease with an option to purchase agreement during this Agreement, Seller shall also pay Broker a separate leasing commission in the amount of $_____ and as follows: _____. Notwithstanding any provision to the contrary contained herein, the payment of a leasing Commission (including in lease/purchase transactions or lease with an option to purchase transactions) shall not relieve Seller from paying the Commission at the closing of a Contract to Sell, as provided elsewhere in this Agreement.

5. **Protected Period.** The length of Protected Period, as that term is herein defined, shall be _____ days.

6. **Agency and Brokerage.** The following are types of agency relationship(s) **NOT** offered by Broker:
☐ seller agency ☐ buyer agency ☐ designated agency ☐ dual agency ☐ sub-agency ☐ tenant agency ☐ landlord agency
Seller ☐ does or ☐ does not consent to Broker acting in a dual agency capacity, as that agency relationship is explained in Section B.6(b) below and in the CB01 ABCs of Agency. Seller expressly consents to Broker acting in any other agency relationship offered by Broker.

7. **Seller Has the Following Special Circumstances That Will Require Third-Party Approval Before Seller Can Do the Following:**
   a. List the Property for Sale:
   ☐ (1) **Bankruptcy:** Seller has filed for bankruptcy protection and this Agreement is made contingent upon the bankruptcy court authorizing the listing of the Property for sale.
   ☐ (2) **Divorce:** Seller has filed for divorce and this Agreement is made contingent upon the court having jurisdiction over the divorce action authorizing the listing of the Property for sale.
   ☐ (3) **Other (Please describe):** _____

   b. Contract to Sell the Property:
   ☐ (1) **Bankruptcy:** Seller has filed for bankruptcy protection. Any purchase and sale agreement for the sale of the Property will need to be conditioned upon the approval of the bankruptcy court.
   ☐ (2) **Divorce:** Seller has filed for divorce. Any purchase and sale agreement for the sale of the Property will need to be conditioned upon the approval of the court having jurisdiction over the divorce.
   ☐ (3) **Short Sale:** The sale of the Property will not generate sufficient proceeds to pay off the Broker's real estate commission and all mortgages or liens on the Property. Therefore, the purchase and sale agreement for the sale of the Property will need to be made contingent upon the mortgage lender(s) and other lien holders agreeing to take less than the face amount of what they are owed.
   ☐ (4) **Seller Not On Title:** Seller does not yet have title to the Property and the purchase and sale agreement for the Property ☐ will or ☐ will not need to be subject to Seller acquiring title to the Property.
   ☐ (5) **Other (Please describe):** _____
   _____
   _____

8. **Negotiation.** Seller ☐ does OR ☐ does not authorize the Broker to assist, to the extent requested by Seller, in negotiating the terms of and filling out a pre-printed form contracts for Seller's review and approval.

B. CORRESPONDING PARAGRAPHS FOR SECTION A.

1. **Exclusive Seller Brokerage Engagement Agreement.** Seller has the full authority to enter into this Agreement for the listing of Seller's Property for sale. This Agreement may not be amended except by the written agreement of Seller and Broker. The failure of the parties to adhere strictly to the terms and conditions of this Agreement shall not constitute a waiver of the right of the parties later to insist on such strict adherence. Seller is not a party to any other exclusive seller brokerage engagement agreement and all such previous agreements, if any, have expired and not been renewed. Seller acknowledges that Seller may have to pay a previous broker a real estate commission if Seller is subject to a current seller brokerage engagement agreement or has terminated a previous seller brokerage engagement agreement without the consent of the previous broker.

2. **List Price and Listing Period.**
   a. **List Price:** Seller agrees to list the Property for sale at the list price specified in this Agreement. The failure of the Property to be shown or sell at the list price may be an indication that the list price for the Property is too high.
   b. **Initial Listing Period When Property Is Under Contract to Sell:** If the Property is under a Contract to Sell, as that term is defined below, during the Listing Period, but the Listing Period expires prior to the closing, then the Listing Period shall be automatically extended through the closing of the Contract to Sell.

c. **Extension:** If during the term of this Agreement, Seller and a prospective buyer enter into: 1) a real property purchase and sale agreement for the Property; 2) a contract to exchange property, including the Property; 3) an option contract for the sale of the Property; or 4) a contract to sell the shares or partnership or membership interests in the legal entity constituting Seller (hereinafter, collectively referred to in this Agreement as a "Contract to Sell") which is not consummated or closed for any reason whatsoever, then the Listing Period may be extended unilaterally by Broker for the number of days that Property was under the Contract to Sell (hereinafter, "Extension Period") by Broker providing written notice of the same to Seller within five (5) days of the Contract to Sell not being consummated but in no event later than prior to the expiration of this Agreement (hereinafter, "Notification Period"). If such written notice is not given before the end of the Notification Period, then the Extension Period for that transaction shall be deemed to have been waived by Broker.

3. **Marketing.**
   a. **Generally:** Broker is authorized to market and advertise Property for sale in any media of Broker's choosing, including the Internet and multiple listing services, and attempt to procure buyers for the Property in cooperation with other real estate brokers and their affiliated licensees. Seller acknowledges that in listing the Property in a multiple listing service, all members of multiple listing services and real estate related third parties will have access to Seller's listing information including images and recordings and the right to use all available technology to create, download, store, supplement and manipulate such listing information to assist Seller in the sale of the Property and for tracking and analyzing real estate transactions. As such, Broker may not always have control over aspects of the marketing of the Property. Any media created or purchased by Broker to be used in the marketing effort shall not belong to or be the property of the Seller and may not be copied, reproduced, or used by Seller or other third parties without the express written permission of the Broker. Seller warrants that any media provided or paid for by Seller is the property of the Seller. Seller agrees to indemnify the Broker for any claim by a third party related to the use of the provided media. Broker shall be allowed to use Seller provided materials, during the term of this Agreement, with any third-party for the purposes of marketing the property, and Seller acknowledges that Broker shall not be liable to Seller for the continued use of media by third-parties after the termination of the Agreement. Seller agrees not to place any advertisements on the Property or to advertise the Property for sale in any media except with the prior written consent of Broker. Broker is also hereby authorized to place Broker's "For Sale" sign on Property. If the Property is sold or a Contract to Sell the Property is entered into during the term of this Agreement, the Broker may advertise the Property (including images thereof) in any media of Broker's choosing as being "under contract" while a sale is pending and as being "sold" upon the closing of the Property (except nothing herein shall permit Broker to place a Sold sign on property no longer owned by Seller except with the written permission of the new owner). Seller acknowledges that buyers and other brokers may take photographs, videos and use other technology to capture images of the Property to assist in marketing the Property and helping buyers remember different properties. Seller agrees to remove any personal property prior to listing the Property of which Seller does not want images to be so captured.
   b. **Multiple Listing Service(s):** Broker agrees to file this Agreement with the above referenced Multiple Listing Service(s) within one (1) business day of the Marketing Commencement Date, which shall be the date the Property is made available to the public. Marketing of the property to the public includes, but is not limited to, flyers displayed in windows, yard signs, digital marketing on public facing websites, brokerage website displays (including IDX and VOW), digital communications marketing (email blasts), multi-brokerage listing sharing networks and applications available to the general public. Seller acknowledges that the MLS(s) is/are not a party to this Agreement and is/are not responsible for errors or omissions on the part of Seller or Broker. Seller agrees to indemnify Service(s) from and against any and all claims, liabilities, damages or losses arising out of or related to the listing and sale of Property. Seller acknowledges that by virtue of listing the Property in MLS(s), all MLS(s) members and their affiliated licensees, will have access to Seller's listing information for the purpose of assisting Seller in the sale of the Property.
   c. **Consent of Seller to be Called:** If Seller is on a "Do Not Call List," Seller expressly consents to Broker calling Seller for any purpose related to the sale of the Property. This paragraph shall survive the termination of this Agreement.
   d. **Lockboxes:** A lockbox may be used in connection with the marketing of Property. There have been isolated instances of reported burglaries of homes on which lockboxes have been placed and for which the lockbox has been alleged to have been used to access the home. In order to minimize the risk of misuse of the lockbox, Broker recommends against the use of lockboxes on door handles that can be unscrewed from the outside or on other parts of the home from which the lockbox can be easily removed. Since prospective buyers and others will have access to Property, Seller agrees to either remove all valuables, prescription drugs and/or keys, or put them in a secure place.
   e. **No Marketing by Seller:** Seller is encouraged to communicate the availability of the Property for sale to friends and other acquaintances. However, since Broker has been hired to exclusively market and show the Property, Seller shall not, with respect to the sale of the Property, prepare and distribute marketing materials, hold open houses, put up signs regarding the Property, create websites for the Property, prepare flyers, brochures or videos or engage in other similar activities without the prior written consent of Broker.

4. **Commission.**
   a. **Obligation to Pay Commission:** In the event that Seller enters into a Contract to Sell or lease, lease/purchase, or lease with an option to purchase the Property or any portion thereof during the term of this Agreement with any buyer, seller agrees to pay Broker's Commission at the closing (regardless of whether the closing is during or after the term of this Agreement), and if applicable, Broker's Leasing Commission prior to the commencement of a lease, lease/purchase, or lease with an option to purchase.
   b. **Sharing of Broker's Commission with Cooperating Broker:** Broker shall share this commission with a cooperating broker, if any, who procures the buyer of Property by paying such cooperating broker at closing the percent (%) of the sales price of Property referenced above **OR** the flat amount referenced herein. There may be times when the Broker may not pay the cooperating broker the full amount of the commission as set forth in Section A.

5. **Protected Period.** The Protected Period shall be the period of time set forth in this Agreement commencing upon the expiration or the unilateral termination of this Agreement by Seller during which Broker shall be protected for its Commission or Leasing Commission, as applicable. If this Agreement is unilaterally terminated by Seller without the consent of the Broker, the Protected Period shall be the number of days remaining on what would have been the original listing as of the date the Seller terminates the Agreement plus the number of days set forth as the Protected Period in Section A.5 of this Agreement. There shall be no Protected Period if Broker and Seller mutually agree to terminate this Agreement. In the event that during the Protected Period, Seller enters into a Contract to Sell or lease, lease/purchase, or lease with an option to purchase of all or any portion of the Property which during the term of this Agreement was submitted to, identified or shown to any buyer (either in person or virtually), was provided specific information about or inquired about the Property, either directly or through a broker working with the buyer, then Seller shall pay Broker at closing or the commencement of the lease, lease/purchase, or lease with an option to purchase, as applicable, the Commission or Leasing Commission set forth above.

   Notwithstanding the above, if this Agreement expires (and is not unilaterally terminated by Seller) an exception to the above Commission obligations shall apply and no Commission or Leasing Commission, as applicable, shall be due, owing or paid to Broker if Seller enters into a Contract to Sell or lease, lease/purchase, or lease with an option to purchase all or any portion of the Property during the Protected Period by or through another licensed broker with whom Seller has signed an exclusive seller brokerage engagement agreement. This exception shall not apply if the Agreement is unilaterally terminated by Seller. The Commission rights and obligations set forth herein shall survive the termination of this Agreement.

   For the purposes of this section, the term "Seller" shall include Seller, all member of the Seller's immediate family, any legal entity in which Seller or any member of Seller's immediately family owns or controls, directly or indirectly, more than ten percent (10%) of the shares or interests therein, and any third party who is acting under the direction or control of any of the above parties. For the purposes of this Agreement, the term "buyer" shall include buyer, all members of the buyer's immediate family, any legal entity in which buyer or any member of buyer's immediate family owns or controls, directly or indirectly, more than ten percent (10%) of the shares or interests therein, and any third party who is acting under the direction or control of any of the above parties.

6. **Agency and Brokerage.**
   a. **Broker's Policy on Agency:** Unless Broker has indicated elsewhere herein that Broker is not offering a specific agency relationship, the types of agency relationships offered by Broker are: seller agency, buyer agency, designated agency, dual agency, sub-agency, landlord agency, and tenant agency.
   b. **Dual Agency Disclosure:** *[Applicable only if Broker's agency policy is to practice dual agency and Seller has consented to Broker acting in a dual agency capacity.]* If Seller and a prospective buyer are both being represented by the same Broker and the Broker is not acting in a designated agency capacity, Seller is aware that Broker is acting as a dual agent in this transaction and hereby consents to the same. Seller has been advised that:
      (1) In serving as a dual agent, Broker is representing two parties, Seller and the buyer, as clients whose interests are or at times could be different or even adverse;
      (2) Broker will disclose all adverse, material facts relevant to the transaction and actually known to the dual agent to all parties in the transaction except for information made confidential by request or instructions from either party which is not otherwise required to be disclosed by law;
      (3) Seller does not have to consent to dual agency. The consent of the Seller to dual agency has been given voluntarily in Section A and the Seller has read and understands this Agreement.
      (4) Notwithstanding any provision to the contrary contained herein, Seller hereby directs Broker, while acting as a dual agent, to keep confidential and not reveal to the other party any information which could materially and adversely affect their negotiating position except as required by law.
      (5) Broker or Broker's affiliated licensees will timely disclose to each party the nature of any material relationship with other party other than that incidental to the transaction. A material relationship shall mean any actually known personal, familial, or business relationship between Broker and a party which would impair the ability of Broker to exercise fair and independent judgment relative to another client. The other party whom Broker may represent in the event of dual agency may not be identified at the time Seller enters into this Agreement. If any party is identified after the Agreement and has a material relationship with Broker, then Broker shall timely provide to Seller a disclosure of the nature of such relationship.
      (6) Upon signing this brokerage engagement with the dual agency disclosures contained herein, Seller's consent to dual agency is conclusively deemed to have been given and informed in accordance with state law, provided that Seller has consented to Broker acting in a dual agency capacity in Section A(6) above.
   c. **Designated Agency Disclosure:** *[Applicable only if Broker's agency policy is to practice designated agency.]* Seller does hereby consent to Broker acting in a designated agency capacity in transactions in which Broker is representing Seller and a prospective buyer, but where Broker assigns one or more of its affiliated licensees exclusively to represent the Seller and one or more of its other affiliated licensees exclusively to represent the prospective buyer.
   d. **No Other Adverse Agency Relationships:** Unless specified herein, Broker has no other known agency relationships with other parties which would conflict with any interests of Seller (except that Broker may represent other buyers, sellers, landlords, and tenants in buying, selling or leasing property).

7. **Special Circumstances.**
   a. The sale of Property is contingent upon a third party's approval as indicated above. It shall be Seller's responsibility to seek to fulfill any contingency or condition selected herein, if any, and ensure that the purchase and sale agreement is made subject to any such contingency or condition.

b. Broker agrees to keep confidential all information which Seller asks to be kept confidential by express request or instruction unless Seller permits such disclosure by subsequent word or conduct or such disclosure is required by law. Seller acknowledges, however, that buyer and buyer's broker may possibly not treat any offer made by Seller (including its existence, terms and conditions) as confidential unless those parties have entered into a Confidentiality Agreement with Seller.
c. Broker may not knowingly give customers false information.
d. In the event of a conflict between Broker's duty not to give customers false information and the duty to keep the confidences of Seller, the duty not to give customers false information shall prevail.

8. **Negotiation.** While Broker may assist Seller in negotiating the terms of a Contract to Sell, if Seller has elected to have Broker assist in this role, all decisions regarding price, terms and other conditions in a Contract to Sell shall still be made by Seller.

C. OTHER TERMS AND CONDITIONS

1. **Seller's Property Disclosure Statement.** Georgia Law (O.C.G.A. §51-6-2) requires that a Seller disclose latent defects in the Property which could not be observed by Buyer upon a reasonable inspection of the Property. This is the case even if the Property is sold in "as-is" condition. Within three (3) days of the date of this Agreement, Seller agrees to provide Broker with a current, fully executed Seller's Property Disclosure Statement or Disclosure of Latent Defects & Fixtures Checklist. In addition, if any dwelling on the Property, or portion thereof, was constructed prior to 1978, Seller agrees, as required by federal law, to additionally provide Broker with a current fully executed Lead-Based Paint Disclosure Exhibit (GAR F316) within the same timeframe so that Broker may provide the same to buyers in accordance with federal law. Broker is hereby authorized to distribute the Seller's Property Disclosure Statement and any Lead-Based Paint Exhibit to buyers interested in Property. Seller agrees to promptly update any of the above-referenced disclosure documents through the Closing should any changes occur.

2. **Hazardous Conditions on Property.** Seller acknowledges that Seller owes a duty of reasonable care to keep the Property safe for prospective buyers and their agents who to view and inspect the Property. Among other things, this includes a duty to warn such invitees of dangerous conditions that would not be obvious to an invitee. Seller is encouraged to inspect the Property for hazardous conditions and correct and eliminate all such conditions. Seller agrees to indemnify and hold Broker harmless from and against any and all claims, causes of action, suits, and damages arising out of or relating to a person or persons being injured or harmed while on the Property.

3. **Limits on Broker's Authority and Responsibility.** Seller acknowledges and agrees that Broker:
    a. may show other properties to prospective buyers who are interested in Property;
    b. shall have no duty to inspect the Property or advise buyer or Seller on any matter relating to the Property which could have been revealed through a survey, appraisal, title search, Official Georgia Wood Infestation Report, utility bill review, septic system inspection, well water test, tests for radon, asbestos, mold, and lead-based paint; inspection of the Property by a licensed home inspector, construction expert, structural engineer, or environmental engineer; review of this Agreement and transaction by an attorney, financial planner, mortgage consultant, or tax consultant; and consulting appropriate governmental officials to determine, among other things and without limitation, the zoning of the Property, the propensity of the Property to flood, flood zone certifications, whether any condemnation action is pending or has been filed or other nearby governmental improvements are planned. Seller acknowledges that Broker does not perform or have expertise in any of the above tests, inspections, and reviews or in any of the matters handled by the professionals referenced above. Seller should seek independent expert advice regarding any matter of concern to Seller relative to the Property and this Agreement. Seller acknowledges that Broker shall not be responsible to monitor or supervise or inspect any portion of any construction or repairs to Property and that such tasks fall outside the scope of real estate brokerages services;
    c. shall owe no duties to Seller nor have any authority on behalf of Seller other than what is set forth in this Agreement;
    d. shall make all disclosures required by law;
    e. shall not be responsible for ensuring that Seller complies with the duties and deadlines contained in any Contract to Sell entered into by Seller and that Seller shall be solely responsible for the same; and
    f. shall be indemnified and held harmless by Seller from any and all claims, causes of action, or damages arising out of or relating to:
        (1) inaccurate and/or incomplete information provided by Seller to Broker;
        (2) earnest money handled by anyone other than Broker;
        (3) Seller's negligence or intentional wrongdoing;
        (4) any loss or theft of valuables, prescription drugs, keys, or other personal property, relating to the use of a lockbox or an open house resulting from Seller's failure to remove or secure the same;
        (5) the existence of undisclosed material facts about the Property or the transaction; and
        (6) any damages or injuries occurring on the Property as a result of dangerous or defective conditions on the Property or the failure to secure or restrain pets.
    g. shall have no authority to bind Seller to any Contract to Sell or give notices on behalf of Seller other than to forward, if requested by Seller, a notice signed by Seller pertaining to a real estate transaction. Under the standard GAR Purchase and Sale Agreement Forms, notice received by the Broker is deemed to be notice received by the Seller.

4. **LIMIT ON BROKER'S LIABILITY. SELLER ACKNOWLEDGES THAT BROKER:**
    a. **SHALL, UNDER NO CIRCUMSTANCES, HAVE ANY LIABILITY GREATER THAN THE AMOUNT OF THE REAL ESTATE COMMISSION PAID HEREUNDER TO BROKER (EXCLUDING ANY COMMISSION AMOUNT PAID TO A COOPERATING REAL ESTATE BROKER, IF ANY) OR, IF NO REAL ESTATE COMMISSION IS PAID TO BROKER, THAN A SUM NOT TO EXCEED $100; AND**
    b. **NOTWITHSTANDING THE ABOVE, SHALL HAVE NO LIABILITY IN EXCESS OF $100 FOR ANY LOSS OF FUNDS AS THE RESULT OF WIRE OR CYBER FRAUD.**

5. **Disclosure of Potentially Fraudulent Activities** as required by the Georgia Residential Mortgage Fraud Act (O.C.G.A. § 16-8-100 et seq.).
   a. To help prevent fraud in real estate transactions, Seller does hereby give Broker permission to report any suspicious, unusual and/or potentially illegal or fraudulent activity (including but not limited to mortgage fraud) to:
      (1) Governmental officials, agencies and/or authorities and/or
      (2) Any mortgage lender, mortgage insurer, mortgage investor and/or title insurance company which could potentially be harmed if the activity was in fact fraudulent or illegal.
   b. Seller acknowledges that Broker does not have special expertise with respect to detecting fraud in real estate transactions. Therefore, Seller acknowledges that:
      (1) Activities which are fraudulent or illegal may be undetected by Broker; and
      (2) Activities which are lawful and/or routine may be reported by Broker as being suspicious, unusual or potentially illegal or fraudulent.

6. **Miscellaneous.**
   a. **Arbitration:** All claims arising out of or relating to this Agreement and the alleged acts or omissions of any or all the parties hereunder shall be resolved by arbitration in accordance with the Federal Arbitration Act 9 U.S.C. § 1 et. seq. and the rules and procedures of the arbitration company selected to administer the arbitration. Upon making or receiving a demand for arbitration, the parties shall work together in good faith to select a mutually acceptable arbitration company with offices in Georgia to administer and conduct the arbitration. If the parties cannot mutually agree on an arbitration company, the company shall be selected as follows. Each party shall simultaneously exchange with the other party a list of three arbitration companies with offices in Georgia acceptable to that party to administer and conduct the arbitration. If there is only one (1) arbitration company that is common to both lists, that company shall administer and conduct the arbitration. If there is more than one arbitration company that is common to both lists, the parties shall either mutually agree on which arbitration company shall be selected or flip a coin to select the arbitration company. If there is not initially a common arbitration company on the lists, the parties shall repeat the process by expanding their lists by two each time until there is a common name on the lists selected by the parties. The decision of the arbitrator shall be final and the arbitrator shall have authority to award attorneys' fees and allocate the costs of arbitration as part of any final award. All claims shall be brought by a party in his or her individual capacity and not as a plaintiff or class member in any purported class or representative proceeding. The arbitrator may not consolidate more than one person's claims, and may not otherwise preside over any form of a representative or class proceeding. Notwithstanding anything to the contrary contained herein, this agreement to arbitrate shall not apply to: (1) any claim regarding the handling and disbursement of earnest money; and (2) any claim of Broker regarding the entitlement to or the non-payment of a real estate commission hereunder.
   b. **Assignability:** As part of a sale of all or substantially all of the assets of Broker to another brokerage firm, Seller consents to this Agreement being assigned by Broker to the other brokerage firm. In such event, the assignee, upon consenting to the assignment, shall: (1) thereafter be responsible for performing all of the duties and responsibilities of the assignor under this Agreement; and (2) have all of the rights of assignor including the right to receive the commissions under the Agreement.
   c. **Attorney's Fees:** In the event this Agreement, or any provision therein, is enforced through or is the subject of a dispute resulting in litigation or arbitration, the prevailing party shall be entitled to recover its actual attorney's fees, reasonably incurred.
   d. **Broker:** Where the context indicates the term "Broker" shall include Broker's affiliated licensees.
   e. **Entire Agreement:** This Agreement represents the entire agreement of the parties with respect to listing of the Property for sale and is intended to supersede all prior written and verbal agreements of the parties hereto. No representation, statement, promise, or inducement not contained herein shall be binding on either party hereto. This Agreement shall be binding on the heirs of the Seller.
   f. **Fair Housing Disclosure:** Seller acknowledges that Broker is committed to providing equal housing opportunities to all persons and that Seller and Broker are obligated to comply with state and federal fair housing laws in selling the Property. Seller and Broker agree not to discriminate in the sale of the Property on the basis of race, color, religion, national origin, sex, familial status, disability, sexual orientation or gender identity.
   g. **GAR Forms:** The Georgia Association of REALTORS®, Inc. ("GAR") issues certain standard real estate forms. These GAR forms are frequently provided to the parties in real estate transactions. No party is required to use any GAR form. Since these forms are generic and written with the interests of multiple parties in mind, they may need to be modified to meet the specific needs of the parties using them. If any party has any questions about his or her rights and obligations under any GAR form, he or she should consult an attorney. Provisions in the GAR Forms are subject to differing interpretations by our courts other than what the parties may have intended. At times, our courts may strike down or not enforce provisions in our GAR Forms, as written. No representation is made that the GAR Forms will protect the interests of any particular party or will be fit for any specific purpose. The parties hereto agree that the GAR forms may only be used in accordance with the licensing agreement of GAR. While GAR forms may be modified by the parties, no GAR form may be reproduced with sections removed, altered or modified unless the changes are visible on the form itself or in a stipulation, addendum, exhibit or amendment thereto.
   h. **Governing Law and Interpretation:** This Agreement may be signed in multiple counterparts each of which shall be deemed to be an original and shall be interpreted in accordance with the laws of Georgia. No provision herein, by virtue of the party who drafted it, shall be interpreted less favorably against one party than another. All references to time shall mean the time in Georgia. If any provision herein is to be unenforceable, it shall be severed from this Agreement while the remainder of the Agreement shall, to the fullest extent permitted by law, continue to have full force and effect as a binding contract.
   i. **Independent Contractor Relationship:** This Agreement shall create an independent contractor relationship between Broker and Seller. Broker shall at no time be considered an employee of Seller. Unless otherwise stipulated, all affiliated licensees of Broker are independent contractors of Broker.
   j. **No Imputed Knowledge:** Seller acknowledges and agrees that with regard to any property which Seller intends to sell, there shall be no knowledge imputed between Broker and Broker's licensees or between the different licensees of Broker. Broker and each of Broker's licensees shall be deemed to have only actual knowledge of such properties.

k. **Notices Between Seller and Broker:**
   (1) **Communications Regarding Real Estate Transactions:** Seller acknowledges that many communications and notices in real estate transactions are of a time sensitive nature and that the failure to be available to receive such notices and communications can have adverse legal, business and financial consequences. During the term of this Agreement, Seller agrees to remain reasonably available to receive communications from Broker.
   (2) **Notices between Broker and Seller Regarding this Agreement:** Seller and Broker agree that communications and notices between them regarding the terms of this Agreement shall be in writing, signed by the party giving the notice, and may be delivered in person or to any address, e-mail address and/or facsimile number to the person to whom the communication or notice is being given specifically set forth in this Agreement. It is the intent of the parties that those means of transmitting notices for which a party has not provided an address or number shall not be used for receiving notices and communications. For example, if a party has not provided an e-mail address in this Agreement, it shall mean that the party is not accepting notices or communications sent by this means.
l. **Referrals:** Seller hereby authorizes Broker to refer Seller to another real estate licensee or broker for brokerage or relocation services not related to the sale of the Property. Seller acknowledges and agrees that Broker may receive a valuable consideration for the referral.
m. **Statute of Limitation:** All claims of any nature whatsoever against Broker and/or their affiliated licensees, whether asserted in litigation or arbitration and sounding in breach of contract and/or tort, must be brought within two (2) years from the date any claim or cause of action arises. Such actions shall thereafter be time-barred.
n. **Survival:** The rights and obligations of Broker to a commission subsequent to the termination or expiration of this Agreement as set forth herein, the limitation of liability, the obligation to arbitrate and indemnify Broker and other similar provisions that by their terms are meant to protect Broker shall survive the termination of this Agreement.
o. **Third Party Vendors:** Broker may provide Seller with the names of vendors to perform services on behalf of Seller relative to real estate transactions involving Seller. Broker does not warrant or endorse the performance of any such vendor and the names of vendors are provided solely as a courtesy and starting point for Seller to identify possible vendors to perform services on behalf of Seller. Seller agrees to do his or her own due diligence regarding the skills, expertise and reputation of all such vendors performing services for Seller and the terms of all contracts with vendors (including whether there is a limitation of liability in such contracts). All decisions regarding which vendor to hire shall be solely that of Seller.
p. **Time of Essence:** Time is of the essence of this Agreement.

7. **Broker's and Seller's Duties.**
   a. **Broker's Duties to Seller.** Broker's sole duties to Seller shall be to:
      (1) make all disclosure required by law;
      (2) use Broker's best efforts to procure a buyer ready, willing, and able to purchase Property at the List Price (which amount includes the Commission herein) or any other price acceptable to Seller;
      (3) comply with all applicable laws in performing its duties hereunder including the Brokerage Relationships in Real Estate Transaction Act, O.C.G.A. § 10-6A-1 et. seq.; and
      (4) if selected in Section A(8) above, assist in negotiating terms or filling out pre-printed real estate purchase and sale agreements and/or counteroffers.
   b. **Seller's Duties.** Seller will do the following:
      (1) cooperate with Broker to sell the Property to prospective buyers and will refer all inquiries concerning the sale of Property to the Broker during the term of this Agreement;
      (2) make the Property available for showing at reasonable times as requested by Broker;
      (3) provide Broker with accurate information regarding the Property (including information concerning all adverse material facts pertaining to the physical condition of Property);
      (4) comply with all local, state and federal laws applicable to the sale of the Property; and
      (5) carefully read all Contracts to Sell before signing them and comply with all duties and all time deadlines contained therein.

8. **Seller Default.**
   a. **Events Constituting a Seller Default.** Seller shall be in breach of this Agreement if Seller:
      (1) Terminates this Agreement prior to the end of the Agreement without the prior written agreement of Broker. Broker removing the listing from multiple listing service(s), taking down Broker's sign, ceasing to market the Property after this Agreement is unilaterally terminated by Seller and other similar activities shall not be evidence of the Broker's agreement to mutually terminate this Agreement, but shall instead merely be an acquiescence by Broker of the unilateral termination by Seller;
      (2) Defaults under any Contract to Sell the Property resulting in such contract not closing;
      (3) Agrees with a buyer of the Property to terminate a Contract to Sell without the consent of Broker; or
      (4) Refuses to accept a lawful, bona fide, written offer to purchase the Property meeting the following terms and conditions at a time when the Property is not otherwise under contract:
         (a) The purchase price in the offer, after deducting all fees, costs and contributions to be paid by the Seller (other than the real estate brokerage commission to be paid by Seller and the Seller's payment of ad valorem real property taxes through the date of closing) is for at least the full listing price set forth herein and is to be paid in cash or cash equivalent at the closing;
         (b) The offer is not subject to contingencies, conditions precedent, due diligence periods, or required terms other than those set forth herein;
         (c) The offer is not subject to Seller warranties or representations other than: (i) those warranties the Seller agrees to provide in any Seller's Property Disclosure Statement the Seller has filled out and made available to prospective buyers for inclusion in any offer, and (ii) the Seller warranting to convey good and marketable title (which for all purposes herein shall have the same meaning as set forth in the GAR Purchase and Sale Agreements) to the Property at closing by limited warranty deed; and

(d) The date of closing in the offer is not less than thirty (30) days nor more than forty-five (45) days from the offer date. Notwithstanding the above, in the event there are multiple offers to purchase the Property meeting the above criteria, Seller shall not be in breach of this Agreement if the Seller first gives the prospective buyers a reasonable opportunity (not exceeding ten (10) days from the date of the first offer) to make their best offer to purchase the Property and Seller accepts one of the offers.

b. **Broker Remedies for Seller Default.** Seller shall immediately pay Broker the Commission referenced herein for any of the Seller defaults above, except for Seller unilaterally terminating this Agreement prior to the end of the Listing Period (as the same may have been extended as provided for herein). With respect to this event of default, Seller's obligation to pay Broker its Commission shall be controlled by the Protected Period sections of this Agreement.

c. **Seller Default.** In the event Seller defaults under this Agreement, Seller shall, in addition to its other obligations set forth elsewhere herein, immediately reimburse Broker for the out-of-pocket costs and expenses incurred by Broker and Broker's affiliated licensees in seeking to market and sell the Property. Such costs and expenses shall include, without limitation, printing, and copying charges, mileage at the highest rate allowed by the IRS as a business deduction and expenses to advertise the Property in various media. Seller shall also pay all costs, fees and charges for removing the listing from any multiple listing service. The payment of these costs, fees, charges and expenses by Seller shall not waive or limit Broker's right to assert any other claim, cause of action or suit (hereinafter collectively, "Claims") against Seller for Broker's Commission and/ or other damages and shall not release Seller from such Claims. Notwithstanding the above, the amount of such fees, charges, costs and expenses paid by Seller to Broker hereunder shall be an offset against any Claim of Broker for a Commission.

9. **WARNING TO BUYERS AND SELLERS: BEWARE OF CYBER-FRAUD.** Fraudulent e-mails attempting to get the buyer and/or seller to wire money to criminal computer hackers are increasingly common in real estate transactions. Specifically, criminals are impersonating the online identity of the actual mortgage lender, closing attorney, real estate broker or other person or companies involved in the real estate transaction. In that role, the criminals send fake wiring instructions attempting to trick buyers and/or sellers into wiring them money related to the real estate transaction, including, for example, the buyer's earnest money, the cash needed for the buyer to close, and/or the seller's proceeds from the closing. These instructions, if followed, will result in the money being wired to the criminals. In many cases, the fraudulent email is believable because it is sent from what appears to be the email address/domain of the legitimate company or person responsible for sending the buyer or seller wiring instructions. The buyer and/or seller should verify wiring instructions sent by email by independently looking up and calling the telephone number of the company or person purporting to have sent them. Buyers and sellers should never call the telephone number provided with wiring instructions sent by email since they may end up receiving a fake verification from the criminals. Buyers and sellers should be on special alert for 1) emails directing the buyer and/or seller to wire money to a bank account in a state other than Georgia; and 2) emails from a person or company involved in the real estate transaction that are slightly different (often by one letter, number, or character) from the actual email address of the person or company.

10. **Brochures.** Brochures referenced herein are prepared courtesy of GAR. The recommendations contained therein are general in nature and may not be applicable to the transaction reflected in this Agreement, and are not intended to either be exhaustive or specific advice that Seller should rely on without first consulting with independent experts and professionals of Seller's own choosing to ensure that Seller is protected.

The following **Brochures have been received by the Seller(s)**. (Check all that apply. Any box not checked means the Seller(s) has not received that brochure or other consumer information)

☐ GAR CB01 – The ABC's of Agency
☐ GAR CB04 – Lead Based Paint Pamphlet
☐ GAR CB07 – Mold Pamphlet
☐ GAR CB08 – EPA Home Buyer's and Seller's Guide to Radon Pamphlet
☐ GAR CB10 – Protect Yourself When Selling a House
☐ GAR CB28 – What Buyers and Sellers Should Know About Short Sales and Distressed Properties
☐ Other: _____

11. **Exhibits and Addenda.** All exhibits and/or addenda attached hereto, listed below, or referenced herein are made a part of this Agreement. If any such exhibit or addenda conflicts with any preceding paragraph (including any changes thereto made by the parties), said exhibit or addendum shall control:

☐ Legal Description Exhibit (F807 or other) * _____
☐ Lead-Based Paint Exhibit (F316) * _____
☐ Retainer Fee Exhibit (F149) * _____
☐ Other: _____
☐ Other: _____

SPECIAL STIPULATIONS: The following Special Stipulations, if conflicting with any exhibit, addendum, or preceding paragraph, shall control:

☐ Additional Special Stipulations are attached.

BY SIGNING THIS AGREEMENT, SELLER ACKNOWLEDGES THAT: (1) SELLER HAS READ ALL PROVISIONS AND DISCLOSURES MADE HEREIN; (2) SELLER UNDERSTANDS ALL SUCH PROVISIONS AND DISCLOSURES AND HAS ENTERED INTO THIS AGREEMENT VOLUNTARILY; AND (3) SELLER IS NOT SUBJECT TO A CURRENT SELLER BROKERAGE ENGAGEMENT AGREEMENT WITH ANY OTHER BROKER.

SELLER'S ACCEPTANCE AND CONTACT INFORMATION

1 Seller's Signature _____ 2 Seller's Signature _____

Print or Type Name _____ Date _____   Print or Type Name _____ Date _____

Seller's Address for Receiving Notice _____   Seller's Address for Receiving Notice _____

Seller's Phone Number: ☐ Cell ☐ Home ☐ Work   Seller's Phone Number: ☐ Cell ☐ Home ☐ Work

Seller's E-mail Address _____   Seller's E-mail Address _____

☐ Additional Signature Page (F146) is attached.

BROKER / BROKER'S AFFILIATED LICENSEE CONTACT INFORMATION

Brokerage Firm _____   MLS Office Code _____   Broker's Phone Number _____   Brokerage Firm License Number _____

Broker/Affiliated Licensee Signature _____   Broker's Address _____

Print or Type Name _____ Date _____   Licensee's E-mail Address _____

Licensee's Phone Number _____   Fax Number _____   REALTOR® Membership _____

GA Real Estate License Number _____

RECEIPT OF A COPY OF THIS AGREEMENT IS HEREBY ACKNOWLEDGED BY SELLER. The above Agreement is hereby accepted _____ o'clock _____ .m. on the date of _____.

FICUS BANK
4321 Random Boulevard • Somecity, ST 12340

Save this Loan Estimate to compare with your Closing Disclosure.

Loan Estimate

DATE ISSUED	2/15/2013
APPLICANTS	Michael Jones and Mary Stone 123 Anywhere Street Anytown, ST 12345
PROPERTY	456 Somewhere Avenue Anytown, ST 12345
SALE PRICE	$180,000

LOAN TERM	30 years
PURPOSE	Purchase
PRODUCT	Fixed Rate
LOAN TYPE	☒ Conventional ☐ FHA ☐ VA ☐ _____
LOAN ID #	123456789
RATE LOCK	☐ NO ☒ YES, until 4/16/2013 at 5:00 p.m. EDT

*Before closing, your interest rate, points, and lender credits can change unless you lock the interest rate. All other estimated closing costs expire on **3/4/2013** at 5:00 p.m. EDT*

Loan Terms

		Can this amount increase after closing?
Loan Amount	$162,000	NO
Interest Rate	3.875%	NO
Monthly Principal & Interest *See Projected Payments below for your Estimated Total Monthly Payment*	$761.78	NO

		Does the loan have these features?
Prepayment Penalty		YES • As high as **$3,240** if you pay off the loan during the first 2 years
Balloon Payment		NO

Projected Payments

Payment Calculation	Years 1-7	Years 8-30
Principal & Interest	$761.78	$761.78
Mortgage Insurance	+ 82	+ —
Estimated Escrow *Amount can increase over time*	+ 206	+ 206
Estimated Total Monthly Payment	**$1,050**	**$968**

		This estimate includes	In escrow?
Estimated Taxes, Insurance & Assessments *Amount can increase over time*	**$206** a month	☒ Property Taxes ☒ Homeowner's Insurance ☐ Other: *See Section G on page 2 for escrowed property costs. You must pay for other property costs separately.*	YES YES

Costs at Closing

Estimated Closing Costs	$8,054	Includes $5,672 in Loan Costs + $2,382 in Other Costs – $0 in Lender Credits. *See page 2 for details.*
Estimated Cash to Close	$16,054	Includes Closing Costs. *See Calculating Cash to Close on page 2 for details.*

*Visit **www.consumerfinance.gov/mortgage-estimate** for general information and tools.*

Closing Cost Details

Loan Costs

A. Origination Charges	$1,802
.25 % of Loan Amount (Points)	$405
Application Fee	$300
Underwriting Fee	$1,097

B. Services You Cannot Shop For	$672
Appraisal Fee	$405
Credit Report Fee	$30
Flood Determination Fee	$20
Flood Monitoring Fee	$32
Tax Monitoring Fee	$75
Tax Status Research Fee	$110

C. Services You Can Shop For	$3,198
Pest Inspection Fee	$135
Survey Fee	$65
Title – Insurance Binder	$700
Title – Lender's Title Policy	$535
Title – Settlement Agent Fee	$502
Title – Title Search	$1,261

D. TOTAL LOAN COSTS (A + B + C)	$5,672

Other Costs

E. Taxes and Other Government Fees	$85
Recording Fees and Other Taxes	$85
Transfer Taxes	

F. Prepaids	$867
Homeowner's Insurance Premium (6 months)	$605
Mortgage Insurance Premium (months)	
Prepaid Interest ($17.44 per day for 15 days @ 3.875%)	$262
Property Taxes (months)	

G. Initial Escrow Payment at Closing		$413
Homeowner's Insurance	$100.83 per month for 2 mo.	$202
Mortgage Insurance	per month for mo.	
Property Taxes	$105.30 per month for 2 mo.	$211

H. Other	$1,017
Title – Owner's Title Policy (optional)	$1,017

I. TOTAL OTHER COSTS (E + F + G + H)	$2,382

J. TOTAL CLOSING COSTS	$8,054
D + I	$8,054
Lender Credits	

Calculating Cash to Close

Total Closing Costs (J)	$8,054
Closing Costs Financed (Paid from your Loan Amount)	$0
Down Payment/Funds from Borrower	$18,000
Deposit	– $10,000
Funds for Borrower	$0
Seller Credits	$0
Adjustments and Other Credits	$0
Estimated Cash to Close	$16,054

APPENDIX E Documents for Review

Additional Information About This Loan

LENDER	Ficus Bank	**MORTGAGE BROKER**	
NMLS/__ LICENSE ID		**NMLS/__ LICENSE ID**	
LOAN OFFICER	Joe Smith	**LOAN OFFICER**	
NMLS/__ LICENSE ID	12345	**NMLS/__ LICENSE ID**	
EMAIL	joesmith@ficusbank.com	**EMAIL**	
PHONE	123-456-7890	**PHONE**	

Comparisons
Use these measures to compare this loan with other loans.

In 5 Years	$56,582	Total you will have paid in principal, interest, mortgage insurance, and loan costs.
	$15,773	Principal you will have paid off.
Annual Percentage Rate (APR)	4.274%	Your costs over the loan term expressed as a rate. This is not your interest rate.
Total Interest Percentage (TIP)	69.45%	The total amount of interest that you will pay over the loan term as a percentage of your loan amount.

Other Considerations

Appraisal	We may order an appraisal to determine the property's value and charge you for this appraisal. We will promptly give you a copy of any appraisal, even if your loan does not close. You can pay for an additional appraisal for your own use at your own cost.
Assumption	If you sell or transfer this property to another person, we ☐ will allow, under certain conditions, this person to assume this loan on the original terms. ☒ will not allow assumption of this loan on the original terms.
Homeowner's Insurance	This loan requires homeowner's insurance on the property, which you may obtain from a company of your choice that we find acceptable.
Late Payment	If your payment is more than *15* days late, we will charge a late fee of *5% of the monthly principal and interest payment.*
Refinance	Refinancing this loan will depend on your future financial situation, the property value, and market conditions. You may not be able to refinance this loan.
Servicing	We intend ☐ to service your loan. If so, you will make your payments to us. ☒ to transfer servicing of your loan.

Confirm Receipt

By signing, you are only confirming that you have received this form. You do not have to accept this loan because you have signed or received this form.

_____   _____   _____   _____
Applicant Signature   Date   Co-Applicant Signature   Date

LOAN ESTIMATE

Closing Disclosure

This form is a statement of final loan terms and closing costs. Compare this document with your Loan Estimate.

Closing Information
- **Date Issued** 4/15/2013
- **Closing Date** 4/15/2013
- **Disbursement Date** 4/15/2013
- **Settlement Agent** Epsilon Title Co.
- **File #** 12-3456
- **Property** 456 Somewhere Ave
  Anytown, ST 12345
- **Sale Price** $180,000

Transaction Information
- **Borrower** Michael Jones and Mary Stone
  123 Anywhere Street
  Anytown, ST 12345
- **Seller** Steve Cole and Amy Doe
  321 Somewhere Drive
  Anytown, ST 12345
- **Lender** Ficus Bank

Loan Information
- **Loan Term** 30 years
- **Purpose** Purchase
- **Product** Fixed Rate
- **Loan Type** ☒ Conventional ☐ FHA ☐ VA ☐ _____
- **Loan ID #** 123456789
- **MIC #** 000654321

Loan Terms

		Can this amount increase after closing?
Loan Amount	$162,000	NO
Interest Rate	3.875%	NO
Monthly Principal & Interest *See Projected Payments below for your Estimated Total Monthly Payment*	$761.78	NO

		Does the loan have these features?
Prepayment Penalty		YES • **As high as $3,240** if you pay off the loan during the first 2 years
Balloon Payment		NO

Projected Payments

Payment Calculation	Years 1-7	Years 8-30
Principal & Interest	$761.78	$761.78
Mortgage Insurance	+ 82.35	+ —
Estimated Escrow *Amount can increase over time*	+ 206.13	+ 206.13
Estimated Total Monthly Payment	**$1,050.26**	**$967.91**

Estimated Taxes, Insurance & Assessments *Amount can increase over time* *See page 4 for details*	$356.13 a month	This estimate includes ☒ Property Taxes ☒ Homeowner's Insurance ☒ Other: Homeowner's Association Dues	In escrow? YES YES NO

See Escrow Account on page 4 for details. You must pay for other property costs separately.

Costs at Closing

Closing Costs	$9,712.10	Includes $4,694.05 in Loan Costs + $5,018.05 in Other Costs – $0 in Lender Credits. *See page 2 for details.*
Cash to Close	$14,147.26	Includes Closing Costs. *See Calculating Cash to Close on page 3 for details.*

Closing Cost Details

Loan Costs		Borrower-Paid At Closing	Borrower-Paid Before Closing	Seller-Paid At Closing	Seller-Paid Before Closing	Paid by Others
A. Origination Charges		**$1,802.00**				
01 0.25 % of Loan Amount (Points)		$405.00				
02 Application Fee		$300.00				
03 Underwriting Fee		$1,097.00				
04						
05						
06						
07						
08						
B. Services Borrower Did Not Shop For		**$236.55**				$405.00
01 Appraisal Fee	to John Smith Appraisers Inc.					
02 Credit Report Fee	to Information Inc.		$29.80			
03 Flood Determination Fee	to Info Co.	$20.00				
04 Flood Monitoring Fee	to Info Co.	$31.75				
05 Tax Monitoring Fee	to Info Co.	$75.00				
06 Tax Status Research Fee	to Info Co.	$80.00				
07						
08						
09						
10						
C. Services Borrower Did Shop For		**$2,655.50**				
01 Pest Inspection Fee	to Pests Co.	$120.50				
02 Survey Fee	to Surveys Co.	$85.00				
03 Title – Insurance Binder	to Epsilon Title Co.	$650.00				
04 Title – Lender's Title Insurance	to Epsilon Title Co.	$500.00				
05 Title – Settlement Agent Fee	to Epsilon Title Co.	$500.00				
06 Title – Title Search	to Epsilon Title Co.	$800.00				
07						
08						
D. TOTAL LOAN COSTS (Borrower-Paid)		**$4,694.05**				
Loan Costs Subtotals (A + B + C)		$4,664.25	$29.80			

Other Costs		Borrower-Paid At Closing	Borrower-Paid Before Closing	Seller-Paid At Closing	Seller-Paid Before Closing	Paid by Others
E. Taxes and Other Government Fees		**$85.00**				
01 Recording Fees	Deed: $40.00 Mortgage: $45.00	$85.00				
02 Transfer Tax	to Any State			$950.00		
F. Prepaids		**$2,120.80**				
01 Homeowner's Insurance Premium (12 mo.) to Insurance Co.		$1,209.96				
02 Mortgage Insurance Premium (mo.)						
03 Prepaid Interest ($17.44 per day from 4/15/13 to 5/1/13)		$279.04				
04 Property Taxes (6 mo.) to Any County USA		$631.80				
05						
G. Initial Escrow Payment at Closing		**$412.25**				
01 Homeowner's Insurance $100.83 per month for 2 mo.		$201.66				
02 Mortgage Insurance per month for mo.						
03 Property Taxes $105.30 per month for 2 mo.		$210.60				
04						
05						
06						
07						
08 Aggregate Adjustment		– 0.01				
H. Other		**$2,400.00**				
01 HOA Capital Contribution	to HOA Acre Inc.	$500.00				
02 HOA Processing Fee	to HOA Acre Inc.	$150.00				
03 Home Inspection Fee	to Engineers Inc.	$750.00				$750.00
04 Home Warranty Fee	to XYZ Warranty Inc.			$450.00		
05 Real Estate Commission	to Alpha Real Estate Broker			$5,700.00		
06 Real Estate Commission	to Omega Real Estate Broker			$5,700.00		
07 Title – Owner's Title Insurance (optional) to Epsilon Title Co.		$1,000.00				
08						
I. TOTAL OTHER COSTS (Borrower-Paid)		**$5,018.05**				
Other Costs Subtotals (E + F + G + H)		$5,018.05				

		Borrower-Paid At Closing	Borrower-Paid Before Closing	Seller-Paid At Closing	Seller-Paid Before Closing	Paid by Others
J. TOTAL CLOSING COSTS (Borrower-Paid)		**$9,712.10**				
Closing Costs Subtotals (D + I)		$9,682.30	$29.80	$12,800.00	$750.00	$405.00
Lender Credits						

CLOSING DISCLOSURE

Calculating Cash to Close

Use this table to see what has changed from your Loan Estimate.

	Loan Estimate	Final	Did this change?
Total Closing Costs (J)	$8,054.00	$9,712.10	YES • See Total Loan Costs (D) and Total Other Costs (I)
Closing Costs Paid Before Closing	$0	− $29.80	YES • You paid these Closing Costs before closing
Closing Costs Financed (Paid from your Loan Amount)	$0	$0	NO
Down Payment/Funds from Borrower	$18,000.00	$18,000.00	NO
Deposit	− $10,000.00	− $10,000.00	NO
Funds for Borrower	$0	$0	NO
Seller Credits	$0	− $2,500.00	YES • See Seller Credits in Section L
Adjustments and Other Credits	$0	− $1,035.04	YES • See details in Sections K and L
Cash to Close	$16,054.00	$14,147.26	

Summaries of Transactions

Use this table to see a summary of your transaction.

BORROWER'S TRANSACTION

K. Due from Borrower at Closing		$189,762.30
01 Sale Price of Property		$180,000.00
02 Sale Price of Any Personal Property Included in Sale		
03 Closing Costs Paid at Closing (J)		$9,682.30
04		
Adjustments		
05		
06		
07		
Adjustments for Items Paid by Seller in Advance		
08 City/Town Taxes	to	
09 County Taxes	to	
10 Assessments	to	
11 HOA Dues 4/15/13 to 4/30/13		$80.00
12		
13		
14		
15		

L. Paid Already by or on Behalf of Borrower at Closing		$175,615.04
01 Deposit		$10,000.00
02 Loan Amount		$162,000.00
03 Existing Loan(s) Assumed or Taken Subject to		
04		
05 Seller Credit		$2,500.00
Other Credits		
06 Rebate from Epsilon Title Co.		$750.00
07		
Adjustments		
08		
09		
10		
11		
Adjustments for Items Unpaid by Seller		
12 City/Town Taxes 1/1/13 to 4/14/13		$365.04
13 County Taxes	to	
14 Assessments	to	
15		
16		
17		

CALCULATION	
Total Due from Borrower at Closing (K)	$189,762.30
Total Paid Already by or on Behalf of Borrower at Closing (L)	− $175,615.04
Cash to Close ☒ From ☐ To Borrower	**$14,147.26**

SELLER'S TRANSACTION

M. Due to Seller at Closing		$180,080.00
01 Sale Price of Property		$180,000.00
02 Sale Price of Any Personal Property Included in Sale		
03		
04		
05		
06		
07		
08		
Adjustments for Items Paid by Seller in Advance		
09 City/Town Taxes	to	
10 County Taxes	to	
11 Assessments	to	
12 HOA Dues 4/15/13 to 4/30/13		$80.00
13		
14		
15		
16		

N. Due from Seller at Closing		$115,665.04
01 Excess Deposit		
02 Closing Costs Paid at Closing (J)		$12,800.00
03 Existing Loan(s) Assumed or Taken Subject to		
04 Payoff of First Mortgage Loan		$100,000.00
05 Payoff of Second Mortgage Loan		
06		
07		
08 Seller Credit		$2,500.00
09		
10		
11		
12		
13		
Adjustments for Items Unpaid by Seller		
14 City/Town Taxes 1/1/13 to 4/14/13		$365.04
15 County Taxes	to	
16 Assessments	to	
17		
18		
19		

CALCULATION	
Total Due to Seller at Closing (M)	$180,080.00
Total Due from Seller at Closing (N)	− $115,665.04
Cash ☐ From ☒ To Seller	**$64,414.96**

CLOSING DISCLOSURE

Additional Information About This Loan

Loan Disclosures

Assumption
If you sell or transfer this property to another person, your lender
- ☐ will allow, under certain conditions, this person to assume this loan on the original terms.
- ☒ will not allow assumption of this loan on the original terms.

Demand Feature
Your loan
- ☐ has a demand feature, which permits your lender to require early repayment of the loan. You should review your note for details.
- ☒ does not have a demand feature.

Late Payment
If your payment is more than *15* days late, your lender will charge a late fee of *5% of the monthly principal and interest payment.*

Negative Amortization (Increase in Loan Amount)
Under your loan terms, you
- ☐ are scheduled to make monthly payments that do not pay all of the interest due that month. As a result, your loan amount will increase (negatively amortize), and your loan amount will likely become larger than your original loan amount. Increases in your loan amount lower the equity you have in this property.
- ☐ may have monthly payments that do not pay all of the interest due that month. If you do, your loan amount will increase (negatively amortize), and, as a result, your loan amount may become larger than your original loan amount. Increases in your loan amount lower the equity you have in this property.
- ☒ do not have a negative amortization feature.

Partial Payments
Your lender
- ☒ may accept payments that are less than the full amount due (partial payments) and apply them to your loan.
- ☐ may hold them in a separate account until you pay the rest of the payment, and then apply the full payment to your loan.
- ☐ does not accept any partial payments.

If this loan is sold, your new lender may have a different policy.

Security Interest
You are granting a security interest in
456 Somewhere Ave., Anytown, ST 12345

You may lose this property if you do not make your payments or satisfy other obligations for this loan.

Escrow Account
For now, your loan
- ☒ will have an escrow account (also called an "impound" or "trust" account) to pay the property costs listed below. Without an escrow account, you would pay them directly, possibly in one or two large payments a year. Your lender may be liable for penalties and interest for failing to make a payment.

Escrow		
Escrowed Property Costs over Year 1	$2,473.56	Estimated total amount over year 1 for your escrowed property costs: *Homeowner's Insurance Property Taxes*
Non-Escrowed Property Costs over Year 1	$1,800.00	Estimated total amount over year 1 for your non-escrowed property costs: *Homeowner's Association Dues* You may have other property costs.
Initial Escrow Payment	$412.25	A cushion for the escrow account you pay at closing. See Section G on page 2.
Monthly Escrow Payment	$206.13	The amount included in your total monthly payment.

- ☐ will not have an escrow account because ☐ you declined it ☐ your lender does not offer one. You must directly pay your property costs, such as taxes and homeowner's insurance. Contact your lender to ask if your loan can have an escrow account.

No Escrow		
Estimated Property Costs over Year 1		Estimated total amount over year 1. You must pay these costs directly, possibly in one or two large payments a year.
Escrow Waiver Fee		

In the future,
Your property costs may change and, as a result, your escrow payment may change. You may be able to cancel your escrow account, but if you do, you must pay your property costs directly. If you fail to pay your property taxes, your state or local government may (1) impose fines and penalties or (2) place a tax lien on this property. If you fail to pay any of your property costs, your lender may (1) add the amounts to your loan balance, (2) add an escrow account to your loan, or (3) require you to pay for property insurance that the lender buys on your behalf, which likely would cost more and provide fewer benefits than what you could buy on your own.

APPENDIX E Documents for Review

Loan Calculations

Total of Payments. Total you will have paid after you make all payments of principal, interest, mortgage insurance, and loan costs, as scheduled.	$285,803.36
Finance Charge. The dollar amount the loan will cost you.	$118,830.27
Amount Financed. The loan amount available after paying your upfront finance charge.	$162,000.00
Annual Percentage Rate (APR). Your costs over the loan term expressed as a rate. This is not your interest rate.	4.174%
Total Interest Percentage (TIP). The total amount of interest that you will pay over the loan term as a percentage of your loan amount.	69.46%

? **Questions?** If you have questions about the loan terms or costs on this form, use the contact information below. To get more information or make a complaint, contact the Consumer Financial Protection Bureau at **www.consumerfinance.gov/mortgage-closing**

Other Disclosures

Appraisal
If the property was appraised for your loan, your lender is required to give you a copy at no additional cost at least 3 days before closing. If you have not yet received it, please contact your lender at the information listed below.

Contract Details
See your note and security instrument for information about
- what happens if you fail to make your payments,
- what is a default on the loan,
- situations in which your lender can require early repayment of the loan, and
- the rules for making payments before they are due.

Liability after Foreclosure
If your lender forecloses on this property and the foreclosure does not cover the amount of unpaid balance on this loan,

☒ state law may protect you from liability for the unpaid balance. If you refinance or take on any additional debt on this property, you may lose this protection and have to pay any debt remaining even after foreclosure. You may want to consult a lawyer for more information.

☐ state law does not protect you from liability for the unpaid balance.

Refinance
Refinancing this loan will depend on your future financial situation, the property value, and market conditions. You may not be able to refinance this loan.

Tax Deductions
If you borrow more than this property is worth, the interest on the loan amount above this property's fair market value is not deductible from your federal income taxes. You should consult a tax advisor for more information.

Contact Information

	Lender	Mortgage Broker	Real Estate Broker (B)	Real Estate Broker (S)	Settlement Agent
Name	Ficus Bank		Omega Real Estate Broker Inc.	Alpha Real Estate Broker Co.	Epsilon Title Co.
Address	4321 Random Blvd. Somecity, ST 12340		789 Local Lane Sometown, ST 12345	987 Suburb Ct. Someplace, ST 12340	123 Commerce Pl. Somecity, ST 12344
NMLS ID					
ST License ID			Z765416	Z61456	Z61616
Contact	Joe Smith		Samuel Green	Joseph Cain	Sarah Arnold
Contact NMLS ID	12345				
Contact ST License ID			P16415	P51461	PT1234
Email	joesmith@ficusbank.com		sam@omegare.biz	joe@alphare.biz	sarah@epsilontitle.com
Phone	123-456-7890		123-555-1717	321-555-7171	987-555-4321

Confirm Receipt

By signing, you are only confirming that you have received this form. You do not have to accept this loan because you have signed or received this form.

_____   _____   _____   _____
Applicant Signature   Date   Co-Applicant Signature   Date

CLOSING DISCLOSURE

APPENDIX E Documents for Review

American Land Title Association	ALTA Settlement Statement - Combined Adopted 05-01-2015

File No./Escrow No.:
Print Date & Time:
Officer/Escrow Officer:
Settlement Location:

Title Company Name
ALTA Universal ID
Title Company Address

Title Company Logo

Property Address:
Buyer:
Seller:
Lender:

Settlement Date:
Disbursement Date:
Additional dates per state requirements:

Seller		Description	Borrower/Buyer	
Debit	Credit		Debit	Credit
		Financial		
		Sales Price of Property		
		Personal Property		
		Deposit including earnest money		
		Loan Amount		
		Existing Loan(s) Assumed or Taken Subject to _____		
		Seller Credit		
		Excess Deposit		
		Prorations/Adjustments		
		School Taxes from (date) to (date)		
		County Taxes from (date) to (date)		
		HOA dues from (date) to (date)		
		Seller Credit		
		Loan Charges to (lender co.)		
		Points		
		Application Fee		
		Origination Fee		
		Underwriting Fee		
		Mortgage Insurance Premium		
		Prepaid Interest		

Copyright 2015 American Land Title Association.
All rights reserved.

File #
Printed on (date) at (time)

		Other Loan Charges		
		Appraisal Fee to _____		
		Credit Report Fee to _____		
		Flood Determination Fee to _____		
		Flood Monitoring Fee to _____		
		Tax Monitoring Fee to _____		
		Tax Status Research Fee to _____		
		Impounds		
		Homeowner's Insurance _____ mo @ $ _____/mo		
		Mortgage Insurance _____ mo @ $ _____/mo		
		City/town taxes _____ mo @ $ _____/mo		
		County Taxes _____ mo @ $ _____/mo		
		School Taxes _____ mo @ $ _____/mo		
		Aggregate Adjustment		
		Title Charges & Escrow / Settlement Charges		
		Owner's Title Insurance ($ amount) to _____		
		Owner's Policy Endorsement(s) _____		
		Loan Policy of Title Insurance ($ amount) to _____		
		Loan Policy Endorsement(s) _____		
		Title Search to _____		
		Insurance Binder to _____		
		Escrow / Settlement Fee to _____		
		Notary Fee to _____		
		Signing Fee to _____		
		Commission		
		Real Estate Commission to _____		
		Real Estate Commission to _____		
		Other		
		Government Recording and Transfer Charges		
		Recording Fees (Deed) to _____		
		Recording Fees (Mortgage/Deed of Trust) to _____		
		Recording Fees (Other) to _____		
		Transfer Tax to _____		
		Transfer Tax to _____		
		Payoff(s)		
		Lender: Payoff Lender Co.		
		Principal Balance ($ amount)		
		Interest on Payoff Loan ($ amount/day)		
		Additional Payoff fees/Reconveyance Fee/Recording Fee/Wire Fee		
		Lender: Payoff Lender Co.		
		Principal Balance ($ amount)		

APPENDIX E Documents for Review

		Interest on Payoff Loan ($ amount/day)		
		Additional Payoff fees/Reconveyance Fee/Recording Fee/Wire Fee		
		Miscellaneous		
		Pest Inspection Fee to _____		
		Survey Fee to _____		
		Homeowner's insurance premium to _____		
		Home Inspection Fee to _____		
		Home Warranty Fee to _____		
		HOA dues to _____		
		Transfer fee to Management Co.		
		Special Hazard Disclosure		
		[Utility] Payment to _____		
		Assessments		
		School Taxes		
		City/town taxes		
		County Taxes/County Property taxes		
		Buyer Attorney fees to _____		
		Seller Attorney fees to _____		
Seller			**Borrower/Buyer**	
Debit	**Credit**		**Debit**	**Credit**
		Subtotals		
		Due From/To Borrower		
		Due From/To Seller		
		Totals		

Acknowledgement

We/I have carefully reviewed the ALTA Settlement Statement and find it to be a true and accurate statement of all receipts and disbursements made on my account or by me in this transaction and further certify that I have received a copy of the ALTA Settlement Statement. We/I authorize _____ *title company name* _____ to cause the funds to be disbursed in accordance with this statement.

_____
Buyer

_____
Buyer

_____
Seller

_____
Escrow Officer

Copyright 2015 American Land Title Association.
All rights reserved.

File #
Printed on (date) at (time)

LEASE FOR RESIDENTIAL PROPERTY

2021 Printing

For and in consideration of $10.00 and other good and valuable consideration, the receipt and sufficiency of which is hereby acknowledged, the undersigned Landlord (_____) and the undersigned Tenant (_____, _____) do hereby agree as follows:

A. PRIMARY TERMS. The primary terms of this Lease are set forth in this Section and are subject to the explanations and clarifications set forth in Corresponding Paragraphs Section B of the Lease.

Lease. Landlord agrees to lease to Tenant, and Tenant agrees to lease from Landlord, the Premises identified herein on this date of _____ on the terms and conditions of which are set forth below.

1. **Property Address:** _____ Unit _____
   City _____ County _____ Georgia, Zip _____ ("Premises")

2. **Lease Start Date:** _____ **Last Day of Lease ("Lease End Date"):** _____
   Tenant may terminate this Agreement without penalty if possession is not granted within _____ days of the Lease Start Date ("Approved Delay Period").

3. **Rent.**
   a. **Rent:** Tenant shall pay monthly rent of $_____. Rent Shall Be Payable To _____ and delivered to: _____ ("Rent Payment Address") unless another address is specified by the above-referenced party receiving the rent following the notice provisions herein.
   b. **Due Date for Rent:** Rent is due by the _____ day of the month. Rent may be paid in any of the forms checked here: ☐ Check ☐ Cash ☐ Certified Check ☐ Money Order ☐ Credit Card ☐ ACH or ☐ EFT.
   c. **Late Date and Additional Rent for Late Payment:** Rent paid after _____ .m. on the _____ day of the month shall be late and must include additional rent of _____ ("Additional Rent for Late Payment").
   d. **Credit Card:** If rent is paid by Credit Card rent must include a credit card convenience fee of _____.
   e. **Service Charge:** Tenant shall immediately pay Landlord a service charge of $_____ ("Service Charge") for all dishonored checks or rejected electronic (ACH) payments.

4. **Security Deposit.**
   a. Tenant shall pay _____ as "Holder" a security deposit of $_____ by: ☐ Check ☐ Cash ☐ Certified Check ☐ Money Order ☐ Credit Card ☐ ACH or ☐ EFT. Security deposit shall be paid not later than the Lease Start Date but not earlier than the date Landlord or Manager has presented Tenant with a copy of the Move-In Inspection. Landlord's or Manager's signature below does not constitute receipt of the security deposit. Landlord or Manager shall provide Tenant with a receipt for the security deposit once said deposit has been paid.
   b. **Security Deposit Bank Account:** The security deposit will be held in:
   ☐ Escrow Account at _____ Bank; OR ☐ General Account at _____ Bank.

5. **Notice Not to Renew Lease.** A party electing not to renew the Lease shall be required to provide _____ days notice of the same to the other party even when the lease becomes a month to month agreement.

6. **Re-Key Fee Paid By Tenant upon Lease Termination:** $ _____

7. **Non-Refundable Administrative Fee Paid by Tenant:** $ _____

8. **Pets.** Tenant ☐ shall or ☐ shall not be allowed to keep pets on the premises. If pets are allowed a separate pet exhibit must be attached hereto and is incorporated into this Lease.

9. **Smoking.** Tenant ☐ shall or ☐ shall not be allowed to smoke, in any form, on or in the Premises.

10. **No Subletting.** No subletting of any kind including, but not limited to, nightly rental services such as AIRBNB.com, or home exchange services such as HomeExchange.com.

11. **Utilities.** Utilities provided by Landlord: ☐ Water ☐ Sewer ☐ Gas ☐ Electricity ☐ Trash Pickup ☐ Cable ☐ None
    ☐ Other: _____

12.	**Early Termination by Tenant.** Tenant ☐ shall OR ☐ shall not have the right to terminate this Lease early. If Tenant has a right to terminate the Lease early, Tenant must pay the lesser of 35% of the sum of the rental payments remaining during the current lease term or the sum of the charges in the subparagraphs c. and d. below. These fees are a reasonable pre-estimate of Landlord's and Manager's additional expenses for unanticipated vacancies, turnkey expenses and re-letting costs. ☐ **a.** Give Landlord no less than _____ days prior notice of the termination. ☐ **b.** Comply in ALL respects with the requirements set out in Paragraph B.12. ☐ **c.** In addition to the rent due, pay as liquidated damages $_____ or _____ % of the total rent that otherwise would have been owed through the Lease End Date, not later than _____ days from the date Notice to Terminate is received. ☐ **d.** Pay an Early Lease Termination Administrative Fee of $_____, not later than _____ days from the date Notice to Terminate is received.
13.	**Early Termination by Landlord.** Landlord shall have the right to terminate the Lease early upon not less than _____ days notice and upon such termination and Tenant vacating the Premises, Landlord shall credit Tenant with the sum of $_____ ("Early Termination Fee to Tenant") which shall first be applied against any monies owing from Tenant to Landlord with the balance thereafter being paid to Tenant by Landlord.
14.	**Holding Over Rate.** The daily rate for holding over beyond the expiration or termination of the Lease is $_____.
15.	**Fee to Prepare Lease Amendment:** $_____
16.	**Use:** Only the following people are authorized to occupy the Premises: _____
17.	**Appliances provided by Landlord:** ☐ Compactor ☐ Dryer ☐ Microwave ☐ Range ☐ Washer ☐ Other:_____ ☐ Dishwasher ☐ Electric ☐ Oven ☐ Built-in ☐ Wine/Drink Cooler ☐ Other:_____ ☐ Disposal ☐ Gas ☐ Electric ☐ Free-standing ☐ Venthood ☐ Other:_____ ☐ Gas ☐ Refrigerator ☐ Other:_____
18.	**Lawn & Exterior Maintenance.** ☐ Tenant OR ☐ Landlord shall maintain the lawn and perform exterior maintenance as described elsewhere herein.
19.	**Pest Control.** Pest Control, as specified elsewhere in the Lease, shall be the responsibility of and paid for by: ☐ Tenant OR ☐ Landlord.
20.	**Propensity of Flooding.** The Premises ☐ have OR ☐ have not flooded at least three (3) times within the past five (5) years.
21.	**Lead Based Paint.** The Premises ☐ were (attach F918 Lead-Based Paint Exhibit) OR ☐ were not built prior to 1978. Tenant ☐ has OR ☐ has not received a copy of the *Lead-Based Paint Pamphlet (CB04)*.
22.	**Other Liquidated Damages Paid By Tenant.** **a. Fee to Halt Dispossessory Action:** The fee paid by Tenant to halt dispossessory actions in certain situations as set forth elsewhere herein shall be $_____ ("Fee to Halt Dispossessory Action") plus an Administrative Fee of $_____ per occurrence. **b. Denial of Access Charge:** Tenant agrees to pay $_____ for each incident where Tenant denies Landlord access to the Premises ("Denial of Access Fee") as described elsewhere herein. **c. Unauthorized Pet Charge:** $_____ per incident. Every day the violation occurs shall be deemed a separate incident. **d. Unauthorized smoking within the Premises charge:** $_____. **e. Utility Disconnection Charge for un-authorized disconnection of utility service:** $_____.
23.	**Renewal.** **a. Term:** The Lease ☐ shall automatically renew in _____ month increments (each of which shall be referred to as a "Renewal Term") or ☐ shall renew on a month to month basis with all other terms and conditions of the Lease remaining the same including, but not limited to, the number of days notice required to terminate the Lease. If the month to month option is selected, then the language below regarding the "Automatic Renewal" of the Lease shall not be applicable or part of this Lease. **b. Automatic Renewal:** Upon the first day of the calendar month following the initial Lease End Date, and every twelve (12) months thereafter, the rent will automatically increase _____% over the immediately preceding rental rate. Landlord shall have the right to increase the rent above this amount upon notice being given to Tenant at least ninety (90) days prior to the end of the then applicable Lease Term or Renewal Term. Upon the receipt of such notice, Tenant shall have thirty (30) days thereafter to notify Landlord of Tenant's decision either to: (1) terminate the Lease effective upon the end of the current term of the Lease; or (2) accept the increase in the rent above the amount set forth elsewhere in the Lease. If Tenant fails to timely respond to the notice of rent increase above the increase set forth elsewhere herein, then Tenant shall be deemed to have accepted the increase in rent for the subsequent Renewal Term. After the expiration of _____ Renewal Terms, the Lease shall automatically become a month-to-month Lease if not otherwise terminated. All other terms and conditions of this Lease, including the notice provisions, shall remain the same and in full force and in effect.

24. **Brokerage Relationships in this Transaction:**
   a. Leasing Broker is _____ and is:
      (1) working with Tenant as a ☐ client or ☐ customer.
      (2) ☐ acting as a dual agent representing Landlord and Tenant.
      (3) ☐ acting as designated agent where:
      _____
      has been assigned to exclusively represent Tenant.

   b. Listing Broker is _____ and is:
      (1) working with Landlord as a ☐ client or ☐ customer.
      (2) ☐ acting as a dual agent representing Tenant and Landlord.
      (3) ☐ acting as designated agent where:
      _____
      has been assigned to exclusively represent Landlord.

25. **Material Relationship Disclosure:** Broker and/or their affiliated licensees disclose the following material relationships:
   _____
   _____

26. **Disclosure of Ownership and Agents.**
   a. **Owner Disclosure:** The name and address of the Owner of record of the Premises or the person authorized to act for and on behalf of the Owner for the purpose of serving of process and receiving demands and notices is as follows:
   _____
   _____

   b. **Manager Disclosure:** The name and address of the person authorized to manage the Premises and Property is as follows:
   Brokerage Firm: _____ (hereinafter "Manager").
   Address of Brokerage Firm: _____
   Contact Person: _____ Phone Number: _____

Tenant(s) Initials _____ Landlord(s) Initials _____

B. CORRESPONDING PARAGRAPHS

1. **Agreement to Lease.** The parties agree to enter into this Lease for the Premises which may be further described in Exhibit "A". The Premises may be part of a larger property ("Property"). If so, Tenant shall have the right to use the common areas of the Property subject to: (a) all rules, regulations and covenants applicable thereto; and (b) the common areas being reduced, modified, altered or being made subject to further use restrictions adopted by Landlord, in its sole discretion, or any community association responsible for the same. While Tenant may use and enjoy the Premises to the fullest extent permitted in this Lease, no estate or permanent legal interest in the Premises is being transferred or conveyed by Landlord to Tenant herein. Landlord shall have the right to assign this Lease to a subsequent owner of the Premises.

2. **Term and Possession.** If Landlord is unable to deliver possession of Premises on the Start Date, rent shall be abated on a daily basis until possession is granted. Neither Owner, Landlord or Broker shall be liable for any delay in the delivery of possession of Premises to Tenant.

3. **Rent.** Tenant shall pay rent in advance to Landlord monthly, and on or before the Due Date during the Lease Term to the Rent Payment Address (or at such other address as may be designated from time to time by Landlord in writing). If the Lease Start Date or the Lease End Date is on the second day through the last day of any month, the rent shall be prorated for that month. Mailing the rent payment shall not constitute payment. Rent must be actually received by Landlord to be considered paid. Tenant acknowledges that all funds received by Landlord will be applied to the oldest outstanding balance owed by Tenant to Landlord. Rent not paid in full by the Due Date shall be late. Landlord may, but shall have no obligation to accept any rent paid after the Due Date. If late payment is made and Landlord accepts the same, the payment must include Additional Rent for Late Payment in the form of cash, cashier's check, certified check or wire transfer of immediately available funds, and if applicable, the Service Charge for any returned check. Landlord reserves the right, upon notice to Tenant, to refuse to accept personal checks from Tenant after one or more of Tenant's personal checks have been returned by the bank unpaid.

4. **Security Deposit.**
   a. **Move-In:** Prior to Tenant tendering a Security Deposit, Landlord shall provide Tenant with a comprehensive list of any existing damages to Premises. Prior to taking occupancy, Tenant will be given the right to inspect Premises to ascertain the accuracy of the form. Both Landlord and Tenant shall sign the form and Tenant shall be entitled to retain a copy of the form. Tenant acknowledges that Tenant has carefully inspected the Premises, is familiar with the same and that the Premises are in a good and habitable condition.
   b. **Deposit of Same:** Holder shall deposit the Security Deposit within five (5) banking days of receiving the same into the bank and account referenced herein. If Landlord is managing the property, the Security Deposit may be deposited in a general account, and it will not be segregated and will be co-mingled with other funds of Holder.
   [NOTE: If Landlord or Landlord's spouse or minor children own more than ten (10) rental units, if Landlord is not a natural person or if Landlord is a real estate licensee or if the management, including rent collection, is performed by third persons, natural or otherwise, for a fee, the Security Deposit must be deposited into an escrow account.]
   All interest earned on the above-referenced account shall belong to the Holder. Holder shall have the right to change the bank in which the Security Deposit is held upon notice to Landlord and Tenant, provided that the type of account remains the same. Landlord shall have the right upon fourteen (14) days prior notice to Holder and Tenant to change the Holder of the Security Deposit and / or the bank account into which the Security Deposit is deposited; provided that the new Holder designated by Landlord is a licensed Georgia real estate broker and the bank account into which the Security Deposit is deposited into is an escrow/trust account.

c. **Security Deposit Check Not Honored:** In the event any Security Deposit check is dishonored, for any reason, by the bank upon which it is drawn, Holder shall promptly notify all parties to this Agreement of the same. Tenant shall have three (3) banking days after notice to deliver good funds to Holder. In the event Tenant does not timely deliver good funds, Landlord shall have the right to terminate this Lease upon notice to Tenant.
d. **Return of Security Deposit:** The balance of the Security Deposit to which Tenant is entitled shall be returned to Tenant by Holder within thirty (30) days after the termination of this Agreement or the surrender of Premises by Tenant, whichever occurs last (hereinafter "Due Date"); provided that Tenant meets the following requirements: (1) the full term of the Lease has expired; (2) Tenant has given the required written notice to vacate; (3) the Premises is clean and free of dirt, trash and debris; (4) all rent, additional rent, fees and charges have been paid in full; (5) there is no damage to the Premises or the Property except for normal wear and tear or damage noted at the commencement of the Lease in the Move-In, Move-Out Condition Report (F910 or F911) signed by Landlord and Tenant; and (6) all keys to the Premises and to recreational or other facilities, access cards, gate openers and garage openers have been returned to Landlord or Manager.
e. **Deductions from Security Deposit:** Holder shall have the right to deduct from the Security Deposit: (1) the cost of repairing any damage to Premises or Property caused by Tenant, Tenant's household or their invitees, licensees and guests, other than normal wear and tear; (2) unpaid rent, utility charges or pet fees; (3) cleaning costs if Premises is left unclean; (4) the cost to remove and dispose of any personal property; (5) late fees and any other unpaid fees, costs and charges referenced herein.
f. **Move-Out Statement:** Holder shall provide Tenant with a statement ("Move-Out Statement") listing the exact reasons for the retention of the Security Deposit or for any deductions there from. If the reason for the retention is based upon damage to Premises, such damages shall be specifically listed in the Move-Out Statement. The Move-Out Statement shall be prepared within three (3) banking days after the termination of occupancy. If Tenant terminates occupancy without notifying the Holder, Holder may make a final inspection within a reasonable time after discovering the termination of occupancy. Tenant shall have the right to inspect Premises within five (5) banking days after the termination of occupancy in order to ascertain the accuracy of the Move-Out Statement. If Tenant agrees with the Move-Out Statement, Tenant shall sign the same. If Tenant refuses to sign the Move-Out Statement, Tenant shall specify in writing, the items on the Move-Out Statement with which Tenant disagrees within three (3) banking days. For all purposes herein, a banking day shall not include Saturday, Sunday or federal holidays.
g. **Delivery of Move-Out Statement:** Holder shall send the Move-Out Statement, along with the balance, if any, of the Security Deposit, to Tenant on or before it is due under state law. The Move-Out Statement shall either be delivered personally to Tenant or mailed to the last known address of Tenant via first class mail. If the letter containing the payment is returned to Holder undelivered and if Holder is unable to locate Tenant after a reasonable effort, the payment shall become the property of Landlord ninety (90) days after the date the payment was mailed.
h. **Right of Holder to Interplead Security Deposit:** If there is a bona fide dispute over the Security Deposit, Holder may, (but shall not be required to), interplead the funds into a court of competent jurisdiction upon notice to all parties having an interest in the Security Deposit. Holder shall be reimbursed for and may deduct from any funds interpleaded its costs and expenses including reasonable attorneys' fees actually incurred. The prevailing defendant in the interpleader lawsuit shall be entitled to collect its attorneys' fees and court costs and the amount deducted by Holder from the non-prevailing party. All parties hereby agree to indemnify and hold Holder harmless from and against all claims, causes of action, suits and damages arising out of or related to the performance by Holder of its duties hereunder. All parties further covenant and agree not to sue Holder for damages relating to any decision of Holder to disburse the Security Deposit made in accordance with the requirements of this Lease or to interplead the Security Deposit into a court of competent jurisdiction.

5. **Notices.**
   a. **Required Notice to Lease Termination or Raising the Rent:** Either party must provide the other party with the number of days notice to terminate the Lease set forth elsewhere herein. Landlord must provide Tenant with the same number of days notice prior to increasing the rental rate.
   b. **Generally:** All notices given hereunder shall be in writing, legible and signed by the party giving the notice. In the event of a dispute regarding notice, the burden shall be on the party giving notice to prove delivery. The requirements of this notice paragraph shall apply even prior to this Agreement becoming binding. Notices shall only be delivered: (1) in person; (2) by courier, overnight delivery service or by certified or registered U.S. mail (hereinafter collectively "Delivery Service"); or (3) by e-mail or facsimile. The person delivering or sending the written notice signed by a party may be someone other than that party.
   c. **Delivery of Notice:** A notice to a party shall be deemed to have been delivered and received upon the earliest of the following to occur: (1) the actual receipt of the written notice by a party; (2) in the case of delivery by a Delivery Service, when the written notice is delivered to an address of a party set forth herein (or subsequently provided by the party following the notice provisions herein), provided that a record of the delivery is created; (3) in the case of delivery electronically, on the date and time the written notice is electronically sent to an e-mail address or facsimile number of a party herein (or subsequently provided by the party following the notice provisions herein). Notice to a party shall not be effective unless the written notice is sent to an address, facsimile number or e-mail address of the party set forth herein (or subsequently provided by the party following the notice provisions herein).
   d. **When Broker Authorized to Accept Notice for Client:** No Broker shall have the authority to accept notice on behalf of a Tenant or Landlord except that a Broker acting as the Manager hereunder shall be authorized to receive notices on behalf of Landlord and notices delivered to Manager shall for all purposes herein be deemed to be notice to Landlord provided that the notice is delivered to Manager following the notice proceedings set forth here to Manager's address, facsimile number or e-mail address of Manager set forth herein (or subsequently provided by the Manager to Tenant following the notice provisions herein).

6. **Re-Key Fee.** Upon vacating the Premises Tenant agrees to pay the fee to rekey the locks set forth elsewhere herein either upon the termination of the Lease or to replace any mailbox keys or access cards not returned by Tenant at move out.

7. **Administrative Fee.** Prior to the commencement of occupancy, Tenant shall pay Holder the non-refundable Administrative Fee set forth elsewhere herein.

8. **Pets.** No pets are allowed or shall be kept in the Premises or on the Property unless a separate pet exhibit is attached to and incorporated into this Lease.

9. **No Smoking.** Unless specifically authorized in this Agreement, Premises shall be a smoke free zone and smoking shall not be permitted therein. This includes electronic cigarettes and vaping.

10. **No Subletting.** Tenant may not sublet Premises in whole or in part or assign this Lease without the prior written consent of Landlord which consent may be withheld for any reason or for no reason. This Lease shall create the relationship of Landlord and Tenant between the parties hereto. Tenant is specifically prohibited from offering all or part of the Premises for short-term rental such as through AirBnB, VRBO, or other such sites or programs, regardless of any local laws that may be or have been enacted. Any advertising or on-line postings as well as actual rentals of the Premises to vacation or short-term guests shall constitute a material breach of this Agreement. Any person who is not a Tenant, as defined herein, who occupies any portion of the Premises, for any period of time whatsoever, for any compensation or consideration whatsoever (including, without limitation, the payment of money and/or trade and/or barter of other goods, services, or property occupancy rights) is NOT a guest, and such occupancy constitutes unauthorized subletting or assignment which is a substantial and material breach of this Agreement.

11. **Utilities.** Landlord shall have no responsibility to connect utilities the responsibility of which to pay for shall be that of the Tenant. Tenant shall select and connect all utilities to be paid for by Tenant within three (3) banking days from the commencement of the Lease and shall keep these utilities on through the completion of the Move-Out Inspection. In the event Landlord fails to disconnect any utilities serving the Premises after completing the move in inspection and Tenant receives the benefit of such utilities paid for by Landlord, Tenant shall, upon receiving a bill for the same, immediately pay the cost thereof as additional rent to Landlord. In addition, Tenant shall immediately cause any such utility to be transferred to Tenant's name so that the bill goes to and is paid directly by Tenant.

12. **Early Termination by Tenant.**
    a. **Right to Terminate Early:** Tenant shall have the right to terminate this Lease early only if Tenant has expressly been given the right to terminate the Lease early as provided elsewhere herein, Tenant is not in default hereunder at the time of giving notice, Tenant has strictly complied with all of the provisions of this paragraph, Tenant continues to pay rent on time and in full for the months prior to the Termination Date, Tenant pays any additional fees due per this section on time as set out in the Primary Terms section, and termination is as of the last day of a calendar month. If all of these conditions have been met, Tenant may terminate this Lease by following the procedures set forth elsewhere herein and returning the Premises in a clean and rent ready condition, ordinary wear and tear excepted. To be effective, any notice for early termination must be signed by all Tenants. Tenant's election of early termination shall not relieve Tenant of responsibilities and obligations regarding damage to Premises and/or Property. Tenant may not apply the security deposit toward the payment of any of Tenant's financial obligations set forth herein.
    b. **Military Activation:** Notwithstanding any provision to the contrary contained herein, if Tenant is called to active duty in the military during the term of this Lease, Tenant shall present to Landlord the official orders activating Tenant; then and in that event, this Lease shall be controlled by the Service Members' Civil Relief Act of 2003 as amended in 50 U.S.C.A. § 50-534 and O.C.G.A. § 44-7-22.
    c. **Active Military:** If Tenant is on active duty with the United States military and Tenant or an immediate family member of Tenant occupying Premises receives, during the term of this Lease, permanent change of station orders or temporary duty orders for a period in excess of three (3) months, Tenant's obligation for rent hereunder shall not exceed: (1) thirty (30) days rent after Tenant gives notice under this section; and (2) the cost of repairing damage to Premises or Property caused by an act or omission of Tenant. If Tenant is active duty military and presents to Landlord a copy of official orders of transfer to another military location, then and in that event, Tenant shall be required to give Landlord the notice to terminate early set forth elsewhere herein but shall have no obligation to pay an Early Lease Termination Administrative Fee or additional rent other than for thirty (30) days after Tenant gives notice under this section in accordance with O.C.G.A. § 44-7-22.
    d. **Victim of Domestic Abuse:** Notwithstanding any provision to the contrary contained herein, if Tenant receives a "Civil family violence order" or a "Criminal family violence order" as defined in O.C.G.A. § 44-7-23, and Tenant provides Landlord with a copy of said order, then and in that event, Tenant shall be required to give Landlord the notice to terminate early set forth elsewhere herein but shall have no obligation to pay an Early Lease Termination Administrative Fee or additional rent other than for thirty (30) days after Tenant gives notice under this section.

13. **Early Termination by Landlord.** Landlord may terminate the Lease prior to the lease expiration date and in such event Tenant agrees to vacate the Premises subject to the following:
    a. Landlord shall give Tenant written notice of the early termination and to vacate (in which case Tenant shall still owe rent through the notice period); and
    b. After Tenant has vacated the Premises, Landlord shall credit to Tenant the Early Termination Fee to Tenant as liquidated damages for disturbing Tenant's quiet enjoyment of the Premises and for the inconvenience of moving early. This credit will be applied to the Tenant account at the time the Tenant vacates the Premises and shall be included with any applicable security deposit refund. The foregoing shall not relieve the Tenant of his or her responsibilities and obligations regarding any damage to the property.

14. **Holding Over.** Tenant shall have no right to remain in the Premises after the termination or expiration of this Lease. Should Tenant fail to vacate the Premises upon the termination or expiration of this Agreement, Tenant shall pay Landlord the per day Holding Over Fee set forth elsewhere herein for every day that Tenant holds over after the expiration or termination of this Lease. Acceptance of the Holding Over Fee by Landlord shall in no way limit Landlord's right to treat Tenant as a tenant at sufferance for unlawfully holding over and to dispossess Tenant for the same.

15. **Fee to Prepare Lease Amendment.** Should Tenant request and Landlord consent to modifying the Lease, Tenant agrees to pay Manager the Fee to Prepare Lease Amendment set forth elsewhere herein.

16. **Use.** Premises shall be used for residential purposes only and shall be occupied only by those persons listed in this Agreement. Premises and Property shall be used by Tenant and Tenant shall cause all occupants of the Premises and their guests, invitees, licensees and contractors of Tenant to use the Premises and Property in accordance with all federal, state, county, and municipal laws and ordinances. A "guest" shall be defined as anyone who visits the Property for no longer than fourteen (14) consecutive days or twenty-eight (28) non-consecutive days in any twelve (12) month period. Any adult that resided in the Property for more than fourteen (14) consecutive days or twenty-eight (28) non-consecutive days in any twelve (12) month period shall be an unauthorized occupant in violation of this paragraph unless such adult undergoes Landlord's application process and is added to this Lease by mutual agreement. Tenant agrees that any violation or noncompliance of the above resulting in fines, sanctions or penalties being imposed against Landlord or Manager shall be the financial responsibility of and immediately paid by the Tenant to Landlord as Additional Rent. Tenant shall be responsible for ensuring that Tenant, all occupants of the Premises and their respective invitees, licensees, contractors and guests comply with the Rules and Regulations set forth below and not engage in any activity while on Property or in Premises that is unlawful, would endanger the health and safety of others or would otherwise create a nuisance. In the event Tenant or any of the above-named parties are arrested or indicted for any unlawful activity occurring on Property or for a felony occurring off of the Property and said charges are not dismissed within thirty (30) days thereafter, Tenant shall be deemed to be in default of this Lease and Landlord may, but shall not be obligated to, terminate this Lease upon notice to Tenant. For the purpose of this Lease, an unlawful activity shall be deemed to be any activity in violation of local, state or federal law.

17. **Appliances.** Only the appliances described elsewhere herein are provided by Landlord as part of this Agreement and included in this Lease. Tenant acknowledges that Tenant has inspected these appliances and that the same are in good working order and repair.

18. **Lawn and Exterior Maintenance.** The party maintaining the lawn shall keep the lawn mowed and edged, beds free of weeds, shrubs trimmed, trash and grass clippings picked up on a regular basis (minimum of once every two weeks in growing season and fall leaf season) and shall keep the Premises, including the yard, lot, grounds, walkways and driveway clean and free of rubbish, trash and debris. Landlord shall be responsible for any other maintenance of the Premises or the Property required under O.C.G.A. 44-7-13.

19. **Pest Control.** Landlord will be responsible for termite and rodent control. The term "pest control" herein means addressing any problems in the Premises with ants, cockroaches, spiders and other insects and preventing the infestation thereof and the party responsible for the same is set forth elsewhere herein). Tenant shall be responsible for the immediate treatment of any bed bugs in the Premises by a licensed Georgia pest control operator and the immediate and permanent removal from the Premises of any mattresses, bedding, clothing and other similar items that may contain bed bugs or bed bug larvae.

20. **Propensity for Flooding.** When the owner of real property, either directly or through an agent, seeks to lease or rent that property for residential occupancy, prior to entering a written agreement for the leasehold of that property, the owner shall, either directly or through an agent, notify the prospective tenant in writing of the property's propensity of flooding if flooding has damaged any portion of the living space covered by the lease or attachments thereto to which the tenant or the tenant's resident relative has sole and exclusive use under the written agreement at least three times during the five-year period immediately preceding the date of the lease. This disclosure set forth elsewhere herein is to fulfill that requirement.

21. **Lead-Based Paint.** For any Premises built prior to 1978, Tenant acknowledges that Tenant has received and read the Lead-Based Paint Pamphlet (CB04), and signed the Lead-Based Paint Exhibit (F918) attached hereto and incorporated herein by reference. Any approved painting or other alterations by Tenant that disturb lead-based paint shall be performed in accordance with the EPA's Renovate Right brochure (http://www.epa.gov/lead/pubs/renovaterightbrochure.com).

22. **Other Liquidated Damages Paid by Tenant.** It is acknowledged by Landlord and Tenant with respect to any reference in the Lease to liquidated damages, that the actual damages of the party being paid such damages are hard to calculate and that the liquidated damages referenced in the Lease are a reasonable pre-estimate of the party's actual damages and not a penalty.
    a. **Amount Paid to Terminate Lease Early:** If the parties have agreed elsewhere herein, Tenant shall have the right to terminate this Lease early by paying amounts set forth in Section A.12 as liquidates damages.
    b. **Fee to Halt Dispossessory Action:** Landlord can file a dispossessory action against Tenant if any rent or other fees and charges owed by Tenant are not paid in full by the Due Date. In the event that a dispossessory action is filed against the Tenant and then dismissed prior to a court hearing because Tenant pays the amounts owed, Tenant shall also pay Landlord, as liquidated damages, the Fee to Halt Dispossessory Action in the amount set forth elsewhere herein. This fee shall immediately be paid as additional rent along with all other amounts paid to halt the dispossessory action.
    c. **Denial of Access, Right of Access, Signage:** Upon 24 hours advance notice to Tenant, Landlord and Landlord's agents shall have the right Monday through Saturday from 9:00 a.m. to 8:00 p.m. and Sunday from 1:00 p.m. to 6:00 p.m. to access the Premises to inspect, repair, and maintain the same and/or to show the Premises to prospective tenants and buyers. In addition, Landlord and Landlord's agents may enter the Premises at any time to investigate potential emergencies. Evidence of water leaks, fire, smoke, foul odors, sounds indicating the possibility of an injured person or animal and other similar evidence of an emergency shall all be sufficient grounds for Landlord and Landlord's agents to enter Premises and Property for this purpose. During the last sixty (60) days of the term of the Lease, and during any period when Premises is being leased month to month, Landlord and Landlord's agents may also place a "for rent" or "for sale" sign in the yard or on the exterior of the Premises or on the Property, may install a lockbox and may show the Premises and the Property to prospective tenants or purchasers during the hours listed above. Tenant agrees to cooperate with Landlord and Landlord's agents who may show the Premises and/or Property to prospective tenants or buyers. In the event a lockbox is installed, Tenant shall secure keys, jewelry, prescription drugs and other valuables and agrees to hold Landlord and Landlord's agents harmless for any loss thereof. For each occasion where the access rights described above are denied, Tenant shall pay Landlord the Denial of Access Fee as liquidated damages in the amount set forth elsewhere herein.

d. **Unauthorized Pet Charge:** Except for those Pets authorized by a Pet Addendum attached to this lease (if applicable), no other animals are authorized to be within the Premises. This includes, but is not limited to, animals which belong to guests or animals which are only staying temporarily. Should Landlord or Manager ever witness an unauthorized animal within the Premises, Tenant agrees to pay Landlord the Unauthorized Pet Charge as liquidated damages in the amount set forth elsewhere herein for each occasion where Landlord/Manager observed the unauthorized animal.
e. **Unauthorized Smoking within Premises:** Many people are very sensitive to the smell of smoke whether cigarette, cigar, or any other substances and removing smoke odor is costly. If Tenant is NOT authorized to smoke within the Premises as set forth elsewhere herein and Landlord or Manager note that smoking has occurred within the Premises, Tenant agrees to pay Landlord the Unauthorized Smoking within the Premises charge as described elsewhere herein.
f. **Utility Connection Charge:** In order for Landlord or Manager to perform an accurate Move-Out Condition Report (F910 or F912), utilities to the Premises need to be on. Should Tenant disconnect the utilities prior to the completion of the Move-Out Condition Report (F910 or F912), thereby interfering with Landlord's ability to perform a complete review of the Premises' condition, Tenant agrees to pay to Landlord the Utility Disconnect Fee as liquidated damages as set forth elsewhere herein.

23. **Renewal Term.** Either party may terminate this Lease at the end of the term by giving the other party the Notice Not to Renew Lease Term. If neither party gives the required notice, the Lease will automatically renew as described elsewhere herein. If the Renewal Term paragraph calls for a percentage increase in the rental rate the rental charge for any Renewal Term shall be rounded up to the next $5.00 increment. All other terms of the existing Lease shall remain the same. The additional term shall begin on the first day following the end of the preceding term unless either party gives notice to the other prior to end of the then current term of that party's decision to terminate the Lease at the end of the current term. If this Lease has not been terminated during the final renewal term, this Lease will continue on a month to month basis until the same is terminated in accordance with Georgia Law.

24. **Agency and Brokerage.**
    a. **Agency Disclosure:** In this Lease, the term "Broker" shall mean a licensed Georgia real estate broker or brokerage firm and, where the context would indicate, the Broker's affiliated licensees and employees. No Broker in this transaction shall owe any duty to Tenant or Owner/Landlord greater than what is set forth in their brokerage engagements and the Brokerage Relationships in Real Estate Transactions Act, O.C.G.A. § 10-6A-1 et. seq.; The Broker(s) that are party(s) to this Agreement are representing the Landlord and/or Tenant.
    b. **Brokerage:** The Broker(s) identified herein have performed valuable brokerage services and are to be paid a commission pursuant to a separate agreement or agreements. Unless otherwise provided for herein, the Listing Broker will be paid a commission by the Landlord, and the Leasing Broker will receive a portion of the Listing Broker's commission pursuant to a cooperative brokerage agreement.

25. **Material Relationship Disclosure.** For the purposes of this Agreement, a material relationship shall mean any actually known personal, familial, or business relationship between the broker or the broker's affiliated licensees and a client which would impair the ability of the broker or affiliated licensees to exercise fair and independent judgment relative to another client. Any such material relationship will be disclosed in Material Relationship Paragraph above.

26. **Disclosure of Ownership and Agents.** At or before the commencement of a tenancy, the Landlord or an agent or other person authorized to enter into a rental agreement on behalf of the Landlord shall disclose to Tenant in writing the names and addresses of the following persons:
    a. **Owner.** The owner of record of the Premises or a person authorized to act for and on behalf of the owner for the purposes of serving of process and receiving and receipting for demands and notice; and (b) The person authorized to manage the Premises. These Parties are named in the Owner Disclosure and Manager Disclosure Paragraph of this Agreement. In the event of a change in any of the names and addresses required to be contained in such statement, the Landlord shall advise Tenant of the change within thirty (30) days after the change either in writing or by posting a notice of the change in a conspicuous place on the Property.
    b. **Manager.** If no Manager is identified in the Manager Disclosure Paragraph above, the Owner shall be deemed to be self-managing the Premises and shall be deemed the Landlord for all purposes herein. If a Manager is identified in Manager Paragraph above as the Manager hereunder, Manager is authorized to manage the Premises on behalf of the Landlord and exercise any and all of the rights and powers granted in this Agreement to Landlord. In such event, Tenant shall communicate with Landlord through the Manager and rely on the notices and communications of Manager as having been fully authorized by Landlord. Manager shall have no rights, duties, obligations or liabilities greater than what is set forth in the Management Agreement between Owner and Manager, a copy of which is incorporated herein by reference. No real estate broker or the broker's affiliated licensees shall be deemed to be responsible for any aspect of managing the Property unless the Broker is identified as the Manager herein and has agreed to serve in that capacity. Any Broker serving as the Manager shall have the authority to either execute this Lease on behalf of Landlord as Landlord's managing agent or to execute this Lease as Manager itself if so authorized by Owner. It shall be presumed that any Manager executing this Lease as a Landlord or as the agent of the Landlord has the authority to do so.

C. OTHER TERMS AND CONDITIONS

1. **Default.**
    a. **Default Generally:** Tenant shall be in default of this Lease upon the occurrence of any of the following:
        (1) Tenant fails to abide by any of the terms and conditions of this Lease.
        (2) Tenant files a petition in bankruptcy (in which case this Lease shall automatically terminate and Tenant shall immediately vacate the Premises leaving it in the same condition it was in on the date of possession, normal wear and tear excepted).
        (3) Tenant fails to timely pay rent or other amounts owed to Landlord under this Lease.
        (4) Tenant fails to reimburse Landlord for any damages, repairs and costs to the Premises or Property (other than normal wear and tear) caused by the actions, neglect or intentional wrongdoing of Tenant or members of Tenant's household and their invitees, licensees and guests.

(5) Prior to the end of the Lease, Tenant either moves out of the Premises or shuts off any of the utilities serving the Premises without the consent of Landlord.

b. **Effect of Default:** If Tenant defaults under any term, condition or provision of this Lease, Landlord shall have the right to terminate this Lease by giving notice to Tenant and pursue all available remedies at law or in equity to remedy the default. All rent and other sums owed to Landlord through the end of the Lease term shall immediately become due and payable upon the termination of the Lease due to the default of Tenant. Such termination shall not release Tenant from any liability for any amount due under this Lease. All rights and remedies available to Landlord by law or in this Lease shall be cumulative and concurrent. Notwithstanding anything to the contrary contained herein, in the event of a non-monetary default by Tenant that is reasonably capable of being cured, Landlord shall give Tenant notice of the same and a three (3) day opportunity to cure the default.

2. **Tenant's Responsibilities.**
   a. **Repairs and Maintenance:** Tenant has inspected Premises and acknowledges that it is in good condition, free of defects and fit for residential occupancy. Tenant shall promptly notify Landlord of any dangerous condition or need for maintenance existing in Premises or on the Property. Upon receipt of notice from Tenant, Landlord shall, within a reasonable time period thereafter, repair the following: (1) all defects in Premises or Property which create unsafe living conditions or render Premises untenable, and (2) to the extent required by state law, such other defects which, if not corrected, will leave Premises or Property in a state of disrepair. Except as provided above, Tenant agrees to maintain Premises in the neat, sanitary and clean condition free of trash and debris. All of Tenant's trash shall be kept in designated trash containers and removed from the Premises at least once each week. Tenant obligation to maintain the Premises includes, but not limited to, replacing any light bulbs which fail during the Lease Term and regularly changing HVAC filters. Tenant shall be responsible for any clogged plumbing within the Premises. Landlord shall be responsible for all other plumbing issues between the Premises and the street or the Premises and the septic tank or in any plumbing line outside of the Premises which exclusively serves the Premises. Tenant shall be responsible for any damages to the Premises and/or Property caused by Tenant's abuse or neglect of the Premises/Property. Any expenses incurred by Landlord to remedy any violations of this provision shall be paid by Tenant to Landlord as additional rent within fourteen (14) days of the receipt of an invoice from Landlord. If Tenant submits a service request or repair request to Landlord, and the contractor responding to this request on behalf of Landlord determines that the item is working correctly, Tenant agrees to reimburse Landlord for the amount for the contractor's invoice.
   b. **Smoke Detector:** Tenant acknowledges that Premises is equipped with a smoke detector(s) that is in good working order and repair. Tenant agrees to be solely responsible to check the smoke detector every thirty (30) days and notify Landlord immediately if the smoke detector is not functioning properly.
   c. **Freezing of Pipes:** To help in preventing the freezing of pipes, Tenant agrees that when the temperature outside falls below 32°F, Tenant shall: (1) leave the thermostat regulating the heat serving Premises in an "on" position and set to a minimum of 60°F; and (2) leave the faucets dripping.
   d. **Mold and Mildew:** Tenant acknowledges that mold and/or mildew can grow in any portion of the Premises or Property that are exposed to elevated levels of moisture and that some forms of mold and mildew can be harmful to their health. Tenant therefore agrees to regularly inspect the Premises for mold and/or mildew and immediately report to Landlord any water intrusion problems mold and/or mildew (other than in sinks, showers, toilets and other areas designed to hold water or to be wet areas). Tenant shall not block or cover any heating, ventilation, or air conditioning ducts located in the Premises. Tenant acknowledges having read the "A Brief Guide to Mold, Moisture in Your Home" found at www.epa.gov and shall follow the recommendations contained herein.
   e. **Access Codes:** Landlord shall provide Tenant with all access codes to all entrance gates and security systems, if any, located on the Premises or the Property. Within three (3) business days of vacating the property Tenant will provide Landlord with all access that are currently in use for entrance gates and security systems located on the Premises or the Property.
   f. **Premises Part of Community Association:** If the Premises or a part of the Property are subject to either a Declaration of Condominium, a Declaration of Covenants, Conditions and Restrictions, rules and regulations adopted pursuant to the Declaration and/or other similar documents (hereinafter collectively "C.A. Documents"). Tenant agrees to strictly comply with all use and occupancy restrictions contained therein in using the Premises and the Property. In the event any fine or specific assessment is levied against the Premises or the Owner thereof as a result of Tenant violating the use and occupancy restrictions set forth in the C.A. Documents, Tenant shall immediately pay the same to Landlord as additional rent.

3. **Rules and Regulations.** Tenant shall be responsible for violations of these Rules and Regulations caused by Tenant, any occupant of the Premises and their guests, invitees, licensees and contractors.
   a. Tenant is prohibited from adding, changing or in any way altering locks installed on the doors of the Premises without prior written permission of Landlord which permission shall not be unreasonably withheld; provided that, Tenant provides Landlord with a key or current code thereto, as the case may be, and uses a type and make of lock approved by Landlord.
   b. Motor vehicles shall only be parked on the paved portions of the Premises and the Property intended for use as parking spaces and whose use is not reserved to others.
   c. Motor vehicles with expired or missing license plates, non-operative vehicles and vehicles which drip oil or antifreeze shall not be parked or kept on the Premises or the Property.
   d. No waterbeds shall be used on the Premises or Property without the prior written consent of the Landlord.
   e. Tenant shall not shower in a shower which does not have a fully operational shower curtain or shower enclosure.
   f. No space heaters or window air conditioning units shall be used to heat or cool Premises except with the written consent of Landlord.
   g. Tenant shall comply with all posted rules and regulations governing the use of any recreational facilities, if any, located on the Premises or Property.
   h. Tenant shall only skateboard, skate, rollerblade or bicycle on paved portions of the Premises or Property and while wearing proper safety equipment.

i. Tenant shall be prohibited from improving, altering or modifying the Premises or Property (including painting and landscaping) during the term of this Agreement without the prior written consent of the Landlord. Any improvements, alterations or modifications approved by Landlord shall be deemed to be for the sole benefit of Tenant and Tenant expressly waives all rights to recover the cost or value of the same. Landlord shall have the right but not the obligation to condition the approval of requested modifications on Tenant removing the same prior to the end of the Lease Term and restoring the affected area to a condition equal to or better than it was prior to the modification.

j. No window treatments currently existing on any windows shall be removed or replaced by Tenant without the prior written consent of Landlord. No sheets, blankets, towels, cardboard, newspaper or other make-shift temporary window treatments shall be used on the Premises or Property.

k. Other than normal household goods in quantities reasonably expected in normal household use, no goods or materials of any kind or description which exceed the normal structural weight loads for the Premises or Property, are combustible or would increase fire risk or increase the risk of other injuries or casualties, shall be kept or placed on the Premises or Property.

l. No nails, screws or adhesive hangers except standard picture hooks, shade brackets and curtain rod brackets may be placed in walls, woodwork or any part of the Premises or Property.

m. Tenant shall not engage in any behavior in the Premises or on the Property, including, but not limited to, yelling, screaming, playing loud music, playing the television at an excessive volume that unreasonably disturbs other tenants in the sole, reasonable opinion of Landlord constitutes a nuisance.

n. All appliances, equipment and systems on or serving the Premises shall only be used in accordance with the manufacturer's operating instructions.

o. Tenant shall not flush down a toilet any sanitary napkins, paper towels, diapers or other item not intended to be disposed of in a toilet.

p. The Premises shall only be used for residential purposes. No trade or business uses shall be permitted except with the prior written consent of Landlord and provided that such use is permitted under applicable zoning laws.

q. Any product or material that is a potential environmental hazard shall only be disposed of in accordance with all applicable federal laws and regulations.

r. Tenant shall not use the Premises or any portion of Landlord's property outside of the Premises for any use or purpose that constitutes a nuisance or attractive nuisance, as determined in the reasonable discretion of Landlord, or materially increases the potential liability or risk of claims against Landlord or Landlord's agents, including, but not limited to, placing a trampoline or aboveground swimming pool on the Premises or on Landlord's property outside of the Premises without the prior written permission of Landlord (excluding a baby pool; provided, that the same is emptied of water at all times when an adult is not present at the baby pool).

4. **Personal Property Loss and Personal Injury; Statute of Limitations.** Storage of personal property by Tenant in Premises or in any other portion of Property shall be at Tenant's sole risk. Tenant has been advised to obtain renter's insurance that provides comprehensive insurance for damage to or loss of Tenant's personal property. Tenant agrees to look solely to Tenant's insurance carrier for reimbursement of losses resulting from such events and hereby indemnifies and agrees to hold Landlord harmless from any claims, causes of action or damages relating to the same. Landlord shall have no responsibility or liability for Tenant's personal property. Any and all claims of Tenant and other occupying the Premises pursuant to the Lease for property damage and/or personal injury sounding in breach of contract and/or tort shall be brought within one (1) year of the date of the damage and/or injury or shall be extinguished.

5. **Disclaimer.**
   a. **General:** Tenant and Landlord acknowledge that they have not relied upon any advice, representations or statements of Brokers and waive and shall not assert any claims against Brokers involving the same. Tenant and Landlord agree that no Broker shall have any responsibility to advise Tenant and/or Landlord on any matter including but not limited to the following except to the extent Broker has agreed to do so in a separately executed Property Management Agreement: any matter which could have been revealed through a survey, title search or inspection of Property or Premises; the condition of the Premises or Property, any portion thereof, or any item therein; building products and construction and repair techniques; the necessity of any repairs to Premises or Property; mold; hazardous or toxic materials or substances; termites and other wood destroying organisms; the tax or legal consequences of this transaction; the availability and cost of utilities or community amenities; any condition(s) existing off the Premises and Property which may affect the Premises or Property; and the uses and zoning of the Premises and Property whether permitted or proposed. Tenant and Landlord acknowledges that Broker is not an expert with respect to the above matters and that, if any of these matters or any other matters are of concern, Tenant should seek independent expert advice relative thereto. Tenant and Landlord acknowledge that Broker shall not be responsible to monitor or supervise any portion of any construction or repairs to the Premises or Property and such tasks clearly fall outside the scope of real estate brokerage services.

   b. **Construction Disclaimer:** Tenant acknowledges that the Premises, or portions thereof, may have been constructed at times when different and less stringent building codes were in place. Tenant shall not assume that the Premises or Property are energy efficient or contain products or features designed to protect residents against injuries or damage that might exist if the Premises and Property had been constructed in accordance with all current building codes.

   c. **Neighborhood Conditions:** Tenant acknowledges that in every neighborhood there are conditions which different tenants may find objectionable. It shall be Tenant's duty to become acquainted with any present or future neighborhood conditions which could affect the Premises or Property including without limitation land-fills, quarries, high-voltage power lines, cemeteries, airports, stadiums, odor producing factories, crime, schools serving the Premises and Property, political jurisdictional maps and land use and transportation maps and plan. If Tenant is concerned about the possibility of a registered sex offender residing in a neighborhood, or if Meth is known to have been manufactured in the house, in which Tenant is interested, Tenant should review the Georgia Violent Sex Offender Registry available on the Georgia Bureau of Investigation Website at www.gbi.georgia.gov and the National Clandestine Laboratory Register – Georgia at www.dea.gov.

6. **Miscellaneous.**
   a. **Time of Essence:** Time is of the essence of this Lease.
   b. **No Waiver:** Any failure of Landlord to insist upon the strict and prompt performance of any covenants or conditions of this Lease or any of the Rules and Regulations set forth herein shall not operate as a waiver of any such violation or of Landlord's right to insist on prompt compliance in the future of such covenant or condition, and shall not prevent a subsequent action by Landlord for any such violation. No provision, covenant or condition of this Lease may be waived by Landlord unless such waiver is in writing and signed by Landlord.
   c. **Definitions:** Unless otherwise specifically noted, the term "Landlord" as used in this Lease shall include its representatives, heirs, agents, assigns, and successors in title to Property and the term "Tenant" shall include Tenant's heirs and representatives. The terms "Landlord" and "Tenant" shall include singular and plural, and corporations, partnerships, companies or individuals, as may fit the particular circumstances. The term "Binding Agreement Date" shall mean the date that this Lease has been signed by the Tenant and Landlord and a fully signed and executed copy thereof has been returned to the party making the offer to lease.
   d. **Joint and Several Obligations:** The obligations of Tenant set forth herein shall be the joint and several obligations of all persons occupying the Premises.
   e. **Entire Agreement:** This Lease and any attached addenda and exhibits thereto shall constitute the entire Agreement between the parties and no verbal statement, promise, inducement or amendment not reduced to writing and signed by both parties shall be binding.
   f. **Attorney's Fees, Court Costs and Costs of Collection:** Whenever any monies due hereunder are collected by law or by attorney at law to prosecute such an action, then both parties agree that the prevailing party will be entitled to reasonable attorney's fees, plus all court costs and costs of collection.
   g. **Indemnification:** Tenant agrees to indemnify and hold Landlord, Broker and Manager harmless from and against any and all injuries, damages, losses, suits and claims against Landlord, Broker and/or Manager arising out of or related to: (1) Tenant's failure to fulfill any condition of this Lease; (2) any damage or injury happening in or to the Premises and the Property or to any improvements thereon as a result of the acts or omissions of Tenant or Tenant's family members, invitees or licensees; (3) Tenant's failure to comply with local, state or federal law; (4) any judgment, lien or other encumbrance filed against the Premises or Property as a result of Tenant's actions and any damage or injury happening in or about the Premises or Property to Tenant or Tenant's family members, invitees or licensees (except if such damage or injury is caused by the intentional wrongful acts of Landlord or Broker); (5) failure to maintain or repair equipment or fixtures, where the party responsible for their maintenance uses commercially reasonable efforts to make the necessary repairs and Tenant covenants not to sue Landlord, Broker or Manager with respect to any of the above-referenced matters. In addition to the above Tenant agrees to hold Broker and Manager harmless from and against Owner of the Property not paying or keeping current with any mortgage, property taxes or home owners association fee's on the Property or not fulfilling the Owner's obligations under this lease. For the purpose of this paragraph, the term "Broker" shall include Broker and Broker's affiliated licensees, employees and if Broker is a licensed real estate brokerage firm, then officers, directors and owners of said firm.
   h. **Keys:** Landlord may release keys to or open the Premises to any of the occupants listed herein.
   i. **Waiver of Homestead Rights:** Tenant for himself and his family waives all exemptions or benefits under the homestead laws of Georgia.
   j. **Governing Law:** This Lease may be signed in multiple counterparts and shall be governed by and interpreted pursuant to the laws of the State of Georgia. This Lease is not intended to create an estate for years on the part of Tenant or to transfer to Tenant any ownership interest in the Premises or Property.
   k. **Security Disclaimer:** Tenant acknowledges that: (1) crime can occur in any neighborhood including the neighborhood in which the Premises and Property is located; and (2) while Landlord may from time to time do things to make the Premises and Property reasonably safe, Landlord is not a provider or guarantor of security in or around the Premises and / or the Property. Tenant acknowledges that prior to occupying Property, Tenant carefully inspected all windows and doors (including the locks for the same) and all exterior lighting and found these items: (a) to be in good working order and repair; and (b) reasonably safe for Tenant and Tenant's household and their invitees, licensees and guests knowing the risk of crime. If during the term of the Lease any of the above items become broken or fall into disrepair, Tenant shall give notice to Landlord of the same immediately.
   l. **Disclosure Rights:** Landlord may disclose information about Tenant to law enforcement officers, governmental officials and for business purposes.
   m. **Rental Application:** Only those people indicated on Tenant's rental application are permitted to reside at the Premises, with the exception of any minor children born to, or adopted by, Tenant. If it is later discovered that the information disclosed on rental application by Tenant was incomplete or inaccurate at the time it was given, Tenant shall be in default of this Lease and Landlord may pursue any and all of Landlord's remedies regarding said default.
   n. **Fair Housing Disclosure:** Landlord, Broker and Manager are committed to leasing and managing the Premises without regard to race, color, national origin, religion, handicap, familial status, sex, sexual orientation or gender identity.

7. **Destruction of Property.** If flood, fire, storm, mold, other environmental hazards that pose a risk to the occupants' health, other casualty or Act of God shall destroy (or so substantially damage as to be uninhabitable) the Premises, rent shall abate from the date of such destruction. Landlord or Tenant may, by written notice, within thirty (30) days of such destruction, terminate this Lease, whereupon rent and all other obligations hereunder shall be adjusted between the parties as of the date of such destruction. If Premises is damaged but not rendered wholly untenable by flood, fire, storm, or other casualty or Act of God, rent shall abate in proportion to the percentage of Premises which has been damaged and Landlord shall restore Premises as soon as is reasonably practicable whereupon full rent shall commence. Rent shall not abate nor shall Tenant be entitled to terminate this Lease if the damage or destruction of Premises, whether total or partial, is the result of the negligence of Tenant or Tenant's household or their invitees, licensees, or guests.

8. **Mortgagee's Rights.** Tenant's rights under this Lease shall at all times be automatically junior and subordinate to any deed to secure debt which is now or shall hereafter be placed on the Premises or Property. If requested, Tenant shall execute promptly any certificate that Landlord may request to effectuate the above.

9. **GAR Forms.** The Georgia Association of REALTORS®, Inc. ("GAR") issues certain standard real estate forms. These GAR forms are frequently provided to the parties in real estate transactions. No party is required to use any GAR form. Since these forms are generic and written with the interests of multiple parties in mind, they may need to be modified to meet the specific needs of the parties using them. If any party has any questions about his or her rights and obligations under any GAR form, he or she should consult an attorney. Provisions in the GAR Forms are subject to differing interpretations by our courts other than what the parties may have intended. At times, our courts may strike down or not enforce provisions in our GAR Forms, as written. No representation is made that the GAR Forms will protect the interests of any particular party or will be fit for any specific purpose. The parties hereto agree that the GAR forms may only be used in accordance with the licensing agreement of GAR. While GAR forms may be modified by the parties, no GAR form may be reproduced with sections removed, altered or modified unless the changes are visible on the form itself or in a stipulation, addendum, exhibit or amendment thereto.

10. **Additional Rules & Regulations.** In addition to the rules and regulations generally listed in this Agreement, the following additional rules also apply:
    _____
    _____
    _____

11. **Beware of Cyber Fraud:** Fraudulent e-mails attempting to get you to wire money to criminal computer hackers are increasingly common in real estate transactions. Under this scam, computer hackers fraudulently assume the online identity of the actual mortgage lender, closing attorney and/or real estate broker with whom you are working in the real estate transaction. Posing as a legitimate company, they then direct you to wire money to them. In many cases, the fraudulent e-mail is sent from what appears to be the authentic web page of the legitimate company responsible for sending the wiring instructions. You should use great caution in sending or receiving funds based solely on wiring instructions sent to you by e-mail. Independently verifying the wiring instructions with someone from the company sending them is the best way to prevent fraud. In particular, you should treat as highly suspect any follow up e-mails you receive from a mortgage lender, closing attorney and/or real estate broker directing you to wire funds to a revised account number. Never verify wiring instructions by calling a telephone number provided along with a second set of wiring instructions since you may end up receiving a fraudulent verification from the computer hackers trying to steal your money. Independently look up the telephone number of the company who is supposed to be sending you the wiring instructions to make sure you have the right one.

12. **Exhibits.** All exhibits attached hereto listed and selected below or referenced herein are made a part of this Lease. If any such exhibit conflicts with any preceding paragraph, said exhibit shall control:
    ☐ Legal Description Exhibit (F807 or other) "_____"
    ☐ Owner's Property Disclosure Statement Exhibit (F907) "_____"
    ☐ Move In/Move Out Condition Report (F910) "_____"
    ☐ Move-In Inspection Report (F911) "_____"
    ☐ Lead-Based Paint Exhibit (F918) "_____"
    ☐ Pet Exhibit (F810) "_____"
    ☐ Consent to Take Pictures and Video of Property Exhibit (F919) "_____"
    ☐ Required Renter's Insurance Exhibit (F920) "_____"
    ☐ Pool on Property Exhibit (F921) "_____"
    ☐ Other _____
    ☐ Other _____
    ☐ Other _____

SPECIAL STIPULATIONS: The following Special Stipulations, if conflicting with any exhibit, addendum, or preceding paragraph (including any changes thereto made by the parties), shall control:

☐ Additional Special Stipulations are attached.

By signing this Agreement, Tenant and Landlord acknowledge that they have each read and understood this Agreement and agree to its terms.

_____
1 Tenant's Signature

_____
Print or Type Name   Date

_____
Tenant's Address for Receiving Notice

_____
Tenant's Phone Number: ☐ Cell ☐ Home ☐ Work

_____
Tenant's E-mail Address

_____
2 Tenant's Signature

_____
Print or Type Name   Date

_____
Tenant's Address for Receiving Notice

_____
Tenant's Phone Number: ☐ Cell ☐ Home ☐ Work

_____
Tenant's E-mail Address

☐ Additional Signature Page (F931) is attached.

Leasing Broker/Affiliated Licensee Contact Information

_____
Leasing Broker

_____
Broker/Affiliated Licensee Signature   Date

_____
Print or Type Name   GA Real Estate License #

_____
Licensee's Phone Number   Fax Number

_____
Licensee's E-mail Address

_____
REALTOR® Membership

_____
Broker's Address

_____
Broker's Phone Number   Fax Number

MLS Listing Number: _____

_____
MLS Office Code   Brokerage Firm License Number

_____
1 Landlord's Signature

_____
Print or Type Name   Date

_____
Landlord's Address for Receiving Notice

_____
Landlord's Phone Number: ☐ Cell ☐ Home ☐ Work

_____
Landlord's E-mail Address

_____
2 Landlord's Signature

_____
Print or Type Name   Date

_____
Landlord's Address for Receiving Notice

_____
Landlord's Phone Number: ☐ Cell ☐ Home ☐ Work

_____
Landlord's E-mail Address

☐ Additional Signature Page (F931) is attached.

Listing Broker/Affiliated Licensee Contact Information

_____
Listing Broker: If adjacent box is checked ☐, Listing Broker is also the Manager herein and shall have the authority to act as the agent of the Landlord hereunder.

_____
Broker/Affiliated Licensee Signature   Date

_____
Print or Type Name   GA Real Estate License #

_____
Licensee's Phone Number   Fax Number

_____
Licensee's Email Address

_____
REALTOR® Membership

_____
Broker's Address

_____
Broker's Phone Number   Fax Number

_____
MLS Office Code   Brokerage Firm License Number

Binding Agreement Date: The Binding Agreement Date in this Lease is the date of _____ and has been filled in by _____.

PURCHASE AND SALE AGREEMENT
Offer Date: _____

Georgia REALTORS®

2021 Printing

A. KEY TERMS AND CONDITIONS

1. **Purchase and Sale.** The undersigned buyer(s) ("Buyer") agree to buy and the undersigned seller(s) ("Seller") agree to sell the real property described below including all fixtures, improvements and landscaping therein ("Property") on the terms and conditions set forth in this Agreement.
   a. **Property Identification:** Address: _____
   City _____, County _____, Georgia, Zip Code _____
   MLS Number: _____ Tax Parcel I.D. Number: _____
   b. **Legal Description:** The legal description of the Property is *[select one of the following below]*:
      ☐ (1) attached as an exhibit hereto;
      ☐ (2) Condominium (attach F204 Condominium Resale Purchase and Sale Exhibit)
      ☐ (3) the same as described in Deed Book _____, Page _____, et. seq., of the land records of the above county; **OR**
      ☐ (4) Land Lot(s) _____ of the _____ District, _____ Section/ GMD, Lot _____, Block _____, Unit _____, Phase/Section _____ of _____ Subdivision/Development, according to the plat recorded in Plat Book _____, Page _____, et. seq., of the land records of the above county.

2. **Purchase Price of Property to be Paid by Buyer.**
   $ _____

3. **Closing Costs.**
   Seller's Contribution at Closing: $ _____

4. **Closing Date and Possession.**
   Closing Date shall be _____ with possession of the Property transferred to Buyer
   ☐ at Closing **OR** ☐ _____ days after Closing at _____ o'clock ☐ AM ☐ PM (attach F219 Temporary Occupancy Agreement).

5. **Holder of Earnest Money ("Holder").** (If Holder is Closing Attorney, F510 must be attached as an exhibit hereto, and F511 must be signed by Closing Attorney.)

6. **Closing Attorney/Law Firm.**

7. **Earnest Money.** Earnest Money shall be paid by ☐check ☐ACH ☐cash or ☐wire transfer of immediately available funds as follows:
   ☐ a. $ _____ as of the Offer Date.
   ☐ b. $ _____ within _____ days from the Binding Agreement Date.
   ☐ c. _____.

8. **Inspection and Due Diligence.**
   a. **Due Diligence Period:** Property is being sold subject to a Due Diligence Period of _____ days from the Binding Agreement Date.
   b. **Option Payment for Due Diligence Period:** In consideration of Seller granting Buyer the option to terminate this Agreement, Buyer:
      (1) has paid Seller $10.00 in nonrefundable option money, the receipt and sufficiency of which is hereby acknowledged; plus
      (2) shall pay Seller additional option money of $_____ by ☐ check or ☐ wire transfer of immediately available funds either ☐ as of the Offer Date; **OR** ☐ within _____ days from the Binding Agreement Date. Any additional option money paid by Buyer to Seller ☐ shall (subject to lender approval) or ☐ shall not be applied toward the purchase price at closing and shall not be refundable to Buyer unless the closing fails to occur due to the default of the Seller.

9. **Lead-Based Paint.** To the best of Seller's knowledge, the residential dwelling(s) on the Property (including any portion thereof or painted fixture therein) ☐ was (attach F316 Lead-Based Paint Exhibit) **OR** ☐ was not built prior to 1978.

10. **Brokerage Relationships in this Transaction.**
    a. **Buyer's Broker is** _____ and is:
       (1) ☐ representing Buyer as a client.
       (2) ☐ working with Buyer as a customer.
       (3) ☐ acting as a dual agent representing Buyer and Seller.
       (4) ☐ acting as a designated agent where: _____ has been assigned to exclusively represent Buyer.
    b. **Seller's Broker is** _____ and is:
       (1) ☐ representing Seller as a client.
       (2) ☐ working with Seller as a customer.
       (3) ☐ acting as a dual agent representing Buyer and Seller.
       (4) ☐ acting as a designated agent where: _____ has been assigned to exclusively represent Seller.
    c. **Material Relationship Disclosure:** The material relationships required to be disclosed by either Broker are as follows: _____

11. **Time Limit of Offer.** The Offer set forth herein expires at _____ o'clock _____.m. on the date _____.

Buyer(s) Initials _____ Seller(s) Initials _____

THIS FORM IS COPYRIGHTED AND MAY ONLY BE USED IN REAL ESTATE TRANSACTIONS IN WHICH _____ IS INVOLVED AS A REAL ESTATE LICENSEE. UNAUTHORIZED USE OF THE FORM MAY RESULT IN LEGAL SANCTIONS BEING BROUGHT AGAINST THE USER AND SHOULD BE REPORTED TO THE GEORGIA ASSOCIATION OF REALTORS® AT (770) 451-1831.

Copyright© 2021 by Georgia Association of REALTORS®, Inc.

B. CORRESPONDING PARAGRAPHS FOR SECTION A

1. **Purchase and Sale.**
   a. **Warranty:** Seller warrants that at the time of closing Seller will convey good and marketable title to said Property by limited warranty deed subject only to: (1) zoning; (2) general utility, sewer, and drainage easements of record as of the Binding Agreement Date and upon which the improvements (other than any driveway or walkway) do not encroach; (3) declarations of condominium and declarations of covenants, conditions and restrictions of record on the Binding Agreement Date; and (4) leases and other encumbrances specified in this Agreement. Buyer agrees to assume Seller's responsibilities in any leases specified in this Agreement.
   b. **Examination:** Buyer may examine title and obtain a survey of the Property and furnish Seller with a written statement of title objections at or prior to the closing. If Seller fails or is unable to satisfy valid title objections at or prior to the closing or any unilateral extension thereof, which would prevent the Seller from conveying good and marketable title to the Property, then Buyer, among its other remedies, may terminate the Agreement without penalty upon written notice to Seller. Good and marketable title as used herein shall mean title which a title insurance company licensed to do business in Georgia will insure at its regular rates, subject only to standard exceptions.
   c. **Title Insurance:** Buyer hereby directs any mortgage lender involved in this transaction to quote the cost of title insurance based upon the presumption that Buyer will be obtaining an enhanced title insurance policy since such a policy affords Buyer greater coverage.

2. **Purchase Price to be Paid by Buyer.** The Purchase Price shall be paid in U.S. Dollars at closing by wire transfer of immediately available funds, or such other form of payment acceptable to the closing attorney.

3. **Closing Costs.**
   a. **Seller's Contribution at Closing:** At closing, Seller shall make the referenced Seller's Monetary Contribution which Buyer may use to pay any cost or expense of Buyer related to this transaction. Buyer acknowledges that Buyer's mortgage lender(s) may not allow the Seller's Monetary Contribution, or the full amount thereof, to be used for some costs or expenses. In such event, any unused portion of the Seller's Monetary Contribution shall remain the property of the Seller. The Seller shall pay the fees and costs of the closing attorney: (1) to prepare and record title curative documents and (2) for Seller not attending the closing in person.
   b. **Items Paid by Buyer:** At closing, Buyer shall pay: (1) Georgia property transfer tax; (2) the cost to search title and tax records and prepare the limited warranty deed; and (3) all other costs, fees and charges to close this transaction, except as otherwise provided herein.
   c. **Prorations:** Ad valorem property taxes, community association fees, solid waste and governmental fees and utility bills for which service cannot be terminated as of the date of closing shall be prorated as of the date of closing. In the event ad valorem property taxes are based upon an estimated tax bill or tax bill under appeal, Buyer and Seller shall, upon the issuance of the actual tax bill or the appeal being resolved, promptly make such financial adjustments between themselves as are necessary to correctly prorate the tax bill. In the event there are tax savings resulting from a tax appeal, third party professional costs to handle the appeal may be deducted from the savings for that tax year before re-prorating. Any pending tax appeal for the year in which the Property is sold shall be deemed assigned to Buyer at closing. The liability to the county in which the Property is located for ad valorem real property taxes for the year in which the Property is sold shall be assumed by Buyer upon the Closing of the Property. Buyer agrees to indemnify Seller against any and all claims of the county for unpaid ad valorem real property taxes for the year in which the Property is sold.

4. **Closing Date and Possession.**
   a. **Right to Extend the Closing Date:** Buyer or Seller may unilaterally extend the closing date for eight (8) days upon notice to the other party given prior to or on the date of closing if: (1) Seller cannot satisfy valid title objections (excluding title objections that: (a) can be satisfied through the payment of money or by bonding off the same; and (b) do not prevent Seller from conveying good and marketable title, as that term is defined herein, to the Property); (2) Buyer's mortgage lender (even in "all cash" transactions where Buyer is obtaining a mortgage loan) or the closing attorney is delayed and cannot fulfill their respective obligations by the date of closing, provided that the delay is not caused by Buyer; or (3) Buyer has not received required estimates or disclosures and Buyer is prohibited from closing under federal regulations. The party unilaterally extending the closing date shall state the basis for the delay in the notice of extension. If the right to unilaterally extend the closing date is exercised once by either the Buyer or Seller, the right shall thereafter terminate.
   b. **Keys and Openers:** At Closing, Seller shall provide Buyer with all keys, door openers, codes and other similar equipment pertaining to the Property.

5. **Holder of Earnest Money.** The earnest money shall be deposited into Holder's escrow/trust account (with Holder being permitted to retain the interest if the account is interest bearing) not later than: (a) five (5) banking days after the Binding Agreement Date hereunder or (b) five (5) banking days after the date it is actually received if it is received after the Binding Agreement Date. If Buyer writes a check or pays with an ACH for earnest money and the same is deposited into Holder's escrow/trust account, Holder shall not return the earnest money until the check or ACH has cleared the account on which the check was written or from which the ACH was sent. In the event any earnest money check is dishonored by the bank upon which it is drawn, or earnest money is not timely paid, Holder shall promptly give notice of the same to Buyer and Seller. Buyer shall have three (3) banking days from the date of receiving the notice to cure the default and if Buyer does not do so, Seller may within seven (7) days thereafter terminate this Agreement upon notice to Buyer. If Seller fails to terminate the Agreement timely, Seller's right to terminate based on the default shall be waived.

6. **Closing Attorney/Law Firm.** Buyer shall have the right to select the closing attorney to close this transaction, and hereby selects the closing attorney referenced herein. In all cases where an individual closing attorney is named in this Agreement but the closing attorney is employed by or an owner, shareholder, or member in a law firm, the law firm shall be deemed to be the closing attorney. If Buyer's mortgage lender refuses to allow that closing attorney to close this transaction, Buyer shall select a different closing attorney acceptable to the mortgage lender. The closing attorney shall represent the mortgage lender in any transaction in which the Buyer obtains mortgage financing (including transactions where the method of payment referenced herein is "all cash"). In transactions where the Buyer does not obtain mortgage financing, the closing attorney shall represent the Buyer.

7. **Earnest Money.**
    a. **Entitlement to Earnest Money:** Subject to the paragraph below, Buyer shall be entitled to the earnest money upon the: (1) failure of the parties to enter into a binding agreement; (2) failure of any unexpired contingency or condition to which this Agreement is subject; (3) termination of this Agreement due to the default of Seller; or (4) termination of this Agreement in accordance with a specific right to terminate set forth in the Agreement. Otherwise, the earnest money shall be applied towards the purchase price of the Property at closing or if other funds are used to pay the purchase price then the earnest money shall be returned to Buyer.
    b. **Disbursement of Earnest Money:** Holder shall disburse the earnest money upon: (1) the closing of Property; (2) a subsequent written agreement of Buyer and Seller; (3) an order of a court or arbitrator having jurisdiction over any dispute involving the earnest money; or (4) the failure of the parties to enter into a binding agreement (where there is no dispute over the formation or enforceability of the Agreement). In addition, Holder may disburse the earnest money upon a reasonable interpretation of the Agreement, provided that Holder first gives all parties at least ten (10) days notice stating to whom and why the disbursement will be made. Any party may object to the proposed disbursement by giving written notice of the same to Holder within the ten (10) day notice period. Objections not timely made in writing shall be deemed waived. If Holder receives an objection and, after considering it, decides to disburse the earnest money as originally proposed, Holder may do so and send notice to the parties of Holder's action. If Holder decides to modify its proposed disbursement, Holder shall first send a new ten (10) day notice to the parties stating the rationale for the modification and to whom the disbursement will now be made. Holder shall disburse the earnest money to Seller by check in the event Holder: (1) makes a reasonable interpretation of the Agreement that the Agreement has been terminated due to Buyer's default; and (2) sends the required ten (10) day notice of the proposed disbursement to Buyer and Seller. The above-referenced check shall constitute liquidated damages in full settlement of all claims of Seller against Buyer and the Brokers in this transaction. Holder may require Seller to sign a W-9 before issuing a check to Seller for liquidated damages of $600 or more. Such liquidated damages are a reasonable pre-estimate of Seller's actual damages, which damages the parties agree are difficult to ascertain and are not a penalty.
    c. **Interpleader:** If an earnest money dispute cannot be resolved after a reasonable time, Holder may interplead the earnest money into a court of competent jurisdiction if Holder is unsure who is entitled to the earnest money. Holder shall be reimbursed for and may deduct its costs, expenses and reasonable attorney's fees from any funds interpleaded. The prevailing defendant in the interpleader lawsuit shall be entitled to collect its attorney's fees, court costs and the amount deducted by Holder to cover Holder's costs and expenses from the non-prevailing defendant.
    d. **Hold Harmless:** All parties hereby covenant and agree to: (1) indemnify and hold Holder harmless from and against all claims, injuries, suits and damages arising out of the performance by Holder of its duties; (2) not to sue Holder for any decision of Holder to disburse earnest money in accordance with this Agreement.

8. **Inspection and Due Diligence.**
    a. **Right to Inspect Property:** Upon prior notice to Seller, Buyer and/or Buyer's representatives shall have the right to enter the Property at Buyer's expense and at reasonable times (including immediately prior to closing) to inspect, examine, test, appraise and survey Property. This right to enter shall include the time period after the end of any Due Diligence Period to, among other things, and without limitation, meet contractors and vendors, measure for renovations and confirm that any agreed upon repairs have been made and the Property otherwise remains in the same condition. Seller shall cause all utilities, systems and equipment to be on so that Buyer may complete all inspections. Buyer agrees to hold Seller and all Brokers harmless from all claims, injuries and damages relating to the exercise of these rights and shall promptly restore any portion of the Property damaged or disturbed from testing or other evaluations to a condition equal to or better than the condition it was in prior to such testing or evaluation. If Buyer is concerned that the Property may have been used as a laboratory for the production of methamphetamine, or as a dumpsite for the same, Buyer should review the National Clandestine Laboratory Register – Georgia at www.dea.gov.
    b. **Duty to Inspect Neighborhood:** In every neighborhood there are conditions which different buyers may find objectionable. Buyer shall have the sole duty to become familiar with neighborhood conditions that could affect the Property such as landfills, quarries, power lines, airports, cemeteries, prisons, stadiums, odor and noise producing activities, crime and school, land use, government and transportation maps and plans. It shall be Buyer's sole duty to become familiar with neighborhood conditions of concern to Buyer. **If Buyer is concerned about the possibility of a registered sex offender residing in a neighborhood in which Buyer is interested, Buyer should review the Georgia Violent Sex Offender Registry available on the Georgia Bureau of Investigation Website at** www.gbi.georgia.gov.
    c. **Warranties Transfer:** Seller agrees to transfer to Buyer, at closing, subject to Buyer's acceptance thereof (and at Buyer's expense, if there is any cost associated with said transfer), Seller's interest in any existing manufacturer's warranties, service contracts, termite treatment and/or repair guarantee and/or other similar warranties which, by their terms, may be transferable to Buyer.
    d. **Property Sold "As-Is" Unless this Agreement is Subject to Due Diligence Period:**
        (1) **General:** Unless the Property is being sold subject to a Due Diligence Period referenced herein, the Property shall be sold "as-is" with all faults. Even if the Property is sold "as-is" Seller is required under Georgia law to disclose to the Buyer latent or hidden defects in the Property which Seller is aware and which could not have been discovered by the Buyer upon a reasonable inspection of the property. The inclusion of a Due Diligence Period herein shall: (a) during its term make this Agreement an option contract in which Buyer may decide to proceed or not proceed with the purchase of the Property for any or no reason; and (b) be an acknowledgement by Seller that Buyer has paid separate valuable consideration of $10 for the granting of the option.
        (2) **Purpose of Due Diligence Period:** During the Due Diligence Period, Buyer shall determine whether or not to exercise Buyer's option to proceed or not proceed with the purchase of the Property. If Buyer has concerns with the Property, Buyer may during the Due Diligence Period seek to negotiate an amendment to this Agreement to address such concerns.
        (3) **Notice of Decision Not To Proceed:** Buyer shall have elected to exercise Buyer's option to purchase the Property unless prior to the end of any Due Diligence Period, Buyer notifies Seller of Buyer's decision not to proceed by delivering to Seller a notice of termination of this Agreement. In the event Buyer does not terminate this Agreement prior to the end of the Due Diligence Period, then: (a) Buyer shall have accepted the Property "as-is" subject to the terms of this Agreement; and (b) Buyer shall no longer have any right to terminate this Agreement based upon the Due Diligence Period.
    e. **Repairs:** All agreed upon repairs and replacements shall be performed in a good and workmanlike manner prior to closing.

9. **Lead-Based Paint.** If any portion of a residential dwelling on the Property was built prior to 1978, the Lead-Based Paint Exhibit (F316) is hereby attached as an exhibit to this Agreement. The term "residential dwelling" includes any painted fixture or material used therein that was built or manufactured prior to 1978.

10. **Brokerage Relationships in this Transaction.**
    a. **Agency Disclosure:** No Broker in this transaction shall owe any duty to Buyer or Seller greater than what is set forth in their brokerage engagements and the Brokerage Relationships in Real Estate Transactions Act, O.C.G.A. § 10-6A-1 et. seq.;
        (1) **No Agency Relationship:** Buyer and Seller acknowledge that, if they are not represented by Brokers in a client relationship, they are each solely responsible for protecting their own interests, and that Broker's role is limited to performing ministerial acts for that party.
        (2) **Consent to Dual Agency:** If Broker is acting as dual agent in this transaction, Buyer and Seller consent to the same and acknowledge having been advised of the following:
            i. **Dual Agency Disclosure:** *[Applicable only if Broker is acting as a dual agent in this transaction.]*
                (a) As a dual agent, Broker is representing two clients whose interests are or at times could be different or even adverse;
                (b) Broker will disclose all adverse material facts relevant to the transaction and actually known to the dual agent to all parties in the transaction except for information made confidential by request or instructions from each client which is not otherwise required to be disclosed by law;
                (c) Buyer and Seller do not have to consent to dual agency and the consent of Buyer and Seller to dual agency has been given voluntarily and the parties have read and understand their brokerage engagement agreements.
                (d) Notwithstanding any provision to the contrary contained herein Buyer and Seller each hereby direct Broker while acting as a dual agent to keep confidential and not reveal to the other party any information which could materially and adversely affect their negotiating position.
            ii. **Designated Agency Disclosure:** If Broker in this transaction is acting as a designated agent, Buyer and Seller consent to the same and acknowledge that each designated agent shall exclusively represent the party to whom each has been assigned as a client and shall not represent in this transaction the client assigned to the other designated agent.
    b. **Brokerage:** Seller has agreed to pay Seller's Broker(s) a commission pursuant to a separate brokerage engagement agreement entered into between the parties and incorporated herein by reference ("Seller Brokerage Engagement Agreement"). The Seller's Broker has agreed to share that commission with the Buyer's Broker. The closing attorney is hereby authorized and directed to pay the Broker(s) at closing, their respective portions of the commissions out of the proceeds of the sale. If the sale proceeds are insufficient to pay the full commission, the party owing the commission shall pay any shortfall at closing. The acceptance by the Broker(s) of a partial real estate commission at the closing shall not relieve the party owing the same from paying the remainder after the closing (unless the Broker(s) have expressly agreed in writing to accept the amount paid in full satisfaction of the Broker(s) claim to a commission). The Brokers herein are signing this Agreement to reflect their role in this transaction and consent to act as Holder if either of them is named as such. This Agreement and any amendment thereto shall be enforceable even without the signature of any Broker referenced herein. The broker(s) are express third-party beneficiaries to this Agreement.
    c. **Disclaimer:** Buyer and Seller have not relied upon any advice or representations of Brokers other than what is included in this Agreement. Brokers shall have no duty to inspect the Property or to advise Buyer or Seller on any matter relating to the Property which could have been revealed through a survey, appraisal, title search, Official Georgia Wood Infestation Report, utility bill review, septic system inspection, well water test, tests for radon, asbestos, mold, methamphetamine, and lead-based paint; moisture test of stucco or synthetic stucco, inspection of the Property by a professional, construction expert, structural engineer or environmental engineer; review of this Agreement and transaction by an attorney, financial planner, mortgage consultant or tax consultant; and consulting appropriate governmental officials to determine, among other things and without limitation, the zoning of Property, the propensity of the Property to flood, flood zone certifications, whether any condemnation action is pending or has been filed or other nearby governmental improvements are planned. Buyer and Seller acknowledge that Broker does not perform or have expertise in any of the above tests, inspections, and reviews or in any of the matters handled by the professionals referenced above. Buyer and Seller should seek independent expert advice regarding any matter of concern to them relative to the Property and this Agreement. Buyer and Seller acknowledge that Broker shall not be responsible to monitor, supervise, or inspect any construction or repairs to Property and such tasks clearly fall outside the scope of real estate brokerage services. If Broker has written any special stipulations herein, the party for whom such special stipulations were written: a) confirms that each such stipulation reflects the party's complete understanding as to the substance and form of the special stipulations; b) hereby adopts each special stipulation as the original work of the party; and c) hereby agrees to indemnify and hold Broker who prepared the stipulation harmless from any and all claims, causes of action, suits, and damages arising out of or relating to such special stipulation. Buyer acknowledges that when and if Broker answers a question of Buyer or otherwise describes some aspect of the Property or the transaction, Broker is doing so based upon information provided by Seller rather than the independent knowledge of Broker (unless Broker makes an independent written disclosure to the contrary).

11. **Time Limit of Offer.** The Time Limit of the Offer shall be the date and time referenced herein when the Offer expires unless prior to that date and time both of the following have occurred: (a) the Offer has been accepted by the party to whom the Offer was made; and (b) notice of acceptance of the Offer has been delivered to the party who made the Offer.

C. **OTHER TERMS AND CONDITIONS**

1. **Notices.**
    a. **Generally:** All notices given hereunder shall be in writing, legible and signed by the party giving the notice. In the event of a dispute regarding notice, the burden shall be on the party giving notice to prove delivery. The requirements of this notice paragraph shall apply even prior to this Agreement becoming binding. Notices shall only be delivered: (1) in person; (2) by courier, overnight delivery service or by certified or registered U.S. mail (hereinafter collectively "Delivery Service"); or (3) by e-mail or facsimile. The person delivering or sending the written notice signed by a party may be someone other than that party.

b. **Delivery of Notice:** A notice to a party shall be deemed to have been delivered and received upon the earliest of the following to occur: (1) the actual receipt of the written notice by a party; (2) in the case of delivery by a Delivery Service, when the written notice is delivered to an address of a party set forth herein (or subsequently provided by the party following the notice provisions herein), provided that a record of the delivery is created; (3) in the case of delivery electronically, on the date and time the written notice is electronically sent to an e-mail address or facsimile number of a party herein (or subsequently provided by the party following the notice provisions herein). Notice to a party shall not be effective unless the written notice is sent to an address, facsimile number or e-mail address of the party set forth herein (or subsequently provided by the party following the notice provisions herein).

c. **When Broker Authorized to Accept Notice for Client:** Except where the Broker is acting in a dual agency capacity, the Broker and any affiliated licensee of the Broker representing a party in a client relationship shall be authorized agents of the party and notice to any of them shall for all purposes herein be deemed to be notice to the party. Notice to an authorized agent shall not be effective unless the written notice is sent to an address, facsimile number or e-mail address of the authorized agent set forth herein (or subsequently provided by the authorized agent following the notice provisions herein). Except as provided for herein, the Broker's staff at a physical address set forth herein of the Broker or the Broker's affiliated licensees are authorized to receive notices delivered by a Delivery Service. The Broker, the Broker's staff and the affiliated licensees of the Broker shall not be authorized to receive notice on behalf of a party in any transaction in which a brokerage engagement has not been entered into with the party or in which the Broker is acting in a dual agency capacity. In the event the Broker is practicing designated agency, only the designated agent of a client shall be an authorized agent of the client for the purposes of receiving notice.

2. **Default.**
   a. **Remedies of Seller:** In the event this Agreement fails to close due to the default of Buyer, Seller's sole remedy shall be to retain the earnest money as full liquidated damages. Seller expressly waives any right to assert a claim for specific performance. The parties expressly agree that the earnest money is a reasonable pre-estimate of Seller's actual damages, which damages the parties agree are difficult to ascertain. The parties expressly intend for the earnest money to serve as liquidated damages and not as a penalty.
   b. **Remedies of Buyer:** In the event this Agreement fails to close due to the default of Seller, Buyer may either seek the specific performance of this Agreement or terminate this Agreement upon notice to Seller and Holder, in which case all earnest money deposits and other payments Buyer has paid towards the purchase of the Property shall be returned to Buyer following the procedures set forth elsewhere herein.
   c. **Rights of Broker:** In the event this Agreement is terminated or fails to close due to the default of a party hereto, the defaulting party shall pay as liquidated damages to every broker involved in this Agreement the commission the broker would have received had the transaction closed. For purposes of determining the amount of liquidated damages to be paid by the defaulting party, all written agreements establishing the amount of commission to be paid to any broker involved in this transaction are incorporated herein by reference. The liquidated damages referenced above are a reasonable pre-estimate of the Broker(s) actual damages and are not a penalty.
   d. **Attorney's Fees:** In any litigation or arbitration arising out of this Agreement, including but not limited to breach of contract claims between Buyer and Seller and commission claims brought by a broker, the non-prevailing party shall be liable to the prevailing party for its reasonable attorney's fees and expenses.

3. **Risk of Damage to Property.** Seller warrants that at the time of closing the Property and all items remaining with the Property, if any, will be in substantially the same condition (including conditions disclosed in the Seller's Property Disclosure Statement or Seller's Disclosure of Latent Defects and Fixtures Checklist) as of the Offer Date, except for changes made to the condition of Property pursuant to the written agreement of Buyer and Seller. At time of possession, Seller shall deliver Property clean and free of trash, debris, and personal property of Seller not identified as remaining with the Property. Notwithstanding the above, if the Property is destroyed or substantially destroyed prior to closing, Seller shall promptly give notice to Buyer of the same and provide Buyer with whatever information Seller has regarding the availability of insurance and the disposition of any insurance claim. Buyer or Seller may terminate this Agreement without penalty not later than fourteen (14) days from receipt of the above notice. If Buyer or Seller do not terminate this Agreement, Seller shall cause Property to be restored to substantially the same condition as on the Offer Date. The date of closing shall be extended until the earlier of one year from the original date of closing, or seven (7) days from the date that Property has been restored to substantially the same condition as on the Offer Date and a new certificate of occupancy (if required) is issued.

4. **Other Provisions.**
   a. **Condemnation:** Seller shall: (1) immediately notify Buyer if the Property becomes subject to a condemnation proceeding; and (2) provide Buyer with the details of the same. Upon receipt of such notice, Buyer shall have the right, but not the obligation for 7 days thereafter, to terminate this Agreement upon notice to Seller in which event Buyer shall be entitled to a refund of all earnest money and other monies paid by Buyer toward the Property without deduction or penalty. If Buyer does not terminate the Agreement within this time frame, Buyer agrees to accept the Property less any portion taken by the condemnation and if Buyer closes, Buyer shall be entitled to receive any condemnation award or negotiated payment for all or a portion of the Property transferred or conveyed in lieu of condemnation.
   b. **Consent to Share Non-Public Information:** Buyer and Seller hereby consent to the closing attorney preparing and distributing an American Land Title Association ("ALTA") Estimated Settlement Statement-Combined or other combined settlement statement to Buyer, Seller, Brokers and Brokers' affiliated licensees working on the transaction reflected in this Agreement for their various uses.
   c. **Duty to Cooperate:** All parties agree to do all things reasonably necessary to timely and in good faith fulfill the terms of this Agreement. Buyer and Seller shall execute and deliver such certifications, affidavits, and statements required by law or reasonably requested by the closing attorney, mortgage lender and/or the title insurance company to meet their respective requirements.
   d. **Electronic Signatures:** For all purposes herein, an electronic or facsimile signature shall be deemed the same as an original signature; provided, however, that all parties agree to promptly re-execute a conformed copy of this Agreement with original signatures if requested to do so by, the buyer's mortgage lender or the other party.

e. **Entire Agreement, Modification and Assignment:** This Agreement constitutes the sole and entire agreement between all of the parties, supersedes all of their prior written and verbal agreements and shall be binding upon the parties and their successors, heirs and permitted assigns. No representation, promise or inducement not included in this Agreement shall be binding upon any party hereto. This Agreement may not be amended or waived except upon the written agreement of Buyer and Seller. Any agreement to terminate this Agreement or any other subsequent agreement of the parties relating to the Property must be in writing and signed by the parties. This Agreement may not be assigned by Buyer except with the written approval of Seller which may be withheld for any reason or no reason. Any assignee shall fulfill all the terms and conditions of this Agreement.
f. **Extension of Deadlines:** No time deadline under this Agreement shall be extended by virtue of it falling on a Saturday, Sunday or federal holiday except for the date of closing.
g. **GAR Forms:** The Georgia Association of REALTORS®, Inc. ("GAR") issues certain standard real estate forms. These GAR forms are frequently provided to the parties in real estate transactions. No party is required to use any GAR form. Since these forms are generic and written with the interests of multiple parties in mind, they may need to be modified to meet the specific needs of the parties using them. If any party has any questions about his or her rights and obligations under any GAR form, he or she should consult an attorney. Provisions in the GAR Forms are subject to differing interpretations by our courts other than what the parties may have intended. At times, our courts may strike down or not enforce provisions in our GAR Forms, as written. No representation is made that the GAR Forms will protect the interests of any particular party or will be fit for any specific purpose. The parties hereto agree that the GAR forms may only be used in accordance with the licensing agreement of GAR. While GAR forms may be modified by the parties, no GAR form may be reproduced with sections removed, altered or modified unless the changes are visible on the form itself or in a stipulation, addendum, exhibit or amendment thereto.
h. **Governing Law and Interpretation:** This Agreement may be signed in multiple counterparts each of which shall be deemed to be an original and shall be interpreted in accordance with the laws of Georgia. No provision herein, by virtue of the party who drafted it, shall be interpreted less favorably against one party than another. All references to time shall mean the time in Georgia. If any provision herein is to be unenforceable, it shall be severed from this Agreement while the remainder of the Agreement shall, to the fullest extent permitted by law, continue to have full force and effect as a binding contract.
i. **No Authority to Bind:** No Broker or affiliated licensee of Broker, by virtue of this status, shall have any authority to bind any party hereto to any contract, provisions herein, amendments hereto, or termination hereof. However, if authorized in this Agreement, Broker shall have the right to accept notice on behalf of a party. Additionally, any Broker or real estate licensee involved in this transaction may perform the ministerial act of filling in the Binding Agreement Date. In the event of a dispute over the Binding Agreement Date, it may only be resolved by the written agreement of the Buyer and Seller.
j. **Notice of Binding Agreement Date:** The Binding Agreement Date shall be the date when a party to this transaction who has accepted an offer or counteroffer to buy or sell real property delivers notice of that acceptance to the party who made the offer or counteroffer in accordance with the Notices section of the Agreement. Notice of the Binding Agreement Date may be delivered by either party (or the Broker working with or representing such party) to the other party. If notice of accurate Binding Agreement Date is delivered, the party receiving notice shall sign the same and immediately return it to the other party.
k. **Statute of Limitations:** All claims of any nature whatsoever against Broker(s) and/or their affiliated licensees, whether asserted in litigation or arbitration and sounding in breach of contract and/or tort, must be brought within two (2) years from the date any claim or cause of action arises. Such actions shall thereafter be time-barred.
l. **Survival of Agreement:** The following shall survive the closing of this Agreement: (1) the obligation of a party to pay a real estate commission; (2) any warranty of title; (3) all written representations of Seller in this Agreement regarding the Property or neighborhood in which the Property is located; (4) the section on condemnation; (5) the obligations of the parties regarding ad valorem real property taxes; and (6) any obligations which the parties herein agree shall survive the closing or may be performed or fulfilled after the Closing.
m. **Terminology:** As the context may require in this Agreement: (1) the singular shall mean the plural and vice versa; and (2) all pronouns shall mean and include the person, entity, firm, or corporation to which they relate. The letters "N.A." or "N/A", if used in this Agreement, shall mean "Not Applicable", except where the context would indicate otherwise.
n. **Time of Essence:** Time is of the essence of this Agreement.

5. **Definitions.**
   a. **Banking Day:** A "Banking Day" shall mean a day on which a bank is open to the public for carrying out substantially all of its banking functions. For purposes herein, a "Banking Day" shall mean Monday through Friday excluding federal holidays.
   b. **Binding Agreement Date:** The "Binding Agreement Date" shall be the date when a party to this transaction who has accepted an offer or counteroffer to buy or sell real property delivers notice of that acceptance to the party who made the offer or counteroffer in accordance with the Notices section of the Agreement. Once that occurs, this Agreement shall be deemed a Binding Agreement.
   c. **Broker:** In this Agreement, the term "Broker" shall mean a licensed Georgia real estate broker or brokerage firm and its affiliated licensees unless the context would indicate otherwise.
   d. **Business Day:** A "Business Day" shall mean a day on which substantially all businesses are open for business. For all purposes herein, a "Business Day" shall mean Monday through Friday excluding federal holidays.
   e. **Material Relationship:** A material relationship shall mean any actually known personal, familial, social, or business relationship between the broker or the broker's affiliated licensees and any other party to this transaction which could impair the ability of the broker or affiliated licensees to exercise fair and independent judgment relative to their client.

6. **WARNING TO BUYERS AND SELLERS: BEWARE OF CYBER-FRAUD.** Fraudulent e-mails attempting to get the buyer and/or seller to wire money to criminal computer hackers are increasingly common in real estate transactions. Specifically, criminals are impersonating the online identity of the actual mortgage lender, closing attorney, real estate broker or other person or companies involved in the real estate transaction. In that role, the criminals send fake wiring instructions attempting to trick buyers and/or sellers into wiring them money related to the real estate transaction, including, for example, the buyer's earnest money, the cash needed for the buyer to close, and/or the seller's proceeds from the closing. These instructions, if followed, will result in the money being wired to the criminals. In many cases, the fraudulent email is believable because it is sent from what appears to be the email address/domain of the legitimate company or person responsible for sending the buyer or seller wiring instructions. The buyer and/or seller should verify wiring instructions sent by email by independently looking up and calling the telephone number of the company or person purporting to have sent them. Buyers and sellers should never call the telephone number provided with wiring instructions sent by email since they may end up receiving a fake verification from the criminals. Buyer and sellers should be on special alert for: 1) emails directing the buyer and/or seller to wire money to a bank or bank account in a state other than Georgia; and 2) emails from a person or company involved in the real estate transaction that are slightly different (often by one letter, number, or character) from the actual email address of the person or company.

7. **LIMIT ON BROKER'S LIABILITY. BUYER AND SELLER ACKNOWLEDGE THAT BROKER(S):**
   a. SHALL, UNDER NO CIRCUMSTANCES, HAVE ANY LIABILITY GREATER THAN THE AMOUNT OF THE REAL ESTATE COMMISSION PAID HEREUNDER TO BROKER (EXCLUDING ANY COMMISSION AMOUNT PAID TO A COOPERATING REAL ESTATE BROKER, IF ANY) OR, IF NO REAL ESTATE COMMISSION IS PAID TO BROKER, THAN A SUM NOT TO EXCEED $100; AND
   b. NOTWITHSTANDING THE ABOVE, SHALL HAVE NO LIABILITY IN EXCESS OF $100 FOR ANY LOSS OF FUNDS AS THE RESULT OF WIRE OR CYBER FRAUD.

8. **Exhibits and Addenda.** All exhibits and/or addenda attached hereto, listed below, or referenced herein are made a part of this Agreement. If any such exhibit or addendum conflicts with any preceding paragraph (including any changes thereto made by the parties), said exhibit or addendum shall control:
   - ☐ All Cash Sale Exhibit (F401) "_____"
   - ☐ Back-up Agreement Contingency Exhibit (F604) "_____"
   - ☐ Closing Attorney Acting as Holder of Earnest Money Exhibit (F510) "_____"
   - ☐ Community Association Disclosure Exhibit (F322) "_____"
   - ☐ Condominium Resale Purchase and Sale Exhibit (F204) "_____"
   - ☐ Conventional Loan Contingency Exhibit (F404) "_____"
   - ☐ FHA Loan Contingency Exhibit (F407) "_____"
   - ☐ Lead-Based Paint Exhibit (F316) "_____"
   - ☐ Lease Purchase and Sale Exhibit (F207) (to be used with F916) "_____"
   - ☐ Lease for Lease/Purchase Agreement (F916) (to be used with F207) "_____"
   - ☐ Legal Description Exhibit (F807 or other) "_____"
   - ☐ Loan Assumption Exhibit (F416) "_____"
   - ☐ Sale or Lease of Buyer's Property Contingency Exhibit (F601) "_____"
   - ☐ Seller's Property Disclosure Statement Exhibit (F301, F302, F304, F307 or F310) "_____"
   - ☐ Survey of Property as Exhibit "_____"
   - ☐ Temporary Occupancy Agreement for Seller after Closing Exhibit (F219) "_____"
   - ☐ USDA-RD Loan Contingency Exhibit (F413) "_____"
   - ☐ VA Loan Contingency Exhibit (F410) "_____"
   - ☐ Other _____
   - ☐ Other _____

SPECIAL STIPULATIONS: The following Special Stipulations, if conflicting with any exhibit, addendum, or preceding paragraph (including any changes thereto made by the parties), shall control:

☐ Additional Special Stipulations are attached.

By signing this Agreement, Buyer and Seller acknowledge that they have each read and understood this Agreement and agree to its terms.

Buyer Acceptance and Contact Information	Seller Acceptance and Contact Information
1 Buyer's Signature _____	**1 Seller's Signature** _____
Print or Type Name _____ Date _____	Print or Type Name _____ Date _____
Buyer's Address for Receiving Notice _____	Seller's Address for Receiving Notice _____
Buyer's Phone Number: ☐ Cell ☐ Home ☐ Work	Seller's Phone Number: ☐ Cell ☐ Home ☐ Work
Buyer's E-mail Address _____	Seller's E-mail Address _____
2 Buyer's Signature _____	**2 Seller's Signature** _____
Print or Type Name _____ Date _____	Print or Type Name _____ Date _____
Buyer's Address for Receiving Notice _____	Seller's Address for Receiving Notice _____
Buyer's Phone Number: ☐ Cell ☐ Home ☐ Work	Seller's Phone Number: ☐ Cell ☐ Home ☐ Work
Buyer's E-mail Address _____	Seller's E-mail Address _____
☐ Additional Signature Page (F267) is attached.	☐ Additional Signature Page (F267) is attached.

Buyer's Broker/Affiliated Licensee Contact Information	Seller's Broker/Affiliated Licensee Contact Information
Buyer Brokerage Firm _____	Seller Brokerage Firm _____
Broker/Affiliated Licensee Signature ____ Date ____	**Broker/Affiliated Licensee Signature** ____ Date ____
Print or Type Name _____ GA Real Estate License # _____	Print or Type Name _____ GA Real Estate License # _____
Licensee's Phone Number _____ Fax Number _____	Licensee's Phone Number _____ Fax Number _____
Licensee's E-mail Address _____	Licensee's Email Address _____
REALTOR® Membership _____	REALTOR® Membership _____
Broker's Address _____	Broker's Address _____
Broker's Phone Number _____ Fax Number _____	Broker's Phone Number _____ Fax Number _____
MLS Office Code _____ Brokerage Firm License Number _____	MLS Office Code _____ Brokerage Firm License Number _____

Binding Agreement Date: The Binding Agreement Date in this transaction is the date of _____ and has been filled in by _____.

APPENDIX E Documents for Review

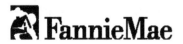

Uniform Residential Loan Application/*Solicitud Uniforme para Préstamo Hipotecario Residencial*

This application is designed to be completed by the applicant(s) with the Lender's assistance. Applicants should complete this form as "Borrower" or "Co-Borrower," as applicable. Co-Borrower information must also be provided (and the appropriate box checked) when ☐ the income or assets of a person other than the Borrower (including the Borrower's spouse) will be used as a basis for loan qualification or ☐ the income or assets of the Borrower's spouse or other person who has community property rights pursuant to state law will not be used as a basis for loan qualification, but his or her liabilities must be considered because the spouse or other person has community property rights pursuant to applicable law and Borrower resides in a community property state, the security property is located in a community property state, or the Borrower is relying on other property located in a community property state as a basis for repayment of the loan.

Esta solicitud se diseñó para ser completada por el solicitante o solicitantes con la ayuda del prestador. Los solicitantes deben completar esta solicitud como "Prestatario" o "Co-Prestatario", según corresponda. La información sobre el Co-Prestatario también debe proporcionarse (marque el cuadro correspondiente) ☐ si el ingreso o los bienes de una persona que no sea el "Prestatario" (incluyendo el cónyuge del prestatario) se emplearán como base para calificar para el préstamo ☐ o los bienes e ingresos del cónyuge del prestatario o de otra persona con derechos de comunidad conyugal de conformidad con la ley estatal no se usarán como base para calificar para el préstamo, pero las deudas de dichas personas tienen que considerarse debido a que el cónyuge u otra persona tienen derechos de comunidad conyugal de conformidad con la ley aplicable y a que el Prestatario reside en un estado en el que rige el régimen de comunidad conyugal, la propiedad que se ofrece como garantía se encuentra en un estado en el que rige el régimen de comunidad conyugal, o el Prestatario depende de otra propiedad que se encuentra en un estado en el que rige el régimen de comunidad conyugal para el pago total del préstamo.

If this is an application for joint credit, Borrower and Co-Borrower each agree that we intend to apply for joint credit (sign below):

Si se trata de una solicitud de crédito conjunto, el Prestatario y Co-Prestatario acuerdan que pretenden solicitar un crédito conjunto (firmar a continuación):

_____ _____
Borrower   Co-Borrower
Prestatario   *Co-Prestatario*

I. TYPE OF MORTGAGE AND TERMS OF LOAN/*TIPO DE HIPOTECA Y CONDICIONES DEL PRÉSTAMO*

Mortgage Applied for/ *Préstamo Hipotecario Solicitado:*	☐ VA/*VA* ☐ FHA/*FHA*	☐ Conventional/*Convencional* ☐ USDA/Rural Housing Service *USDA/Servicio Rural de Vivienda*	☐ Other (explain)/ *Otro (explique):*	Agency Case Number/ *Nº de Préstamo de la Agencia*	Lender Case Number/ *Nº de Préstamo del Prestador*
Amount/*Cantidad Total del Préstamo* $	Interest Rate/ *Tasa de Interés* %	No. of Months/ *Plazo (Meses)*	**Amortization Type/** *Tipo de Amortización:*	☐ Fixed Rate/*Tasa Fija* ☐ GPM/*GPM*	☐ Other (explain)/ *Otro (explique):* ☐ ARM (type)/*ARM (tipo)*

II. PROPERTY INFORMATION AND PURPOSE OF LOAN/*INFORMACIÓN SOBRE LA PROPIEDAD Y PROPÓSITO DEL PRÉSTAMO*

Subject Property Address (street, city, state & ZIP)/ *Dirección de la Propiedad (calle, ciudad, estado y código postal)*	No. of Units/ *Nº de Unidades*
Legal Description of Subject Property (attach description if necessary)/ *Descripción Legal de la Propiedad (adjunte descripción si es necesario)*	Year Built/ *Año de Construcción*

Purpose of Loan/ *Propósito del Préstamo*	☐ Purchase/*Compra* ☐ Refinance/*Refinanciamiento*	☐ Construction/*Construcción* ☐ Construction-Permanent/ *Financiamiento Permanente de Construcción*	☐ Other (explain): *Otro (explique)*	Property will be/*La propiedad será:* ☐ Primary Residence/ *Residencia Principal*	☐ Secondary Residence/ *Residencia Secundaria*	☐ Investment/ *Inversión*

Complete this line if construction or construction-permanent loan./ *Complete esta línea si es un préstamo para construcción o financiamiento permanente de construcción.*

Year Lot Acquired/ *Año en que se Adquirió el Lote*	Original Cost/ *Costo Original* $	Amount Existing Liens/ *Monto de los Gravámenes Actuales* $	(a) Present Value of Lot/ *Valor Actual del Lote* $	(b) Cost of Improvements/ *Costo de las Mejoras* $	Total (a + b)/ *Total (a + b)* $

Complete this line if this is a refinance loan./ *Complete esta línea si es un préstamo de refinanciamiento.*

Year Acquired/ *Año en que se Adquirió*	Original Cost/ *Costo Original* $	Amount Existing Liens/ *Monto de los Gravámenes Actuales* $	Purpose of Refinance/ *Propósito del Refinanciamiento*	Describe Improvements/ *Descripción de las Mejoras* Cost/*Costo*: $	☐ made/ *realizadas*	☐ to be made/ *por realizarse*

Title will be held in what Name(s) /*Nombre(s) que se Registrará(n) en el Título*	Manner in which Title will be held/ *Manera en que se Registrará el Título*	Estate will be held in/ *La propiedad se mantendrá en:* ☐ Fee Simple/ *Pleno Dominio* ☐ Leasehold (show expiration date)/ *Arrendamiento (indique fecha de vencimiento)*
Source of Down Payment, Settlement Charges, and/or Subordinate Financing (explain)/ *Origen de Pago Inicial, Costos de Cierre y/o Financiamiento Subordinado (explique)*		

Uniform Residential Loan Application
Freddie Mac Form 65s 7/05 (rev.6/09)

Fannie Mae Form 1003s 7/05 (rev.6/09)

APPENDIX E Documents for Review

Borrower/*Prestatario*				III. BORROWER INFORMATION/ *INFORMACIÓN SOBRE EL PRESTATARIO*	Co-Borrower/*Co-Prestatario*			
Borrower's Name (include Jr. or Sr. if applicable)/ *Nombre del Prestatario (indique Jr., o Sr. si aplica)*					Co-Borrower's Name (include Jr. or Sr. if applicable)/ *Nombre del Co-Prestatario (indique Jr., o Sr. si aplica)*			
Social Security Number/ *Número de Seguro Social*	Home Phone (incl. area code)/ *Teléfono de la Casa (incluya código de área)*	DOB (mm/dd/yyyy)/ *Fecha de nacimiento (mm/dd/aaaa)*	Yrs. School/ *Años de Educación*	Social Security Number/ *Número de Seguro Social*	Home Phone (incl. area code)/ *Teléfono de la Casa (incluya código de área)*	DOB (mm/dd/yyyy)/ *Fecha de nacimiento (mm/dd/aaaa)*		Yrs. School/ *Años de Educación*
☐ Married *Casado* ☐ Separated *Separado*	☐ Unmarried (include single, divorced, widowed)/ *No está casado (incluye soltero, divorciado, viudo)*	Dependents (not listed by Co-Borrower)/ *Dependientes (no incluidos por el Co-Prestatario)* No./*N°* Ages/*Edades*		☐ Married *Casado* ☐ Separated *Separado*	☐ Unmarried (include single, divorced, widowed)/ *No está casado (incluye soltero, divorciado, viudo)*	Dependents (not listed by Borrower)/ *Dependientes (no incluidos por el Prestatario)* No./*N°*		Ages/*Edades*
Present Address (street, city, state, ZIP)/ *Dirección Actual (calle, ciudad, estado, código postal)*		☐ Own/ *Propietario* ☐ Rent *Inquilino* ___No. Yrs./ *N° de Años*		Present Address (street, city, state, ZIP)/ *Dirección Actual (calle, ciudad, estado, código postal)*		☐ Own *Propietario* ☐ Rent *Inquilino*		___No. Yrs./ *N° de Años*
Mailing Address, if different from Present Address/ *Dirección donde recibe su correspondencia, si es diferente de su dirección actual*				Mailing Address, if different from Present Address/ *Dirección donde recibe su correspondencia, si es diferente de su dirección actual*				

If residing at present address for less than two years, complete the following:/Si habita en dicha dirección hace menos de dos años, por favor complete:

Former Address (street, city, state, ZIP) Yrs. *Dirección Anterior (calle, ciudad, estado, código postal)*	☐ Own *Propietario*	☐ Rent *Inquilino*	___No. *N° de Años*	Former Address (street, city, state, ZIP) *Dirección Anterior (calle, ciudad, estado, código postal)*	☐ Own *Propietario*	☐ Rent *Inquilino*	___No. Yrs. *N° de Años*

Borrower/*Prestatario*			IV. EMPLOYMENT INFORMATION/ *INFORMACIÓN SOBRE EL EMPLEO*	Co-Borrower/*Co-Prestatario*		
Name & Address of Employer/ *Nombre y Dirección del Empleador*	☐ Self Employed/ *Empleado por Cuenta Propia*	Yrs. on this job/ *Años en este trabajo* Yrs. employed in this line of work/profession/ *Años de empleo en este tipo de trabajo/profesión*		Name & Address of Employer/ *Nombre y Dirección del Empleador*	☐ Self Employed/ *Empleado por Cuenta Propia*	Yrs. on this job/ *Años en este trabajo* Yrs. employed in this line of work/profession/ *Años de empleo en este tipo de trabajo/profesión*
Position/Title/Type of Business/ *Posición/Título/Tipo de Negocio*	Business Phone (incl. area code)/*Teléfono en el lugar de trabajo (incluya código de área)*			Position/Title/Type of Business/ *Posición/Título/Tipo de Negocio*	Business Phone (incl. area code)/*Teléfono en el lugar de trabajo (incluya código de área)*	

If employed in current position for less than two years or if currently employed in more than one position, complete the following:/ Si ha estado trabajando en la posición actual menos de dos años o si actualmente está empleado en más de una posición, complete lo siguiente:

Name & Address of Employer/ *Nombre y Dirección del Empleador*	☐ Self Employed/ *Empleado por Cuenta Propia*	Dates (from – to)/ *Fechas de empleo (desde – hasta)* Monthly Income/ *Ingreso Mensual* $	Name & Address of Employer/ *Nombre y Dirección del Empleador*	☐ Self Employed/ *Empleado por Cuenta Propia*	Dates (from – to)/ *Fechas de empleo (desde – hasta)* Monthly Income/ *Ingreso Mensual* $
Position/Title/Type of Business/ *Posición/Título/Tipo de Negocio*	Business Phone (incl. area code)/ *Teléfono en el lugar de trabajo (incluya código de área)*		Position/Title/Type of Business/ *Posición/Título/Tipo de Negocio*	Business Phone (incl. area code)/ *Teléfono en el lugar de trabajo (incluya código de área)*	
Name & Address of Employer/ *Nombre y Dirección del Empleador*	☐ Self Employed/ *Empleado por Cuenta Propia*	Dates (from – to)/ *Fechas de empleo (desde – hasta)* Monthly Income/ *Ingreso Mensual* $	Name & Address of Employer/ *Nombre y Dirección del Empleador*	☐ Self Employed/ *Empleado por Cuenta Propia*	Dates (from – to)/ *Fechas de empleo (desde – hasta)* Monthly Income/ *Ingreso Mensual* $

Uniform Residential Loan Application
Freddie Mac Form 65s 7/05 (rev.6/09)

Fannie Mae Form 1003s 7/05 (rev.6/09)

APPENDIX E Documents for Review

Borrower/*Prestatario*		IV. EMPLOYMENT INFORMATION/ *INFORMACIÓN SOBRE EL EMPLEO* (cont'd)		Co-Borrower/*Co-Prestatario*	
Position/Title/Type of Business/ *Posición/Título/Tipo de Negocio*		Business Phone (incl. area code)/ *Teléfono en el lugar de trabajo (incluya código de área)*	Position/Title/Type of Business/ *Posición/Título/Tipo de Negocio*		Business Phone (incl. area code)/ *Teléfono en el lugar de trabajo (incluya código de área)*

V. MONTHLY INCOME AND COMBINED HOUSING EXPENSE INFORMATION/
INFORMACIÓN SOBRE EL INGRESO Y LOS GASTOS MENSUALES COMBINADOS DE VIVIENDA

Gross Monthly Income *Ingreso Bruto Mensual*	Borrower *Prestatario*	Co-Borrower *Co-Prestatario*	Total	Combined Monthly Housing Expense/*Gastos Mensuales Combinados de Vivienda*	Present *Actual*	Proposed *Propuesto*
Base Empl. Income* *Ingreso Básico del Empleado**	$	$	$	Rent *Alquiler*	$	
Overtime *Horas extra*				First Mortgage (P&I) *Hipoteca Principal (Principal e Interés)*		$
Bonuses *Pagas Extras*				Other Financing (P&I) *Otro Financiamiento (Principal e Interés)*		
Commissions *Comisiones*				Hazard Insurance *Seguro Contra Riesgos*		
Dividends/Interest *Dividendos/Intereses*				Real Estate Taxes *Impuestos Sobre Bienes Raíces*		
Net Rental Income *Ingreso Neto por Alquiler*				Mortgage Insurance *Seguro de Hipoteca*		
Other (before completing, see the notice in "describe other income", below) *Otros (antes de llenar, vea el aviso en "describa otros ingresos", a continuación)*				Homeowner Assn. Dues *Cuotas de la Asociación de Propietarios* Other: *Otro:*		
Total	$	$	$	Total	$	$

* Self Employed Borrower(s) may be required to provide additional documentation such as tax returns and financial statements.

* *Se podrá requerir al Prestatario o Prestatarios que trabajan por cuenta propia que proporcionen documentos adicionales, tales como declaraciones y planillas de impuestos y estados financieros.*

Describe Other Income/ *Describa Otros Ingresos*

Notice: Alimony, child support, or separate maintenance income need not be revealed if the Borrower (B) or Co-Borrower (C) does not choose to have it considered for repaying this loan.

Aviso: La pensión conyugal, pensión para el sustento de los hijos o ingreso de mantenimiento por separación, no tienen que declararse si el Prestatario (B) o Co-Prestatario (C) no desea que se considere para el pago de este Préstamo.

B/C		Monthly Amount *Cantidad Mensual*
		$

VI. ASSETS AND LIABILITIES/*BIENES Y PASIVOS*

This Statement and any applicable supporting schedules may be completed jointly by both married and unmarried Co-Borrowers if their assets and liabilities are sufficiently joined so that the Statement can be meaningfully and fairly presented on a combined basis; otherwise, separate Statements and Schedules are required. If the Co-Borrower section was completed about a non-applicant spouse or other person, this Statement and supporting schedules must be completed about that spouse or other person also.

Esta Declaración y cualquier anexo respaldatorio pertinente pueden llenarse conjuntamente tanto por Co-Prestatarios casados como no casados si sus bienes y deudas están suficientemente unidos de manera que la Declaración pueda presentarse con sentido sobre una base combinada y de una forma fiel; o de lo contrario, se requieren Declaraciones y Anexos por separado. Si en la sección del Co-Prestatario se completó la parte sobre el cónyuge, no solicitante u otra persona, esta Declaración y los anexos respaldatorios también deben completarse para dicho cónyuge u otra persona.

Completed/*Se completó* ☐ Jointly/*En Conjunto* ☐ Not Jointly/*Por Separado*

ASSETS/*BIENES* Description/*Descripción*	Cash or Market Value/ *Valor en Efectivo o Valor en el Mercado*	Liabilities and Pledged Assets. List the creditor's name, address, and account number for all outstanding debts, including automobile loans, revolving charge accounts, real estate loans, alimony, child support, stock pledges, etc. Use continuation sheet, if necessary. Indicate by (*) those liabilities, which will be satisfied upon sale of real estate owned or upon refinancing of the subject property.
Cash deposit toward purchase held by:/ *Depósito en efectivo para la compra en poder de:*	$	***Deudas y Bienes Gravados.*** *Indique el nombre, la dirección y el número de cuenta de todas las deudas pendientes, incluyendo préstamos para autos, cuentas de poder de: crédito rotativo, préstamos de bienes raíces, pensión conyugal, pensión para el sustento de hijos, valores gravados, etc. Si es necesario, use una hoja adicional. Indique con un (*) aquellas deudas que se satisfarán al venderse o refinanciarse la propiedad inmobiliaria en cuestión.*

Uniform Residential Loan Application
Freddie Mac Form 65s 7/05 (rev.6/09)

Fannie Mae Form 1003s 7/05 (rev.6/09)

APPENDIX E Documents for Review   613

VI. ASSETS AND LIABILITIES/*BIENES Y PASIVOS* (cont'd)

		LIABILITIES/*PASIVOS*	Monthly Payment & Months Left to Pay/ *Pago Mensual y N° de Pagos Mensuales que quedan por pagar*	Unpaid Balance/ *Balance Pendiente*
List checking and savings accounts below/ Indique abajo las cuentas de cheques y de ahorros		Name and address of Company/ *Nombre y dirección de la Compañía*	$ Payment/Months $ *Pagos/Meses*	$
Name and address of Bank, S&L, or Credit Union/ *Nombre y dirección del Banco, Asociación de Ahorro y Préstamo o Cooperativa de Crédito*				
		Acct. no./*N° de Cuenta*		
Acct. no./*N° de Cuenta*	$	Name and address of Company/ *Nombre y dirección de la Compañía*	$ Payment/Months $ *Pagos/Meses*	$
Name and address of Bank, S&L, or Credit Union/ *Nombre y dirección del Banco, Asociación de Ahorro y Préstamo o Cooperativa de Crédito*				
		Acct. no./*N° de Cuenta*		
Acct. no./*N° de Cuenta*	$	Name and address of Company/ *Nombre y dirección de la Compañía*	$ Payment/Months $ *Pagos/Meses*	$
Name and address of Bank, S&L, or Credit Union/ *Nombre y dirección del Banco, Asociación de Ahorro y Préstamo o Cooperativa de Crédito*				
		Acct. no./*N° de Cuenta*		
Acct. no./*N° de Cuenta*	$	Name and address of Company/ *Nombre y dirección de la Compañía*	$ Payment/Months $ *Pagos/Meses*	$
Name and address of Bank, S&L, or Credit Union/ *Nombre y dirección del Banco, Asociación de Ahorro y Préstamo o Cooperativa de Crédito*				
		Acct. no./*N° de Cuenta*		
Acct. no./*N° de Cuenta*	$	Name and address of Company/ *Nombre y dirección de la Compañía*	$ Payment/Months $ *Pagos/Meses*	$
Stocks & Bonds (Company name/number and description)/ *Acciones y Bonos (Nombre de la compañía/número y descripción de los valores y bonos)*	$	Acct. no./*N° de Cuenta*		
Life insurance net cash value/ *Valor en efectivo neto del seguro de vida* Face amount: *Monto de la póliza:* $	$	Name and address of Company/ *Nombre y dirección de la Compañía*	$ Payment/Months $ *Pagos/Meses*	$
Subtotal Liquid Assets/ ***Subtotal de los Bienes Líquidos***	$			
Real estate owned (enter market value from schedule of real estate owned)/ *Propiedad inmobiliaria de la cual es dueño (indique el valor en el mercado según el anexo de la propiedad inmobiliaria)*	$			
Vested interest in retirement fund/ *Intereses adquiridos en el fondo de retiro*	$			
Net worth of business(es) owned (attach financial statement)/ *Valor neto de negocio(s) propio(s) (incluya estados financieros)*	$	Acct. no./*N° de Cuenta*		
Automobiles owned (make and year)/ *Automóviles de los cuales es dueño (marca y año)*	$	Alimony/Child Support/Separate Maintenance Payments Owed to:/ *Pensión Alimenticia/Pensión Para el Sustento de los Hijos/Manutención por Separación:*	$	
Other Assets (itemize)/ *Otros Bienes (detalle)*	$	Job-Related Expense (child care, union dues, etc.)/ *Gastos Relacionados con el Empleo(cuidado de los hijos, cuotas de sindicatos, etc.)*	$	
		Total Monthly Payments/ ***Total de Pagos Mensuales***	$	
Total Assets a./ ***Total de Bienes a.***	$	Net Worth ▶ (a minus b) *Valor Neto (a menos b)*	$	**Total Liabilities b.** ***Total de Pasivos b.*** $

Uniform Residential Loan Application
Freddie Mac Form 65s 7/05 (rev.6/09)

Fannie Mae Form 1003s 7/05 (rev.6/09)

APPENDIX E Documents for Review

VI. ASSETS AND LIABILITIES/*BIENES Y PASIVOS* (cont'd)

Schedule of Real Estate Owned (If additional properties are owned, use continuation sheet.)
Anexo de Propiedades Inmobiliarias (Si es dueño de más propiedades, use la hoja a continuación.)

Property Address (enter S if sold, PS if pending sale or R if rental being held for income)/ *Dirección de la Propiedad (ponga una S por vendida, una PS por venta pendiente o una R si recibe ingreso por alquiler)*	Type of Property/ *Tipo de Propiedad* ▼	Present Market Value/ *Valor Actual en el Mercado*	Amount of Mortgages & Liens/ *Cantidad de Hipotecas y Gravámenes*	Gross Rental Income/ *Ingreso Bruto por Alquiler*	Mortgage Payments/ *Pagos Hipotecarios*	Insurance, Maintenance, Taxes & Misc./ *Seguro, Mantenimiento, Impuestos y Otros*	Net Rental Income/ *Ingreso Neto por Alquiler*
		$	$	$	$	$	$
	Totals/ *Totales*	$	$	$	$	$	$

List any additional names under which credit has previously been received and indicate appropriate creditor name(s) and account number(s):/
Indique otros nombres bajo los cuales ha recibido crédito anteriormente, así como los nombres de los acreedores y el número de las cuentas.

Alternate Name/*Otro Nombre*	Creditor Name/*Nombre del Acreedor*	Account Number/*Número de Cuenta*

VII. DETAILS OF TRANSACTION/ *DETALLES DE LA TRANSACCIÓN*

a.	Purchase price/*Precio de compra*	$
b.	Alterations, improvements, repairs/ *Remodelaciones, mejoras, reparaciones*	
c.	Land (if acquired separately)/ *Terreno (si fue adquirido por separado)*	
d.	Refinance (incl. debts to be paid off)/ *Refinanciamiento (incluya deudas que se pagarán)*	
e.	Estimated prepaid items/ *Estimado de partidas prepagadas*	
f.	Estimated closing costs/ *Estimado de los costos de cierre*	
g.	PMI, MIP, Funding Fee/ *Seguro de hipoteca privado (PMI), Primas de seguro de hipoteca (MIP), Costos de Financiamiento*	
h.	Discount (if Borrower will pay)/ *Descuento (si el Prestatario lo pagará)*	
i.	Total costs (add items a through h)/ *Total de costos (sume las líneas "a" hasta la "h")*	
j.	Subordinate financing/ *Financiamiento subordinado*	
k.	Borrower's closing costs paid by Seller/ *Costos de cierre del Prestatario pagados por el Vendedor*	
l.	Other Credits (explain)/ *Otros Créditos (explique)*	

VIII. DECLARATIONS/ *DECLARACIONES*

If you answer "Yes" to any questions a through i, please use continuation sheet for explanation. /
Si responde "Sí" a cualquier de las preguntas de la "a" a la "i", debe utilizar una hoja adicional para dar una explicación.

	Borrower/*Prestatario*		Co-Borrower/*Co-Prestatario*	
	Yes/*Sí*	No	Yes/*Sí*	No
a. Are there any outstanding judgments against you? *¿Existe alguna sentencia o fallo judicial pendiente en contra suya?*	☐	☐	☐	☐
b. Have you been declared bankrupt within the past 7 years? *¿Se ha declarado en bancarrota durante los últimos 7 años?*	☐	☐	☐	☐
c. Have you had property foreclosed upon or given title or deed in lieu thereof in the last 7 years? *¿Se le ha entablado una ejecución hipotecaria o ha transferido el título de propiedad en sustitución de una ejecución hipotecaria en los últimos 7 años?*	☐	☐	☐	☐
d. Are you a party to a lawsuit? *¿Es usted parte en una demanda judicial?*	☐	☐	☐	☐
e. Have you directly or indirectly been obligated on any loan which resulted in foreclosure, transfer of title in lieu of foreclosure, or judgment? *¿Ha estado usted obligado, directa o indirectamente, en algún préstamo que provocó una ejecución hipotecaria, transferencia de título en sustitución de una ejecución hipotecaria, o alguna sentencia, o fallo en su contra?* (This would include such loans as home mortgage loans, SBA loans, home improvement loans, educational loans, manufactured (mobile) home loans, any mortgage, financial obligation, bond, or loan guarantee. If "Yes," provide details, including date, name, and address of Lender, FHA or VA case number, if any, and reasons for the action.) *(Esto incluye préstamos tales como préstamos hipotecarios para vivienda, préstamos SBA, préstamos para mejoras en la casa, préstamos educacionales, préstamos para casa móviles, cualquier hipoteca, obligación financiera, bono o préstamo garantizado. Si la respuesta es "Sí", incluya la fecha, el nombre y la dirección del Prestador, o el número de caso de FHA o VA, si lo hubiera, y las razones de la acción.)*	☐	☐	☐	☐
f. Are you presently delinquent or in default on any Federal debt or any other loan, mortgage, financial obligation, bond, or loan guarantee? If "Yes," give details as described in the preceding question. *¿Se encuentra atrasado, moroso o en incumplimiento con alguna deuda federal o cualquier otro préstamos, hipoteca, obligación finaciera, bono o garantía de préstamos? Si la respuesta es "Sí", provea detalles según se describe en la pregun ta anterior.*	☐	☐	☐	☐
g. Are you obligated to pay alimony, child support, or separate maintenance? *¿Está obligado a pagar por pensión alimenticia, pensión para el sustento de los hijos, o manutención por separación?*	☐	☐	☐	☐
h. Is any part of the down payment borrowed? *¿Le prestaron alguna parte del pago inicial?*	☐	☐	☐	☐

APPENDIX E Documents for Review

VII. DETAILS OF TRANSACTION/ *DETALLES DE LA TRANSACCIÓN*		VIII. DECLARATIONS/ *DECLARACIONES*				
m.	Loan amount (exclude PMI, MIP, Funding Fee financed)/ *Cantidad del Préstamo (excluya PMI, MIP, Costos de Financiamiento financiados)*	i. Are you a co-maker or endorser on a note? *¿Es usted co–prestatario o fiador de un pagaré?*	☐	☐	☐	☐
		j. Are you a U.S. citizen? *¿Es usted ciudadano de los Estados Unidos?*	☐	☐	☐	☐
n.	PMI, MIP, Funding Fee financed/ *Seguro de hipoteca privado (PMI), Primas de seguro de hipoteca (MIP), Costos de Financiamiento financiados*	k. Are you a permanent resident alien? *¿Es usted un residente extranjero permanente de los Estados Unidos?*	☐	☐	☐	☐
		l. Do you intend to occupy the property as your primary residence? If "Yes," complete question m below. *¿Tiene usted la intención de ocupar la propiedad como su residencia principal? Si la respuesta es "Sí" conteste la pregunta "m".*	☐	☐	☐	☐
o.	Loan amount (add m & n) / *Cantidad del Préstamo (sume líneas "m" y "n")*					
p.	Cash from/to Borrower (subtract j, k, l & o from i)/ *Dinero del / para el Prestatario (reste j, k, l & o de i)*	m. Have you had an ownership interest in a property in the last three years? *¿Ha tenido usted participación como dueño en una propiedad en los últimos 3 años?* (1) What type of property did you own—principal residence (PR), second home (SH), or investment property (IP)? *¿De qué tipo de propiedad era usted dueño–residencia principal (PR), reisdencia secundaria (SH) o propiedad de inversion (IP)?* (2) How did you hold title to the home—solely by yourself (S), jointly with your spouse (SP), or jointly with another person (O)? *¿Cómo estaba registrado el título–a nombre suyo solamente (S), conjuntamente con su cónyuge (SP), o conjuntamente con otra persona (O)?*	☐ ___ ___	☐ ___ ___	☐ ___ ___	☐ ___ ___

IX. ACKNOWLEDGEMENT AND AGREEMENT/*RECONOCIMIENTO Y ACUERDO*

Each of the undersigned specifically represents to Lender and to Lender's actual or potential agents, brokers, processors, attorneys, insurers, servicers, successors and assigns and agrees and acknowledges that: (1) the information provided in this application is true and correct as of the date set forth opposite my signature and that any intentional or negligent misrepresentation of this information contained in this application may result in civil liability, including monetary damages, to any person who may suffer any loss due to reliance upon any misrepresentation that I have made on this application, and/or in criminal penalties including, but not limited to, fine or imprisonment or both under the provisions of Title 18, United States Code, Sec. 1001, et seq.; (2) the loan requested pursuant to this application (the "Loan") will be secured by a mortgage or deed of trust on the property described in this application; (3) the property will not be used for any illegal or prohibited purpose or use; (4) all statements made in this application are made for the purpose of obtaining a residential mortgage loan; (5) the property will be occupied as indicated in this application; (6) the Lender, its servicers, successors or assigns may retain the original and/or an electronic record of this application, whether or not the Loan is approved; (7) the Lender and its agents, brokers, insurers, servicers, successors, and assigns may continuously rely on the information contained in the application, and I am obligated to amend and/or supplement the information provided in this application if any of the material facts that I have represented herein should change prior to closing of the Loan; (8) in the event that my payments on the Loan become delinquent, the Lender, its servicers, successors or assigns may, in addition to any other rights and remedies that it may have relating to such delinquency, report my name and account information to one or more consumer reporting agencies; (9) ownership of the Loan and/or administration of the Loan account may be transferred with such notice as may be required by law; (10) neither Lender nor its agents, brokers, insurers, servicers, successors or assigns has made any representation or warranty, express or implied, to me regarding the property or the condition or value of the property; and (11) my transmission of this application as an "electronic record" containing my "electronic signature," as those terms are defined in applicable federal and/or state laws (excluding audio and video recordings), or my facsimile transmission of this application containing a facsimile of my signature, shall be as effective, enforceable and valid as if a paper version of this application were delivered containing my original written signature.

Cada uno de los suscritos representa específicamente al Prestamista y a los verdaderos o posibles agentes, corredores, procesadores, abogados, aseguradores, administradores, sucesores y cesionarios del Prestamista, y está de acuerdo y acepta que: (1) la información que se proporciona en esta solicitud es exacta y correcta a partir de la fecha expuesta en la línea opuesta a mi firma, y que toda distorsión, intencional o negligente, de esta información contenida en esta solicitud pudiera resultar en una penalidad civil, incluyendo daños monetarios, hacia cualquier persona que sufra alguna pérdida debido a la toma de decisiones hecha en base a cualquier declaración falsa que yo haya hecho en esta solicitud, o en castigos penales, incluyendo, pero sin limitar a, multa o arresto o ambos, de acuerdo con las disposiciones del Título 18, del Código de los Estados Unidos, Sec. 1001, et seq.; (2) el préstamo solicitado de acuerdo a esta solicitud (el "Préstamo") estará asegurado por una hipoteca o escritura de fideicomiso sobre la propiedad descrita en la presente solicitud; (3) la propiedad no se utilizará para ningún propósito o uso ilegal o prohibido; (4) todas las declaraciones realizadas en esta solicitud se hacen con el fin de obtener un préstamo hipotecario residencial; (5) la propiedad se ocupará de acuerdo con lo indicado en la presente solicitud; (6) el Prestamista, sus administradores, sucesores o cesionarios pudieran retener los registros originales o electrónicos contenidos en esta solicitud, se apruebe o no el Préstamo; (7) el Prestamista y sus agentes, corredores, aseguradores, administradores, sucesores y cesionarios, pueden tomar decisiones constantemente en base a la información contenida en esta solicitud, y yo estoy obligado a corregir y complementar la información proporcionada en esta solicitud si alguno de los hechos significativos que he declarado en la presente cambia antes del cierre del Préstamo; (8) en el caso de que mis pagos al Préstamo se atrasen, el Prestamista, sus administradores, sucesores o cesionarios pudiera, además de cualquier otro derecho y recurso que pueda tener relacionado a dicho atraso, reportar mi nombre e información de cuenta a una o más agencias de información de crédito del consumidor; (9) la propiedad del Préstamo o la administración de la cuenta del Préstamo pudiera transferirse otorgando la notificación que requiera la ley; (10) ningún Prestamista ni sus agentes, corredores, aseguradores, administradores, sucesores o cesionarios me han hecho alguna manifestación de garantía, expresa o implícita, respecto a la propiedad, o la condición o el valor de la propiedad; (11) mi transmisión de esta solicitud como un "registro electrónico" que contenga mi "firma electrónica", como se definen esos términos en las leyes federales y estatales correspondientes (excluyendo grabaciones de audio y video), o mi transmisión de facsímil de esta solicitud que contenga un facsímil de mi firma, deberá ser tan eficaz, acatable y válida como si se hubiera entregado una versión en papel de esta solicitud que contenga mi firma escrita original.

Acknowledgement. Each of the undersigned hereby acknowledges that any owner of the Loan, its servicers, successors and assigns, may verify or reverify any information contained in this application or obtain any information or data relating to the Loan, for any legitimate business purpose through any source, including a source named in this application or a consumer reporting agency.

Reconocimiento. Cada uno de los abajo firmantes reconocen por la presente que el titular del Préstamo, sus administradores, sucesores y cesionarios pueden verificar y reverificar cualquier información incluida en esta solicitud u obtener cualquier información o datos relacionados con el Préstamo, para cualquier propósito comercial legítimo, a través de cualquier fuente, incluida una fuente mencionada en esta solicitud o una agencia de crédito del consumidor.

THE SPANISH TRANSLATION IS FOR CONVENIENCE PURPOSES ONLY. IN THE EVENT OF AN INCONSISTENCY BETWEEN THE ENGLISH AND SPANISH LANGUAGE VERSIONS OF THIS FORM, THE ENGLISH LANGUAGE VERSION SHALL PREVAIL.
LA TRADUCCIÓN AL ESPAÑOL ES PARA SU CONVENIENCIA ÚNICAMENTE. EN CASO DE QUE EXISTA UNA INCONSISTENCIA ENTRE LA VERSIÓN EN INGLÉS Y LA VERSIÓN EN ESPAÑOL DE ESTE FORMULARIO, PREVALECERÁ LA VERSIÓN EN INGLÉS.

LEA ESTO PRIMERO: Este documento contiene una traducción al español de su texto en inglés.

APPENDIX E Documents for Review

Borrower's Signature/*Firma del Prestatario*	Date/*Fecha*	Co-Borrower's Signature/*Firma del Co-Prestatario*	Date/*Fecha*
X		X	

X. INFORMATION FOR GOVERNMENT MONITORING PURPOSES/*INFORMACIÓN PARA FINES DE VERIFICACIÓN POR EL GOBIERNO*

The following information is requested by the Federal Government for certain types of loans related to a dwelling in order to monitor the lender's compliance with equal credit opportunity, fair housing and home mortgage disclosure laws. You are not required to furnish this information, but are encouraged to do so. The law provides that a lender may not discriminate either on the basis of this information, or on whether you choose to furnish it. If you furnish the information, please provide both ethnicity and race. For race, you may check more than one designation. If you do not furnish ethnicity, race, or sex, under Federal regulations, this lender is required to note the information on the basis of visual observation and surname if you have made this application in person. If you do not wish to furnish the information, please check the box below. (Lender must review the above material to assure that the disclosures satisfy all requirements to which the lender is subject under applicable state law for the particular type of loan applied for.)

La siguiente información la solicita el gobierno Federal para ciertos tipos de préstamos relacionados con una vivienda, con el fin de verificar el cumplimiento del Prestador con las leyes de igualdad de Oportunidades de Crédito, "fair housing" y las leyes de divulgación de hipotecas para viviendas. Usted no está obligado a proporcionar esta información, pero le instamos a hacerlo. La ley dispone que un Prestador no puede discriminar en base a esta información ni por el hecho de que decida o no proporcionarla. Si usted decide proporcionarla debe indicar grupo étnico y raza. Usted puede indicar más de una raza. Si usted no desea suministrar la información, de acuerdo a las reglamentaciones federales el Prestador debe anotar la raza y el sexo basado en una observación visual y de acuerdo a su apellido si usted preparó esta solicitud en persona. Si usted no desea proporcionar la información, sírvase marcar en el cuadro ubicado en la parte inferior. (El Prestador debe evaluar el material arriba mencionado para asegurarse de que la información proporcionada cumple con todos los requisitos a los que está sujeto el Prestador bajo la ley estatal pertinente para el tipo de préstamo en particular que se ha solicitado.)

BORROWER/*PRESTATARIO* ☐ I do not wish to furnish this information / *No deseo proporcionar esta información*	CO-BORROWER/*CO-PRESTATARIO* ☐ I do not wish to furnish this information / *No deseo proporcionar esta información*
Ethnicity: / *Grupo étnico* ☐ Hispanic or Latino/ *Hispano o Latino* ☐ Not Hispanic or Latino/ *No Hispano o Latino*	**Ethnicity:** / *Grupo étnico* ☐ Hispanic or Latino/ *Hispano o Latino* ☐ Not Hispanic or Latino/ *No Hispano o Latino*
Race/*Raza***:** ☐ American Indian or Alaska Native/ *Indio Americano o Nativo de Alaska* ☐ Asian/ *Asiático* ☒ Black or African American/ *Negro o Afroamericano* ☐ Native Hawaiian or Other Pacific Islander/ *Nativo de Hawai o de otra isla del Pacífico* ☐ White/*Blanco*	**Race/***Raza***:** ☐ American Indian or Alaska Native/ *Indio Americano o Nativo de Alaska* ☐ Asian/ *Asiático* ☐ Black or African American/ *Negro o Afroamericano* ☐ Native Hawaiian or Other Pacific Islander/ *Nativo de Hawai o de otra isla del Pacífico* ☐ White/*Blanco*
Sex/*Sexo***:** ☐ Female/*Femenino* ☐ Male/*Masculino*	**Sex/***Sexo***:** ☐ Female/*Femenino* ☐ Male/*Masculino*

To be Completed by Loan Originator:
A COMPLETARSE POR EL ORIGINADOR DEL PRÉSTAMO

This information was provided:
Esta informacion fue proporcionada a través de:
☒ In a face-to-face interview / *Entrevista en persona*
☐ In a telephone interview/*Entrevista por teléfono*
☐ By the applicant and submitted by fax or mail/*El solicitante y enviado por fax o por correo*
☐ By the applicant and submitted via e-mail or the Internet/*El solicitante y enviado por correo electrónico o por el Internet*

Loan Originator's Signature / *Firma del Originador del Préstamo* X	Date/ *Fecha*
Loan Originator's Name (print or type) / *Nombre del Originador del Préstamo (use en letra de imprenta o a máquina)*	Loan Originator Identifier / *Identificación del Originador del Préstamo*	Loan Originator's Phone Number (including area code) / *Nº de Teléfono del Originador del Préstamo (incl. código de área)*
Loan Origination Company's Name / *Nombre de la Compañía Originadora del Préstamo*	Loan Origination Company Identifier / *Identificación de la Compañía Originadora del Préstamo*	Loan Origination Company's Address / *Dirección de la Compañía Originadora del Préstamo*

Uniform Residential Loan Application
Freddie Mac Form 65s 7/05 (rev.6/09)

Fannie Mae Form 1003s 7/05 (rev. 6/09)

CONTINUATION SHEET/RESIDENTIAL LOAN APPLICATION/*HOJA DE CONTINUACIÓN/SOLICITUD PARA PRÉSTAMO HIPOTECARIO RESIDENCIAL*		
Use this continuation sheet if you need more space to complete the Residential Loan Application. Mark **B** f or Borrower or **C** for Co-Borrower. *Utilice esta hoja si necesita más espacio para completar la aplicación para hipoteca residencial. Escriba "B" para Prestatario y "C" para Co–Prestatario.*	Borrower/*Prestatario*:	Agency Case Number/ *Número de Préstamo de la Agencia*:
	Co-Borrower/*Co-Prestatario*:	Lender Case Number/ *Número de Préstamo del Prestador*:

I/We fully understand that it is a Federal crime punishable by fine or imprisonment, or both, to knowingly make any false statements concerning any of the above facts as applicable under the provisions of Title 18, United States Code, Section 1001, et seq.
Entiendo/Entendemos que es un crimen federal penado con multa o encarcelamiento, o ambos, el hacer declaraciones falsas con respecto a cualquiera de los hechos arriba declarados, según sea pertinente de acuerdo con las disposiciones del Título 18 del Código de los Estados Unidos, Artículo 1001, et seq.

Borrower's Signature/*Firma del Prestatario*	Date/*Fecha*	Co-Borrower's Signature/*Firma del Co-Prestatario*	Date/*Fecha*
X		X	

Uniform Residential Loan Application
Freddie Mac Form 65s 7/05 (rev.6/09)

Fannie Mae Form 1003s 7/05 (rev. 6/09)

Instructions

Uniform Residential Loan Application (Spanish)

The lender may use this form to record relevant financial information about a Spanish-speaking applicant who applies for a conventional one- to four-family mortgage, if the applicant is more comfortable responding to questions in that language.
Lenders must use this revised form on and after 1/1/06.

Copies

Original, plus one.

Printing Instructions

We provide Form 1003S in an electronic format that prints as a letter size document. However, lenders may print Form 1003S as a legal size document or with different fonts or margins that may affect pagination; we have no specific standards for the number or size of pages the form may have. Consequently, the number and size of pages will not affect compliance with Fannie Mae requirements pertaining to use of the Uniform Residential Loan Application, provided that the content of the form has not been materially altered. When printing this form, you must use the "shrink to fit" option in the Adobe Acrobat print dialogue box.

Instructions

All instructions related to the completion of the standard Uniform Residential Loan Application (Form 1003) apply to this bilingual (Spanish-English) version of the form.

This bilingual form was developed solely as an accommodation for Spanish-speaking borrowers. Its use is optional. A lender should bear in mind that if the Spanish translation of this form results in a different interpretation of a specific Fannie Mae requirement than that which is apparent from reading the Selling Guide, no modification to our requirements was intended. A lender that chooses to use this bilingual form in connection with a mortgage application must be able to make all of our standard representations and warranties with respect to compliance with all applicable laws and the requirements specified in our Mortgage Selling and Servicing Contract and Guides. By making this form available, we make no representation or warranty regarding its suitability for use in any jurisdiction. Before using this bilingual form, a lender should consult with its own legal and compliance advisors to ensure that its use is not prohibited or regulated. A lender should verify that the laws of any jurisdiction allow the use of this form in connection with a mortgage transaction and make sure that its use does not impair any of the borrower's obligations or the lender's rights under the mortgage and applicable law.

After Recording Return To:

_____

_____

_____

_____

_____[Space Above This Line For Recording Data]_____

SECURITY DEED

DEFINITIONS

Words used in multiple sections of this document are defined below and other words are defined in Sections 3, 11, 13, 18, 20 and 21. Certain rules regarding the usage of words used in this document are also provided in Section 16.

(A) **"Security Instrument"** means this document, which is dated _____, _____, together with all Riders to this document.

(B) **"Borrower"** is _____. Borrower is the grantor under this Security Instrument.

(C) **"Lender"** is _____. Lender is a _____ organized and existing under the laws of _____. Lender's address is _____ _____. Lender is the grantee under this Security Instrument.

(D) **"Note"** means the promissory note signed by Borrower and dated _____, _____. The Note states that Borrower owes Lender _____ _____ Dollars (U.S. $_____) plus interest. Borrower has promised to pay this debt in regular Periodic Payments and to pay the debt in full not later than _____.

(E) **"Property"** means the property that is described below under the heading "Transfer of Rights in the Property."

(F) **"Loan"** means the debt evidenced by the Note, plus interest, any prepayment charges and late charges due under the Note, and all sums due under this Security Instrument, plus interest.

(G) **"Riders"** means all Riders to this Security Instrument that are executed by Borrower. The following Riders are to be executed by Borrower [check box as applicable]:

☐ Adjustable Rate Rider   ☐ Condominium Rider   ☐ Second Home Rider
☐ Balloon Rider   ☐ Planned Unit Development Rider   ☐ Other(s) [specify] _____
☐ 1-4 Family Rider   ☐ Biweekly Payment Rider

GEORGIA--Single Family--Fannie Mae/Freddie Mac UNIFORM INSTRUMENT   Form 3011   1/01

(H) **"Applicable Law"** means all controlling applicable federal, state and local statutes, regulations, ordinances and administrative rules and orders (that have the effect of law) as well as all applicable final, non-appealable judicial opinions.

(I) **"Community Association Dues, Fees, and Assessments"** means all dues, fees, assessments and other charges that are imposed on Borrower or the Property by a condominium association, homeowners association or similar organization.

(J) **"Electronic Funds Transfer"** means any transfer of funds, other than a transaction originated by check, draft, or similar paper instrument, which is initiated through an electronic terminal, telephonic instrument, computer, or magnetic tape so as to order, instruct, or authorize a financial institution to debit or credit an account. Such term includes, but is not limited to, point-of-sale transfers, automated teller machine transactions, transfers initiated by telephone, wire transfers, and automated clearinghouse transfers.

(K) **"Escrow Items"** means those items that are described in Section 3.

(L) **"Miscellaneous Proceeds"** means any compensation, settlement, award of damages, or proceeds paid by any third party (other than insurance proceeds paid under the coverages described in Section 5) for: (i) damage to, or destruction of, the Property; (ii) condemnation or other taking of all or any part of the Property; (iii) conveyance in lieu of condemnation; or (iv) misrepresentations of, or omissions as to, the value and/or condition of the Property.

(M) **"Mortgage Insurance"** means insurance protecting Lender against the nonpayment of, or default on, the Loan.

(N) **"Periodic Payment"** means the regularly scheduled amount due for (i) principal and interest under the Note, plus (ii) any amounts under Section 3 of this Security Instrument.

(O) **"RESPA"** means the Real Estate Settlement Procedures Act (12 U.S.C. §2601 et seq.) and its implementing regulation, Regulation X (24 C.F.R. Part 3500), as they might be amended from time to time, or any additional or successor legislation or regulation that governs the same subject matter. As used in this Security Instrument, "RESPA" refers to all requirements and restrictions that are imposed in regard to a "federally related mortgage loan" even if the Loan does not qualify as a "federally related mortgage loan" under RESPA.

(P) **"Successor in Interest of Borrower"** means any party that has taken title to the Property, whether or not that party has assumed Borrower's obligations under the Note and/or this Security Instrument.

TRANSFER OF RIGHTS IN THE PROPERTY

This Security Instrument secures to Lender: (i) the repayment of the Loan, and all renewals, extensions and modifications of the Note; and (ii) the performance of Borrower's covenants and agreements under this Security Instrument and the Note. For this purpose, Borrower does hereby grant and convey to Lender and Lender's successors and assigns, with power of sale, the following described property located in the _____

[Type of Recording Jurisdiction]

of _____:

[Name of Recording Jurisdiction]

which currently has the address of _____
[Street]
_____, Georgia _____ ("Property Address"):
[City] [Zip Code]

TO HAVE AND TO HOLD this property unto Lender and Lender's successors and assigns, forever, together with all the improvements now or hereafter erected on the property, and all easements, appurtenances, and fixtures now or hereafter a part of the property. All replacements and additions shall also be covered by this Security Instrument. All of the foregoing is referred to in this Security Instrument as the "Property."

BORROWER COVENANTS that Borrower is lawfully seised of the estate hereby conveyed and has the right to grant and convey the Property and that the Property is unencumbered, except for encumbrances of record. Borrower warrants and will defend generally the title to the Property against all claims and demands, subject to any encumbrances of record.

THIS SECURITY INSTRUMENT combines uniform covenants for national use and non-uniform covenants with limited variations by jurisdiction to constitute a uniform security instrument covering real property.

UNIFORM COVENANTS. Borrower and Lender covenant and agree as follows:

1. Payment of Principal, Interest, Escrow Items, Prepayment Charges, and Late Charges. Borrower shall pay when due the principal of, and interest on, the debt evidenced by the Note and any prepayment charges and late charges due under the Note. Borrower shall also pay funds for Escrow Items pursuant to Section 3. Payments due under the Note and this Security Instrument shall be made in U.S. currency. However, if any check or other instrument received by Lender as payment under the Note or this Security Instrument is returned to Lender unpaid, Lender may require that any or all subsequent payments due under the Note and this Security Instrument be made in one or more of the following forms, as selected by Lender: (a) cash; (b) money order; (c) certified check, bank check, treasurer's check or cashier's check, provided any such check is drawn upon an institution whose deposits are insured by a federal agency, instrumentality, or entity; or (d) Electronic Funds Transfer.

Payments are deemed received by Lender when received at the location designated in the Note or at such other location as may be designated by Lender in accordance with the notice provisions in Section 15. Lender may return any payment or partial payment if the payment or partial payments are insufficient to bring the Loan current. Lender may accept any payment or partial payment insufficient to bring the Loan current, without waiver of any rights hereunder or prejudice to its rights to refuse such payment or partial payments in the future, but Lender is not obligated to apply such payments at the time such payments are accepted. If each Periodic Payment is applied as of its scheduled due date, then Lender need not pay interest on unapplied funds. Lender may hold such unapplied funds until Borrower makes payment to bring the Loan current. If Borrower does not do so within a reasonable period of time, Lender shall either apply such funds or return them to Borrower. If not applied earlier, such funds will be applied to the outstanding principal balance under the Note immediately prior to foreclosure. No offset or claim which Borrower might have now or in the future against Lender shall relieve Borrower from making payments due under the Note and this Security Instrument or performing the covenants and agreements secured by this Security Instrument.

    2.   **Application of Payments or Proceeds.** Except as otherwise described in this Section 2, all payments accepted and applied by Lender shall be applied in the following order of priority: (a) interest due under the Note; (b) principal due under the Note; (c) amounts due under Section 3. Such payments shall be applied to each Periodic Payment in the order in which it became due. Any remaining amounts shall be applied first to late charges, second to any other amounts due under this Security Instrument, and then to reduce the principal balance of the Note.

    If Lender receives a payment from Borrower for a delinquent Periodic Payment which includes a sufficient amount to pay any late charge due, the payment may be applied to the delinquent payment and the late charge. If more than one Periodic Payment is outstanding, Lender may apply any payment received from Borrower to the repayment of the Periodic Payments if, and to the extent that, each payment can be paid in full. To the extent that any excess exists after the payment is applied to the full payment of one or more Periodic Payments, such excess may be applied to any late charges due. Voluntary prepayments shall be applied first to any prepayment charges and then as described in the Note.

    Any application of payments, insurance proceeds, or Miscellaneous Proceeds to principal due under the Note shall not extend or postpone the due date, or change the amount, of the Periodic Payments.

    3.   **Funds for Escrow Items.** Borrower shall pay to Lender on the day Periodic Payments are due under the Note, until the Note is paid in full, a sum (the "Funds") to provide for payment of amounts due for: (a) taxes and assessments and other items which can attain priority over this Security Instrument as a lien or encumbrance on the Property; (b) leasehold payments or ground rents on the Property, if any; (c) premiums for any and all insurance required by Lender under Section 5; and (d) Mortgage Insurance premiums, if any, or any sums payable by Borrower to Lender in lieu of the payment of Mortgage Insurance premiums in accordance with the provisions of Section 10. These items are called "Escrow Items." At origination or at any time during the term of the Loan, Lender may require that Community Association Dues, Fees, and Assessments, if any, be escrowed by Borrower, and such dues, fees and assessments shall be an Escrow Item. Borrower shall promptly furnish to Lender all notices of amounts to be paid under this Section. Borrower shall pay Lender the Funds for Escrow Items unless Lender waives Borrower's obligation to pay the Funds for any or all Escrow Items. Lender may waive Borrower's obligation to pay to Lender Funds for any or all Escrow Items at any time. Any such waiver may only be in writing. In the event of such waiver, Borrower shall pay directly, when and where payable, the amounts due for any Escrow Items for which payment of Funds has been waived by Lender and, if Lender requires, shall furnish to Lender receipts evidencing such payment within such time period as Lender may require. Borrower's obligation to make such payments and to provide receipts shall for all purposes be deemed to be a covenant and agreement contained in this Security Instrument, as the phrase "covenant and agreement" is used in Section 9. If Borrower is obligated to pay Escrow Items directly, pursuant to a waiver, and Borrower fails to pay the amount due for an Escrow Item, Lender may exercise its rights under Section 9 and pay such amount and Borrower shall then be obligated under Section 9 to repay to Lender any such amount. Lender may revoke the waiver as to any or all Escrow Items at any time by a notice given in accordance with Section 15 and, upon such revocation, Borrower shall pay to Lender all Funds, and in such amounts, that are then required under this Section 3.

Lender may, at any time, collect and hold Funds in an amount (a) sufficient to permit Lender to apply the Funds at the time specified under RESPA, and (b) not to exceed the maximum amount a lender can require under RESPA. Lender shall estimate the amount of Funds due on the basis of current data and reasonable estimates of expenditures of future Escrow Items or otherwise in accordance with Applicable Law.

The Funds shall be held in an institution whose deposits are insured by a federal agency, instrumentality, or entity (including Lender, if Lender is an institution whose deposits are so insured) or in any Federal Home Loan Bank. Lender shall apply the Funds to pay the Escrow Items no later than the time specified under RESPA. Lender shall not charge Borrower for holding and applying the Funds, annually analyzing the escrow account, or verifying the Escrow Items, unless Lender pays Borrower interest on the Funds and Applicable Law permits Lender to make such a charge. Unless an agreement is made in writing or Applicable Law requires interest to be paid on the Funds, Lender shall not be required to pay Borrower any interest or earnings on the Funds. Borrower and Lender can agree in writing, however, that interest shall be paid on the Funds. Lender shall give to Borrower, without charge, an annual accounting of the Funds as required by RESPA.

If there is a surplus of Funds held in escrow, as defined under RESPA, Lender shall account to Borrower for the excess funds in accordance with RESPA. If there is a shortage of Funds held in escrow, as defined under RESPA, Lender shall notify Borrower as required by RESPA, and Borrower shall pay to Lender the amount necessary to make up the shortage in accordance with RESPA, but in no more than 12 monthly payments. If there is a deficiency of Funds held in escrow, as defined under RESPA, Lender shall notify Borrower as required by RESPA, and Borrower shall pay to Lender the amount necessary to make up the deficiency in accordance with RESPA, but in no more than 12 monthly payments.

Upon payment in full of all sums secured by this Security Instrument, Lender shall promptly refund to Borrower any Funds held by Lender.

4.　Charges; Liens. Borrower shall pay all taxes, assessments, charges, fines, and impositions attributable to the Property which can attain priority over this Security Instrument, leasehold payments or ground rents on the Property, if any, and Community Association Dues, Fees, and Assessments, if any. To the extent that these items are Escrow Items, Borrower shall pay them in the manner provided in Section 3.

Borrower shall promptly discharge any lien which has priority over this Security Instrument unless Borrower: (a) agrees in writing to the payment of the obligation secured by the lien in a manner acceptable to Lender, but only so long as Borrower is performing such agreement; (b) contests the lien in good faith by, or defends against enforcement of the lien in, legal proceedings which in Lender's opinion operate to prevent the enforcement of the lien while those proceedings are pending, but only until such proceedings are concluded; or (c) secures from the holder of the lien an agreement satisfactory to Lender subordinating the lien to this Security Instrument. If Lender determines that any part of the Property is subject to a lien which can attain priority over this Security Instrument, Lender may give Borrower a notice identifying the lien. Within 10 days of the date on which that notice is given, Borrower shall satisfy the lien or take one or more of the actions set forth above in this Section 4.

Lender may require Borrower to pay a one-time charge for a real estate tax verification and/or reporting service used by Lender in connection with this Loan.

    5. Property Insurance. Borrower shall keep the improvements now existing or hereafter erected on the Property insured against loss by fire, hazards included within the term "extended coverage," and any other hazards including, but not limited to, earthquakes and floods, for which Lender requires insurance. This insurance shall be maintained in the amounts (including deductible levels) and for the periods that Lender requires. What Lender requires pursuant to the preceding sentences can change during the term of the Loan. The insurance carrier providing the insurance shall be chosen by Borrower subject to Lender's right to disapprove Borrower's choice, which right shall not be exercised unreasonably. Lender may require Borrower to pay, in connection with this Loan, either: (a) a one-time charge for flood zone determination, certification and tracking services; or (b) a one-time charge for flood zone determination and certification services and subsequent charges each time remappings or similar changes occur which reasonably might affect such determination or certification. Borrower shall also be responsible for the payment of any fees imposed by the Federal Emergency Management Agency in connection with the review of any flood zone determination resulting from an objection by Borrower.

    If Borrower fails to maintain any of the coverages described above, Lender may obtain insurance coverage, at Lender's option and Borrower's expense. Lender is under no obligation to purchase any particular type or amount of coverage. Therefore, such coverage shall cover Lender, but might or might not protect Borrower, Borrower's equity in the Property, or the contents of the Property, against any risk, hazard or liability and might provide greater or lesser coverage than was previously in effect. Borrower acknowledges that the cost of the insurance coverage so obtained might significantly exceed the cost of insurance that Borrower could have obtained. Any amounts disbursed by Lender under this Section 5 shall become additional debt of Borrower secured by this Security Instrument. These amounts shall bear interest at the Note rate from the date of disbursement and shall be payable, with such interest, upon notice from Lender to Borrower requesting payment.

    All insurance policies required by Lender and renewals of such policies shall be subject to Lender's right to disapprove such policies, shall include a standard mortgage clause, and shall name Lender as mortgagee and/or as an additional loss payee. Lender shall have the right to hold the policies and renewal certificates. If Lender requires, Borrower shall promptly give to Lender all receipts of paid premiums and renewal notices. If Borrower obtains any form of insurance coverage, not otherwise required by Lender, for damage to, or destruction of, the Property, such policy shall include a standard mortgage clause and shall name Lender as mortgagee and/or as an additional loss payee.

    In the event of loss, Borrower shall give prompt notice to the insurance carrier and Lender. Lender may make proof of loss if not made promptly by Borrower. Unless Lender and Borrower otherwise agree in writing, any insurance proceeds, whether or not the underlying insurance was required by Lender, shall be applied to restoration or repair of the Property, if the restoration or repair is economically feasible and Lender's security is not lessened. During such repair and restoration period, Lender shall have the right to hold such insurance proceeds until Lender has had an opportunity to inspect such Property to ensure the work has been completed to Lender's satisfaction, provided that such inspection shall be undertaken promptly. Lender may disburse proceeds for the repairs and restoration in a single payment or in a series of progress payments as the work is completed. Unless an agreement is made in writing or Applicable Law requires interest to be paid on such insurance proceeds, Lender shall not be required to pay Borrower any interest or earnings on such proceeds. Fees for public adjusters, or other third parties, retained by Borrower shall not be paid out of the insurance proceeds and shall be the sole obligation of Borrower. If the restoration or repair is not economically feasible or Lender's security would be lessened, the insurance proceeds shall be applied to the sums secured by this Security Instrument, whether or not then due, with the excess, if any, paid to Borrower. Such insurance proceeds shall be applied in the order provided for in Section 2.

If Borrower abandons the Property, Lender may file, negotiate and settle any available insurance claim and related matters. If Borrower does not respond within 30 days to a notice from Lender that the insurance carrier has offered to settle a claim, then Lender may negotiate and settle the claim. The 30-day period will begin when the notice is given. In either event, or if Lender acquires the Property under Section 22 or otherwise, Borrower hereby assigns to Lender (a) Borrower's rights to any insurance proceeds in an amount not to exceed the amounts unpaid under the Note or this Security Instrument, and (b) any other of Borrower's rights (other than the right to any refund of unearned premiums paid by Borrower) under all insurance policies covering the Property, insofar as such rights are applicable to the coverage of the Property. Lender may use the insurance proceeds either to repair or restore the Property or to pay amounts unpaid under the Note or this Security Instrument, whether or not then due.

6. Occupancy. Borrower shall occupy, establish, and use the Property as Borrower's principal residence within 60 days after the execution of this Security Instrument and shall continue to occupy the Property as Borrower's principal residence for at least one year after the date of occupancy, unless Lender otherwise agrees in writing, which consent shall not be unreasonably withheld, or unless extenuating circumstances exist which are beyond Borrower's control.

7. Preservation, Maintenance and Protection of the Property; Inspections. Borrower shall not destroy, damage or impair the Property, allow the Property to deteriorate or commit waste on the Property. Whether or not Borrower is residing in the Property, Borrower shall maintain the Property in order to prevent the Property from deteriorating or decreasing in value due to its condition. Unless it is determined pursuant to Section 5 that repair or restoration is not economically feasible, Borrower shall promptly repair the Property if damaged to avoid further deterioration or damage. If insurance or condemnation proceeds are paid in connection with damage to, or the taking of, the Property, Borrower shall be responsible for repairing or restoring the Property only if Lender has released proceeds for such purposes. Lender may disburse proceeds for the repairs and restoration in a single payment or in a series of progress payments as the work is completed. If the insurance or condemnation proceeds are not sufficient to repair or restore the Property, Borrower is not relieved of Borrower's obligation for the completion of such repair or restoration.

Lender or its agent may make reasonable entries upon and inspections of the Property. If it has reasonable cause, Lender may inspect the interior of the improvements on the Property. Lender shall give Borrower notice at the time of or prior to such an interior inspection specifying such reasonable cause.

    8. Borrower's Loan Application. Borrower shall be in default if, during the Loan application process, Borrower or any persons or entities acting at the direction of Borrower or with Borrower's knowledge or consent gave materially false, misleading, or inaccurate information or statements to Lender (or failed to provide Lender with material information) in connection with the Loan. Material representations include, but are not limited to, representations concerning Borrower's occupancy of the Property as Borrower's principal residence.

    9. Protection of Lender's Interest in the Property and Rights Under this Security Instrument. If (a) Borrower fails to perform the covenants and agreements contained in this Security Instrument, (b) there is a legal proceeding that might significantly affect Lender's interest in the Property and/or rights under this Security Instrument (such as a proceeding in bankruptcy, probate, for condemnation or forfeiture, for enforcement of a lien which may attain priority over this Security Instrument or to enforce laws or regulations), or (c) Borrower has abandoned the Property, then Lender may do and pay for whatever is reasonable or appropriate to protect Lender's interest in the Property and rights under this Security Instrument, including protecting and/or assessing the value of the Property, and securing and/or repairing the Property (as set forth below). Lender's actions can include, but are not limited to: (a) paying any sums secured by a lien which has priority over this Security Instrument; (b) appearing in court; and (c) paying reasonable attorneys' fees to protect its interest in the Property and/or rights under this Security Instrument, including its secured position in a bankruptcy proceeding. Securing the Property includes, but is not limited to, making repairs, replacing doors and windows, draining water from pipes, and eliminating building or other code violations or dangerous conditions. Although Lender may take action under this Section 9, Lender does not have to do so and is not under any duty or obligation to do so. It is agreed that Lender incurs no liability for not taking any or all actions authorized under this Section 9.

    Any amounts disbursed by Lender under this Section 9 shall become additional debt of Borrower secured by this Security Instrument. These amounts shall bear interest at the Note rate from the date of disbursement and shall be payable, with such interest, upon notice from Lender to Borrower requesting payment.

    If this Security Instrument is on a leasehold, Borrower shall comply with all the provisions of the lease. If Borrower acquires fee title to the Property, the leasehold and the fee title shall not merge unless Lender agrees to the merger in writing.

    10. Mortgage Insurance. If Lender required Mortgage Insurance as a condition of making the Loan, Borrower shall pay the premiums required to maintain the Mortgage Insurance in effect. If, for any reason, the Mortgage Insurance coverage required by Lender ceases to be available from the mortgage insurer that previously provided such insurance and Borrower was required to make separately designated payments toward the premiums for Mortgage Insurance, Borrower shall pay the premiums required to obtain coverage substantially equivalent to the Mortgage Insurance previously in effect, at a cost substantially equivalent to the cost to Borrower of the Mortgage Insurance previously in effect, from an alternate mortgage insurer selected by Lender. If substantially equivalent Mortgage

Insurance coverage is not available, Borrower shall continue to pay to Lender the amount of the separately designated payments that were due when the insurance coverage ceased to be in effect. Lender will accept, use and retain these payments as a non-refundable loss reserve in lieu of Mortgage Insurance. Such loss reserve shall be non-refundable, notwithstanding the fact that the Loan is ultimately paid in full, and Lender shall not be required to pay Borrower any interest or earnings on such loss reserve. Lender can no longer require loss reserve payments if Mortgage Insurance coverage (in the amount and for the period that Lender requires) provided by an insurer selected by Lender again becomes available, is obtained, and Lender requires separately designated payments toward the premiums for Mortgage Insurance. If Lender required Mortgage Insurance as a condition of making the Loan and Borrower was required to make separately designated payments toward the premiums for Mortgage Insurance, Borrower shall pay the premiums required to maintain Mortgage Insurance in effect, or to provide a non-refundable loss reserve, until Lender's requirement for Mortgage Insurance ends in accordance with any written agreement between Borrower and Lender providing for such termination or until termination is required by Applicable Law. Nothing in this Section 10 affects Borrower's obligation to pay interest at the rate provided in the Note.

Mortgage Insurance reimburses Lender (or any entity that purchases the Note) for certain losses it may incur if Borrower does not repay the Loan as agreed. Borrower is not a party to the Mortgage Insurance.

Mortgage insurers evaluate their total risk on all such insurance in force from time to time, and may enter into agreements with other parties that share or modify their risk, or reduce losses. These agreements are on terms and conditions that are satisfactory to the mortgage insurer and the other party (or parties) to these agreements. These agreements may require the mortgage insurer to make payments using any source of funds that the mortgage insurer may have available (which may include funds obtained from Mortgage Insurance premiums).

As a result of these agreements, Lender, any purchaser of the Note, another insurer, any reinsurer, any other entity, or any affiliate of any of the foregoing, may receive (directly or indirectly) amounts that derive from (or might be characterized as) a portion of Borrower's payments for Mortgage Insurance, in exchange for sharing or modifying the mortgage insurer's risk, or reducing losses. If such agreement provides that an affiliate of Lender takes a share of the insurer's risk in exchange for a share of the premiums paid to the insurer, the arrangement is often termed "captive reinsurance." Further:

(a) **Any such agreements will not affect the amounts that Borrower has agreed to pay for Mortgage Insurance, or any other terms of the Loan. Such agreements will not increase the amount Borrower will owe for Mortgage Insurance, and they will not entitle Borrower to any refund.**

(b) **Any such agreements will not affect the rights Borrower has - if any - with respect to the Mortgage Insurance under the Homeowners Protection Act of 1998 or any other law. These rights may include the right to receive certain disclosures, to request and obtain cancellation of the Mortgage Insurance, to have the Mortgage Insurance terminated automatically, and/or to receive a refund of any Mortgage Insurance premiums that were unearned at the time of such cancellation or termination.**

11. Assignment of Miscellaneous Proceeds; Forfeiture. All Miscellaneous Proceeds are hereby assigned to and shall be paid to Lender.

If the Property is damaged, such Miscellaneous Proceeds shall be applied to restoration or repair of the Property, if the restoration or repair is economically feasible and Lender's security is not lessened. During such repair and restoration period, Lender shall have the right to hold such Miscellaneous Proceeds until Lender has had an opportunity to inspect such Property to ensure the work has been completed to Lender's satisfaction, provided that such inspection shall be undertaken promptly. Lender may pay for the repairs and restoration in a single disbursement or in a series of progress payments as the work is completed. Unless an agreement is made in writing or Applicable Law requires interest to be paid on such Miscellaneous Proceeds, Lender shall not be required to pay Borrower any interest or earnings on such Miscellaneous Proceeds. If the restoration or repair is not economically feasible or Lender's security would be lessened, the Miscellaneous Proceeds shall be applied to the sums secured by this Security Instrument, whether or not then due, with the excess, if any, paid to Borrower. Such Miscellaneous Proceeds shall be applied in the order provided for in Section 2.

In the event of a total taking, destruction, or loss in value of the Property, the Miscellaneous Proceeds shall be applied to the sums secured by this Security Instrument, whether or not then due, with the excess, if any, paid to Borrower.

In the event of a partial taking, destruction, or loss in value of the Property in which the fair market value of the Property immediately before the partial taking, destruction, or loss in value is equal to or greater than the amount of the sums secured by this Security Instrument immediately before the partial taking, destruction, or loss in value, unless Borrower and Lender otherwise agree in writing, the sums secured by this Security Instrument shall be reduced by the amount of the Miscellaneous Proceeds multiplied by the following fraction: (a) the total amount of the sums secured immediately before the partial taking, destruction, or loss in value divided by (b) the fair market value of the Property immediately before the partial taking, destruction, or loss in value. Any balance shall be paid to Borrower.

In the event of a partial taking, destruction, or loss in value of the Property in which the fair market value of the Property immediately before the partial taking, destruction, or loss in value is less than the amount of the sums secured immediately before the partial taking, destruction, or loss in value, unless Borrower and Lender otherwise agree in writing, the Miscellaneous Proceeds shall be applied to the sums secured by this Security Instrument whether or not the sums are then due.

If the Property is abandoned by Borrower, or if, after notice by Lender to Borrower that the Opposing Party (as defined in the next sentence) offers to make an award to settle a claim for damages, Borrower fails to respond to Lender within 30 days after the date the notice is given, Lender is authorized to collect and apply the Miscellaneous Proceeds either to restoration or repair of the Property or to the sums secured by this Security Instrument, whether or not then due. "Opposing Party" means the third party that owes Borrower Miscellaneous Proceeds or the party against whom Borrower has a right of action in regard to Miscellaneous Proceeds.

Borrower shall be in default if any action or proceeding, whether civil or criminal, is begun that, in Lender's judgment, could result in forfeiture of the Property or other material impairment of Lender's interest in the Property or rights under this Security Instrument. Borrower can cure such a default and, if acceleration has occurred, reinstate as provided in Section 19, by causing the action or proceeding to be dismissed with a ruling that, in Lender's judgment, precludes forfeiture of the Property or other material impairment of Lender's interest in the Property or rights under this Security Instrument. The proceeds of any award or claim for damages that are attributable to the impairment of Lender's interest in the Property are hereby assigned and shall be paid to Lender.

All Miscellaneous Proceeds that are not applied to restoration or repair of the Property shall be applied in the order provided for in Section 2.

12. Borrower Not Released; Forbearance By Lender Not a Waiver. Extension of the time for payment or modification of amortization of the sums secured by this Security Instrument granted by Lender to Borrower or any Successor in Interest of Borrower shall not operate to release the liability of Borrower or any Successors in Interest of Borrower. Lender shall not be required to commence proceedings against any Successor in Interest of Borrower or to refuse to extend time for payment or otherwise modify amortization of the sums secured by this Security Instrument by reason of any demand made by the original Borrower or any Successors in Interest of Borrower. Any forbearance by Lender in exercising any right or remedy including, without limitation, Lender's acceptance of payments from third persons, entities or Successors in Interest of Borrower or in amounts less than the amount then due, shall not be a waiver of or preclude the exercise of any right or remedy.

13. Joint and Several Liability; Co-signers; Successors and Assigns Bound. Borrower covenants and agrees that Borrower's obligations and liability shall be joint and several. However, any Borrower who co-signs this Security Instrument but does not execute the Note (a "co-signer"): (a) is co-signing this Security Instrument only to mortgage, grant and convey the co-signer's interest in the Property under the terms of this Security Instrument; (b) is not personally obligated to pay the sums secured by this Security Instrument; and (c) agrees that Lender and any other Borrower can agree to extend, modify, forbear or make any accommodations with regard to the terms of this Security Instrument or the Note without the co-signer's consent.

Subject to the provisions of Section 18, any Successor in Interest of Borrower who assumes Borrower's obligations under this Security Instrument in writing, and is approved by Lender, shall obtain all of Borrower's rights and benefits under this Security Instrument. Borrower shall not be released from Borrower's obligations and liability under this Security Instrument unless Lender agrees to such release in writing. The covenants and agreements of this Security Instrument shall bind (except as provided in Section 20) and benefit the successors and assigns of Lender.

14. Loan Charges. Lender may charge Borrower fees for services performed in connection with Borrower's default, for the purpose of protecting Lender's interest in the Property and rights under this Security Instrument, including, but not limited to, attorneys' fees, property inspection and valuation fees. In regard to any other fees, the absence of express authority in this Security Instrument to charge a specific fee to Borrower shall not be construed as a prohibition on the charging of such fee. Lender may not charge fees that are expressly prohibited by this Security Instrument or by Applicable Law.

If the Loan is subject to a law which sets maximum loan charges, and that law is finally interpreted so that the interest or other loan charges collected or to be collected in connection with the Loan exceed the permitted limits, then: (a) any such loan charge shall be reduced by the amount necessary to reduce the charge to the permitted limit; and (b) any sums already collected from Borrower which exceeded permitted limits will be refunded to Borrower. Lender may choose to make this refund by reducing the principal owed under the Note or by making a direct payment to Borrower. If a refund reduces principal, the reduction will be treated as a partial prepayment without any prepayment charge (whether or not a prepayment charge is provided for under the Note). Borrower's acceptance of any such refund made by direct payment to Borrower will constitute a waiver of any right of action Borrower might have arising out of such overcharge.

15. Notices. All notices given by Borrower or Lender in connection with this Security Instrument must be in writing. Any notice to Borrower in connection with this Security Instrument shall be deemed to have been given to Borrower when mailed by first class mail or when actually delivered to Borrower's notice address if sent by other means. Notice to any one Borrower shall constitute notice to all Borrowers unless Applicable Law expressly requires otherwise. The notice address shall be the Property Address unless Borrower has designated a substitute notice address by notice to Lender. Borrower shall promptly notify Lender of Borrower's change of address. If Lender specifies a procedure for reporting Borrower's change of address, then Borrower shall only report a change of address through that specified procedure. There may be only one designated notice address under this Security Instrument at any one time. Any notice to Lender shall be given by delivering it or by mailing it by first class mail to Lender's address stated herein unless Lender has designated another address by notice to Borrower. Any notice in connection with this Security Instrument shall not be deemed to have been given to Lender until actually received by Lender. If any notice required by this Security Instrument is also required under Applicable Law, the Applicable Law requirement will satisfy the corresponding requirement under this Security Instrument.

16. Governing Law; Severability; Rules of Construction. This Security Instrument shall be governed by federal law and the law of the jurisdiction in which the Property is located. All rights and obligations contained in this Security Instrument are subject to any requirements and limitations of Applicable Law. Applicable Law might explicitly or implicitly allow the parties to agree by contract or it might be silent, but such silence shall not be construed as a prohibition against agreement by contract. In the event that any provision or clause of this Security Instrument or the Note conflicts with Applicable Law, such conflict shall not affect other provisions of this Security Instrument or the Note which can be given effect without the conflicting provision.

As used in this Security Instrument: (a) words of the masculine gender shall mean and include corresponding neuter words or words of the feminine gender; (b) words in the singular shall mean and include the plural and vice versa; and (c) the word "may" gives sole discretion without any obligation to take any action.

17. Borrower's Copy. Borrower shall be given one copy of the Note and of this Security Instrument.

18. Transfer of the Property or a Beneficial Interest in Borrower. As used in this Section 18, "Interest in the Property" means any legal or beneficial interest in the Property, including, but not limited to, those beneficial interests transferred in a bond for deed, contract for deed, installment sales contract or escrow agreement, the intent of which is the transfer of title by Borrower at a future date to a purchaser.

If all or any part of the Property or any Interest in the Property is sold or transferred (or if Borrower is not a natural person and a beneficial interest in Borrower is sold or transferred) without Lender's prior written consent, Lender may require immediate payment in full of all sums secured by this Security Instrument. However, this option shall not be exercised by Lender if such exercise is prohibited by Applicable Law.

If Lender exercises this option, Lender shall give Borrower notice of acceleration. The notice shall provide a period of not less than 30 days from the date the notice is given in accordance with Section 15 within which Borrower must pay all sums secured by this Security Instrument. If Borrower fails to pay these sums prior to the expiration of this period, Lender may invoke any remedies permitted by this Security Instrument without further notice or demand on Borrower.

19. Borrower's Right to Reinstate After Acceleration. If Borrower meets certain conditions, Borrower shall have the right to have enforcement of this Security Instrument discontinued at any time prior to the earliest of: (a) five days before sale of the Property pursuant to any power of sale contained in this Security Instrument; (b) such other period as Applicable Law might specify for the termination of Borrower's right to reinstate; or (c) entry of a judgment enforcing this Security Instrument. Those conditions are that Borrower: (a) pays Lender all sums which then would be due under this Security Instrument and the Note as if no acceleration had occurred; (b) cures any default of any other covenants or agreements; (c) pays all expenses incurred in enforcing this Security Instrument, including, but not limited to, reasonable attorneys' fees, property inspection and valuation fees, and other fees incurred for the purpose of protecting Lender's interest in the Property and rights under this Security Instrument; and (d) takes such action as Lender may reasonably require to assure that Lender's interest in the Property and rights under this Security Instrument, and Borrower's obligation to pay the sums secured by this Security Instrument, shall continue unchanged. Lender may require that Borrower pay such reinstatement sums and expenses in one or more of the following forms, as selected by Lender: (a) cash; (b) money order; (c) certified check, bank check, treasurer's check or cashier's check, provided any such check is drawn upon an institution whose deposits are insured by a federal agency, instrumentality or entity; or (d) Electronic Funds Transfer. Upon reinstatement by Borrower, this Security Instrument and obligations secured hereby shall remain fully effective as if no acceleration had occurred. However, this right to reinstate shall not apply in the case of acceleration under Section 18.

20. Sale of Note; Change of Loan Servicer; Notice of Grievance. The Note or a partial interest in the Note (together with this Security Instrument) can be sold one or more times without prior notice to Borrower. A sale might result in a change in the entity (known as the "Loan Servicer") that collects Periodic Payments due under the Note and this Security Instrument and performs other mortgage loan servicing obligations under the Note, this Security Instrument, and Applicable Law. There also might be one or more changes of the Loan Servicer unrelated to a sale of the Note. If there is a change of the Loan Servicer, Borrower will be given written notice of the change which will state the name and address of the new Loan Servicer, the address to which payments should be made and any other information RESPA requires in connection with a notice of transfer of servicing. If the Note is sold and thereafter the Loan is serviced by a Loan Servicer other than the purchaser of the Note, the mortgage loan servicing obligations to Borrower will remain with the Loan Servicer or be transferred to a successor Loan Servicer and are not assumed by the Note purchaser unless otherwise provided by the Note purchaser.

Neither Borrower nor Lender may commence, join, or be joined to any judicial action (as either an individual litigant or the member of a class) that arises from the other party's actions pursuant to this Security Instrument or that alleges that the other party has breached any provision of, or any duty owed by reason of, this Security Instrument, until such Borrower or Lender has notified the other party (with such notice given in compliance with the requirements of Section 15) of such alleged breach and afforded the other party hereto a reasonable period after the giving of such notice to take corrective action. If Applicable Law provides a time period which must elapse before certain action can be taken, that time period will be deemed to be reasonable for purposes of this paragraph. The notice of acceleration and opportunity to cure given to Borrower pursuant to Section 22 and the notice of acceleration given to Borrower pursuant to Section 18 shall be deemed to satisfy the notice and opportunity to take corrective action provisions of this Section 20.

21. Hazardous Substances. As used in this Section 21: (a) "Hazardous Substances" are those substances defined as toxic or hazardous substances, pollutants, or wastes by Environmental Law and the following substances: gasoline, kerosene, other flammable or toxic petroleum products, toxic pesticides and herbicides, volatile solvents, materials containing asbestos or formaldehyde, and radioactive materials; (b) "Environmental Law" means federal laws and laws of the jurisdiction where the Property is located that relate to health, safety or environmental protection; (c) "Environmental Cleanup" includes any response action, remedial action, or removal action, as defined in Environmental Law; and (d) an "Environmental Condition" means a condition that can cause, contribute to, or otherwise trigger an Environmental Cleanup.

Borrower shall not cause or permit the presence, use, disposal, storage, or release of any Hazardous Substances, or threaten to release any Hazardous Substances, on or in the Property. Borrower shall not do, nor allow anyone else to do, anything affecting the Property (a) that is in violation of any Environmental Law, (b) which creates an Environmental Condition, or (c) which, due to the presence, use, or release of a Hazardous Substance, creates a condition that adversely affects the value of the Property. The preceding two sentences shall not apply to the presence, use, or storage on the Property of small quantities of Hazardous Substances that are generally recognized to be appropriate to normal residential uses and to maintenance of the Property (including, but not limited to, hazardous substances in consumer products).

Borrower shall promptly give Lender written notice of (a) any investigation, claim, demand, lawsuit or other action by any governmental or regulatory agency or private party involving the Property and any Hazardous Substance or Environmental Law of which Borrower has actual knowledge, (b) any Environmental Condition, including but not limited to, any spilling, leaking, discharge, release or threat of release of any Hazardous Substance, and (c) any condition caused by the presence, use or release of a Hazardous Substance which adversely affects the value of the Property. If Borrower learns, or is notified by any governmental or regulatory authority, or any private party, that any removal or other remediation of any Hazardous Substance affecting the Property is necessary, Borrower shall promptly take all necessary remedial actions in accordance with Environmental Law. Nothing herein shall create any obligation on Lender for an Environmental Cleanup.

NON-UNIFORM COVENANTS. Borrower and Lender further covenant and agree as follows:

22. Acceleration; Remedies. Lender shall give notice to Borrower prior to acceleration following Borrower's breach of any covenant or agreement in this Security Instrument (but not prior to acceleration under Section 18 unless Applicable Law provides otherwise). The notice shall specify: (a) the default; (b) the action required to cure the default; (c) a date, not less than 30 days from the date the notice is given to Borrower, by which the default must be cured; and (d) that failure to cure the default on or before the date specified in the notice may result in acceleration of the sums secured by this Security Instrument and sale of the Property. The notice shall further inform Borrower of the right to reinstate after acceleration and the right to bring a court action to assert the non-existence of a default or any other defense of Borrower to acceleration and sale. If the default is not cured on or before the date specified in the notice, Lender at its option may require immediate payment in full of all sums secured by this Security Instrument without further demand and may invoke the power of sale granted by Borrower and any other remedies permitted by Applicable Law. Borrower appoints Lender the agent and attorney-in-fact for Borrower to exercise the power of sale. Lender shall be entitled to collect all expenses incurred in pursuing the remedies provided in this Section 22, including, but not limited to, reasonable attorneys' fees and costs of title evidence.

If Lender invokes the power of sale, Lender shall give a copy of a notice of sale by public advertisement for the time and in the manner prescribed by Applicable Law. Lender, without further demand on Borrower, shall sell the Property at public auction to the highest bidder at the time and place and under the terms designated in the notice of sale in one or more parcels and in any order Lender determines. Lender or its designee may purchase the Property at any sale.

Lender shall convey to the purchaser indefeasible title to the Property, and Borrower hereby appoints Lender Borrower's agent and attorney-in-fact to make such conveyance. The recitals in the Lender's deed shall be prima facie evidence of the truth of the statements made therein. Borrower covenants and agrees that Lender shall apply the proceeds of the sale in the following order: (a) to all expenses of the sale, including, but not limited to, reasonable attorneys' fees; (b) to all sums secured by this Security Instrument; and (c) any excess to the person or persons legally entitled to it. The power and agency granted are coupled with an interest, are irrevocable by death or otherwise and are cumulative to the remedies for collection of debt as provided by Applicable Law.

If the Property is sold pursuant to this Section 22, Borrower, or any person holding possession of the Property through Borrower, shall immediately surrender possession of the Property to the purchaser at the sale. If possession is not surrendered, Borrower or such person shall be a tenant holding over and may be dispossessed in accordance with Applicable Law.

23. Release. Upon payment of all sums secured by this Security Instrument, Lender shall cancel this Security Instrument. Borrower shall pay any recordation costs. Lender may charge Borrower a fee for releasing this Security Instrument, but only if the fee is paid to a third party for services rendered and the charging of the fee is permitted under Applicable Law.

24. Waiver of Homestead. Borrower waives all rights of homestead exemption in the Property.

25. Assumption Not a Novation. Lender's acceptance of an assumption of the obligations of this Security Instrument and the Note, and any release of Borrower in connection therewith, shall not constitute a novation.

26. Security Deed. This conveyance is to be construed under the existing laws of the State of Georgia as a deed passing title, and not as a mortgage, and is intended to secure the payment of all sums secured hereby.

BORROWER ACCEPTS AND AGREES to the terms and covenants contained in this Security Instrument and in any Rider executed by Borrower and recorded with it.

IN WITNESS WHEREOF, Borrower has signed and sealed this Security Instrument.

Signed, sealed and delivered in the presence of:

_____   _____(Seal)
Unofficial Witness   - Borrower

_____   _____(Seal)
                                                                                             - Borrower

Notary Public, _____ County_____

_____**[Space Below This Line For Acknowledgment]**_____

INDEX & GLOSSARY

Abstract of title [a summary of all recorded documents affecting title to a given parcel of land], 424–425
Acceleration clause [allows the lender to demand immediate payment of the entire loan if the borrower defaults], 306–307
Accession, 411
Accountability, of brokers, 145–146
Accredited resident manager (ARM), 444, 521
Accretion [a gradual addition to land], 411
Accrued interest, prorating, 380–381
Acknowledgment [a formal declaration by a person signing a document that s/he did, in fact, sign the document], 419–420, *421*
Acre [43,560 square feet], 43–44, *44*
Act of the parties, termination of agency by, 158
Actual age, 358
Actual eviction [the removal of a defaulting tenant through legal proceedings], 442
Actual notice [knowledge gained from what one has actually seen, heard, read, or observed], 417
ADA (Americans with Disabilities Act) [a federal law giving disabled individuals the right to access commercial facilities open to the public], 97–99
Addendums, 206
Adjustable-rate mortgages (ARMs) [mortgages on which the interest rate rises and falls with changes in prevailing interest rates], 240, 279–283, *280*
Adjusted market price, *346*, 348–349
Adjusted sales price, 330
Adjustment period, 281
Adjustment process, 345
Administrator/administratrix, 407
Ad valorem taxes [taxes charged according to the value of a property], 322
Advance cost listings, 186–187
Advance fee listings [listings in which a broker gets paid in advance and charges an hourly rate], 186–187
Adverse Action, Notice of, 102
Adverse possession [acquisition of land through prolonged and unauthorized occupation], 408–409, *410*
Advertising
 blind, 494
 of loans, 245–246
 property, 492–494
Affordable housing loans [an umbrella term that covers many slightly different loans that target first-time home buyers and low- to moderate-income borrowers], 287–288
Age
 building, *346*, 347
 in credit application evaluation, 101
Age/life method, 358
Agency [created when the principal delegates to the agent the right to act on behalf of the principal], 480
 accountability for actions and funds received in, 145–146
 authority of, 140–141
 buyer, 151–152
 confidentiality of, 144
 coupled with an interest, 141
 designated, 155, 505, 507–508
 disclosure, 155–156
 divided, 154–155
 dual, 154–155, 480, 505, 507
 by estoppel, 141
 full disclosure to, 144–145
 honesty, fairness, and integrity in, 146–147
 loyalty in, 142–143
 obedience in, 143–144
 in purchase contracts, 203
 by ratification, 141
 reasonable care in, 146
 representation problems of, 155–156
 single, 506–507
 termination of, 156–158, 192–193
 types of, 140
Agent [the person empowered to act by and on behalf of the principal], 140–141
 closing duties of, 374–375
 principal's obligations to, 152–153
 tax advice and liability of, 334
Agreement
 compromise, VA loans and, 238
 fixtures and, 34
 property management, 485–486, 520
 termination of agency by, 157
Agreement of sale, 208–211
Agricultural Credit Act of 1987, 271
Air lots, 48, *48*
Air rights, 29, *29*

Alienation clause [requires immediate repayment of the loan if ownership transfers], 275, 306
Alienation of title, 413
Alimony, in credit application evaluation, 101
Allodial system, 53, 55
Alluvion [the increase of land caused by the gradual depositing of water borne soil], 411
ALTA Settlement Statement-Combined, 393
Alternative business models, 193–194
Amendatory language clause, 205
Amendment, 129–130
American Land Title Association, 393
Americans with Disabilities Act (ADA) [a federal law giving disabled individuals the right to access commercial facilities open to the public], 97–99
Amortization tables, 224–226, *226*
Amortized loans, partially, 227–228, *228*
Amortized loans [loans requiring periodic payments that include both interest and partial repayment of principal], 223–227, *224–226*
Amount financed, 246
Amount realized [the sales price of a property less commissions and closing costs; also called adjusted sales price], 330
AMP (Applied Measurement Professionals, Inc.), 14–15
Annexation, 411
Annexing party, intentions of, 33–34
Annual meetings, of condominium owners' associations, 113
Annual percentage rate (APR) [calculated under the federal Truth in Lending Act by combining the interest rate with other costs of the loan], 246
Anticipation, principle of, 340
Antitrust laws, 159–161, 528–531
Appealing an assessment, 325

Applied Measurement Professionals, Inc. (AMP), 14–15
Apportionment, 329
Appraisal [an estimate of the value of something], 7–8, 322–323
  approaches to, 363–364
  best estimate in, 364–365
  CMA for, 350–352, *351*
  of condominiums, townhouses, and cooperatives, 349–350
  cost approach for, 343, *354*, 354–359, *357*, 363–364
  formal/informal, 339
  income approach for, 343, 359–364, *360*, *363*
  market comparison approach for, 343–354, *346*, *351*, *353*, *354*, 363–364
  purpose and use of, 339
  reconciliation of approaches for, 364
  of vacant land, 350
  value in, 340–343
Appraisal reports, copies of, 102–103
Appropriation process, 322
Appurtenances [improvements, rights, or privileges that are part of the land and pass with the ownership], 30, 35
APR (annual percentage rate) [calculated under the federal Truth in Lending Act by combining the interest rate with other costs of the loan], 246
ARM (accredited resident manager), 444, 521
Arm's-length transactions, 339
ARMs (adjustable-rate mortgages) [mortgages on which the interest rate rises and falls with changes in prevailing interest rates], 240, 279–283, *280*
"As is," 150–151, 201, 511–512
Assemblage [combining two or more adjacent properties into one larger parcel], 342
Assessed value [a value placed on a property for the purpose of taxation], 323, 342

Assessment appeal board [local governmental body that hears and rules on property owner complaints of over-assessment], 325
Assessment districts, 327–328
Assessment rolls, 325, 328
Assessor's parcel number/maps, 46–47, *47*
Asset and liability analysis, 251–252
Assignee/assignor, 441
Assigning contracts, 175
Assignment [the total transfer of the lessee's rights to another party], 441
Associate brokers [licensees who meet all the requirements to be a broker of a firm but choose to work for the brokerage firm], 13, 153, 450
  independent contractor compared to, 22–23
Association dues, 113–114
Associations, professional real estate, 24–26
Assumability, 233, 240
Assumed name certificate, 17
Assumption, 309
Attachment, of fixtures, 33
Attachments, in purchase contracts, 206
Attorney-in-fact, 168
Automated underwriting systems [computerized systems for loan approval communication between a loan originator and the investor], 273–274
Avulsion [a sudden washing away of land which does not typically alter the property lines], 411

Balloon loans [any loan in which the final payment is larger than the preceding payments], 227
Banks, 480
  commercial, as mortgage lenders, 261–262
Bare title, 303
Bargain and sale deed [a deed that contains no covenants but does imply that the grantor owns the property being conveyed], 404, *404*
Baselines, *40*, 40–41

Basis [the price paid for property; used in calculating income taxes], 329–330
Benchmarks, 39–40
Beneficiary [one for whose benefit a trust is created; the lender in a deed of trust], 303
Beneficiary statement, 373
Bequest, 407
Best estimate, in appraisal, 364–365
Best evidence rule, 517
Bilateral contract [a promise exchanged for a promise], 165. See also Purchase contracts
Bill of sale, 30
Binders [short purchase contracts used to secure a real estate transaction until more formal contracts can be signed], 206–207
Biweekly payments, 229
Blanket mortgages [mortgages secured by two or more properties], 284–285
Blended-rate loans, 286
Blind ads, 494
Blind advertising, 494
Blockbusting, [the illegal practice of inducing panic selling in a neighborhood for financial gain], 95
Board of directors, of condominium owners' associations, 112–113
Board of equalization, 325
BOMA (Building Owners and Managers Association), 523
BOMI International (originally Building Owners & Managers Institute), 444
Bonds, 328
Borrower analysis, 250
Boycotting [two or more people conspiring to restrain competition], 160, 529
Branch offices, 17
Breach of contract [failure, without legal excuse, to perform as required by a contract], 176–179
Broad market, 343
Brokerage, types, 193

Brokerage agreement [the written contract between a broker and a client; also called a brokerage engagement], 450
Brokerage engagement, 480, 501–502
Brokerage firms, management of, 458–459
Brokerage relationships, 485–486
Brokerage Relationships in Real Estate Transactions Act (BRRETA) [governs real estate agency in Georgia], 184, 501–506
Broker's license, 453, 455
Brokers [those who act as agents for others in negotiating contracts or sales], 450
  accountability of, 145–146
  affiliating with, 19–22
  compensation and, 20–21, 190–192
  cooperating, 153–156
  designated agency of, 505, 507–508
  disclosure by, 144–145, 147–148, 503–504
  dual agency of, 154–155, 505, 507
  fees, 159
  honesty, fairness, and integrity of, 146–147
  legal interpretations of, 146
  listing, 203
  listing agreement and, 183–185
  locating, 21–22
  misrepresentations by, 147–148
  mortgage, 263
  obligations to client, 503
  obligations to principal, 141–147
  obligations to third parties, 147–149
  principal, 25
  qualifying, 17, 485–487
  reasonable care of, 146
  red flags and, 148–149
  sales staff of, 153
  selling, 203
  support from, 21
  training from, 20
  transaction, 154, 494–495, 508–509
  trust account management and, 489–492
BRRETA (Brokerage Relationships in Real Estate Transactions Act) [governs real estate agency in Georgia], 184, 501–506
Budgeting, in property management, 522–523
Budget mortgage, 227
Buffer zones, 131
Building age, 346, 347
Building codes [local and state laws that set minimum construction standards], 132
Building Owners and Managers Association (BOMA), 523
Bush, George H. W., 261
Business brokerage, 495
Business firm licensing, 17
Buyer agency, 151–152
Buyer appeal, 352–353
Buyer brokerage engagement agreement [the agreement between a buyer and a brokerage firm hired to represent the interests of the buyer], 187–188
Buyer representation, 513–518
Buyers, categories of, 513–515
Buyer's brokerage, 151–152
Buyer's market, 343
Bylaws [rules that govern how an owners' association will be run], 111–112

Call, 214
Call clause [requires immediate repayment of the loan if ownership transfers], 275, 306
CAM (community association management) [management of owners' associations rather than property], 527–528
Canons, 25
Capital gains tax, 331–332
Capitalize [to convert future income to current value], 359
Capitalizing income, 361–362, 363
Career opportunities, 5–10, 443
Case law, 71
Cash value, 251
Cause, 173
Caveat emptor, 150, 179

CC&Rs (covenants, conditions, and restrictions), 112
CDs (certificates of deposit), 260
CDs (closing documents), 393
Certificate of eligibility, 237
Certificate of occupancy [a government-issued document that states that a structure meets local zoning and building code requirements and is ready for use], 132
Certificate of reasonable value (CRV), 237
Certificate of reduction, 309
Certificate of sale, 315, 324–325
Certificate of title, 425, 431
Certificates of deposit (CDs), 260
Certified property manager (CPM), 444, 521
Cession deeds, 406
CFPB (Consumer Financial Protection Bureau), 245, 392
Chain of title [the linkage of property ownership that connects the present owner to the original source of title], 422–424, *423*
Change, principle of, 341
Character loans, 273–274
Chattel [an article of personal property], 30, 71
Chattel mortgage, 71, 311
Checks, *40*, 41
Children, in credit application evaluation, 101
Child support, in credit application evaluation, 101
Chunking, 293
Citations [issued by the commission as a penalty instead of imposing a sanction], 496
Civil Rights Act of 1866 [federal law that prohibits discrimination in buying, holding, or inheriting real estate], 91
Claims, title insurance, 428–429
Client [a person who has entered into a brokerage engagement], 480, 501–503, 513–515
CLO (computerized loan origination) [originating loans through the use of a networked computer system], 264
Close into escrow, 375
Closing agent [the person placed in charge of closing a real estate transaction], 389
Closing [a meeting at which the buyer pays for the property and receives a deed, and at which all other matters pertaining to the sale are concluded], 518–519
  agent's duties in, 374–375
  buyer's responsibilities at, 374
  coordination of, 519
  delays and problems with, 376
  dry, 375
  in Georgia, 372–373
  location of, 373
  prorating at, 377–388
  reporting requirements in, 376–377
  RESPA governing, 519
  seller's responsibilities at, 373–374
  statement, 375
Closing date, 372
Closing disclosure [includes a detailed accounting of the final terms of the mortgage transaction], 519
Closing documents (CDs), 393
Cloud on the title [any claim, lien, or encumbrance that impairs title to property], 405, 430
CMA (competitive market analysis), 350–352, *351*
CMBS (commercial mortgage-backed securities), 272
Code of ethics, 25–26
Codicil [an amendment or change to a will rather than a complete re-creation], 408
Coldwell Banker, 23
Color of title [some plausible but not completely clear-cut indication of ownership rights], 409–410
Commercial banks, as mortgage lenders, 261–262
Commercial brokerage careers, 5–6
Commercial finance companies, as mortgage lenders, 259, 265
Commercial mortgage-backed securities (CMBS), 272
Commercial Real Estate Broker Lien Act [a Georgia Act that allows a broker to lien a property to protect a commission right], 512–513
Commingling [the mixing of clients' or customers' funds with an agent's personal funds], 145
Commissioner [full-time employee of the commission who supervises the department], 18, 450, 451
Commissions, sales, 20–21
Commission [the Georgia Real Estate Commission, which is made up of six members], 14, 450
  creation of, 451
  operations of, 481
  organization of, 479–480
Commitments, Fannie Mae, 268–269
Common elements [those parts of a condominium that are owned by all the unit owners], 111
Common law, 71
Common law dedication, 412
Community association management (CAM) [management of owners' associations rather than property], 527–528
Community association manager's license, 452
Community property [spouses are treated as equal partners, with each owning one-half interest], 67, *81–82*, 83–84
Community Reinvestment Act (CRA) [a federal statute encouraging federally regulated lenders to increase their participation in low-income areas], 103–104
Community Solutions Program, Fannie Mae, 287
Comparables [properties similar to the subject property that have sold recently], 344, 345
Compass directions, in land descriptions, *39*, 39–40

Compensation, 20–21, 152, 190–192
Competent party [person considered legally capable of entering into a binding contract], 167–168
Competitive market analysis (CMA), 350–352, *351*
Comprehensive plan, 133–134
Compromise agreement, VA loans and, 238
Computerized loan origination (CLO) [originating loans through the use of a networked computer system], 264
Computerized MLS, 189
Computing depreciation, 358
Concurrent ownership [ownership by two or more persons at the same time]
  community property, 67, *81–82*, 83–84
  joint tenancy, 78–80, *81–82*
  tenancy by the entirety, 80, *81–82*, 83
  tenants in common, 76–78, *81–82*
Condemnation, 53–54, 59, 131
Conditional sales contracts, 208–211
Conditional-use permits, 130
Condition precedent estate, 64
Condition subsequent estate, 64
Condominium conversions, 115–116
Condominiums [individual ownership of a particular airspace plus undivided ownership of the common elements], 107
  advantages of, 116–117
  annual meetings of, 113
  appraisal of, 349–350
  board of directors of, 112–113
  bylaws of, 111–112
  CC&Rs of, 112
  common elements in, 111
  cooperatives compared to, 120
  creation of, 110
  deeds in, 112
  disadvantages of, 117
  financing of, 114–115
  land division in, *109*, 110
  maintenance fees of, 113–114
  management of, 113
  owners' associations and, 111–113
  pre-purchase considerations for, 117–118
  property taxes and insurance for, 114
  reserves for, 114
  separate elements in, 111
  voting rules of, 112
Condominium subdivision, 111
Conduits, 272
Confidentiality
  of agency, 144
  between parties, 154–155
Conformity, principle of, 341
Consent
  informed, 156
  notice of, 16
Consequential damages, 54
Consideration [the promise or payment of something good or valuable], 172–173, 399
Constitutional concepts, fair housing and, 90–91
Construction costs, estimating, 355–356, *357*
Construction loans [short-term loans for new construction or remodeling of an existing structure], 285–286
Construction regulations, on FHA loans, 235
Constructive eviction [for all intents and purposes, typically because of an action or inaction of the landlord, the tenant cannot use the property for the intended purpose], 442
Constructive notice [notice given by the public records and by visible possession, coupled with the legal presumption that all persons are thereby notified], 416, 431
Consulting careers, 9
Consumer Financial Protection Bureau (CFPB), 245, 392
The Consumer Handbook on Adjustable Rate Mortgages, 282
Consummation, 393
Contingency fees, 186–187
Continuing education, 14, 453, 484
Contour maps, 48, *48*
Contract contingencies, 518
Contract for deed, 208–211, 291
Contracts [an agreement to do (or not to do) a particular thing], 164
  assigning, 175
  bilateral, 165
  breach of, 176–179
  conflicting information in, 516–517
  employment, 22
  enforceable, 166, 167, 169, 172, 174–176
  essential elements of, 166–175
  expressed, 165
  implied, 165
  implied obligations of, 179
  installment, 208–211, 291
  invalid, 166
  "no sale, no commission," 191
  option, 211–214
  performance and discharge of, 175–176
  purchase, 198–208, 210–211
  purpose of, 174–175, 197–198
  unenforceable, 166
  unilateral, 165–166
  valid, 166, 167
  void, 166, 167
  voidable, 166, 167
  written, 174–175, 177, 179
Contribution, principle of, 342
Conventional loans [real estate loans that are not insured by the FHA or guaranteed by the VA], 227
Conversion, 145
Conveyance
  of property after death, 406–408
  taxes, 334–335
  in tenants in common, 77
Cooperating brokers, 153–156
Cooperatives [land and building owned or leased by a corporation that, in turn, leases space to its shareholders], 118
  appraisal of, 349–350
  condominiums compared to, 120
  default in, 119

financing of, 119
governing of, 120
land division in, *109*, 110
resale and, 120
Cooperators, 119
Corner lots, 49, *49*
Corporations, as parties to a contract, 168
Correction deeds, 406
Correction lines, *40*, 41
Corrective maintenance, 521
Correlation process, *346*, 349
Cost approach [land value plus current construction costs minus depreciation], 343, *354*, 354–359, *357*, 363–364
Cost handbooks, 356, *357*
Counteroffer [an offer made in response to an offer], 169–170, 517–518
County occupational tax, 463
Covenants [written agreements or promises], 400–402
Covenant against encumbrances, 401
Covenant of further assurance, 401
Covenant of good repair, 306
Covenant of quiet enjoyment, 400–401, 439
Covenant of seizin, 400
Covenants, conditions, and restrictions (CC&Rs), 112
Covenant to pay insurance, 305–306
Covenant to pay taxes, 305
CPM (certified property manager), 444, 521
CRA (Community Reinvestment Act) [a federal statute encouraging federally regulated lenders to increase their participation in low-income areas], 103–104
Credit application evaluation, 100–101
Credit denial, 102
Credit history, in credit application evaluation, 101
Credit report [a report reflecting the creditworthiness of a borrower by showing credit history], 253–255
Credit scoring, 254

Credit unions, as mortgage lenders, 265
Crops, ownership of, 34–35
CRV (certificate of reasonable value), 237
Cul-de-sac, 49, *49*
Curable depreciation, 357
Curtesy, 66, 80
Custodial maintenance, 520
Customer [a person who has not entered into a brokerage engagement], 480, 501–502, 515
Cyber fraud, 374

Datum, 48
DBA (doing business as), 17
Death
conveyance of property after, 406–408
termination of agency by, 157
Debt cancellation/deed transfer, 294
Debt priorities, 309–311
Debt service, 301
Deceased party, 176
Deceased's intentions, protection of, 407–408
Declarations, 252
Decreasing returns, principle of, 341
Dedication, 412
Deed covenants, 61
Deed in lieu of foreclosure, 316
Deed of confirmation, 406
Deed of trust [a document that conveys naked title to a neutral third party (a trustee) as security for a debt], 300, 303–304, 406
Deed restrictions, 61, 132–133
Deeds [written documents that, when properly executed and delivered, convey title to land]. *See also* Security deed
bargain and sale, 404, *404*
cession, 406
in condominiums, 112
correction, 406
essential elements of, 398–402, *400*
executor's, 407
general warranty, 402, *403*
gift, 405–406
guardian's, 406

interspousal, 406
quitclaim, 404–405, *405*
sheriff's, 314–315, 406
special warranty, 402
Deed to secure debt, 406. *See also* Security deed
Deed transfer tax, 344
Default [failure to perform a legal duty, such as failure to carry out the terms of a contract], 202
in cooperatives, 119
on deed of trust, 304
notice of, 315
on promissory note, 302
Defeasance clause [lender must cancel the security instrument upon full payment], 307
Defeasible fee estate, 64–65
Deficiency judgment [a judgment against a borrower if the foreclosure sale does not bring enough to pay the balance owed], 314
Delinquent loans, 311–312
Demand, 340
Denial, credit, 102
Department of Housing and Urban Development (HUD), 96, 148, 158–159, 234–235, 269, 287, 523–524. *See also* Fair housing laws
Department of Veterans Affairs (VA), 232, 236–240, *239*, 282
Depreciation [loss in value due to deterioration and obsolescence]
computing, 358
curable, 357
fictional, 362–363
incurable, 357
physical, 356
Designated agency, 155, 505, 507–508
Desktop Underwriter˚/Desktop Originator˚, 273
Determinable estate, fee simple, 64
Development, advance planning, 133–134
Devise/devisee, 407
Disaffirm, 167, 171
Disclosures
agency, 155–156
in ARMS, 282

of brokerage relationships, 486
by brokers, 144–145, 147–148, 503–504
closing, 519
dual agency, 155
insulation, 205
lead-based paint, 148, 205
lending, 246–247
seller disclosure form, 149–151
Discount points, 231–232
Discrimination. *See also* fair housing laws
by creditors, 99–103
against handicapped, 97–99
in housing, 90–99, 495–496
Disintermediation [the process of individuals investing funds directly, often in government funds, instead of placing their money in banks and other such institutions, thus creating a scarcity of money available for traditional lending], 260
Distributees, 406
Divided agency, 154–155
Dividing land, of estates, *109*, 110
Divorce, in tenancy by the entirety, 83
Doctrine of capture, 35–36
Doctrine of prior appropriation, 35
Documentary tax [a fee or tax on deeds and other documents payable at the time of recordation], 334–335
Documents, other than maps, 46
Dodd, Christopher, 392
Dodd-Frank (Wall Street Reform and Consumer Protection Act), 245, 392
Doing business as (DBA), 17
Dominant estate, 59
Dower, 66, 80
Down payment calculation, 382–383
Downzoning [rezoning of land from a higher-density use to a lower-density use], 130
Dry closing, 375
Dual agency [representation of two or more principals in a transaction by the same agent], 154–155, 480, 505, 507
Due diligence period, in purchase contracts, 201

Due-on-sale clause [requires immediate repayment of the loan if ownership transfers], 275, 306
Duress, 172

Early payoff of loans, 229–230
Earnest money [money that accompanies an offer to purchase as evidence of good faith; earnest money is NOT consideration or required by contract law], 199, 202–203, 489, 491, 516
Easements [the right or privilege one party has to use land belonging to another for a special purpose not inconsistent with the owner's use of the land]
appurtenant, 59
by condemnation, 59
examples of, *58*, 58–64
by grant, 58
in gross, 60
by necessity, 59
party wall, 60
by prescription, 59, 410–411
by reservation, 58
termination of, 60
ECOA (Equal Credit Opportunity Act) [federal law that provides for equal credit to borrowers], 99–103, 250
Economic life, 358
Economic obsolescence [a loss in value that comes from factors outside the subject property, such as noise pollution], 357–358
Economic survey, 133
Education
careers, 9
continuing, 14, 453, 484
home buyer, 288
for licensing, 14
post-license, 483
Effective yield, 231
Efficiency, land-use, 108
Electronic Signatures in Global and National Commerce Act (E-Sign), 215–216, 418
Ellwood Tables, 362

Emblements, 34–35
Eminent domain [the right of government to take privately held land for public use, provided fair compensation is paid], 53–54, 442
Employment contract, 22
termination of, 192–193
Enabling declaration, 111
Encroachments [the unauthorized intrusion of a building or other improvement onto another person's land], 61, *61*, 410
Encumbrances [any impediment to a clear title, such as a lien, lease, or easement]
covenant against, 401
to ownership, 56–58, *57*
Enforceable contracts, 166, 167, 169, 172, 174–176
Entry and possession, 316
E&O (errors and omissions) insurance, 161
Equal Credit Opportunity Act (ECOA) [federal law that provides for equal credit to borrowers], 99–103, 250
Equitable mortgages, 318
Equitable redemption, 306
Equitable title [the legally assured future interest in legal title], 210–211
Equity mortgages, 286
Equity of redemption, 313–314
Equity sharing [an arrangement whereby a party providing financing gets a portion of the ownership graduated payment], 283–284
Equity [the market value of a property less the debt against it], 230–231
Equivalent usefulness, 355
Errors and omissions (E&O) insurance, 161
Escalator clause, 440
Escheat [when ownership of abandoned property reverts to the state], 55
Escrow, 115, 372
close into, 375
tax escrow proration, 386

Escrow account, 227
E-Sign (Electronic Signatures in Global and National Commerce Act), 215–216, 418
Estate in severalty [owned by one person; sole ownership], 76
Estate [one's legal interest or rights in land], 56
   at will, 69, 437
   for years, 68, 437
   from year to year, 69
Estate tax value, 342
ESTIMATED NET TO SELLER worksheet, 389, *391*
ESTIMATED PURCHASER COST worksheet, 389, *390*
Estoppel certificate, 309
Ethics, code of, 25–26
Eviction, 442
Exact replica, 355
Examination, in licensing, 13–14, 482–483
Exchange of promises, 172
Exclusion, income tax, 331
Exclusive agency listings, 185
Exclusive Buyer Brokerage Agreement, 188
Exclusive right-to-sell [a listing that gives the broker the right to collect a commission no matter who sells the property during the listing period], 185
Exclusive Seller Listing Agreement (Form F1), 183–185, 188
Executed, 175
Executor/executrix, 407
Executor's deed, 407
Executory, 175
Exemptions from property taxes, 325–326
Expense forecasting, 359–360, *360*
Expenses, 522–523
Expiration, termination of agency by, 157
Expressed contract [an agreement in which the parties to the contract declare their intentions—either orally or in writing—to do a particular thing], 165

Extinction of subject matter, termination of agency by, 157–158

Face amount, 251
Failure to disclose, 247–248
Fair Business Practices Act of 1975 (FBPA), 530
Fair Credit Reporting Act [federal law giving an individual the right to inspect his/her file with the credit bureau and correct any errors], 253
Fair Housing Act [federal law that specifies protected classes who are protected from discrimination; also called Title VIII], 91–97
Fair housing constitutional concepts, 90–91
Fair housing laws
   acts not covered by, 95–96
   agent's duties in, 97
   amendments to, 92–94
   blockbusting in, 95
   enforcement of, 96–97
   housing types covered by, 95
   protected classes in, 91–92
   state laws, 97, 495–496
   steering in, 94–95
Fair Isaac Corporation (FICO), 254
Fair market value, 339, 342
Fairness, of brokers, 146–147
Faithful performance, to principal, 143–144
Familial status [occurs when one or more individuals under the age of 18 are domiciled with a parent or other person having custody], 93–94
Fannie Mae (FNMA) [a real estate industry nickname for the Federal National Mortgage Association], 268–269, 272, 285, 287–288
Farm brokerage careers, 6
Farm Credit System Reform Act of 1996, 271
Farmer Mac (Federal Agricultural Mortgage Corporation), 271

Farmers Home Administration (FmHA), 241
FBPA (Fair Business Practices Act of 1975), 530
Federal Agricultural Mortgage Corporation (Farmer Mac), 271
Federal Bankruptcy Reform Act of 1978, 67
Federal clauses, in purchase contracts, 205–206
Federal Consumer Credit Protection Act. *See* Truth in Lending Act
Federal Home Loan Mortgage Corporation (FHLMC), 270–272, 295
Federal Housing Administration (FHA), 232–235, 254, 282
Federal Housing Finance Agency (FHFA), 272–273
Federal National Mortgage Association (FNMA), 268–269, 272, 285, 287–288
Federal Trade Commission (FTC), 247–248
Fee simple [the largest, most complete bundle of rights one can hold in land; land ownership]
   bundle of rights, 55–56, *56*
   upon condition precedent, 64
   determinable estate, 64
   encumbrances to, 56–58, *57*
   resort time sharing as, 122
   subject to condition subsequent, 64
FHA (Federal Housing Administration), 232–235, 254, 282
FHFA (Federal Housing Finance Agency), 272–273
FHLMC (Federal Home Loan Mortgage Corporation), 270–272, 295
Fiat money, 274
FICO (Fair Isaac Corporation), 254
Fictional depreciation [an accounting device allowed by governments as an incentive to invest in property; for tax purposes, the property is considered to be depreciating, even if it is actually going up in value], 362–363

Fictitious business name statement, 17
Fidelity insurance, 486
Fiduciary, 142
Fiduciary relationship, 141–142
15-year loan, 229
Fifth Amendment, 90
Finance charge [the total amount the credit will cost over the life of the loan], 246
Financial Institutions Reform, Recovery, and Enforcement Act (FIRREA), 261
Financial liability, VA loans and, 238
Financial Services Modernization (FSM) Act, 261
Financing
   of condominiums, 114–115
   of cooperatives, 119
   Georgia real estate, 524–526
   "rich uncle," 284
   seller, 288–290, *290*
   sources of, 258–276
   types of, 278–297
Financing contingency period, 200
Financing statements, 311
Firm [any individual or entity licensed by the commission as a broke], 450, 480
   management responsibilities of, 486–489
FIRREA (Financial Institutions Reform, Recovery, and Enforcement Act), 261
First mortgage [the mortgage loan with highest priority for repayment in the event of foreclosure], 310
Fixed expenses, 522
Fixity, of land, 32
Fixture [an object that has been attached to land physically so as to become real estate]
   agreement and, 34
   attachment of, 33
   determining, 32
   intentions of annexing party and, 33–34
   modification of, 32
   plants, trees, and crops and, 34–35
   prior liens against, 34

   relationship of the parties for, 33
   trade, 33
Flag lots, 49, *49*
Flat-fee brokerage, 193
Flat fee listings, 187
Flipping, illegal, 293
Floating interest rates, 234
FmHA (Farmers Home Administration), 241
FNMA (Federal National Mortgage Association), 268–269, 272, 285, 287–288
Forbearance, 166
Forecasting, income and expense, 359–360, *360*
Foreclosure [the procedure by which a person's property can be taken and sold to satisfy an unpaid debt], 300
   deed in lieu of, 316
   delinquent loans and, 311–312
   judicial, 312–315
   lease termination and, 443
   nonjudicial, 315–316
   overview of, *317*
   process of, 311–312
   referee's deed in, 314–315, 406
   on security deed, 307–308, 526
   short sales and, 526
   strict, 315
Forfeiture of title, 412
Form 1099-S, 376–377
Formal appraisal, 339
Formal wills, 407–408
Form F1 (Exclusive Seller Listing Agreement), 183–185, 188
Four unities [for joint tenancy, unities of possession, interest, title, and time must be present; represented by the acronym PITT], 78–79
Franchise name, 480
Franchisers, 23–24
Frank, Barney, 392
Fraud [an act intended to deceive for the purpose of inducing another to give up something of value], 168, 170
   cyber, 374
   mortgage, 292–295
   statute of, 174, 398, 416

Freddie Mac (FHLMC) [a real estate industry nickname for the Federal Home Loan Mortgage Corporation], 270–272, 295
Freehold estates, 67–68
Front-foot basis, 329
FSM (Financial Services Modernization) Act, 261
FTC (Federal Trade Commission), 247–248
Full covenant and warranty deeds, 402, *403*
Full disclosure, in agency, 144–145
Full reciprocity, 16
Full-service real estate firms, 24
Full-time investor careers, 9–10
Functional obsolescence [a loss in value due to a change in consumer demand, such as outdated kitchens and baths], 356–357
Funding fees, VA loans and, 238, *239*
Funds disbursement, from trust accounts, 491–492
Further assurance, covenant of, 401

Gain on sale, *330*, 330–331
GAR (Georgia Association of REALTORS'), 438
Garage, *346*, 347
GAR F201 Purchase and Sale Agreement, 198
GCIC (Georgia Crime Information Center) report, 15, 483
GE Capital Mortgage Insurance Corporation, 287
GEI (gross effective income), 522
General agency, 140
General liens, 62
General plan, 133–134
General warranty deeds [grantor makes full guarantee to buyer against defects of title], 402, *403*
Georgia Association of REALTORS' (GAR), 438
Georgia Crime Information Center (GCIC) report, 15, 483
Georgia Housing and Finance Authority (GHFA), 264
Georgia law practice, 500–531

Georgia license law, 449–473
Georgia Property Owners' Association Act [the Georgia law that may be used to govern a homeowners' association], 528
Georgia Real Estate Commission (GREC). *See* Commission
Georgia real estate financing, 524–526
Georgia Residential Mortgage Fraud Act, 293
Georgia Rules and Regulations, 478–496
Georgia Superior Court Clerks Cooperative Authority (GSCCCA), 420
Georgia Time-Share Act [the Georgia law that regulates the sale of properties in time increments], 531
Gift deeds, 405–406
Ginnie Mae (GNMA) [a federal agency that has some low-income housing functions but is best known for its mortgage-backed securities program], 269–270, 295
Good consideration, 173
Good repair, covenant of, 306
Google Earth, 190
Google Street View, 190
Government land rights, 53–55
Government National Mortgage Association (GNMA), 269–270, 295
Government service careers, 8
Government survey, 40–44, *40–44*
GPI (gross potential income), 522
Graduated payment mortgage [a mortgage with an interest rate and maturity that are fixed, but with a monthly payment that gradually rises because the initial monthly payments are insufficient to fully amortize the loan], 283
Graduate REALTOR® Institute (GRI), 26
Grantee [the person named in a deed who acquires ownership], 398

Grantor and grantee indexes, 421
Grantor [the person named in a deed who conveys ownership], 398, 399
Great Depression, 223, 232
GREC (Georgia Real Estate Commission). *See* Commission
GRI (Graduate REALTOR® Institute), 26
GRI (gross rent income), 522
GRM (gross rent multiplier), *353*, 353–354
Gross effective income (GEI), 522
Gross lease [tenant pays a fixed rent and the landlord pays all property expenses], 440
Gross potential income (GPI), 522
Gross rent income (GRI), 522
Gross rent multiplier (GRM), *353*, 353–354
Groundwater, 36
GSCCCA (Georgia Superior Court Clerks Cooperative Authority), 420
Guardian's deed, 406
Guide meridians, *40*, 41

Habendum clause, 401
Handicapped [having a physical or mental impairment that substantially limits one or more life activities, or having a record of such impairment], 92–93, 97–99
Handicapped person provision, 93
Hazard insurance, prorating, 379–380
Hearing [the formal process that must be offered to a person prior to imposing a sanction], 470, 479
Heirs, 406
Highest and best use [that use of a parcel of land that will produce the greatest current value], 341
HOLC (Home Owners' Loan Corporation), 223, 232
Holdover tenants, 69, 437
Holographic wills [handwritten wills with no witnesses], 408

Home Owners' Loan Corporation (HOLC), 223, 232
Homestead Act of 1862, 412
Homestead exemption, 67, 326
Homestead protection laws, 67
Honesty
 of brokers, 146–147
 in licensing, 11
House rules, 112
Houses, land division in, *109*, 110
House size, *346*, 346–347
HUD (Department of Housing and Urban Development), 96, 148, 158–159, 234–235, 269, 287, 523–524. *See also* Fair housing laws
Hypothecation, 302

Identity theft, 293–294
IDX (Internet Data Exchange), 493
Illegal flipping, 293
Illiquid, 251
Immigration residency, in credit application evaluation, 101
Immovability, of land, 30
Implied authority, 141
Implied contract [an agreement made by neither words nor writing but by actions of the parties, which indicate that they intend to create a contract], 165
Implied obligations, 179
Impound account [an account into which the lender places monthly tax and insurance payments], 227
Improvability, of land, 31
Improvement districts, 327–328
Improvements [any form of land development, such as buildings, roads, fences, and pipelines], 30
Incapacity, termination of agency by, 157
Income
 capitalizing, 361–362, *363*
 in credit application evaluation, 101
 forecasting, 359–360, *360*

gross effective/gross potential/gross rent, 522
loan application analysis of, 250–251
median, 287
net operating, 361–362
Income approach [a method of valuing a property based on the monetary returns it can be expected to produce], 343, 359–364, *360*, *363*
Income-producing properties, 5–6
Income taxes, on sale of residence, 329–332
Increasing returns, principle of, 341
Incurable depreciation, 357
Indemnification, 152–153
Independent contractor [one who contracts to do work according to his/her own methods and is responsible to employer only for the results of that work], 22–23
Indestructibility, of land, 30
Indexes, for public records, 420–424
Index leases [rent payments are adjusted periodically according to an index], 440–441
Index rate, 280
Indicated value, 349
Industrial brokerage careers, 6
Influence, undue, 172
Informal appraisal, 339
Informal reference, in land descriptions, 46
Informed consent, 156
Innocent misrepresentation, 170, 171
Inquiry notice [information the law presumes a reasonably diligent person would obtain by making further inquiry], 416–417
Inside lot, 49, *49*
Inspection
of property, 372
in purchase contracts, 200–201
right to, 518
Installment contract [a method of selling and financing property whereby the seller retains title but the buyer takes possession while making the payments], 291
equitable title and, 210–211
protections for, 209–210
public criticism of, 209
uses of, 208
vendors/vendees in, 209
Installment method [sale of real estate in which the proceeds of the sale are deferred beyond the year of sale], 332
Institute of Real Estate Management (IREM), 444, 522
Insulation disclosures, 205
Insurance
for condominiums, 114
covenant to pay, 305–306
errors and omission, 161
fidelity, 486
hazard, 379–380
mortgage, 385–386
private mortgage, 240–241, 385
prorating, 386–387
title, 425–430, *427*
Insurance value, 342
Intangibles tax proration, 388
Integrity, of brokers, 146–147
Intent, contractual, 172
Intentions of annexing party, 33–34
Interest, unity of, 78
Interest adjustments, 383–384
Interest conveyance, in notes, 300–301
Interest deductions, property taxes and, 333
Interest rate cap, 281
Interest-rate-reduction refinancing loans (IRRRLs), 239
Interest rates, 239, 280
Interim loans [short-term loans for new construction or remodeling of an existing structure], 285–286
Internal Revenue Code, 329, 331, 333, 376–377
Internal Revenue Service (IRS), 22, 330–331
Internet, visual tours and, 190
Internet Data Exchange (IDX), 493
Interspousal deeds, 406
Interstate land sales disclosure statements, 158–159
Intestate succession [when a person dies without a lasting will and testament, it directs how the deceased's assets will be distributed], 406
Intoxicated person, effect on contract, 167
Invalid contracts, 166
Inverse condemnation, 54, 131
Investment pools, 267
Investment properties, careers in, 9–10
Involuntary liens, 62
IREM (Institute of Real Estate Management), 444, 522
IRRRLs (interest-rate-reduction refinancing loans), 239
IRS (Internal Revenue Service), 22, 330–331

Joint tenancy [a form of property co-ownership that features the right of survivorship], 78–80, 81–82
Jones v. Alfred H. Mayer Company, 91
Judgment liens, 64
Judgment rolls, 424
Judicial foreclosure, 312–315
Junior mortgage [any mortgage on a property that is subordinate to the first mortgage in priority], 310

Kelo v. City of New London, 54
Key lots, 49, *49*

Laches, 167
Land
attachment to, 33
definition of, 29, *29*
dividing, of estates, *109*, 110
economic characteristics of, 31–32
fixity of, 32
government rights in, 53–55
immovability of, 30
improvability of, 31
improvements, 30
Indestructibility of, 30

interests and rights in, 52–72, *70*
modification of, 32
nonhomogeneity of, 31
physical characteristics of, 30–31
plants, trees, and crops and, 34–35
scarcity of, 31
situs of, 31
Land contracts, 208–211, 291
Land descriptions
    assessor's parcel number/maps in, 46–47, *47*
    compass directions in, *39*, 39–40
    informal reference in, 46
    legal description for, 36
    metes and bounds for, 37–38, *38*, *39*
    recorded plat in, 44–45, *45*
    rectangular survey system for, 40–44, *40–44*
    reference to documents other than maps in, 46
    vertical, 48, *48*
Land development careers, 8
Land leases, 296–297
Landlords, 68
Landlord-tenant laws, 439–440
Land patent, 412
Landscaping, 34–35, *346*, 348
Land-use control [a broad term that describes any legal restriction that controls how a parcel of land may be used]
    court cases on, 127–128
    long-run continuity for, 134
    planning, 133–134
    private, 132–133
    zoning and, 128–131
Land-use efficiency, desire for, 108
Latent defect [concealed, hidden, or could only be identified by a trained eye; a seller is always required to disclose if s/he has knowledge of a latent defect], 149
Latitude lines, *40*, 40–42
Lawful objective, 172
Law sources, 71
Lawsuits, comparison between, 177–178
Lead-based paint, 148, 201, 205

Leasehold estate [a tenant's right to occupy land and/or buildings thereon], 68–69, 437
Lease-option [allows the tenant to buy the property at a preset price and terms for a given period of time], 212–214
Lease restrictions, 132–133
Leases
    elements of, 438
    gross, 440
    index, 440–441
    landlord-tenant laws and, 439–440
    negotiating, 523
    net, 440
    option clause in, 441
    percentage, 440
    provisions of, 438–439
    rents-setting in, 440–441
    subleases, 441
    termination of, 441–443
    valid, creating, 437–438
Lease with option to buy, 441
Leasing real estate, 296–297
Legacy, 407
Legal consideration, 173
Legal description [a method of identifying a property geographically exclusive of any other property on the face of the earth], 36, 516
Legal interpretations, of brokers, 146
Legal notice, 416
Legatee, 407
LEMs (location efficient mortgages), 251
Lender's title policy, 428
Lending disclosures, 246–247
Lending practices, 221–241. *See also* Loans
Lessees [tenants], 68, 437
Lessors [landlords], 68, 437
Letter of intent [an outline of the proposal with language to the effect that the letter is only an expression of mutual intent, and that no liability or obligation is created by it], 207

Licensees [one who holds a license], 12, 450, 495
Licensee transferal, 459–460, 487
License/licensing, 71
    acting without, 473
    activation of, 484–485
    broker's, 453, 455
    business firm, 17
    CAM, 528
    courses, 452–453
    education for, 14
    examination in, 13–14, 482–483
    exceptions to, 470–473
    fees, 451, 455–457, 481
    form of, 455
    jurisdiction, 482
    loyalty, honesty, and truthfulness in, 11
    maintaining, 483–485
    nonresident, 15–16, 453–455
    notice of consent and, 16
    obtaining, 481–483
    people required to have, 11–13
    procedures for, 14–16
    qualifications for, 13–14, 452–453
    rationale for, 10–11
    reciprocity and, 16
    reinstatement of, 484–485
    relocation and, 16
    renewal, 15, 453
    requirements of, 10
    salesperson's, 452
    securities, 19
    testing for, 14–15
License reciprocity [when one state honors another's license], 16
License revocation [to recall and make void a license], 18–19, 457–458
License suspension [to temporarily make a license ineffective], 18–19, 457–458
Licensing laws, 10–12, 449–473
    violations of, 464–470
Lienee/lienor, 62
Liens
    chattel, 311
    general, 62
    judgment, 64
    mechanic's, 63, 424

mortgage, 64
perfecting, 63
prior, against fixtures, 34
property tax, 62–63
special, 62
tax, 324
voluntary/involuntary, 62
Lien theory, 307
Life estates, 65
Life insurance companies, as mortgage lenders, 262
Life tenant, 65
Limited common elements, 111
Limited-service brokerage, 193
Limited warranty deeds, 402
Liquid assets [assets that are in cash or are readily convertible to cash], 251
Liquidated damages [an amount of money specified in a contract as compensation to be paid if the contract is not satisfactorily completed], 178
Lis pendens, notice of, 313
Lis pendens index, 424
Listing agreement, 183–185
Listing brokers, 203
Listing presentation [the organized presentation of information to a seller organized in five sections], 509–511
Listings
advance fee/cost, 186–187
exclusive agency, 185
exclusive right-to-sell, 185
flat fee, 187
net, 186
open, 185–186
termination of, 192–193
Littoral rights [right of landowners to use and enjoy the water touching their land], 35
Loan balance table, 228, *228*
Loan estimates [give a summary of applicable loan terms and estimates of loan and closing costs consumers can expect to pay at closing], 519

Loan origination fees [the expenses a lender incurs in processing a mortgage loan], 231
Loan points, 231–232
Loan Prospector program, 273
Loans. *See also* Mortgages
advertising of, 245–246
affordable housing, 287–288
amortized, 223–227, *224–226*
application and approval of, 248–255
balloon, 227
blended-rate, 286
budget mortgage, 227
character, 273–274
computerized origination of, 264
construction, 285–286
conventional, 227
delinquent, 311–312
early payoff of, 229–230
FHA, 232–235, 254, 282
15-year, 229
interest-rate-reduction refinancing, 239
interim, 285–286
new, 382–383
no down payment, 236–237
partially amortized, 227–228, *228*
participation, 262
predatory, 255
purpose of, 249–250
repayment of, 223–225, *224, 225*
standardized procedures for, 267–273
subprime, 255
term, 222–223
VA, 232, 236–240, *239*, 282
Loan-to-value ratio (L/V or LTVR) [a percentage reflecting what a lender will lend divided by the sale price or market value of the property, whichever is less], 230, 252–253, 382
Loan value, 342
Location efficient mortgages (LEMs), 251
Longitude lines, *40*, 40–42
Long-run continuity, for land-use control, 134

Loose money, 232
Lot-block-tract system, 44–45, *45*
Lot features and location, *346*, 348
Lot types, 49, *49*
Loyalty, in licensing, 11
L/V or LTVR (loan-to-value ratio), 230, 252–253, 382

Maintenance fees, condominium, 113–114
Management, condominium, 113
Map books, 45
Mapping, metes and bounds, 39, *39*
Mapping requirements, 131
Margin, 280–281
MARIA tests, 32–34
Marital status, in credit application evaluation, 102
Marketable title act, 432
Marketable title [title that is reasonably free from litigation], 430
Market analysis, 521–522
Market comparison approach [a method of valuing property based on recent sales of similar properties], 343–354, *346*, *351*, *353*, *354*, 363–364
Market exposure of property, 188–189
Marketing, 521
Market value [the cash price that a willing buyer and a willing seller would agree upon, given reasonable exposure of the property to the marketplace, full information as to the potential uses of the property, and no undue compulsion to act], 339, 342
Marriage, property ownership and, 83–84
Master Deed, 111
Master plan [a comprehensive guide for the physical growth of a community], 133–134
Material facts, 502
Maturity [the end of the life of a loan], 222
MBS (mortgage-backed securities), 269–270

Mechanic's liens, 63, 424
Median income, 287
Meeting of the minds, 168
Menace, 172
Menu of services, 194
Meridians [imaginary lines running north and south, used as references in mapping land], 40, 40–41
MERS® (Mortgage electronic registration system), 417–418
Metes and bounds [a detailed method of land description that identifies a parcel by specifying its shape and boundaries], 37–38, 38, 39
MGIC (Mortgage Guaranty Insurance Corporation), 240–241, 287
Middleman [a person who brings two or more parties together but does not represent either party (known as a transaction broker in Georgia)], 154
Middleman principle, 154
Mill rate [property tax rate that is expressed in tenths of a cent per dollar of assessed valuation], 323
Ministerial acts [acts that do not required discretion or adjudication], 480, 502
Minors, 167
Misrepresentations
   by brokers, 147–148
   innocent, 170, 171
Mistake, in contract law, 171
MLS (multiple listing service) [organization of member brokers agreeing to share listing information and share commissions], 188–190
Modification, of fixtures, 32
Money damages, 177–178
Monopoly [created when one business has no competition], 160, 528–530
Monthly income, 250–251
Monument [an iron pipe, stone, tree, or other fixed point used in making a survey], 36–38, 38
Mortgage [a document that makes property security for the repayment of a debt], 300, 302. *See also* Loans
   adjustable-rate, 240, 279–283, *280*
   blanket, 284–285
   budget, 227
   chattel, 71, 311
   contract for deed, 291
   customized, 278–279
   equitable, 318
   equity, 286
   first, 310
   graduated payment, 283
   investing in, 295
   junior, 310
   location efficient, 251
   package, 284
   PMI and, 240–241
   primary market, 259
   purchase money, 289
   reverse-annuity, 285
   second, 310
   secondary market, 259, 262–263, 265–267, *266*, 270–273
   senior, 310
   shared appreciation, 283–284
   subordination, 290
   UFMIP, 233–234
   variable rate, 279
   wraparound, 289–290, *290*
Mortgage-backed securities (MBS), 269–270
Mortgage bankers, 262
Mortgage Bankers Association, 255
Mortgage broker [one who brings together borrowers and lenders], 263
Mortgage companies [firms that make mortgage loans and then sell them to investors], 262–263
Mortgage electronic registration system (MERS®), 417–418
Mortgage-equity tables, 362, *363*
Mortgagee [the party receiving a mortgage; the lender], 302
Mortgage financing careers, 8–9
Mortgage fraud, 292–295
Mortgage Guaranty Insurance Corporation (MGIC), 240–241, 287
Mortgage insurance, prorating, 385–386
Mortgage lenders
   primary market, 259
   secondary market, 259, 262–263, 265–267, *266*, 270–273
Mortgage liens, 64
Mortgage pools, computerization of, 272–273
Mortgagor/mortgagee index, 424
Mortgagor [the party giving a mortgage; the borrower], 302
Multifamily living, 108–109
Multiple listing service (MLS) [organization of member brokers agreeing to share listing information and share commissions], 188–190
Municipal bonds, 264
Municipality occupational tax, 463
Mutual agreement, 168–172, 192
Mutual rescission, 178–179
MyCommunityMortgage Program, Fannie Mae, 287–288

Naked title [title that lacks the rights and privileges usually associated with ownership], 303
NAR. *See* National Association of REALTORS®
National Association of Real Estate Brokers (NAREB), 24, 26
National Association of REALTORS® (NAR), 23, 493
   code of ethics of, 25–26
   GRI designation and, 26
   local boards of, 24
National Association of Securities Dealers, 19
National Housing Act, 232
National real estate firms, 23–24
Negative amortization [accrual of interest on a loan balance so that, as loan payments are made, the loan balance rises], 281–282
Negotiation, of purchase contracts, 206
Net engagement, 485
Net lease [tenant pays a base rent plus maintenance, property taxes, and insurance], 440

Net liisting [a listing agreement that pays the broker an uncertain amount of commission, generating the principal net proceeds from the sale], 186
Net operating income, 361–362
Networking, 6
Net worth, 252
New loans, 382–383
No down payment loans, 236–237
Nonconforming use [an improvement that is inconsistent with current zoning regulations], 129
Nondisturbance clause [an agreement found in a mortgage where a lender forgoes the right to terminate a valid lease of a performing tenant], 443
Nonhomogeneity, of land, 31
Nonjudicial foreclosure, 315–316
Nonresident licensing, 15–16, 453–455
"No sale, no commission" contract, 191
Notaries public, 419–420, *421*
Note, 300–302, *301*
Notice of Adverse Action, 102
Notice of consent, 16
Notice of default, 315
Notice of lis pendens, 313
Novation, 175–176, 178, 309
"Nuisance cases," 161
Nuncupative wills [oral or spoken wills made in anticipation of death], 408

Obedience, to principal, 143–144
Obligations, implied, 179
Obligees/obligors, 300
Occupational tax, county or municipality, 463
Offer, revocation of, 169–170
Offer and acceptance, 169
Offeree/offeror, 169
Office brokerage policy, 504–505
Office of Thrift Supervision (OTS), 279
Offset statement, 373
100% commission, 21
Open listings, 185–186
Operating expense ratio, 361

Operating expenses [expenditures necessary to maintain the production of income], 360, *360*, 361
Operation of law, termination of agency by, 158
Opinion of title, 425
Option [a right, for a given period of time, to buy, sell, or lease property at a specified price and terms], 291
Option clause [gives the right at some future time to purchase or lease a property at a predetermined price], 441
Option contract [a person has a right, but not an obligation, to perform under agreed-upon terms, price, and time period]
 exercising, 211
 lease-options, 212–214
 on multiple properties, 211–212
Optionee/optioner, 211, 214
Oral wills, 408
Ordinary life estate, 65
Origination fees, loan, 231
Ostensible authority [an agency relationship created by the conduct of the principal], 141
OTS (Office of Thrift Supervision), 279
Overall rates, 362, *363*
Over-encumbered property, 292
Owners' associations, 111–113, 527–528
Ownership. *See also* Liens
 by accession, 411
 concurrent, 67, 76–84, *81–82*
 conveyance of, 397–413
 encumbrances to, 56–58, *57*
 fee simple, 55–56, *56*, 64, 122
 marriage and, 83–84
 protecting, 55
 sole, 76
Owner's title policy, 428

Package mortgages [mortgages that secure personal property in addition to real property], 284
Parol evidence rule, 175

Partially amortized loans, 227–228, *228*
Partial performance, 176–177
Partial reciprocity, 16
Partial take, 442
Participation certificates [certificates representing undivided interests in a Freddie Mac pool], 270
Participation clause, 440
Participation loans, 262
Partition, 78
Part-time income, in credit application evaluation, 101
Party, 165
 competent, 167–168
 deceased, 176
Party wall easement, 60
Patent defect [in the open and would not take training or specific expertise to recognize the problem], 149
Patio, *346*, 347
Payment cap, 281
Pending lawsuits, 424
Pension funds, as mortgage lenders, 265
Percentage lease [tenant pays a percentage of sales as all or a portion of the rent owed to the landlord], 440
Percolating water, 36
Perfecting the lien, 63
Performance, 153
Performance fees, 186–187
Periodic estates, 69, 437
Periodic tenancy, 69
Permanent monuments, 37–38, *38*
Person, unity of, 80
Personal property [a right or interest in things of a temporary or movable nature; anything not classified as real property; also known as personalty or chattel], 30
Personal representative, 407
Personalty, 30
Physical deterioration/depreciation [a loss in value due to wear and tear, such as rotted wood, age, worn carpet, and peeling paint], 356

Physical life, 358
Physical survey, 133
PITI payment [a loan payment that combines principal, interest, taxes, and insurance], 227, 251
Planned unit developments (PUDs) [individually owned lots and houses with community ownership of common areas], *109*, 110, 120–121
Plan of condominium ownership, 111
Plants, ownership of, 34–35
Plat, recorded, 44–45, *45*
Pledging, 302
Plottage [assemblage with a value increase greater than the cost], 342
Plottage value [the amount of the value increase due to plottage], 342
PMI (private mortgage insurance) [a source to insure lenders against foreclosure loss], 240–241, 385
PMM (purchase money mortgage), 289
Point [1% of the loan amount], 231
Point of beginning, in surveying, 37–38, *38*
Police power [the right of government to enact laws and enforce them for the order, safety, health, morals, and general welfare of the public], 53
Policy premium, 427–428
Poolers, 267
Pooling, 269, 272
"Poor man's will," 79–80
Possession, unity of, 78
Post-license education [the 25-hour course of study that must be completed within one year by all original salesperson licensees], 483
Power of attorney [a document by which one person authorizes another to act on his/her behalf], 168
Power of sale [allows a mortgagee to conduct a foreclosure sale without first going to court], 315–316
Predatory lending, 255

Preliminary decision [issued by the commission after proper request of a licensure candidate to help determine the candidate's eligibility to receive a license], 483
Prepayment penalty, 276, 301–302
Prepayment privilege, 301–302
Preprinted clauses, in purchase contracts, 205–206
Preventive maintenance, 521
Price fixing [two or more people conspiring to charge a fixed fee, having an anticompetitive effect], 159, 529
Primary mortgage market [the market in which lenders originate loans and make funds available to borrowers], 259
Principal [the balance owing on a loan], 223
Principal [a person who authorizes another to act], 140
  broker's obligations to, 141–147
  full disclosure to, 144–145
  loyalty to, 142–143
  obedience to, 143–144
  obligations to agent, 152–153
Principal broker [the broker in charge of a real estate office], 25
Principal meridians, *40*, 40–41
Principles of value [the key factors that determine value in real estate], 340–342
Printing press money, 274
Priority position of lenders, 310
Private mortgage insurance (PMI) [a source to insure lenders against foreclosure loss], 240–241, 385
Private mortgage packagers, 272
Probate court, 407
Procuring cause, 191–192
Professional real estate associations, 24–26
Projected operating statement, 359–360, *360*
Projected gross [the estimated rent a fully occupied property can be expected to produce on an annual basis], 359–360, *360*

Promises, exchange of, 172
Promissory note [a written promise to repay a debt; usually referred to simply as a note], 300–302, *301*
Property advertising, 492–494
Property damages, 176
Property management
  agreement, 485–486, 520
  budgeting in, 522–523
  functions of, 520
  job requirements and responsibilities in, 7
  lease negotiation in, 523
  maintenance in, 520–521
  market analysis in, 521–522
  marketing in, 521
  rent collection in, 523–524
  retaining tenants in, 524
  tenant selection in, 523
Property reports, 158–159
Property rights. *See* Fair housing laws
Property taxes
  appraisal and assessment for, 322–323
  assessment appeal for, 325
  budget and appropriation process for, 322
  for condominiums, 114
  exemptions from, 325–326
  history of, 54–55
  interest deductions and, 333
  prorating, 378–379
  rate calculation of, 323, *324*
  special assessments on, 327–329
  unpaid, 324–325
  variations in, 326–327
Property tax liens, 62–63
Proprietary lease [a lease issued by a cooperative corporation to its shareholders], 119
Prorating [the division of ongoing expenses and income items between the buyer and the seller]
  of accrued interest, 380–381
  assumptions in, 377–378
  of hazard insurance, 379–380
  of insurance, 386–387
  of intangibles tax, 388
  interest adjustments and, 383–384

of mortgage insurance, 385–386
new loans and down payment calculation and, 382–383
of property taxes, 378–379
of rent, 384–385
of tax escrows, 386
of transfer tax, 387–388
Prospecting listings, 509
Protected class [a class of people that by law is protected from discrimination], 91–92
Psychologically impacted properties, 512
Public auction, 313
Public grants, 411–412
Public recorder's office [a government-operated facility wherein documents are entered in the public records], 417
Public records, 416–422, *418*, *421*
Public trustee, 304
PUDs (planned unit developments) [individually owned lots and houses with community ownership of common areas], 109, 110, 120–121
Puffing [statements a reasonable person would recognize as nonfactual or extravagant], 146, 151
Pur autre vie (for the life of another), 65
Purchase contracts
  agency and brokerage in, 203
  agency in, 203
  binders for, 206–207
  closing attorney in, 200
  closing date and transfer of possession in, 199
  disclaimer in, 203
  due diligence period in, 201
  earnest money in, 199, 202–203
  equitable title and, 210–211
  exhibits and addenda in, 204–205
  federal clauses in, 205–206
  inspection in, 200–201
  lead-based paint in, 201, 205
  letter of intent and, 207
  negotiation of, 206
  notices in, 203–204
  other provisions in, 204
  payment method in, 200
  practice of law and, 207–208
  purchase and sale in, 198–199
  purchase price in, 199
  riders in, 206
  risk of damage section in, 202
  seller's contributions at closing in, 199–200
  taxes in, 202
  warranty in, 202
Purchase money mortgage (PMM), 289

Quadrangle, *40*, 41
Qualified fee estate [a fee estate that is subject to certain limitations imposed by the person creating the estate], 64–65
Qualifying brokers, 17, 485–487
Quantity survey method, 355, *357*
Quarter-section, 43, *44*
Quiet enjoyment [the right of possession and use of property without undue disturbance by others], 400–401, 439
Quiet title suits [court-ordered hearings held to determine landownership], 409, 430
Quitclaim deed [a legal instrument used to convey whatever title the grantor has; it contains no covenants, warranties, or implication of the grantor's ownership], 404–405, *405*

RAMs (reverse-annuity mortgages) [loans to the homeowner whereby periodic payments are made TO the borrower from the lender; typically for people 62 or older], 285
Range, in rectangular survey system, 42, *42*
Ready, willing, and able buyer [a buyer who is ready to buy at the seller's price and terms and who has the financial capability to do so], 190–191
Real estate [any interest in real property, freehold or non-freehold; tangible or intangible], 450
Real estate appraising, 7–8
Real estate broker [one who acts as an agent for others in negotiating contracts or sales], 12. *See also* Brokers
Real Estate Buyer's Agent Council (REBAC), 187
Real estate commission [a state board that advises and sets policies regarding real estate licensees and transaction procedures], 18. *See also* Commission
Real estate consulting, 9
Real estate department [civil service employees who handle paperwork, arrange for examinations, collect fees, and issue licenses], 18
Real Estate Education, Research and Recovery Fund [a fund that provides an avenue of protection to members of the public harmed by the illegal acts of a licensee], 461–463
Real estate [land and improvements in a physical sense, as well as the rights to own or use them], 29
Real estate listing [a contract wherein a broker is employed to find a buyer or tenant], 183–185
Real estate regulation, 17–18, 124, 235
Real estate salesperson [a person employed by a broker to list, negotiate, sell, or lease real property for others], 12–13
Real Estate Settlement Procedures Act (RESPA) [a federal law that deals with procedures to be followed in certain types of real estate closings], 245, 263, 386, 529
  CFPB and, 245, 392
  closing governed by, 519
  penalties under, 394
  restrictions of, 389, 392
  TRID and, 392–394
Real property administrators (RPA), 444

Real property [land and improvements in a physical sense, as well as the rights to own or use them], 29
Real savings, 274
Realtist [trade name for a member of the National Association of Real Estate Brokers (NAREB)], 26
REALTOR® [a registered trademark owned by the National Association of REALTORS® for use by its members], 25
REALTOR®-ASSOCIATE®, 25
Reamortized, 282
Reasonable care, of broker, 146
REBAC (Real Estate Buyer's Agent Council), 187
Receiver, 315
Reciprocity, 16
Reconveyance deed [used to reconvey title to property back to the borrower once a debt has been paid on a deed of trust; also called a release deed], 303–304
Recorded map, 44–45, 45
Recorded plat [a subdivision map filed in the county recorder's office that shows the location and boundaries of individual parcels of land], 44–45, 45
Recorded survey, 44–45, 45
Recording acts, 417, 418
Records, sales, 344–345
Rectangular survey system [also known as the government survey or U.S. public land survey, describes land based on longitude and latitude], 40–44, 40–44
Red flags, 148–149
Redlining [a lender's refusal to make loans in certain neighborhoods], 252
Referee's deed in foreclosure, 314–315, 406
Registrar of titles, 431
Regulated lenders, 259
Regulation, 17–18, 124, 235
Regulation Z [federal regulations that implement the Truth in Lending Act], 245, 282

Reimbursement, 152
Reissue rates, 428
Relationship of the parties, for fixtures, 33
Release dead, 304
Release of liability, 309
Reliction [the permanent receding of water, exposing dry land], 411
Relocation, to new state, 16
Remainderman/remainderperson, 64
Remaining balance table, 228, 228
Remise, 405
Renewal, licensing, 15, 453
Rent
   collection, 523–524
   proration, 384–385
   setting, 440–441
Rental listing services, 7
Rental value, 342
Renunciation, termination of agency by, 157
Repayment, of loans, 223–225, 224, 225
Replacement cost, 355
Replacement value, 342
Reporting requirements, for closing, 376–377
Reproduction cost, 355
Request for notice of default, 316
Resale, cooperatives and, 120
Rescission, 170, 176
   mutual, 178–179
   right to, 171, 245, 248
   unilateral, 177
Research and education careers, 9
Reservation, life estate by, 65
Reserve accounts [accounts into which the lender places monthly tax and insurance payments], 227
Reserves
   for condominiums, 114
   for replacement, 361, 522–523
Residential brokerage careers, 5
Resort timesharing [the exclusive use of a property for a period of time each year]
   benefits of, 122–123
   commitment in, 123
   costs of, 122

   fee simple format for, 122
   Georgia Time-Share Act and, 531
   right-to-use format for, 121–122
   state regulation of, 124
RESPA. See Real Estate Settlement Procedures Act
Restrictive covenants [clauses placed in deeds and leases to control how future owners and lessees may or may not use the property], 133
Retaining tenants, 524
Retaliatory eviction [the illegal removal of a tenant by a landlord because of complaints or actions against the landlord by the tenant], 442
Reverse-annuity mortgages (RAMs) [loans to the homeowner whereby periodic payments are made TO the borrower from the lender; typically for people 62 or older], 285
Reversion [the right to retake possession at a future date], 68, 437
Revised Regulation Z (RRZ), 245
Revocation
   license, 18–19, 457–458
   of offer, 169–170
   termination of agency by, 157
RHS (Rural Housing Service), 241
"Rich uncle" financing, 284
Rider [any addition annexed to a document and made a part of the document by reference; also known as an addendum or attachment], 206
Right of first refusal [the right to match or better an offer before the property is sold to someone else], 214–215
Right of survivorship [a feature of joint tenancy whereby the surviving joint tenants automatically acquire all the rights, title, and interest of the deceased joint tenant], 77, 79
Right to inspect, 518
Right to rescission, 171, 245, 248
Right-to-use, 121–122

Riparian right [the right of a landowner whose land borders a river or stream to use and enjoy that water], 35
Roommate listing services, 7
RPA (real property administrator), 444
RRZ (Revised Regulation Z), 245
Rules and Regulations, for Georgia, 478–496
Rural Economic and Community Development Program, 241
Rural Housing Service (RHS), 241

Safe Drinking Water Act, 237
Sale and leaseback arrangements, 296
Sale by advertisement, 315–316
Salesperson [a person employed by a broker to list, negotiate, sell, or lease real property for others], 12–13, 450
  compensation for, 20–21
Salesperson's license, 452
Sales records, 344–345
Sales staff, of brokers, 153
Salvage value, 342
SAMs (shared appreciation mortgages), 283–284
Savings and loan (S&L) associations, 259–261
Scarcity
  of land, 31
  for value, 340
Scheduled gross [the estimated rent a fully occupied property can be expected to produce on an annual basis], 359–360, *360*
Secondary market delivery system, *266*, 266–267
Secondary mortgage market [a market in which mortgage loans can be sold to investors], 259, 262–263, 265–267, *266*, 270–273
Second mortgage [a mortgage in which property is used to secure another note before the first mortgage is fully satisfied], 310
Section [one square mile (A township is made up of 36 sections.)], *42*, *43*, *44*

Securities and syndications, careers in, 9
Securities license, 19
Security deed [a document used in Georgia to secure a note; replaces a mortgage or deed of trust], 300, 302, 406
  foreclosure on, 307–308, 526
  provisions of, 305–307
  purpose of, 304–305
  satisfaction of, 307
Seizin, covenant of, 400
Seller disclosure form, 149–151
Seller financing [a note accepted by a seller instead of cash], 288–290, *290*
Seller representation, 509–513
Seller's market, 343
Seller's Property Disclosure Form, 511–512
Selling brokers, 203
Senior mortgage [the mortgage loan with highest priority for repayment in the event of foreclosure], 310
Separate elements [areas in the condominium that are exclusively owned and used by the individual owners], 111
Separate property, 84
Servient estate, 59
Settlement, 372
Settlement funds, 249
Settlement meeting, 373–375
Settlement statement [an accounting of funds given to the buyer and the seller at the completion of a real estate transaction], 375
Severalty, estate in, 76
Severance damages, 54
Sex, in credit application evaluation, 101
Shared appreciation mortgages (SAMs), 283–284
Shelley v. Kraemer, 91
Sheriff's deeds, 314–315, 406
Sherman Antitrust Act, 159–161, 528–529
Short sales, foreclosure and, 526
Silent second, 293

Simple interest, 301
Single agency, 506–507
Situs, 31
Size, of house, *346*, 346–347
S&L (savings and loan) associations, 259–261
SMA (Systems Maintenance Administrator), 444
Soldier and sailor wills, 408
Sole ownership, 76
Sole proprietorship, 17
Southern Building Code, 132
Special agency, 140
Special assessments, on property taxes, 327–329
Special liens, 62
Special warranty deed [grantor warrants title only against defects occurring during the grantor's ownership], 402
Specific performance [contract performance according to the precise terms agreed upon], 177–178
Spot zoning, 130
Square-foot method, 355
Standardized loan procedures, 267–273
Standard parallels, *40*, 41
Standards of conduct, 25
Standards of practice, 25
Statute of frauds, 174, 398, 416
Statute of limitations, 179
Statutory dedication, 412
Statutory estates, 66–67
Statutory law, 71–72
Statutory redemption, 306, 314–315
Steering [practice of directing home seekers to particular neighborhoods based on race, color, religion, sex, national origin, handicapped status, or adults-only status], 94–95
Step-up rentals, 296–297
Stigmatized Property Act, 512
Straight-line method, 358
Straight loans, 222–223
Strict foreclosure, 315
Subagency co-op, 508

Subdivision regulations, 131–132
Subject property, 343–344
"Subject to," 308–309
Sublessee [a lessee who rents from another lessee], 68, 441
Sublessor [a lessee who rents to another lessee], 68, 441
Sublet [to transfer only a portion of one's lease rights], 68, 441
Subordination [voluntary acceptance of a lower mortgage priority than one would otherwise be entitled to], 290, 310
Subprime loans, 255
Substantive regulations, 478–496
Substitute liability, 309
Substitution, principle of, 340–341
Subsurface rights, 29, *29*
Sufferance, tenancy at, 69
Supply and demand, principle of, 341
Support person, employment/duties of, 488–489
Surface rights, 29, *29*
Surplus money action, 312–313
Surrogate court, 407
Survey books, 45
Survey systems, *41*, 41–42
Suspension, license, 18–19, 457–458
Systems Maintenance Administrator (SMA), 444

Tacking, 409
Taking, 130–131
TARP (Troubled Asset Relief Program), 262
Tax certificate [a document issued at a tax sale that entitles the purchaser to a deed at a later date if the property is not redeemed], 324–325
Tax deeds, 324
Taxes, 321
　ad valorem, 322
　agent's liability for advice on, 334
　capital gains, 331–332
　conveyance, 334–335
　covenant to pay, 305
　deed transfer, 344
　documentary, 334–335
　Form 1099-S and, 376–377
　income, on sale of residence, 329–332
　intangibles, 388
　interest deductions and, 333
　occupational, county or municipality, 463
　property, 54–55, 62–63, 114, 322–329, *324*, 333, 378–379
　in purchase contracts, 202
　transfer, 387–388
Tax escrow proration, 386
Tax lien [a charge or hold by the government against property to ensure the payment of taxes], 324
Taxpayer Relief Act of 1997, 377
Teaser rate ARMs, 282–283
Technology Open to Approved Lenders (TOTAL), 254
Tenancy at sufferance, 69, 437
Tenancy by the entirety, 80, *81–82*, 83
Tenants, 68
　holdover, 69, 437
　life, 65
　retaining, 524
　selection of, 523
Tenants in common [shared ownership of a single property among two or more persons; interests need not be equal and no right of survivorship exists], 76–78, *81–82*
Term loans, 222–223
Terms and conditions of sale, *346*, 348
Testate [when a person dies leaving a last will and testament], 406–407
Testator/testatrix, 406–407
Tester [an individual or organization that responds to advertising and visits real estate offices to test for compliance with fair housing laws], 97
Testing, for licensing, 14–15
Thin market, 343
Third parties [persons who are not parties to a contract but who may be affected by it], 140
　broker's obligations to, 147–149
Thirteenth Amendment, 90–91
Tie-in agreements [tying one contract to another and forcing a business relationship], 160–161, 530
Tight money, 232
TIL or TILA (Truth in Lending Act) [a federal law that requires certain disclosures when extending or advertising credit], 244–248, 392
TILSRA (Truth in Lending Simplification and Reform Act), 245
Time, unity of, 79
Time adjustments, 346, *346*
"Time is of the essence" [a phrase that means the time limits of a contract must be faithfully observed or the contract is voidable], 204
Timely, 481
Timesharing, resort, 121–124, 531
T intersections, 49, *49*
Title by descent, 406
Title cloud, 405, 430
Title commitment, 426–427, *427*
Title defects, 405, 430
Title insurance [an insurance policy against defects in title not listed in the title report or abstract], 425–430, *427*
Title plants, 429
Title policies, 426–427
Title search, 422–424, 429, 432
Title searchers, 424, 426
Title [the right to or ownership of something; also the evidence of ownership, such as a deed or bill of sale], 56, 79
Title transferal, 397–413
T lots, 49, *49*
"Too big to fail," 261–262
Torrens system [a state-sponsored method of registering land titles], 430–432
TOTAL (Technology Open to Approved Lenders), 254
Townhouses
　appraisal of, 349–350
　land division in, *109*, 110

Township [a 6-mile square made up of 36 square miles or sections], *42*, 42–43
Tract indexes, 421
Trade associations, agent, 160
Trade fixtures, 33
Traditional mortgage loan delivery system, *266*, 266–267
Training, 20, 443–444
Transaction brokers, 154, 494–495, 508–509
Transactions, in E-Sign, 215
Transferability, 340
Transferring title, 397–413
Transfer tax proration, 387–388
Trees, ownership of, 34–35
TRID (Truth in Lending, Real Estate Settlement Procedures Act Integrated Disclosure), 392–394
Trigger terms, 245
Triple net lease, 440
Troubled Asset Relief Program (TARP), 262
True copy, 485
Trust accounts, 145, 460–461, 489–492
Trust deed. *See* Deed of trust
Trustee [one who holds property in trust for another; the third party in a deed of trust], 303, 304
Trust funds, 265, 489–492
Trustor [one who creates a trust; the borrower in a deed of trust], 303
Truthfulness, in licensing, 11
Truth in Lending, Real Estate Settlement Procedures Act Integrated Disclosure (TRID), 392–394
Truth in Lending Act (TIL or TILA) [a federal law that requires certain disclosures when extending or advertising credit], 244–248, 392
Truth in Lending Simplification and Reform Act (TILSRA), 245
Two-year use rule, 331

UDTPA (Uniform Deceptive Trade Practices Act), 530–531
UETA (Uniform Electronic Transactions Act), 216, 418

UFMIP (up-front mortgage insurance premium) [a one-time charge by the FHA for insuring a loan], 233–234
Underwriting systems, automated, 273–274
Undivided interest [ownership by two or more persons that gives each the right to use the entire property], 76
Undue influence, 172
Unenforceable contracts, 166
Unfair trade practices and violations, 464–470
Uniform Commercial Code, 174
Uniform Deceptive Trade Practices Act (UDTPA), 530–531
Uniform Electronic Transactions Act (UETA), 216, 418
Uniform Residential Loan Application, 248
Uniform Standards of Professional Appraisal Practice (USPAP), 340
Uniform Vendor and Purchaser Risk Act, 176
Unilateral contracts [a promise exchanged for performance], 165–166. *See also* Option contracts
Unilateral rescission, 177
Unit in place method, 355–356
Unity of interest, 78
Unity of person, 80
Unity of possession, 78
Unity of time, 79
Unity of title, 79
Universal agency, 140
Unrecorded interests, 418
Unregulated lenders, 259
Upfront fees, 194
Upfront mortgage insurance premium (UFMIP) [a onetime charge by the FHA for insuring a loan], 233–234
Urban planning careers, 8
USPAP (Uniform Standards of Professional Appraisal Practice), 340
U.S. public land survey, 40–44, *40–44*
Usury [charging an interest rate that is in excess of the legal rate], 260, 275
Utility, 340

VA (Department of Veterans Affairs), 232, 236–240, *239*, 282
Vacancy and collection losses (V&C), 359–360, *360*, 522
Vacant land valuation, 350
Valid contracts, 166, 167
Valuable consideration, 173
Valuation process, 340
Value, 340–343
Variable expenses, 522
Variable rate mortgages, 279
Variance [allows an individual landowner to vary from zoning requirements], 130
Variations in property taxes, 326–327
V&C (vacancy and collection losses), 359–360, *360*, 522
Vendors/vendees, in installment contracts, 209
Vertical land descriptions, 48, *48*
Vested, 423
Violations of licensing laws/rules, 464–470
Visual tours, MLS files and, 190
Voidable contract [a contract with a defect that can be voided by one of its parties], 166, 167
Void contract [a contract that is missing an essential element and has no binding effect on the parties], 166, 167
Voluntary liens, 62
Voting rules, of condominium owners' associations, 112

Walk-through [a final inspection of the property just prior to settlement], 372
Wall Street Reform and Consumer Protection Act (Dodd-Frank), 245, 392
Warranties [assurances or guarantees that something is true as stated], 400–402
Warranty deeds, 402, *403*
Warranty forever, 401
Waste, prohibition of, 65
Water rights, 35–36
Water table, 36

Wills
    codicil to, 408
    conveyance of property after death and, 406–408
    estate at, 69, 437
    formal/witnessed, 407–408
    holographic, 408
    nuncupative, 408
    "poor man's," 79–80
Witnessed wills, 407–408
Witnesses, in public document recording, 419, *419*
Worksheets, buyer and seller, 389, *390*, *391*
Wraparound mortgages [mortgages that encompass any existing mortgages and is subordinate to them], 289–290, *290*
Written contracts, 174–175, 177, 179

Zoning laws [public regulations that control the specific use of land], 128–131